Stuat Bell

ENVIRONMENTAL A$

Environmental Assessment

The Regulation of Decision Making

JANE HOLDER

OXFORD
UNIVERSITY PRESS

OXFORD
UNIVERSITY PRESS

Great Clarendon Street, Oxford OX2 6DP

Oxford University Press is a department of the University of Oxford.
It furthers the University's objective of excellence in research, scholarship,
and education by publishing worldwide in

Oxford New York

Auckland Cape Town Dar es Salaam Hong Kong Karachi
Kuala Lumpur Madrid Melbourne Mexico City Nairobi
New Delhi Shanghai Taipei Toronto

With offices in

Argentina Austria Brazil Chile Czech Republic France Greece
Guatemala Hungary Italy Japan Poland Portugal Singapore
South Korea Switzerland Thailand Turkey Ukraine Vietnam

Oxford is a registered trade mark of Oxford University Press
in the UK and in certain other countries

Published in the United States
by Oxford University Press Inc., New York

© J. Holder, 2004

British Library Cataloguing in Publication Data
Data available

Library of Congress Cataloging in Publication Data
Data available

Typeset by Newgen Imaging Systems (P) Ltd., Chennai, India
Printed in Great Britain
on acid-free paper by
Biddles Ltd., King's Lynn

ISBN   978–0–19–826772–0
ISBN   978–0–19–920758–9 (Pbk.)

3 5 7 9 10 8 6 4 2

For Don

Preface and Acknowledgements

For several years I was fortunate enough to serve as a trustee for the Environmental Law Foundation. It soon became clear to me that much of the Foundation's referral and advisory work was related to environmental assessment. During this time I was also greatly impressed by the sense, on the part of my fellow trustees and 'clients', of what environmental law could accomplish in terms of securing and protecting natural resources as well as improving the environments in which people lived, particularly when threatened by noise, pollution, and unsightly and potentially harmful development. I began to more generally appreciate that environmental assessment provides a valuable viewpoint from which to evaluate the development, effectiveness, and potential of environmental law. This is because the major stages in the development of environmental law—the growth of the guiding principles of integration, precaution, and sustainable development; the shift towards the use of less prescriptive, more flexible regulatory instruments; the creation of conditions for enhanced deliberation; and accommodation of the expansion of the scale of environmental concern in decision making—are all present in environmental assessment. As an inherently interdisciplinary inquiry, environmental assessment also provides an opportunity to examine how law is involved in the gathering, formulation, and presentation of scientific information on which essentially political decisions are based. Considering individual cases of decision making supported by environmental assessment makes the sometimes overwhelming conflict between environmental protection and development conceptually manageable, and so provides a way in to the big issues raised by the 'greening' of governance and political agendas, whilst also making apparent the part played by law in the resolution or otherwise of this conflict. In these various respects, environmental assessment provides a lesson in legal environmental protection. But more valuable than this (and opportunistic involvement by lawyers aside), environmental assessment represents the aim of introducing standards, rigour, and environmental principle into decision making which is often obscure and economically motivated.

My main motive in writing this book was to scrutinize the effectiveness of environmental assessment in practice in order to assess whether this aim had been realized. For this reason, I hope that the book will prove interesting and of some use to environmental lawyers, be they students, academics, or practitioners (as well as to non-lawyers) who already have a grasp of environmental assessment law and procedure, and are interested in the broader questions about decision making and regulation that they raise. I therefore do not aim to provide a comprehensive, step-by-step guide to the law relating to environmental assessment (I refer the reader looking for this to S. Tromans and K. Fuller, *Environmental Impact*

Assessment: Law and Practice (London: Butterworths, 2003) which offers an excellent and thorough legal exposition of the procedure) but intend to elucidate, using empirical research as well as selected reported cases, key parts of the assessment process in an attempt to contribute to larger questions about the socio-legal operation of a regulatory technique latterly accorded the status of reflexive law.

In writing this book I have relied on the help and support of many colleagues and friends at UCL and elsewhere. First amongst these is Ray Purdy, Centre for Law and the Environment at the Faculty of Laws, UCL, who is an expert in the implementation of environmental assessment procedures and kindly helped me find and update many of my sources. Special thanks go also to Sue Elworthy for sharing her insights, commenting on my work, for her tireless enthusiasm for intellectual inquiry, and her admirable quality of getting the job done with vigour and panache. I would also like to recognize Davina Cooper's involvement in various projects over the years, and her originality in conceiving land use and governance issues. I extend this to the Board of the *Social and Legal Studies* journal, the members of which have (probably unwittingly) created a stimulating and supportive academic community. I would like to thank John Louth and Gwen Booth at Oxford University Press for their patience and quiet encouragement and Fiona Barry and Virginia Williams for carrying out production and copy editing so efficiently. I like to think that the book's lengthy gestation gave my ideas time to develop. This is true particularly of the law and geography interface in environmental assessment which I attribute to my work with Carolyn Harrison at the Geography Department, UCL, and the influence of work by amongst others Nick Blomley, David Delaney, and John Adams. The lengthy period spent writing this book is also due to the rapid development of the field. When I submitted my doctoral thesis on environmental assessment to Warwick University in 1995, there was only one judgment from the European Court of Justice of any significance on this subject, and only rudimentary analysis of this, then, new instrument in the United Kingdom courts. By the time I had finished writing this book several years (and three children) later, the case law and related theoretical literature on environmental governance had grown enormously. I have particularly benefited from the way in which Joanne Scott and Liz Fisher have made sense of these developments in the European Union context.

I would also like to recognize the valuable contribution to my thinking about this subject made by undergraduate and postgraduate students at UCL and other colleges in the University of London over many years. Several stand out as excellent students and, more importantly, have made significant contributions to environmental law: Joseph Chun, Maria Adebowale, Darren Abrahams, Caroline Blatch, Oren Perez, Hugh Wilkins, Ainne Ryall, Charles Butler, Chris Dodwell, and Bruce Monnington. It has been particularly gratifying to draw upon their work when writing this book. Over many years, I have found the environmental statement archives maintained at the EIA Centre, University of Manchester, a valuable resource. The Centre has made a great contribution to both academic reflection and the practice of environmental assessment (thanks also to Kevin Anderson for much appreciated hospitality when working in Manchester). I have also benefited from my correspondence with practising lawyers, particularly Stephen Hockman, William Upton, Gregory Rose, Denzil Millichap, and Morag Ellis. Ludwig Krämer's help was invaluable in drawing up the case study on the internal use of environmental assessment at the European Commission. Tim Jewell at DEFRA, Nigel Baker at the Environment Agency, Peter Clibbon at Global Renewable Energy Partners, Jon Curson at English Nature, Mike Wood and Lloyd Austin at RSPB (Scotland), and Alan Todd of the Highland Council all helped enormously with the other case studies. Many thanks also to Jessica Hughes for keeping me on the administrative straight and narrow, and helping me to compile the appendices, bibliography, and figures.

Importantly, I would like to recognize the support, financial and otherwise, given to me by the Faculty of Laws, UCL in terms of research grants and sabbatical leave and for an enlightened maternity leave policy. I would like to thank my academic colleagues, in particular Michael Freeman, my mentor for many years (and whose energy and enthusiasm continues to astound me), David O'Keeffe and Margot Horspool, for making a great teaching team, Jeffrey Jowell, for stimulating my interest in planning law and policy, William Twining, for his encouragement and guidance over the years, Richard Macrory, who has created a dynamic Centre for Law and Environment at the Faculty, and Philippe Sands, also an invaluable member of the Centre, who has generously shared his expertise on environmental assessment with me. I extend my grateful thanks to colleagues beyond UCL with whom I have taught and from whom I have learnt much, in particular Maria Lee, Antonia Layard, Jurgen Lefevere, Michael Purdue, and William Howarth (who additionally read the manuscript and so deserves special thanks). My greatest thanks though go to Donald McGillivray, who provides intellectual stimulation, encouragement, principled standards (in life as in work), and music on a daily basis.

The law is generally stated on the basis of sources available on 1 March 2004. I have not covered in any great detail the provisions of the Planning and Compulsory Purchase Bill because of the possibility that these will be amended or abandoned. At the time of going to press, the Environmental Assessment of Plans and Programmes Regulations (SI 2004, No. 1633) were adopted (see http://www.hms. gov.uk/si/si2004/20041633.htm).

All author's royalties will go to the Environmental Law Foundation.

JH

Barcombe
March 2004

Contents—Summary

Contents

List of Tables

List of Figures

Table of Cases

Table of Cases

European Court of Justice and Court of First Instance

United States of America

Table of Statutes

UNITED KINGDOM STATUTES

UNITED KINGDOM STATUTORY INSTRUMENTS

EUROPEAN COMMUNITY LEGISLATION

Directives

Table of Conventions and International Declarations

1

Introduction: Law, Governance, and Environmental Assessment

Environmental assessment[1] describes a process of predicting the likely effects of a proposed project, plan, or policy on the environment prior to a decision being made about whether these should proceed. Environmental assessment has become a constant refrain in the language of environmental law. The development and refining of this legal form reflects and has also shaped key developments in other areas of environmental law, particularly the move towards integration of legal controls. This gathering of environmental law around environmental assessment may be seen as an example of the convergent evolution of environmental law,[2] with the maturing of environmental assessment regimes signifying the growing conceptual coherence of environmental law as a discipline, worthy of its own principles, regimes, and methodologies and distinct from related areas such as planning law. Whilst the emergence and development of environmental assessment as a regulatory mechanism is therefore of interest in itself, it may also be considered as a mainframe of environmental law, onto which current thinking and concerns are projected and given practical expression.

Environmental assessment has a long history in the United Kingdom, but it may be said to have fully penetrated social and political life when references to it appeared on both the front *and* back pages of the *Evening Standard* one day. On the front page the paper declared 'Car Charges Get Go-Ahead', describing the London Mayor's victory in the High Court over implementing his plan to impose a daily charge to drive into central London. The judge rejected the objectors' call for a public inquiry and a more detailed analysis of the likely environmental impacts of the plan, finding that the Mayor had acted within the law.[3] He did

---

[1] On terminology, I refer to 'environmental assessment' when discussing collectively the environmental impact assessment (of projects) and 'strategic environmental assessment' (of plans, programmes, and policies). For a definition and outline of the environmental assessment process, see Ch. 2, pp. 33–42.

[2] O. A. Houck, 'Of Bats, Birds and B-A-T: The Convergent Evolution of Environmental Law' (1994) 63 *Miss L J* 403. This refers to the convergence of environmental law around one approach, a tendency seen also in the evolution of species, according to the principle that 'over time, the job will select the tool' (at 407).

[3] *R v Mayor of London ex parte Preece and Adamson* [2002] EWHC 2440, QBD, reported in the *Evening Standard*, 31 July 2002, Maurice Kay J. This issue was also the subject of a Parliamentary question (Hansard, 5 March 2002 187W). It elicited the following answer from the Minister of Transport, John Speller, MP: 'The proposed London congestion charging scheme does not fall

comment that 'a more cautious mayor' may have tried to support his judgment with a public inquiry and, by implication, a voluntary environmental statement. Environmental assessment was at the hub of public concern in this case, even in a counter-intuitive sense, since the objectors, Westminster Council and Kennington Association residents' group, argued that the charge was a breach of their human rights, would turn routes on the edge of the charging zone into 'rat-runs', and would do little to curb pollution. They considered that a more detailed environmental assessment might have *qualified* the environmental arguments supporting the Mayor's scheme.

Over on the sports pages, the lead story was Fulham Football Club's failure to redevelop their Craven Cottage ground, and their search for alternative premises.[4] Local residents had already made two bids to force a reappraisal of the club's plans to build a 28,000-seat stadium, financed by building a block of flats on its boundary overlooking the River Thames and, arguably, damaging the habitats of plants, invertebrates, fish, and birds in the river. One such attempt had reached the House of Lords in a case concerning whether the Secretary of State's grant of planning permission for the development of the site should be quashed on the ground that he had not considered whether there should have been an environmental assessment of the proposal.[5] In giving the judgment, Lord Hoffman underlined that the key function of the environmental assessment process is not merely the provision of information (in which case a 'paper chase' could be treated as the equivalent of an environmental statement), but ensuring adequate public participation. The judge, somewhat disparagingly, held that 'the directly enforceable right of the citizen which is accorded by the [EC Environmental Impact Assessment (EIA)] Directive[6] . . . requires the inclusive and democratic procedure prescribed by the Directive in which the public, however misguided or wrong headed its views may be, is given an opportunity to express its opinion on the environmental issues'.[7] The legality of Fulham Football Club's development of its site, as enshrined in *Berkeley No. 1*, reached to the heart of environmental assessment as a regulatory mechanism; that is, whether it is capable

within the scope of Directive 85/337/EEC (as amended by Directive 97/11/EC) on the assessment of the effects of certain public and private projects on the environment'.

[4] 'Fulham Search for New Ground', *Evening Standard*, 31 July 2002.

[5] *Berkeley* v *Secretary of State for the Environment and Fulham Football Club* ('*Berkeley No. 1*') [2000] WLR 420, [2001] AC 603, (2001) 13 *JEL* 89, discussed in Ch. 7, at pp. 220–1, and also see commentary by W. Upton, 'The EIA Process and the Directly Enforceable Rights of Citizens' (2001) 13 *JEL* 98. This case was followed by *Berkeley* v *Secretary of State for the Environment, Transport and the Regions and Fulham Football Club (Berkeley No. 2)* (1998) *The Times*, 7.4.1998, CA (concerning costs which were not awarded, as an expression of disapproval of anything but the highest standards of administrative behaviour). See also *Berkeley* v *Secretary of State for the Environment, Transport and the Regions (Berkeley No. 3)* (2002) 14 *JEL* 331, (2002) JPL 224 [2002] Env LR 14, discussed further in Ch. 4, pp. 121–3, which, although not directed at Fulham Football Club, concerns the application of environmental assessment procedures in the same part of London, and brought by the same applicant.

[6] Directive 85/337/EEC on the assessment of the effects of certain public and private projects on the environment, OJ 1985 L 175, p. 40, as amended by Directive 97/11/EC OJ 1997 L 73, p. 5, hereafter the EC EIA Directive.   [7] *Berkeley No. 1*, at 430.

of bringing about a fundamental change in the quality, nature, and culture of decision making.

In these cases law was engaged in dilemmas about the appropriate balance between nature and development, and the meaning of environmental protection, through a regulatory mechanism which on its face represents a common-sense, even mundane search for information about the likely effects on the environment of a particular project, plan, or policy, but which also provides an opportunity for participation and protest. In this book I attempt to analyse this engagement. Athough seemingly a thoroughly modern endeavour, stories of environmental assessment may also be drawn from historical sources which nevertheless address similar developmental or conservatory dilemmas. For example, the ancient writ of *ad quod damnum* provided a means of examining whether public works such as land drainage and channel dredging (carried out by individual undertakers or adventurers with a licence from the Crown) could proceed and whether compensation was required for those who had suffered damage. The writ originated in the general requirement that the Crown ascertain whether gifts of land to religious institutions would adversely affect its right to receive income from the land. This then developed in the different context of public works, so that whenever a person planned to build a public work, such as a sea wall, they had to bring an action '*ad quod damnum* to know what damage it shall be to the king and others'.[8] In this respect the Crown represented the public interest. When the writ was issued, a jury was called together and asked to determine the nature of such damage. Rudimentary notice was also to be given to other affected people. The practice of the *ad quod damnum* writ of the thirteenth and fourteenth centuries suggests a very early type of environmental assessment rule exercised by the Crown. The impulses for modern forms of environmental assessment are all present—precaution, balance between competing interests, procedural fairness—as well as some of the guiding ideas of contemporary environmental thought such as valuing nature, defining the public benefit, and empowering and engaging the public via citizen juries. There are also parallels in terms of the writ's main mechanism, the compensation for the loss of a natural resource, and the attempts on the part of modern economists to evaluate the value of such resources using compensation as a hypothetical measure.

The following accounts of the writ, written by William Dugdale in 1662,[9] are taken from Bosselman's pioneering and scholarly work on land development in English wetlands.[10] The objective of including these is to put the various theories and expositions of environmental assessment discussed in this book into perspective. Rules to shape decisions about potentially harmful development have existed for

---

[8] F. P. Bosselman, 'Limitations in the Title to Wetlands at Common Law' (1996) *15 Stan L J* 247 at 292.

[9] W. Dugdale, *The History of the Imbanking and Drayning of Divers Fenns and Marshes 17* (London: Alice Warren, 1662), at 42. Quoted in Bosselman, 'Limitations in the Title to Wetlands' at 294.

[10] Bosselman, 'Limitations in the Title to Wetlands' 247.

a long time. They have evolved functionally, and often reflect a pragmatic, rather than scientific or justiciable approach to the allocation of natural resources.

In 20 Edward II the Prior of Bilsyntone representing to the King; that whereas *John Maunsell,* the founder of that monastery, had given to the Canons of that House and their Successors, the Mannour of Over Bilsyntone, with the appurtenances; whereunto a certain salt Marsh situate in Lyde, neer Romenale, containing 60 Acres, did belong: which both at the time of the said grant, and since, had alwayes drowned by the flowings of the Sea humbly petitioned, that he would please to grant licence for the drayning thereof; and that it might be reduced to culture, by the defence of Banks, according to the Marsh Law. Whereupon the said King issued forth a Writ of *Ad quod damnum* to his Escaetor or his County, commanding him to enquire whether the same might be effected without prejudice to himself or others. Upon which enquiry, the Jury certified upon their Oaths, that it might: and that the said Marsh contained of itself 240 perches in length, and 40 perches in bredth; and that it was of no value before the drayning, and banking thereof; but that being so banked and drayned, it might be yearly worth 30 shillings every Acre prized at 6 pence . . .

In II Edward III upon a Writ of *Ad quod damnum,* the Jury certified, that it would not be prejudicial to the King or any other, if licence were given to John then Archbishop of Canterbury, and to the Prior of *Christs-Church* in Canterbury, to suffer an antient Trench, leading from an arm of the Sea called Apuldre, towards the town of Romeney, which passed through the proper soyl of the said Archbishop and Prior, and which was then newly so obstructed by the Sea-sands, that Ships could not passe thereby, to the said town of Romeney, as they used; to be wholly stopped up and filled, so that they the said Archbishop and Prior might make their benefit there of as they thought fit; in regard that there then was a certain other Trench, leading from the said arm unto Romeney, lately made by the force of the Sea, by which Ships and Boats might passe, without impediment to the said town, as they had wont to do by the other, before it was so filled up. And they said moreover, that the said antient Trench was the proper soyl, of the before-specified Archbishop, Prior, and *Margaret de Basynge;* and that it had been obstructed in such a sort, by the space of 30 years and more then last past, by the Silt and Sea-sands, as that Ships could not conveniently passe that way: And that the new Trench was more proper and sufficient, whilst it was open, than the said old one, for the passage of Ships to Romeney above-mentioned; and did so remain at that time: And moreover, that the same new Trench was the soyl of the said Archbishop, Prior, and Covent, *Margaret de Basynges,* and the Abbott of Robertswigge. And lastly, that the said old Trench contained in length *viiC.* perches, and in bredth x. And the new one *vC.* perches in length, and in bredth xx.

Also seen in the history of the writ is the gradual codification of environmental inquiry and decision making: *ad quod damnum* was gradually replaced over time by Private Acts of Parliament and the appointment of special courts ('Courts of Sewers' or 'Commissioners of Sewers') to administer wetland management projects and deal with wetland disputes. Such Acts were described as 'Parliamentary *ad quod damnum*',[11] although a fundamental difference was that affected

[11] *R* v *Inhabitants of Flecklow,* 1 Butt 461, 466, 97 Eng Rep 403 (1758).

parties were not compensated, as had been the case with the writ of *ad quod damnum*. The replacement of the writ with the parliamentary procedure and specialized courts was described by Robert Callis in 1622:[12]

And whereas it is formerly alleged, that the wariness of the common law was such in these cases, that it admitted not one such new trench, river, or new cut to be made, without the awarding out of the writ of *ad quod damn'* directed to the ascheator, an officer sworn to enquire, first, what damage it might be if such a new cut or drain were made? and then upon his inquisition it were found convenient, else not to, be proceeded farther in. But in answer thereto, being the argument set down in the said case of the Isle of Ely, I am of the opinion that there may be more wary and circumspect proceedings by this commission, than in the *ad quod damn'* by the escheator; for there be many Commissioners which be all sworn, and in the *ad quod damn'* there is but one, the escheator . . . and in my opinion, it is much better to commit this weighty business to many Commissioners of great gravity, experence, learning, wisdom and integrity, than to one escheator, who may perhaps want all these virtues.

It is possible to overstate the similarities between the *ad quod damnum* writ and modern environmental assessment procedures. In particular, perceptions of what is 'potentially harmful development' have changed greatly over time, for example historic concerns about land drainage seem remarkably concrete compared to the uncertainties of many modern 'environmental' concerns. Nevertheless it is worth taking account of Bosselman's observations on the writ, particularly considering its parallels to modern environmental assessment procedures: 'practice under the writ of *ad quod damnum* seems to have provided a flexible procedure by which development could be allowed to proceed on condition that the developer pay damages to persons who would suffer economic loss . . . the writ was not designed to prevent changes to wetlands but to ensure that the changes were consistent with the public interest'.[13]

In this book modern environmental assessment provides a focal point for examining the relationship between law, environmental governance, and the regulation of decision making.[14] The related evolution of a body of environmental law is particularly important. The development of environmental law is a legal success story (which may be compared with its *environmental* 'success' or effectiveness). Environmental law has grown as a discipline, with its own professional groupings, legal language (albeit one littered with acronyms), and conceptual apparatus. The establishment of environmental law as a settled legal discipline is in part recognition of the potential role of law in the anticipation and regulation of

---

[12] R. Callis, *Reading upon the Statute of Sewers* 137 (William John Broderip ed., 4th edn., 1824).

[13] Bosselman, 'Limitations in the Title to Wetlands', at 296.

[14] In this book, I attribute a broader meaning to decision making than others. See, for example, Richardson's simple classification of public decision making as 'policy formation, policy application, and policy validification', in G. Richardson, 'The Legal Regulation of Process', in G. Richardson and H. Genn (eds.) *Administrative Law and Government Action* (Oxford: Clarendon, 1994), 105. This book includes within the scope of decision making, standard setting (e.g. thresholds and criteria) and consent procedures from which legal, and practical, effects flow (i.e. permission to develop an area of land).

the repercussions of human activities on the environment. The great expansion of models of environmental assessment is a clear expression of this because, very simply, environmental assessment forces explicit consideration of the potential effects of such activities. By doing this, environmental assessment provides a procedural framework for decision making but, formally at least, does not regulate the substance of the decision—the outcome. This may be considered its essential, or defining, characteristic. Equally importantly, it provides opportunities for a broad constituency of people and groups to become informed and to a limited extent engage in the decision-making process. Law contributes to these functions by demarcating the limits of discretion (as to when to conduct an assessment, according to the likelihood of significant environmental effects), offering opportunities for involvement by interested groups, and specifying the manner in which information ascertained in the assessment process is to be used in decision making.

Environmental assessment allows for an exchange of information between government, industry, environmentalists, and the public, and indeed relies on this for its effectiveness. An important example of this is the enhanced responsibility of the developer or proponent conferred by the environmental assessment process to provide information on which a decision is based (also to monitor continuing impacts and identify areas for improving conduct) and thereby shape in some manner the outcome of that decision. This suggests some conjoining of the roles of the consenting authority and the developer in environmental assessment.

This combination of characteristics in environmental assessment and law exemplifies many of the key strains attributed to new forms of governance, including enhanced opportunities for participation in decision making, with many sites and scales of interaction between government and non-governmental bodies, and the blurring of traditional divisions between the public regulation of environmental problems, and the role of private actors. The legal and administrative complexity of environmental assessment, and the opportunities for interest in the form of regulation that it represents, are well described by Ost:

It is intended to supply scientific illumination for a decision of a political nature. This implies bringing about a dialogue between two largely heterogeneous discourses—each presenting, for instance, their own spatio-temporal framework. But it is also asked to bring out questions and objections of a 'popular' nature during an administrative procedure. And still more fundamentally, it is supposed to allow the expression of a democratic logic (broad information, public enquiry, adversary debate) in the course of a process which is more of a private, technocratic nature.[15]

Although Ost tends to suggest a disjunction between science and popularism which is now increasingly questioned, the quotation importantly highlights how environmental assessment, as an inherently interdisciplinary mechanism, clearly bears upon areas of scientific, social, political, and legal life.

---

[15] F. Ost, 'A Game Without Rules? The Ecological Self-Organisation of Firms', in G. Teubner, L. Farmer, and D. Murphy (eds.) *Environmental Law and Ecological Responsibility* (Chichester: Wiley, 1994), at 351.

Environmental assessment is therefore well placed as an analytical tool to examine aspects of the relationship between law, environmental, governance, and the regulation of decision making. However, it is currently an undertheorized phenomenon. Excusing the tendency to hyperbole, as Bartlett points out, '[A]lthough impact assessment is one of the major innovations in policy making and administration of the twentieth century, so far it has received little attention from political or policy theorists, who have tended to underestimate and misread its power, complexity, and subtlety'.[16] It is a rare introduction that does not include such sentiments. Nevertheless, that environmental assessment has received so little attention from theorists is remarkable because of its high profile within environmental law, representing as it does the apogee of an integrated and interdisciplinary approach, and because of the sheer quantity of case law now being generated on the subject (although relatively recently described as 'legal territory of some obscurity and considerable technicality'[17]). Much of this is the 'bread and butter' of legal practice, before courts in the United Kingdom and before the European Court of Justice. Should an environmental assessment be conducted?[18] Do revived permissions trigger an assessment process?[19] Can one development be split into several projects, neither of which individually requires environmental assessment but which together are likely to have significant environmental and social impacts?[20] What is the meaning of 'development consent' for the purposes of applying environmental assessment rules?[21]

In the context of such questions, the battles of environment and development are played out. Decisions about how and where we live and work, how we travel, what landscapes we see, and the effect of all these issues on the state of our health are supported or refuted by information derived from the environmental assessment process, much of which is not subject to legal scrutiny.[22] Admittedly, the framework for environmental assessment is legally determined, and is frequently

---

[16] R. V. Bartlett, 'Ecological Reason in Administration: Environmental Impact Assessment and Administrative Theory', in R. Paehlke and D. Torgerson (eds.) *Managing Leviathan: Environmental Politics and the Administrative State* (London: Belhaven, 1990), 82.

[17] *Berkeley No. 1* [1998] Env LR 741, 759, per Thorpe LJ (CA).

[18] For example, *Berkeley No. 1; Twyford Parish Council v Secretary of State for Transport* (1992) 4 *JEL* 273, on which see Ch. 6, pp. 219–20 and Ch. 7, pp. 257–8.

[19] As in *R v North Yorkshire County Council ex parte Brown and Cartwright* (1999) JPL 616, on which see Ch. 6, at pp. 207–8.

[20] As in the cases of *R v Swale Borough Council ex parte Royal Society for the Protection of Birds* (1991) 3 *JEL* 135, and Case C-392/96 *Commission v Ireland* [1999] ECR I-5901, see Ch. 4.

[21] *R v London Borough of Hammersmith and Fulham ex parte CPRE ('White City')* [2000] Env LR 532 (HL); *R (Barker) v London Borough of Bromley ('Crystal Palace')* [2002] Env LR 638, and others, see Ch. 6, at pp. 211–18. The Secretary of State has issued a note on this area of environmental assessment law so that local authorities and developers may avoid the 'pitfalls' of controversial case law; Office of the Deputy Prime Minister, 'A Government Note on the Environmental Impact Assessment Directive', (2002) JPL 1067.

[22] Although important work in this area has been done, for example, W. Sheate, *Environmental Impact Assessment: Law and Policy* (London: Cameron May, 1996) and S. Tromans and K. Fuller, *Environmental Impact Assessment: Law and Practice* (London: Butterworths, 2003). The latter in particular provides a comprehensive guide to law relating to environmental assessment and current good practice.

the subject of legal dispute, but what takes place within the environmental assessment process, and what type of knowledge is fed into decision making, has not been the subject of sustained legal and critical scrutiny. My aim in writing this book is to contribute to this scrutiny. My main finding is simple: environmental assessment is highly material to the outcome of a decision. This challenges the presentation of environmental assessment as an example of legal reflexivity, particularly that it operates as an indirect, abstract form of legal control because of its inherently procedural nature. This argument in the book suggests the rematerialization of this aspect of environmental assessment law. By this I mean that environmental assessment engages the developer or proponent of a project or policy in the decision-making process, and may be used to express or pursue particular interests or values in the final decision. The main point here is that, contrary to understanding, environmental assessment is *not* entirely procedural. It has important substantive consequences, suggesting that the procedural–substantive dichotomy is not so clear as has been supposed. This is not to use theories about the rematerialization of law[23] to describe law directly regulating social behaviour by defining substantive prescriptions or substantive standards, but rather to describe the not infrequent use of environmental assessment procedures as a means to advance and legitimize a particular project on a particular site.[24] In advancing this argument I aim to highlight particular uses of environmental assessment, not to discredit the procedure, nor deny the existence of good practice in the area.[25]

This conclusion gives me good reason to be dubious about some of the functions of environmental assessment and to suggest that it is capable of assimilating developers' interests into decision-making procedures, rather than necessarily improving the environmental quality of outcomes. This argument draws upon an examination of the nature of environmental knowledge which is gathered during the assessment process, particularly how that knowledge is shaped by law. This finding is informed by analysis of case studies which help also to bring to life the practice and purpose of decision making using environmental assessment.[26] These case studies are on several developments *du jour*, most of which are ongoing: a flood defence strategy in Lewes, East Sussex;[27] an offshore windfarm to provide renewable energy on the Kentish Flats;[28] the development of internal assessment procedures in the European Commission;[29] the development of a 'global' port at Dibden Bay, Hampshire;[30] and a tourist development to encourage skiing in the Cairngorms.[31] The function of these case studies is not to represent a larger

[23] For example as expressed by G. Teubner, 'Substantive and Reflexive Elements in Modern Law' (1983) *L and Soc Rev* 239.   [24] See in particular Ch. 7, pp. 240–1.

[25] Examples of good practice are issued by the Institute of Environmental Management and Assessment, for example, IEMA, *Perspectives: Guidelines on Participation in Decision Making* (Lincoln: IEMA, 2002).

[26] In adopting this use of the case study, I follow the approach advanced by J. C. Mitchell, 'Case and Situation Analysis' (1983) *Sociol Rev* 188, at 207.   [27] See Ch. 3, pp. 86–94.

[28] See Ch. 4, pp. 140–6.   [29] See Ch. 5, pp. 164–76.

[30] See Ch. 6, pp. 227–9.   [31] See Ch. 7, pp. 272–81.

population of project or development, but rather to establish some essential features which characterize the cases studied and permit analysis of how theories or principles of environmental assessment may manifest themselves in a particular set of events.

The pluralist nature of the environmental assessment process, in terms of the range and roles of the participants, the sites in which it operates, and the disciplines that it draws upon have influenced the methodology of this research. For example, I accordingly broadened the focus of my inquiry beyond reported case law, to take in other legal texts such as development plans and decision letters,[32] and attended inquiries and public planning and consultation meetings. More unusually in a legal work, I have paid particular attention to the environmental statement and representations made about this by interested parties and statutory consultees. This is in recognition that, whilst the overall environmental assessment is conducted by the consenting or governing authority, this is necessarily based upon an environmental statement, generally produced by the developer or proponent of a policy. This means that in practice the centre of gravity of the environmental assessment process is the proponent's statement (Lord Bingham has described it as the 'cornerstone' of the environmental assessment regime[33]) ensuring that responsibility for information gathering in the environmental assessment process, and arguably wider decision making, is shared.

The provision of information on the likely significant effects of a project or plan on the environment in the form of an environmental statement is the central *legal* requirement of environmental assessment regimes, but the nature of this information is multidisciplinary—natural science, geography, engineering, and sociology all play an important part (the environmental statement or report is normally written by a number of experts working in different fields, and overseen by an environmental consultant). This text especially is a product of the pluralism of the environmental assessment process and also contributes to it, creating a necessary focal point for interdisciplinary inquiry. Notwithstanding the opportunities for interdisciplinarity, the bulk of information included within the environmental statement is quantitative and describes the extrapolation of baseline data using models. Importantly, even this type of information is no more than a prediction, frequently presented as fact. In contrast, qualitative judgments included in an environmental statement are usually derived from limited participation requirements. In this context, an important finding is that such judgments (or participative subjectivity)—values, local opinion, perceptions—may be marginalized according to criteria which appear to be objective, such as compliance with an existing hierarchy of law,[34] resulting in the possible devaluation of 'non-expert' opinion. This is because impacts which can be measured tend to receive more

[32] On the variety of legal texts in the planning system, see G. Myerson and Y. Rydin, 'Environment and Planning: A Tale of the Mundane and the Sublime' (1994) 12 *Environmental and Planning D: Space and Society* 432.   [33] *Berkeley No. 1*, at 423.
[34] See case study on Lewes Flood Defence Strategy, Ch. 3, pp. 86–94.

weight in decision making than less tangible (though no less important) non-quantifiable information.

My further aim in basing empirical work upon a range of legal texts, but particularly the environmental statement, is to refocus the attention that lawyers have tended to pay to the rapidly growing body of case law on environmental assessment, generated from the ambiguities, inconsistencies, and lacunas of the governing legislation at various levels. Whilst an appreciation of that growth is appropriate in a book of this kind, discussion of case law is restricted to the key legal determinants of environmental assessment—discretion, significance of environmental impacts, alternatives, rights of participation, and procedural control of decision making. I keep in view that reported cases are the decontextualized accidents of litigation rather than representations of environmental assessment in practice. In addition, very little environmental information may be garnered from case law, particularly when compared with 'developmental' information such as that on the likely delays and costs to be incurred should environmental assessment procedures be invoked; the imbalance between the two categories of information suggesting that the inherent restrictiveness of judicial review procedures is not entirely responsible for this. With some exceptions,[35] a more rounded view of the dilemmas faced was obtained from reading a broader range of texts, including (but not exclusively) environmental statements, in the course of compiling the illustrative case studies.[36]

In terms of the scope of the book, I develop a broadly drawn concept of 'environmental assessment' as a mechanism for regulating decision making having environmental effects, so that I include for analysis several sites of decision making: land use, pollution control, habitat protection, and policy making. This is to take a cue from *ad quod damnum*, the medieval form of environmental assessment which was called upon to deal with a great variety of (proposed and actual) development (sea defences, wetland activities such as draining and channelling, road and bridge building).[37] This approach differs from the more restrictive view of the purview of modern environmental assessment which has hitherto prevailed in the United Kingdom, so that analysis of environmental assessment has tended to focus upon its employment in town and country planning. The breadth of sites of assessment also reflects the growing tendency of environmental assessment to be applied to a range of contexts other than development control, an evolution I refer to as the colonization of decision making by environmental assessment.[38]

---

[35] For example, the European Court of Justice is unusually fulsome in its explanation of the environmental consequences of afforestation, peat extraction, land reclamation, and sheep farming in Case C-392/96 *Commission v Ireland* [1999] ECR I-5091, at paras. 78–81.

[36] As outlined above, p. 8.   [37] See above, pp. 3–5.

[38] As outlined in Ch. 2. On the broadening scope of applications of environmental assessment in the European Union, see H. Vedder, 'The New Community Guidelines on State Aid for Environmental Protection: Integrating Environment and Competition' (2001) *Eur Comp L Rev* 365. Further afield, see G. Bates, 'Environmental Assessment: Australia's New Outlook under the Environment and Biodiversity Conservation Act 1999' (2000) 4 *Env L Rev* 203, on the broadening scope of 'controlled actions' under Australian environmental law.

The argument in favour of producing an environmental assessment to determine the consequences of the introduction of congestion charges discussed at the beginning of this chapter[39] attests to this. Also in terms of the scope of the book, the analysis is rooted in the United Kingdom, and draws particularly upon the law and policy of environmental assessment in England and Wales, though I have sought to reflect the situation in Scotland. My hopeful expectation is that the analysis is more broadly applicable, and will be of interest to academics, students, and lawyers beyond the United Kingdom.

Having explained the influences on the research methodology that I have used, and the effect of this on the scope of the book and the use of texts which formed the basis of analysis, I wish to acknowledge a limitation of this book. I have tried (unsuccessfully) for many years to answer (usually in response to students' questions) what is perhaps the most important question in this area: What *difference* has environmental assessment made? Because an essential characteristic of environmental assessment is that it does not sanction a particular outcome, the contribution of environmental information to a final decision is difficult to determine. When answering the 'What Difference?' question I have therefore had to rely upon my own evaluation of its contribution, based upon my impression of decision-making processes, through analysis of cases and other legal and planning texts, and having talked to those involved in making decisions. In this book, I respond to the question by rephrasing it (which is easier to do than when facing a class of students) so that I address how law deals with and, most importantly, sanctions environmental change through environmental assessment. This is not to ignore the question about the difference that environmental assessment law has made to environmental protection but rather, through empirical analysis, to consider the ways in which environmental assessment, shaped by law, provides certain conditions, or expectations for decision making. This aim accords with Bartlett's warning about studying environmental assessment:

the theorist or analyst who looks only for dramatic impacts or only for obvious direct effects is likely to be unimpressed. Comprehending the significance and potential of EIA requires appreciation of the complexity of ways that choices are shaped, channeled, learned, reasoned, and structured before they are officially made. When EIA succeeds in making far-reaching modifications in the substantive outcomes of social activities, it does so by changing formally, and informally, the premises and rules for arriving at legitimate decisions.[40]

In summary, the interconnected nature of law, environmental governance, and decision making within the context of environmental assessment forms the subject of this book, particularly Chapters 5, 6, and 7, in which I undertake to show the linkages between participatory democracy, regulatory theory, and the practicalities of decision making, based upon several illustrative case studies.

[39] *Ex parte Preece and Adamson.*
[40] Bartlett, 'Ecological Reason in Administration', at 91. Although, see also arguments, Ch. 6, p. 186.

Because the boundaries and connections between these areas are not easy to differentiate, I here outline the relevance of each of these areas to environmental assessment. This is done in the course of identifying the key characteristics of the generic legal form of environmental assessment, and mapping out the structure of the book, particularly marking the relevance of case studies on environmental assessment. In summary, I use environmental assessment as a way into the potentially huge subject of the 'greening' of governance. In this respect, I follow the lead of previous writers,[41] particularly those who have considered the impact of an environmental agenda on decision making,[42] but depart from these by making a sustained critique on a single instrument (albeit broadly defined), beyond the more familiar view of environmental assessment in national law, driven by developments in the European Union.

Even accounting for substantial variations between definitions of assessment and correspondingly different laws on environmental assessment,[43] a generic legal form may be identified. This is characterized by the prediction of significant effects on the environment, the consideration of alternatives, and the inclusion of environmental criteria in broader decision making (the ecologization of decision making), providing a forum for participation, negotiation, and protest, and establishing a framework for decision making (the regulation of decision making). The legal form of environmental assessment is also the subject of a process of standardization in both public fora (best practice guidelines, international treaties) and private realms (for example, in contracts for construction). The identification of these characteristics, outlined below, and elaborated in subsequent chapters, corresponds to the stages of a model environmental assessment process, and reflects also the basic structure of the book, thus combining a conceptual analysis of environmental assessment with a structural understanding of the process.

The Generic Legal Form

Prediction

The central characteristic of the legal form of environmental assessment is the requirement that a prediction be made about the likely significant effects (both

---

[41] For example, H. Heinelt, T. Malek, and A. E. Toller (eds.) *European Union Environmental Policy and New Forms of Governance* (Aldershot: Ashgate, 2001) use environmental assessment and the Eco-Management and Audit Scheme to explore governance; A. Weale, G. Pridham *et al.*, *Environmental Governance in Europe: An Ever Closer Ecological Union?* (Oxford: Oxford University Press, 2000), Ch. 10, similarly refer to case studies in the policy process. This methodological approach was first adopted by J. Scott, in respect of Directive 61/96/EC on Integrated Pollution Prevention and Control in 'Flexibility, "Proceduralisation" and Environmental Governance in the EU', in G. de Búrca and J. Scott (eds.) *The Changing Constitution of the EU: From Uniformity to Flexibility* (Oxford: Hart, 2000).

[42] J. Steele, 'Participation and Deliberation in Environmental Law: Exploring a Problem-Solving Approach' (2001) *OJLS* 415; and L. Fisher, 'Is the Precautionary Principle Justiciable?' (2001) 13 *JEL* 315.   [43] These form the subject of Ch. 2.

positive and negative) of a project, plan, or piece of legislation. The prediction of environmental effects is required only in circumstances defined by law, usually in the form of thresholds, which to some extent reduce the discretion available to the decision maker as to whether an assessment should be conducted or not. However, there is a vague quality to these thresholds; the test of the likelihood of 'significant' environmental effects contained in the EC EIA Directive is a prime example of this.[44] I therefore discuss how techniques, particularly environmental modelling, are used to predict these likely effects and thus provide an apparently acceptable basis for making decisions.[45] The hallowed preventative and (possibly) precautionary qualities of environmental assessment flow from this requirement. It is, however, inevitable that uncertainty enters the assessment process because the accurate futuristic interpretation of data to provide predictions is difficult, sometimes impossible.[46] In short, environmental assessment deals 'with events which have not yet occurred, may not occur, and whose chance of occurrence may be changed by the very statement that they may occur'.[47] From a legal perspective there is also a circularity about this general requirement because an assessment of sorts must be made as to the likely effects of the policy or development prior to the assessment being formally conducted. The necessarily predictive quality of the decision whether to conduct an assessment in the first place is possibly the 'central conundrum' of environmental assessment.[48]

A guiding theme of the tension between objectivity and subjectivity in the collection and interpretation of information emerges from the legal requirement that a prediction must be made of the likely environmental effects of a change in physical circumstances brought about by land development, policy, or legislation. A disjuncture emerges between the apparent objectivity of the prediction of environmental effects, which forms the basis of the environmental assessment process in pursuance of an idea of ecological rationality,[49] and the real nature of environmental assessment steeped in subjective opinion.[50] Subjectivity is also referred to positively, in the sense of the attribution of meaning and values to statistics. A key question here is whether the varied forms of participation described in contemporary deliberative theories are capable of substantially reducing the reliance upon

---

[44] Art. 2(4) of the EIA Directive. The test is similar in the case of the assessment of plans and programmes, as provided for in Art. 3 of EC Directive 2001/42/EC [2001] OJ L 197, p. 30 (hereafter the EC Directive on SEA) and in the case of environmental impact assessment in a transboundary context, as required by Art. 2 of the Espoo Convention. See further Ch. 4, at p. 101.

[45] In Ch. 3.

[46] R. B. Gibson, 'Respecting Ignorance and Uncertainty', in E. Lykke (ed.) *Achieving Environmental Goals: The Concept and Practice of Environmental Performance Review* (London: Belhaven, 1992), 170–1; see also P. de Jongh, 'Uncertainty in Environmental Impact Assessment', in P. Wathern (ed.) *Environmental Impact Assessment: Theory and Practice* (London: Routledge, 1988).

[47] E. Ashby, 'Background to Environmental Impact Assessment', in T. O'Riordan and R. D. Hey (eds.) *Environmental Impact Assessment* (Farnborough: Saxon House, 1976), at 3–4.

[48] On which, see further S. Bell and D. McGillivray, *Ball and Bell on Environmental Law* (Oxford: Oxford University Press, 6th edn., 2005).

[49] On the ecological rationality thesis, see Bartlett, 'Ecological Reason in Administration'.

[50] See Ch. 3, pp. 94–9.

apparently objective, or quantitative, knowledge in environmental assessment. This involves evaluating the contribution and possible complicity of law in the presentation of information as an objective evaluation of the likely environmental change, or risk, to flow from a development, change of policy, or legislation. In the context of a case study on the Lewes Flood Defence Strategy, I discuss how law performs the important function of objectifying information ascertained in the assessment process, sanctioned by the fulfilment of quite limited participation requirements. In this case, an apparently objective process of evaluating various strategic options was in practice derived from simplistically applying a hierarchy of law. The Environment Agency's drawing up of a list of possible strategies was not a product of fully 'engaging the public',[51] but rather derived from a simplistic fidelity to a pre-established hierarchy of norms (in practice by attributing greater weight to centrally set legislative objectives, and less to local or regional policy).[52] This case study questions the conceptual underpinnings of environmental governance approaches,[53] raising issues about when (at what stage) the public should be engaged, but also the effectiveness of this participation in terms of the outcomes of decision making.

Significance

Prediction, whether at the stage of deciding whether an assessment should be conducted, or at the stage at which the assessment *is* conducted, is directed towards judging the likely *significance* of the effects of a development, policy, plan or programme on the environment. This judgment is central to the entire environmental assessment, but is also highly contingent and variable, being dependent upon the effectiveness of mitigating measures, and the cumulative effects of development.[54] The legal treatment of 'significance' raises a central argument in the book: the apparent self-constraint of law in relation to environmental assessment. Although central to many of the decisions and dilemmas concerning environmental assessment, until recently the courts in the United Kingdom have been reluctant to comment upon the meaning of the significance of environmental change (or 'significant environmental effects' as stated in the EC Directive on EIA) necessary to trigger the assessment process, and as the central means by which potential harm is measured. This may be attributed to judicial deference to decision makers, or, more probably, the sheer difficulty of translating such a concept into a legal test, reliant as it is upon interdisciplinary inquiry (an exercise nevertheless conducted with some rigour by state courts in the United States). This raises the issue of whether significance may be better tethered to some legal standard, for example an existing environmental quality

---

[51] As advocated by the Royal Commission on Environment and Pollution, Twenty-first Report, *Setting Environmental Standards*, Cm 4053 (London: HMSO, 1998), ch. 7.
[52] Cf. Ch. 3, pp. 88–9.   [53] See below, pp. 17–19.
[54] Both of these are discussed in relation to significance in Ch. 4, pp. 130–40.

standard.[55] Additionally, findings of significance may be made the subject of enhanced public participation. Analysis of significance in this book is based upon a case study on the proposed offshore windfarm on the Kentish Flats,[56] in which the meaning and manipulation of significance was central to the proponent's case for development consent to be granted. Also in this case, local residents' concerns about changes to the landscape were marginalized in the environmental statement, by the setting of boundaries within which the issue of significance was analysed.

By critically considering the legal framework and role of law, acting through environmental assessment, I offer another explanation for the apparent restraint of law in matters such as the significance of environmental effects. This is that environmental assessment law operates as a frame for sanctioning development with a view to the environmental consequences. Departing from the accepted view of environmental assessment as a necessary conduit for information, environmental assessment may act as a 'battleground' between nature and development (frequently portrayed as progress) so that the role of law in mediating or obscuring conflict, in curtailing the options, or just smoothing out the lumps and bumps of 'participative subjectivity', becomes vital. By concealing the open-ended nature of the concept of significance—by not engaging with it—the law does not acknowledge the subjectivity of the decisions taken and the interests which affect them.

Alternatives

A third, usually sequential, characteristic of the general legal form of environmental assessment is the requirement to consider alternatives to the proposed project, policy, or legislation proposed, discussed in Chapter 5 of this book. I look at this in the context of new approaches to governance and the related search for corresponding forms of regulation. This is closely associated with the twin imperatives of integration[57] and anticipatory control in environmental law. This is because when pollution problems are approached predominantly as problems of air, water, or waste, the traditional solution is usually to move the pollutant to the least protected parts of the environment, whereas integrated systems of pollution control ideally allow alternative processes and products to be judged in the light of all the possible paths or cycles of pollutants in the environment. Environmental harm may therefore be prevented or reduced by identifying

[55] As occurs in the United States, cf. Ch. 7, pp. 239–40. This has been interpreted as providing a link between the substantive and procedural elements of environmental assessment, although the quotation tends to suggest a disjunction between science and popularism which is now discredited.

[56] Ch. 4, pp. 140–6.

[57] 'Integration' is taken to mean integration as between environmental media, or a holistic approach. Of course, 'integration' may also mean making environmental protection a component of other policies, as expressed in Article 6 EC. The latter is discussed in Ch. 5 in the context of the European Union.

possible alternative sites, designs, or technology at an early stage in the process.[58] Recognizing the extent of damage caused by transfers of pollutants between media also provides an incentive to prevent pollution in the first place. At the apogee of this legal requirement is the consideration of alternative policies in strategic environmental assessment which, whilst not representing a complete methodological departure from project-based assessment, operates at a far more abstract level, and is less geographically determined (although it may remain sectorally restricted). Assessment at this level considerably extends the alternatives to be studied, and allows this to take place at a time when it could make a real difference to decision making at lower levels. Too often in project-based environmental assessment the choice of alternatives has been narrowed by prior decisions on the overall strategy to be pursued, for example in transport or energy policy, which in practice restricts the scope of alternatives to a choice between a number of given routes, or processes, and fails to address the cumulative effects of policy choices.[59] A tiered environmental assessment structure may instead operate in which assessments of higher-order policy or plans are conducted first at national or regional level; lower-order programme and project assessments may then be implemented locally.[60] The requirement that alternatives be considered in an integrated and anticipatory manner (across different environmental media and policy sectors and in advance of a final decision) contributes to what may be called, albeit clumsily, the ecologization of governance. To return briefly to the proposed windfarm off the Kentish Flats as a key case on the meaning of alternatives in environmental assessment, the project was itself hailed as an alternative to traditional sources of energy. However, realistic alternatives to the individual project, such as energy conservation programmes, and efficiency savings for existing energy production installations, were not considered beyond a cursory assessment of the appropriateness of the location of the windfarm. Rather, the environmental statement provided the developer with the opportunity to publicize 'The Need for the Kentish Flats Project', particularly with regard to contributing to the United Kingdom's duty under international law to increase the use of renewable forms of energy. The failure to consider 'alternative' options in this case demonstrates the practical limitations of this requirement, particularly when private investment is at stake.

In this book, the main case study on the search for alternatives in the development of strategic environmental assessment is the development of an assessment procedure for reviewing policies *within* the European Commission. This provides a key plank of new methods of 'better regulation' and governance.[61] I also identify the two-edged nature of this development, including the potential use of assessment

[58] This is similarly the case with the principle of the Best Practicable Environmental Option (s. 7(4)(a) Environmental Protection Act 1990).

[59] R. Therivel and E. Wilson *et al.*, *Strategic Environmental Assessment* (London: Routledge, 1993); Department of the Environment, *Policy Appraisal and the Environment* (London: HMSO, 1992).

[60] N. Lee and C. Wood, 'Environmental Impact Assessment: A European Perspective' (1978) 42 *Built Env* 101–10.   [61] Ch. 5, pp. 164–76.

of policy and instrument choices as a braking mechanism for further and possibly more onerous regulation.

The ecologization of governance, particularly through the use of strategic environmental assessment enabling an examination of alternatives, raises a theme pursued throughout this book of the scale and sites of decision making. This idea advances an understanding of environmental assessment as a legal and cultural amplification of environmental concern, so that the measure of environmental planning extends beyond the confines of an individual parcel of property, and traditional conceptions of geographical boundaries in law. In early planning law, for example, the focus of regulation, the unit of planning, was the building. This was made subject to quite precise and onerous building regulations in order to ensure rudimentary sanitation. The later requirement that local plans be drawn up which embraced broader concerns and allowed for regulation on a larger, though still local, scale extended the purview of planning.[62] Contemporary environmental assessment has further enlarged the scale of concern by requiring the consideration of the cumulative impacts of development, and alternative sites for development[63] as relevant or material considerations in decision making. Questions still remain about the appropriate scope of environmental assessment, for example whether it should encompass consideration of a range of impacts on still larger spatial and temporal scales, for example consumption patterns, and trade. An accompanying shift is seen in the scale of concern accommodated by environmental assessment so that there is now a legal base, not just for project-based environmental assessment, but more wide-ranging assessment of policy.[64] The enlargement of the scale of concern through environmental assessment is seen in the case of the proposed offshore windfarm, upheld as a mark of global environmental concern by the developers. The presentation and management of information in that case, however, supports an argument that this may be to the detriment of the locale.

With regard to the theme of the expansion of the scale and sites of decision making, this book makes particularly clear that there is a functional fit between new forms of governance which stress the need for multiple levels of activity and participation and regulation by environmental assessment, precisely because it is capable of responding on several different but related levels (individual sites, larger areas and regions, and policy areas) and in theory at least engages a range of participants in its procedures.[65] More generally, the complex nature of environmental problems—the combining and cumulation of pollution, the breadth of known and unknown effects, and the integrated and entrenched nature of the sources of harm—arguably demands more flexible and precautionary methods of

---

[62] The Housing, Town Planning, Etc Act 1909, discussed in S. Elworthy and J. Holder, *Environmental Protection: Text and Materials* (London: Butterworths, 1997), ch. 7.

[63] Discussed in Ch. 4, pp. 130–6 and Ch. 5, pp. 153–8 respectively.

[64] Notably, Directive 2001/42/EC on the assessment of the effects of certain plans and programmes on the environment, OJ 2001 L 197, p. 30 (see Appendix III) and the Draft Protocol on strategic environmental assessment to the Convention on environmental impact assessment in a transboundary context, Kiev, May 2003 (see Appendix V).   [65] Ch. 5, pp. 150–2.

regulation, such as that represented by environmental assessment. This suggests correspondence between the objectives and methods of new forms of environmental governance, environmental assessment, and law.

Participation

The fourth general characteristic of environmental assessment is the legal requirement that expert and non-expert groups and affected individuals be provided with the opportunity to participate in the assessment process.[66] This derives from the conceptual basis of environmental assessment that the introduction of environmental information from diverse sources into a decision-making process encourages an informed choice between environmental and other objectives, possibly resulting in less environmentally harmful decisions. The underlying deliberative assumption is that changing the rules governing the generation and application of knowledge will change the intellectual and political context of decision making.[67] Parallels may be drawn here with the legal concept of due process which is regarded as a desirable component of public decision making because it allows proper regard for all affected interests and ensures that decisions are based upon a reliable assessment of fact, thus affirming 'reason'.[68] In particular the element of public participation may be considered to democratize development consent procedures by allowing conflicting views about the relevance and adequacy of environmental information to be expressed.[69] The recent extension of participation requirements in environmental assessment by Directive 2003/35/EC[70] indicates a more general concern with environmental democracy. In most forms of assessment, though, the degree of public participation is quite limited, typically granting the opportunity to be consulted, or to scrutinize a developer's statement, and make representations upon it. This leads to the problem that environmental assessment may be too reliant upon a cadre of scientific experts, and have little relevance to the public's perception of environmental harm. This last aspect is borne out by the limited opportunities for the form of environmental assessment to be adapted to evaluate an individual's environmental impact, using energy or carbon audits. The forthcoming amendment of European Community forms of environmental assessment by Directive 2003/35/EC (the EC Directive on participation)[71] will not fundamentally affect this critique, but is designed to bolster existing participation requirements.

[66] This forms the basis of Ch. 6.

[67] S. Taylor, *Making Bureaucracies Think: The Environmental Impact Statement Strategy of Administrative Reform* (Stanford, Calif.: Stanford University Press, 1984).

[68] J. Jowell, 'The Legal Control of Administrative Discretion' (1977) PL 178 at 219, following P. Selznick, *Law, Society and Industrial Justice* (New York: Russell Sage, 1969).

[69] L. K. Caldwell, *Between Two Worlds: Science, the Environmental Movement and Policy Choice* (Cambridge: Cambridge University Press, 1992), 72.

[70] OJ 2003 L 156, p. 17, providing for public participation in respect of the drawing up of certain plans and programmes relating to public participation and access to justice Council Directives 85/337/EEC and 96/61/EC. See Appendix VIII.   [71] ibid.

Related to the participation requirement is the characteristic that environmental assessment provides a forum for negotiation and bargaining about the design of a project, and mitigating measures to be taken, between interest groups and within and between agencies.[72] The reality is that a combination of political resources and circumstances empowers some to negotiate and bargain more effectively than others in the environmental assessment process.[73] The opportunities and shortcomings for public participation in the environmental impact assessment process are examined in the context of the Dibden Bay Port case study which is notable for involving very complex scientific information, presented in a fragmented and inaccessible manner.[74] Combined with the opportunity offered to developers to pursue their own interests, this practical example casts doubt on the theoretical identification of environmental assessment, and other participatory techniques, as representative of a new approach to governance.[75] The identification of a 'legitimacy gap' in the deliberative procedures for national and European Community policy making,[76] discussed above, highlights the disparity between the deliberative idea of public participation and the reality of 'everyday' decision making, particularly when constrained by limits of time and scale, as experienced in development consent regimes. One outcome of this disparity is the use of environmental assessment as a protest 'strategy' by groups and individuals wishing to highlight the environmental (or other[77]) aspects of their case in an instrumental or popular manner, in order to secure delay of the project whilst gaining support for their cause through publicity.

Regulation of Decision Making

The fifth general characteristic of environmental assessment law[78] is that environmental information from the assessment process (including that provided by the developer, as well as representations made about this) must be taken into account before a consent is granted. This procedural requirement is the central control mechanism of environmental assessment. Clearly, a particular objective, standard, or outcome is not pursued. Rather, in formal terms all that is required is that the

---

[72] Taylor, 'Making Bureaucracies Think', at 208; see also B. Sadler, *The Place of Negotiation in Environmental Assessment* (Quebec: Canadian Environmental Assessment Research Council, 1987).

[73] G. Wandesforde-Smith and J. Kerbavaz, 'The Co-evolution of Politics and Policy: Elections, Entrepreneurship and EIA in the United States', in Wathern, *Environmental Impact Assessment*, 161–2. This is also apparent using regulatory space analysis, since information held by developers is an important resource, as advanced by C. Scott, 'Analysing Regulatory Space: Fragmented Resources and Institutional Design' (2001) *PL* 329, amongst others.

[74] Discussed in Ch. 6, pp. 227–32.

[75] As suggested, along with a list of other characteristics of 'new governance', by J. Scott and D. Trubeck, 'Mind the Gap: Law and New Approaches to Governance in the European Union' (2002) 8 *ELJ* 1.   [76] Ch. 5, pp. 167–8 and Ch. 6, pp. 189–94.

[77] For example, the applicants in *ex parte Preece and Adamson* (the *London Congestion Charges* case) might be seen to have invoked environmental assessment to *challenge* measures aimed at improving air quality in central London.   [78] Analysed in Ch. 7, pp. 237–43.

decision maker, the determining authority, is availed of all the information derived from the procedures, and takes this into account prior to reaching a decision. The basic legal form of environmental assessment offers a prime example of a procedural technique of environmental law.

In the early stages of development, this procedural quality meant that environmental assessment was seen to occupy the middle ground between command and control-type regulation and so-called alternative approaches, such as the use of economic incentives and environmental agreements or covenants. Such 'alternatives' are now more commonly described as belonging, variously, to a category of 'reinvented', 'smart', or more responsive regulation.[79] This change in nomenclature describes the assimilation of more flexible and coordinated (between regulator and regulated) legal forms into the mainstream of environmental regulatory methods and marks a vital shift in environmental law, as elsewhere, in favour of law which, arguably, allows for negotiation and deliberation between government, industry, and the public, and makes room for innovation and creativity in decision making. This shift has led to a breakdown of the rigid bipartite character of regulatory strategies, encouraged by analysis which takes account of the paradox of deregulation (that this requires great legal investment to set up), and the 'slippery', and possibly creative, nature of command and control mechanisms (due to the gap between the reality of the regulatory process, and public, formally binding, standards required by law).[80] A central theme is that what is now called 'reinvented regulation' has long existed in the form of environmental assessment. Environmental assessment, then, provides a long-range study of environmental regulation which encourages a critical evaluation of current reinvention efforts, particularly in the context of the more general effort to redesign the job of government.

The apparently procedural nature of environmental assessment means that it has been associated with a pattern of legal reflexivity in which 'the legal control of social action is indirect and abstract, for the legal system only determines the organizational and procedural premises of future action'.[81] Several of the case studies demonstrate how the legal form of environmental assessment is capable of being highly material to the outcome of a decision. Notwithstanding the emphasis on procedure in descriptions of this type of law, reflexive law proves to be not incapable of inducing material change, but it accomplishes this in a more selective,

---

[79] I. Ayres and J. Braithwaite, *Responsive Regulation: Transcending the Deregulation Debate* (Oxford: Oxford University Press, 1992); and with regard to environmental regulation, D. Farber, *Eco-Pragmatism* (Chicago: Chicago University Press, 1999).

[80] D. Farber, 'Taking Slippage Seriously: Noncompliance and Creative Compliance in Environmental Law' (1999) 23 *Harv Env L Rev* 297, at 318.

[81] As G. Teubner describes reflexive law, in 'Substantive and Reflexive Elements in Modern Law', at 255. With specific reference to environmental assessment, see E. Orts, 'Reflexive Environmental Law' (1995) 89 *Northwestern ULR* 1227 and Heinelt *et al.*, *European Union Environmental Policy*. A useful survey of these approaches is given in S. E. Gaines and C. Kimber, 'Redirecting Self-Regulation' (2001) 13 *JEL* 157.

nuanced way than more traditional mechanisms, and may consequently be more nimble and appropriately respectful of social change and diversity. However, the Cairngorm funicular railway project[82] underlines the potential for developers to use environmental assessment to shape the outcome of the decision whether or not to grant development consent in a material, and ultimately favourable, way. The assessment process is capable of acting as a conduit for the (public or private) proponent's or developer's needs, which may be redefined and articulated as constituting a public, or even environmental, benefit. For example, in the case of the Cairngorm funicular railway development, the developer's Environmental Statement (and particularly the description of mitigating measures therein) strongly influenced the content of the planning agreement struck between the local authority and the developer. The planning agreement then allowed objections to the development (on environmental grounds) to be overcome. This supports a finding that the assessment process may operate as a form of developmental advocacy and challenges the presentation of environmental assessment as an exemplar of reflexive law. Unusually, therefore, analysis of environmental assessment drawn from empirical evidence suggests a rematerialization of environmental assessment law. Admittedly this is not rematerialization in the sense that the law directly regulates social behaviour by defining substantive prescriptions, but rather by communicating and accommodating the needs of the proponent of a major project (usually via the environmental statement) and by legitimizing a particular policy choice or decision. This relates directly to issues of governance and participation. The key plank of modern environmental governance, the allocation of responsibility for environmental management to a broader constituency of participants, simultaneously opens up a 'regulatory space' for the proponents of development which may be used by them to further their own interests, particularly when coupled with the currently limited scope for lay participation, and government-sanctioned privatization of the planning agenda.[83] In summary, the case study suggests the continuing relevance of property and developmental interests in this area of environmental law.

The academically well-trodden theme of a public–private distinction is raised by this issue. This identifies very clearly the gulf between the positions of interest within the environmental assessment process, and also the complexity and combinations of responsibility held by those involved. Take, for example, a private developer responsible for providing information on the potential environmental consequences of a mining development as part of the environmental assessment process. This offers him the opportunity to outline the benefits of the development, and in so doing define the public benefit, an apparently objective standard of desirability. The great opportunities for water sports recreation may be detailed, since the pits left from mining for aggregates will be flooded. The loss of

---

[82] Discussed in Ch. 7, pp. 272–80.
[83] See, for example, DLTR, Planning Green Paper, *Planning: Delivering a Fundamental Change* (London: HMSO, 2002).

species will be mitigated by the translocation of species and compensation schemes. Many volumes of the brightly coloured and glossy statement will seek to alleviate the concerns of locals, ramblers, and wildlife conservation groups. All this apart, considerable tensions will continue to exist between private property or developmental interests in the specific parcel of land, and more wide-ranging, *communautaire*, interests in the protection of the wider environment, even though these may appear in the developer's environmental statement to be perfectly reconcilable.

To summarize, environmental assessment may be located at the interstices of key legal distinctions: of objectivity/subjectivity, the scale and sites of decision making, and the public/private divide. Law sometimes operates to conflate these. For example, the compilation of the environmental statement as a legal text in the environmental assessment process lends an appearance of objectivity which may be used advantageously by the proponent of a development. In other cases, the legitimacy of environmental assessment relies upon the opportunity to transcend such distinctions, for example the public–private divide, through such ideas as shared responsibility for environmental change. One important example of such shared responsibility is the provision of information by the developer, to be used by the regulatory body, so that, in other words, the regulated tells the regulator what the problem is and how to solve it.[84] In this book I therefore focus upon the regulation of the final decision, through analysis of the substantive-procedural nature of environmental assessment, but this discussion is inevitably broadened to consider also the form and type of regulation represented by environmental assessment, particularly as these may be indicative of more general regulatory shifts.

An Initial Evaluation

Two main broad theories have been developed to make sense of the role of environmental assessment as a regulatory technique. First, quite simply, environmental assessment may be regarded as a means of informing decision makers of the possible environmental consequences of a proposed project or action. It ensures that planners and developers have available to them relevant information and representations when making a decision which may have adverse effects upon the environment (information theories). Second, culture theories[85] propose, more fundamentally, that environmental assessment inculcates environmental protection values amongst those taking decisions: 'it brings about changes in attitude

---

[84] Paraphrasing E. Bregmann and A. Jacobsen, 'Environmental Performance Review: Self-Regulation in Environmental Law', in G. Teubner, L. Farmer, and D. Murphy (eds.) *Environmental Law and Ecological Responsibility: The Concept and Practice of Ecological Self-Organization* (Chichester: Wiley, 1994), 82.   [85] Advocated strongly by Taylor, *Making Bureaucracies Think*.

Table 1.1   Theoretical approaches to environmental assessment

	Information theories	Culture theories
Claims	• Ensures developers and planners have available to them relevant information and representations about possible environmental consequences of a proposed project or policy when making a decision which may have adverse effects upon the environment	• Process inculcates environmental protection values amongst those taking decisions • Changes attitudes towards the need for and design of new development, and contributes to the development of a 'new administrative logic' or form of ecological 'common law' • Continuing influence of environmental concerns, even beyond decision
Detracting claims	• Contributes to an *idea* of analytically rational planning decisions (in accordance with idea of 'ecological rationality' and due process), and rational choice theory • In effect no more than a balancing act allowing environmental factors to be 'traded off' • 'Symbolic reassurance'/legitimacy functions—combining of project with public interest requirements: a confusion of public and private logics (Ost, 1994) raising legitimacy questions, particularly that public involvement may grant tacit approval • 'Ecological snapshot'	• Political and economic realities and the ethos of strong support for development means that decision makers will continue to incorporate developmental interests in their evaluation of environmental information • Legitimacy/'therapy' function of assessment; may help to mask impact of environmental effects

toward the need for, and design, of new development',[86] and thereby contributes to the development of a 'new administrative logic'.[87] To this extent culture theories of environmental assessment comply with a basic idea of reflexive environmental law, the encouragement of internal self-critical reflection within institutions about their environmental performance.[88] These sets of theories provide the basis of analysis in this book. Although I elaborate aspects of these theories in subsequent chapters, it is helpful at this stage to discuss them in outline. A simplified version of these theories is given in Table 1.1.

Information Theories

With regard to the first set of theories, environmental assessment offers an opportunity for environmental considerations to be taken into account in decision-making

---

[86] J. Herington, 'Environmental Values in a Changing Planning System', in M. Clark and J. Herington (eds.) *The Role of Environmental Impact Assessment in the Planning Process* (London: Mansell, 1998), at 159.   [87] Ost, 'A Game without Rules'.

[88] Orts, 'Reflexive Environmental Law', at 1232.

processes, most commonly development consent systems. As discussed above, it does this by forecasting likely impacts and identifying those areas most susceptible to adverse impacts. Environmental assessment may also allow values to be expressed which are difficult to quantify in substantive environmental standards, for example the quality and value of landscape. Notwithstanding the potential for environmental assessment to assist decision making by contributing environmental information, questions have arisen about the type and quality of information elicited by the procedures and the use to which the information might be put. One concern is that the environmental assessment process constitutes no more than a balancing act. The absence of clear, positive, environmental standards means that, understandably, the ultimate decision whether or not to proceed with a development project will depend on economic judgments and political perspectives, as well as environmental factors.[89] Whilst there is an expectation that information about environmental effects will influence the substance of decision making, its contribution to environmental protection by means of arresting environmentally harmful development is entirely unenforceable in terms of the environmental assessment procedure (although the option of refusing development consent remains). This means that a negative environmental assessment will not necessarily lead to a project failing to gain development consent. More problematically, a 'positive' statement may work to secure development consent, acting as a presumption in favour of development.

Following this assertion, it is significant that environmental assessment contributes to an *idea* of analytically rational planning decisions. This idea may be conferred in two main ways. First, as Sandbach argues in his work on the use of scientific evidence in the environmental debate, the reliance on scientific techniques in the environmental assessment process lends an air of neutrality to decision making in planning. Whilst others see the enlistment of science by decision makers as central to the effectiveness of environmental assessment,[90] Sandbach explains that environmental assessment may be used to convert political and normative issues into bogus scientific and technical ones. His view is that developers are amply capable of ensuring that the evaluation of environmental impacts operates in their favour. Furthermore, the procedure lends approval to a belief that the state of the environment may be measured and predictions made about its future state.[91] Implicitly, environmental concerns may therefore be 'traded off' against other criteria. A second means by which environmental assessment contributes to an idea of neutral and rational planning decisions is discussed by Parkin in his analysis of language in development plans and texts such as environmental statements. He argues that the use of the language of environmental

---

[89] Herington, 'Environmental Values in a Changing Planning System', p. 154; J. Parkin, *Judging Plans and Projects* (Aldershot: Avebury, 1993), 6, concurs.

[90] Notably, Caldwell, *Between Two Worlds*, and Taylor, *Making Bureacracies Think*.

[91] F. Sandbach, *Environmental, Ideology and Policy* (Oxford: Basil Blackwell, 1980), 96–100.

discourse, in particular 'public interest' terminology, contributes to an appearance of rationality.[92] Bregmann and Jacobsen similarly describe how environmental assessment embeds an idea of the public interest in decision-making procedures, thus making the project appear more attractive.[93]

More specifically, environmental statements tend to refer to the visual quality of a project, the character of a local area and collective practices, such as the recreational and cultural opportunities created by the proposed project,[94] and rely upon a liberal use of references to ecology, environment, and nature. These references may act to combine the positive meanings of environment and nature with the proposed project in environmental statements, and thereby lend legitimacy to it. This promotion is clearly evident in cases in which the environmental statement outlines environmental gains likely to accrue from a project. These seek to compensate for the loss of environmental resources arising from a development and may assuage concern that the proposed development will adversely affect the environment. Similarly to planning gain, this information may form the basis of planning obligations negotiated by the developer and planning authority. The inclusion in environmental statements of officially sanctioned[95] environmental 'gain' juxtaposes two contradictory value systems: the ethics of the market and environmental ethics, in a manner inimical to the protection of natural environmental systems: the interdependent, and often irreplaceable, properties of ecological systems run counter to a view that natural resources may be interchanged and compensated.[96] In other words, things that are valued for their 'naturalness' cannot be replaced by human-constructed environments—the two are incommensurable.

An emphasis upon the mitigation of harmful environmental impacts in environmental statements performs a similar function to securing environmental 'gain'. Mitigation allows some environmental impacts to be regarded as side-effects or inconvenient intrusions which may be minimized by the use of suitable techniques. In identifying mitigating measures there is a tacit expectation that environmental management will allow the development to proceed.[97] The tendency to consider development proposals in terms of their environmental effects and to

[92] Parkin, *Judging Plans and Projects*.

[93] Bregman and Jacobson, 'Environmental Performance Review', 231.

[94] See typology of the use of environmental terms in planning developed in Myerson and Rydin, 'Environment and Planning', 437.

[95] See DTLR, Circular 1/97, *Planning Obligations* (London: HMSO, 1997), Annex B, para. 11: 'examples of appropriate planning obligations may include arrangements . . . to offset (through substitution, replacement, or regeneration) the loss of or impact on a resource present on a site or nearby, for example the loss of a wetland habitat on a site offset by opening up a culverted stream or river . . . to protect or reduce harm to protected sites or species, acknowledged to be of importance . . . the Department welcomes initiatives taken by some developers in creating nature reserves, planting trees, establishing wildlife ponds and providing other nature conservation benefits'. See also *Planning Obligations*, consultation document at http://www.planning.dtlr.gov.uk/consult/planoblg/index.htm.

[96] S. Boucher and S. Whatmore, 'Green Gains? Planning by Agreement and Nature Conservation' (1993) 36 *JEPM* 33, at 38.

[97] N. Evernden, *The Social Creation of Nature* (Baltimore: Johns Hopkins University Press, 1993), 9.

negotiate measures to compensate or mitigate for those effects in the environmental assessment process follows a technicist idea of environmental protection. This centres upon the rational and instrumental identification and valuation of stocks of environmental assets. In contrast, calls for the establishment of more precise standards and thresholds for the environmental effects of development represent a move away from a notion of balance to a more absolute sense of environmental quality as something to be protected and which emphasizes constraints in the capacity of ecological systems to absorb pollutants and other stresses, and the difficulty of replicating ecological conditions.[98] From a different, though no less critical, perspective, it may be questioned whether the creation of a replica habitat elsewhere is ever capable of mitigating the loss of a habitat or a colony of a species on the site of a proposed development project, or that compensation may ever be appropriate. This is not just because of the difficulty of recreating ecological conditions but because of sensitivity shown to the 'sense of place' felt by some groups or individuals, the value of which cannot be accurately captured, or even defined, and is therefore incapable of replication.[99]

A related concern is that the very procedural nature of the environmental assessment process confers an idea of due process which may legitimate decisions favouring developmental interests, and thereby encourage the acceptance of projects. Submitting decisions to procedural due process where substantive due process is not possible may result in 'symbolic reassurance', whereby the myths and symbols of law are invoked in order to achieve acquiescence to a decision.[100] In relation to environmental assessment, this danger is increased when environmental statements are compiled solely by the proposed developer or sponsoring agency since there is a possibility that they may become propagandist documents.[101] The acceptance of a project may also be secured through public participation requirements in the environmental assessment process because differing views may be registered, even though decisions may still be taken with little regard to them. The vital role environmental impact assessment could play in securing greater public support for proposed developments was foreseen by the Royal Town Planning Institute in its memorandum to the House of Lords Select Committee on the European Communities on the draft European Community Directive on environmental assessment.[102] More critically, public participation in

---

[98] For example, a heavy-handed and unrealistic approach was taken to translocating snail species from the path of the Newbury bypass, as discussed in Ch. 6, pp. 223–5.

[99] J. Burgess and C. Harrison, 'Capturing Values for Nature: Ecological, Economic, and Cultural Perspectives', in J. Holder and D. McGillivray (eds.) *Locality and Identity: Environmental Issues in Law and Society* (Aldershot: Dartmouth, 1999).

[100] Jowell, 'The Legal Control of Administrative Discretion', at 217.

[101] As suggested by Brookes, in E. Brookes, 'On Putting the Environment in its Place: A Critique of Environmental Impact Assessment', in O'Riordan and Hey, *Environmental Impact Assessment*, 167–77, at 172. On this point, see the case study discussed in Elworthy and Holder, *Environmental Protection*, ch. 10.

[102] House of Lords Select Committee on the European Communities, Eleventh Report, *Environmental Assessment of Projects*, Session 1980–81 (London: HMSO, 1981), 107.

the assessment process may have the effect of granting tacit approval to projects and, furthermore, dissipating environmental interests, by engaging the public in challenging complex documents.[103] A final point is that most assessment procedures do not require post-assessment monitoring. Instead, an ecological snapshot is produced. In such cases, environmental assessment fails to appreciate the dynamics of ecological systems.[104] This factor, combined with an emphasis upon mitigating measures in many statements and the opportunity for securing environmental gains that this confers, as described above, means that environmental assessment may be used to help secure development consent.[105]

This cluster of issues relating to the use and abuse of information suggests that as a regulatory mechanism environmental assessment may encourage acceptance of projects. Furthermore, in representing the procedural safeguard that environmental information has been collected and reviewed, environmental assessment may also lend unjustified legitimacy to the outcome of decision-making processes.

Culture Theories

Culture theories of environmental assessment suggest that environmental assessment instils environmental values amongst decision makers and participants, and indeed relies upon this for its effectiveness.[106] As such, it appreciates a potentially more complex dimension to environmental assessment than information theories suggest. To elaborate, environmental assessment is considered capable of reforming the culture of administrative decision making in, for example, local planning authorities, government departments, and environmental agencies, by enhancing the administration's concern about environmental effects.

Environmental assessment may foster awareness about which projects or policies are less environmentally harmful than others, within an administration, and

---

[103] S. K. Fairfax, 'A Disaster in the Environmental Movement' (1978) 99 *Science* 743–8.

[104] This approach may be compared with other developments in EC law, for example the GMO authorization procedures under Directive 2001/18/EC on the deliberate release into the environment of GMOs, OJ L 106, p. 1 which stipulates procedures where any new information becomes available regarding risks of the product to human health or the environment. An exception is Directive 2001/42/EC on the assessment of the effects of certain plans and programmes on the environment, OJ L 175, p. 30, Art. 10 of which requires Member States to monitor the significant environmental effects of the implementation of plans and programmes in order to identify any unforeseen adverse effects and to take remedial action. On enhancing ecological thinking through environmental assessment, see Ch. 3, pp. 92–4.

[105] R. Bissett and P. Tomlinson, 'Monitoring and Auditing of Impacts', in Wathern, *Environmental Impact Assessment*, 117–28, at 126.

[106] Taylor, *Making Bureaucracies Think*, is a main proponent of culture theories of environmental assessment. See also Bartlett, 'Ecological Reason in Administration', at 82: '[T]he "creative third alternatives" that may hold the most promise, for both action and analysis, are what might be called either "subversive" or "worm in the brain" strategies. Such strategies involve dismantling or transmogrifying the administrative state from within—gradually and not entirely predictably—while remaking individual values and patterns of thinking and acting and, perhaps, while promoting "the preconditions for more substantial institutional innovation". I argue that mandatory environmental impact assessment may often be, in potential and in realization, a policy strategy of this kind.'

even in the wider community. One view is that this characteristic of fostering social awareness approximates to the practices of the scientific community—continuous improvements in knowledge by empirical testing within an environment of detection of error. Environmental assessment may therefore be seen to import scientific norms and procedures into a political setting,[107] except that the process of fostering awareness is governed by informal social rules and expectations shared by those involved in the environmental assessment process. This aspect introduces an element of self-regulation which makes environmental assessment particularly appropriate in cases in which public bodies may cause or facilitate environmental damage, but where they are not subject to traditional regulatory structures.

Underpinning the cultural importance of environmental assessment is an idea that it encourages a particular type of ecological rationality—a rationality 'of living systems, an order of relationships among living systems and their environments'.[108] This may be regarded as a form of practical reason that is quite distinct from other prominent forms, such as technological, economic, social, legal, and political rationality. Since environmental assessment forces explicit consideration of environmental concerns, it holds promise, in Bartlett's words, as a way of 'transmogrifying the administrative state from within—gradually and not entirely predictably—while remaking individual values and patterns of thinking and acting and, perhaps, while promoting "the preconditions for more substantial institutional innovation" '.[109]

A related explanation for the cultural role of environmental assessment is that, through public discussion and debate in an environmental assessment process, people move beyond strict self-interest, or administratively determined interests, to seeing their private or individual interest linked with other, shared, interests, and thus make decisions based on the common good.[110] The idea is that environmental assessment provides a temporary forum in which individuals and groups can exchange their particular views and perspectives, but from which longer-term, collective, environmental discourse can be generated. There is much optimistic thinking on this point: Wilkins, for example, states: 'Common understandings of community and environmental needs can evolve through environmental impact assessments that include all interested people, giving them equal opportunities to participate, and the free and open exchange of information. As such environmental impact assessments provide fora to initiate social learning.' He continues: 'Through the environmental impact assessment process, discourse can therefore assist in promoting community decisions and understandings and

---

[107] Taylor, *Making Bureaucracies Think*, 161–91, at 165.

[108] See J. S. Dryzek, *Rational Ecology: Environment and Political Ecology* (New York: Basil Blackwell, 1987).

[109] Bartlett, 'Ecological Reason in Administration', at 82, drawing upon Dryzek, *Rational Ecology*, at 247.

[110] J. Bohman, *Public Deliberation* (Boston: MIT Press, 2000), 238. On this process see further Ch. 6, pp. 197–9.

over time may affect the values held by individuals as they are exposed to new experiences and beliefs.'[111] A more mundane aspect of culture theory is the gradual development of a type of 'common law' of environmental assessment, in which a form of precedent (related to the significance of likely effects of a particular type of development) operates by the accretion of knowledge by those involved in the process—developers, groups opposing development, environmental consultants, competent authorities, and environment agencies.[112]

There is a great degree of scepticism, however, about the more elaborate claims of culture theories of environmental assessment, that the process contributes to changing the culture in which decisions are made and thus leads to social learning.[113] A less consensual view is that political and economic realities mean that decision makers will continue to prioritize developmental interests when taking decisions, even those governed by environmental assessment procedures.

A Map of this Book

In terms of structure, I first explain in Chapter 2 the roots and development of environmental assessment, alongside the development of environmental law. I explain how environmental assessment offers a functional fit with key developmental stages in environmental law, in particular how it relates to modern environmental governance strategies, such as securing participation of a broad range of actors and conferring responsibility on them for environmental protection. Such characteristics mean particularly that environmental assessment bears the hallmarks of the sustainable development agenda. I then review a range of applications of environmental assessment in various contexts. From this, the theme of standardization emerges, in both private and public fora. I describe also the process of colonization of decision making by environmental assessment as a pervasive form of law, and argue that it is precisely the weakness of its substantive core that has made its adaptation to widely different contexts and jurisdictions possible, but that this is problematic from the perspective of securing satisfactory environmental protection.

The rest of the book then roughly corresponds with the stages of progression of a model environmental assessment process—the prediction of likely effects on the environment (Chapter 3), in particular the judgment as to the *significance* of likely effects (Chapter 4), the consideration of alternatives in an integrated manner in pursuance of the ecologization of governance (Chapter 5), the participation and consultation of experts and members of the public, as well as the strategic use of environmental assessment as a form of protest (Chapter 6), and

---

[111] H. Wilkins, 'The Need for Subjectivity in Environmental Impact Assessment' (2003) 23 *EIA Rev* 401.
[112] As Taylor, *Making Bureaucracies Think*, describes this as occurring in the United States, at 84.
[113] Herington, 'Environmental Values', 150–2.

Table 1.2 A map of this book

Functions of EA (Chapter 1)	EA and environmental law (Chapter 2)	Nature of prediction (Chapter 3)	Judgments of significance (Chapter 4)	Alternatives (Chapter 5)	Model of participation (Chapter 6)	Regulatory form (Chapter 7)	EA and environmental governance (Chapter 8)
Information theories	Outline of general procedure to ascertain information	*Objective* ('science') Absolute information *Fact*	Thresholds/criteria (screening) Future (modelling)	Integrationist: cross-media Restricted alternatives	Instrumental: accurate decision making Exclusion: expert-led/professional judgment Legitimacy	Procedural control Accurate decisions	Multiple levels of governance Information provision Enlargement of information scales
Culture theories	Persuasiveness of EA in various jurisdictions and settings	*Subjective* ('art') Relativity of information *Values*	Locatedness: present/past connections with local environment	Holistic: broader range of alternatives Organizational learning/ ecologization of governance	Dignitarian: protection of values Inclusion/lay knowledge Social learning	Substantive outcome Protection of values	Civil society: responsibility/ partnership Environmental democracy
Empirical analysis	Lewes Flood Defence Strategy: role of law in objectifying opinion and values		Kentish Flats windfarm: meaning of 'significance' and assessment of qualitative information on landscape	European Commission: internal policy assessment of policy and legislative proposals	Dibden Bay Global Port: public participation involving complex scientific information	Cairngorm Funicular: enhanced role of developer in determining options and presentation of information	

taking account of this information in decision making (Chapter 7). These stages are represented in Table 1.2 which also represents the interaction of theories of environmental assessment with the objective-subjective nature of information in environmental assessment, particularly as it is concerned with judgments of significance. In the course of these chapters I aim to indicate the linkages, and also the inconsistencies, between these stages, representing central elements of the environmental assessment process. For example, an emphasis on 'objective' information into environmental assessment, and the consequential relegation of qualitative information in environmental assessment, has had detrimental effects on the involvement of a range of participants in assessing the significance of the likely effects of development on the environment. In turn, analysis of the case studies suggests that law plays an important part in objectifying information which may have the effect of restricting the consideration of alternative policies and projects. A further example is that undue emphasis on the information provision function of environmental assessment, rather than engaging the public in a fully participative, iterative process of environmental assessment, is reflected in case law as a misguided inquiry into whether a body of information already in the public domain will suffice in terms of fulfilling environmental assessment requirements, irrespective of whether a proper assessment process has been conducted.

I do not intend to be overly prescriptive about the linkages between these parts of the book, but rather to propose a scheme by which the bearings and points of influence between theories of governance, and the reality of the regulation of decision making may be explored. Table 1.2 also indicates aspects of the case studies which form the basis of the analysis. Naturally, the case studies raise several, interrelated issues but I tend to highlight particular aspects at a time, leaving the general importance of these to be discussed in the concluding Chapter 8, in which I advocate strengthening environmental assessment by building upon its subjective elements, for example by including a broader range of judgments on matters of significance, likelihood, and alternatives, but also resisting the rush to incorporate 'sustainability criteria' into environmental assessment, which threatens to dilute its specific environmental protection orientation.

2

Tracking Environmental Assessment

Integration, precaution, participation, prevention, proceduralization, sustainability: these are the bywords of environmental law which have recently been attributed to environmental assessment. In this chapter I give an account of the evolution of environmental assessment within the overall development of environmental law, particularly as a means of giving effect to the concept of sustainable development. The focus is upon the development of environmental impact assessment in the United Kingdom, which has been strongly influenced by the EC model of assessment contained in the EIA Directive. Tracing this development allows me to pinpoint the origin of information theories of environmental assessment in the idea that environmental assessment was inherent in the town and country planning system because planning authorities could avail themselves of a power to request 'additional information' from developers. Adopting a broader scope, I then relate the development of environmental assessment to the ascendancy of the sustainable development concept. In particular, the enlargement of environmental assessment to encourage the integration of different policy areas in strategic environmental assessment may be seen as an expression of this concept. This brings me to critically view attempts to further develop environmental assessment as a form of sustainability analysis.

From this development of different levels of environmental assessment (project- and policy-based) the analysis shifts to *sites* of decision making engaging environmental assessment. I survey some of the legal variations of environmental assessment that have evolved in different jurisdictional and functional contexts—land use planning and control, conservation for biodiversity, pollution controls, and development assistance. This analysis suggests that environmental assessment has contributed to the standardization of decision making with respect to environmental concerns. These key aspects (the practical implementation of sustainable development via environmental assessment, and the pervasiveness and adaptability of environmental assessment in various contexts) are linked by an essential characteristic of environmental assessment, that as a highly procedural mechanism it contains no absolute standards, suggesting that it is capable of adjusting to the conceptual and legal frames in operation. Environmental assessment incorporates environmental concerns or criteria into different contexts, but in a flexible and accommodating way and without the 'hard edges' of substantive standards, or the conferral of enforceable rights relating to environmental quality.[1] This has implications for the roles performed by law in environmental assessment—as a framework for interdisciplinary inquiry, as a means of incorporating environmental values or principles in a standardized way into decision making and planning, or, more critically, permitting 'lip-service' to be paid to environmental ideals. In summary, considering a broad range of applications of environmental assessment helps to pinpoint its legal core. First, though, I broadly define the environmental assessment process, building upon the identification of its main characteristics in Chapter 1.[2]

Defining Environmental Assessment

Environmental assessment practice and literature has developed apace, but there is no general and universally accepted definition of the procedure. A traditional starting point is the United States' National Environmental Policy Act (NEPA) 1969 which defines environmental assessment as 'a systematic interdisciplinary approach which will insure the integrated use of the natural and social sciences and the environmental design arts in planning and in decision making which may have an impact on man's environment'.[3] More specifically, policy guidance for England and Wales currently defines environmental impact assessment as:

. . . a means of drawing together, in a systematic way, an assessment of projects likely to have significant environmental effects. This helps to ensure that the importance of the predicted effects, and the scope for reducing them, are properly understood by the public and the relevant competent authority before it makes its decision.[4]

A more rounded definition, also applicable to strategic environmental assessment (of plans and programmes), explains environmental assessment as a process for identifying the likely consequences for the biological, geological, and physical environment and human health and welfare of implementing particular activities, policy, and plans, particularly arising from the participation of those likely to be affected, and for conveying this information to those responsible for sanctioning the

---

[1] However, the right to participate in decision making governed by environmental assessment is now recognized and enforceable. On human rights approaches and environmental assessment, see Ch. 8, pp. 291–4. [2] See pp. 12–22.
[3] S.102(a) 42 USC 4321–4361. See Appendix I.
[4] Department of Environment, Transport and the Regions, Circular 02/99, *Environmental Impact Assessment* (London: HMSO, 1999), para. 9. See the change in emphasis from Department of the Environment, Circular 15/88 (Welsh Office 23/88), *Environmental Assessment* (London: HMSO, 1988), para. 7: 'essentially a technique for drawing together in a systematic way expert quantitative analysis and qualitative assessment of a project's environmental effects, and presenting the results in a way which enables the importance of the predicted effects, and the scope for modifying or mitigating them, to be properly evaluated by the relevant decision making body before a decision is given'.

proposal at a stage when it can materially affect their decision, or their ongoing regulation.[5] This concentrates not so much on a final decision, but rather recognizes environmental assessment to be a process with several stages—negotiation, participation, and monitoring. The description of the social effects of environmental assessment also recognizes that qualitative as well as quantitative data may be used to assess the likely significance of impacts and that value judgments are (and should be) engaged in identifying and predicting impacts.[6]

Questions remain about the exact subject matter of environmental assessment procedures, particularly what is meant by 'environment' and 'impact'. There is, for example, some debate about whether 'the environment' refers to the human (or 'man's')[7] environment in cases such as *Hanly* v *Kleindienst*[8] (concerning the building of a jail in Lower Manhattan) or whether this is restricted to the natural environment. In the United Kingdom, the purpose of the 1999 Regulations[9] (as well as that of the EC EIA Directive[10] implemented by the 1999 Regulations) has been interpreted as the protection of the environment in the public interest. Whilst the Regulations may have the effect of avoiding harm to residential amenity, they may not be applied specifically to protect the amenity of individual buildings.[11] The likelihood of severe shadowing from the development of a football stadium was therefore considered not to have a potential effect upon the environment.[12] Such an interpretation suggests some narrowing of the meaning of 'environment' in the law relating to environmental assessment, particularly when compared to a definition of 'environment' as surroundings, whether these be urban, rural, 'man-made', or 'natural' .

'Impact' has been taken to mean the environmental consequences of a particular activity compared with what might otherwise have occurred. An impact may be both spatial and temporal, as well as positive or negative in environmental terms. The possibly positive nature of impacts was at issue in the *BT* case[13] in which the High Court decided that a local authority should have considered whether there were likely to be any significant effects, adverse or otherwise, by requiring an environmental assessment of a proposed project. This interpretation was based upon a textual reading of the EC EIA Directive as well as an argument that individuals should form their own judgments about the nature of a potential impact through their participation in the environmental assessment process. It is also clear that the term 'impact' may include indirect impacts. For example, building a dam may

[5] Based on a definition given by R. E. Munn (ed.) *Environmental Impact Assessment: Principles and Procedures* (New York: John Wiley, 1979).

[6] See P. McAuslan's argument about the importance of value judgments in planning decisions more broadly, in *Ideologies of Planning Law* (Oxford: Pergamon Press, 1980).

[7] S. 102(a) NEPA.

[8] 471 F2d 823, 4 ERC 1785, 2 *Envtl L Rep* 20, 717 (1972). For discussion of this case, see Ch. 4, p. 105.

[9] Town and Country Planning (Environmental Impact Assessment) (England and Wales) Regulations 1999 (SI 1999, No. 293).

[10] Directive 85/337/EEC, OJ 1985 L 175, p. 40, as amended by Directive 97/11/EC, OJ L 73, p. 5.

[11] *R (Malster)* v *Ipswich Borough Council* [2001] EWHC 711 (Sullivan J).   [12] ibid.

[13] [2001] EWHC Admin 1001 (Elias J). See further Ch. 4, pp. 136–7.

have direct implications for migratory fish movement up a river for spawning, but its indirect effects—on recreational fishing or coastal commercial fisheries—due to the possible decline in fish stocks, should also be appreciated.[14] Arguably, such indirect impacts (or 'flow-on' effects) should be made as obvious as direct effects by the environmental assessment process. After all the failure of more traditional methods of pollution control to deal with the indirect effects of activities was a major trigger for the initial development of environmental assessment.[15]

Legal interpretations of 'environment' and 'impact' (and related terms such as 'significance' and 'likelihood') tend to be limited in scope. On the contrary, the varying and contingent meanings of these terms suggest that they are socially defined and interpreted rather than physically or technically determined. The broader legal and social meanings attributed to terms such as these are discussed in the following chapters.[16] The more practical meanings of terms used in environmental assessment are considered below.

The Procedure in Outline

The environmental impact assessment process is the main subject of this book and also provides its structure since in each of the following chapters I critically and thematically analyse an important stage in the process—predicting impacts,[17] evaluating the significance of these,[18] considering alternatives,[19] engaging in consultation and deliberation,[20] and making a final and informed decision.[21] Because of the centrality of environmental assessment as a *process* I here outline the key stages (mainly using the example of the EC EIA Directive)[22] and explain the terminology used to describe these. A summary is provided in Figure 2.1 which matches each stage of the process with its rationale and leading actor. The assessment of plans and programmes by strategic environmental assessment (governed by the EC SEA Directive)[23] broadly follows the procedural pattern of environmental impact assessment (of proposed projects). Whilst focusing on environmental impact assessment, I explain how and where strategic environmental assessment departs from the EIA model later in this chapter.[24]

Screening and Scoping

Screening is generally the first stage of the environmental assessment process.[25] This involves differentiating between projects and policy proposals that should

---

[14] R. K. Morgan, *Environmental Impact Assessment: A Methodological Perspective* (Dordrecht: Kluwer, 1998), 40.   [15] ibid. See further Ch. 4, pp. 130–6.
[16] See Ch. 3, pp. 76–80 and Ch. 4, pp. 102–8.   [17] Ch. 3.   [18] Ch. 4.
[19] Ch. 5.   [20] Ch. 6.   [21] Ch. 7.   [22] Directive 85/337/EEC, as amended.
[23] Directive 2001/42/EC on the assessment of the effects of certain plans and programmes on the environment, OJ 2001 L 197, p. 30. See Appendix III.   [24] See pp. 60–5.
[25] As required by Arts. 2 and 4 of the EC EIA Directive.

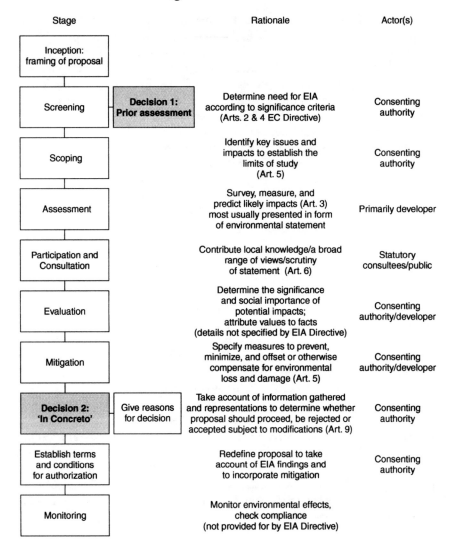

Stage		Rationale	Actor(s)

Inception: framing of proposal

Screening — **Decision 1: Prior assessment** — Determine need for EIA according to significance criteria (Arts. 2 & 4 EC Directive) — Consenting authority

Scoping — Identify key issues and impacts to establish the limits of study (Art. 5) — Consenting authority

Assessment — Survey, measure, and predict likely impacts (Art. 3) most usually presented in form of environmental statement — Primarily developer

Participation and Consultation — Contribute local knowledge/a broad range of views/scrutiny of statement (Art. 6) — Statutory consultees/public

Evaluation — Determine the significance and social importance of potential impacts; attribute values to facts (details not specified by EIA Directive) — Consenting authority/developer

Mitigation — Specify measures to prevent, minimize, and offset or otherwise compensate for environmental loss and damage (Art. 5) — Consenting authority/developer

Decision 2: 'In Concreto' — Give reasons for decision — Take account of information gathered and representations to determine whether proposal should proceed, be rejected or accepted subject to modifications (Art. 9) — Consenting authority

Establish terms and conditions for authorization — Redefine proposal to take account of EIA findings and to incorporate mitigation — Consenting authority

Monitoring — Monitor environmental effects, check compliance (not provided for by EIA Directive)

Figure 2.1   The environmental impact assessement process
Based upon the structure of the EC EIA Directive, with departures marked.

be made subject to the full environmental assessment process on the basis of the likelihood of significant harm. The screening of proposals is therefore defined by the potential for actual harm (although potential environmental benefits may also be assessed) which creates a trigger for the entire process. This creates a circular inquiry because it is only by carrying out a preliminary screening assessment that the decision maker can decide whether it is necessary formally to go through the process, in compliance with the rules relating to the environmental assessment process.

Looking more specifically at the trigger for the process, the harm-based assessment of *significant* environmental impacts is a highly subjective and difficult evaluation.[26] As Hertz states '[V]erbal descriptions of "significance" are not very illuminating and mathematical ones are generally impossible. Moreover it is no mean feat to evaluate the significance of an impact that has not occurred or been studied'.[27] Notwithstanding the inherently subjective nature of determining whether impacts are likely to be significant, environmental assessment procedures are designed to manage the discretionary nature of this judgment, in the case of the EIA Directive by listing projects which must be subject to assessment,[28] combined with thresholds and indicative criteria. Following research which found that the number of environmental assessments being conducted varied widely (a dozen or fewer in Denmark and Portugal, a couple of hundred in the United Kingdom, 1,000 in Germany, 5,500 in France),[29] the EIA Directive was amended more carefully to structure judgment of significance, in accordance with a list of selection criteria.[30] Since these amendments, local planning authorities in the United Kingdom no longer appear to be avoiding the need for environmental impact assessment wherever possible and there is some evidence of a more considered and transparent approach to screening.[31]

In the case of the United Kingdom procedures designed to implement the EIA Directive, the decision whether or not an environmental impact assessment is required can take place at a number of stages, including when the developer submits an environmental statement for the purposes of the 1999 Regulations.[32] Where there is uncertainty about whether a full environmental assessment is required, a developer may request a 'screening opinion' from the local planning authority before submitting an application for planning permission.[33] A planning authority may request an environmental statement where one has not previously been provided, even though a negative screening opinion has already been given. In contrast, a screening opinion provides a determinative judgment where a planning authority decides that an environmental impact assessment is required.[34]

---

[26] On the nature of this prediction, see Ch. 3, pp. 76–80, 94–7.

[27] M. Hertz, 'Parallel Universes: NEPA Lessons for the New Property' (1993) *Columbia L Rev* 1668, at 1712.

[28] See Annexes I and II of Directive 85/337/EEC, to be read in conjunction with Arts. 2 and 4 (see Appendix I). See further Ch. 4, pp. 108–16.

[29] European Commission, *Report from the Commission on the Implementation of Directive 85/337/EEC on the Assessment of the Effects of Certain Public and Private Projects on the Environment*, COM(93)28, 2.4.1993 (Brussels: CEC, 1993), 37–8. On the national disparities in initial implementation of the Directive, see discussion of varying application of thresholds at the screening stage, Ch. 4, pp. 116–23.

[30] Annex III of Directive 85/337/EEC (amended by Directive 97/11/EC OJ 1997 L 73, p. 73) to be read in conjunction with Art. 4(3). See Appendix II. On this judgment, see further Ch. 4, pp. 106–8.

[31] G. Wood and J. Becker, *Screening Decision-Making under the Town and Country Planning (Environmental Impact Assessment) (England and Wales) Regulations 1999* (Oxford: Oxford Brookes University, 2003).

[32] Reg. 4(2)(a) Town and Country Planning (Environmental Impact Assessment) (England and Wales) Regulations 1999.

[33] Reg. 5(1). This opinion is subject to a direction from the Secretary of State (reg. 4(3)).

[34] *R (Fernback)* v *Harrow London Borough Council* [2002] Env LR 10 (Richards J).

Once a decision has been taken to embark upon a formal environmental assessment procedure, the extent of the study to be made, and therefore the onus upon the developer (or policy maker in the case of strategic environmental assessment) must be evaluated. This is referred to as the exercise of 'scoping'.[35] In the case of environmental impact assessment, scoping includes identifying potential receptors, impacts, alternatives, and mitigation measures (as well as relationships between these), and deciding what methodologies to use and who to consult. It may also involve determining the geographical and temporal boundaries of the assessment. This is particularly the case with potential indirect and cumulative impacts which may well extend beyond the given site boundaries of a project, and may only be discerned over a period of time.

At the stage of scoping, characterizing the baseline condition of a receiving environment is necessary to predict the likely state of the environment in the absence of the proposed activity or development, and thus in predicting the main impacts which are likely to flow from these. Taking an ecological approach to impact assessment shows up the inadequacy of one-off surveys to establish baselines, since these provide only a snapshot of current conditions.[36] However, even extending the 'lead times' for such surveys may not fully overcome the difficulty that the variability of biological phenomena makes it difficult to confidently establish baseline conditions.[37]

Under the 1999 Regulations,[38] a developer may request a 'scoping opinion' from the local planning authority (or 'scoping direction' from the Secretary of State)[39] which outlines what are considered to be the main likely effects of the development and therefore the topics on which the environmental statement should focus. This is often drawn up after consulting other authorities with environmental responsibilities, thus compelling an exchange between the authorities and developer and other groups. The identification of potential impacts forms the principal focus of scoping (with landscape and visual impact considered to be by far the most important impact). In comparison, the role of alternatives tends to be given relatively less attention at this stage.[40] Most importantly, decisions about scoping (as well as screening) are typically made by experts, with little input from the public or interest groups.[41] This has led to the suggestion that parallel scoping exercises might be

---

[35] As required by Art. 5(2) EC EIA Directive. This provision was added by Directive 97/11/EC, following research which found that the content of environmental statements, submitted by developers, varied greatly; see *Report from the Commission on the Implementation of Directive 85/337/EEC*. See Reg. 10 of the 1999 Regulations. See generally, P. Morris and R. Therivel (eds.) *Methods of Environmental Impact Assessment* (London: Spon, 2001).

[36] See further Ch. 3, pp. 92–4.

[37] See J. Treweek, *Ecological Impact Assessment* (Oxford: Blackwell, 1999), 131–2.

[38] See n. 9.

[39] Regs. 10 and 11 of the 1999 Regulations.

[40] J. Becker and G. Wood, *Scoping Decision-Making under the Town and Country Planning (Environmental Impact Assessment) (England and Wales) Regulations 1999* (Oxford: Oxford Brookes University, 2003).

[41] See further Ch. 4, pp. 145–6 on judgments of significance.

carried out which employ conventional methods (public meetings, displays, advertisements) as well as more focused small group consultation.[42]

Information Provision, Consultation, and Decision Making

Following the screening and scoping stages, responsibility falls to the developer to provide information about the likely environmental effects of the proposed development in the form of an environmental statement.[43] At the very least this statement should include descriptions of the project, the measures envisaged to mitigate (avoid, reduce, and, if possible, remedy) adverse effects, the data used to ascertain this information, and an outline of the main alternatives considered,[44] all of which should be accompanied by a non-technical summary of these descriptions. This obligation is subject to the qualification that the developer 'may reasonably be required to compile this information having regard *inter alia* to current knowledge and methods of assessment'.[45] This gathering of information also relies upon a freedom of information requirement of sorts, since any authorities holding relevant information must make this available to the developer, subject to some exceptions.[46] Policy guidance makes clear that there is no obligation on public bodies to undertake research or otherwise to take steps to obtain information which they do not already have.[47] This reasonably low standard of obligation on the part of authorities means that there is frequently a lack of baseline information for the purpose of measuring potential impacts.[48]

The developer (in practice the environmental consultant) may use several methods to identify and predict the severity or otherwise of impacts, each of which is underpinned by differing assumptions about the measurability of the environment and the predictability and nature of impacts. At their simplest, these methods may consist of checklists to ensure that key impacts are not overlooked and statutory thresholds are taken into account. Looking to the future, sustainability checklists, involving a broader range of criteria than environmental protection, are likely to be used more frequently.[49] Matrices are similarly used to identify potential impacts which may be weighted or ranked to encourage evaluation of their significance,

---

[42] Becker and Wood, *Scoping Decision-Making*, para. 2.5.8.

[43] Art. 5(1) of the EIA Directive, implemented by Reg. 2(1) and Sch. 4 of the 1999 Regulations (see Appendix VII).   [44] On alternatives, see further Ch. 5, pp. 149–50.

[45] Art. 5(1)(b) EIA Directive.

[46] Art. 5(4) EIA Directive. Exceptions include defence projects (Art. 10). In the United Kingdom, the general regime of freedom of information is governed by the Environmental Information Regulations (SI 1992, No. 1447).

[47] Department of the Environment, Transport and the Regions, Circular 02/99, *Environmental Impact Assessment*, para. 99.

[48] Although, in the case of the Lewes Flood Defence Strategy, English Nature commissioned extensive baseline surveys in order to ascertain the existence of sites with similar ecological conditions to those threatened by flood defence works. See further Ch. 3, pp. 89–92.

[49] For a critique of this methodological and conceptual development see below, pp. 57–9, and for a practical example, see Ch. 5, pp. 164–76.

and may additionally show cause-effect links between impacts and their sources when plotted on axes.[50] The most common method for predicting impacts is the use of models based upon mathematical or statistical functions which are applied to calculate the probability of quantitative values from data. Modelling may be carried out on computer spreadsheets, but more complex models are capable of incorporating many variables.[51] This method relies primarily upon the availability of baseline data which, as mentioned above, may simply be unavailable or may be questioned in terms of accuracy and representativeness. A further method, network and systems analysis, is used particularly to determine the nature of cumulative and indirect impacts. This is based on the concept that there are links and interaction pathways between individual elements of the environment and that when one element is specifically affected this will have an effect on those elements which interact with it. The results of this method are often portrayed in flow diagrams which are liable to become complex.[52] More simply, maps are frequently used to indicate the features of areas subject to the likely impacts and the location of receptors. Overlay maps or picture imaging can integrate several layers, often to represent the effect of different impacts. Increasingly, geographical information systems (GIS) are used to analyse a number of layers, and to manipulate quantitative information derived from modelling. GIS may also allow for a project's effects to be superimposed on selected receptors to establish areas where impacts would be most significant. Furthermore, carrying capacity analysis, based on the recognition that thresholds exist in the environment, addresses the accumulation of impacts against thresholds and identified trends.

Most of the methods described so far elicit quantitative information. More qualitative categories of information may instead be articulated in public opinion surveys, consultation exercises, public inquiries and, more recently, by focus groups, citizens' juries, and consensus conferences[53] in order to ascertain what values may be held by those affected or interested in the project. These exercises in consultation and participation are more often carried out by public authorities than private entities.

Taking a further look at these specifications, detailing mitigation methods is an important part of compiling an environmental statement. Mitigation includes any deliberate action taken to alleviate adverse effects, either by controlling the sources of impacts or the exposure of species and habitats. The description of mitigating measures is important because without this the decision maker cannot properly evaluate the severity, or significance, of the potential effects.[54] However,

[50] See generally the descriptions of techniques in Morris and Therivel, *Methods* 7–8.

[51] ibid.

[52] European Commission, *Indirect and Cumulative Impacts and Impact Interactions* (CEC, Brussels, 2002).

[53] See further Royal Commission on Environmental Pollution, *Setting Environmental Standards*, ch. 7.

[54] The correspondence between judgments of significance and the offer, or acceptance, of mitigation measures is discussed in Ch. 4, pp. 136–40. This interrelationship is also considered in the context of the Cairngorm funicular railway project: Ch. 7, pp. 272–83.

as a matter of law, developers need only *recommend* suitable mitigating measures. There is no formal obligation to demonstrate that they can and will be undertaken, or to conduct post-assessment monitoring, aside from controls imposed under planning legislation, for example by conditions.[55]

Mitigation comes in many forms, ranging from avoidance (for example, avoiding areas during sensitive periods such as breeding seasons), moderation (emission controls, noise barriers), rescue (translocation of animals), repair (reinstatement of plants or animals), and compensation (donating or creating substitute habitat areas or 'shadow projects').[56] These forms of mitigation are commonly seen as technical exercises, about which there is some optimism that the adverse effects of development may be reduced and beneficial effects increased, thus rendering the project or policy more acceptable in environmental terms. Along these lines, Morgan states:

In its extreme form, the use of environmental impact assessment can be seen as fine-tuning proposals to a particular environment, to avoid the worst excesses of development. There may not be any doubt about the project going ahead, nor any need to consider alternative sites or project designs. Consequently, in that sense, environmental impact assessment becomes a technical tool for designing mitigation measures.[57]

The suggestion is that the mitigation of adverse effects defines and explains the entire environmental assessment process. However, the adequacy of mitigation by the replication of habitats and translocation of species, and even the appropriateness of trying to 'compensate' for environmental loss should be questioned.[58]

The next stage of the environmental assessment process is the consultation of 'a larger audience' which recognizes the public interest nature of activities with environmental effects.[59] Comments on the developer's environmental statement and any other information arising from the assessment process may be provided by statutory consultees (an extensive list of consultees is contained in the 1999 Regulations)[60] and sought from members of the public, particularly those living near to a proposed project.[61] As indicated by Figure 2.1 the opportunity for statutory consultees and members of the public to contribute to the assessment process is a relatively narrow window when compared to the more significant roles of the consenting authority and developer.

---

[55] Treweek, *Ecological Impact Assessment*, 239. A different approach is taken in the Netherlands in which consenting authorities must carry out post-assessment monitoring of projects, and report the findings to the independent EIA Commission and statutory consultees; remedial action may be taken, for example by tightening up licence conditions.
[56] As listed by Treweek, *Ecological Impact Assessment*.
[57] Morgan, *Environmental Impact Assessment*, 13.   [58] See discussion in Ch. 1, pp. 25–6.
[59] Art. 6 of the EIA Directive. See further Ch. 6, pp. 189–94.
[60] Statutory consultees according to the 1999 Regulations (various provisions) include any principal council for the area where the development is situated, other than the consenting planning authority, the Countryside Commission and English Nature, the Environment Agency, and the Countryside Commission for Wales and the Secretary of State for Wales.
[61] See Regs 13–18 of the 1999 Regulations.

When deciding whether or not to grant development consent, or grant this subject to conditions, the planning authority must take into account information provided by the developer as well as representations about the proposed project made by statutory consultees and members of the public. Making this decision involves a final evaluation of environmental effects on the part of the authority. The exact form of this evaluation is not prescribed, except that it must be capable of forming the basis of reasons for the decision.[62] Although not yet a feature of the EIA Directive, post-assessment monitoring offers an opportunity to analyse the realization of predicted impacts and possibly adjust conditions in the light of these.

Roots and Evolution

Environmental assessment of sorts has existed for centuries. The *ad quod damnum* writ, first documented in the seventeenth century, was an early form of assessment in which those who might 'be damned' by certain works were identified and possibly compensated.[63] The aim of the writ was to protect the Crown's interest in land development, which later developed as representative of the public interest. That the writ was inevitably concerned with the effects of works *beyond* the location in which they were taking place has provided an important legacy for the development of environmental assessment.

The modern forms of the EIA and SEA procedures evolved as a response to the increasing recognition of the harmful environmental impacts of post-war development schemes such as dams and motorways, and an upsurge in public environmental activism.[64] Sheate, for example, considers that the development of environmental impact assessment was 'a natural consequence of the politicisation of the environment'.[65] Whatever the exact nature of the initial impulse, this development has been analysed according to discrete and broadly chronological stages. First, procedures were established to formally assess a project's viability on the basis of engineering and economic factors. The second stage saw the employment of conventional cost-benefit analysis in which an emphasis was placed upon efficiency within a broad context of economic development, but which effectively ignored environmental and social costs. At the next stage of innovative cost-benefit analysis, pricing mechanisms were used in which economic development became just one of a number of objectives. Finally, at the (current) stage of environmental assessment, the concern is with describing the impact of policy or project proposals on the biological and physical systems which make up the environment.[66] The

---

[62] On the duty to give reasons, see Ch. 7, pp. 269–72.   [63] See Ch. 1, pp. 3–5.

[64] B. D. Clark, 'Environmental Impact Assessment: Scope and Objectives', in B. D. Clark, R. Bissett, and A. Gilad (eds.) *Perspectives on Environmental Impact Assessment* (New York: Reidel, 1984), 3–13.

[65] W. Sheate, 'From Environmental Impact Assessment to Strategic Environmental Assessment: Sustainability and Decision-Making', in J. Holder (ed.) *The Impact of EC Environmental Law in the United Kingdom* (Chichester: Wiley, 1997), 268.

[66] J. Garner and T. O'Riordan, 'Environmental Impact Assessment in the Context of Economic Recession' (1982) 148 *Geog J* 343.

appropriate relationship between environmental assessment and these other forms of project and policy evaluation is still a matter of concern.[67]

In legal terms, modern environmental assessment originated in the United States' NEPA 1969,[68] which has since provided a template for environmental assessment regimes the world over. NEPA required federal agencies to formally document how they considered the environment when making decisions to authorize works and pursue policies. These agencies are still required to include a detailed environmental impact statement in every recommendation or report on proposals for legislation and other major public developments and actions *significantly* affecting the quality of the human environment. When planning an action or policy, an agency must first determine whether an EIS (Environmental Impact Statement) is required. It does this by applying regulations which identify actions which almost always require an EIA and those which the agency has determined never have significant environmental impacts. If the action falls into neither category the agency must prepare an Environmental Assessment (EA). If on the basis of this assessment the agency finds that the action will not have a significant environmental impact, the process is completed. Otherwise, an EIS must be prepared which considers the likely environmental impacts of the proposal. This begins with 'scoping' to determine what issues the EIS will address, in part through public meetings. The agency then prepares the EIS itself, first as a draft for circulation to the public and all interested agencies and then in a final form which reflects and responds to the specific comments received. The statement must describe the state of the present environment and detail changes that the proposed action is likely to cause, both direct and indirect. There is also an obligation to discuss alternatives to the proposal, including a 'do-nothing' alternative, and to evaluate the variability and likely environmental harm of other options. Finally, once the agency has decided to proceed with a particular action, it must prepare a record of decision. This states the agency's final decision, explains how it reached this, and identifies the main alternatives and reasons for rejecting these.[69] The entire procedure is overseen by a Council of Environmental Quality which establishes guidelines for good practice. Although views differ, it has been argued that the process has significantly altered federal decision making because agencies are exposed to criticism from 'outsiders' based on the content of environmental statements, and must respond to these.[70]

---

[67] For example, Petts now calls for greater integration between cost-benefit analysis and environmental assessment, in 'EIA: Overview of Purpose and Process', in J. Petts (ed.) *Handbook of Environmental Impact Assessment: Vol. 1 Process, Methods and Potential* (Oxford: Blackwell, 1999). See also I. J. Bateman, 'Environmental Impact Assessment, Cost-Benefit Analysis and the Valuation of Environmental Impacts', in Petts, *Handbook*, 93.

[68] S. 102(2)(c) NEPA 1969, 42 USC 4321–4361. See Appendix I.

[69] Described by M. Hertz, 'Parallel Universes: NEPA Lessons for the New Property' (1993) *Columbia L Rev* 1668, at 1678.

[70] Taylor, *Making Bureaucracies Think*, 80–1. See also L. K. Caldwell, *Science and the National Environmental Policy Act: Redirecting Policy through Procedural Reform* (Alabama: Alabama University Press, 1982). See further Ch. 7, pp. 251–6 on the nature of decision making governed by environmental assessment procedures in the United States.

The United States' legislation influenced a number of international organizations to adopt similar forms of environmental assessment. In the mid-1970s the Organization for Economic Cooperation and Development recommended that member countries establish procedures for assessing environmental impacts of significant public and private projects and exchanging information on forecasting environmental effects.[71] Similarly, the United Nations Environment Programme produced guidelines on conducting environmental assessment which stressed also the evaluation of possible social and economic effects.[72] As a body specifically concerned with environmental change giving rise to health hazards, the World Health Organization recommended that environmental and health impact assessment studies be carried out prior to the implementation of all major economic development projects, particularly dams, and offered guidance to member countries to encourage them to undertake environmental health assessments at national level.[73] In line with these initiatives, environmental appraisal was also developed in various development assistance programmes,[74] for example, the OECD issued guidelines for assessing assistance projects[75] and the World Bank began to categorize development assistance projects which required full-scale environmental assessment.[76] These few examples suggest the initial adoption of environmental assessment procedures by organizations hitherto primarily concerned with economic, development, and human health agendas. It also suggests the beginning of a process of standardizing environmental assessment procedures.

The operation of environmental assessment procedures in the United States, and the recommended use of the technique by international organizations stimulated interest in environmental assessment in Europe. Environmental impact assessment had become a frequently litigated area in the United States and this acted as a warning to European countries engaged in introducing similar legislation,

[71] *Environmental Consequences of Significant Public and Private Projects* C(74)216 (Paris: OECD, 1974); *Coordinated Methods of Assessing the Potential Environmental Effects of Chemical Compounds* C(74)215, 14.11.74 (Paris: OECD, 1974); *Coordination Guidelines in Respect of Procedures and Requirements for Anticipating the Effects of Chemicals on Man and the Environment* C(77)97 final, 7.6.77 (Paris: OECD, 1977); *The Assessment of Projects with Significant Impact on the Environment* C(79)116 (Paris: OECD, 1979).

[72] United Nations Environment Programme, *Guidelines for Assessing Industrial Environmental Impact and Criteria for the Siting of Industry* (Paris: UNEP, 1980); see M. N. Htun, 'Development of United Nations Environment Programme Guidelines for Assessing Industrial Criteria for the Siting of Industry', in Clark *et al.*, *Perspectives on Environmental Impact Assessment*, 253–63.

[73] World Health Organization, *Rapid Assessment of Sources of Air, Water and Land Pollution Resolution* WHO/35.17 (Geneva: World Health Organization, 1982); see also E. Giroult, 'World Health Organisation Interest in Environmental Health Impact Assessment', in Wathern, *Environmental Impact Assessment*, 258–71, at 258.

[74] W. V. Kennedy, 'Environmental Impact Assessment and Bilateral Development Aid: An Overview', in Wathern, *Environmental Impact Assessment*, 272–85, at 272.

[75] Organization for Economic Cooperation and Development, *Recommendation of the Council on Measures Required to Facilitate the Environmental Assessment of Development Assistance Projects and Programmes*, C(86)26 (Paris: OECD, 1986).

[76] World Bank, *The World Bank and the Environment: First Annual Report* (Washington: World Bank, 1990). See further below, pp. 71–2.

even though the American and European contexts were essentially different. NEPA was imposed upon a land use planning system in which there were few existing procedures for predicting a proposed development's environmental impacts.[77] In contrast, when the (then) EEC adopted the EIA Directive in 1985 most Member States had established land use laws, including in some cases procedures for predicting environmental effects of development proposals. One of the most comprehensive of these was the French regime, introduced by the Protection de la Nature 1978 which mandated the preparation of environmental assessments for all major public or private development projects requiring authorization. The role of environmental assessment in other European countries varied considerably.[78] Initially, the United Kingdom, the Federal Republic of Germany, and the Nordic countries adapted their already well-developed land use planning systems to take account of the effects of development on the environment. The United Kingdom was later obliged to introduce specific legislation on environmental assessment in order to comply with Community law. Over a period of about ten years, this has involved wide-ranging amendments of planning and environmental law to fill the gaps in legislation which have allowed for opportunistic as well as well-founded legal action by groups wishing to oppose development.[79]

Developing Environmental Impact Assessment in the United Kingdom

In addition to the influences already mentioned, the introduction of environmental impact assessment in the UK took place against a background of growing disillusionment with the public planning inquiry system. This was because its adversarial approach tended to inhibit agreement on matters of fact prior to the inquiry and discouraged witnesses from making evidence known in advance. The additional practical difficulties of combining national policy and local issues in the single inquiry procedure (with political resistance to analysing national policy in this forum), and the limited scope for effective public participation that the inquiry system appeared to offer[80] were shown up by the Windscale (later to become Sellafield) inquiry.[81] Idealistically, some writers considered that inquiry

[77] K. Von Moltke, 'Environmental Impact Assessment in the United States and Europe', in Clarke *et al.*, *Perspectives on Environmental Impact Assessment*, at 28.

[78] See the review of European responses to environmental assessment in A. Gilpin, *Environmental Impact Assessment: Cutting Edge for the Twenty-First Century* (Cambridge: Cambridge University Press, 1995) which surveys these countries in chs. 6, 8, and 9; P. Wathern, 'The EIA Directive of the European Community' in Wathern, *Environmental Impact Assessment*, 194–200 also describes the position in France and other Member States prior to the adoption of the EIA Directive.

[79] See further Ch. 6, pp. 206–18.

[80] N. Hutton, *Lay Participation in a Public Inquiry: A Sociological Case Study* (London: Gower, 1986); see also J. Herington, 'Environmental Values in a Changing Planning System', in M. Clark and J. Herington (eds.) *The Role of Environmental Impact Assessment in the Planning Process* (London: Mansell, 1988), 145.

[81] R. Kemp, 'Planning, Legitimation and the Development of Nuclear Power: A Critical Theoretic Analysis of the Windscale Inquiry' (1986) 14 *Policy and Politics* 350, at 351. Some of these

procedures would be greatly improved by the onset of an environmental impact assessment regime:

... a fully informed inquiry process could only be achieved if preceded by some form of environmental impact assessment which would consider all the diverse effects of a particular proposal upon the natural environment. Such an examination could be interpreted as the optimum stage of instrumental or purposive rationality and therefore of fundamental value to practical decision making on major planning proposals.[82]

Particular faith was placed in the ability of environmental assessment procedures to strengthen the hand of environmental and conservationist groups:

[Environmental impact assessment] will ensure that inquiry participants are fully prepared and that common ground and areas of dispute have been identified in advance. It will help all the parties with information and allow the public to be well informed and it should add a further element of objectivity to hearings.[83]

However, empirical evidence suggests poor integration of environmental impact assessment and planning inquiry procedures in practice, mainly because little consideration was given as to how environmental impact assessment would be integrated into planning inquiry procedures.[84] The consequence was an uneasy relationship between the European model of environmental assessment and the British inquiry procedure, which may still be discerned, particularly in relation to major projects.[85]

This concern with the planning inquiry system was combined with private initiatives to develop environmental assessment. For example, during the 1970s environmental impact assessment methodologies were developed by companies operating in the newly discovered oil fields of the North Sea.[86] This form of environmental assessment was not particularly transparent, but the financial risks involved in oil exploration meant that environmental assessment acted as a genuine search for the best option amongst alternative sites (but on economic as well as environmental grounds).

criticisms were addressed in the House of Commons Environment Committee, Fifth Report, *Planning Appeals and Call-in and Major Public Inquiries*, Session 1985–1986 HC 181, Cm 43.

[82] Kemp, 'Planning, Legitimation and the Development of Nuclear Power', at 364.

[83] M. Clark, 'Environmental Impact Assessment: An Ideology for Europe' (1978) *TCP* 395, at 388.

[84] See J. Holder, 'An Analysis of Council Directive 85/337/EEC on the Assessment of the Effects of Certain Public and Private Projects on the Environment and the Development of Environmental Law in the United Kingdom' (Ph.D., University of Warwick, 1995), ch. 7.

[85] On which, see J. Popham and M. Purdue, 'The Future of the Major Inquiry' [2002] *JPL* 137, at 144, which describes as particularly problematic the environmental assessment of projects subject to Hybrid Bills since there are no legal requirements as to the content of the environmental statement provided to Parliament. See further on the relationship between environmental assessment and the planning inquiry, Ch. 6. pp. 229–32.

[86] See also R. Smith, 'The Implementation of EIA in Britain', in H. Heinelt, T. Malek, R. Smith and A. E. Toller, *European Union Environment Policy and New Forms of Governance* (Aldershot: Ashgate, 2001).

Literature in this early period of development gave guidance on methods of assessment,[87] although there were also theoretical appraisals of assessment as a regulatory technique.[88] The scope of application of environmental impact assessment then expanded beyond its use as a management tool for investment, but instead became closely identified with the planning system as a technique for controlling the harmful effects of pollution by influencing the siting of industrial activities. Miller and Wood,[89] for example, concluded that environmental impact assessment could help identify and possibly remedy environmental harm which ensued after planning permission was granted for industrial projects, and that this would additionally reduce unjust social distribution of pollution. Their work influenced the European Commission's proposals for a Community-wide environmental impact assessment regime, and the authors helped to draft a directive.[90]

Following the implementation of the EC EIA Directive in the town and country planning system in England and Wales, environmental assessment became a central part of development consent requirements in the planning system.[91] Environmental assessment procedures have since been applied to a wide range of policy issues and operate in a number of contexts—nature conservation, pollution control, development assistance[92]—but they have been developed most fully in the planning system. This is because environmental impact assessment was initially project-based and the need to obtain development consent for projects provided a trigger for the application of assessment rules. This compares to procedures in the United States in which agency *policies* were also subject to environmental assessment from the outset.

The adoption of the EIA Directive by the European Economic Community in 1985 represented the first incursion of European Community law into the planning systems of the Member States. In England and Wales this formalized existing methods of taking environmental effects into account in decision making.[93] Prior to the implementation of the Directive, information about the environmental effects of a proposed development was obtained in a number of ways. A type of environmental

[87] Munn, *Environmental Impact Assessment*; B. D. Clark *et al.*, 'Methods of Environmental Analysis' (1978) 4 *Built Env* 111. More recently, see Morris and Therivel *Methods of Environmental Impact Assessment.*   [88] O'Riordan and Hey, *Environmental Impact Assessment.*

[89] C. Miller and C. Wood, *Planning and Pollution: An Examination of the Role of Land Use Planning in the Protection of the Environmental Quality* (Oxford: Oxford University Press, 1983), 216–22.; see also M. J. Ledger, 'An Assessment of the Effectiveness of Land Use Planning Powers to Control Pollution' (Ph.D., University of Manchester, 1982); and C. Wood, *Planning Pollution Prevention: A Comparison of the Siting Controls over Air Pollution in Great Britain and the USA* (Oxford: Heineman Newnes, 1989).

[90] Commission of the European Communities, *Draft Directive 7972/80 on Environmental Assessment* COM(80) 313 final.

[91] For example, see Herington, 'Environmental Values,' at 159, on the role of environmental assessment in the town and country planning system.   [92] Discussed below, pp. 65–72.

[93] N. Haigh, 'The EEC Directive on Environmental Assessment of Development Projects' (1983) JPL 585; R. Macrory, 'Environmental Assessment: Critical Legal Issues in Implementation', in D. Vaughan (ed.) *EC Environmental and Planning Law* (London: Butterworths, 1986); M. Grant, 'Implementation of the EC Directive on Environmental Impact Assessment' (1989) 4 *Conn J of Int L* 463; J. Salter, 'EIA: The Question of Implementation' [1992] JPL 313.

assessment was first required by the Town and Country Planning Act 1971. This stipulated that the written statement of a structure plan should include measures for the improvement of the physical environment, reinforced by Department of Environment guidance that the local planning authority should set out in the development plan how environmental considerations had been taken into account, including measures for reducing water, air, and noise pollution.[94] Environmental information could also be obtained under the procedure set out in the General Development Order 1977.[95] This gave planners powers to request further information from a prospective developer beyond that contained in their planning application 'to enable them to determine the application'. However, this national precursor to environmental impact assessment did not entitle the local authority to insist upon the submission of environmental information and analysis as a formal assessment.[96] The effect of this procedure was that environmental impacts were assessed according to information provided solely by the developer (although the usual forms of consultation in the planning system also applied). An assessment of sorts was also to be conducted in the case of special categories of development.[97] At the same time, environmental assessments were conducted outside the town and country development consent system when a proposed project fell outside the statutory definition of 'development',[98] or became the subject of a public planning inquiry.[99]

These various procedures ensured that environmental appraisal was clearly a feature of the land use planning system prior to the adoption of the EIA Directive. Use of the 'further information' power by local authorities meant that assessments could be made beyond those which formed the subject of specific policy guidance. But planning legislation and policy guidance still imposed few constraints upon the internal procedures for judging the weight to be given to environmental information derived from the various procedures. Studies of pre-statutory environmental assessment in the planning system found an absence of any rigorous

[94] Department of the Environment, Circular 4/79 *Memorandum on Structure and Local Plans* (London: HMSO, 1979).

[95] Reg. 5 Town and Country Planning General Development Order 1977 (SI 1977, No. 289) (enacted under s. 25 Town and Country Planning Act 1971 as amended).

[96] For example, supplementary written analysis of the House of Lords report on the proposed Directive, Eleventh Report, *Environmental Assessment of Projects*, Session 1980–81, at p. 149: 'there is doubt whether local authorities can require all the information now specified in the proposed directive, but in any event, this provision (Reg. 5 General Development Order 1977) is discretionary'.

[97] According to Department of Environment guidance, an assessment of harm was to take place if the proposed project involved the storage of hazardous materials (Circular 1/72 *Development Involving the Use of Storage in Bulk of Hazardous Material*), was likely to be a noisy development (Circular 10/73 *Planning and Noise*) or was a small business sited in a residential area (Circular 61/72 *Small Firms*).

[98] e.g. a *de facto* environmental assessment arose from the statutory requirement that official notices about a road building project 'shall state the general effect of the proposed scheme', Highways Act 1959, Sch. 1, para. 7.

[99] T. O'Riordan, 'Beyond Environmental Impact Assessment' in O'Riordan and Hey (eds.) *Environmental Impact Assessment*, 207: 'The present method of assessing environmental impacts is the planning inquiry'. On the relationship between the planning inquiry and environmental assessment, see further Ch. 6, pp. 229–32.

environmental appraisal on the part of local planning authorities and considerable variation in the structure, content, and role of environmental assessments.[100] While not denying that the informal assessment procedures conducted as part of the development consent system generally permitted the impact of a proposed development on the surrounding area, this assessment was generally carried out in relation to a specific site. In contrast, the EIA Directive was designed explicitly to require an assessment with respect to the wider environment, including in terms of the cumulative, indirect, and integrated effects of development.

The existence of these various non-statutory and loosely prescribed forms of environmental assessment meant that the initial attempt to implement the Directive proved a tricky affair. Faced with a draft Directive on environmental assessment,[101] the government's view was that environmental assessment was 'implicit in the United Kingdom's town and country planning system'[102] and thus mandatory assessment should be avoided. From this perspective, the consequence of statutory environmental assessment was the removal of discretion and in its place an arbitrary classification system. In line with its policy of 'lifting the burden' on developers, the government considered that the EIA Directive would also impose unreasonable costs on developers. The Commons concurred.[103] The government's view that environmental assessment was already to be found in the planning system led it to attempt to achieve the Directive's results by absorbing its requirements into existing legislation and administrative arrangements for applying for development consent. Tellingly, the working party set up by the Department of the Environment to explore the means of implementation concluded principally: '[T]he requirements of the Directive can be met within the context of the existing planning system without imposing significant new burdens on either developers or planning authorities'.[104] This view expresses information theories of environmental assessment, since the power to request 'additional information' from developers on the part of local authorities was considered to adequately reflect the purpose and content of the EIA Directive, although this interpretation effectively ignored the advances made in the Directive to encourage participation and consultation in decision making.

A minimalist approach to implementation was therefore pursued by absorbing the Directive's requirements into existing planning procedures by means of secondary legislation,[105] primarily the Town and Country Planning (Assessment of

[100] P. H. Selman, 'The Use of Ecological Evaluations by Local Planning Authorities' (1982) 15 *J of Env Plg and Management* 1; Royal Commission on Environmental Pollution, *Air Pollution Control: An Integrated Approach* Cmnd 6371 (London: HMSO, 1976).

[101] Draft Directive 7972/80 Com(80) 313 final.

[102] House of Commons Select Committee on the European Communities, Eleventh Report, *Environmental Assessment of Projects*, Session 1980–81 (London: HMSO, 1981), para. 31.

[103] Department of the Environment, *Implementation of the European Directive on Environmental Assessment* (London: HMSO, 1986), para. 6.

[104] House of Lords Select Committee on European Legislation, Twelfth Report, Session 1980–81. This Report warmly welcomed the Directive.

[105] By powers contained in s. 2 European Communities Act 1972.

Environmental Effects) Regulations 1988 ('the 1988 Regulations')[106] in the case of applications for development consent in the town and country planning system. This was incongruent with the breadth of purpose of the principle that 'projects which are likely to have significant effects should be granted only after prior assessment of the likely significant effects has been carried out'.[107] This discrepancy is illustrated by the environmental impact assessment of projects designed to intensively farm semi-natural or uncultivated land. Though listed in Annex II of the Directive, this category of project fell outside the scope of the implementing 1988 Regulations because these were based upon the existing categories of 'development' requiring planning permission,[108] which excludes certain agriculture and forestry projects.[109] This, and other gaps, led the European Commission to question the adequacy of the implementing provisions. Lengthy negotiations between the Commission and the Secretary of State took place against a political background of the United Kingdom opting out of the Social Chapter of the Treaty on European Union, and invoking the subsidiarity principle in respect of individual projects which also formed the basis of the Commission's enforcement action. The United Kingdom government eventually conceded in 1992 (in exchange for the Commission terminating legal proceedings on five specific projects)[110] that environmental impact assessment procedures should apply to cases involving the use of semi-natural and uncultivated areas for intensive agriculture.[111] Separate sets of Regulations requiring the environmental impact assessment of such projects likely to have significant effects on the environment were not issued until 2001 (2002 in the case of Scotland).[112] This and other examples suggest that the initial implementation effort had the effect of narrowing the scope of the

[106] (SI 1988, No. 1199). J. Salter, 'EIA: The Challenge from Brussels' [1992] JPL 14, at 14 recounts that the Directive was also implemented by contract in those cases in which the assessment of projects relates to land lying below the low water mark—within the scope of Community law, but outside the jurisdiction of the local planning authority.

[107] Ninth recital, preamble to the EIA Directive, to be read in conjunction with Arts. 5 and 8 of the Directive.

[108] S. 55(1)(e) Town and Country Planning Act 1990. On this regulatory gap and the regime introduced to remedy this, see further Royal Commission on Environmental Pollution, Twenty-third Report, *Environmental Planning* Cm 5459 (London: HMSO, 2002), paras. 9.48–9.53.

[109] Other notable gaps included those projects which do not constitute 'development', such as those permitted under a development order. The filling of such gaps was completed in stages, for example by the Town and Country Planning (Assessment of Environmental Effects) (Amendment) Regulations 1990 (SI 1990, No. 367), the Town and Country Planning (Assessment of Environmental Effects) (Amendment) Regulations 1992 (SI 1992, No. 1494) and the Town and Country Planning (Assessment of Environmental Effects) (Amendment) Regulations 1994 (SI 1994, No. 677).

[110] These included the extension of the M3 motorway through Twyford Down, on which see further Ch. 6, p. 223, and Ch. 7, pp. 257–8.

[111] HC Written answers, 16.12.1992, Cols. 319–20.

[112] Environmental Impact Assessment (Uncultivated Land and Semi-natural Areas) (England) Regulations 2001 (SI 2001, No. 3966); Environmental Impact Assessment (Uncultivated Land and Semi-natural Areas) (Northern Ireland) Regulations 2001 (SI 2001, No. 435) and Environmental Impact Assessment (Uncultivated Land and Semi-natural Areas) (Scotland) Regulations 2002 (SI 2002, No. 6).

environmental assessment process as set out in the Directive, and that this has taken a long time to rectify.[113]

In summary, the implementation of the EIA Directive was influenced in an immediate sense by political events, but more fundamentally by the existence in the United Kingdom of a long-standing, informal, and discretionary approach to environmental assessment. Several conclusions can be drawn from the process of implementation. Primarily, 'indigenous' procedures for predicting the effects of development on the environment were formalized and codified as a result of the EIA Directive's implementation. The Directive provided for the formal introduction of expert and public opinion on the effects of development on the environment into essentially political planning procedures. Notwithstanding the formal nature of assessment, fragmentation in the administration of assessment procedures still exists because of the piecemeal absorption of the Directive's provisions into existing planning procedures by means of many different sets of regulations.[114] It was therefore perhaps inevitable that the legal and administrative features of the ad hoc and largely informal pre-statutory environmental assessment procedures came to be combined with those designed to give legal effect to the EIA Directive, in particular that an onus was placed upon the developer to provide information about the effects of development on the environment and that, in eliciting and presenting this information, the developer should enjoy discretion. For this reason also, the planning system's existing lacunae, notably the exclusion of all but a handful of agricultural and forestry projects from the need for development consent, similarly prevailed in law designed to implement the Directive.

In terms of the exercise of discretion, the 1988 Regulations and other implementing Regulations have continued to confer considerable discretion on planners to determine the application of environmental assessment rules, the adequacy of environmental statements submitted by developers with an application for planning permission (despite overall responsibility for the implementation of a statutory and uniform assessment system lying with central government), and, of course, the final decision. Unlike the procedures existing prior to the implementation of the EIA Directive, this discretion is now subject to the requirement that a project likely to have significant effects upon the environment must be subjected to an environmental assessment,[115] which has involved the establishment of statutory and judicial boundaries on judgments of significance.[116] However, similarly to pre-statutory assessment, the implementing Regulations grant discretion to the

---

[113] Although the enactment of s. 15 of the Planning and Compensation Act 1991, which inserted s. 71 into the Town and Country Planning Act 1990 enabled the Secretary of State to require environmental impact assessment of planning projects other than those listed in the European Directive, for example motorway service stations and golf courses.

[114] There are currently 37 sets of regulations in force for this purpose (with more planned). See Appendix X.

[115] As confirmed by *Berkeley* v *Secretary of State for the Environment and Fulham Football Club* (*Berkeley No. 1*) [2000] WLR 420, [2001] AC 603, (2001) 13 *JEL* 89. HL.

[116] See Ch. 4, pp. 108–30.

developer with respect to the selection and presentation of information. Such control over information on the effects of development on the environment entering the decision-making procedures of the planning system is particularly important in cases in which the developer's environmental statement is mistakenly treated as though it were an account of the full assessment process.

The initial attempts to implement the Directive led to research being conducted on its legal implications, as well as more practical concerns about its administration by various professional and interest groups, not least the European Commission.[117] The relative neglect of legal aspects of environmental assessment at the time of the adoption of the Directive on environmental assessment was partially remedied by works which highlighted the inadequacies of English law in accommodating its aims and methods, something which came to light through analysis of judicial review cases on environmental assessment.[118] Since the bulk of this research was conducted, there has been an explosion of governance literature which has considerably advanced theories on participation, deliberation, and the regulation of decision making. The existing literature on environmental assessment fails almost entirely to recognize this. This is striking when the general characteristics of environmental assessment, outlined in Chapter 1,[119] are considered. In particular, environmental assessment contributes to the sharing of responsibility for providing environmental information on which decisions may be based and, in formal terms at least, provides opportunities for the consultation of a broad range of participants. These features suggest that environmental assessment is capable of relating the style and premises of modern forms of environmental governance to the regulation of decision making,[120] and in so doing expressing aspects of the concept of sustainable development. The interpretation of environmental assessment as a means of putting into operation the concept of sustainable development can be explained to a large extent by its development as an instrument of international environmental law and custom.

---

[117] E. Gouge, 'The UK Implementation of Environmental Assessment: Organisational and Political Implications' (1989) *Local Government Policy Making* 55; W. Sheate, *The Environmental Assessment Directive: Five Years On* (London: Council for the Protection of Rural England, 1991); Institute of Environmental Assessment, *Practical Experience of Environmental Assessment in the United Kingdom* (East Kirkby: Institute of Environmental Assessment, 1993), Royal Institute of Chartered Surveyors, *Environmental Assessments* (London: RICS, 1989); C. Wood and C. Jones, *Monitoring Environmental Assessment and Planning* (London, HMSO, 1990); C. Wood and C. Jones, 'The Impact of Environmental Assessment on Local Planning Authorities' (1992) 35 *JEPM* 115–27; C. Wood, 'Five Years of British Environmental Assessment', in D. Cross and C. Whitehead (eds.) *Development and Planning* (Cambridge: Cambridge University Press, 1994); Wathern, *Environmental Impact Assessment*; European Commission, *Report from the Commission on the Implementation of Directive 85/337/EEC on the Assessment of the Effects of Certain Public and Private Projects on the Environment* COM(93) 28, 2.4.1993 (Brussels: CEC, 1993).

[118] J. Alder, 'Environmental Impact Assessment: The Inadequacies of English Law', (1993) 5 *JEL* 203; A. Ward, 'The Right to an Effective Remedy in European Community Law: A Case Study of United Kingdom Decisions Concerning the Environmental Assessment Directive' (1993) 5 *JEL* 221 also examines this case law, but from a different perspective—the effectiveness of remedies in Community law.   [119] See pp. 12–22.   [120] See particularly Chs. 6 and 7.

International Law and Custom

The position of environmental assessment in international law has been slowly enhanced to the extent that it has reached the status of a general principle of international law, and possibly even a requirement of customary international law. This progression has been reflected in the gaining in significance of environmental assessment in national legal systems, and in the European Community. It begins, though, with statements about the desirability of environmental assessment governing decision making in several non-binding instruments.[121] One such early formulation was contained in the 1982 World Charter for Nature which called for an exhaustive examination and assessment of activities likely to pose a significant risk to nature and required that activities should either not proceed (if likely to cause irreversible damage to nature based on an assessment's findings) or proceed with minimal potential effects.[122] This also (unusually at this time) detailed that such assessments were to be disclosed to the public to allow for effective consultation and participation and that all persons, in accordance with national legislation, were to be given an opportunity to participate in the formulation of decisions of direct concern to their environment.[123] In this respect, the Charter was prophetic in its reinforcement of participatory democracy by environmental assessment. For example, this idea formed the core of Agenda 21 in 1992 in which references to environmental assessment abound,[124] but in particular requires the signatory states to ensure that relevant decisions are preceded by environmental impact assessments and take into consideration the costs of development in terms of its ecological consequences.[125] The most influential of non-binding references (in terms of initiating national measures on environmental assessment) is Principle 17 of the Rio Declaration which states that: 'Environmental impact assessment, as a national instrument, shall be undertaken for proposed activities that are likely to have a significant adverse impact on the environment and are subject to a decision of a competent national authority'.[126] Arguably the mandatory language of Principle 17 is consistent with the view that environmental impact

---

[121] Described in detail by P. Sands, *Principles of International Environmental Law* (Cambridge: Cambridge University Press, 2nd edn., 2003), ch. 16. Notably, an early draft of the Stockholm Declaration contained a reference to environmental impact assessment (Principle 20) but this was withdrawn, only to be revived as Principle 5 of the 1978 UNEP Draft Principles of Conduct, on which see Sands, *Principles*, 801. Gray's interpretation of the withdrawal of Principle 20 was because this was perceived by developing countries to offer a means by which developed countries could impede projects; see K. Gray, 'International Environmental Impact Assessment: Potential for a Multilateral Environmental Agreement' (2000) *Col J of Int Env L and Policy* 83, at 105–6. The opposite appears to be true; see below, pp. 71–2.

[122] World Charter for Nature, (1982) 23 ILM 455, p. 11 (a)–(c).   [123] At pp. 16–23.

[124] See specifically Sands, *Principles*, 802–3.

[125] UNCED, Agenda 21: Programme of Action for Sustainable Development (1992), Ch. 8 of which is devoted to integrating environmental protection and development in decision making.

[126] UNCED (1992) 31 ILM 874.

assessments are now required as a general principle of international law, particularly in respect of environmentally harmful activities which may have transboundary consequences.[127]

Unsurprisingly, binding instruments tend to be less prescriptive,[128] for example the United Nations Convention on the Law of the Sea (1982)[129] sets out requirements for environmental assessment as follows:

> When states have reasonable grounds for believing that planned activities under their jurisdiction or control may cause substantial pollution of or significant and harmful changes to the marine environment, they shall, as far as practicable, assess the potential effects of such activities on the marine environment and shall communicate reports of the results of such assessments at appropriate intervals to the competent international organisations, which should make them available to all states.[130]

Whilst conferring an obligation to carry out an assessment of activities that have potential effects on the marine environment, this is clearly restricted to what is practicable. In addition, there is no binding requirement on states to take the results of an environmental impact assessment procedure into account when authorizing an activity.[131]

In contrast, instruments negotiated by United Nations Economic Commission of Europe on transboundary environmental assessment[132] and strategic environmental assessment,[133] and on participation, public access to environmental information, and access to justice in environmental matters[134] have provided an important impetus in the European Community's development of enforceable environmental assessment legislation. In particular, the Espoo Convention creates obligations to take appropriate and effective measures to prevent, reduce, and control significant adverse transboundary environmental impacts from proposed development and other activities, and to provide for public participation in such cases.[135] This required the EIA Directive to be strengthened in several respects.[136]

With varying degrees of precision, these declarations and instruments forge a potential alliance between the principle of sustainable development and the use of

---

[127] Sands, *Principles*, 800.

[128] On the nature of these instruments, see generally, Gray, 'International Environmental Impact Assessment'.

[129] United Nations Convention on the Law of the Sea (1982) 21 ILM 1261.

[130] Arts. 205 and 206. See further comment by Gray, 'International Environmental Impact Assessment', at 92.

[131] See further comment by Gray, op. cit. at 92. See also reliance on UNCLOS in *Ireland* v *United Kingdom (the MOX case)* ITLOS Order, 41 ILM 405 (2002), discussed below, p. 56.

[132] Convention on environmental impact assessment in a transboundary context (Espoo Convention) 30 ILM 802 (1991).

[133] Protocol on strategic environmental assessment (Kiev) 21 May 2003 (not yet in force).

[134] Aarhus Convention, 38 ILM 517 (1999). For the set of EC measures designed to implement Aarhus, see Ch. 6, pp. 192–4.

[135] See further Ch. 6, pp. 186–7 and 191. See also Gray, 'International Environmental Impact Assessment', 100 ff. and J. Beggs, 'Combating Biospheric Degradation: International Environmental Impact Assessment and the Transboundary Pollution Dilemma' (1995) *Fordham Env L J* 379.

[136] By its amendment in 1997 by Directive 97/11/EC OJ 1997 L 73, p. 5.

environmental assessment.[137] The accomplishment of environmental assessment as a general principle of international law, as foreseen by the Legal Experts Group on Environmental Law of the WCED,[138] has been realized in the course of several judgments of the International Court of Justice. In *New Zealand* v *France*[139] New Zealand challenged France's decision to resume underground nuclear tests in the Pacific Atolls on the ground that France was under an obligation in customary international law to conduct an environmental impact assessment of the potential effects of this before carrying out the tests.[140] Amongst the *dissenting* judgments, Judge Palmer advocated the recognition of environmental limits via such mechanisms as environmental assessment, 'otherwise the paradigm of sustainable development enhanced by the world at the Rio Conference cannot be achieved'.[141] Judge Weeramantry also expressed a dissenting opinion that the principle of environmental impact assessment, being ancillary to the precautionary principle, 'was gathering strength and international acceptance and had reached a level of general recognition such that the Court should take notice of it'.[142]

The International Court of Justice revisited the status of environmental impact assessment *vis-à-vis* sustainable development in the *Gabčíkovo-Nagymaros Project* case[143] which concerned a dispute between Hungary and Slovakia over the breakdown of agreement between the states to cooperate in the building of the barrages on the River Danube contained in a 1977 Treaty between the parties. Hungary had unilaterally suspended construction of a barrage at Nagymaros (ostensibly due to evidence of environmental harm), but the Slovak government had continued to build a new dam at Gabčíkovo within their territory but with effects upon the flow of the river. The majority view of the Court in this case was that there was imposed on the states a duty of continuous environmental impact assessment in the light of developments in knowledge, and that this duty influenced the provisions of the Treaty governing their cooperation in this field. Judge Weeramantry (now in the majority) stated:

... Environmental law in its current state of development would read into treaties which may reasonably be considered to have a significant impact upon the environment, a duty of environmental impact assessment and this means also, whether the treaty expressly so provides or not, a duty of monitoring the environmental impacts of any substantial project during the operation of the scheme.[144]

Judge Weeramantry additionally argued that sustainable development is not merely a concept but a recognized principle of customary international law, albeit

[137] Discussed below, pp. 56–60.

[138] Environmental assessment was identified as a legal principle of sustainable development and international law by the World Commission on Environment and Development's Experts Group on Environmental Law, *Legal Principles for Environmental Protection and Sustainable Development* (Dordrecht: Martinus Nijhoff, 1987), 58.   [139] (1995) ICJ Reports, 288.

[140] New Zealand also based its case on Art. 16 of the Convention for the Protection of the Natural Resources and Environment of the South Pacific Region (Noumea Convention) 26 ILM (1987).

[141] At para. 68.   [142] (1995) ICJ Reports, 344.   [143] (1997) ICJ Reports, 7.

[144] (1997) ICJ Reports, 7, at 11.

one which suggests procedural rather than substantive obligations. The case suggests a stringent obligation of continuous monitoring of the environmental impacts of a project, which has not been as fully accepted on the domestic front.[145]

The third significant case heard before the International Court of Justice is ongoing. *Ireland* v *United Kingdom* was brought on the basis that the United Kingdom had violated its obligations under the United Nations Convention on the Law of the Sea[146] by authorizing a new nuclear plant in 2001 (on the existing Sellafield site) to manufacture mixed oxide (MOX) fuel on the basis of an environmental impact assessment from 1993. This statement failed to take into account the potential effects of the manufacturing process on the marine environment of the Irish Sea,[147] suggesting also that the customary principle of 'continuous environmental impact assessment' established by the International Court had been infringed. In the preliminary stages of the case on provisional measures before the International Tribunal, Ireland failed to have the works suspended, but secured a minority view that the inadequate environmental impact assessment would have warranted this on the grounds that this 'is a central tool of the international law of prevention'.[148]

Relating Environmental Assessment and Sustainable Development

The profound shift in environmental discourse and environmental law by which sustainable development became an organizing theme and objective of international environmental law (and environmental law more generally) has been reflected in the functions ascribed to environmental assessment. As mentioned above, environmental impact assessment was originally considered to assist mainly with pollution control (though also habitat and landscape concerns) through informing decisions about siting industrial development, thus performing a technicist function in environmental law. It has since been acknowledged to have a far broader role in implementing the principle of sustainable development by influencing decision makers to take account of the quality of development and its effects upon the conservation of natural resources, as well as still influencing locational issues. This parallel shift in the perceived function of environmental impact assessment reflects the rejection of purely technocratic practices in favour of a more general reformist environmental strategy (although more extreme interpretations

---

[145] Instead a pragmatic approach to continuous monitoring, and the application of environmental assessment throughout the lifetime of a project has been taken by British courts, with the effect that a narrower version of environmental assessment prevails. See e.g. *R (Prokopp)* v *LUL* [2003] EWCA 960 (Admin), cf. Ch. 6, p. 209.   [146] Art. 206.
[147] See further, Sands, *Principles*, 806–7.
[148] ITLOS Order, 3 December 2001, 41 ILM 405 (2002). Opinion of Judge Szekely, paras. 12–17.

of sustainable development have advanced economic methodologies which are similarly technicist).[149] Encouraging popular participation in environmental decision making formed an important part of this strategy. In this vein, the World Commission on Environment and Development specifically identified environmental assessment of projects and policies as offering a means to achieve sustainable industrial development, alongside the use of economic instruments,[150] a role similarly identified for environmental assessment in the Rio Declaration (1992)[151] and Agenda 21[152] which followed the WCED's report. The potential contribution of environmental assessment to sustainable development has since been described by, amongst others,[153] Pearce in his blueprint for 'implementing' sustainable development,[154] and Jacobs who welcomed environmental assessment as 'a reasonably considered and open approach to mediating conflict within the sustainability framework by allowing those most likely to be affected by a project's environmental effects to communicate their views to decision makers'.[155]

Environmental assessment is clearly thought capable of being further developed to include the assessment of environmental impacts on communities,[156] human health,[157] and habitats.[158] Moving further beyond environmental protection, the prediction of impacts prior to decision making may be used to reflect a range of concerns, for example human rights,[159] and the burden of regulation on administration.[160] This expansion may ultimately lead to an all-embracing sustainability assessment, a development which reflects the adoption of the sustainable development agenda in environmental law. Relating the evolution of environmental assessment to the ascendancy of the concept of sustainable development in law and policy offers an explanation for this. For example in the context of the European Union, the sustainable development principle has undergone a process

---

[149] For an excellent review of this shift, see M. A. Hajer, *The Politics of Environmental Discourse: Ecological Modernisation and the Policy Process* (Oxford: Oxford University Press, 1997), ch. 3.

[150] World Commission on Environment and Development, *Our Common Future* (Oxford: Oxford University Press, 1987), 221–4.   [151] UNCED (1992) 31 ILM 874.

[152] UNCED, 1992.

[153] For example. A. Blowers, *Planning for a Sustainable Future* (London: Earthscan, 1993), 23; Council for the Protection of Rural England, *Sense and Sustainability: Land Use Planning and Environmental Sustainable Development* (London: CPRE, 1993), 15; and T. Clarke, 'Environmental Assessment and Sustainable Development' (1991) 6 *EIA* at 2–3.

[154] D. W. Pearce, *Blueprint for a Green Economy* (London: Earthscan, 1989), 120–30.

[155] M. Jacobs, *The Green Economy* (London: Pluto Press, 1993), 220–1.

[156] On the evaluation of social impacts of development, see N. Lichfield, *Community Impact Evaluation: Principles and Practice* (London: University College Press, 1996).

[157] See e.g. the Royal Commission on Environmental Pollution's recommendation that human health issues be incorporated explicitly in the environmental impact assessment process. *Environmental Planning*, paras. 7.36–7.38.

[158] For example, M. Montini, 'Habitats Impact Assessment: An Effective Instrument for Biodiversity Conservation?' (2001) 9 *Env Liab* 182.

[159] As discussed by S. I. Skegly, *The Human Rights Obligations of the World Bank and Monetary Fund* (London: Cavendish, 2001).

[160] B. Morgan, 'The Economisation of Politics' (2003) 12 *SLS* 489.

of 'mainstreaming' which describes its adoption as a guiding principle, informing the formation and fulfilment of all policies pursued by the Union,[161] not just those with an environmental purview. Since sustainable development is predicated upon the integration of environmental considerations in decision making in exactly the manner achieved by environmental assessment instruments, this suggests some inevitability about the remit of environmental assessment being extended (as impact assessment or sustainability analysis) and being placed at the centre of policy making.

Sadler[162] offers an evangelical view of the expansion of the remit of environmental assessment as a means to take fuller account of social and economic (as well as environmental) factors in decision making. He predicts a transition from environmental impact assessment ('a first-generation' process typically concerned with mitigating the impacts of major developments rather than maintaining the capacity and integrity of natural systems')[163] and strategic environmental assessment ('a second generation process that addresses both the sources and symptoms (or effects) of environmental damage')[164] towards a third generation form of ESA (Environmental Sustainability Assessment) involving a 'full cost analysis' of social, economic, and environmental impacts. Sadler considers that, where critical and 'high value' environmental functions and areas may be affected by development, the acceptability of potential environmental effects should be evaluated against the composition and value of natural capital stock.[165] He considers that the current focus on mitigation in traditional forms of environmental assessment (EIA and SEA) is misplaced in cases of 'medium and low environmental value' and instead that compensation, whether to offset impacts or provide 'like for like' compensation for the residual impacts that cannot be mitigated or avoided, should be pursued in such cases.[166] In elaborating the importance of compensation, and approving the making of 'trade-offs' in this manner, Sadler tends to skirt over the diversity of human values by simplistically categorizing environmental 'value' as high, medium, and low. His following analysis of 'compensation packages' inevitably raises questions about the valuation of 'naturalness', discussed previously,[167] raised here in the context of sustainable development.

Based on an impact damage assessment, different compensation-packages can be identified, e.g. *in full (no trade-off)* to identically offset high-value loss incurred, e.g. for key species or wetland functions; *equal replacement* to generally offset the high-medium-value

---

[161] Art. 2 EC Treaty, as amended, states: 'The Community shall have as its task, by establishing a common market and an economic and monetary union and by implementing common policies or activities . . . to promote throughout the Community a harmonious and balanced sustainable development of economic activities . . . a high level of protection and improvement of the quality of the environment'. Art. 2 Treaty on European Union similarly states that the Union shall 'promote economic and social progress to achieve balanced and sustainable development'.

[162] B. Sadler, 'Environmental Sustainability and Assurance', in J. Petts (ed.) *Handbook of EIA: Vol. 1 Process, Methods and Potential* (Oxford: Blackwell, 1999).   [163] At p. 27.

[164] ibid.   [165] At p. 30. On the nature of 'in-kind' compensation, see Ch. 1, p. 25.

[166] Sadler, 'Environmental Sustainability and Assurance', 31.   [167] See Ch. 1, p. 26.

loss, e.g. so that habitat units can be traded across important species; *relative replacement* for medium-value loss to ensure other types of habitat or wetland functions are improved or rehabilitated in areas of concern; *flexible trading* to compensate for low-value loss of abundant resources or where there is no equivalency, e.g. carbon sequestering for carbon dioxide emissions. Undoubtedly, this type of asset-trading and replacement will be crude and imprecise. As such, impact compensation will need to be promoted and implemented pragmatically.[168]

The enthusiasm for environmental assessment as a means to secure a weak form of sustainable development (even without its development into 'environmental sustainability assessment') demonstrates a key characteristic of the procedure—an ability to absorb other concerns, be they environmental, economic, or social—and thus encourage recognition of diverse concerns, and the connections between them.[169] From a more critical standpoint, environmental assessment facilitates the balancing of competing interests, or rather contributes to an impression of balance, or mediation (rather than absolute environmental protection) which similarly underlies the concept of sustainable development. Of course, this also facilitates the identification of 'trade-offs' that may be made. A key point, however, is that having secured the integration of environmental concerns in land use systems, and policy making, the further inclusion within the scope of environmental assessment of other indicators or indices may lead to the marginalization of environmental impacts as against a broader spectrum of concern.[170]

In conceptual terms, the development of environmental assessment is in accordance with aspects of the efficiency-oriented ecological modernization agenda[171] of which sustainable development is an important part. This is particularly the case with moves to integrate environmental concerns into broader social and political issues (and to facilitate the identification of trade-offs) and correspondingly encourage shared responsibility for environmental *management*, as opposed to protection. The mainstreaming of 'alternative' regulatory forms, such as environmental agreements and taxes, stems from this development. The underlying self-regulatory mode of control of these mechanisms has also come to be identified with environmental assessment.[172]

[168] Sadler, 'Environmental Sustainability and Assurance', 30.

[169] For example, the Royal Commission on Environmental Pollution discusses the prospects for sustainability appraisal which would extend appraisal to include social and economic criteria as being of equal concern to environmental criteria, See Twenty-Third Report, paras. 7.43–7.45. See, already, Department of the Environment, Transport and the Regions, *Proposals for a Good Practice Guide on Sustainability Appraisal of Regional Planning Guidance* (London: DETR, 2000).

[170] See e.g. case study on the European Commission's development of a form of sustainability assessment to review policy choices, Ch. 5, pp. 164–81.

[171] Hajer, *The Politics of Environmental Discourse*. On the ecological modernization justification for EU environmental policy, see also Weale *et al.*, *Environmental Governance in Europe*, ch. 1.

[172] As identified by E. Bregman and A. Jacobsen, 'Environmental Performance Review: Self-Regulation in Environmental Law' in G. Teubner , L. Farmer, and D. Murphy (eds.) *Environmental Law and Ecological Responsibility: The Concept and Practice of Ecological Self-Organisation* (Chichester: Wiley, 1994) and more generally, Heinelt *et al.*, *European Union Environmental Policy*.

The association of environmental assessment with the ideas of ecological modernization and sustainable development may be further explained by the influence of ecological science, and the changing paradigms within the discipline.[173] Early environmental assessment was held up as an example of 'ecological science in action', synthesized with law in the United States' NEPA 1969.[174] The conception of ecology at the time of this enactment was one based upon the dominant paradigm of homeostasis or equilibrium between organisms and the environment—a 'balance of nature'—which could be maintained only by resistance to change.[175] Although not prescribing a particular environmental standard, environmental assessment was a culturally significant evocation of the importance of such ecological concerns in decision making, so that the fairly strict environmental assessment requirements contained within the 1969 Act (alongside the development of nature reserves, biodiversity preservation strategies, and the setting of emission standards) suggest the absorption of some of this thinking into environmental law. In the meantime, the equilibrium paradigm underwent a revolution, with the result that ecological science now stresses change and instability of ecosystems, and no longer upholds as ideal the withdrawal of humankind from nature. This 'New Ecology' recognizes instead the inevitability of interactions between humans and the natural environment,[176] and thus the management of ecosystems, rather than their preservation, or restoration. The reformed perspective of ecology inevitably informed the evolution of the political concept of sustainable development by providing a scientific basis for it, and the associated drive for the integration of environmental factors in all decision making. Bosselman and Tarlock sum this up: 'Environmentalism's initial objective was to make environmental quality a relative quality to be considered. This battle has now largely been won and the movement's focus has shifted to the assured comprehensive and long-term integration, if not dominance, of this perspective in all resource decision making'.[177] A triumvirate of law, ecology, and politics therefore acted to reconceive environmental assessment as a legal expression of sustainable development, particularly giving practical effect to the more integrative aspects of this concept, so that environmental concerns are taken into account in decision making, but do not (by design) necessarily predominate.

Expanding Environmental Impact Assessment: Strategic Environmental Assessment

To recap, with the rapid evolution and expansion in the function and form of environmental assessment, law has attempted to keep pace with, and control, its development. Taking the United Kingdom as an example, relatively weak statutory

---

[173] F. P. Bosselman and A. D. Tarlock, 'The Influence of Ecological Science on American Law' (1994) 69 *Chicago-Kent L Rev* 847.   [174] See Appendix I.

[175] Bosselman and Tarlock, 'The influence of Ecological Science', at 866.

[176] This paradigm shift is attributed to several ecologists: B. T. McKibben, *The End of Nature* (New York: Random House, 1989); D. B. Botkin, *Discordant Harmonies: A New Ecology for the Twenty-First Century* (Oxford: Oxford University Press Inc, 1990).

[177] 'The Influence of Ecological Science', at 872.

provisions, codes of practice, and guidelines on taking account of environmental considerations have been replaced with a formal legislative requirement to conduct environmental assessment in certain cases, accompanied by indicative and prescriptive thresholds which narrow discretion on the part of the decision maker. This is largely the consequence of European Community legislation, although procedures conceptually similar to environmental assessment were also given a legislative base without a European impetus.[178] Law has also provided a basis for the expansion of the remit of environmental assessment—from project-based procedures to the broader scope of strategic level of assessment. This is because, although the environmental impact assessment of projects was initially considered a way of giving effect to the concept of sustainable development, fairly soon it became clear that this level of assessment was too limited in scope to achieve this because decision making at the project level was often superseded by higher-level policy decisions. The development of strategic environmental assessment is a response to the need for multiple levels of assessment (to reflect different levels and scales of environmental decision making) and suggests a deeper level of integration and policy coordination than is the case with project-based assessment.[179]

An early form of strategic environmental assessment was developed in the United States under NEPA which required agencies to make a detailed assessment of the environmental implications of any action (be it a development project or policy) significantly affecting the quality of the human environment.[180] This influenced the European Commission's proposal for a similar model of assessment (though additionally applying to the private sector) in 1980.[181] Strong resistance by some Member States to the proposed element of policy appraisal in the instrument led to the exclusion of this element from the final Directive, even though it had been strongly favoured by the European Parliament. This meant that the scope of the resulting EIA Directive was severely restricted,[182] in keeping with its portrayal as an instrument for fostering competitive conditions,[183] rather than aiding forward planning.[184] Shaving off the policy element inevitably resulted in a strong focus on

[178] For example, best practicable environmental option assessments (s. 7(4) Environmental Protection Act 1990), on which see further below, p. 70.

[179] For example, see arguments made for strategic environmental assessment in European Commission, *SEA and the Integration of the Environment into Strategic Decision Making* (Brussels: CEC, 2001).   [180] See above, p. 43.

[181] Draft directive on environmental assessment, 7972/80 COM(80) 313 final.

[182] The final draft directive (there were several versions) also included provisions on post-assessment monitoring and the supervision of conditions made following environmental assessment.

[183] This rationale for the draft directive was given in its preamble: 'beyond environmental protection . . . significant divergence in the principles and criteria of assessment at present in the Community may well produce disparities in investment conditions between one region of the Community and another and thus create distortion of competition with negative effects on the functioning of the Common Market'. Such a rationale was needed because of the lack of a specific legal base in the EEC Treaty for environmental measures.

[184] Although a policy commitment to policy appraisal was made in the Fourth Environmental Action Programme, COM(86) 485 final (Brussels: CEC, 1987) which stated that EIA 'will also be extended, as rapidly as possible, to cover policies and policy statements, plans and their implementation, procedures,

'the project', with an accordingly weaker emphasis placed upon cumulative and indirect effects, and alternative options. To some extent this focus has been retained in the current SEA Directive[185] (which is due to be fully implemented in the Member States in 2004) since this requires the environmental assessment of certain plans and programmes *in order* to provide a framework for the future development consent of projects. The omission of 'policies' from the scope of this Directive reflects the concerns of Member States that its inclusion would severely restrict their discretion in policy making. These concerns had resulted in a legislative stalemate on this proposal for several years. So, although the SEA Directive is admittedly broader in scope than previous versions (one of which, controversially, limited environmental assessment requirements to plans and programmes for town and country planning purposes)[186] it nevertheless remains a European apology for a more complete, strategic, assessment regime. The further development of environmental assessment by the UNECE Kiev Protocol to the Espoo Convention to include (fairly weak) strategic elements is unlikely to detract fundamentally from this criticism.[187]

Although strategic environmental assessment has been presented as an advance on project-based appraisal, particularly in terms of encouraging the consideration of alternatives, in practice it is sometimes difficult to pinpoint exactly where environmental impact assessment ends and strategic environmental assessment begins.[188] For example, strategic environmental assessment has been advocated as a means to assess the overall impact of licensing regimes (e.g. oil and gas development) in which individual consents are made subject to environmental impact assessment, but the full, cumulative effects of many such licences are not examined. However, the gradual strengthening of the requirements to consider alternatives,[189] and cumulative effects[190] in project-based environmental assessment detract from this argument in favour of SEA. Similarly, a strategic assessment of the ecological impacts of transport networks may use geographical information systems to identify areas designated for conservation of birds which would be within several kilometres of proposed routes. Such an assessment is remote from a particular site, but remains tied to the physical condition of a specified area so that it appears more like a 'bundle of environmental impact assessments'.[191] This

programmes . . . as well as individual projects'. This was reiterated in the Fifth Environmental Action Programme, *Towards Sustainability: A European Programme of Policy and Action in Relation to the Environment and Sustainable Development*, COM(92) 23 final (Brussels: CEC, 1992) in the context of achieving sustainable development.

[185] Directive 2001/42/EC on the assessment of the effects of certain plans and programmes on the environment, OJ 2001 L 197, p. 30.

[186] Art. 2(a) Commission proposal for a Council Directive on the assessment of the effects of certain plans and programmes on the environment, COM(96) 511 final, OJ C 129, p. 14. On which see critical commentary, S. Tromans and C. Roger-Machart, 'Strategic Environmental Assessment: Early Evaluation Equals Efficiency?' [1997] JPL 993.

[187] UNECE Draft Protocol on Strategic Environmental Assessment (Kiev Protocol). See Appendix V.

[188] This was the case with the Lewes Flood Defence Strategy case study; see Ch. 3, pp. 86–9.

[189] See Ch. 5, pp. 149–50.   [190] See Ch. 4, pp. 130–6.

[191] J. Treweek, *Ecological Impact Assessment* (Oxford: Blackwell, 1999), 26.

is particularly the case when compared to an assessment of alternatives to road transport—air, rail, or local production programmes—which is spatially unlimited by the condition of a particular site, or sites, and may span policy on local, regional, and national scales. The latter example of strategic environmental assessment genuinely represents a sea-change in decision making. Whereas most environmental impact assessments are triggered by a proposed development, and are most often underpinned by a private (usually property) interest, strategic environmental assessment is by its very nature conducted by public bodies or agencies of government with the aim of better administration or governance. A further genuine difference between the forms of assessment is that environmental impact assessment is a reactive device, responding to a developer's application for development consent concerning an individual site whereas strategic environmental assessment may be used as a mechanism for forward planning.

To summarize, environmental impact assessment and strategic environmental assessment have different rationales, and operate on different levels, but they remain closely related and may overlap in subject matter and methodologies, because an important aim of strategic environmental assessment is to provide a framework for decisions about development consent on individual sites. This is borne out by the EC SEA Directive[192] which explicitly states:

... an environmental assessment shall be carried out for all plans and programmes for agriculture, forestry, fisheries, energy, industry, transport, waste management, water management, telecommunications, tourism, town and country planning, or land use and which set the framework for future development consent of projects listed in Annex I and II to the EIA Directive, or which, in view of the likely effect on sites, require an assessment under the Habitats Directive.[193]

The potentially fruitful (but also possibly problematic) relationship between environmental impact assessment and strategic environmental assessment has been acknowledged by the Environment Directorate of the European Commission:

It is very likely that the strong link of Directive 2001/42/EC, referred to as 'the SEA Directive' with the EIA Directive . . . will strengthen the administrative capacities of the respective authorities in the Member States in their assessment procedures and will complement in many cases the application and better implementation of the EIA Directive. Implementation is also likely to reveal some difficulties (e.g. the boundary with the EIA Directive and the definition of project).[194]

The relationship with other forms of environmental assessment is also addressed:

Looking ahead, the 2006 review of the operation of the SEA Directive ought to address the relationship between it and the EIA Directive and the other directives which require

---

[192] Art. 3(2) SEA Directive 2001/42/EC OJ 2001 L 197, p. 30 on the assessment of the effects of certain plans and programmes on the environment.
[193] Arts. 6 and 7 Habitats Directive 92/43/EC OJ 1992 L 206, p. 7.
[194] Internal note to the Policy Group, DG Environment, on the *Five Years Report to the European Parliament and the Council on the Effectiveness of the EIA Directive* (Brussels: CEC, 2002), 12.

environmental assessments of some kind (for example, IPPC and Habitats). It may be that by then the time will be ripe for clarification of these relationships.[195]

The future convergence of forms of environmental assessment,[196] envisaged by the Commission and the subject of research,[197] is to some extent already provided for by the SEA Directive, which allows Member States to provide for coordinated or joint procedures fulfilling the requirements of other pieces of Community legislation in order to avoid the duplication of assessment procedures.[198] Further in terms of scope, the SEA Directive also applies to plans and programmes concerned with the use of small areas at local level and modifications to plans and programmes where Member States consider that they are likely to have significant environmental effects, and to those plans and programmes not listed in the EIA and Habitats Directives but which set the framework for future development consent concerning projects likely to have significant effects upon the environment.[199] The Directive does not apply to plans and programmes financed under the structural funds (until 2007).[200] The official reason for this is that such plans and programmes have already been put in place. In practice this provides scope for disintegrated policy making, at least until that date. However, even a broad-ranging model of strategic environmental assessment is not a panacea for the limitations of project-based assessment. Methodological problems experienced with environmental impact assessment are compounded when applied to higher level considerations. For example, it has proved difficult to separate out different stages in the formulation of a policy as discrete steps in a hierarchical or even chronological sequence and to identify boundaries to complex and often open-ended policy-making processes. Moreover, even where boundaries are set and discrete stages are identified, the dynamic nature of the policy process means that the implementation stage may well be critical in interpreting and thereby formulating policy. These amount to important conceptual problems in undertaking policy appraisal.[201] These are general observations. There are also more specific problems difficulties associated with strategic environmental assessment, such as securing meaningful participation.[202]

In summary, environmental assessment is now applied in many different contexts, but in the United Kingdom at least, it has been developed most fully in the planning system and remains closely tied to planning procedures and objectives. Within planning, environmental assessment has survived a substantial expansion of its remit: in early literature it was identified almost exclusively as a means of

---

[195] Internal note to the Policy Group, DG Environment, on the *Five Years Report to the European Parliament and the Council on the Effectiveness of the EIA Directive* (Brussels: CEC, 2002), 12.

[196] Discussed below pp. 73–4.

[197] IMPEL, *Report on the Interrelationship between the IPPC, EIA and SEVESO Directives and EMAS Regulation* (Brussels: CEC, 1998).   [198] Art. 11.

[199] Arts. 3(3) and 3(4).   [200] Art. 3(9).

[201] E. Wilson, 'Progress towards Strategic Environmental Assessment of Policies, Plans and Programmes', paper delivered at the IRNES conference on Perspectives on the Environment, September 1992.   [202] See particularly Ch. 6, p. 191.

controlling the harmful effects of pollution by influencing the siting of industry; in recent years it has been acknowledged as a means by which the principle of sustainable development may be 'implemented'. The development of environmental assessment may therefore be seen in light of its use as a mechanism for integrating environmental concerns into policy making in response to growing pressure from international organizations and the public that such concerns be given greater prominence. This development reflects many of the broader developments taking place simultaneously in the evolution of environmental law more generally.

Sites of Environmental Assessment

Above I traced the development of different levels of environmental assessment (project- and policy-based) by focusing upon the expansion of environmental impact assessment into strategic environmental assessment in the context of Community law (the EIA and SEA Directives). Here the analysis shifts to multiple *sites* of decision making engaging environmental assessment by surveying some of the legal variations of environmental assessment that have evolved in different jurisdictional and functional contexts—land use control and planning, bio-diversity conservation, pollution control regimes, and development assistance.[203] In Chapter 1, I outlined the general characteristics of environmental assessment by reference to the EC EIA Directive. This was necessarily a simplified account of the form of environmental assessment, but other types of assessment follow a similar pattern, suggesting some convergence of the form of assessment and the adoption of common methodologies, at least with regard to these core requirements. Further sites of decision making not considered below include procedures concerning climate change[204] and activities in Antarctica.[205] Other relevant Conventions include the 1986 Noumea Convention[206] and the 1982 United Nations Convention on the Law of the Sea,[207] discussed in the context of the development of environmental assessment in international law.[208] On the domestic front, environmental assessment is becoming a feature of decision making in the utilities sector, for example a duty may be imposed on the Gas and Electricity Markets Authority to carry out impact assessments when 'proposing to do anything for the purposes of, or in connection with, the carrying out of any function exercisable by it . . . '.[209] This is a prime example of statutory backing for environmental assessments through primary legislation.

[203] I discuss the development of environmental assessment by the European Commission separately, as an example of the ecologization of governance; Ch. 5, pp. 164–81.

[204] Under the Climate Change Convention 31 ILM 849 (1992).

[205] Antarctic Environment Protocol 30 ILM 1461 (1991).

[206] Noumea Convention for the Protection of the Natural Resources and Environment of the South Pacific Region 26 ILM 38 (1986).   [207] 21 ILM 1261 (1982).

[208] See above, pp. 53–6.

[209] Sustainable Energy Bill, Clause 6, which would insert a new s. 5A into the Utilities Act 2000.

Land Use

As discussed earlier in this chapter, land use control is the main and traditional site of decision making using environmental assessment instruments, within which environmental assessment methodologies and guidance have been developed because of the clear repercussions for environmental protection of decisions about the nature and location of development. In addition the inherently anticipatory nature of the planning system (due to the need to obtain development consent prior to development taking place—the licence) is reinforced by the predictive nature of environmental assessment. This compatibility is borne out by the Royal Commission on Environmental Pollution's presentation of environmental assessment as part of a suite of techniques of environmental planning, including also state of the environment reports, and auditing.[210]

Under the development control regimes of the United Kingdom, 363 environmental statements were prepared in 2002, divided between the main categories of project controlled by the town and country planning system.[211] In the case of England and Wales, these Regulations prohibit the grant of planning permission without consideration of environmental information for projects defined as 'EIA development'.[212] As Table 2.1 shows, this category makes up over half of all statements submitted. However, there has also been an increase in the number of statements submitted outside this system, particularly offshore oil and gas projects which were brought under the EIA regime in 1999.[213] The progression of proposals for which development consent is sought and which are subject to environmental assessment is considered in later chapters, including the determination of the proposed development's likely significance,[214] the requirement to consider alternatives, and to consult statutory consultees and public,[215] so that this is a necessarily truncated account of environmental assessment within decision making on land use.

Related to the specific application of environmental assessment rules in development-consent procedures is the environmental appraisal of development plans used to guide decision making at local and county levels.[216] This has been 'good practice' for several years,[217] reflecting that to some extent the process of

[210] Royal Commission on Environmental Pollution, Twenty-third Report, *Environmental Planning*, Cm 5459 (London: HMSO, 2002).

[211] Town and Country Planning (Environmental Impact Assessment) (England and Wales) Regulations 1999 (SI 1999, No. 293) (the 1999 Regulations), the Environmental Impact Assessment (Scotland) Regulations 1999 (SI 1999, No. 1), the Planning (Environmental Impact Assessment) Regulations (Northern Ireland) 1999 (SR 1999, No. 73). See further Appendix X.   [212] Reg. 3.

[213] Offshore Petroleum Production and Pipelines (Assessment of Environmental Effects) Regulations 1999 (SI 1999, No. 360).   [214] Ch. 4   [215] Ch. 6

[216] S. 54A Town and Country Planning Act 1990, as amended. The Planning and Compulsory Purchase Bill will overhaul the system of development planning in England and Wales by replacing the existing local and structure plans with local development documents and regional spatial strategies (see Parts I and II of the Bill).

[217] DETR, *Proposals for a Good Practice Guide on Sustainability Appraisal of Regional Planning Guidance* (GPG 25) (London: DETR, 2000). See generally, B. Dalal-Clayton, *Getting to Grips with Green Plans: National Level Experience in Industrial Countries* (London: Earthscan, 1996).

Table 2.1 Environmental statements under different authorization regimes, 2002

	Number	% of total	% change over 2000
Planning, England	363	52	−1
Planning, Scotland	69	10	+15
Planning, Wales	53	8	+66
Land drainage	34	5	+100
Fish farms	32	5	+146
Offshore oil and gas	23	3	+15
Highways	21	3	+600
Power stations/overhead lines	16	2	+14
Forestry	8	1	+14
Transport	7	1	−13
Offshore wind/water generating	7	1	N/A[1]
Pipelines (gas)	5	1	−38
Harbour works	4	0.5	−67
Nuclear reactors	2	0.5	N/A[1]
Northern Ireland, all	50	7	+28

[1]N/A = not applicable (0 in 2000).

environmental appraisal of plans at the policy level is conceptually and practically similar to 'high level' environmental impact assessment, particulary in terms of making opportunities for public participation.[218] As discussed above, the EC SEA Directive now makes the process of environmental appraisal of development plans mandatory.[219] A related development is that the review of proposals in plans according to sustainability criteria looks set to move from 'good practice' to a statutory requirement,[220] the implications of which are discussed in Chapter 5.[221] With the broader 'sustainability' appraisal of development plans now likely, it is important that existing practice in appraising plans is patchy, with innovative approaches being taken by a number of local authorities, but also omissions in terms of procedures (for example, consideration of alternative policies) and content, such as a failure to describe the baseline condition of the environment, or to describe environmental objectives.[222] Predictably, environmental

[218] An examination in public for structure plans roughly corresponded to requirements in environmental assessment regimes. This mode of participation is retained by the Planning and Compulsory Purchase Bill in the case of regional spatial strategies. The Bill will additionally require a statement of community involvement in the formation of local development documents (s. 17).

[219] See above, pp. 60–5. On the relationship between the EIA Directive and development planning, see Case C-81/96 *B en W Haarlemmerliede en Spaarnwoude and Others* v *GS van Noord-Holland* [1998] ECR I-3923.   [220] S. 5(4) Planning and Compulsory Purchase Bill.

[221] Pp. 60–5.

[222] J. M. Curran, C. Wood, and M. Hilton, 'Environmental Appraisal of UK (Local) Plans: Current Practice and Future Directions' (1998) *25 Environment and Planning B: Planning and Design* 411.

appraisal of plans at the local level has been instrumental in shaping the proposed strategy and policies rather than in recommending radical changes.[223]

Conservation of Biological Diversity

The above account of the development of environmental impact assessment points to the fact that this was designed primarily as an instrument for environmental planning rather than for the conservation of biodiversity.[224] Nevertheless, the UN Convention on Biological Diversity[225] requires impact assessment studies to be conducted on 'proposed projects that are likely to have significant adverse effects on biological diversity in order to minimise their effects'.[226] Furthermore it requires parties to promote the exchange of information and consultation on activities under their jurisdiction or control which are likely to significantly affect the biological diversity of other states or areas beyond their jurisdiction and to provide immediate notification in the event of any imminent danger or damage to biodiversity.[227] This marks the utility of environmental assessment in identifying potential risks to biodiversity from development projects.[228] However, difficulties exist in this process of identification, for example the paucity of criteria for assessing the significance of impacts on biodiversity, particularly when compared with the employment of quality and emission standards in pollution control,[229] means that what constitutes a critical level for biodiversity loss is uncertain. A further difficulty is that in practice the onus of assessment tends to be on threatened species, whereas non-listed or endangered species also need to be taken into account to arrest any early decline.[230] Overall, though, it may be that the development of an information base through the assessment process may strengthen action taken to secure biodiversity in the long run.[231]

Within the European Union, the Habitats Directive[232] has impinged directly upon land use and development controls in the Member States. In order to fulfil Article 6 of this Directive,[233] in the United Kingdom a competent authority must make an 'appropriate assessment' in order to predict the implications of a project or plan for the conservation status of a 'European' site,[234] before deciding whether to grant planning permission for a project which is likely to have a significant

[223] J. M. Curran, C. Wood, and M. Hilton, 'Environmental Appraisal of UK (Local) Plans: Current Practice and Future Directions' (1998) *25 Environment and Planning B: Planning and Design* 429.

[224] On the ecological and biodiversity premises of environmental impact assessment, see Treweek, *Ecological Impact Assessment*.   [225] 31 ILM 822 (1992).

[226] Art. 14(1)(a).   [227] Art. 14(1)(c) and (d).

[228] As recognized, for example by G. Wynne (ed.) *Biodiversity Challenge: An Agenda for Conservation Action in the UK* (Sandy: RSPB, 1993) which advocates that environmental appraisal should be widely carried out as a guiding principle of biodiversity.

[229] Treweek, *Ecological Impact Assessment*, 36.   [230] ibid.

[231] For example by providing baseline information for biodiversity action plans, as discussed by Treweek, *Ecological Impact Assessment*.

[232] Council Directive 92/43/EC on the conservation of natural habitats and of wild fauna and flora (OJ L 206, 21.5.1992).   [233] See Appendix IX.

[234] The term 'European site' includes both Special Protection Areas, as defined by Directive 79/409/EEC on the conservation of wild birds, OJ L 103, 25.12.1979, and Special Areas of Conservation designated for the purposes of the Habitats Directive.

effect.[235] In the absence of alternative solutions and notwithstanding a negative assessment of the implications of the plan or project for the site's conservation objectives, a local planning authority may grant planning permission for a project if they are satisfied that it must be carried out for imperative reasons of overriding public interest, which may be of a social or economic nature, and if compensatory measures are taken. However, where the site concerned hosts a so-called priority, or particularly endangered, natural habitat type or species, then the planning authority may only grant planning permission for reasons relating 'to human health or public safety, to beneficial consequences of primary importance for the environment, or further to an Opinion from the Commission, to other imperative reasons of overriding public interest'.[236] A two-tier system of protection therefore operates with the effect that greater weight in decision making is given to information relating to a priority European habitat site or species, thus making development consent more difficult to obtain. The main point to take from this is that species and habitats of European conservation importance should be accorded substantive respect and protection in the national legal systems of the European Union.

The trigger for an assessment under the Habitats Regulations is almost identical to that for the purposes of the 1999 Regulations (for environmental impact assessment for the purposes of the town and country planning system)[237]—the likely significant effects of the proposed plan or project on the environment—except that these effects are more closely prescribed in the Habitats Regulations as affecting a site's 'conservation objectives'. The obligations contained in the Habitats Directive do not replicate exactly the provisions of the EIA Directive, the procedural details of which are more extensively described, particularly with regard to participation requirements. The European Commission has provided guidance that where an 'appropriate assessment' takes the form of an assessment under national legislation on EIA (in line with the EC EIA Directive), this will 'provide obvious assurances in terms of records and transparency'.[238] However, this raises the question as to what may be considered an 'appropriate assessment' where an assessment for the purposes of the Habitats Regulations does not take the form of assessment under the EIA regime. The Commission's answer is that an 'appropriate assessment' should be capable of being recorded, that it should be reasoned (in the light of particular information relating to the environment) and timely, taking place before the decision to approve or refuse the plan or project.[239] The relationship between appropriate assessments under the Habitats Regulations 1994 and the 1999 (EIA) Regulations

[235] Reg 48 Conservation (Natural Habitats &c.) Regulations 1994 (SI 1994, No. 2716) ('the Habitat Regulations 1994').
[236] Reg. 49 of the Habitats Regulations 1994, implementing Art. 6(4) of the Habitats Directive. On the Commission's Opinions on imperative reasons, see Ch. 5, pp. 158–62.
[237] Reg. 48 (1)(a) requires that 'a competent authority, before deciding to undertake, or give any consent, permission or other authorisation for, a plan or project which is likely to have a significant effect on a European site in Great Britain . . . shall make an appropriate assessment of the implications for the site in view of that site's conservation objectives'.
[238] European Commission, *Managing Natura 2000 Sites* (Brussels: CEC, 2000), para. 4.5.1.
[239] ibid.

is further complicated by guidance issued by the Environment Agency.[240] This advises that in carrying out an 'appropriate assessment', the applicant may be required to carry out a full environmental impact assessment under the 1999 Regulations (to 'aid the appropriate assessment process').[241] This variance in guidance strongly suggests the practicality of conducting a single assessment for the fulfilment of biodiversity and environmental planning objectives.

Pollution Controls and Water Resources

A similar conclusion is reached when considering the potential for overlaps in carrying out environmental assessments for pollution control and water resource purposes. Under the system of pollution prevention and control established by the 1999 Act,[242] an application for a permit to operate an industrial (or in certain circumstances, agricultural) activity, must be accompanied by a wide variety of information, including information on the condition of the site and any associated pollution risks, the raw materials and energy used in carrying out the activity, waste minimization and prevention measures, the foreseeable emissions and environmental effects of the activity, information on the technology and other techniques used for reducing emissions and other environmental impacts and arrangements for monitoring impacts. This body of information must be accompanied by a non-technical summary. These requirements echo those under the 1999 (EIA) Regulations. This was perhaps more clearly the case with the previous integrated pollution control regime in which an explicit reference to the 'best practicable environmental option'[243] required an assessment of the various pathways and environmental effects of different operating options, thus bringing the concept into line with environmental assessment. Although the Pollution Prevention and Control regime under the 1999 Act does not have any corresponding requirement to undertake an assessment of the best practicable environmental option for an activity, an operator has to consider all of the environmental impacts of an activity (including a wide-ranging obligation to return a site to a satisfactory state after an installation has closed). It has recently been confirmed that a planning authority (but equally the Environment Agency) must base its decision about an application for waste disposal facilities (whether for a waste management licence, a pollution prevention and control permit, or planning permission) on the outcome of a properly structured process which identifies the best practicable environmental option for the waste stream involved.[244]

---

[240] Environment Agency, Habitats Directive: Executive Summary (providing guidance for English Nature and the Countryside Council for Wales, both of which constitute a 'competent authority' for the 1994 Regulations).   [241] At p. 4.

[242] Pollution Prevention and Control Act 1999, augmented by the Pollution Prevention and Control (England and Wales) Regulations 2000 (SI 2000, No. 1973).

[243] S. 7(7) Environmental Protection Act 1990.

[244] *Blewett* v *Derbyshire County Council* [2003] EWHC 2775 (Admin), Sullivan J. On the implications of this, see D. Wolfe, 'A Duty to Find the Least Worst Option?' (2004) 17e-law(u.k. environmental law association e-journal).

More specific environmental assessment requirements exist with regard to water resources, as a result of the need to implement the provisions of the amended EIA Directive, which extended the range of projects to which the Directive applies to include groundwater abstraction, artificial recharge of groundwater, or the transfer of water resources between river basins. In terms of overlap with existing environmental assessment requirements, where planning permission is required for a project involving water resources, the need for an assessment is linked to the planning process, but where no planning permission is required, the need for an environmental assessment will be linked to the need to obtain a licence from the Environment Agency.[245] The similarities in the relative duties of the planning authorities and Environment Agency suggest that a unified approach to environmental assessment within the two systems of environmental control appears likely.

Development Assistance

Instruments such as the Espoo Convention, and other environmental impact assessment regimes have been considered to be the product of developed countries, reflecting a common outlook that projects having significant environmental impacts in another country must be reviewed.[246] This observation is difficult to sustain when the nature of disputes heard before the International Court of Justice (particularly the *MOX* case)[247] is considered. It is even more difficult to support when the application of environmental assessment is addressed in the context of development assistance in which the environmental consequences of projects (particularly large-scale infrastructure development) are more easily obscured by donor countries and lending institutions. However, as mentioned above in the context of the development of environmental assessment regimes,[248] it is now commonplace for multilateral development banks to incorporate environmental assessment into their approval procedures. Notwithstanding a slow process of standardization, such procedures vary greatly between institutions. There is, for example, no international set of guidelines for use by all such banks (and development assistance agencies) in conducting an environmental assessment. This means that when lending or development assistance is at stake 'EIA requirements are often eased if not exempted'.[249] Perez, for example, highlights in this context the advent of the 'Pseudo-EIA' which is carried out with the single objective of securing a project, irrespective of its true environmental costs.[250]

---

[245] By virtue of the Water Resources (Environmental Impact Assessment) (England and Wales) Regulations 2003 (SI 2003, No. 164).

[246] Gray, 'International Environmental Impact Assessment', at 104.

[247] See above, p. 56.

[248] See pp. 44–5 on the accommodation of environmental impact assessment procedures in international organizations and multinational banks.

[249] Gray, 'International Environmental Impact Assessment', at 196.

[250] O. Perez, 'Using Private-Public Linkages to Regulate Environmental Conflicts: The Case of International Construction Contracts' (2002) 29 *JLS* 77, at 94, which further examines the content of construction contracts for enforceable environmental obligations.

In the case of the World Bank, environmental assessment procedures have been applied since 1989.[251] These now include an Operation Policy which requires an environmental assessment of projects to be financed by the Bank. The extent and type of environmental impact assessment to be conducted in each case depends upon a judgment of a project's likely significance. The scope of assessment is broad, in keeping with the 'mainstreaming' of environmental considerations; an environmental impact assessment should cover 'the natural environment (air, water and land), human health and safety; social aspects (involuntary resettlement, indigenous people and cultural property); and transnational and global environmental aspects'.[252] A sticking point in the procedures for assessment is public participation, with World Bank project personnel often failing to solicit a variety of cultural perspectives and adjusting the process in a way that is amenable to the values of the community likely to be affected by a project.[253] A necessary review procedure was introduced in 1993 by the establishment of an Inspection Panel with the authority to make recommendations to the Board of the Bank, and ensure compliance with the Operational Policy. An inescapable conclusion, however, is that approval of projects, even those subject to the Bank's internal environmental assessment rules, will result in funds being allocated to private construction corporations often operating on a global scale, and governed by contractual obligations which rarely feature environmental considerations.[254]

The WCED Experts Group[255] suggested that an international assessment body be created to help developing countries assess the environmental impact of planned development projects, but no such body was established. This suggestion has recently been revived in the form of an international Commission for Environmental Impact Assessment, proposed by the Dutch EIA Commission. The Commission envisages a membership organization, by which experts are called upon to judge the completeness and quality of environmental information supporting decision making (but with no say upon the social and environmental acceptability of an intended project or policy).[256] Attempts such as this suggest not just the widespread use of environmental assessment, but also the need to implement generally agreed minimum standards for environmental assessment.

Conclusions

The evolution of environmental assessment has spanned several decades and has taken place in greatly varying contexts. One aim of this chapter was to give a sense

[251] For a critique of the early form of assessment, including the failure of the assessment regime to mandate public participation of those affected by the Bank's decisions, see Sands, *Principles of International Environmental Law*, 821.

[252] Operational Policy 4.01 (1991) 5P3. See World Bank, *Mainstreaming the Environment: The World Bank Group and the Environment since the Rio Earth Summit* (Washington: World Bank, 1995).   [253] Gray, 'International Environmental Impact Assessment', at 112.

[254] Perez, 'Using Private-Public Linkages'.   [255] *Legal Principles*.

[256] This proposal is still at the formative stages, see http://www.geocities.com/iciaos/Mission1.html.

of the panorama of environmental assessment—informal assessment, statutory assessment, public and private forms, wide-ranging assessment, and assessment applied to specific concerns—from which three trends can be identified. First, is the convergence of the form of environmental assessment. Notwithstanding the many different applications and sites of environmental assessment, the process[257] is remarkably consistent, as seen by the similarity of various forms of assessment (contained in national, European Union, and international law).[258] This means that in practice a single project, or policy area, may be subject to several similar forms of environmental assessment operating at different levels. For this reason there are indications of the development of a unitary environmental assessment procedure, at least for obtaining development and pollution control consents.[259] For example, the preamble to the SEA Directive permits that where the obligation to carry out assessments of the effects on the environment arises simultaneously from the SEA Directive and other Community legislation such as the Wild Birds Directive, Habitats Directive, or Water Framework Directive, in order to avoid duplication of the assessment, Member States may provide for coordinated or joint procedures fulfilling the requirements of the relevant Community legislation.[260] This raises an issue of the responsiveness of environmental assessment, when engaging common assessment methodologies, to different legal and political contexts. Second, there has been a clear expansion of the remit of environmental assessment, so that the environmental assessment process is increasingly being used to take account of social and economic impacts, in recognition of the indivisible and interrelated nature of environmental problems, popularized by the concept of sustainable development. Ultimately, a form of 'sustainability assessment' may override the more specific forms of environmental impact assessment and strategic environmental assessment.[261] A less amenable consequence of this expansion is the identification of potential trade-offs between social, economic, and environmental 'resources' which may be acted upon in decision making. This absorption of the concept of sustainable development in environmental assessment clearly reflects the more general evolution and mainstreaming of environmental law. The third trend, related to the expansion of subject matter in environmental assessment, is the accommodation of multiple levels of decision making, seen most clearly in the development of strategic environmental assessment at European Union and international levels.

I continue to track the parallel development of environmental assessment and environmental law in the following chapters by considering environmental assessment as a gauge for the arrival and fulfilment of new forms of environmental

[257] Outlined in Figure 2.1, p. 36.

[258] Several of which are reproduced in the Appendices to this book.

[259] For example, in EC law, the assessment of effects upon the environment required by Directive 96/61/EC OJ L 275, also suffices for the purposes of the EC Directive on EIA, as urged by UKELA, *Overlaps in the Requirements for Environmental Assessment* (London: UKELA, 1993).

[260] See also Art. 2a of the EIA Directive with regard to a joint procedure for the purpose of fulfilling EIA and IPPC procedural requirements.

[261] I consider this process in greater detail in Ch. 5, pp. 164–82.

regulation. In particular, I highlight aspects of environmental assessment which serve to demonstrate the broader development of environmental law—recognition of the need for interdisciplinary inquiry,[262] expansion of environmental concern to take into account social and economic conditions,[263] and enhancing opportunities for participation.[264] I explain how the environmental assessment process gives rise to these issues by analysing its main constituent parts, the first of which is the central requirement that the effects of development be predicted prior to consent being granted, or a policy or programme being adopted.

[262] Ch. 3.   [263] Ch. 5.
[264] Ch. 6.

3

Prediction

In the previous chapter I introduced environmental assessment as having developed from many sources and influences and surveyed the different forms of environmental assessment that exist in various sites of decision making and jurisdictions. The anticipation of a diverse range of effects on the environment of a development, plan, or policy lies at the heart of each of these environmental assessment regimes. This quality is encapsulated in the requirement to predict the 'likely significant effects', common to many environmental assessment instruments. Usually, 'likelihood' is considered in terms of the probability of an impact in environmental or ecological terms, and it is thought possible accurately to gauge the magnitude of the impact. Conversely the assessment of the *significance* of such impacts is thought to require an evaluative judgment of this prediction, according to several further factors. This perceived line between the objective and subjective categories of predictions has contributed to a debate along the lines of 'objectivity equals good; subjectivity equals bad', dissipating more useful attempts to explore the role of values in the collection and interpretation of facts.[1] An aim of this chapter is to question these assumptions by considering the type and source of information entering the environmental assessment process. Following analysis of case studies, I argue that apparently scientific assessments are also subject to subjective or value-laden judgments.

A key issue is the role of law in objectifying environmental knowledge which is capable of adding 'weight' to information. I suggest that the main case study considered, the Lewes Flood Defence Strategy, offers an example of this role of law. In this case, the options for various flood defence works were judged according to a set hierarchy of laws, rather than by reference to local preference and deliberation, suggesting deference to law and to 'objective' knowledge. This case study also provides an example of the difficulty in practice of distinguishing between strategic environmental assessment (of plans and programmes) and environmental impact assessment (of projects): although presented as a strategic assessment of various flood defence options, the statement, prepared for the Environment Agency, considered these options by assessing the constituent projects.

---

[1] Based on work in the United States; see S. Jasanoff, *The Fifth Branch: Science Advisers as Policy Makers* (Cambridge, Mass.: Harvard University Press, 1989) and L. K. Caldwell, *Between Two Worlds: Science, The Environmental Movement and Policy Choice* (Cambridge: Cambridge University Press, 1992), 8 which traces the growing discipline of environmental science as a mediator between science and policy.

In this chapter I use the literature on the objectivity-subjectivity of information as an opportunity to examine the interdisciplinarity of environmental assessment (environmental assessment as science *and* culturally based evaluation) because this provides the practical and conceptual basis for the integrated nature of control that it offers. To this effect I first discuss the nature of knowledge in environmental assessment from environmental, ecological, and legal perspectives, and with reference to the objective-subjective debate. In this discussion I employ the traditional distinction between 'environmental' in the sense of related to the quality of environmental media (air, water, and land) and 'ecological' meaning related to the living constituents of those media (species, habitats) and their interrelationships. I consider in particular how law governs the gathering and application of environmental knowledge and also shapes the creation of that knowledge by its interaction with other disciplines. I then relate the interdisciplinarity of environmental assessment to integrationist thinking within environmental law and policy, suggesting that conceptually at least these are mutually reinforcing. In the following chapter I continue to analyse the legal requirement of prediction but with a focus upon how law structures discretion in decisions about whether an environmental assessment should be conducted or not, through the setting of thresholds and indicative criteria, and by judicial interpretation of the meaning of 'significant effects'.

A further issue raised by considering the type of information entering the assessment process is the relationship between law and ecology which was a motor for the development of environmental assessment in the United States.[2] Enhancing environmental assessment to better reflect ecological understandings of linkages and relationships between habitats and species calls for an expansion of the scales of time and space within which environmental assessment usually operates and ideally replacing the emphasis upon an individual process, site, or development, with a more complex picture of natural dependency, variation, and resilience.

The Nature of Knowledge in Environmental Assessment

Prediction and Likelihood

Overall the environmental assessment procedure is anticipatory. It allows predictions made about likely impacts and their significance to enter decision-making processes before a final decision has been made. The primary characteristic of information in environmental assessment is therefore its predictive quality, dealing with events that have not yet occurred, indeed that might never occur[3]—the

---

[2] See also discussion in Ch. 2, p. 60.

[3] The nearest form of information of this type is that ascertained in the inquiry process. I discuss the place and role of environmental assessment within planning inquiries in Ch. 6, pp. 229–32.

likely significant effects.[4] This exercise in prediction can be traced to the development in the eighteenth century of methods of collection, measurement, and analysis in the fields of time measurement, astrological observation, anatomy, navigation, chemical substance analysis, and mathematics,[5] all of which took place in an intellectual climate of scientific determinism and market expansionism. The impetus for the development of each of these areas was the idea of nature as observable. This required adherence to an idea of dualism—the fundamental separation between man and nature, mind and matter, subject and object—in which nature came to be understood as a portion of the world, as one aspect of everything (and as a resource) rather than, as previously understood, as 'an invisible medium through which each moved'.[6] The empirical methods of observation and analysis of data were used to uncover universal principles, or laws of nature. Such enlightenment thinking also enabled the 'environment' as an amorphous and uncertain thing to be categorized, parcelled, and possessed in law, and subjected to more effective exploitation than previously.[7] However, only part of the evolving empirical method involved prediction, for example of future lunar eclipses.[8] The overwhelming aim was the discovery of existing rules of nature, not the potential of development or progress to disrupt nature, as is the case with modern environmental assessment. It is also important that evidential rules in this period entrenched the sentiments and practice of scientific determinism in law, and were correspondingly restrictive. Such rules coped uneasily with the uncertainty which arises from prediction. In contrast, in recent years a key development of environmental law has been the acceptance of the inevitability of uncertainty in evidence relating to potential effects upon the environment, through environmental assessment and the development of the precautionary principle.

Although problematic in evidential terms, the predictive nature of extrapolation from information is responsible for the anticipatory control offered by environmental assessment. Providing information about potential impacts at an early stage in decision-making processes (most obviously the development consent stage of planning procedures) allows the possibility of imposing conditions about the siting of development and the mitigation of harmful environmental effects

---

[4] A similar predictive exercise is required in considering the role of mitigation measures in judgments of significance (Ch. 4, pp. 136–40) and in the case of outline planning applications, with matters reserved (Ch. 6, pp. 211–18).

[5] Told creatively by L. Jardine, *Ingenious Pursuits: Building the Scientific Revolution* (London: Little, Brown and Co., 1999), 7 ff.

[6] Evernden, *The Social Creation of Nature*, 6. I further describe this process in J. Holder, 'New Age: Rediscovering Natural Law' (2000) 53 *CLP* 151, at 160–3. See also D. Delaney, *Law's Nature* (Cambridge: Cambridge University Press, 2003), ch. 4, particularly 81–7.

[7] The idea that 'knowledge of nature is needed for domination' still holds, for example, D. Harvey, *Justice, Nature and the Geography of Difference* (Oxford: Blackwell, 1996), 123. From this perspective, environmental assessment allows for the 'measure' of nature for exploitative purposes.   [8] Jardine, *Ingenious Pursuits*, 178–84.

prior to harm occurring: environmental harm may therefore be controlled at its source. In the event that such anticipatory measures are not taken, enforcement action may ensue even though harm may not have occurred.[9]

This type of control compares markedly with retrospective regulation which specifies an environmental quality standard or quantity of pollution, environmental harm, or nuisance, which must not be exceeded. Such controls may only be enforced after the occurrence of a harmful incident and are reliant upon proof beyond all reasonable doubt, or on a balance of probabilities, of a causal link between the acts of a person and the harm that has occurred. The rules developed to manage the collection and use of such evidence, and the existence of a solid body of case law which has developed to assist with what 'cause' means,[10] suggest relative ease in dealing with such *ex post facto* information. The need to establish a causal link differs fundamentally from the type of impact or risk assessment which forms the focus of inquiry in environmental assessment. Clear legal rules for the collection and use of *predictive* information in environmental assessment have not yet been developed, possibly because of the uncertainties inherent in this category of information, even allowing for the growing acceptance of the precautionary principle in environmental law, and elsewhere.[11] For instance, the common statutory term for the prediction of the effects of an activity, proposed development, or policy on the environment—likelihood—has not been the subject of much legal scrutiny, even though it describes the core inquiry of the environmental assessment process. It is not clear, for example, whether 'likely' means possible, probable, or even potential. Guidance of sorts is given in *Hardy No. 1*[12] which concerned the level of detail required in an environmental statement to support a prediction. An environmental statement on a proposed landfill development indicated that there might be bats (a protected species under the Habitats Directive),[13] badgers, and liverwort species on the site that might be affected. Planning permission was granted subject to a condition that further, more detailed surveys should be carried out to ascertain the exact effects of the development on the conservation interest of the site and to propose mitigation measures (as recommended by English Nature). The approach of the local planning authority was found by Harrison J to have been flawed because until the detailed

---

[9] On the preventative (and possibly precautionary) nature of environmental assessment, see A. Sifakis, 'Precaution, Prevention, and the EIA Directive' [1998] *EELR* 349.

[10] For example, in the context of water pollution, particularly the meaning of s. 85 of the Water Resources Act 1991, see W. Howarth and D. McGillivray, *Water Quality and Water Pollution Law* (London: Shaw and Sons, 2001), 527–42.

[11] For example, a precautionary approach was adopted by the European Commission in the banning of British beef exports, in Commission Decision 94/474/EEC, OJ 1994 L 194, 29 July 1994. See also European Commission, *Communication on Precaution* (Brussels: CEC, 2001) and T-13/99, *Pfizer Animal Health SA v Council of the EU* [2002] ECR II-3305.

[12] *R v Cornwall CC ex parte Hardy (Hardy No. 1)* [2001] Env LR 25, [2001] JPL 786, Harrison J.

[13] Directive 92/42/EC on the conservation of natural habitats and of wild fauna and flora, OJ L 206, p. 7.

surveys had been carried out, it was not possible to ascribe the likelihood of the significant effects. He stated:

> The bats are European protected species. They and their roosts, or resting places, are subject to strict protection under the Habitats Directive. There was evidence in the ecological report that bats or resting places may be found in the mine shafts if surveys were carried out . . . The respondent [local planning authority] concluded that those surveys should be carried out. They could only have concluded that those surveys should be carried out if they thought that bats or their resting places might, or were likely, to be found in the mine shafts. If their presence were found by the surveys and if it were found that they were likely to be adversely affected by the proposed development, it is, in my view, an inescapable conclusion, having regard to the system of strict protection for these European protected species, that such a finding would constitute a 'significant adverse effect' and a 'main effect' within the meaning of paragraphs 2 and 3 of Part II of Schedule 4 to the Regulations,[14] with the result that the information required by those two paragraphs would have to be contained in the environmental statement and considered by the Planning Committee before deciding whether to grant planning permission.[15]

A counterpoint to this judgment is provided by the Court of Appeal judgment in *Jones*[16] on the point whether the conclusion of a planning authority that a development would be unlikely to have significant effects on the environment can only be reached after a comprehensive assessment. Even though there were gaps in the information provided about the potential environmental impacts of the housing development (on Golden Plovers and bats) Dyson LJ confirmed the first instance decision that whether a proposed development is likely to have significant effects on the environment involves an exercise of judgment or opinion; it is not a question of hard fact to which there can only be one possible correct answer in any given case. The uncertainties in the information available did not invalidate the exercise of that judgment: 'the uncertainties may or may not make it impossible reasonably to conclude that there is no likelihood of significant environmental effects even if certain details are not known and further surveys are to be undertaken. Everything depends upon the circumstances of the individual case'.[17]

Other opinions suggest that 'the likelihood of significant environmental harm requires that the risk is probable, not simply possible' and that the inclusion of the 'likelihood' formulation in the EC EIA Directive renders it a preventative, rather than precautionary, instrument.[18] Guidance on the meaning of likelihood may be obtained from other areas, such as conservation law. In the *North Uist Fisheries* case,[19] concerning the notification of owners and occupiers of land of operations which are

---

[14] Town and Country Planning (Environmental Impact Assessment) Regulations 1999 (SI 1999, No. 293).   [15] At para. 61.

[16] R *(Jones)* v *Mansfield District Council* [2003] EWCA (Civ) 1408. See further Ch. 4, pp. 125–6.   [17] At para. 39.

[18] Sifakis, 'Precaution, Prevention, and the EIA Directive', at 351.

[19] *North Uist Fisheries Ltd* v *Secretary of State for Scotland* [1992] SLT 333, (1992) 4 *JEL* 241, including commentary by C. Reid.

likely to damage features of special interest,[20] Lord Cullen suggested, *obiter dictum*, that the use of the word 'likely' required any potential damage to land of special interest to be probable rather than a bare possibility,[21] an interpretation which, if correct, 'would undermine the whole of the legislation on protection of sites of special scientific interest'.[22] These cases demonstrate the unclear relationship between ecological circumstances, particularly the uncertainties about the present and future state of the environment, and definitions of possibility and probability in law. This suggests an important role for environmental assessment in ascertaining a fuller range of information on ecological change in a legal process.

A further area of tension arises from prediction as the central objective of environmental assessment, because lay participants tend to contribute local and historic knowledge, based upon past experience as well as present connections with an area, whereas the prediction of impacts using models is forward looking, although frequently based upon baselines surveys.[23] This temporal misalignment in environmental assessment means that local groups often cannot comment on, or formulate, predictions using equivalent methodological language.[24] This suggests the need for a reappraisal of mechanisms for determining significance based upon the public's existing perceptions of the environment.[25]

The relative lack of guidance in law and policy about the meaning of 'likelihood' is seen also with the concept of 'significance'.[26] A possible explanation for the reluctance to define in precise legal terms the predictive duty under environmental assessment is because the 'likelihood' (and significance) tests are drawn from inquiries within and across disciplines. A legal definition ideally has to accommodate the differing meanings of 'likely' attributed by the social sciences, as well as the physical sciences, and this requires a high level of multidisciplinary and interdisciplinary expertise.

Interdisciplinarity and Integration

Environmental assessment has developed according to a number of different influences which are represented by literature on technical and scientific matters

---

[20] Under s. 29 of the Wildlife and Countryside Act (now repealed in England).

[21] The case concerned the carrying out of fish farming on Loch Obisary. The Judge questioned the Reporter's analysis of the likely harm from this activity that this was more than a 'bare possibility', stating that 'this was evidently based on a subjective judgment of the "ecological risk" which he considered unacceptable . . . ' (at 245).

[22] S. Bell and D. McGillivray, *Environmental Law* (Oxford: Oxford University Press, 5th edn., 2000), 630. See also H. J. Peters, 'The Significance of Environmental Precaution in the Environmental Impact Assessment Directive' (1996) *EELR* 210.

[23] See S. Shackley, 'Mission to Model Earth', in S. Elworthy *et al.* (eds.) *Perspectives on the Environment 2* (Aldershot: Avebury, 1995).

[24] An observation drawn from the case study on Dibden Bay discussed in Ch. 6, pp. 227–32 is that there is a tendency for effects that can be measured to receive more weight than less tangible, though perhaps more important, non-quantifiable, local knowledge and information.

[25] See Ch. 4, pp. 145–6.   [26] See Ch. 4, pp. 104–8.

such as the identification of impacts, modelling, and scoping,[27] and literature on the legal and political framework of decision making in pollution control and development consent systems (culturally based evaluations).[28] This division reflects two main issues in analysing environmental assessment: the evaluation of the environmental impact of a given project, and the consideration of environmental information in a legal framework, the latter being the focus of this book. These diverse influences have contributed to the interaction of a wide range of disciplines within environmental assessment, particularly in relation to the exercise of prediction. As a consequence, interdisciplinarity is a defining characteristic of knowledge in environmental assessment, drawing as it does on perspectives and methodologies from (predominantly) the physical sciences, but also the social sciences. The assessment of impacts across different environmental media and the breadth of potential impacts on health, cultural heritage, landscape and habitats, further encourages connections to be made between disciplines and sub-disciplines, and means that the expertise of biological scientists, architects, ecologists, archaeologists, and engineers may each be called upon to help compile the environmental statement and evaluate environmental information.

The interdisciplinary quality of environmental assessment was first made evident in the United States' NEPA 1969[29] which required all Federal agencies to 'utilize a systematic, interdisciplinary approach which will insure the integrated use of the natural and social sciences and the environmental design arts in planning and decision making which may have an impact on man's environment'. Caldwell, the principal drafter of this provision, described it as requiring a synthesis of the 'natural' sciences and engineering, social, and behavioural sciences, economics, law, and ethics.[30] The interdisciplinary quality of the EC EIA Directive flows from the requirement in Article 3 that the direct and indirect effects of a project on human beings, fauna and flora; soil, water, air, climate and the landscape, material assets and the cultural heritage, and the interaction between these categories must be assessed,[31] although this falls short of the United States' model of environmental assessment which overtly calls for interdisciplinarity in terms of policy making and methodology.

At a basic level, then, environmental assessment encourages an assessment of the likely emission of pollutants and their transfer between environmental media

[27] See generally, Ch. 2, pp. 42–5. Examples of literature on these technical aspects include Morgan, *Environmental Impact Assessment*; W. E. Westman, *Ecology, Impact Assessment and Environmental Planning* (Chichester: John Wiley, 1985); C. S. Holling (ed.) *Adaptive Environmental Assessment and Management* (Chichester: John Wiley, 1978); see also Wathern, *Environmental Impact Assessment*.
[28] e.g. O'Riordan and Hey, *Environmental Impact Assessment*; M. Clark and J. Herington, (eds.) *The Role of Environmental Impact Assessment in the Planning Process* (London: Mansell, 1988); B. D. Clark, R. Bissett, and A. Gilad, *Perspectives on Environmental Impact Assessment* (New York: Reidel, 1984).
[29] S. 102 National Environmental Policy Act (NEPA) 1969. See further Ch. 2, p. 43 and Appendix I.   [30] Caldwell, *Between Two Worlds*, 8.
[31] Art. 3 Directive 85/337/EEC (the EC EIA Directive). For a sense of the interdisciplinarity of the Directive as a whole, see Appendix II.

and, more broadly, the environmental effects of different policies. This approach was novel to the United Kingdom's regulatory apparatus. Hitherto, the predominant approach was sectoral in the sense of regulating individual industrial sectors (as with the Alkali Acts 1863 and 1874), or environmental media (as with the Rivers Pollution Prevention Act 1876 and the subsequent Rivers (Prevention of Pollution) Act 1951 and the Water Resources Act 1991). Even until relatively recently,[32] laws relating to the environment were to be found in an array of statutes and statutory instruments, with dispersed responsibilities for their promulgation, administration, and enforcement. Furthermore, the sectoral nature of pollution controls was exacerbated by the treatment of environmental policy as a discrete policy area which was often overlaid upon other concerns.[33] This was mainly because historically the environment was conceived, if at all, as the sum of media—air, water, and land—and scant attention was given to devising integrated and coordinated institutions which would allow environmental considerations to affect a wide range of policy concerns. The result was a highly fragmented regulatory system. The sometimes disastrous effects on the environment of this approach have been well documented from a legal perspective.[34]

Environmental assessment works against this trend of fragmentation of controls by establishing procedures for more integrated decision making, both in the sense of taking account of the effects of a development on a range of environmental issues (Article 3 of the EIA Directive) and, at a higher level, of the effects of policy, so that environmental concerns may be integrated into a broader sweep of policy concerns. This accords with the principle of integration, which has formed the strapline of environmentalism over the last twenty years or so. This principle, encouraged first by holistic theories,[35] sought to achieve a closer fit to the interrelated nature of ecosystems. It has since been influenced by the demands of sustainable development, which, having contributed to the identification of linkages between the social, environmental, and economic spheres, required the development of mechanisms to act upon these. Environmental assessment, in its various forms, is one important response to this need, because it is capable of forging interdisciplinary connections (in terms of cross-media controls and policy appraisal), and because, as a horizontal measure, it cuts across traditional legal and administrative boundaries, most obviously as between pollution controls and land use development controls.[36] To restate Ost's description of the hybrid nature

[32] With the onset of the Environmental Protection Act 1990 (particularly Part I), the Environment Act 1995 (which established the Environment Agency), and the Pollution Prevention and Control Act 1999 (which implemented Directive 96/61/EC on Integrated Pollution Prevention and Control, OJ 1996 L 257, p. 26).

[33] A. Weale, *The New Politics of Pollution* (Manchester: Manchester University Press, 1992), 20.

[34] M. Purdue, 'Integrated Pollution Control in the Environmental Protection Act 1990: A Coming of Age of Environmental Law?' (1991) 54 *MLR* 534 and Bell and McGillivray, *Environmental Law*, ch. 13.   [35] For example, B. Commoner, *The Closing Circle* (London: Cape, 1972).

[36] On the incorporation of mitigating measures, outlined in environmental statements, in conditions for planning permission, see Ch. 7, p. 280; in relation to this, I discuss the role of mitigating measures in judging the likely significance of projects, see Ch. 4, pp. 136–40.

of environmental assessment,[37] environmental assessment represents the integration of technical and scientific information on the effects of development in what are essentially political processes (although geographical[38] and social elements[39] are also vitally important to the assessment process). There now exist more clearly established conceptual linkages between such integrationist thinking and the design of regulatory instruments, particularly those seen as capable of operationalizing sustainable development by the inclusion of environmental considerations into other policy areas. (This forms the basis of the discussion in Chapter 5.)

To summarize, environmental assessment represents a marked departure from a traditional approach to environmental regulation which centred upon specific, substantive, and remedial measures to protect discrete environmental media or to regulate a single industrial sector, thus contributing to (and marking the transition from) fragmented to integrated methods of pollution control and policy appraisal in environmental law. As the principle of integration has been developed beyond the recognition of cross-media transfers of pollutants, to take in higher-level and more wide-ranging policy appraisal, so environmental assessment has kept pace with this. As yet, however, the main developments in terms of integration have occurred in the case of the former, rather than in the more wide-ranging sense of policy integration, which represents a more holistic approach to decision making, and relies more on cultural changes within and between organizations and institutions, as I discuss in the context of the European Commission's development of impact assessment for its internal policy making and legislative proposal procedures.[40]

Ecology in Environmental Assessment

Although undoubtedly drawing upon several disciplines, the driving force of environmental assessment, and indeed of environmental law, has been ascribed to ecological science, based upon 'a concept of an ecosystem as a functioning, holistic, and inherently stable system, vulnerable to serious and long-term assaults

---

[37] Ch. 1 p. 6, citing Ost, 'A Game without Rules?' at 351.

[38] The traditional, and most basic, role for geography in environmental assessment is creating representations of land, through mapping, the envisaging of changed landscapes, and the use of Geographical Information Systems (GIS) to establish baseline surveys of the ecological state of an area. On GIS and environmental law, see R. Goldstein, 'Putting Environmental Law on the Map: A Spatial Approach to Environmental Law Using GIS', in J. Holder and C. Harrison (eds.) *Law and Geography* (Oxford: Oxford University Press, 2002).

[39] For example, the dissection of a community by the building of a bypass in a town may be analysed by social scientists; sociology in environmental assessment. On sociological perspectives in environmental assessment, see N. Lichfield, *Community Impact Evaluation: Principles and Practice* (London: University College Press, 1996), L. Pelizzoni, 'Sociological Aspects of Environmental Impact Assessment', in A. G. Columbo (ed.) *Environmental Impact Assessment* (Dordrecht: Kluwer, 1992); C. J. Barrow, *Environmental and Social Impact Assessment* (London: Arnold, 1997); and, more generally, F. Vanclay and D. A. Bronstein (eds.) *Environmental and Social Impact Assessment* (Chichester: Wiley, 1995).   [40] Ch. 5, pp. 164–81.

from a wide variety of human activities'.[41] The best example of this, the United States' NEPA 1969, which mandated federal agencies to conduct environmental assessment of their policies and activities, has been described as 'the most enduring legal application of ecology . . . the first piece of federal legislation to raise ecology to a star status'[42] because it rests on the premise that ecological information could guide administrative action,[43] triggering the 'coevolution of ecology and environmental law'.[44] Such sentiments were enhanced by judgments such as in *Calvert Cliffs*[45] in which it was held that NEPA's requirement of federal agencies to produce an environmental statement also required them to consider environmental issues just as they consider other matters within their mandate.[46] This was interpreted as 'a legally mandated linkage between ecology as reflected in the environmental impact statement and government action'.[47] In short, 'ecology and law could meet in the Environmental Impact Statement'.[48] Despite the celebratory tone of such remarks, even in the most general terms environmental assessment stresses the interdependence of ecological systems by a presumption that the effects of environmental harm will be felt beyond their immediate source. However, ecological science is not a monolithic discipline and so its influence upon environmental law, and environmental assessment in particular, has varied in its intensity and in its message. For example, as I discussed previously,[49] an ecological paradigm of equilibrium, which emphasized the stability and balance of nature, was influential in the development of environmental laws such as environmental assessment, particularly in the United States. This has since been superseded by an understanding of the dynamic and unstable nature of ecological systems, alongside some acceptance of accelerating interaction between humans and the natural environment,[50] and the inevitability of the accompanying developmental strains. As a consequence, a broadening of analysis of environmental connections to take into account human–environmental relationships, including analysis of human behaviour, attitudes, and values, may be seen in the development of environmental science. This change in emphasis is reflected in the expanding scope of environmental assessment, which serves also to give expression to the multiple concerns and objectives of sustainable development.

---

[41] Bosselman and Tarlock, 'The Influence of Ecological Science on American Law', at 861. R. O. Brooks, R. Jones, and R. A. Virginia, *Law and Ecology: The Rise of the Ecosystem Regime* (Aldershot: Ashgate, 2002) simply define ecology as the study of organisms and their environments (p. 7), but then make finer distinctions between various branches, and levels of ecology in ch.1.

[42] Bosselman and Tarlock, 'The Influence of Ecological Science', at 864. See L.K. Caldwell, *Science and the National Environmental Policy Act: Redirecting Policy through Procedural Reform* (Alabama: Alabama University Press, 1982).   [43] ibid.

[44] Brooks *et al.*, *Law and Ecology*.

[45] *Calvert Cliffs' Coordination Committee, Inc.* v *US Atomic Energy Commission* 449 F2d 1109 (1971). See further pp. 252–3 below.   [46] At 1112.

[47] Brooks *et al.*, *Law and Ecology*, at 159.   [48] ibid.   [49] Ch. 2, p. 60.

[50] e.g. Botkin, *Discordant Harmonies*.

In practice though, the influence of ecological science in environmental assessment, and particularly in the scope and structure of environmental statements submitted by developers, is limited. In several of the case studies discussed in this book,[51] individual species tend to be dealt with in isolation, with little appreciation of their place in an integrated ecosystem. Potential impacts are frequently treated in a fragmented manner, so that their significance on the integrity of an ecosystem as a whole is lost. The prevailing approach is distinctly environmental, with a focus upon the impacts of development upon the quality of human life—pollution of various sorts, nuisance, and visual disturbances, rather than an ecological systems approach which would necessarily entail an examination of broad, cumulative effects, the interrelation of species and habitats, and the effects of development on this. The prevailing tendency for an atomistic treatment of issues in some environmental assessment procedures, such that nature is presented as a collection of units, amounts to a rejection of the tenets of ecology,[52] and recalls the early treatment of the environment as no more than the sum of its constituent media. This suggests that currently the integrationist quality of environmental assessment exists primarily in terms of the regulation of cross-media pollution and to a lesser extent in policy appraisal, rather than in a more complex and holistic sense of appreciating the interconnectedness of nature. This is supported by the experience of the United States' regime in which environmental statements are reduced in some cases to a collection of checklists, matrices of activities and environmental components, and other devices for identifying, organizing, and displaying the numerous effects of a complex project.[53] NEPA and its accompanying Regulations have apparently produced a traditional comprehensive planning approach to assessment, classed as a lukewarm 'embrace' of ecology.[54] Recent developments in environmental assessment law in the United States appear to have enhanced the ecological content of environmental statements, for example by introducing specific ecological concepts, such as the importance of biological diversity and cumulative impacts to ecosystems into NEPA's functions.[55] Such reforms apart, the current minimalist approach to ecology in environmental assessment practice, as opposed to its genesis, has led to arguments for the use of specialist sub-assessments such as on biodiversity,[56]

[51] As seen particularly clearly in the case of the Kentish Flats windfarm proposal, the Environmental Statement dealt with species quite separately, even when there are clear patterns of dependence, e.g. as between bird and fish species. See further Ch.4, pp. 140–6.

[52] This point is made more generally by Delaney in *Law's Nature*, ch. 9 in which he discusses wilderness and law, and by D. Wilkinson, 'Using Environmental Ethics to Create Ecological Law', in J. Holder and D. McGillivray (eds.) *Locality and Identity: Environmental Issues in Law and Society* (Aldershot: Ashgate, 1999).

[53] This minimalist approach may also be an antidote to the extensiveness of early environmental statements which triggered a backlash against environmental assessment and made European legislators wary of replicating the experience.   [54] Brooks *et al.*, *Law and Ecology*, 159.

[55] ibid. 165–82.

[56] See generally Treweek, *Ecological Impact Assessment*. On biodiversity impact assessments, see specifically Montini, 'Habitats Impact Assessment', in which he proposes a hierarchy of assessment,

within a broad environmental assessment framework. The case of the Lewes Flood Defence Strategy supports this argument, and also serves to illustrate the respective and related roles of law and ecology within the environmental assessment process. One less obvious but nevertheless important function of law in environmental statements, the objectification of environmental information, is also seen in this case.

Space for Law: The Case of the Lewes Flood Defence Strategy

The potential contribution of ecological science to environmental assessment is apparent. The process may be viewed as a product of this discipline, but other disciplines also play a major part, particularly geography, sociology, and engineering. As for law, it is clear that one role of law in the environmental assessment process is to establish a framework for procedures, culminating in the legal authorization of a project, policy, or piece of legislation. On an initial reading of environmental statements, one could be forgiven for assuming that this is the only role law performs in the assessment process. Although law manages the interrelationship between those involved in writing the statement by specifying minimum standards for the potential impacts to be studied, and (more vaguely) the form in which these are to be presented, law is rarely considered in any detail or depth, in terms of methods of regulation, or implementation strategies, and appears quite separate from other disciplines engaged in assessing impacts. Where European Community proposals for an explicitly stronger role for law have been advanced, for example by linking post-assessment monitoring of conditions with assessments made in the developer's environmental statement, these have been resisted by Member States.[57] In terms of the content of environmental statements, law tends to be portrayed simplistically, typically in the form of lists of relevant legislation which demonstrate the authors' awareness of legal requirements and offer a guarantee of sorts of legislative compliance.[58] This suggests deference to the law, but also limited appreciation of practical implementation issues of applying laws

with the findings of biodiversity habitat assessments (under Art. 6 of the Habitats Directive) taking precedence over more general environmental assessments. To a limited extent this fragmentation of environmental assessment occurs in practice, for example, in the case of English Nature conducting their own ecological surveys, for example in the case of the Lewes Flood Defence Strategy, discussed below.

[57] As proposed in the Draft Directive on environmental assessment, 7972/80 COM(80)313 final, and resisted by the House of Commons Select Committee on the European Communities, Eleventh Report, *Environmental Assessment of Projects*, Session 1980–81 (London: HMSO, 1981), at para. 77: 'the further measures being proposed in the Directive should be dealt with under specific legislation such as pollution control legislation, rather than through the planning system'.

[58] Legislation is usually listed at length. In the case of the Lewes Flood Defence Strategy, an 1847 Act of Parliament, which aimed to prevent the flooding of the Parish of Southease, was considered to be relevant in terms of the Environmental Agency's statutory duties.

to certain circumstances. Of course, law does far more than this in environmental assessment. There is evidence to suggest that law is highly material to the way in which assessments of significance of effects of projects and policies are made, particularly in terms of how information is collected and presented.[59]

In October 2000 the River Ouse flooded[60] and more than 1,000 properties were flooded in the river's catchment area, mainly in the town of Lewes.[61] This is not a new occurrence—the river, which is tidal beyond Lewes, has habitually flooded since Roman times and various plans have been proposed to deal with this. The prime causes of the 2001 flooding were narrowly described by the Environment Agency as housing development on the floodplain through Lewes which prevents it from performing its natural function of storing and absorbing the tidal waters, and the constriction of the river channel within the town.[62] In response to calls by local people to prevent a reoccurrence of the effects of such flooding, the Environment Agency, which has statutory responsibility for the River Ouse (due to its definition as a 'main river')[63] identified a floodplain south of Lewes (the Lewes Brooks) as a suitable site for storing the tidal waters. As a Site of Special Scientific Interest (SSSI),[64] the identification of Lewes Brooks for this function was controversial because the storage of tidal waters would irretrievably change its conservation 'interest' from freshwater ditches to saltwater marsh. The conservation status of the Brooks meant that the East Sussex branch of English Nature also became involved (as a statutory consultee) in the development of a strategy for flood defences in the area, but with the Environment Agency taking the lead. Central government's role (Department of Environment, Food, and Regional Affairs) was to provide funding for the chosen scheme.

An environmental assessment of the various options was prepared for the Environment Agency by consultants in accordance with the EC SEA Directive. This was done even though the Directive was not in force at the time, suggesting that a lengthy planning period was envisaged. As mentioned above, there is some uncertainty about the strategic nature of this document: the 'Strategy' included a set of preliminary options for flood defence management, the analysis of which required consideration of such projects as wall raising, downstream storage, and upstream storage. A further option was to 'do nothing', so that flood warnings

[59] This is the main finding of Ch. 4, see particularly Kentish Flats windfarm case study, pp. 140–6.

[60] Locally called 'The Great River of Lewes', describing the part of the Sussex Ouse between Lewes and the sea.

[61] Environment Agency, *Sussex Ouse Flood Management Strategy Executive Summary* (Worthing: Environment Agency, 2002).

[62] For example the possible contribution from climate change was not explored. On the implications of this for flooding in the South East of England, see W. Howarth, *Flood Defence Law* (London: Shaw and Sons, 2002), 13–17.

[63] S. 165(1) Water Resources Act 1991. On the powers and responsibilities of the Environment Agency, see Howarth, *Flood Defence Law*, ch. 4.

[64] As originally notified under s. 28 Wildlife and Countryside Act 1981. This notification suggests that the site is a wetland of national importance.

would not be given, in contrast to the current position. This operated as an incentive for choosing one of the other options. These options were then 'refined', by assessing them against a set of environmental objectives, as required by the Department of Environment, Food, and Rural Affairs and the Environment Agency's internal guidance notes. These 'environmental' objectives were identified following external consultation with stakeholders, the district and county councils affected, and following public meetings. The objectives included 'improving the quality of life', 'enhancing wildlife', preserving agricultural land, and so on. The relevance of this strategic environmental assessment is referred to elsewhere.[65] For the purpose of this chapter, the case study is important because of the use of law in refining or screening the options against certain environmental objectives. This was done by giving a numerical weighting to the type of objective against which the options were to be judged. In this environmental statement,[66] a scheme of assessment was used in which a statutory requirement (i.e. required under legislation) was given a weight of 5, a DEFRA guideline was 4, an Environment Agency requirement 3, a planning requirement (such as in a development plan) 2, and a non-statutory requirement was given a weight of 1. The high regard given to legislative and centrally determined requirements may be seen in that duties and responsibilities as a result of UK legislation, such as the Environment Act 1995, were considered as statutory requirements and given a weighting of 5, whereas those objectives which are part of the Agency's powers but are not a statutory requirement were assigned a weight of 3. Each key objective identified in the consultation process was then given a weight, for example, the objective of reducing the risk of flooding to people and their properties was given a weight of 4, whereas the objective of preserving the development of the lower Ouse Valley as an agriculturally productive and environmentally beneficial resource was accorded a weight of 1, the discrepancy between these objectives resulting from the imposed hierarchy of law and guidance. A further example of this is that creating opportunities for habitat creation (statutorily defined) was given a weighting of 5, whereas preventing encroachment on the river channel and consequential narrowing of the channel was gauged at 1. Some peculiarities exist in this exercise; for example, whilst no mention is made of climate change as a contributory factor to the flooding problem, an objective to ensure that flood defences do not contribute to climate change was attributed a score of 3. According to the Strategy report, the scoring and weighting system provided a quantitative basis upon which the Agency could then assess the degree to which each flood defence option had achieved the identified environmental objectives.

The role of public consultation and participation is therefore considered important at the stage of identifying a range of environmental *objectives* to be

[65] Ch. 5, p. 164.
[66] This Strategy was also likely to be used to determine prioritization for the purpose of funding from the Department for the Environment, Food, and Rural Affairs, on which see Howarth, *Flood Defence Law*, 100–2.

considered by the Environmental Agency when assessing its various options. Thereafter, these options are given a weight by the Environment Agency in a quantitative fashion by applying a hierarchy of law. It remains unclear exactly how each option was assigned a score that reflects the degree to which it achieves the objectives. Importantly, this is not a calculation in which participants, or stakeholders, are involved, even though they were initially involved in identifying the objectives to be achieved. Rather, a hierarchy of law was used to filter the various options according to environmental criteria, with special regard paid to legislative, and centrally sanctioned, environmental objectives, and less attention paid to local interests. The predicted significant effects of various policy options were thereby fitted into a framework of legislative requirements. This is capable of creating a legal 'full stop', so that, for example, habitats identified as important by statute are given enhanced protection, whereas local interests are less fully protected. A real concern therefore lies with the imperfections of the scoring system, as well as the application of this in a particular context.

Integrating Law and Ecology in Environmental Assessment

A feature of the Environment Agency's Strategy was uncertainty about the presence of alternative sites, having similar habitats and species to the Lewes Brooks. Several further surveys were commissioned by English Nature to reduce this uncertainty. These surveys offer an example of the potential utility of combining legal requirements and ecological survey techniques[67] through the environmental assessment process. As mentioned above, the proposal of storing tidal waters on Lewes Brooks (the so-called 'saline downstream storage option') emerged from the process of conducting the strategic environmental assessment as the preferred option. This was considered by the Agency to be the most 'sustainable' approach because hard engineering options for water management, such as the raising of existing sea walls, could be avoided, particularly as these were likely to require further work if freshwater and tide levels continue to rise as a result of climate change. The Strategy Report concluded:

In terms of achieving ecological objectives, the saline downstream storage will result in the loss of the Lewes Brooks SSSI, unless mitigation measures are employed . . . This option does not allow for the provision of flood alleviation and conservation benefits through water level management, as no water control structures would be constructed. However, the saline storage option does provide a greater opportunity to renaturalise the river valley system, which would allow the Lower Ouse river valley to function as a floodplain. It also allows a greater opportunity to create new habitat, such as saline wetland habitats. Saltmarsh and mudflat are listed in Annex I of the Habitats Regulations; any extension of

---

[67] On ecological survey techniques, see Morris and Therivel, *Methods of Environmental Impact Assessment*, Appendix G.

this habitat would therefore help contribute to overall biodiversity targets locally and nationally . . . However, in the short- to medium-term the saline option presents a number of serious questions that would need to be addressed, most critical being the alteration to a site protected under UK law and the level of uncertainty associated with the habitat that would develop under a saline regime . . . it is recommended that a detailed study of the options for, and likely outcome of, managed realignment be undertaken.[68]

As an adviser to the Environment Agency on matters of conservation, English Nature conducted a baseline survey of the ecological condition of Lewes Brooks. This survey,[69] produced by a number of specialist consultants, included fauna and flora surveys of the key taxa in the wet grassland fields and in sample ditches in the 5-mile Brooks area. The results of this were compared with the original notification of the site as an SSSI in 1988. The reason given for the notification at that time was that the area 'produces a mosaic of habitats which, together with the cyclical clearing of ditches, supports a wide diversity of invertebrates'. A range of aquatic plant species were also found to exist, including rigid and rarer soft horn-worts, fennel pondweeds, and other emergent and local species. The waterbeds to the north of the site were considered to be of great entomological interest, sup-porting several rare flies, uncommon moths, the uncommon hairy dragonfly, and the variable damselfly.

The baseline survey commissioned for English Nature in 2002 found that this rich habitat had partially declined in diversity since notification, with several species on the original list not recorded. The boundaries of the SSSI were described as now encompassing not only those areas of the site of greatest ecologi-cal interest but also large areas that were now quite degraded and appeared to have much lower biodiversity. Nevertheless, the invertebrate interest of the site was still described as high, and several additional species of conservation interest were dis-covered in the course of the survey.[70] Although the objective of the survey was to provide a baseline for modelling purposes, the consultants also predicted the effects of changing the area to saltmarsh on the existence of several species. The survey thus approximated to a specialist environmental impact assessment of the pro-posed option, with the main emphasis upon the biological state of the site, but with some account taken of the ecology of the area, for example, the interdepend-ence of different communities and as between the species and management prac-tices on the site.

This biological survey was then followed by the commissioning of a series of further surveys in the Ouse Valley (currently ongoing) in order to ascertain whether similar ecological conditions prevailed elsewhere:

Extending the biological survey effort in the Lower Ouse Valley beyond the area covered by this project would yield valuable information about the comparative importance of this

[68] At p. 57 of the Strategy.
[69] English Nature, *Baseline Biological Survey of the Lower Ouse Valley* (Lewes: English Nature, 2002).
[70] At p. 93.

part of the floodplain. For example, land to the east of the river and northwards along the Glynde Reach contains significant amounts of floodplain grassland and a network of ditches that are probably comparable to the Lewes Levels and may support similar biological communities.[71]

These extended surveys are likely to be useful in ecological terms because the areas mentioned have never been surveyed for the purpose of SSSI notification. However, the main reason for conducting further research in these areas was because English Nature needed to satisfy itself that there were other sites in the area which might act as mitigation for the 'changed' conservation status of this SSSI, before agreeing that the Lewes Brooks should be flooded with tidal water (the so-called 'managed realignment' of the freshwater habitat).[72] To elaborate, the proposed strategy of flooding the Lewes Brooks with tidal water, arrived at following a strategic environmental assessment process conducted for the Environment Agency, presented English Nature with a serious dilemma, hinged upon the respective requirements of law and policy that it is subject to. Whilst English Nature is charged with a duty to notify SSSIs,[73] as a matter of internal policy, it seeks to encourage naturally flowing rivers. Applying such policy to this case meant supporting the 'renaturalization' of Lewes Brooks to a saltmarsh. Along these lines, English Nature was careful to emphasize the current, unnatural, state of the habitat of ditches and fields of arable and grazed farmland, a product of human intervention, and to describe the proposed option as likely to result in a 'change of conservation status', rather than the wholesale loss of the majority of species on the site. English Nature expected that, in time, the site would regain its SSSI status, but for quite a different reason—the creation of an inter-tidal habitat, thus maintaining the number of SSSI sites in East Sussex overall.

The finding of alternative sites sharing similar ecological qualities to Lewes Brooks was therefore vitally important. Whereas environmental assessment is often portrayed as a means by which alternative policies and sites to those proposed may be appraised,[74] unusually in this case the environmental assessment process triggered the search for alternatives sites which might be used to justify, or facilitate, the favoured option. Ecological information, as an integral part of the environmental assessment process, therefore provided potential support for the proposed strategy. This suggests the combining of law and ecology through environmental assessment, since the ecological baseline surveys were commissioned only because of the strategic environmental assessment (English Nature officials confirmed that this would have been a very low priority otherwise). The case thereby demonstrates the variability of the requirement to consider alternatives, so that here this requirement was used to find alternative sites, sharing similar

---

[71] At p. 95.   [72] Pers. comm. Jon Curson, English Nature, Lewes, 22.5.03.
[73] S. 28(1) Wildlife and Countryside Act 1981, as amended. There is no specific duty on English Nature to *protect* SSSIs, but there exist important mechanisms to compel landholders to take protective actions.   [74] See, further, Ch. 5 at pp. 148–53.

ecological qualities, to *support* the preferred option, and to act as mitigation for the loss of the freshwater wetland site, rather than as a genuine option available to the Agency.[75]

This case study makes clear the usually latent role of law in conducting environmental assessment. The use of hierarchies of law by which to judge various options suggests that the law has a role in objectifying judgments and values. In addition, it demonstrates that there is clearly a link between law and ecology in environmental assessment, but with the qualification that in this case a body of ecological information was gathered outside the scope of the formal requirements of the EC SEA Directive. This was prompted by uncertainty about the opportunity for maintaining 'conservation interest' in the County, revealed by the Strategy. This suggests that whilst criticism levelled against the environmental assessment processes as 'unecological' in approach and method (particularly as reflected in environmental statements) still holds, the assessment process encourages more extensive ecological studies to be carried out. In addition, the information gathered from the ecological surveys informed English Nature's representations about the preferred option, and this was fed into decision making. This provides support for carrying out specialist ecological assessments which do not in practice constitute a balance between technical, economic, and environmental factors.

Enhancing Ecological Thinking in Environmental Assessment

The environmental assessment process may be further enhanced to reflect ecological thinking by focusing upon linkages and relationships between habitats and species. The study of such relationships requires that 'artificial' (or unecological) constraints be overcome, for example timescales for the determination of development consent, or administrative and geographical boundaries.[76] Ideally this means that there should be repeated surveys to establish patterns and limits of seasonal variation in population numbers, and that this study should accord with the habitat, and even migratory range, of species.[77] Transcending boundaries of time and space requires expansion of the scale of assessment, far beyond that normally undertaken, and flexibility in terms of timing. Whilst representing a considerable advance on the atomistic 'collect and count' approach to assessing the impact of a proposal on individual species which currently dominates environmental impact assessment practice, such expansive studies fit uneasily in the contexts within which environmental assessment takes place, particularly those relating to development consent, and which inevitably determine the timeframe of such inquiries. It does, however, make sense for there to be a more ecological approach to the

---

[75] The requirement to consider alternatives as part of the environmental assessment process is discussed further in Chapter 5.   [76] Treweek, *Ecological Impact Assessment*.
[77] ibid. 49–50.

characterization of the baseline condition of an area in the absence of a proposed development, an approach which is implicit in the legal requirement to predict the likely impact of a project.[78] This is because the commonplace one-off survey to establish an environmental baseline provides only a snapshot of current conditions and fails to take into account natural spatial and temporal variation.[79] Treweek, for example, describes how many natural systems have moving baselines so that if only short runs of data are available it may be difficult to distinguish underlying trends from superimposed impacts, particularly when compared to apparently more straightforward estimates, such as noise levels. Longer 'lead times' should therefore be allowed for when trying to characterize natural systems.[80] One example of constructing baselines for impact assessment which takes into account natural variation is the United States' habitat evaluation procedure developed by the Fish and Wildlife Service. This acts as a continuous field survey, with the boundaries of study influenced by knowledge gathered on the site-specific behaviour of species, once the process of assessment has begun.[81]

An ecological perspective on environmental assessment may elucidate the likely effectiveness of the proposals for the mitigation of impacts. The general issue of surveying as part of the predictive process of environmental assessment is discussed above in relation to the *Hardy No.1* and *Jones* cases.[82] More specifically, information about vegetation changes, the likelihood of colonization by particular species, and the necessary size of recipient sites may reduce the occurrence of insensitive translocation of species. Studies of compensatory mitigation,[83] such as the creation of new habitat, also suggest that this is rarely successful in ecological terms. Treweek points out that it is not always possible to locate suitable alternative, and 'ecologically equivalent', sites in industrialized areas, a problem which is less acute in the more rural areas of Sussex.[84] At the very least, a more ecologically aware approach to mitigation might guard against accepting as mitigation 'benefits' unrelated to the ecology of a site in either scale or kind. For example in *Smith*[85] Sedley LJ quite rightly criticized as a Trojan horse a planning inspector's approval of a unilateral undertaking which included payments made by a developer for traffic safety measures in the nearby town, landscaping, and the formation of a local liaison committee as 'providing significant environmental and community benefits which would mitigate the impact of the development'.[86]

[78] On establishing baselines, see Ch. 2, pp. 39–40.
[79] For example, some varieties of plants such as orchids do not appear annually.
[80] Treweek, *Ecological Impact Assessment*, 131.   [81] ibid. 164–5.   [82] At pp. 78–80.
[83] e.g. C. A. Simenstad and R. M. Thom, 'Functional Equivalency Trajectories of the Restored Gog-Le-Hi-Te Estuarine Wetland' (1996) 6 *Ecological Applications*, 38, cited in Treweek, *Ecological Impact Assessment*, 226–7. Treweek notes that in the United Kingdom there has been so little follow-up of mitigation projects that it is difficult to judge the extent to which compensatory mitigation has replaced lost ecosystem function (at 226).   [84] ibid. 227.
[85] *Smith* v *Secretary of State for the Environment, Transport and the Regions* [2003] EWCA Civ 262, discussed further in Ch. 6, pp. 216–17.
[86] At para. 62. Although this issue feeds into the more general problem of planning obligations, discussed in the context of the effects of such practices for public participation; Ch. 6, p. 217.

Treweek's main argument when advocating a type of ecological impact assessment is that its effectiveness depends on the extent to which legislative frameworks are supportive. Although there are now several environmental assessment provisions relating to biodiversity,[87] the governing legal instruments on environmental assessment fail to reflect a strongly ecological approach to matters such as cumulative effects and mitigation[88] and alternatives,[89] beyond a fairly basic requirement to take account of impacts in an integrated manner. Referring to the position in the United States, Brooks, Jones, and Virginia consider that environmental law and ecology have episodically co-evolved, and that in particular the growing trend of ecologists to look at the interaction of different levels of biological organization (individuals, populations, ecosystems) will lead to environmental laws becoming further integrated and more responsive to natural, rather than administrative, or geographical boundaries.[90] This is not yet a feature of environmental law in the United Kingdom. However, the case of the Lewes Flood Defence Strategy suggests that environmental assessment is capable of accommodating the incorporation of ecological criteria in decision making.

Between Two Worlds:[91] Fact and Value in Environmental Assessment

In terms of the types of information entering the environmental assessment process, the interdisciplinary nature of environmental assessment produces a mix of quantitative and qualitative analysis, although the correct balance between these is frequently contested. What is regarded as the correct balance between the 'science' (generally meaning the physical or natural sciences), and the attribution of values and judgments is largely dependent upon ideas of the function of environmental assessment, portrayed in this book as theories of information provision, and theories of culture, or social learning.[92]

An argument that information in environmental assessment should be objective displays a modernist concern with accuracy, predictability, and expert risk assessment. However, as I discuss below, this supposed objectivity jars with the subjective nature of the central concepts of likelihood and significance. In contrast, from the perspective of a culture theory of assessment, the value-laden, relativist nature of information in environmental assessment is unproblematic, even desirable. This is because subjective judgments testify to layers of meanings

---

[87] See Ch. 2, pp. 68–70.   [88] See Ch. 4, pp. 130–40.   [89] Ch. 5, pp. 148–62.
[90] Brooks *et al., Law and Ecological,* 7.
[91] From Caldwell, *Between Two Worlds,* 8, referring to the growing discipline of 'environmental science', located between science and policy. On this theme, see also E. L. Hyman, *Combining Facts and Values in Environmental Impact Assessment* (New York: Westview Publications, 1986).
[92] See Ch. 1, pp. 22–9.

and values attributed to environmental protection through the environmental assessment process, and suggest a process of dialogue which may encourage social learning.[93]

There is an argument for making subjective, or qualitative judgments a core part of the assessment process, for example by using a broader constituency of participants to define the likely significant impacts in any given case.[94] Such an argument was discounted by the House of Commons Select Committee on the European Communities in its deliberations about the nature of environmental assessment as 'science', and whether social and economic impacts should be included within the scope of environmental assessment. While accepting that on many occasions 'complete objectivity may be difficult to attain and value judgments will have to be made',[95] the Committee was of the opinion that judgments in environmental assessments about social and economic impacts should be restricted. It recommended treating environmental assessment as an objective exercise.

A practical example of the prevalence of the idea that objective assessments can and should be conducted may be seen in the Countryside Commission's guidance on the treatment of landscape.[96] This draws a distinction between assessing the magnitude of impacts and evaluating their significance in an environmental statement: 'Everything to be included in an environmental statement under the heading of "magnitude" should be a presentation of quantitative, factual, information. Value judgments relating to the significance or a project's effects are best considered under a different heading'.[97] In practice, the two categories are combined, as illustrated by the case of the Kentish Flats windfarm,[98] in which the magnitude of the visual impact was entirely dependent upon the boundary chosen by the developer to determine this.[99] More accurately, then, the very nature (and value) of the predictive exercise of environmental assessment renders an objective, or 'scientific', assessment unlikely, even in the case of determining the magnitude of an impact. As Wilkins points out, the core of environmental assessment, the need for prediction, makes subjectivity unavoidable because 'knowledge of the environment will never be sufficient to accurately predict the exact impacts of a project'.[100] Ost considers the consequences of this, particularly that the redundancy of simplistic ontological dualism (thought-matter, observer-observed) means 'we need notions of multiple and circular causality, the interweaving of elements and the involvement of the observer, and the idea of uncertainty'.[101]

---

[93] As I discuss further in Ch. 6, pp. 197–9.

[94] This forms the main conclusion of Ch. 4, pp. 145–6.

[95] House of Lords Select Committee on the European Communities, Eleventh Report, para. 45.

[96] Countryside Commission, *Environmental Assessment: The Treatment of Landscape and Countryside Recreation Issues* (Manchester: Countryside Commission, 1991).   [97] At p. 33.

[98] See Ch. 4, pp. 140–4.   [99] At p. 141.

[100] Wilkins, 'The Need for Subjectivity in Environmental Assessment', 401.

[101] Ost, 'A Game Without Rules?' at 339.

This approach has led some to talk of a chimera of objectivity in relation to environmental assessment. Beattie, for example, describes the assessment process as follows:

... data of varying degrees of quantity and quality are gathered, causal explanations with varying degrees of validity and robustness are applied to the data, and projections for different scenarios of action are created. Each of these steps requires the practitioner to make assumptions, to select certain approaches, and to limit the inquiry.[102]

Hence, there is room for politicized evaluations, narrow setting of boundaries, and simplified assumptions.[103] Wilkins counters the criticism that environmental assessment is an uncertain and inaccurate regulatory device, because of its subjective elements, by arguing that this subjectivity reflects discourse and debate and the attribution of values of facts, which in turn fortifies the assessment process. This also means that the lack of precision in predicting the type and significance of impacts is not a concern, an argument he relates to the achievement of sustainable development:

Subjectivity in EIA is an important source of discourse by which social values fostering sustainable development may be inspired. To achieve the long-term objectives of sustainable development, social values must change toward a long-term focus. As a forum for discourse, EIA provides the tools by which changes in social values may evolve. Thus, the value of EIA may not lie solely in its predictive capacities (or lack thereof) but in its role as a mechanism for promoting sustainable development ... The legitimacy of EIA lies in the subjective basis upon which it is rooted.[104]

In practice a choice cannot be made between the objective and subjective elements of environmental assessment because the 'scientific' parts of the process, at least as defined by the House of Commons Select Committee, such as the assessment of the potential significance of impacts, are inevitably combined with qualitative and subjective components, including the choice of impacts to be assessed and the selection of alternatives to be studied. The optimal achievement of objectivity proves to be elusive. However, the presentation of objectivity as obtainable is reminiscent of Habermas's description of the 'scientization' of politics in which political decisions, practice, and opinion are camouflaged by using science to make them appear objective, and thereby increase the legitimacy of power.[105]

---

[102] R. Beattie, 'Everything You Already Knew about EIA (But Don't Often Admit)' (1995) 15 *EIA Rev*, 109, at 110.

[103] Further on the illusion of a distinction between subjective/objective and qualitative/quantitative knowledge in environmental assessment, see D. Lawrence, 'Quantitative versus Qualitative Evaluation: A False Dichotomy' (1993) 13 *EIA Rev*, 2.

[104] Wilkins, 'The Need for subjectivity in Environmental Assessment'.

[105] J. Habermas, *Towards a Rational Society* (London: Heinemann, 1971).

'Fluffing' the Assessment

A strong subjective element may also enter the process as bias, the opportunities for which are enhanced by the practice of considering the environmental assessment process to be encapsulated by the proponent's environmental statement. The basis for this in the United Kingdom is the manner of implementation of the EC Directive on EIA. The original implementing measure for environmental assessment of projects requiring consent under the town and country planning legislation,[106] the 1988 Environmental Effects Regulations,[107] prohibited the authority from granting planning permission without having considered the developer's environmental statement, any representations, and the views of various statutory consultees (referred to collectively in the Regulations as environmental information). This had the effect of giving weight to the environmental statement, compiled by the developer, and placing this text at the core of the assessment procedures. This is now replicated in the current 1999 Regulations which require that the planning authority, Secretary of State, or inspector shall not grant planning permission unless they have first taken environmental information into consideration, and they shall state in their decision that they have done so.[108] 'Environmental information' is defined as the environmental statement, including any further information, any representations made by any body required by these Regulations to be invited to make representations, and any representations duly made by any other person about the environmental effects of the development.[109] Although no strict hierarchy operates, the tenor of the definition is such as to prioritize the developer's environmental statement.

This departs from the process of environmental assessment envisaged in the Directive, in which the competent authority carries out an assessment *on the basis* of the environmental information provided by the developer and from other sources, importantly representations from the public and statutory consultees.[110] Aware of this discrepancy, the European Commission raised in 1992 an 'issue of principle' whether a developer's environmental statement can properly constitute an environmental assessment.[111] It considered that the United Kingdom's implementation in

---

[106] S. 55(1) Town and Country Planning Act 1990.

[107] Reg. 4 and Regs. 8–15 Town and Country Planning (Assessment of Environmental Effects) Regulations 1988 (SI 1988, No. 1199). A similar emphasis is seen in the current set of implementing Regulations, the Town and Country Planning (Environmental Impact Assessment) (England and Wales) Regulations 1999 (SI 1999, No. 293), Reg. 3.

[108] Sheate, *The Environmental Assessment Directive*, para. 3.11.

[109] Reg. 2 of the 1999 Regulations.   [110] See the ninth recital, preamble to the Directive.

[111] Along with other questions concerning the United Kingdom's implementation of the Directive, which formed a letter of formal notice (31 July 1992). On this, and other aspects of implementation of the Directive, see European Commission, *Report from the Commission on the Implementation of Directive 85/337/EEC on the Assessment of the Effects of Certain Public and Private Projects on the Environment* COM(93) 28, 2.4.1993.

this respect compromised the independent appraisal of environmental impacts. Research conducted soon after the implementation of the Directive in the United Kingdom supports the European Commission's claim that the environmental assessment process was capable of being used by developers to ease the project through procedures for gaining planning permission. In some cases developers voluntarily submitted an environmental statement with their application, and used this to publicize the need for the project and assuage local concerns about a proposed development.[112] Winter accords with this analysis, and additionally implicates planning officers:

[I]n terms of the professional integrity of Environmental Statements (and those who produce them) it has to be said that very often an Environmental Statement may read (at least in parts) as a justification for a project rather than a robust and professionally objective assessment of it. Similarly, the officers of local planning authorities, in their approach to such Environmental Statements, sometimes appear to gloss over the issues in the interests of a Council's overall political objectives in relation to a particular strategic project.[113]

However, it should be noted that research by Jones, Wood, and Dipper suggests a more thorough approach to assessing information contained in environmental statements is taken by planners.[114]

One effect of the developer providing an environmental statement which may be considered as representative of the full environmental assessment process is a conflict in the roles a developer is expected to perform in the assessment process: as an interested proponent of a particular development and as an objective assessor of the effects of that development upon the wider environment notwithstanding possible adverse consequences. In the single text of the developer's environmental statement, developmental interests are combined with environmental interests which are public or communitarian in nature. A tension also exists on the spatial level: a developer must make an assessment of the effects of a project beyond the limits of a parcel of land defined by the developmental interest. This conflict is mediated in practice by an emphasis in the environmental statement upon developers' intentions to mitigate the effects of the project and, in some cases, by enhancing the local environment in some way. These statements of intent tend to denote general, shared, and public interests such as the provision of recreation areas or extensive landscaping, thereby reducing objections to potentially harmful development. Combined with the procedural safeguard offered by the *form* of environmental assessment, statements also prove capable of justifying or rationalizing development. In particular, the zealous identification of mitigating measures and environmental gains in developers' environmental statements compares markedly with the low priority accorded to identifying

---

[112] Elworthy and Holder, *Environmental Protection*, ch. 10.
[113] P. Winter, 'EIA: Getting it Right' [2000] JPEL 18, at 42.
[114] C. E. Jones, C. M. Wood, and B. Dipper, 'Environmental Assessment in the Planning Process' (1998) 69 *T P Rev* 315.

alternative sites and processes, examining pollution control measures at the planning stage, and committing to conduct post-assessment auditing. These features may also be products of the 'double allegiance' felt, as the authors of such reports, by consultants, who must demonstrate a certain independence and supply the public with reliable information, whilst also being retained by the proponent.[115] That this state of affairs is so problematic may be seen in the recommendation of the Royal Commission on Environmental Pollution to establish an independent commission to provide a rigorous check on the assessment process, carry out evaluations of a sample of statements, and issue guidance on best practice,[116] a recommendation which has not found favour with the present government.[117]

The opportunities to persuade, publicize, or assuage public concern by using the environmental assessment process may be seen as falling short of bias, operating rather as a 'power to seduce'. This term is used by Ost to describe a symptom of organizations engaged in a range of contemporary legal practices—environmental agreements, eco-auditing, eco-labelling, as well as environmental assessment. Ost locates such behaviour in the changing nature of regulatory structures in environmental governance, particularly the move towards self-regulation, coupled with 'euphoric deregulation' strategies. Ost similarly identifies a confusion in the controlling logics of environmental assessment: as between the logic of public service, as expressed through requirements to provide impartial information, and the private logic of the promoter's freedom of enterprise, in which case the assessment process appears either as an additional legal formality or obstacle.[118] This confusion may not be overcome simply by the appointment of an independent commission to oversee the various processes involved, so engrained are the ideas of the ethics of responsibility, self-organization, and partnership, which are essential to current forms of governance and are so neatly expressed in the theoretical foundations of sustainable development.

Conclusions

In order to achieve 'ecological rationality',[119] environmental assessment relies upon the twin fictions of predictability and objectivity, both of which are wedded to modernist forms of knowledge. This creates the potential for incompatibility

---

[115] On the consultancy profession, see Environmental Data Services Ltd, *Environmental Consultants in the UK: A Market Analysis* (London: ENDS Ltd, 1995). As an aside, no 'taxi rank' principle operates amongst environmental consultants—instead firms of consultants appear to work for one 'side' (public interest groups or developers) or another.

[116] Royal Commission on Environmental Pollution, *Environmental Planning*, Twenty-Third Report, Cm 5459 (London: ESO, 2002), para. 7.35. See further Ch. 8, pp. 296–7.

[117] UK Government's Response to the RCEP's Twenty-third Report *Environmental Planning* Cm 5887.   [118] Ost, 'A Game without Rules?', 351.

[119] On ecological rationality, see further Ch. 7, pp. 244–5.

between the distinctly modernist ideal of objective information, the *fact* (concerning the environmental impact, its magnitude, direction, probability, and quantifica- tion) which feeds environmental assessment, and the presentation of the legal form of environmental assessment as a participative, communicative, and *values*- led technique, as discussed further in Chapter 6. The exclusion in practice of lay participants from the environmental assessment process, particularly in attribut- ing weight to a given set of objectives (as in the case of the Lewes Flood Defence Strategy) or, as discussed in the following chapter, in defining the significance of potential impacts (as well as the criteria by which such significance is deter- mined), means that the opportunities for attributing values to fact, according to experience and local knowledge, are narrowed. One conclusion is that environ- mental assessment is an inherently interdisciplinary mechanism, permitting disciplinary connections to be made, but that the expression of a very broad base of environmental knowledge, including local opinion, is limited in practice. Importantly, law may be used to further limit the range of contributions, by tightly prescribing lay participation, and by objectifying environmental know- ledge in favour of a particular developer, proponent, or proposal.

Law and ecology have provided an important interdisciplinary connection in the development of environmental assessment. This has, for example, encouraged the integrated analysis of different sectors and processes. However, the further contribution of ecological thinking and method, as suggested by the Lewes Flood Defence Strategy, appears currently to be unexplored. A more thorough engage- ment of law and ecology in environmental assessment would necessitate a review of the scales of time and space within which assessment currently works. In the following chapters I highlight the potential influence of ecological approaches to matters of significance, including cumulative impacts and mitigating measures and the consideration of alternatives.

4

Significance

In the previous chapter, I broadly analysed the engagement of ecology and law in predicting the impacts of projects, and policies, upon the environment. More specifically in this chapter, I consider the central determination in decision making regulated by environmental assessment—predicting the potential *significance* of such impacts. This is an exercise in evaluating risk (but also potential benefits)[1] to the environment. Significance also operates as a threshold for determining whether an environmental assessment process should be conducted in a particular circumstance. As such, it is the core feature of legal provisions governing the assessment process. In the United States, NEPA 1969[2] requires Federal agencies to make a detailed statement on the environmental impact of any proposed action likely to significantly affect the quality of the human environment. In the case of European Community legislation, the EIA Directive applies to 'those public and private projects which are likely to have significant effects on the environment',[3] and, in the context of the assessment of plans and programmes, the SEA Directive similarly applies to those 'which are likely to have significant effects on the environment'.[4] For the purpose of nature conservation, the EC Habitats requires that '[A]ny plan or project not directly connected with or necessary to the management of the site but likely to have a significant effect thereon . . . shall be subject to appropriate assessment of its implications for the site in view of the site's conservation objectives'.[5] In international law, the Espoo Convention requires parties to 'take all appropriate and effective measures to prevent, reduce and control significant adverse transboundary environmental impact from proposed activities',[6] and the Aarhus Convention uses a similar formulation.[7] The Convention on Biological Diversity

---

[1] Positive and negative impacts are encompassed by the EC EIA Directive; see Ch. 2, p. 34.

[2] S. 102 National Environmental Policy Act 1969. See Appendix I.

[3] Art. 1 Directive 85/337/EEC, OJ 1985 L 175, p. 40, as amended by Directive 97/11/EC, OJ 1997 L 73, p. 5. See Appendix II.

[4] Art. 1 and Art. 3 EC Directive 2001/42/EC on SEA, OJ 2001 L 197, p. 30. See Appendix III.

[5] Art. 6 Directive 92/43/EC on the conservation of natural habitats and of wild fauna and flora, OJ 1992 L 206, p. 7. See Appendix IX.

[6] Art. 1 UN/ECE Convention on Environmental Impact Assessment in a Transboundary Context. See Appendix IV.

[7] Art. 6 UN/ECE Convention on Access to Information, Public Participation in Decision Making and Access to Justice in Environmental Matters sets out public participation requirements in decisions on whether to permit certain listed activities, and activities which 'may have a significant effect on the environment'. See Appendix VI.

requires that impact assessment studies should be conducted on 'proposed projects that are likely to have significant effects on biological diversity' in order to minimize their effects.[8] These various applications beg the question, addressed in this chapter, whether 'significant' means the same thing in different contexts.

In the previous chapter I examined the nature of knowledge in environmental assessment with reference to the objectivity-subjectivity debate. Here, I apply this analysis by focusing upon how law structures discretion in decisions about whether an environmental assessment should be conducted or not, through the legal meanings attributed to the term significant, and the setting of thresholds and criteria to help determine significance. Notwithstanding its obvious centrality to the substance and procedure of decision making, significance has not been the subject of much sustained legal analysis. Case law provides some guidance on this matter, although generally with regard to the decision whether an environmental assessment should be conducted in the first place, less so on the actual assessment which takes place following an affirmative decision. Although often presented as an objective exercise, for example derived from models of baseline figures, the case study of a proposed windfarm discussed in this chapter suggests that determining significance may also be a matter of subjective interpretation, and may express particular interests and value judgments. This case study, and a growing set of thorny case law on significance, raises the question of the degree of influence that developers' interpretations of significance may have upon a decision whether to grant development consent, particularly when compared to judgments of significance arrived at by lay participants. The issue of the seriousness with which local impacts are treated by decision makers is related to this concern. For example, the point at which courts *would* review a decision of the local authority as unreasonable on the basis that it ignored the significance of local impacts of a proposed project (which falls below relevant thresholds) is still not clear. The underlying question about how participation in environmental assessment procedures may be enhanced to foster lay judgments of significance, particularly concerning local impacts, is considered elsewhere,[9] but in this chapter I review the strides being taken in the protective regime for the historic environment to more fully engage the public in decisions about significant monuments and buildings. A further issue, raised initially in the previous chapter,[10] is how might 'quality control' of environmental statements be improved, for example by a system of independent review?

Judgments of Significance: Matters of Fact and Law

Mass whale strandings have regularly occurred in the Canary Islands in recent years. Each of these has coincided with NATO exercises in the area. Similar whale

---

[8] Art. 14 Convention on Biological Diversity (1992) 31 ILM 818. See further Ch. 2, pp. 68–70.
[9] Ch. 6, pp. 194–205.　　　[10] Ch. 3, pp. 97–9. See also Ch. 8, pp. 296–7.

beachings and deaths have occurred in Greece and the Bahamas, all following the use of powerful acoustic sonar systems by the US navy and NATO. In response to protests by conservation groups, such as the National Resources Defence Council, the US navy conducted an environmental assessment, observing the reaction of whales to their use of sonar. It concluded that the reactions did not add up to a 'significant biological impact' that may interfere with mating, feeding, or migrating. Conservation groups considered that judgment arbitrary.[11] Different findings of significance formed the core of the dispute in this case, underlining that in practice the concept is open to differing interpretations. It is also one reason why many different jurisdictions have been able to interpret and adapt environmental assessment regimes to their own political and legal contexts,[12] for example the EIA Directive has proved broadly compatible with divergent national land use legislation of the Member States of the European Union.[13]

Significance is a complex concept, and yet it is frequently presented in environmental statements as a simplistic or unitary finding of often intricate and differentiated projects, or policies. Although practically problematic, the assessment of the likely significance of the impact of an activity or policy (not, yet, of an omission) underlies the gathering, and analysis, of information in the environmental assessment process. At a basic level, environmental assessment duplicates the traditional role of planning, ensuring that the *location* of environmentally harmful activities is taken into account in the decision-making process, but environmental assessment extends this considerably by requiring a formal evaluation of the likely *significance* of those activities when a decision about whether to confer or deny planning permission, or whether to adopt certain plans or confirm a policy change is taken. Lately, the European Court of Justice has conflated the two functions by requiring that issues of significance be determined in relation to the sensitivity of the location of a project, as further discussed below.[14]

A judgment about the potential significance of an impact includes several elements,[15] in particular, consideration of the state of the receiving environment, and the intensity of the impacts. It also involves an analysis of the likely amount of change to the environment perceived to be acceptable to a community,[16]

---

[11]   O. Dyer, 'Death Knell', *The Guardian*, 30 October 2002.

[12]   B. Sippe, 'Criteria and Standards for Assessing Significant Impact', in J. Petts (ed.) *Handbook of Environmental Impact Assessment: Vol. 1 Process, Methods and Potential* (Oxford: Blackwell, 1999), 74. To support this argument, Sippe refers to 200 environmental assessment regimes worldwide, but cites several specific uses of significance in environmental assessment legislation, for example, in Australia the (Commonwealth) Environmental Protection (Impact of Proposals) Act 1974, s. 5(1): 'The object of this Act is to ensure, to the greatest extent that is practicable, that matters affecting the environment to a significant extent are fully examined and taken into account'; and in the United States the National Environmental Protection Act 1969 s. 102(2)(c).

[13]   Ost, 'A Game without Rules?' 351.

[14]   See discussion of Case C-392/96 *Commission* v *Ireland* [1999] ECR I-5901, below, at 120.

[15]   Sippe, 'Criteria and Standards for Assessing Significant Impact', at 79–80.

[16]   A variant of this element is seen in *Twyford Parish Council* v *Secretary of State for Transport* (1992) 4 *JEL* 273 in which McCullogh J makes an assessment of the significance of harm suffered by

including cumulative change. Context is therefore vitally important in judgments about significance, suggesting that 'environmental significance is an unashamedly anthropocentric concept'.[17] The contextual aspect of environmental assessment may be enhanced in the future by the further incorporation of human health issues in the environmental assessment process since this will extend the inquiry of significant effects of a proposal to the receiving population, as well as the environment.[18] Context also has a strong bearing on the extent to which significance is considered to be a value judgment, as opposed to a scientific, or statistical, exercise. A finding of significance may, for example, be influenced by the likely reaction of the decision maker and by the degree of public, or media, furore which surrounds a proposed project or policy.[19] As Sadler states:

In the final analysis, recognise that the evaluation of significance is subjective, contingent upon values, and dependent upon the environmental and community context. Often scientists evaluate significance differently. The intrusion of wider public concerns and social values is inescapable and contentions will remain even with well-defined criteria and a structured approach.[20]

Legal Meanings of Significance

There is no single, precise definition of the concept of significance in any of the environmental assessment instruments mentioned above. Whilst this has aided the acceptance and adaptability of environmental assessment in different jurisdictions, it has also led to the setting of thresholds and criteria which imperfectly but pragmatically give effect to the concept (as discussed below),[21] and has prompted courts and administrations to advance their own understandings of this term. In the United States in *Grant*[22] the standard 'significantly affecting the quality of the human environment' was construed as:

. . . having an important or meaningful effect, direct or indirect upon a broad range of aspects of the human environment. The cumulative impact with other projects must be considered.

the applicants for the failure to conduct an environmental assessment, without recognizing that an environmental assessment exercise might have adduced evidence of the significance of harm suffered.

[17] Sippe, 'Criteria and Standards', at 75.

[18] As recommended by the Royal Commission on Environmental Pollution, *Environmental Planning*, Twenty-third Report, para. 7.38.

[19] Gilpin, *Environmental Impact Assessment*, 6–7. Although as a matter of policy guidance Circular 02/99 states that these should not be relevant considerations: 'the amount of opposition or controversy to which a development gives rise is not relevant to this determination, unless the substance of the opponents' arguments reveals that there are likely to be significant effects on the environment' (at para. 34).

[20] B. Sadler, *Environmental Assessment in a Changing World: Evaluating Practice to Improve Performance*, Final Report of the International Study of the Effectiveness of Environmental Assessment and Canadian Environmental Assessment Agency, Ministry of Supply and Services (Ottawa, 1996).   [21] See pp. 106–10.

[22] *Natural Resources Defence Council, Inc* v *Grant* (1972) 341 FSupp 356, DCNC, 3 ERC 1883, 2 Env LR 20, 185.

Any action that substantially affects, beneficially or detrimentally, the depth or course of streams, plant life, wildlife, habitats, fish and the soil and air 'significantly affects the quality of the human environment'.[23]

Also in the United States, the Court of Appeals in *Kleindienst*[24] was called upon to decide whether an Agency proposing to build a jail in Lower Manhattan was the appropriate body to make the 'threshold determination' whether the action was one 'significantly affecting the quality of the environment so as to require an environmental impact statement' under NEPA. The Court held that to decide whether a major federal action will 'significantly' affect the quality of the human environment, the agency should review the proposed action in the light of at least two relevant factors: first, the extent to which the action will cause adverse environmental effects in excess of those created by existing uses in the area affected by it, and second, the absolute quantitative adverse environmental effects of the action itself, including the cumulative harm that results from its contribution to existing adverse conditions or uses in the affected area. The Court elaborated that where conduct conforms to existing uses, its adverse consequences will usually be less significant than when it represents a radical change:

Absent some showing that an entire neighbourhood is in the process of redevelopment, its existing environment, though frequently below an ideal standard, represents a norm that cannot be ignored. For instance, one more highway in an area honeycombed with roads usually has less impact than if it were constructed through a roadless public park.[25]

The latter part of the judgment appears to advocate a type of locality doctrine with regard to establishing significance, except that the Court qualifies a strict approach to this:

Although the existing environment of the area which is the site of a major federal action constitutes one criterion to be considered, it must be recognised that even a slight increase in adverse conditions that form an existing environmental milieu may sometimes threaten harm that is significant. One more factory polluting air and water in an area zoned for industrial use may represent the straw that breaks the back of the environmental camel. Hence the absolute, as well as comparative, effects of a major federal action must be considered.[26]

Judge Friendly's punchy dissent should also be noted. He concludes, with some frustration, that 'significant effect lies somewhere in between "not trivial" and "momentous" '.[27]

---

[23] At 185.

[24] *Hanly* v *Kleindienst* (1972) 471 F2d 823, 4 ERC 1785, 2 Env LR 20, 717. Interestingly, broad applications of s. 102 NEPA 1969 were considered, particularly taking account of the urban nature of the development, so that the lower court in this case construed the Act to include protection of the quality of life for city residents: 'Noise, traffic, overburdened mass transportation systems, crime, congestion, and even availability of drugs all affect the urban "environment" and are surely results of the profound influences of . . . high density urbanisation and industrial expansion' (at 647).

[25] At 831.   [26] ibid.   [27] Quoted in Orts, 'Reflexive Environmental Law', at 1272.

In the European Union, the concept of significance has been considered by the European Court of Justice in relation to nature conservation.[28] In *Commission* v *Spain*,[29] Advocate General van Gerven interpreted the requirement in the Wild Birds Directive[30] that Member States must take appropriate steps to avoid pollution or deterioration of habitats 'in so far as these would be significant having regard to the objectives of this Article'[31] as follows:

[I]n my view the Council intended . . . to indicate that no pollution, deterioration or disturbance which significantly affects the quality of the living conditions of the birds may take place in the protection area concerned. It thus also covers negative aspects which, although they do not endanger the survival and reproduction of the birds, do significantly affect their survival and reproduction in most suitable circumstances.[32]

The Advocate General rejected Spain's argument that, because the number of birds had not decreased, the test of significant harm was not fulfilled. Rather, he considered that certain activities such as waste-water discharges could have significant effects on the very survival and reproduction of the birds because of their long-term and cumulative effects. Significance may therefore denote consideration of both present and future effects, and potential as well as actual harm.

In practice the place and importance of this concept offers an interesting example of a self-limitation exercise in law, since the governing instrument on environmental assessment, the EIA Directive, does not define significance (apart from the indications and presumptions provided by the thresholds and criteria in Annexes I–III) and, importantly, does not detail the implications of a finding of significance in substantive, as opposed to procedural, terms, even though a finding of significance of impacts is clearly central to the working of the environmental assessment process as envisaged by the Directive.[33] Article 2(1) of the EIA Directive provides: 'Member States shall adopt all measures necessary to ensure that, before consent is given, projects likely to have significant effects on the environment by virtue, *inter alia*, of their nature, size or location are made subject to a requirement for development consent and an assessment with regard to their effects'. The potential significance of the effects provides a threshold for action required under the Directive, and also defines the nature of that action. Article 4(1) and (2), read in conjunction with Article 2(1), elaborates on those projects *considered* to have significant effects. These are listed under Annex I, and include, by way of example and subject to various quantitative thresholds, major installations (crude-oil refineries, thermal power stations, nuclear power stations, chemical

---

[28] As pointed out by C. Butler, 'The Judicial Interpretation of the EIA Directive in Ireland' (LLM dissertation, UCL, 2002).   [29] [1993] ECR I-4221.
[30] Directive 79/409/EEC OJ 1979 L 103, p. 1.
[31] Art. 4(4) Directive 79/409/EC OJ 1979 L 103, p. 1.   [32] At para. 33.
[33] This is mirrored in The Town and Country Planning (Environmental Impact Assessment) (England and Wales) Regulations 1999 (SI 1999, No. 293) which does not define significance.

manufacture, waste disposal, livestock), infrastructure works (motorways, airports, railway lines, ports), and water abstraction. Projects such as these must be made subject to an assessment in accordance with the Directive.[34] The more varied categories of projects listed in Annex II are those which are thought likely to have significant effects on the environment, taking into account their nature, size, and location (agricultural, silviculture and aquaculture projects, extractive, energy, and tourism industry projects, metal processing, chemical production, food manufacture, and textile, leather, wood and paper production and treatment). Member States must determine the likely significance of these projects either by conducting a case-by-case examination or according to thresholds or criteria set by the Member States (or a combination of the two methods).[35] The ample scope for Member States to determine the likely significance of a project by setting and applying criteria and thresholds by reference to its 'nature, size, and location' therefore arises from the structure of the Directive, particularly the interplay of Articles 2(1) and 4(2). In each of these cases, the Member State must take into account the set of selection criteria given in Annex III of the Directive, which states the potential impacts and locations of projects which are likely to lead to the realization of significant impacts. There is a strong argument that once a proposal has been deemed likely to lead to significant effects on the environment then an environmental assessment must be conducted, in a similarly mandatory fashion to Annex I projects.[36]

The concept of significance is therefore relevant to two related stages in the Directive:[37] first, determining whether to do an assessment in the first place (the screening of proposed projects), the circumstances for which are set out in Articles 2 and 4 and Annex III of the Directive; and secondly, evaluating the actual assessment of significance, as provided for by Articles 5 to 10 of the Directive. This evaluation is fed into decision making, but does not lead to a particular, substantive outcome.[38] The circularity of establishing significance in environmental assessment may be seen here since the likely significance of a project must be established before the actual assessment is conducted. Some duplication of the function of assessment and prejudging of the main issues is therefore an inevitable feature of the assessment process. However, it is possible to distinguish between these two stages of assessment, at least in formal terms. Advocate General Pergola[39] has considered that 'prior assessment' concerns the characteristics of projects viewed in terms of their effects. Article 3 of the Directive states that prior assessment is meant to *identify* the direct and indirect effects of *every* such project on all the environmental factors listed in that article (including fauna and flora, soil, water, air, climate, and so on). The next stage of the environmental assessment

---

[34] Article 4(1).   [35] Article 4(2).   [36] R. Williams, '*Twyford Down*' [1991] *CLJ* 382.

[37] For a diagrammatic representation of the environmental assessment process, see Figure 2.1, Ch. 2, p. 236.   [38] As discussed in Ch. 7, pp. 237–43.

[39] Case C-392/96 *Commission* v *Ireland* [1999] ECR I-5901, AG Opinion, at para. 40.

procedure is one of verification *in concreto*, in which the potential effects are attributed to the *individual* project under scrutiny. Importantly, though, even the assessment or verification *in concreto* is a predictive exercise.

Prior Assessment: 'Screening'

Turning to the first stage of judging significance (or 'prior assessment')—screening proposals for the likely significance of their effects on the environment to decide whether they should be subject to a full assessment procedure[40]—decisions about significance are replaced by (in the case of Annex I projects) or supplemented with (in the case of Annex II projects) a prescribed list of projects in the Directive attracting the application of environmental assessment procedures. In addition, as mentioned above, there are criteria for screening projects (now contained in Annex III, but summarized by the 'nature, size and location' test contained in Article 2(1)) and/or quantitative thresholds for the same purpose (for example, crude-oil refineries and installations for the gasification and liquefaction of 500 tonnes or more of coal or bituminous shale per day). In the case of Annex II projects, the criteria and thresholds set in the Directive may be further elaborated by the Member States,[41] offering decision makers a path to help them determine significance. This may be seen as an institutionalized response to knowledge acquired through the environmental assessment process, a legal interpretation of 'social learning'.[42] Importantly, this also preserves Member States' discretion in decision making, because the determination of significance at the screening stage by a case-by-case examination of the project, or by the application of criteria, or thresholds, set by the Member States themselves, offers considerable opportunities for flexible application of the Directive's requirements in line with the principle of subsidiarity. In the Environmental Impact Assessment Regulations 1999[43] ('the 1999 Regulations') the setting of indicative thresholds and criteria for Schedule 2 projects (to implement Annex II of the Directive) is done simply to exclude projects from the application of environmental assessment rules, with elaboration provided in the form of official guidance contained in Circular 02/99.[44] The main factor in determining whether a Schedule 2 project[45] is excluded from the application of the rules is the area taken up by it. For example, the threshold for projects for the use of uncultivated land or semi-natural areas for intensive agricultural purposes is 0.5 hectare, as is the threshold for urban

---

[40] The screening process is considered in detail in Ch. 2, pp. 35–7.   [41] Art. 4(2).

[42] Sippe, 'Criteria and Standards', 84–5.

[43] Sch. 2 Town and Country Planning (Environmental Impact Assessment) (England and Wales) Regulations 1999 (SI 1999, No. 293). See Appendix VI.

[44] Department of Environment, Transport and the Regions, Circular 02/99, *Environmental Impact Assessment*.

[45] Should the project fall within Schedule 1 of the 1999 Regulations, an environmental impact assessment is always required.

development projects.[46] The output of the development is a further determinant, for example the threshold for intensive fish farming is an installation resulting from the development which is designed to produce more than 10 tonnes of dead-weight fish per year.[47] In certain cases (reclamation of land from the sea, and certain extractive industry projects) no thresholds are stated, so that all developments are potentially subject to the Regulations. Those projects which fall below a particular threshold may be 'screened out', unless, according to criteria set out in Schedule 3 to the Regulations, they are located wholly or in part in a 'sensitive area',[48] are considered major developments which are of more than local importance, or are developments with unusually complex and potentially hazardous environmental effects. With regard to the sensitive location criteria, a general observation of Circular 02/99 is that '[F]or any given development proposal, the more environmentally sensitive the location the more likely it is that the effects will be significant and will require EIA'.[49] But Circular 02/99 also stresses that 'development in a sensitive area should only be considered to be Schedule 2 development if it falls within a description in Schedule 2'.[50] This means that the mere location of a project in a sensitive area does not mean that it will automatically be subject to environmental assessment rules, although it must be screened in order to determine whether it is indeed a Schedule 2 project. The number of cases complying with these criteria is considered to be a very small proportion of the total number of Schedule 2 developments, so that 'the basic test of the need for an EIA in a particular case is the likelihood of significant effects on the environment'.[51] Those Schedule 2 projects falling below a particular threshold and which are not sited in a sensitive area need not be subject to environmental assessment, although, as *Berkeley No. 3*[52] demonstrates, this is limited to statutorily defined areas, so that the local significance of a site may be downplayed. In conjunction with the quantitative thresholds, criteria for screening Schedule 2 development[53] require a subjective evaluation of, for example, the risk of accidents, the absorption

---

[46] On the application of this threshold, see *Berkeley v Secretary of State for the Environment, Transport and the Regions (Berkeley No. 3)* [2002] Env LR 14, (2002) 14 *JEL* 331. Interestingly, the threshold for urban development projects (which tend to be high rather than expansive in terms of acreage) are judged according to hectares rather than volume, although this has now been picked up by the courts, for example, *R v Kingston Upon Hull ex parte Roplas* CO/2897/2001, discussed in J. Pugh-Smith, 'Environmental Impact Assessments: The Continuing Jurisprudence' [2002] JPL, 1316, at 1317, in which the local planning authority submitted to judgment because it had failed to screen an urban development project of just over 0.5 hectare comprising 1,000 sq m of retail and 3,000 sq m of a health centre.   [47] Sch. 2 of the 1999 Regulations, 1(d).
[48] As defined in Reg. 2(1) of the 1999 Regulations, which includes, *inter alia*, land notified as an SSSI under s. 28 of the Wildlife and Countryside Act 1981, as amended, 'European sites' (special protection areas and special areas of conservation), National Park land, and areas of outstanding natural beauty.   [49] Circular 02/99, para. 36.   [50] ibid., para. 30.
[51] ibid., para. 34.
[52] *Berkeley v Secretary of State for the Environment, Transport and the Regions (Berkeley No. 3)*, considered further below, pp. 121–3.
[53] Contained in Sch. 3 of the 1999 Regulations (following exactly those set out in Annex III of the Directive).

capacity of the natural environment, and the duration, frequency, and reversibility of the impact. Emphasis is also placed upon the quality of the development itself, for example the nature of farming techniques, or the use of alternative technology to minimize waste production.[54]

For the purpose of analysing case law on the initial stage of screening projects to be subject to full assessment in the United Kingdom's environmental impact assessment regime set out under the 1999 Regulations,[55] it is useful to stagger the judgments to be made by the local authority or Secretary of State.[56] The first judgment which must be made is whether the proposed project falls within Schedules 1 or 2 of the 1999 Regulations, or neither of these. The second is whether the proposed project may be 'screened out' because it falls below the relevant threshold for Schedule 2 and the criteria in Schedule 3 as to sensitive locations do not apply. Finally, even when the proposed project exceeds the relevant thresholds, it must be judged whether that project is likely to have significant effects on the environment. If so, the development is referred to as 'EIA development'.[57] The last is because the local planning authority or Secretary of State must not grant planning permission for an application to which the 1988 or 1999 Regulations apply unless they have first taken the environmental information into consideration and state in their decision that they have done so.[58] This requirement applies to development mentioned in Schedule 2 which 'would be likely to have significant effects on the environment by virtue of factors such as its nature, size or location'.[59] The nature of these decisions, in relation to matters of fact and law, is set out in Figure 4.1. This indicates also how the margin of discretion (referred to as 'discretionary judgment' in several of the cases) broadly increases when judgments about the significance of the proposed project are considered by the courts to be a matter of fact, rather than law and are thus categorized as reviewable decisions.

Judgment 1

The discretion available to decision makers to determine whether a project falls within Schedules 1 or 2, or neither of these, was initially found to be broad and not easily reviewable by the courts, although this is no longer the case (Fig. 4.1). The early response to the matter of discretion is seen in the *Swale* case[60] in which the

[54] Circular 02/99, Annex A.

[55] Many of the cases which follow have been decided under the Town and Country Planning (Assessment of Environmental Effects) Regulations 1988 (SI 1988, No. 1199) ('the 1988 Regulations), which suggests that litigation in this area is a lengthy exercise; additionally, at least one local authority wrongly applied the 1988 Regulations (in *R (Goodman)* v *London Borough of Lewisham ('Big Yellow')* [2003] Env LR 28).

[56] This is the approach taken in Circular 02/99, 7.

[57] See Reg. 2(1) of the 1999 Regulations which defines 'EIA development' as either Schedule 1 development or Schedule 2 development likely to have significant effects in the environment by virtue of factors such as its nature, size, or location.   [58] Reg. 4(2) 1999 Regulations.

[59] Reg. 2(1) 1999 Regulations. Note that projects which serve a national defence purpose are exempt from the Regulations.

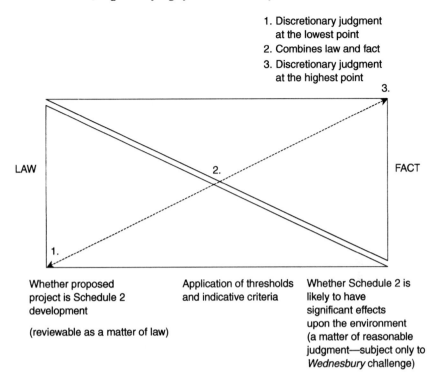

Figure 4.1   Representations of judicial review concerning judgments of significance for screening potential Schedule 2 projects

Royal Society for the Protection of Birds (RSPB) sought to challenge a grant of planning permission issued by the Borough Council for reclamation of 125 acres of mudflats in the Medway Estuary to provide a storage area for a nearby trading port, on the grounds that an environmental assessment had not been conducted of the potential effects of the project, contrary to the Town and Country Planning (Assessment of Environmental Effects) Regulations 1988[61] and because the Royal Society had not been consulted on the planning application despite a written assurance that they would be. Simon Brown J rejected the Royal Society's argument that the 1988 Regulations should apply in this case, and stated that the decision whether any particular project is or is not within the descriptions of projects set out in schedules to the Regulations (which accord with the Annexes of the EC Directive on EIA) is exclusively for the planning authority in question, subject only to *Wednesbury*[62] challenge. He concluded that questions of classification 'are essentially questions of fact and degree, not

---

[60] *R* v *Swale Borough Council and Medway Ports Authority ex parte The Royal Society for the Protection of Birds* (1991) 3 *JEL* 135.   [61] SI 1988, No. 1199.
[62] *Associated Provincial Picture Houses Ltd* v *Wednesbury Corporation* [1948] 1 KB 223.

of law',[63] and accordingly disapproved of the applicant's submission that the only possible view open to Swale Borough Council was that the project should be subject to environmental assessment. It is particularly interesting that Simon Brown J was not inclined to the view that the court was entitled upon judicial review to act effectively as an appeal court and to reach its own decision so as to ensure that 'our EEC obligations are properly discharged',[64] since the European Court of Justice later established this as a principle of environmental assessment law.[65] However, in his list of broad conclusions he did, in effect, exactly that, stating that he was quite satisfied that on the information before it the Borough Council was well entitled to regard this development, for one reason or another, as falling outside either Schedule.[66] He continued:

Even, moreover, had they categorised it as being prima facie within schedule 2 they cannot be faulted for concluding that it would not have a significant environmental effect on the environment. After all, not only had such reclamation work not previously given rise to environmental concern on anyone's part but the NCC (Nature Conservancy Council) themselves . . . responded to express consultation by advising that they had no objection.[67]

This was notwithstanding that the 'largest conservation charity', the RSPB, had pointed out early on in the planning stages that the proposals might potentially have direct or indirect effects on the estuarine complex of the Medway Marshes and the Swale, sites which had already been designated, or were candidate sites for designation, under the Ramsar Convention and the EC Wild Birds Directive. This judgment gave planning authorities considerable discretion to decide whether a Schedule 2 project requires environmental assessment. As such it has been considered a good example of deference to administration in English legal culture,[68] combined with a traditional resistance towards purposive interpretations of claims in reliance upon the Directive,[69] legal characteristics which have been placed under strain from the acceptance in policy of the precautionary principle, and the need to make participation in decision making more effective.

---

[63] *R* v *Swale Borough Council.*   [64] ibid.

[65] Particularly Case C-72/95 *Aannemersbedrijf P. K. Kraaijeveld BV* v *Gedeputeerde Staten van Zuid-Holland* [1996] ECR I-5403, discussed below, pp. 117–18.

[66] A key problem was that the project did not fall precisely into either Schedule I or Schedule 2 of the Regulations (akin to Annex I and Annex II of the Directive). It was not strictly an operation to provide a trading port, or a modification of a trading port, as provided for in Schedule 1 (although clearly essential to the workings of the port), but neither did it constitute 'reclamation of land from the sea for the purposes of agriculture', as provided in Schedule 2. Simon Brown J's view was that the applicant's 'best bet' was to define the project as 'a site for depositing sludge', with the help of the Oxford English Dictionary's definition of sludge as mud! This view is at odds with the enabling, purposive approach adopted by the European Court of Justice to similar issues of interpretation in cases concerning modifications to development projects, such as in *Kraaijeveld,* discussed further below, and Case C-431/92 *Commission* v *Germany* [1995] I-2189, at paras. 34–6.

[67] *R* v *Swale Borough Council,* at 143.   [68] Alder, 'Environmental Impact Assessment', 203.

[69] M. Stallworthy, *Sustainability, Land Use and Environment: A Legal Analysis* (London: Cavendish, 2002), 139.

More specific points arising from this judgment about the relationship between law and environmental assessment may also be made. In particular the judgment gives a strong impression of the withdrawal of law from decisions about significance. After all, the classification of a project as either presumed to have significant environmental effects (Schedule 1), or having the potential to have significant environmental effects (Schedule 2) is considered to be a matter of fact and degree, not *law*. Whereas, as Grant asserts, whether the development falls within either Schedule 1 or Schedule 2 is 'a straight question of law . . . and this is so even in the case of the more subjectively defined schedule 2 development, which includes "development which is not exempt development and which would be likely to have significant effects on the environment by virtue of factors such as its nature, size, or location" '.[70] Grant continues: 'The proper application of the Regulations may indeed involve issues of fact and degree, but underlying them (as with the definition of "development" in the Act) are broad principles of law and interpretation'.[71] The apparent withdrawal of law from the categorization of the project, and thus the application of the Regulations, avowedly prevents the judge from reaching his own decision, although in *Swale* the judge's views on the likely environmental significance of the project were then almost immediately advanced. The Court's treatment of environmental assessment in this respect leads to a blurring of the two uses of the concept of 'significance' in the Directive: first, as a threshold for action, or screening exercise (prior assessment) relating to the potential impacts of all similar projects, and, secondly, as a definition of the nature and objective of that action when conducting the assessment (assessment or 'verification *in concreto*') on the individual project actually proposed. Also apparent is the acceptance of 'information' before the Borough Council as sufficient to discount the need for a more rigorous assessment, conforming to established rules of procedure, particularly on participation and consultation. Such an approach is an expression of information theories of environmental assessment, which emphasize the importance of decision makers having available relevant information and representations when making a decision which may have adverse environmental effects, rather than viewing environmental assessment as a means to engage a range of participants in an exercise which may inculcate environmental values in those participants and the decision maker. As Simon Brown J himself noted, had he quashed the planning permission and remitted the matter to the Borough Council, 'Importantly . . . the applicants would then have the opportunity, as previously they have not, to seek to influence that decision both as to the appropriate categorisation of the development and as to its environmental significance'.[72]

---

[70] M. Grant, 'Development and the Protection of Birds: The *Swale* Decision' (1991) 3 *JEL* 150.

[71] ibid., at 151. However, the view of the High Court in *Swale* has prevailed, as seen in official guidance: Circular 02/99, at para. 13 states: 'It remains the task of the local planning authority to judge each application on its merits within the context of the Development Plan, taking account of all material considerations, including the environmental impacts'.

[72] *R* v *Swale Borough Council ex parte RSPB* (1991) 3 *JEL* 135, at 143.

In this case, the information that was available was almost certainly inadequate as a basis for the decision taken by the Borough Council, since the failure to consult the RSPB left the authority without environmental information which the organization would have supplied.[73]

The judgment in *Swale* was seemingly approved in *ex parte Preece and Adamson*,[74] in which the applicants sought to challenge, *inter alia*, the London Mayor's decision to introduce a congestion charging scheme in central London without carrying out a full environmental assessment. One problem was that such a scheme for managing traffic could not properly be called a 'project' for the purposes of the EIA Directive (the 1999 Regulations were inapplicable in this case, because there was no grant of development consent), but it then fell to be decided whether the Mayor could properly hold that the scheme would not fall within Annex II of the Directive since it was argued that it was an 'urban development project'. Maurice Kay J considered that it would strain the words of the Directive beyond a purposive construction (such as that advanced in *Kraaijeveld*)[75] to hold that the scheme was such a project, but nevertheless went on to consider the applicability of the *Swale* judgment in the light of Lord Hoffmann's judgment in *Berkeley No. 1*[76] that 'If no reasonable Secretary of State could have considered that the . . . application [for planning permission] was a Schedule 2 application, the judge would of course have been entitled to rule that no EIA could have been required'.[77] This was taken to mean that the Court will defer in the first instance to the decision maker, whose decision can only be challenged on *Wednesbury* grounds. *Berkeley No. 1* was then distinguished on the basis that in that case the Secretary of State had simply not applied his mind to the question. Whereas, the decision of the Mayor not to call for an EIA, embracing the conclusion that Article 4(2) of the Directive did not bite because of a lack of significant effects, was not susceptible to challenge on the basis of irrationality, misdirection, or otherwise. The Mayor was therefore entitled to conclude that an EIA was not required by the Directive.

The view of the court in *Swale*, that it is a matter of 'fact and degree' on the part of the local authority whether a proposed project falls within either of the Schedules of the Regulations (followed in *ex parte Preece and Adamson*) was finally overturned in '*Big Yellow*'[78] in which a company wished to redevelop a site by building a warehouse and self-storage building. The Borough Council did not screen the development for the applicability of the 1999 Regulations (having wrongly applied the 1988 Regulations),[79] but contended that whether the

---

[73] A point made by Grant, 'Development and Protection of Birds', at 152.

[74] *R v Mayor of London ex parte Preece and Adamson* [2002] EWHC 2440, [2002] 2 All ER (D) 494 (Jul).   [75] Case C-72/95, para. 39 Judgment, para. 21 AG Elmer.

[76] *Berkeley v Secretary of State for the Environment (Berkeley No. 1)*. For the facts of this case, see, Ch. 1, pp. 2–3, and Ch. 7, pp. 258–63.   [77] At 430.

[78] *R (Goodman) v London Borough of Lewisham ('Big Yellow')*, 140.

[79] Described by Buxton LJ, at para. 11, thus: 'In the event, nothing in the case turns on that error, but it was not a good start'.

proposed development is, or is not, within Schedule 2 (which depended upon an interpretation of the admittedly broad terms 'infrastructure projects', including 'urban development projects'[80] described as 'statutory expressions') is entirely a matter for them to decide, subject only to challenge on the grounds of *Wednesbury* unreasonableness (on the facts, Lewisham had decided that storage and distribution, as carried out by the company in this case, could not *as a category* fall within Schedule 2). In other words, the Borough Council argued that this was not a question of law at all, but a question of fact and planning judgment. The Court of Appeal disagreed. Buxton LJ giving judgment stated:

However fact-sensitive such a determination may be, it is not simply a finding of fact, nor of discretionary judgment. Rather it involves the application of the authority's understanding of the meaning in law of the expression used in the Regulation. If the authority reaches an understanding of those expressions that is wrong as a matter of law, then the court must correct that error; and in determining the meaning of the statutory expressions the concept of reasonable judgment as embodied in *Wednesbury* simply has no part to play.[81]

But the judge did envisage a situation in which the meaning in law may itself be sufficiently imprecise that in applying it to the facts, as opposed to determining what the meaning was in the first place, a range of different conclusions may be legitimately available, in which case the court is entitled to substitute its own opinion.[82] Buxton LJ allowed the appeal, giving a purposive interpretation of the scheme of the EIA Directive, albeit one which mistakenly confused the developer's environmental statement for an entire, assessment process, including public participation:

[T]he whole aim and object of the system introduced by Directive 85/337 is that there should be sequential and transparent consideration of the environmental implications of a project; and that decisions whether or not to grant planning permission should be taken by planning authorities in the light either of the information contained in an environmental statement or of the reasons why such a statement is not required. The local authority, when presented with this planning application, did not receive that assistance in proper form. It must now be given the opportunity to re-take the decision whether to grant planning permission in the light of an analysis that accords with the requirements of the Regulations.[83]

The Court's interpretation of Schedule 2 of the Regulations (point 10(b)) as including the construction of a storage and distribution facility within the category of 'infrastructure projects' and 'urban development project', was informed also by the European Court of Justice's approach to the interpretation of Annex II of the EIA Directive in *Kraaijeveld*,[84] particularly the Court's statement that '[T]he wording of the directive indicates that it has a wide scope and a broad

---

[80] For the purpose of para. 10(b) of Schedule 2 of the 1999 Regulations.   [81] Para. 8.
[82] ibid.   [83] Para. 14.   [84] Case C-72/95 [1996] ECR I-5403.

purpose',[85] which was in that case deemed capable of overriding narrower linguistic versions of the Annex.

Judgment 2

Although in practice contemporaneous with 'judgment 1', a second judgment in screening projects is whether relevant thresholds and criteria exclude the project from the application of a full environmental assessment. In making this decision, British courts have been influenced by case law of the European Court of Justice. This has had the effect of restricting the scope of discretion available, or assumed, by the government to set thresholds and establish criteria in order to guide decision making on the likely significant effects on the environment of certain projects (although not defining significance in as precise a manner as courts in the United States). In this category of decision, matters of 'discretionary judgment' describe government action on a grand scale, as much as decisions of the local planning authority or Secretary of State with respect to individual applications for planning permission. The Court of Justice has also granted national courts power (not yet tantamount to a duty) to review cases in which such discretion appears to have been exceeded. With just a few exceptions,[86] the Court has generally upheld the importance and centrality of the concept of significance, and tightened its application, mainly through a purposive interpretation of the Directive's requirements. In so doing, it pursues quite different 'missions' and performs different functions from those of national courts. As Bell and McGillivray state:

> For the European Court of Justice . . . the main concern has been to prevent Member States from putting an unduly light burden on their own developers (and administrators) and in so doing frustrate one of the key aims of the Directive: harmonisation. For the national courts, however, the concern has tended to be to avoid being dragged into arguments about the merits of whether an environmental impact assessment should, or should not, be required, and maintaining the position that matters of discretion, and rules of procedure, are generally not to be interfered with, even where EC case law suggests that they should exercise a closer degree of scrutiny.[87]

In the Court of Justice's first judgment on the matter of significance, *Commission* v *Belgium*,[88] it interpreted Belgium's wholesale exclusion in its implementing legislation of certain classes of project from Annex II of the EIA Directive as a failure to fulfil its obligations under that Directive. The Belgian government had argued that, in the light of the state of the environment in Flanders, only some categories

---

[85] Para. 3 of the ECJ Judgment, cited by Morland J in *Big Yellow*, at para. 21.
[86] These exceptions relate to the use of environmental assessment in internal EU decision making in the context of judicial review of acts and omissions of the institutions, e.g. Case C-321/95P *Greenpeace* v *Commission* [1998] ECR I-1651, and Case C-461/93 *An Taisce and WWF (UK)* v *Commission* [1994] ECR II-733, on which see further Ch. 5, p. 168.
[87] Bell and McGillivray, *Environmental Law*, 362.
[88] Case C-133/94 [1996] ECR I-2323, para. 41.

of project mentioned in Annex II which come within the threshold and other criteria that it established ought to be subjected to environmental assessment, and, implicitly, that all of the other projects need not undergo assessment. Belgium thus considered in the abstract and in advance that the characteristics of certain projects listed in Annex II would not render any such project likely to have significant effects upon the environment. The Court disagreed. It confirmed that Member States may specify certain types of projects as being subject to assessment, or may establish criteria and/or thresholds for determining which projects are to be subject to assessment, but that that power is conferred within each of the classes listed in Annex II. The Court's interpretation of the purpose of the Directive was that all of the classes of projects listed in Annex II may possibly have significant effects on the environment depending on the characteristics exhibited by those projects at the time when they were drawn up. The criteria and/or thresholds mentioned in the Directive (Article 4(2)) are designed to facilitate this examination, *not* to exempt in advance from that obligation certain whole classes of project listed in Annex II which may be envisaged in the territory of a Member State.[89]

Similar cases followed.[90] In *Kraaijeveld*[91] Dutch implementing legislation had fixed thresholds for canalization or flood relief works at such a level that in practice all projects relating to dykes, such as those which formed the subject of this case, were exempted in advance from the requirement to conduct an environmental assessment (although it should be noted that the project at issue was small by Dutch standards). Basing its judgment on *Commission v Belgium*,[92] the Court of Justice pronounced that 'the wording of the Directive indicates that it has a wide scope and broad purpose',[93] and held that although Article 4(2) of the Directive confers a measure of discretion to specify certain types of projects which will be subject to an assessment or to establish the criteria or thresholds applicable, the limits of that discretion are to be found in the obligation set out in Article 2(1) that projects likely, by virtue *inter alia* of their nature, size, or location, to have significant effects upon the environment must be made subject to an assessment.[94] The Court concluded that a Member State which established criteria or thresholds at a level such that, in practice, all projects relating to dykes would be

---

[89] ibid., para. 42.

[90] See also on this point Case C-301/95 *Commission v Germany* [1998] ECR I-6135 in which it was held that, by excluding in advance whole classes of projects listed in Annex II to the Directive, Germany had failed to fulfil its obligations under the Directive, and Case C-435/97 *World Wildlife Fund (WWF) v Autonome Provinz Bozen* [1999] I-5613 in which the Court of Justice interpreted the Directive as not conferring on a Member State the power either to exclude, from the outset and in their entirety, from the environmental impact assessment procedure certain classes of project falling within Annex II to the Directive, including modifications to those projects, or to exempt from such a procedure a specific project, such as the project of restructuring an airport with a runway shorter than 2,100 m, either under national legislation or on the basis of an individual examination of that project, unless those classes of projects, in their entirety, or the specific project could be regarded on the basis of a comprehensive assessment as not being likely to have significant effects on the environment.

[91] Case C-72/95 [1996] ECR I-5403.   [92] Case C-133/94 [1996] ECR I-2323.

[93] At para. 31.   [94] At para. 50.

exempted in advance from the requirement of an impact assessment would exceed the limits of its discretion under Articles 2(1) and 4(2) of the Directive.[95] In this regard the Court followed the Advocate General's lead in referring to the purpose of the Directive as being to ensure that there is a prior assessment of the likely environmental effects of projects, and that this purpose means that 'in the interpretation of Annex II significant importance must in cases of doubt be attached to the actual effects on the environment which may be regarded as bound up with various categories of projects'.[96] The possibility of significance therefore remained the central consideration. Curiously, the Court did envisage that the prior exclusion of whole classes of projects listed in Annex II may be permissible when all the excluded projects, viewed as a whole, could be regarded as not being likely to have significant effects on the environment, which is a very difficult assessment to carry out in practice,[97] but which, correctly, imposes a burden of proof upon Member States. Most importantly, the Court of Justice interpreted the obligation of Member States to take all the measures necessary to achieve the result prescribed by a directive as binding on all the authorities of the Member States, including the courts. This aspect of the judgment, as well as providing a 'case study in purposive interpretation',[98] means that, although Member States have a discretion under Articles 2(1) and 4(2) of the Directive, this does not preclude judicial review of the question whether the national authorities have exceeded the limits of this discretion. The Court of Justice therefore imposed a duty on national courts to examine on their own behalf whether the authorities of a Member State remained within the limits of their discretion under Articles 2(1) and 4(2) of the Directive.[99] According to the *Kraaijeveld* judgment, if it is found that that discretion has been exceeded, the national court must set aside the measure and the authorities of the Member States and ensure that projects are examined in order to determine whether they are likely to have significant effects on the environment and, if so, that they are subject to a full impact assessment.[100] This judgment requires that Member States must make a specific estimate as to whether the project is likely to have significant effects on the environment and, where appropriate, carry out an impact assessment which is judicially reviewable. An implication of this is the need for a 'reasoned decision', including a duty to give reasons, in line with general principles of Community law.[101]

The Court of Justice, when faced in *Bozen*[102] with the similar situation of the exemption from the outset of projects (in this case the restructuring of an airport

[95] At para. 53.   [96] At para. 21 of the A-G's Opinion.   [97] At para 53.

[98] C. Boch, 'The Enforcement of the Environmental Assessment Directive in the National Courts: A Breach in the "Dyke"?' (1997) 9 *JEL* 129, at 130.

[99] This is restricted to those jurisdictions in which a court may raise of its own motion pleas in law which were not put forward by the parties as a matter of national law.

[100] Case C-72/95, paras 59–61.

[101] As argued, unsuccessfully, in *R v Secretary of State for the Environment, ex parte Marson* (CA) [1998] JPL 869. On the duty to give reasons under environmental assessment law, see Ch. 7, pp. 269–72.   [102] Case C-435/97 *World Wildlife Fund* v *Autonome Provinz Bozen*.

with a runway shorter than 2,100 m) from the scope of the Directive, confirmed that the discretion conferred by Article 4(2) to set thresholds or criteria by which to determine whether an assessment should be conducted, is subject to 'the obligation set out in Article 2(1) that projects likely, by virtue of their nature, size or location, to have significant effects on the environment are to be subject to an environmental impact assessment'.[103] The Court of Justice summarized its position:

Whatever the method adopted by Member States to determine whether a specific project needs to be assessed, be it by legislative designation or following an individual examination of the project, the method adopted must not undermine the objective of the Directive, which is that no project likely to have significant effects on the environment, within the meaning of the Directive, should be exempt from assessment, unless the specific project excluded, could, on the basis of a comprehensive assessment, be regarded as not being likely to have such effects.[104]

With these last two cases, the Court of Justice swept away the apparent judicial reluctance of the British courts to 'interfere' with administrative judgments of 'fact and degree' in terms of establishing the potential significance of a project through the process of categorization. Rather than presenting the 'withdrawal of law', as in *Swale*, the Court of Justice sanctioned the direct involvement of national courts in deciding whether discretion has been exceeded and, related to this, whether significant environmental effects are likely to ensue in a particular case, following a rather straightforward interpretation that the Directive's objectives must not be thwarted. The approach of the Court in *Kraaijeveld* and *Bozen* also circumvents some of the difficulties associated with a finding that the Directive has a direct effect,[105] since the effect is to impose an onus on a national court to raise and to decide whether a national authority has exceeded its discretion, rather than confirming that the Directive creates rights for individuals which may be enforced in their national courts.[106]

---

[103] At para. 36.   [104] At para. 62.

[105] As Boch discusses, 'The Enforcement of the Environmental Assessment Directive', at 134, much of the substance of the Directive concerns obligations imposed upon a private developer against whom the Directive cannot be enforced. In addition, it has been held in national courts that the discretion vested in administrative authorities for Annex II projects by Article 4(2) deprived the article of direct effect and therefore prevented judicial review of the discretionary powers granted (per Lord Coulsfield, *Kincardine and Deeside District Council* v *Forestry Commissioners* (1992) 4 *JEL* 289. See on this issue, Ward, 'The Right to An Effective Remedy'.

[106] However, the language of direct effect is also used, in combination with the 'public law effect' of the *Kraaijeveld* judgment, in Case C-435/97 *Bozen*, at para. 71: 'where the discretion conferred by the Directive has been exceeded by the legislative or administrative authorities of a member state, individuals may rely on those provisions before a court of that member state against the national authorities and thus obtain from the latter the setting aside of the national rules or measures incompatible with those provisions. In such a case, it is for the authorities of the member state to take, according to their relevant powers, all the general or particular measures necessary to ensure that projects are examined in order to determine whether they are likely to have significant effects on the environment and, if so, to ensure that they are subject to an impact assessment'. The Court of Justice

Ireland also fell foul of the European Commission in exercising its discretion in setting thresholds and criteria to help administrators judge the potential significance of several projects.[107] The Irish government had set 'absolute thresholds' which had the effect that the full range of characteristics of a project were not taken into account when deciding whether or not the project should be subject to an environmental assessment. This meant that combinations of projects likely to have significant effects upon the environment escaped the assessment requirement because individually they did not reach the thresholds set. The European Court of Justice ruled that 'a Member State which established criteria or thresholds taking account only of the size of projects, without also taking their nature and location into consideration, would exceed the limits of discretion under Articles 2(1) and 4(2) of the Directive',[108] and elaborated that even a small-scale project may have significant effects where, because of its nature, there is a risk that it will cause a substantial or irreversible change in those environmental factors, irrespective of its size.[109] Taking the Irish example, when afforestation is carried out in areas of active blanket bog it is likely to destroy the bog ecosystem and lead to the irreversible loss of biotopes. This judgment also furnishes a *de facto* definition of significance by the Court of Justice, as 'substantial or irreversible change'[110] to the environmental factors set out in Article 3 of the Directive, such as fauna and flora, soil, water, climate, or cultural heritage. Its further ramifications are seen clearly in current guidance for England and Wales, which states:

... the criteria and thresholds in this Annex are only indicative. In determining whether significant effects are likely, the location of a development is of crucial importance. The more environmentally sensitive the location, the lower will be the threshold at which significant effects will be likely.[111]

The Court of Justice's approach to the matter of significance provides a key to its interpretation of the entire Directive because of the centrality of the concept to the effectiveness of the instrument. The British courts have slowly accommodated the European Court of Justice's purposive interpretation of the Directive, based on its broad reading of 'significant effects', less so its elegant broadening and deepening of the legal effect of the Directive. For example, the Court of Justice's requirement in *Kraaijeveld* and *Bozen* that purposive construction of the Directive overcome narrow linguistic and technical hurdles informed Lord Hoffmann's *dictum* in *Brown*,[112] concerning whether an environmental assessment was required on the

therefore considers that the Directive confers directly enforceable rights upon citizens. On this point, see J. Scott, *EC Environmental Law* (London: Longmans, 1998), 123–4. The 'horizontality' trap is also raised by this case. On which, see the illuminating judgment by Sedley LJ in *R v Durham County Council ex parte Huddleston* (CA) [2000] Env LR 488.

[107] Case C-392/96 *Commission v Ireland* [1996] ECR I-5901.   [108] At para. 65.
[109] At para. 66.   [110] At para. 67, read in conjunction with para. 66.
[111] Department of the Environment, Transport and the Regions, Circular, 02/99.
[112] *R v North Yorkshire County Council ex parte Brown and Cartwright* [1999] 2 WLR 452, at 454.

imposition of conditions for an old mining permission, which had the effect of activating the permission:

[The EIA] Directive was adopted to protect the environment throughout the European Union by requiring member states to ensure that planning decisions likely to have a significant environmental effect were taken only after a proper assessment of what those effects were likely to be. It requires that before a grant of 'development consent' for specified kinds of project, member states should ensure that an environmental impact assessment is taken.

He approved the judgment of the Court of Justice in *Kraaijeveld* to the effect that if discretion under the Directive has been exceeded so that the national provisions must be set aside, it is for the authorities of the Member State to take all the measures necessary to determine whether projects are likely to have a significant effect on the environment and, if so, to ensure that they are subject to an impact assessment.[113] Lord Hoffmann further pursued this reasoning in *Berkeley No. 1*,[114] deciding that '[I]t is arguable that the development was an "urban development project" within paragraph 10(b) of Schedule 2',[115] and imposing a fairly low burden of proof on the applicants to show that a project was likely to have significant effects for the purpose of Schedule 2 of the 1999 Regulations:

... the conflicting evidence on the potential effect on the river is enough in itself to show that it was arguably likely to have significant effects on the environment. In those circumstances, individuals affected by the development had a directly enforceable right to have the need for an environmental assessment considered before the grant of planning permission by the Secretary of State and not afterwards by a judge.[116]

This had the important consequence that the House of Lords was then unable to dispense retrospectively with the requirement to conduct a full environmental assessment process on the ground that the outcome would have been the same. In particular, Lord Hoffmann took the opportunity to emphasize the importance of the public's role in the assessment process,[117] though not in terms of contributing to judgments about significance.

The main detractor from this approach to the Directive's requirements is the Court of Appeal judgment in *Berkeley No. 3*[118] which amounts to a view that 'The amended directive is not intended to *prevent* all developments which are likely to have a *significant* effect on the environment'.[119] This suggests a misreading of the Directive because, although it is quite accurate to say that the Directive is not

---

[113] At para. 61 of the *Kraaijeveld* judgment.
[114] [2000] WLR 420, at 430. See further Ch. 7, pp. 258–62.   [115] At 430 C.
[116] At 430 C.
[117] See Upton, 'The EIA Process'. See analysis of this aspect of the judgment in Ch. 6, pp. 188–9 and 220–1.
[118] *Berkeley v Secretary of State for the Environment, Transport and the Regions (Berkeley No. 3)* (2002) 14 *JEL* 331. See commentary by W. Upton, 'The Use of Minimum Size Thresholds in EIA' (2002) 14 *JEL* 346.   [119] At para. 47 (emphasis added).

intended to prevent all developments which are likely to have a significant effect on the environment, Article 2(1) of the Directive does require that all development which is likely to have a significant effect on the environment be subject to an environmental assessment procedure. The proposed project which formed the subject of the case, the erection of a building containing some 30 one- or two-bedroom flats on a site by the River Thames, was found by the Court of Appeal to fall outside the scope of the 1999 Regulations[120] because the area to be developed did not exceed 0.5 hectare, the relevant threshold set for such urban development projects. The applicant had argued that the site was in a sensitive location, and that this, and the possibility of an accumulation of such projects in the area, rendered the project likely to have significant effects and that this should be taken into account, as required by Articles 2(1) and 4(2) of the Directive. The applicant also appealed to the judgment of the Court of Justice in *Commission* v *Ireland*[121] which had established that 'a member State which establishes criteria or thresholds taking account only of the size of a project, without also taking their nature and location into consideration, would exceed the limits of its discretion under Articles 2(1) and 4(2) of the Directive'.[122] Schiemann LJ responded that *Berkeley No. 3* could be distinguished from the 'Irish case' in which the national legislation infringed Community law, because the relevant thresholds and criteria properly took into account both size and sensitivity, and the proposed development was accordingly exempted from the remit of the Regulations by these.[123] One difficulty with judging the validity of this view is that Schiemann LJ chose not to lengthen the judgment by setting out all the relevant material.[124] Nevertheless, the Court's narrow interpretation of the sensitivity of the location may be questioned here since, as an *urban* development, it was unlikely in any event that this could be judged purely according to the 'sensitive area' criteria set out in the 1999 Regulations,[125] that is whether the area was a Site of Special Scientific Interest, a National Park, an area of outstanding natural beauty, or a European site for the purposes of the Habitats Directive. This meant that the impact on an important location, as defined locally (within Mortlake Conservation Area and a River Thames Area of Special Character), though not in a sensitive area as defined by law, was disregarded, alongside the argument that the cumulative effects of such projects should be taken into account.[126] In other words, the Court of Appeal confirmed in this case that size does matter, apparently to the exclusion of other considerations such as the sensitivity of the location, as locally, rather than statutorily, defined. In particular, Shiemann LJ's statement of 'settled law' that the purpose of thresholds and criteria is to render unnecessary an assessment of each individual project that comes forward, will possibly have the effect that 'some projects likely to have a significant effect on the environment can slip through

---

[120] Town and Country Planning (Environmental Impact Assessment) (England and Wales) Regulations 1999 (SI 1999, No. 293), sch. 2.   [121] Case C-392/96.
[122] At para. 65.   [123] At para. 50.   [124] ibid.   [125] Reg. 2(1).
[126] On cumulative effects, see further below, pp. 130–6.

the net'.[127] A restrictive, and strictly irrelevant, reading of the purpose of the Directive appears to underlie the Court of Appeal's approach in this case: 'there seems to us no reason to suppose that the quality of the decision-making process in relation to this block of flats would be significantly improved by the carrying out of an EIA'.[128] This is at odds with both the decision, and purposive reasoning, of the House of Lords in *Berkeley No. 1* that a court may not dispense with an assessment on such 'grounds',[129] and as such offers a clear example of the continuing relevance of information theory approaches to environmental assessment.

The setting and application of thresholds and criteria may be described as a mix of fact and law: although considered to be 'statutory expressions',[130] they are also factual assumptions about the nature of significance in certain cases, predicated mainly on the size and function of particular projects. *Berkeley No. 3* confirms that if a project is excluded by the operation of thresholds in Schedule 2, then the inquiry as to its 'residual' likely significance, according to the set of criteria in Schedule 3, is a rather straightforward affair, with the focus upon whether, as a matter of law, the project is planned to take place in a prescribed, sensitive, place, and less so upon its potential cumulative effects, or even precedent value. This is highly relevant to the issue of effective participation in environmental assessment,[131] particularly whether judgments of significance and related to this, sensitivity, should be broadened to take account of local opinion.

Judgment 3

Even if the decision maker finds that a proposed project falls within the scope of certain thresholds and criteria in Schedule 2 ('Schedule 2 development), a judgment about whether the project is 'likely to have significant effects on the environment, by virtue of factors such as its nature, size, or location' must be made; if so, the development is then defined as 'EIA development'. Schedule 3 is designed to assist the decision maker in making this decision.[132] In terms of this decision, the lower English courts (and confirmed by the Court of Appeal) have been reluctant to interfere with the judgment of local authorities, as a matter of fact. In *Malster*,[133] a challenge to a decision not to require an environmental impact

---

127 Pugh-Smith, 'Environmental Impact Assessments', at 1318.
128 Berkeley No. 3, at para. 51.
129 On which, see further Ch. 7, pp. 261–2.
130 As in *R (Goodman)* v *London Borough of Lewisham* ('*Big Yellow*'), para. 8.
131 Discussed further in Ch. 6, pp. 189–94.
132 By Reg. 4(5) of the 1999 Regulations: 'Where a local authority or the Secretary of State has to decide under these Regulations whether Schedule 2 development is EIA development the authority or Secretary of State shall take into account in making that decision such of the selection criteria set out in Schedule 3 as are relevant to the development'. Schedule 3 is headed Selection Criteria for Screening Schedule 2 Development and groups the criteria under three headings: characteristics of development, location of development, and characteristics of the potential development. See further Appendix VII.
133 *R (Malster)* v *Ipswich Borough Council and Ipswich Town Football Club* [2001] EWHC Admin 711 (Sullivan J).

assessment of the redevelopment of a football ground raised the broader question whether the judgment of likely significant effects of the project was a question of jurisdictional fact for the court to decide, if necessary by substituting its view for that of the planning authority. Sullivan J rejected this argument and its basis in *dicta* of the New South Wales Court of Appeal on the ground that the NSW Land and Environment Court comprised judges with specialist knowledge, and the jurisdiction, to enable it to deal with environmental disputes on their merits.[134] Rather, he stated, 'the 1999 Regulations made it clear that it is for the Secretary of State or the local planning authority to decide whether Schedule 2 development is EIA development'.[135] Sullivan cited with approval the judgment of Simon Brown J in *Swale* that '[Q]uestions of classification are essentially questions of fact and degree, not of law', even though this case dealt with the different decision of whether the proposed development was Schedule 2 development in the first place, not whether it was likely to have significant effects on the environment.

Malster makes clear that the decision about significance is relevant in terms of effects upon the natural, rather than the built, environment, (several houses were likely to be placed in shadow by the redevelopment). This is an important statement on the purview of the Regulations: '[T]he 1999 Regulations are concerned to protect the environment in the public interest. Whilst this may have the effect of avoiding harm to residential amenity, the purpose of the 1999 Regulations is not to protect the amenity of individual dwellinghouses. There may be a significant impact upon a particular dwelling or dwellings, without there being any likely significant effect on the environment for the purposes of the Regulations'[136] (although this seems to overlook the other, undeniably 'environmental', impacts referred to in the case such as on a local nature reserve). Also at issue in this case was the potential importance of locality in judging significance, notwithstanding that policy guidance in Circular 02/99 states that, in the light of Schedule 3, and in general, environmental assessment will be required for 'major developments which are of more than local significance'.[137] In *Malster* the proposed project was likely to produce a severe, but highly localized, shadowing effect upon a relatively few properties. This was found not to amount to a likely significant effect on the environment such as to warrant a full assessment process.[138]

The issue of local significance similarly arose in *ex parte Walton*[139] in which the decision not to require an environmental assessment of a planned access road (across water meadows) was challenged. The local authority had considered that the project was not of more than local importance, since its impacts were likely to be confined to the development site itself and its immediate environs. Hooper J considered that the authority had attached too much weight in deciding whether the effect is 'significant' to the fact that the road was only of local importance, and

[134] *Timbarra Protection Coalition* v *Ross Mining* [1999] NSWCA 8.   [135] At para. 9.
[136] ibid.   [137] At para. 35 of Circular 02/99.   [138] ibid.
[139] *R* v *Edmundsbury Borough Council ex parte Walton* [1999] JPL 805.

that, instead, a road may have a significant effect even though its effect is local. Nevertheless, the judge confirmed that a planning authority acting reasonably and applying the correct test to the facts of this case would be entitled to reach the conclusion that it was not likely that the effects on the environment of the proposed road would be 'significant'.

The Court of Appeal judgment in *Jones*[140] is now authority on the reviewability of the decision whether Schedule 2 development is likely to have significant effects on the environment.[141] The case was brought to challenge a local authority's decision to grant planning permission for an industrial estate on the basis that the authority had not properly considered whether an environmental impact assessment should have been carried out. The applicants' argument was that, construing the Directive and Regulations so as to give effect to the broad scope and purpose of the Directive, Schedule 2 projects which may have significant environmental effects must be the subject of an EIA, and that a conclusion that a development would be unlikely to have significant effects can be properly reached only after a comprehensive assessment. In short, where there is any uncertainty about the environmental effects of a development, it cannot be said that it would be unlikely to have significant effects on the environment, and an EIA will be required. At first instance Richards J denied this precautionary aspect of environmental assessment, and held that the decision as to whether a proposed development was likely to have significant effects on the environment called for an exercise of judgment on the part of the planning committee even when that committee was faced with uncertainties or gaps in the information about the potential environmental impacts of the proposed development. However, in the event, the committee's judgment about the significance of the likely environmental impacts was held up for legal scrutiny, in this case favourably. Richards J considered 'although there might have been some impact on Golden Plovers or bats, the impact was minor and was not significant enough to warrant an environmental report (or more correctly an environmental statement). In addition there was nothing in the course of the representations such as about the loss of habitats or other wildlife, that had made it unreasonable for the committee to proceed as to a decision on an environmental impact report or to have concluded that there was no likelihood of significant environmental effects'.[142] At the Court of Appeal, Dyson LJ confirmed:

[W]hether a proposed development is *likely* to have *significant* effects on the environment involves an exercise of judgment or opinion. It is not a question of hard fact to which there can only be one possible correct answer in any given case. The use of the word 'opinion' in regulation 2(2) is, therefore, entirely apt. In my view, that is in itself a sufficient reason for concluding that the role of the court should be limited to one of review on *Wednesbury* grounds.[143]

[140] *R (Jones)* v *Mansfield District Council* [2003] EWCA Civ 1408.
[141] [2003] EWHC (Admin) 711.   [142] ibid., para. 5.
[143] [2003] EWHC Civ 1408, para. 16.

On the matter of gaps in information, Dyson LJ considered:

> ... the uncertainties may or not make it impossible reasonably to conclude that there is no likelihood of significant environmental effects. It is possible in principle to have sufficient information to enable a decision reasonably to be made as to the likelihood of significant environmental effects even if certain details are not known and further surveys are to be undertaken. Everything depends on the circumstances of the individual case.[144]

Before coming to this conclusion, Dyson LJ noted that it was unfortunate that the question, raised by Carnwarth LJ, whether the development would be likely to have significant effects on the environment by virtue of factors such as its nature, size, or location might be for the court to decide as a question of primary fact was 'the subject of only the most exogenous argument'.[145] Overall, Carnwarth LJ agreed that 'within the statutory framework set by the legislature, determination of "significance" (for Annex II projects) is a matter for the administrative authorities, subject only to judicial review on conventional "Wednesbury" grounds',[146] taking the opportunity to state that this interpretation also made practical sense, allowing an authoritative decision as to the procedure to be made at the outset and without risk of subsequent challenge except on legal grounds. Carnwarth LJ concluded:

> ... the word 'significant' does not lay down a precise legal test. It requires the exercise of judgment, on technical or other planning grounds, and consistency in the exercise of that judgment in different cases. That is a function for which the courts are ill-equipped, but which is well suited to the familiar role of local planning authorities, under the guidance of the Secretary of State.[147]

In summary, the position of the Court of Appeal in '*Big Yellow*' and *Jones* are not mutually exclusive. As Buxton LJ described in '*Big Yellow*', having decided whether a development is a Schedule 2 development, which is broadly a matter of law—determining statutory expressions in which the concept of reasonable judgment as embodied in *Wednesbury* has no part to play—the local authority or Secretary of State has then to go on and decide whether that 'Schedule 2 development' is also 'EIA development' by determining whether it is likely to have significant effects on the environment by virtue of factors such as its nature, size, or location. In the case of such an inquiry, Buxton LJ stated, the *Wednesbury* principle does apply,[148] as confirmed by the Court of Appeal in *Jones*. Returning to the representation of this decision in Figure 4.1,[149] it is at this stage that discretionary judgment, or 'opinion' is at its highest.

This survey of recent case law suggests that the role of the courts in the determination of significance (as opposed to the initial inquiry as to whether a project falls within or outwith Schedule 2) is one of pragmatic withdrawal in the sense that it is considered to be a matter of the exercise of judgment on the part of

---

[144] At para. 39.   [145] At para. 14.   [146] At para. 60.   [147] At para. 61.
[148] At para. 9.   [149] See p. 111.

a local authority, according to the facts of individual cases, and unhampered by the prospect of judicial review. This also means that a potentially 'action-forcing' role of the courts, such as that seen in the United States,[150] is not adopted. This approach also fails to uphold the precautionary sentiments of European judgments such as *Kraaijeveld*. In *Jones*, for example, it was held that a local council was *not* subject to the so-called 'bounding principle' whereby it had to require an environmental assessment of the development of an industrial estate unless it was confident that the proposed development would not have significant effects on the environment, and that any uncertainty had to be resolved in favour of requiring an environ-mental assessment. Notwithstanding this apparent withdrawal from determining the matter of significance, the courts have been instrumental in defining the remit of the 1999 Regulations, particularly with regard to local impacts. Although to some extent following the lead of policy guidance in Circular 02/99 (that major projects which are of more than local importance are likely to have significant effects on the environment), the courts have tended to take an unecological view of local impacts, such as those likely to compromise the 'green buffers' at stake in *Jones* and *Walton*. An unresolved issue is the point at which courts would review a decision of the local authority as unreasonable on the basis that it ignored the significance of local impacts of a proposed project. This is illustrated by Sharpston's example in *Berkeley No. 3* of the London Eye, a large and visually significant project which is accommodated on a site of less than 0.5 hectare and is thus exempted from the Regulations by the relevant threshold for urban development.[151]

An issue related to the interpretation of the significance threshold of the Directive is whether national time limits remain valid in cases in which significant effects are likely to be produced by a Schedule 2 development. For instance, in *CPRE*[152] Richards J stated that European judgments such as *Kraaijeveld* do not deprive the national court of its discretion in relation to time limits: 'the fact that there exists an arguable breach of Community law does not mean that normal procedural safeguards, including those that are there to protect legal certainty, have to be thrown out of the window', even, presumably, in cases in which significant, and adverse, effects upon the environment are likely to ensue.

Assessment *in Concreto*

Above, I analysed the limits of discretion to set indicative thresholds and criteria, and to make judgments of significance in order that authorities may screen projects for the application of environmental assessment rules, as a form of prior

---

[150] See Ch. 7, at pp. 251–6.   [151] *Berkeley No. 3*, para. 40.

[152] *R v London Borough of Hammersmith and Fulham ex parte Council for the Protection of Rural England* [2000] Env LR 532, affd [2000] Env LR 549, CA (on which see further, Ch. 6, pp. 211–12). This judgment was followed in *R v North West Leicestershire District Council ex parte Moses* [2000] Env LR 443, CA.

assessment. Turning to the stage of ascertaining the likely significance of a proposal (verification *in concreto*), a difficult question arises about whether a finding that a project is not likely to have significant effects should, or could, be subject to judicial review within the scope of the existing rules at national level, and failing that, as a matter of Community law.[153] Such a review might include analysis of the quality of an environmental statement and consultations, the examination of alternatives, and the failure to act on opinions expressed in the environmental assessment process.

As yet, this question has not been addressed explicitly by the Court of Justice or courts in the United Kingdom, although a more limited inquiry along these lines may be seen in several classes of case. First, there are those cases in which the information to hand, or in the public domain, is compared with that likely to be elicited from a prescribed environmental assessment process, and which inevitably involves discussion about the quality of the 'assessment of sorts' actually conducted.[154] Secondly, are cases concerning the grant of outline planning permission which necessarily involve deficient environmental statements because reserved matters must still be worked out, creating difficulties in relating the description of the development in the environmental statement to the development as it will finally be carried out, and raising questions about whether the environmental information provided is adequate to support a prediction of the likely significance of the proposal.[155] Thirdly, the European Court of Justice has conferred a duty on the national courts to raise on their own behalf and review the exercise of discretion of authorities in determining the likely significance of the effects of certain projects on the environment. This duty is clearly not restricted to the prior assessment stage and may possibly be applied in future in order to review the environmental assessment conducted *in concreto*.[156] Fourthly, there are cases in which the courts have taken a strict view of mistakes made by the authorities in interpreting the 1999 Regulations. This may influence a finding of the likelihood of significance, though it would not amount to a complete review of that finding.[157] Finally, planning authority decisions have been challenged on the

---

[153] On this point, see Boch, 'The Enforcement of the Environmental Assessment Directive', at 90.

[154] For example Case C-431/92, *Commission* v *Germany* [1995] ECR I-2189, at para. 43, which informed the Court of Appeal's judgment in *Berkeley No. 1* [1998] Env LR 741, per Pill LJ, at 754.

[155] For example, *R* v *Rochdale Metropolitan Borough Council ex parte Tew* [1999] 3 PLR 74 in which Sullivan J held that it was necessary in order to assess the likely effects that there should be an adequate description of the development and that this could not be provided by a bare outline application or by the reserved matters procedure or use of conditions. But, in the subsequent case, *R* v *Rochdale MBC, ex parte Milne ('Tew II')* (2001) 81 P and CR 365, [2001] Env LR 22, [2001] JPL 470, Sullivan J accepted that the issue of whether sufficient information had been provided was for the planning authority, as a matter of planning judgment, rather than the courts. See discussion of reserved matters with regard to participation requirements in Ch. 6, pp. 211–18.

[156] For example, as stated in Case C-435/97 *World Wildlife Fund* v *Autonome Provinz Bozen* [1999] ECR I-5613, at para. 71.

[157] For example, in *BT* v *Gloucester City Council* [2001] EWHC Admin 1001 (Elias J) in which it was argued that the authority should have considered whether an environmental impact assessment

ground of inadequate environmental statements, although the applicants have hitherto been unsuccessful.[158]

Essentially though this second stage of assessment is characterized by minimal legal scrutiny with regard to judgments of significance. The lead is taken from the governing legal provisions in England and Wales which, reflecting the terms of EIA Directive, make no specific allowance for judicial review of the substance of the assessment actually conducted on the basis that there is a dispute about the likelihood, or non-likelihood, of significant effects or related matters, such as the quality of the assessment conducted, or the manner in which alternative options are dealt with. The apparent reluctance of the courts to explicitly attend to such matters may be because of the procedural objective and content of the Directive, even though each of the above matters may influence a finding of the likely significance of the effects of a project.

Of course, litigation upon environmental assessment is still maturing, as is its methodology and practice, as a review of the 'generations' of environmental assessment case law to date suggests. Early litigation, following the adoption of the EIA Directive by the EEC in 1985, was primarily concerned with the application of assessment rules to 'pipeline' cases[159] (those which had been in the planning pipeline before the date for implementation of the EIA Directive in 1988) and, similarly, with the legality of transitional arrangements.[160] This subject matter was inevitably surpassed by matters of categorizing projects as requiring environmental assessment or not (typically, *Swale*), and the correct exercise of discretion in setting thresholds and criteria for screening purposes (setting levels for the purpose of prior assessment). The last made up the core of case law in the latter part of the 1990s, notably *Kraaijeveld*,[161] and *Bozen*.[162] The future occurrence of cases

---

was needed under the 1999 Regulations. The authority's Director of Environment had informally determined that no such assessment was needed. This decision was held to be defective for a number of reasons, including that he had considered that there were likely to be no significant adverse effects, whereas under the Regulations, he should have considered whether there were likely to be any significant effects, adverse or otherwise, in order to give the public the opportunity to form their own view on whether the effects were beneficial or adverse. A possible mistake on the part of the defendant planning authority was also at stake in *R (Vetterlein)* v *Hampshire County Council* [2002] Env LR 8 in which Sullivan J dismissed the argument that the prospective developer's environmental statement had been inaccurately summarized by the authority's report presented to its planning committee on the ground, *inter alia*, that it was 'questionable' whether an error relating to 'a particular aspect of one of the many topics covered in the report could sensibly be said to invalidate the committee's decision to grant planning permission'.

[158] See *R (Bedford and Clare)* v *London Borough of Islington and Arsenal Football Club plc* [2002] EWHC 2044 (Admin) and *R (Burkett)* v *London Borough of Hammersmith and Fulham* [2003] EWHC 1031 (Admin). For analysis of these cases, see Tromans and Fuller, *Environmental Impact Assessment*, 4.32–4.39.

[159] For example, *Twyford Parish Council* v *Secretary of State for Transport* (1992) 4 *JEL* 273.

[160] For example, Case C-396/92 *Bund Naturschutz in Bayern E.V.* v *Freistaat Bayern* [1994] ECR I-1097, Case C-431/92 *Commission* v *Germany* [1995] ECR I-2189, para. 28; Case C-150/97 *Commission* v *Portugal* Judgment of the Court of Justice 21 Jan 1999; and Case C-81/96 *Burgemeester en Westhouders van Haarlemmerliede en Spaarunoude* v *Gedeputeerde Stan van Noord-Holland* [1998] ECR I-3923, paras. 23–8.   [161] Case C-72/95.   [162] Case C-435/97.

concerned with more substantive matters, such as the quality of the environmental assessment actually conducted, may be an indicator of a maturing legal regime for environmental assessment, one signal of which is *Medway Council*,[163] concerning the proper consideration of alternatives to building an airport as part of the assessment process (although not amounting to authority for judicial review of a decision such as this on its merits). Interestingly, in the United States, case law has already featured a similar debate about the substantive review of decisions regulated by environmental assessment procedures, with differences of opinion expressed by the Federal and state judiciary.[164]

Indirect, Cumulative, and Interrelated Impacts

The potential indirect, cumulative, and interrelated impacts[165] of a proposed development have a direct bearing upon judgments of its 'likely significance', both at the screening stage, and in terms of the assessment *in concreto*. This is because, when viewed narrowly in terms of its component parts, separated by space ('sliced up' projects) and/or time (in the case of 'staged' projects), a project may fall below a threshold for significance, but when these parts are viewed together they may have considerable, or significant, effects. Environmental assessment procedures potentially provide an opportunity to consider a development as a whole—in terms of the wider impacts of an entire project (including all its component parts), and in combination with related projects, so that the effects of incremental damage from ribbon development, in-filling, and associated projects such as road building, and damage from synergistic effects (the reaction of one impact with another) are not neglected.[166] For example, an environmental assessment of a proposed extension to a power station may include analysis of emissions from cooling towers carrying saline material, in addition to the estuarine water already used (an example of indirect and cumulative impacts), as well as emissions of sulphur dioxide and nitrogen dioxide measured in the light of similar

---

[163] *R* v *Secretary of State for Transport ex parte Medway Council* [2002] EWHC 2516. Discussed further in Ch. 5, p. 155.   [164] On US case law on alternatives, see Ch. 7, pp. 250–6.

[165] This is a category of impacts beyond those directly related to the project, as defined by the European Commission, *Guidance on Indirect, Cumulative and Impact Interactions* (Brussels: CEC, 2001). This defines these impacts as follows, at (iii): 'indirect impacts: Impacts on the environment, which are not a direct result of the project, often produced away from or as a result of a complex pathway. Sometimes referred to as second or third level impacts, or secondary impacts; cumulative impacts: Impacts that result from incremental changes caused by other past, present or reasonably foreseeable actions together with the project; impact interactions: the reactions between impacts whether between the impacts of just one project or between the impacts of other projects in the areas'. There are clearly overlaps between these categories and different interpretations of them.

[166] On the opportunities in environmental assessment to take account of cumulative effects, see N. C. Sontag and R. R. Everitt *et al.*, *Cumulative Effective Assessment: A Context for Further Development and Research* (Quebec: Canadian Environmental Assessment Research Centre, 1987).

emissions from existing power stations in the vicinity of the proposed development (cumulative impact), and the increased generation of ozone through chemical reactions (the interaction of impacts).[167]

The common factor of each of these impact types is that they require consideration of the effects of a project *beyond* a particular site, or a particular process. The recognition that such impacts may be significant when viewed in association is in line with ecological thinking in which delayed or indirect impacts, as well as linked impacts which occur beyond an immediate project site, are recognized as sources of stress which can permanently reduce the ability of an ecosystem to absorb impacts, or recover from them,[168] or reduce environmental quality. In conceptual terms an appreciation of cumulative impacts is also to accept the vital interrelationships of what may otherwise be considered component parts of the environment. Environmental assessment should therefore entail gauging the relationship of projects with one another, and their collective impact.

The cumulative effect of projects is one part of the more general problem of setting and applying thresholds to determine the significance of likely effects. This was pointed out by Advocate General Pergola in *Commission* v *Ireland*[169] in which he clarified the necessary relationship between setting thresholds to determine the potential significance of impacts, and taking into consideration the cumulative effects of these, an approach followed implicitly by the European Court of Justice in this case. Approving the European Commission's argument, the Advocate General considered that thresholds set by Member States are correlated to a sufficient extent with the environmental factor of sensitivity of location, only if they are *applied* having regard to both the *individual* projects (planned for the area in question, which may affect relatively small areas) and all the projects which *as a whole* affect the same area. He stated: 'the important factor for the purposes of prior assessment is therefore the full impact of the operation to which the pro-jects, viewed individually or collectively, subject a section of the environment which is recognised as deserving special protection'[170] (although a difficulty here is that neither the scope of the 'same area', nor 'a section of the environment' is defined). In contrast, a reluctance to take account of the cumulative or synergistic effects of development leads to a narrow assessment of the effects of development on the environment. This state of affairs is particularly pronounced in the United Kingdom because the prevalence of interests of private property in the planning system has long been manifested in an emphasis upon a particular site for the purposes of development consent.[171] A demonstrably narrow approach on the part

---

[167] This example is the Killingholme CCGT Power Station Extension, cited in European Commission, *Guidance on Indirect, Cumulative and Impact Interactions*, 39 ff.

[168] Treweek, *Ecological Impact Assessment*, 154.

[169] Case C-392/96 [1996] ECR I-5901, AG Opinion, at para. 36.   [170] At para. 37.

[171] The main consequence of this characteristic of the planning system is the reluctance to consider alternatives, in terms of sites, projects, and technology. On the development of a requirement to consider alternatives prompted by the tenor of the EC Directive on EIA, if not its specific provisions, see Ch.5, pp. 149–53.

of the English courts to the question of the cumulative effects of development arising from staged applications was taken in *Lewin*,[172] concerning the construction of the M1–A1 link road. The High Court held that a side road order could be treated as a separate project and therefore fell only within Schedule 2 of the 1988 Regulations, whereas treating the side road as part of the main road project would have brought the whole project within the ambit of Schedule 1 of the Regulations, thus making an environmental assessment of the likely environmental effects mandatory.[173] More specifically, in the development consent system in England and Wales, a 'project' is commonly equated with a particular application for planning permission, whereas the EIA Directive defines 'project' broadly to include a whole enterprise that is proposed.[174] This issue was raised before the Court of Appeal in *Swale*,[175] since, after the original application was lodged, associated applications concerning larger development schemes were submitted. The RSPB argued that the applicants should have submitted an integrated planning consent application, accompanied by an environmental statement. The importance of potential cumulative effects for a finding of significance was acknowledged to a limited extent by Simon Brown J in a judgment which upheld the planning authority's argument that 'the question whether or not the development is of a category described in either schedule must be answered strictly in relation to the development applied for, not any development contemplated beyond that'.[176] A large (Schedule 1) project that as a whole might require assessment could thus be broken up into separate smaller applications, escaping the 1988 Environmental Effects Regulations.[177] Simon Brown J then distinguished such circumstances from those in relation to Schedule 2 (discretionary) projects: 'The proposal should not then be considered in isolation if in reality it is properly to be regarded as an integral part of an inevitably more substantial development . . . the existence of the smaller development of itself promoting the larger development and thereby likely to carry in its wake the environmental effects of the latter'.[178] The rationale for this approach is that developers could otherwise defeat the object of the Regulations by piecemeal development proposals.

The potential for a development to be broken up into separate components with the effect that a sense of the cumulative impacts of the development as a whole is lost was not recognized in the original EC EIA Directive. Amendments

[172] *Lewin and Rowley* v *Secretary of State for Transport* (1990) 2 *JEL* 216.
[173] A similar difficulty of whether the environmental impact is to be assessed solely for the section of a road link for which development consent has been sought, or in addition to the area covered by that section, for the road as a whole, arose in Case C-396/92 *Bund Naturschutz in Bayern* v *Freistaat Bayern* [1994] ECR I-3713, but the Court of Justice considered that there was no need to address this issue.
[174] Article 1 of the EIA Directive defines 'project' as: the execution of construction or other installation or schemes, and other interventions in the natural surroundings and landscape including those of extraction of mineral resources.
[175] *R* v *Swale Borough Council and Medway Ports Authority ex parte the Royal Society for the Protection of Birds* (1991) 3 *JEL* 135.   [176] At 142.   [177] SI 1988, No. 1199.   [178] ibid.

to this Directive in 1997[179] required that the cumulative effects with other projects be considered when screening a project for the application of environmental assessment rules,[180] and that the developer must supply information on any indirect, secondary, and cumulative effects. In contrast, the EC Directive on SEA[181] is inherently more concerned with cumulative effects because it is designed to more accurately appreciate the impact of plans and programmes, which in turn are made up of individual projects.[182] Specifically, this Directive requires that an environmental report must be prepared in which the relationship of the plan and programme with others must be described.

A clear lead on the need to consider the cumulative effects of projects when reaching a decision about the likely significance of a project was given by the Court of Justice in *Commission* v *Ireland*.[183] This case concerned not so much the level of certain thresholds adopted in Ireland, but rather their application which the European Commission regarded as contrary to the EIA Directive because incremental, and cumulative, effects were not taken into account. The Court cited in particular the cumulative effect of land reclamation projects: 'limestone pavement, which is characteristic of the area, has been destroyed, as have vegetation and archaeological remains, giving way to pasture. Considered together, these interventions were likely to have significant effects'.[184] Since the national provisions on environmental assessment did not countenance the cumulative effect of such projects, which, individually, fell below the various thresholds set, Ireland had exceeded the limits of its discretion provided in the Directive. The Court held that Member States must ensure that the objective of the Directive was not circumvented by the splitting of projects into their component parts: 'Not taking account of the cumulative effect of projects means in practice that all projects of a certain type may escape the obligation to carry out an assessment when, taken together, they are likely to have significant effects on the environment within the meaning of Article 2(1) of the Directive'.[185] Interestingly, the approach of the Court in this case was not followed by the Court of Appeal in *Berkeley No. 3* in which it roundly dismissed the applicant's argument about the cumulative effect of urban development: 'It is manifest that one can always conceive of possible situations in which by an accumulation of notional sites and notional development a devastating effect on the environment could be produced'.[186] In this case there was a very real likelihood of similar development in this area, after all the applicants had long been occupied in staving off applications for development on the banks of the River Thames which were far from

---

[179] By Directive 97/11/EC OJ 1997 L 73, p. 5.

[180] See Annex III, point 1 of the EIA Directive as amended by Directive 97/11/EC: 'The characteristics of projects must be considered having regard, in particular, to . . . the cumulation with other projects' (see Appendix II of this book for the context of this provision).

[181] EC Directive on SEA. [182] See further, Ch. 2, pp. 60–5.

[183] Case C-392/96 [1996] ECR I-5901. [184] At para. 80. [185] At para. 76.

[186] At para. 49.

'notional',[187] although this development may be more accurately described as having precedent value, rather than synergistic, or cumulative, effects.

An unsympathetic approach to taking into account cumulative effects is seen also in the Court of Appeal's judgment in *ex parte Moses*,[188] an application for judicial review in connection with two related extensions (the subject of two applications for planning permission) to the runway of an airport. Planning permission was granted before an environmental statement on the cumulative effects of the extensions was conducted and submitted to the planning authority. Although the Secretary of State for the Environment and the planning authority considered that the entire development should be subject to environmental assessment (as a matter of Article 3 of the EC Directive), Simon Brown LJ decided that there was room for doubt as to whether a cumulative assessment was strictly appropriate. In any event, the case was decided on the grounds of hardship, prejudice (in particular operational difficulties and loss of income on behalf of the airport and contractors), 'detriment to good administration', and delay in bringing the application for judicial review.[189] The European Court of Justice's interpretation of the extent of the duty to see that an environmental assessment is carried out, in cases of staged applications, or after the normal period for judicial review has expired, was not sought in this case.

A similar story is seen in *ex parte Surrey County Council*,[190] concerning various widening 'improvements' to the M25 motorway encircling London. The development was proposed in phases, each of which was subject to an environmental statement. The Council sought judicial review of the Department of Transport's approach on the grounds that, under the EC Directive, the schemes should be treated as one project, not several. MacPherson J distinguished between the construction of a new road, in which case the project should be looked at in its entirety and is not capable of being dealt with by separate stages, and the facts of this case, where several improvements to a road are proposed. In such circumstances, he stated, the natural and ordinary meaning of the word 'project' is that which is about to be done, rather than that envisaged in the future: 'improvements of traffic flow on the M25, which is the overall plan and the overall package which the government is addressing, can sensibly and rightly and legally be divided into separate stages and steps, each of which is its own project'. The judge placed great faith in the inquiry system to take a broader view of the potential impacts of the programme of improvements as a whole.

This, and the other judgments referred to, highlight that environmental assessment forms part of national development consent systems which are rooted in the

187 The key example of which is *Berkeley No. 1*, which dealt with Fulham Football Club's attempt to redevelop their grounds, financed by building a block of flats on the banks of the river.

188 *R v North West Leicestershire District Council ex parte Moses* [2000] Env LR 443 (CA).

189 On the aligning of the public interest with such concerns, see Ch. 6, at pp. 218–22.

190 *R v Secretary of State for Transport ex parte Surrey County Council* (1993) High Court, 24 November 1993, unreported.

concept of the project. Although conceiving of 'projects' broadly,[191] the EIA Directive similarly draws upon the project as the central unit of environmental assessment, because of the way in which it ties environmental assessment to an application for development consent. This can lead to the (ecological) 'tyranny of small decisions'.[192] EC Directive 2001/42/EC on the environmental assessment of plans and programmes[193] will possibly prove more capable of addressing a broader range of impacts, in temporal as well as spatial terms, so that future phases of work may be taken into account when judging the significance of a plan or programme overall. A more ecological approach to cumulative impacts, translated into law and policy, and against which existing environmental assessment rules may be compared, is the Florida courts' ruling on permits for land development in wetlands.[194] This explicitly links the impact of a permit with the achievement of environmental quality standards. In the United Kingdom, some developers currently strive to demonstrate the compliance of a proposed project with particular quality standards and conservation objectives,[195] but this is not yet a requirement of environmental assessment law, or policy. The Florida ruling also highlights the 'equitable independence of several projects—past, present, and future',[196] and their effects on coastal water quality *in toto*, both of which are arguably more easily achieved in the case of permits for discharges (from developments which already exist) than development consents for projects which have yet to be formally proposed.

In order to show entitlement to a dredge and fill permit, an applicant must show that he has provided reasonable assurance that water quality standards will not be violated and that the project is not contrary to the public interest, and both of these tests must take into consideration the cumulative impacts of similar projects which are existing, under consideration, or reasonably expected in the future.

. . . The applicant's burden of proof includes the burden of giving reasonable assurance that cumulative impacts do not cause a project to be contrary to the public interest or to violate quality standards.

. . . The purpose of cumulative impact analysis is to distribute equitably that amount of dredging and filling activity which may be done without resulting in violations of water quality standards and without being contrary to the public interest. In order to determine whether the allocation to a particular applicant is equitable, the determination of the cumulative is based in part on the assumption that reasonably expected similar future applications will also be granted.

. . . Specifically in the context of permitting access roads and bridges, it has been the policy of the Department to consider what will be at the end of the bridge or road.

---

[191] i.e. Art. 1(1) and Annex II, point 13.   [192] Treweek, *Ecological Impact Assessment*, 151.
[193] See Ch. 2, pp. 60–5 and Ch. 5, pp. 162–4.
[194] *Peebles* v *State of Florida, Department of Environmental Regulation*, 12 FALR 1961 (1990), cited in Brooks *et al.*, *Law and Ecology*, 171.
[195] As in the case of the Lewes Flood Strategy, discussed in Ch. 3, pp. 86–9.
[196] Brooks *et al.*, *Law and Ecology*, 172.

Notwithstanding the vast differences between pollution permits (for substances which in ecological terms are capable of obvious synergistic effects), and land use development, such an example demonstrates the relatively low standard required of developers to explain the likely effects of their proposal, in combination with others, under existing environmental assessment rules in the United Kingdom. Although official guidance recognizes that '[Q]uantified thresholds cannot easily deal with this kind of "incremental" development', and advocates consideration of cumulative effects in cases of multiple applications and changes or extensions to existing or approved development,[197] a minimalist approach is still taken on this matter. For example, in line with the 1999 Regulations, Circular 02/99 stresses that only the 'main' or 'significant' environmental effects to which a development is likely to give rise need be considered in the environmental statement,[198] less so indirect, or secondary effects. This considerably lightens the onus on the developer to explain what lies 'at the end of the bridge or road' and so forth.

Mitigating Measures

As discussed in Chapter 2,[199] mitigating measures of various types (including avoidance strategies, barriers, relocation, restoration, and compensation) may allow objections to a development to be overcome. For example, in the case of the Cairngorm funicular railway project the developer's proposed mitigation strategy, described in the environmental statement, formed the basis of a planning agreement which persuaded the local authority to allow the project to proceed.[200] Following faithfully the provisions of the EC EIA Directive,[201] the 1999 Regulations require that developers include in their environmental statement '[A] description of the measures envisaged to prevent, reduce and where possible offset any significant adverse effects on the environment'.[202] This much is clear, but the issue has arisen whether mitigating measures are capable of rendering the likely significant effects of a project insignificant for *screening* purposes. In *BT*[203] Elias J considered whether a council had wrongly taken into account the effect of mitigating measures (protecting Roman remains even though the development entailed the demolition or alteration of listed buildings in the same area) when deciding whether there would be significant impacts on the archaeology of an area earmarked for redevelopment as a 'multiplex', and thus whether an environmental assessment process should be triggered. The claimants' argument on this point was that it should not be assumed that the mitigation strategy would be successful in eliminating any detrimental consequences. Elias J decided this

---

[197] Circular 02/99, para. 46.   [198] Para. 82.   [199] See pp. 40–1.
[200] Discussed in Ch. 7, at pp. 272–81.   [201] Art. 5(3) and Annex IV, point 5.
[202] Sch. 4.
[203] *BT plc and Bloomsbury Land Investments* v *Gloucester City Council* [2002] JPL 993.

matter, not on whether mitigation could, or could not, successfully alleviate significant harm, but rather that the consideration of mitigating measures at the screening stage pre-empted public discussion on whether the measures suggested would be successful, compared to other measures. Adopting Lord Hoffmann's approach in *Berkeley No. 1* on the importance of public participation,[204] he stated: '[T]he purpose is surely to enable public discussion to take place about whether the measure will be successful, or perhaps whether more effective measures can be taken than those proposed to ameliorate the anticipated harm'.[205] He concluded that 'the question whether or not there are likely to be significant environmental effects should be approached by asking whether these would be likely to result, absent some specific measures being taken to ameliorate or reduce them. If they would, the environmental statement is required and the mitigating measures must be identified in it'.[206] Otherwise, 'if a decision runs two issues together [significance and remediation] and rests in the view that remediation measures will be effective to prevent otherwise significant effects, it deprives the public of the opportunity to make informed representations in accordance with the EIA procedures about the adequacy of such measures'.[207]

This judgment, indicative of 'a warmer approach to the Directive',[208] was then followed by Sullivan J in *R (Lebus)*,[209] but was tempered by the Court of Appeal in *Gillespie*[210] which concerned a housing development on the site of an old gasworks, contaminated 'to a significant degree' according to the inspector who led an inquiry into the application. The inspector's recommendation that the scheme would provide an opportunity to bring the site back into beneficial use, in line with policy on using brownfield sites for housing development, was accepted by the Secretary of State who decided that an environmental assessment was not required because, taking into consideration the proposed measures to decontaminate the site, the project would be unlikely to have 'significant effects on the environment by virtue of factors such as its nature, size or location'. Pill LJ underlined the view of the first instance judge, Richards J, that such cases will turn upon their own particular facts (referring in particular to 'standard' environmental effects—noise and dust generation which can properly be controlled by the operation of standard conditions and a reasonably managed development).

---

[204] See discussion above, Ch. 7, pp. 258–62.   [205] *Berkeley No. 1*, para. 73.

[206] ibid.   [207] ibid., para. 74.

[208] R. McCracken, 'Environmental Assessment: From Technocratic Paternalism to Participatory Democracy?', Paper given at the Enforcement of EC Environmental Law Seminar, King's College London, June 2003.

[209] *R (Lebus)* v *South Cambridgeshire District Council* [2003] Env LR 17. At para. 46 Sullivan J states: 'It is not appropriate for a person charged with making a screening opinion to start from the premise that although there may be significant impacts, these can be reduced to insignificance as a result of the implementation of conditions of various kinds. The appropriate course in such a case is to require an environmental statement setting out the significant impacts and the measures which it is said will reduce their significance'.

[210] *Bellway Urban Renewal Southern* v *Gillespie* [2003] EWHC 400.

The Lord Justice then considered that the exhaustive and comprehensive enquiries into remedial measures that had been undertaken could properly be regarded by the Secretary of State,[211] and that he was entitled to decide that an environmental assessment was not required as a matter of his 'practical judgment' as to whether the project would be likely to have significant effects on the environment: 'When making his screening decision, the Secretary of State was not in my judgment obliged to shut his eyes to the remedial measures submitted as a part of the planning proposal', and that '[T]hat would apply whatever the scale of the development and whether (as in *BT*) some harm to the relevant environment is inevitable or whether (as is claimed in the present case) the development will actually produce an improvement in the environment'.[212] European authority in *Bozen*[213] appears to support this position, since the Court of Justice decided that no project likely to have significant effects on the environment should be exempt from assessment 'unless the specific project excluded could, on the basis of a comprehensive assessment, be regarded as not being likely to have such effects'.[214] Pill LJ elaborated that in some cases the remedial measures will be modest in scope, or so plainly achievable that the project would not be likely to have significant effects on the environment even though, in the absence of the proposed remedial measures, it would be likely to have such effects. Furthermore, the judgment of the Secretary of State should not be predetermined by the complexity of the project or whether the remedial measures are controversial, although these are important factors for consideration.[215] Importantly, the judge ultimately accepted that devising a condition which is capable of bringing the development below the relevant threshold does not necessarily lead to a decision that an environmental assessment is unnecessary.[216]

In the event the appellant developer was unsuccessful because the Secretary of State was found to have erred in assuming that the investigations and mitigation works could be treated, at the time of the screening decision, as having had a successful outcome. In practice, on the material available to the Secretary of State, the contingencies and uncertainties of mitigation meant that a decision that the project is unlikely to have significant effects on the environment could not be reached. Although this case at first appears to turn on technicalities—the complexity of the project, and predictions about the success or otherwise of the remedial measures, the judgment broadly achieves the preservation of discretion on the part of the decision maker, in this case the Secretary of State, to take into account proposed mitigating measures at the stage of screening the project for likely significant effects.[217] This is desirable to the extent that it encourages the use of technology-forcing 'solutions' to reduce adverse environmental effects, even before an application for planning permission is submitted. However, this approach may also have the effect of curtailing public discussion on the effectiveness, and moral

[211] Para. 28.   [212] Para. 36.   [213] Case C-435/97 [1999] ECR I-5613.
[214] ibid., para. 59.   [215] *Gillespie*, para. 37.   [216] Para. 39.   [217] Paras. 41 and 42.

value, of a range of mitigation measures which may include 'standard' remediation measures, such as methods of construction which normally form the content of planning conditions, but which may also include more controversial forms of mitigation such as the translocation of species, or compensation for the loss of a site or species, and about which public debate should take place. Some appreciation of this is seen in Laws LJ's judgment in *Gillespie* to the effect that if prospective remedial measures are not plainly established and not plainly uncontroversial then the case calls for an environmental assessment. Otherwise, the very form of enquiry contemplated by the Directive and Regulations would be pre-empted,[218] and the deployment of conditions (requiring, as in this case, a site investigation and scheme of remediation before work could commence) could effectively act as a surrogate for the entire EIA process.[219]

This problem of taking mitigating measures into account at the screening stage may be seen in terms of the progression of the environmental assessment process, illustrated in Figure 2.1.[220] This clearly shows the two-stage nature of decision making in environmental assessment: a prior assessment ('decision 1') for the purposes of screening the project, according to the typical impacts produced by all such projects; and second, an assessment *in concreto* ('decision 2') at which the impacts specific to the proposed project are evaluated, taking into account the information provided by the developer (including a description of the measures envisaged in order to avoid, reduce, and if possible remedy significant adverse effects) and representations on such measures by members of the public and environmental organizations and statutory consultees. Investing the first decision on screening with information on mitigation, properly designed to inform the second decision, may thereby result in circumventing participation requirements by permitting a decision that a 'second stage' environmental assessment is unnecessary.

Screening projects for environmental assessment, whilst taking into account the possible effectiveness of mitigating measures, highlights the complexity of predictions in the entire environmental assessment exercise[221] and raises also the issue of the extent to which local authorities may consider the adequacy of pollution and other controls in assessing the likely significant effects of a project. This is a '*Gateshead*-type'[222] issue since the overlapping nature of the planning and pollution control regimes needs to be considered In *Gateshead*, Sullivan J held that 'just as the environmental impact of such emissions is a material planning consideration, so also is the existence of a stringent regime under the Environmental Protection Act 1990 for preventing or mitigating that impact and for rendering

---

[218] Para. 46.   [219] Para. 48.   [220] p. 36.

[221] As discussed in Ch. 3. Cf. *R v Cornwall County Council ex parte Hardy* (*Hardy No. 1*) [2001] Env LR 25, [2001] JPL 786, per Harrison J.

[222] *Gateshead Metropolitan Borough Council* v *Secretary of State for the Environment* [1995] Env LR 36.

any emissions harmless'.[223] The same judge adopted a similar stance in *Milne* (*Tew II*):[224]

Any major development project will be subject to a number of detailed controls, not all of them included within the planning permission. Emissions to air, discharges into water, disposal of the waste produced by the project, will all be subject to controls under legislation dealing with environmental protection. In assessing the likely significant environmental effects of a project the authors of the environmental statement and the local planning authority are entitled to rely on the operation of controls of those controls with a reasonable degree of competence on the part of the responsible authority . . . The same approach should be adopted to the local planning authority's power to approve reserved matters. Mistakes may occur in the system of detailed controls, but one is identifying and mitigating the 'likely significant effects', not every conceivable effect, however minor or unlikely, of a major project.[225]

Similar considerations about the nature of prediction, but additionally the importance of public participation in making judgments of significance,[226] are further illustrated by the following case study.

Subjectivity and Significance: The Kentish Flats Windfarm

The concept of significance was the central issue in an application to build a windfarm off the north Kent coast, located on the southern side of the outer Thames estuary, north of Herne Bay and Whitstable on the north Kent coast.[227] Global Renewable Energy Partners, a private consortium, sought to develop the windfarm, consisting of 30 turbines about 8.5 km out to sea. An environmental impact assessment was required because, as an 'installation for the harnessing of wind power for energy production (wind farms)', as described in Schedule 2 of the 1999 Regulations, the project exceeded the thresholds set, and was additionally considered by the local authority likely to have significant effects upon the environment.[228] In this case, an 'appropriate assessment' was also required of the

---

[223] At 44.

[224] *R v Rochdale Metropolitan Borough Council ex parte Milne* (*Tew II*) [2001] Env LR 22. See further Ch. 6, pp. 212–13.   [225] At para. 28.

[226] Similar issues arise when screening projects on the basis of incomplete information, in cases in which outline planning permission is granted, subject to reserved matters, as discussed in Ch. 6, pp. 211–17.

[227] This individual project should be seen in the context of the increasing popularity of this mode of energy production. Many similar projects are planned in Denmark, Germany, and Scotland.

[228] Additionally, all offshore power generating facilities fall within the scope of the Electricity Works (Environmental Impact Assessment) (England and Wales) Regulations 2000 (SI 2000, No. 1927), and most are likely to require an environmental impact assessment. Other statutory requirements must be complied with, mainly in the form of obtaining consents under the Electricity Works Act 1989, s. 36, the Food and Environment Protection Act 1985, s. 5, and the Coast Protection Act 1949, s. 34.

likely significant effect of the windfarm on any European nature conservation site.[229] These various requirements indicate the territorial reach of the EIA Directive.[230] The Environmental Statement[231] submitted with the application for planning permission to Canterbury County Council performed several functions other than compliance with statutory requirements, including explaining 'The Need for the Kentish Flats Project',[232] described in terms of the '*significant* role this and other offshore projects will play in helping to achieve Government targets in relation to climate change and commitments of the Kyoto Protocol', and thereby aligning the project with the fulfilment of international commitments. Other important functions of the Statement were to describe the mitigating measures 'offered' to alleviate the negative impacts of the project on wildlife in the vicinity, and the positive impacts which might flow from the project, such as offering new structures for colonization by marine animals, and to describe the extensive consultation exercises which preceded the application.

The key part of the Environmental Statement, though, dealt with the significance of the visual impacts of the project. As the central issue in this proposal, landscape (in terms of individuals' perceptions of landforms, rather than physical topography) is highly subjective because it differs with individuals' differing perspectives, cultural backgrounds, and experiences. The proposal therefore provides a good example of how such issues are dealt with in the assessment process. Defining the concept of significance was central to the developer's arguments about the impact of the project on the landscape, and indeed for its case that development consent be granted. In particular, local residents' appreciation of change to the landscape was marginalized in the Environmental Statement, mainly because of the setting of boundaries within which the issue of significance was analysed (or 'the zone of visual intrusion').[233] Not surprisingly, many of the residents in the immediate area (8–9 km away from the proposed windfarm) considered the project would have significant effects, less so in the case of residents living 30 km away, the outer limit set by the developer for assessment purposes. The Statement concludes on this point:

'[A]ny offshore windfarm development may result in significant effects on the landscape, seascape or visual amenity of the locality. Within the 30km radius covered by the assessment of the proposed offshore windfarm at the Kentish Flats, significant effects are limited to a stretch of the North Kent coast between Whitstable and Birchington. Significant effects on the landscape, seascape and visual amenity of the study area will be limited to this short stretch of coastline.[234]

---

[229] For the purposes of Reg. 48 of the Conservation (Natural Habitats, &c) Regulations 1994 (SI 1994, No. 2716) which aims to implement Art. 6 of EC Directive 92/43/EC on the conservation of habitats and flora and fauna, OJ 1992 L 206, p. 7, see Ch 2, pp. 68–70, and below, p. 142.

[230] See further G. Plant [2003] 'Offshore Wind Energy Development: The Challenges for English Law', JPL 939.

[231] Global Renewable Energy Partners, *Environmental Statement: Kentish Flats Offshore Windfarm* (Durley, Hants: GREP 2002).　　　[232] ibid. Non-technical summary, p. 3.

[233] On methologies for landscape assessment, see Morris and Therivel, *Methods of Environmental Impact Assessment*, ch. 6, which fails to see drawing the boundaries of the landscape to be analysed as controversial.　　　[234] *Environmental Statement*, pp. 8–81.

Choosing a 'visual envelope' of this size (30 km)[235] permitted the developer to emphasize that, for the most part, the effects of the project on the landscape were insignificant. In addition, the Statement illustrated the visual impact of the wind-farm by using technologically enhanced and altered images of the landscape, par-ticularly on the stretch of coastline most likely to be affected by the project. These images were presented as particular viewpoints, for example as though looking entirely to the left and right as one walks along the beach at Whitstable. In reality, of course, a landscape is never looked at from one perspective only. This approach departs from guidance issued by the Countryside Commission on the treatment of landscape in environmental assessment that '[C]are should be taken to ensure visual presentations are neutral and so do not give a false impression by distorting perspective or selecting unrepresentative viewpoints'.[236]

A further issue of boundary drawing in determining significance is seen in the case of the 'appropriate assessment' conducted for the purposes of the Habitats Directive. This, included within the main body of the Environmental Statement, indicates that the windfarm is encircled by important, or sensitive, sites for con-servation, for example the Swale Ramsar site (10 km away from the proposed windfarm), Thanet Coast and Sandwich Bay Ramsar site (8 km away), and the Thames Estuary and Marshes Special Protection Area and Ramsar site (21 km away). A narrow approach to the issue of significance was adopted in this respect, so that it was concluded that 'no *direct* impacts on any of these sites will occur as a result of construction, operation or decommissioning',[237] effectively ignoring indirect, or secondary, effects of the development, such as loss of feed for birds because of fish avoiding noisy areas during operation of the turbines.

The treatment of landscape in this Environmental Statement serves to demon-strate that the dimension of scale is vitally important in making judgments about significance: '[W]hilst the scale of the proposed turbines will be large, they will form a group of clean lined, simple structures, which translates at nearly all viewpoints into a satisfactory, well balanced composition'.[238] An 'irony of scale' seems to oper-ate here, so that the localized nature of effects allows for the project, having more broadly positive impacts, to be advanced. The case study also underlines the impor-tance of context in judging significance, as discussed in theoretical terms above:[239]

[T]here may be significant effects on visual amenity for people boating or sailing off the north Kent coast, although the wind turbines will be seen in the context of a busy com-mercial sea channel . . . This is one of the busiest waterways around the UK and there is constant movement of vessels of all kinds, as well as permanent installations such as the

[235] The size of this radius is in line with guidance on windfarm development in English Nature, RSPB, WWF, BWEA, *Windfarm Development and Nature Conservation* (Peterborough: English Nature, 2001) and Centre for Environment, Fisheries and Aquaculture Science, *Offshore Wind Farms: Guidance Note in Respect of Food and Environment Protection Act 1985 and Coast Protection Act 1949* (London: DEFRA, 2001).
[236] Countryside Commission, *Environmental Assessment*, p. 34.
[237] Non-technical summary, p. 9.   [238] ibid., 13.   [239] At pp. 103–4.

Maunsell forts[240] and various navigational marks, and the development must be viewed in this context.

The discussion of both scale and context, as part of the process of determining the significance of the visual impacts on the landscape and seascape, enabled the developer to assert that 'significant effects of the type described are not necessarily unacceptable'.[241]

The overall presentation of fact and judgment in the Statement is in positive terms, and this is informed by the developer's treatment of significance in this as a simplistic, and unitary matter, particularly when considering the potential diversity of environmental impacts. Importantly, the developer also engages social and economic criteria in the assessment of significance:

[I]n the case of windfarms, the actual development itself provides a wide range of environmental benefits, nationally and globally, because of its important contribution to reducing the emission of greenhouse gases. This in turn brings with it a range of social benefits which are not always associated with development such as cleaner air, potentially healthier populations, reduced risk from sea level rise or climate change and a more sustainable and renewable source of energy generation, as well as the more normal benefits of development such as employment opportunities.[242]

The developer clearly saw this positive and, at times, campaigning approach, as entirely justified by guidance alluded to. In particular, one such guidance note states: 'these benefits, the avoidance of pollutant gases and the preservation of raw material like gas and coal should be clearly stated in the Environmental Impact Assessment . . . the emphasising of these *positive* environmental impacts is crucial in relation to the public and political acceptance of wind energy'.[243] The Statement then quantifies the positive contribution of the particular project, the displacement of up to 8,736,760 tonnes of carbon dioxide over the life of the project, equivalent to almost 60 per cent of annual UK CO_2 emissions in 1998. Although such potential savings are to be commended, the overwhelmingly positive spin may also be seen in the assessment of cumulative effects, which is a key determinant in judging the significance of the likely effects of a project such as this. In determining the likely cumulative effects of this and other projects, the developer adopts a narrow approach, by restricting analysis to the Thames Estuary region (in which one other similar development is planned) and, beyond this, to other similar offshore projects. This limited scope of assessment allows the developer to conclude that 'The key cumulative effect that will occur will be as a result of the cumulative generation of clean, renewable, sustainable electricity from the proposed 18 offshore windfarms around the UK, and indeed in-combination [sic]

---

[240] Disused buildings previously used for wartime defence.
[241] Non-technical summary, p. 13.   [242] *Environmental Statement*, at para. 8.2.
[243] Greenpeace, *North Sea Offshore Wind—A Powerhouse for Europe: Technical Possibilities and Ecological Considerations* (London: Greenpeace, 2000) identifies the need to consider the positive effects of the project on the global environment (e.g. climate) as part of the site-specific EIA process.

with all other renewable energy projects. This will lead to a cumulative impact on air quality, reducing greenhouse gas emissions and representing a significant cumulative effect on the targets set by the UK government'.[244] This evaluation is far removed from official guidance issued by DEFRA[245] which requires that the assessment of cumulative impacts must include projects in the past, present, and foreseeable future, and should include not only other potential windfarms but also other types of projects taking place in the marine environment. The positive tone of the Statement may further be qualified by considering the potential significance of the decommissioning process to take place in approximately 20 years.

In summary, this case illustrates the many functions which may be performed by a developer's environmental statement as a legal text in the environmental assessment process: as an explanatory document, a means of demonstrating compliance with statutory requirements, and a campaigning, or public relations, tool for securing acceptance of a particular project and, as in this case, an emergent sector of industry. The developer's use of the concept of significance suggests the need for more inclusive, and subjective, judgments of significance. Whereas there is a marked tendency in some statements to emphasize the infallibility of information, and the objectivity of the assessment process,[246] in this example the developer utilized the subjectivity inherent in determining the significance of the visual impact of the development. Paradoxically, subjectivity is used both in a dismissive sense, but also to support the developer's case: 'public consultation has demonstrated that in fact the majority of residents have shown very little concern with regard to the potential visual impacts, whilst another, smaller group do consider it a potentially significant concern. It is then, an entirely subjective matter'.[247] Most clearly, the Kentish Flats windfarm case emphasizes that judgments of significance are dependent upon the drawing of boundaries, as well as the widely acknowledged factors of context, scale, cumulative effects, and mitigating measures, discussed earlier in this chapter. Particularly in the case of visual impact, the likely significance of an impact for those affected is influenced by the breadth of the constituency chosen to represent those potentially affected, both in terms of human perception of the environment, and conservation.

The private consortium has now been granted authorization from the Department of Trade and Industry to build and operate the main generating development.[248] Several other authorizations (for example, for pipelines) are in the course of being decided by the local authority. The consent letter from the Department specifically refers to the environmental information contained in the developer's statement (as well as the comments made by the local planning authority, those designated as statutory consultees, and other consultees and objectors).

---

[244] Non-technical summary, p. 14.
[245] Centre for Environment, Fisheries and Aquaculture Science, *Offshore Wind Farms*, p. 16.
[246] e.g., in the case of the Dibden Bay development, discussed in Ch. 6, pp. 227–32.
[247] Non-technical summary, p. 13.
[248] Under s. 36 of the Electricity Works Act 1989.

This case study, and many of the litigated cases discussed in this chapter, highlight that significance is a contested concept, a subject of argument and debate involving subjective judgments, notwithstanding the existence of thresholds and criteria designed to streamline decisions about the likely significance of effects arising from proposed projects, plans, and programmes. Using the example of the recent reappraisal of mechanisms for determining the significance of historic sites in the law and policy relating to listed buildings and monuments, it is possible to more explicitly draw upon the subjective elements of significance, in order to involve more fully those affected by a proposed development. A central theme of English Heritage's report of the Review of the Historic Environment, *Power of Place*,[249] is that the historic environment is seen by most people as a totality—they value places, not a series of individual sites and buildings. This has implications for the way in which they identify and evaluate significance as a matter of context, and surroundings. A more inclusive approach to the significance of environmental effects may then recognize that this depends upon the connections, or identities, associated with a place, or landscape. This shift in approach appears to have been accepted by government,[250] since its statement of heritage policy now accepts the need for a wider range of views and values, whilst emphasizing the continued relevance of the existing statutory framework of designation for historic monuments and buildings based upon scheduled criteria.[251] The reappraisal of methods for valuing the historic environment provides a useful example because of the centrality of 'significance' in establishing what monuments should be scheduled under the Ancient Monuments and Archaeological Areas Act 1979. In addition, the approach of evaluating significance in this context has hitherto been viewed as an objective, clinical, exercise of applying criteria, notably representativeness and national importance, whereas other grounds for ascribing significance were devalued, particularly the significance of ancient monuments for a particular locality.[252]

Applying a similar approach to judgments of significance to be made in the environmental assessment process is not mere conjecture. In *Environmental Planning*,[253] the Royal Commission on Environmental Pollution recommends that a mandatory stage in environmental assessment be introduced in which the planning authority will prescribe the scope of a particular assessment after public consultation. This draws upon similar suggestions made in the environmental assessment literature:

Determining which criteria are relevant to assessing significance for specific impacts should be open to greater stakeholder involvement, the scoping stage providing

---

[249] (London: HMSO, 2000). Discussed in detail by P. English, 'The Genius Loci of Ancient Places', in Holder and Harrison, *Law and Geography*.

[250] Department of Culture, Media and Sport, *The Historic Environment: Force for our Future* (London: HMSO, 2001).   [251] English, 'The Genius Loci of Ancient Places', 482.

[252] ibid., 475.   [253] At para. 7.31.

a significant opportunity in this regard. However this determination requires dialogue, not least where more qualitative criteria relating to social, economic and cultural impacts are concerned.[254]

The Royal Commission's recommendation is potentially far-reaching because the logic of this recommendation may be extended beyond the scoping exercise to the initial stage of predicting significance for the purposes of screening projects, and also in making the final determination of the likely significance of a proposal. This may furnish lay participants with a vital role, lay bare the inherent subjectivity of assessing significance, and open up the assessment of significance to a plurality of meanings. This is not to deny the need for scientific assessments about significance, for example in the form of ecological baseline surveys,[255] but to argue that these may usefully be coupled with a further, more inclusive, inquiry of significance. A similar two-stage approach, in which facts are ascertained and values then attributed to them by a process of public consultation was advocated by the Royal Commission on Environmental Pollution in the context of setting environmental standards.[256] The possible advantages of such an approach are made clear by considering the deficiencies in the environmental assessment conducted for the purposes of the Kentish Flats windfarm. In Chapter 6 I explore more generally the mechanisms by which more inclusive assessment of significance may be advanced through participation strategies.

Conclusions

'Significance' and 'likelihood',[257] as the central terms of art in environmental assessment, require subjective evaluation, even though their conceptual premises lie in environmental and ecological science. Both concepts have been translated into law, with the effect that they have assumed an appearance of objectivity. For example, significance has been judged according to the application of thresholds and criteria and has long been considered a matter of 'fact and degree', rather than values, and the definition of 'likelihood' has turned on the legal differentiation of possibilities and probabilities. A growing body of case law on significance for the purposes of screening developments, discussed in this chapter, suggests considerable doctrinal development in the field of environmental assessment law. In particular, the pragmatic withdrawal of the courts from this decision means in effect that 'discretionary judgment' is enjoyed by the local authority and Secretary of State. There is, however, a tendency for a *developer*'s view of the likely significance of a project to inform this decision, particularly when an environmental statement

---

[254] Sippe, 'Criteria and Standards', p. 10.

[255] As I discuss in the context of the Lewes Flood Defence Strategy, Ch. 3, at pp. 89–92.

[256] Royal Commission on Environmental Pollution, *Setting Environmental Standards*, Twenty First Report, particularly ch. 7, 'Articulating Public Values'.   [257] Discussed in Ch. 3.

is treated as representative of a full environmental assessment process.[258] In this chapter the Kentish Flats windfarm illustrates that developers' judgments about significance may predominate. This allows for subjectivity in making judgments about significance to be enshrined in law, though also to be masked by it. This raises a question about the narrow range of participants in making judgments about significance, addressed more fully in Chapter 6.

To summarize, in this chapter I have attempted to show how law structures judgments about the likely significance of impacts by constraining discretion in decision making about whether an environmental assessment should be conducted or not, primarily through the use of indicative thresholds and criteria. The Court of Justice has consistently held that discretion to set such thresholds and criteria is subject to the overwhelming duty contained in Article 2(1) of the EC Directive on environmental assessment that, 'before consent is given, projects likely to have significant effects on the environment by virtue, *inter alia*, of their nature, size or location are made subject to a requirement for development consent and an assessment with regard to their effects'. The English courts are also closely involved in making judgments about significance, particularly in terms of deciding the correct remit of the 1999 Regulations, and the issue of 'local significance', so that their upholding of the discretion of decision makers,[259] and their apparent pragmatic withdrawal from decisions about significance, is only partial. Inroads have also been made in this approach, particularly by judgments of the European Court of Justice and, most recently, by the requirement in the Aarhus Convention, that the substantive review of decisions involving public participation be available,[260] a point I return to in Chapters 6 and 7.

---

[258] For example, Buxton LJ in the *Lewisham (Big Yellow)* case mistakenly considers that the decision of the local authority should be made in the light of information contained in the developer's environmental statement, at para. 14.

[259] As seen in other areas, for example, in cases arising under the Human Rights Act, on which, see R. A. Edwards, 'Judicial Deference under the Human Rights Act' (2002) 65 MLR 859.

[260] On the implementation of this requirement, see Directive 2003/53/EC on public participation in respect of the drawing up of certain plans and programmes relating to the environment and amending Council Directives 85/37/EEC and 96/61/EC.

5

Alternatives

In the previous two chapters, I examined the process of environmental assessment, from various sources and disciplinary backgrounds, but focused on the core requirement of the prediction of the likely significant effects of development on the environment. In particular I identified the subjective (and latent) nature of this prediction, as well as the prospect of making the subjective dimension more explicit, in recognition of the valuable part that this may play in providing a more rounded assessment. I also considered the means by which the subjective elements of an environmental assessment may be used by a developer or proponent of a plan or policy. Following the prediction of the likely significant effects of a development, plan, or policy on the environment comes the next stage of a model environmental assessment process—the consideration of alternatives, either in a limited sense of alternative sites, designs, or technologies, or a more far-reaching assessment of alternative policy options. In both cases, the consideration of alternatives in order to find the optimal site, route, or policy in ecological terms provides an important rationale for the development and use of environmental assessment and is facilitated by its interdisciplinary, and (in administrative terms) horizontal, nature.

Analysis of alternatives is considered a key element of environmental assessment, perhaps even the most important,[1] because it encapsulates a preventative approach. Early recognition of the importance of considering both alternative options—sites, designs, facilities—and mitigating measures, or 'alterations' to the plans for a project, was spelt out judicially in *Calvert Cliffs*,[2] an early landmark case on the extent of the duty to carry out an assessment under NEPA 1969.[3] In the United States' Court of Appeals, District of Columbia Circuit, Judge Skelly

[1] Hertz, 'Parallel Universes', at 1679, considers the alternatives discussion to be 'the heart of the environmental impact statement'.

[2] *Calvert Cliffs' Coordinating Committee Inc* v *United States Atomic Energy Commission* 449 F2d 1109 (1971). See further Ch. 7, pp. 252–4.

[3] S. 102(D) of NEPA requires all agencies of the Federal government specifically to 'study, develop, and describe appropriate alternatives to recommended courses of action in any proposal which involves unresolved conflicts concerning alternative uses of available resources'; and s.102(C) requires such agencies to include in every recommendation or report on proposals for legislation and other major Federal actions significantly affecting the quality of the human environment, a detailed statement on . . . alternatives to the proposed action'. For the statutory context of these provisions, see Appendix I.

Wright referred to the importance of a prior licensing system as a means of controlling development, in this case the construction of nuclear power facilities, and paid particular attention to the role of environmental assessment in the consideration of alternatives:

The special importance of the pre-operating license stage is not difficult to fathom. In cases where environmental costs were not considered in granting a construction permit, it is very likely that the planned facility will include some features which do significant damage to the environment and which could not have survived the rigorous balancing of costs and benefits. At the later operating licence proceedings, this environmental damage will have to be fully considered. But by that time the situation will have changed radically. Once a facility has been completely constructed, the economic cost of any alteration may be great. In the language of NEPA, there is likely to be an 'irreversible and irretrievable commitment of resources' which will inevitably restrict the Commission's options. Either the licensee will have to undergo a major expense in making alterations in a completed facility or the environmental harm will have to be tolerated. It is all too probable that the latter result would come to pass.

By refusing to consider the requirement of alterations until construction is completed, the Commission may effectively foreclose the environmental protection desired by Congress. It may also foreclose rigorous consideration of environmental factors at the eventual license proceedings. If 'irreversible and irretrievable commitment[s] of resources' have already been made, the licence hearing (and any public intervention therein) may become a hollow exercise. This hardly amounts to consideration of environmental values 'to the fullest extent possible'.[4]

A full NEPA considerations of alternatives in the original plans of a facility, then, is both important and appropriate well before the operating license proceedings.[5]

The prior consideration of alternatives is obviously important in environmental terms, even to the limited extent of redesigning a site, facility or processes, as described in *Calvert Cliffs*, and even more so when alternative policy options are considered. However, in the European Union's governing instrument for project-based assessment, the EIA Directive,[6] the requirement on the part of the developer 'to provide an outline of the main alternatives studied by the developer and an indication of the main reasons for his choice, taking into account the environmental effects'[7] is relatively weak, even with its recent strengthening.[8] The SEA

[4] This is a reference to s.102 NEPA which requires that 'to the fullest extent possible: (1) the policies, regulations, and public laws of the United States shall be integrated and administered in accordance with the policies set forth in this Act, and (2) all agencies of the Federal Government shall—(A) utilize a systematic, interdisciplinary approach which will insure the integrated use of the natural and social sciences and the environmental design arts in planning and decision making which may have an impact on man's environment. . .'   [5] At 1128.

[6] Directive 85/337/EEC OJ L 175, p. 40, as amended by Directive 97/11/EC OJ L 73, p. 5.

[7] Art. 5(3), repeated in Annex IV.

[8] Prior to Directive 97/11/EC amending Directive 85/337/EEC, such a requirement was relegated to the category of 'additional information' that a developer might supply (Art. 5 and Schedule III of the 1985 Directive), and was qualified by the words 'where appropriate'. The UN/ECE Convention on

Directive[9] offers an opportunity for a more genuine consideration of a range of policy alternatives by requiring that reasonable alternatives are identified, described, and evaluated, taking into account the objectives and the geographical scope of the plan or programme,[10] but most importantly, requiring Member States to also make available the reasons for choosing the plan or programme in the light of the other reasonable alternatives dealt with, which suggests that the developer must more fully internalize the requirement, rather than paying lip-service to it.[11] In the context of European conservation law, substantive effects may flow from such a requirement to consider alternatives, as discussed below.[12] Current environmental assessment law and policy in the United Kingdom adopts a lukewarm approach to alternative considerations. The 1999 Regulations[13] now require that 'where alternative approaches have been considered' the developer is to include in the environmental statement an outline of the main alternatives and the main reasons for the choice. Reflecting pre-existing planning law, policy guidance (Circular 02/99)[14] states that '[A]lthough the Directive and Regulations do not expressly require the developer to study alternatives, the nature of certain developments and their location may make the consideration of alternative *sites* a material consideration' for the purposes of development consent.[15] The need to consider a broader category of alternatives (including choice of process, and the phasing of construction, as well as alternative sites) is relegated in the guidance to 'good practice' which may 'result in a more robust application for planning permission'.[16]

A fuller consideration of alternatives has been hampered by a conceptual, and practical, resistance to considering the environmental effects of a development beyond a particular site, usually defined by a property interest, and, more generally, by the inherent limitations created by the consideration of alternatives in project-based environmental assessment, in which decisions are usually made within the context of an already decided policy. For these reasons, strategic, or higher-order, environmental assessment provides an opportunity for a genuine assessment of alternatives and, implicitly, less harmful (in environmental protection terms) policy choices, which may provide a framework for individual projects and clusters of development. It is this search for alternative policy choices,

---

access to information, public participation in decision making and access to justice in environmental matters (Aarhus Convention) does not significantly extend this provision.

[9] Directive 2001/42/EC OJ L 197, p. 30.   [10] Art. 5.

[11] Contrast with Art. 9 of the EIA Directive, as amended, which requires more limited reasons for the decision to be made available.

[12] Directive 92/43/EEC on the conservation of natural habitats and of wild fauna and flora, OJ 1992 L 206, p. 7, Art. 6.

[13] The Town and Country Planning (Environmental Impact Assessment) (England and Wales) Regulations 1999, para. 2 of Part II of Sched. 4.

[14] Department of the Environment, Transport and the Regions, Circular 02/99, *Environmental Impact Assessment*, para. 83.   [15] Town and Country Planning Act 1990, s. 70(2).

[16] Circular 02/99, para. 83.

engaging different administrative sectors, and requiring shifts in organizational structures, which in theory encourages the absorption of the ideas and language of environmental policy into the core of law- and policy-formation, a process described as the 'ecologization of governance',[17] or environmental policy integration. This process is a response to a more general sustainable development strategy which seeks to make apparent, and act upon, linkages between social, economic, and environmental factors and problems, and furthermore sees these as reconcilable.[18] The enlargement of environmental assessment to take on board a broad range of policy considerations and sectors indicates also how environmental assessment has simultaneously responded to, and in turn further encouraged, the expansion of the sites and scales of decision making so that environmental assessment is still relevant to a particular site, but is no longer tethered to this.

The mainstreaming of environmental law within the European Union (the process of ecologization) through environmental assessment, and other mechanisms such as the imposition of general duties upon the Community institutions,[19] has led to important (but not terribly effective) institutional changes.[20] For this reason, the element of environmental assessment requiring consideration of alternatives is explored in this chapter by analysing the development of strategic environmental assessment *within* the European Commission, albeit that this is still at an early stage. This case study demonstrates that the consideration of alternatives offers a test for the claims of culture theories of environmental assessment, particularly that the process of conducting environmental assessment may encourage the inculcation of environmental values in an organization. But the case study also illustrates the double-edged nature of the requirement to identify alternative policy and legislative options, particularly that it may be used as a brake on regulation, by requiring the consideration of less onerous policy and regulatory instruments. In such circumstances, the process of assessment may act as a conductor for existing deregulatory strains within an organization or administration, while giving the appearance that an environmental agenda is being pursued. I consider this case study in relation to the overriding theme of the public/private divide in the application of environmental assessment, concluding that both public and private entities may use the consideration

---

[17] See e.g. D. Chalmers, 'Inhabitants in the Field of EC Environmental Law', in P. Craig and G. de Búrca (eds.) *The Evolution of EU Law* (Oxford: Oxford University Press, 1999), and D. McGillivray and J. Holder, 'Locating EC Environmental Law' (2001) 20 *Yearbook of European Law* 139. On the related development of the 'Europeanization' of environmental policy, see A. Weale *et al.* (eds.) *Environmental Governance in Europe: An Ever Closer Ecological Union* (Oxford: Oxford University Press, 2000). [18] See Ch. 2, pp. 56–60.

[19] Primarily Art. 2 EC which specifies the achievement of sustainable development as a fundamental objective of the EU, and Art. 6 EC which requires that environmental protection requirements must be integrated into the definition and implementation of the Community policies and activities in particular with a view to promoting sustainable development.

[20] A. Lenschow, 'New Regulatory Approaches in "Greening" EU Policies' (2002) 8 *ELJ* 19.

of alternatives to facilitate particular outcomes. Finally, environmental assessment attests to the fact that due process matters, not so much because of ecologization, but as a concern with human rights. Towards the end of this chapter I therefore consider the parallels between the requirement to consider alternatives, and classic proportionality analysis with regard to fundamental rights.

Consideration of Alternatives

In the United Kingdom, the genuine consideration of a broad range of alternatives—sites, technologies, policies—has long been hampered by an emphasis placed upon a particular site, as the subject of an application for development consent. This is related to a reluctance to consider cumulative effects on the environment which necessarily involves an assessment of other sites and projects. This situation arose because the protection of specific, easily defined, property was—and remains—a primary function of the common law of nuisance. An individual's ability to be free from nuisance and to obtain redress when subjected to pollution was tied to a property interest in a specific parcel of land. This was incorporated by judicial interpretation into the post-war planning (and land settlement) system, so that the principle of the protection of private property continued to exist as rights of development.[21] A right to develop land, and be involved in planning decisions, remains closely linked to the possession of a property or developmental interest in a particular parcel of land, manifestations of which include the long-held presumption in favour of development, even in the face of sustainability arguments to the contrary, and continued official resistance to affording third parties rights of appeal. The last is, of course, under pressure for change, though as a part of human rights reform rather than the dynamic of ecologization.[22]

The specificity of property rights in a parcel of land in the planning system has, however, proved incompatible with the expression of abstract, and public, rights of access to information, and participation in decision making shaped by environmental assessment, even when these are advanced in a fledgling form in instruments such as the EIA Directive. Such rights are in line with doctrines of good public administration and, typically, European principles of environmental law such as precaution and are unrelated to the protection of private property. Hence, in pursuing a system of environmental assessment, there is some scope for circumventing property interests, most spectacularly by refusing development consent, the practical corollary of taking account of the public, and environmental,

[21] As told by McAuslan, *Ideologies of Planning Law*. However, such rights of development were no longer compensatable, as was the case prior to the nationalization of development rights in the Town and Country Planning Act 1947.

[22] CPRE, RSPB, WWF *et al.*, *Third Party Rights of Appeal* (London: CPRE, 2002). See also M. Purdue, 'The Case for Third Party Planning Appeals' (2001) 3 *Env L Rev* 83.

effects of development being a reduced role for private property considerations. Moreover, by broadening environmental concerns beyond a particular site to the wider ecological system by a presumption that the effects of environmental harm will be felt beyond their source, environmental assessment represents a conceptual understanding of the environment as integrated and interdependent, which transcends the division of land into parcels or sites denoting ownership.

Bearing this in mind, it is perhaps inevitable that the absorption of the EIA Directive into the property-oriented planning system of England and Wales (the chosen model of implementation) led to discordance between the European Community model of environmental assessment in the Directive and existing assessment procedures in the planning system.[23] For example, the traditional onus on developers to provide information on the effects of development has meant that statutory environmental assessment procedures depart from the objective of the Directive (at least as expressed in the Directive's preamble) that the 'competent authority' conduct an environmental assessment on the basis of information provided by the developer.[24] The existence of property and developmental rights continues to play a key role in understanding the uses to which the environmental assessment process is put by developers in the planning system. This also explains the weakness of the requirement to search for valid alternatives to a proposal that necessarily involves making inquiries beyond a particular site.

Geographical Boundaries and Alternative Sites

A potential for conflict exists between traditional proprietorial boundaries respected in planning law and a key conceptual premise of environmental assessment, that the effects of development may be felt beyond their source and must be taken into account in decision-making processes. This is seen clearly in *Velcourt*[25] in which one of the applicants' grounds of leave to quash the decision of a planning inspector was that he had failed to give due weight to the absence of an adequate environmental assessment of the effects of the *off-site* disposal of chicken litter from the site of a proposed extension to a poultry farm (it was not made clear how this fell to be assessed). The inspector stated in his decision letter that 'what happens to it [the disposal of waste on the second site] afterwards is another matter and not one which is before me to consider . . . It becomes a separate operation which may or may not require planning permission'. Tucker J considered

---

[23] Alder, 'Environmental Impact Assessment', discusses the incompatibility of aspects of English legal culture with the EIA Directive.

[24] Although this depends on what exactly is meant by environmental assessment, as discussed in Ch. 2, pp. 97–8. There also seems to be no obstacle in Community law to a competent authority being a private party, except that there has been some dispute about whether Crown Estate Commissioners were an appropriate body to conduct environmental assessment for salmon farms given their commercial interest in the outcome of a favourable assessment.

[25] *Wychavon District Council* v *Secretary of State for the Environment and Velcourt Ltd* (1994) 6 *JEL* 352.

that the inspector had properly directed himself in law on this matter because the sites (for the development and the disposal of chicken litter) were not linked physically and were not dependent on each other for planning permission.[26] The inspector's easy acceptance that the effects of the off-site disposal of chicken litter need not be subject to the 1988 Environmental Effects Regulations[27] relied on a narrow conception of environmental assessment since the disposal of such wastes can clearly have significant environmental consequences.[28] The outcome of this case highlights that the biases of the planning system have traditionally been directed by a concern with planning consent for an immediate geographical area, most commonly defined by property ownership. A more encompassing approach to the issue of off-site effects has been taken by the courts in conservation law, in which property and commercial interests are not quite so sharply defined. It has, for example, been held permissible for land of lesser intrinsic scientific interest to be designated as an SSSI if it is part of the same environmental unit as land which is of genuine interest, thus creating a surrounding buffer.[29]

A resistance to off-site issues in planning decisions is seen specifically in the limited legal requirements for considering alternative sites,[30] although the courts have accepted that where a proposal has severe environmental implications, consideration of alternative sites may be necessary, and may constitute a material consideration.[31] In one such case,[32] for example, the local council challenged the Secretary of State's decision to grant permission for office development on the ground that the Secretary of State had failed to have regard to a material consideration by not examining the other comparable sites. In the Court of Appeal, Oliver LJ considered that comparability was appropriate in cases in which *inter alia* there was a clear public convenience or advantage in the proposal, but that this was also combined with the existence of inevitable adverse effects or disadvantages to the public or a section of the public where there was the existence of an alternative site for the same project which would not have those effects or would not have them to the same extent.

---

[26] At 356–7.

[27] Town and Country Planning (Assessment of Environmental Effects) Regulations 1988 (SI 1988, No. 1199).

[28] See comment by B. Fitzpatrick, 'Redressing the Late Implementation of the Environmental Impact Assessment Directive' (1994) 6 *JEL* 351, at 368.

[29] For example, *Sweet* v *Secretary of State for the Environment and Nature Conservancy Council* (1989) 1 *JEL* 245. S. 28C of the 1981 Act, as amended by Schedule 9 of the Countryside and Rights of Way Act 2000, appears to allow for buffers, although there remains some uncertainty about this.

[30] See *R* v *Carlisle City ex parte Cumbria Cooperative* [1986] *JPL* 206, as noted by R. Carnwath, 'The Planning Lawyer and the Environment', (1991) 3 *JEL* 56, at 62. See further, M. Billot, 'Implementing the Effective Treatment of Alternatives into the UK EIA Process' (2002) (MA dissertation, EIA Centre, University of Manchester).

[31] A similar requirement exists in guidance relating to development on green-belt sites: the owner of a green-belt site is required to take pains to ensure that there are no other (non-green-belt) sites on which the proposed development might be located.

[32] *GLC* v *Secretary of State and Cablecross Projects Ltd* [1986] JPL 183.

Several of these factors were present in *ex parte Medway Council*,[33] concerning the consideration of alternatives to building an airport at Cliffe in North Kent, particularly the expansion of Gatwick airport, an option 'conspicuous by its absence' from the Department of Transport's consultation document on the development of air transport in the South East of England. This case took place prior to an environmental impact assessment process being triggered for development consent purposes, and therefore provides an example of the consideration of alternatives at the level of policy making. One ground on which the application (made by councils and individuals opposing the building of an airport at Cliffe) succeeded was that the consultation procedure was unfair. This was because the applicants in effect lost their only real opportunity to present their case about the desirability of the alternative option at a time when options could genuinely be considered (the government's adherence to a legal agreement not to further develop Gatwick airport before 2017 presented an insurmountable hurdle to such consideration). The relevant part of the case was the judicial categorization of the need to consider alternatives. Mr Justice Maurice Kay accepted that 'fairness in this context is synonymous with procedural fairness rather than substantive fairness which concerns the effect of a decision as opposed to the way in which it was reached . . . However it is important not to be too schematic in considering this distinction'.[34] This is some acknowledgement that, although the requirement to consider alternatives is a procedural one, substantive effects flow from it. As with making judgments about the significance of environmental effects,[35] United Kingdom courts have been reluctant to attend to matters of substance relating to environmental assessment, particularly the adequacy of considering alternative options, solutions, or sites. Whilst the *Medway* case clearly does not amount to a review of the merits of the decision to exclude Gatwick airport from the consultation procedure on air transport in the South East, it suggests at the very least an acceptance that procedural requirements, including the need to take a hard look at the matter of alternatives, are highly relevant to any particular outcome, and that environmental assessment may act as a vector for the adequate consideration of alternative options. Other grounds were also relied upon in this case, including Habitats Directive issues.[36]

Further cases suggest that the resistance to considerations of alternatives is being overcome.[37] In another case concerning the destruction of Twyford Down, *ex parte Murray* (*No. 2*),[38] the applicant sought to quash decisions which allowed the local authority to build a car park on land which had been turned back into

---

[33] *R v Secretary of State for Transport ex parte Medway Council and Kent County Council* [2002] EWHC 2516 (Admin), Maurice Kay J.   [34] At para. 32.   [35] See Ch. 4.

[36] Discussed further below, pp. 158–62.

[37] See also *Elmbridge Borough Council* v *Secretary of State for the Environment, Transport and the Regions* [2002] Env LR 1 which concerned the availability of alternative sites, but was decided as a 'reserved matters' case, on which see Ch. 6, p. 213.

[38] *R v Hampshire County Council ex parte Murray* (*No. 2*) [2002] EWHC 2491.

open grassland as part of an undertaking by the government to mitigate for land lost as a result of the expansion of the M3 motorway.[39] The planning permission was subject to a condition that development should not take place until a scheme for the provision and management of alternative grassland in mitigation for the development site was submitted to, and approved by, the local planning authority. The Secretary of State had specified five possible 'mitigation sites'. The applicant contested that, in approving the scheme, the local authority had failed to properly consider the ecological value of the proposed development site, as compared to other sites identified by the Secretary of State. Ousley J held that the local authority had erred in failing to consider the comparison between the potential ecological value of the development site, and the potential ecological value of the other possible mitigation sites, thus giving weight to the approach to alternatives contained in environmental assessment instruments, even though specific environmental assessment provisions were not at stake in this case.

The issue of the availability of an alternative site was also raised in *ex parte Adriano*.[40] The applicant in this case successfully challenged a decision of the local authority to grant planning permission for an incinerator at a landfill site on several grounds, including that the authority had failed to reassess the issue of need in the light of planning permission being granted for an alternative site and that this was a material consideration, even though the alternative site was designed to deal with different categories of waste.

Notwithstanding the possible future extension of the requirement to consider alternatives via judicial review suggested by cases such as these, as mentioned above the provision to consider alternatives (whether they be alternative sites, designs, or technologies) remains weak under the EC EIA Directive. Originally, the requirement on the part of the developer to give 'an outline of the main alternatives studied by the developer and an indication of the main reasons for his choice, taking into account the environmental effects' formed part of the category of 'additional information' to be provided in the developer's environmental statement.[41] The provision of this information was dependent upon whether a Member State considered that this was relevant to a given stage of the consent procedure and to the specific characteristics of a particular project or type of project and of the environmental features likely to be affected, and that the developer might reasonably be required to compile this information having regard, *inter alia*, to current knowledge and methods of assessment.[42] Although not purely discretionary, this requirement formed no more than an adjunct to the central but basic body of information which *shall* be provided by the developer, such as a description of the site and the project.[43]

---

[39] The subject of *Twyford Parish Council* v *Secretary of State for Transport* (1992) 4 *JEL* 273.
[40] *R* v *Surrey County Council ex parte Adriano* [2002] EHWC 2471.
[41] Art. 5(1) in conjunction with Annex III, para. 2 of Directive 85/337/EEC.
[42] Art. 5(1).   [43] Art. 5(2).

'The failure on the part of developers to take account of alternatives where this would be justified'[44] was recognized by the European Commission as a major deficiency in the quality of environmental statements in its first review of the implementation of the Directive which also highlighted the discrepancy between the substantive weakness of the requirement to consider alternatives and the fundamental nature of the need to do so. Directive 97/11/EC, which was drafted in the light of the Commission's concerns on this and other points of implementation, elevated the status of this category of information to a mandatory requirement.[45] However the onus of considering alternatives rests firmly on the potential developer, with no requirement on the part of the authorities to demonstrate that alternatives have been considered, and to make this available to the public, such as exists in the case of the consideration of mitigating measures.[46] The burden, such as it is, may be difficult to discharge fully because of the problems involved in obtaining comprehensive information about alternative sites, or the feasibility of alternative designs or technology.

An example of the currently limited nature of the requirement to consider alternatives is found in the case of the Kentish Flats windfarm,[47] in which the developer, Global Renewable Energy Partners, failed to comprehensively describe alternatives to the building of 30 turbines, citing the project itself as an alternative to traditional means of energy generation.[48] The obvious alternatives, energy saving and efficiency improvements, were not considered. Instead, 'Project Alternatives', listed in the non-technical summary accompanying the Environmental Statement, were restricted to a narrow consideration of alternative *sites*, particularly in the Thames Estuary. This was limited, however, by the need for a suitable point for the distribution of the electricity to be generated. The location of the proposed windfarm, off the Whitstable coast, provided this in the form of an existing electricity substation at Herne Bay, to which the windfarm could be connected. The assessment of alternative locations by the developer was therefore predetermined by technical feasibility, rather than ecological criteria. The Kentish Flats windfarm proposal demonstrates also the obvious difficulty of considering 'real' alternatives to a project, in the face of approved policy. Providing the policy context in this case was the government's environmentally favourable (on a national, rather than local, scale) policy to promote the development of 'clean, sustainable' sources of power generation, which was bolstered by the target to generate 10 per cent of electricity from renewables by the year 2010. Arguably, this presented the developer with the

---

[44] European Commission, *Report from the Commission on the Implementation of Directive 85/337/EEC*, COM(93) 28, 2.4.1993, p. 43.

[45] Art. 5(3) of Directive 85/337/EEC as amended by Directive 97/11/EC.

[46] Art. 9(1). On this point, compare the provision in Directive 2001/42/EC on the environmental assessment of plans and programmes, as discussed below, at pp. 162–4.

[47] See Ch. 4, pp. 140–6.

[48] Global Renewable Energy Partners, *Environmental Statement*.

opportunity to align the entire project with 'alternative' approaches to energy production, and pre-empted a fuller consideration of genuinely alternative ways of doing this. To some extent, given the development of strategic environmental assessment, this omission of discussion of policy alternatives might be seen as defining the limits of project-specific environmental impact assessment.[49] Recognizing the different levels of environmental assessment has the counterpart that some issues are appropriately dealt with at one level rather than another.

Alternatives and the Habitats Directive

A further requirement to consider alternatives arises in the Habitats Directive[50] with, potentially, some important substantive effects. The Directive provides a number of procedural safeguards in the event that a plan or project likely to have a significant effect upon a European conservation site (a Special Protection Area[51] or Special Area of Conservation[52]) is proposed. The plan or project must first be the subject of a preliminary 'appropriate assessment' of its implications for the site in view of its conservation objectives.[53] In the case of this assessment being negative, alternative *solutions* must be considered, in the absence of which the plan or project may be carried out for 'imperative reasons of overriding public interest, including those of a social or economic nature', so long as the Member State takes all compensatory measures necessary to ensure the overall coherence of the network of such sites.[54] Such alternatives could include alternative locations (or routes), different scales or designs of development, alternative processes, as well as a 'zero-option'.[55] The Commission has interpreted this obligation accordingly: 'alternative solutions have to be sought in case the assessment is negative; if alternative solutions exist, they have to be realised. Only in the absence of alternative solutions does Article 6(4) of the Habitats Directive allow for derogations',[56] which makes clear the centrality of the requirement to consider alternatives in this context. The Commisson's interpretive guidance further states that the reference

---

[49] On the interrelationship between environmental impact assessment and strategic environmental assessment, see Ch. 2, pp. 62–5.

[50] Directive 92/43/EEC on the conservation of natural habitats and of wild fauna and flora OJ 1992 L 206, p. 7.

[51] Established under Art. 4(4) of Directive 79/409/EEC OJ 1979 L 103, p. 1.

[52] As provided for under Arts. 3 and 4 of the Habitats Directive.

[53] Art. 6(3). Further on this procedure, see Ch. 2, pp. 68–70.

[54] Art. 6(4). See Appendix IX.

[55] European Commission, *Managing Natura 2000 Sites* (Brussels: CEC, 2000), 43.

[56] This possibility for an exception is restricted if the site concerned hosts a priority natural habitat type and/or priority species. In that case, reasons other than human health and public safety may only be raised further to an opinion from the Commission as described in Commission Opinion 95/C of 27 April on the planned A20 motorway (Germany) which will intersect the Trebel and Recknitz Valley pursuant to Article 6(4) of Directive 92/43/EEC on the conservation of natural habitats and of wild fauna and flora, OJ 1995 C 178, p. 3, para. 2.2.

parameters for the national authorities to make the necessary comparisons between different options deal with the conservation of the site and its ecological functions. Because of this, other criteria such as economic criteria 'cannot be seen as overruling ecological criteria' in this phase of assessment.[57] Other kinds of factors which may be accepted as rendering an alternative unsuitable, such as technical feasibility, are not listed, possibly to give the national authorities some leeway in conformity with the principle of subsidiarity. At the stage of the second assessment made by the authorities (in the absence of alternative solutions—or in the presence of solutions having even more negative environmental effects on the site concerned) the authorities may examine the existence of imperative reasons of overriding public interest which may justify the loss of the site or its ecological 'integrity'; these may include economic reasons, so long as some long-term public (rather than entirely private) benefit is promoted by the plan or project, sufficient to outweigh the long-term conservation interests produced by the Directive.

The Commission's application of the requirement to advance alternative solutions, (prior to its publication of guidance on this point) is illustrated in two of its Opinions, required in the event that the endangered sites are host to priority (or particularly vulnerable) habitat types or species. Both Opinions hail from the German plan to build a motorway linking the eastern and western parts of the country, a policy supported financially by the Community through the deployment of structural funds to help 'lagging behind' areas, and thus strengthen the social and economic cohesion of the Community. The planned motorway also forms part of the trans-European road network, the aim of which is 'to ensure the functioning of the internal market and to enable citizens of the Union, economic operators and regional and local communities to benefit from an area without internal frontiers'.[58] Issues concerning the enlargement of the European Union were also at stake. The motorway plan was therefore firmly grounded in the core economic, political, and social objectives of the Union. As a matter of law, the success of the plan was, though, dependent upon the Commission's view of it as necessary as a matter of 'overriding public interest', since the motorway was to dissect several important conservation areas. And, also as a matter of law, the consideration of alternatives should be central to this determination. In practice, the influence of the existence of 'alternative solutions' on the final decisions of the Commission is difficult to make out, mainly because the Commission accepts a low standard of what is meant by this requirement, permitting its restriction to a mere comparison of routes, rather than more expansive, and admittedly more difficult to evaluate, alternatives, such as rail travel, or other ways of economically

---

[57] ibid.
[58] Commission Opinion 96/15/EC of 18 December 1995 on the intersection of the Peene Valley (Germany) by the planned A20 motorway pursuant to Article 6(4) of Council Directive 92/43/EEC on the conservation of natural habitats and of wild fauna and flora, OJ 1995 L 6, p. 14, para. 1.4.

regenerating the area concerned. This is then followed by the Commission's acceptance of a narrow review of alternative routes, largely based upon information provided by the developer, the German government, although admittedly going beyond the developer's initial geographical remit. As Nollkaemper states: 'The Commission's Opinions take only a soft glance at how Member States use their discretion'.[59] In the case of the motorway's intersection of the Peene Valley, the Commission first details the political, structural, and economic influences on the initial curtailing of alternative options:

For the Peene crossing, the Federal Republic examined as main alternative solutions the area west of Loitz and the areas east and west of Jarmen. For economic and structural reasons, in particular the time-saving linking of Grimmen and Greifswald with other economic centres, the Federal Republic favoured the crossing east of Jarmen.

On 20 January 1995 the Federal Ministry of Transport decided that the route should be east of Jarmen. The Ministry of Economic Affairs of Mecklenburg-Western Pomerania was instructed to seek a solution for the Peene crossing which would ensure compliance with national and European environmental objectives.

Thus alternative routes located west of Jarmen or Loitz could no longer be considered by the authorities of Mecklenburg-Western Pomerania. The Commission, however, has to ensure that adverse effects on a site are only accepted in the absence of alternative solutions. It has therefore to evaluate whether a solution less damaging than the route proposed for east of Jarmen exists.[60]

The Commission then conducted a brief survey of four possible crossings inside the protection areas, including the original preferred option which was rejected on the grounds that it would adversely affect a priority habitat type. The process of conducting this assessment of alternatives on the part of the Commission led Germany to propose a further route for ecological reasons, which was accepted by the Commission since the new negative effects of this route would be combined with existing industrial and infrastructure strains in the area.[61] Significantly, the proposed mitigation and compensation measures (including the creation or restoration of seven different habitat types and engineering solutions to lessen the impact of the motorway, including barriers to mitigate the light attraction and disturbance of nocturnal animals by the headlights of cars) were highly influential in the Commission's judgment about the least damaging alternative solution in this case. Whereas, according to the structure of Article 6(4) of the Directive, such influences should impinge on decision making only after a decision has been made about the least damaging alternative solution. The Commission concluded that, taking into account these measures and considering that (eventually) the least damaging alternative solution had been chosen, the adverse effects on the protection area under threat were justified by imperative

---

[59] A. Nollkaemper, 'Habitat Protection in European Community Law: Evolving Conceptions of a Balance of Interests' (1997) 9 *JEL* 271, at 272.   [60] Opinion 96/15/EC.
[61] ibid., paras. 4.1 and 4.3.

reasons of overriding public interest,[62] even though these reasons were pro-foundly economic in nature.

This Opinion suggests that there is some value in the Commission supervising the consideration of alternative options, but that additionally there is a need for information from sources other than the proposed developer[63] in order to broaden the range of alternatives considered, rather than as initially in this case deriving from political edict, and with a priority given to economic influences, including 'time-saving' linkages between economically important towns. An overly optimistic interpretation of this Opinion is that the analyses of alternatives for projects covered by Article 6(4) of the Habitats Directive will now be super-vised by the Commission. Additionally, it is argued that the Habitats Directive transforms consideration of alternatives into a more substantive, and reviewable, requirement than currently exists in assessment procedures for development con-sent purposes, such as under the EIA Directive (which in practice would be con-ducted contemporaneously).[64]

Such conclusions appear unduly confident in the Commission's ability to properly scrutinize alternatives when the Opinion on the crossing of the Valley of the Trebel and Recknitz is taken into account.[65] In this Opinion, the Commission readily agreed with Germany that no better alternative existed, and accepted the need for the road as a given ('an east-west link has to be created in Mecklenburg Western Pomerania in order to link it with central regions of the Community')[66], notwithstanding a finding that the affected area played host to two priority natural habitats. The offer of certain compensatory measures was coupled with the finding that alternatives did not exist. Striking for its apparent lack of analysis of alternatives, it remains unclear even what this negative finding is referring to, for example alternative routes, designs, technologies, or even a 'do nothing' option. This Opinion highlights the desirability of alternative solutions being assessed more strictly according to ecological criteria, rather than with regard to the offer of compensatory and mitigatory measures, and the technical feasibility of these. A starting point, though, would be for the Commission to make explicit the range, scale, and type of alternatives that it has considered, particularly if it is to habitually perform a supervisory role in the carrying out of environmental assessments for conservation purposes.[67]

The *Medway* case,[68] discussed above, hardens the requirement to consider alternatives in Article 6(4) of the Habitats Directive into a ground of judicial

---

[62] ibid., para. 4.3.

[63] Although the Commission did conduct a site visit for the purposes of writing the Opinion 96/15/EC, this did not amount to an independent appraisal.

[64] Nollkaemper, 'Habitat Protection', at 282. The optimism is misplaced when one considers that the Commission has no supervisory function in the case of Art. 6(4) first indent cases.

[65] Opinion 95/C.   [66] ibid., para. 4.3.

[67] Although this seems unlikely, given the Commission's current reluctance to publish even those Opinions that it has given.   [68] [2002] EWHC 2516 (Admin), Maurice Kay J.

review. The applicants' challenge, based upon so-called 'conservation obligations' was derived from the importance of the Cliffe site in conservation and environmental terms: the site includes the Thames Estuary and Medway Marshes Special Protection Area and the Northwood Hall Site of Special Scientific Interest and National Nature Reserve. It is also a site designated as having exceptional value as a wetland of international importance, under the Ramsar Convention on Wetlands of International Importance. Precise obligations, though, flow from the Habitats Directive, as implemented by Regulations 48 and 49 of the Conservation (Habitats &c.) Regulations 1994[69] which provides that prior to undertaking or giving consent for development on a European site, the competent authority shall make an appropriate assessment of the implications for the site in view of that site's conservation objectives. Replicating the test set out in Article 6(4) of the Habitats Directive, if the competent authority is satisfied that, there being no alternative solutions, the plan must be carried out for imperative reasons of overriding public interest, the authority may agree to the plan or project notwithstanding a negative assessment of the implications for the site. Medway and Kent Councils argued that this amounts to an obligation to consider any reasonable alternatives, including the extension of runway capacity at Gatwick. Mackay J agreed: 'if it may be the case that Gatwick, by itself or with one or both of the others, would be an, or the, alternative solution, that would have the potential to impact upon the question whether or not there were imperative reasons of overriding public interest in favour of Cliffe',[70] concluding that it was therefore irrational to exclude all Gatwick options from the consultation process at the stage of policy making. This judgment makes clear the possible, and logical, leakage of legal requirements concerning environmental assessment for development consent into policy formation, and the necessary interplay between project-based and policy-based environmental assessment, as highlighted by EC Directive 2001/42/EC, discussed below.

Strategic Environmental Assessment and the Consideration of Alternative Options

In theory, the development of strategic environmental assessment (the assessment of policies, plans, and programmes)[71] considerably extends the alternatives which may be considered in a decision-making process by allowing a broad range of criteria to be incorporated, for example by the assessment of policy options.[72] For

---

[69] SI 1994, No. 2716.   [70] At para. 36.

[71] Directive 2001/42/EC on the assessment of the effects of certain plans and programmes on the environment OJ 2001 L 197, p. 30, the development of which is discussed in Ch. 2, pp. 60–5.

[72] M. Partidario, 'Strategic Environmental Assessment: Principles and Potential', in J. Petts (ed.) *Handbook of Environmental Impact Assessment: Vol. 1 Process, Methods and Potential* (Oxford: Blackwell, 1999), 67.

this reason also, strategic environmental assessment encourages the integration of sectors, and policy areas, which explain the association of strategic environmental assessment with the implementation of sustainable development. This is particularly the case when compared to project-based environmental assessment in which the choice of alternatives has often been narrowed by prior decisions taken at a higher level, and which tends to require a more limited cross-sectoral assessment of the effects of a project upon environmental media and other factors, with the focus upon the particular site on which the project is planned.[73] As Morgan describes: 'SEA is the link between the EIA of projects, as it is presently being carried out, and the achievement of a level of human activities that maintains the quality of the environment'.[74]

General points about the relationship between environmental impact assessment and strategic environmental assessment are discussed elsewhere.[75] In this chapter, the key issue is whether strategic environmental assessment realizes real alternatives to proposed policies, plans, and programmes, and thus promotes changes in the culture of decision making.

Certainly a notable feature of the EC SEA Directive is the potential for enhanced attention to be given to the consideration of alternatives, particularly when compared with the EIA Directive which establishes a project-based environmental assessment procedure. Where an environmental assessment is required under the SEA Directive, an environmental report must identify, describe, and evaluate the likely significant effects on the environment of implementing the plan or programme, and 'reasonable alternatives' to it, taking into account the objectives and the geographical scope of the plan or programme.[76] There is also a requirement to describe the 'zero-option', or do-nothing alternative.[77] When a plan or programme is adopted, the authority must provide a statement of how the assessment was conducted and the reasons for not adopting the alternatives considered.[78] A similar requirement exists in the Draft Protocol on Strategic Environmental Assessment (the Kiev Protocol, 2003), a Protocol to the Espoo Convention, so that 'the reasonable alternatives of a plan or programme must be included in an environmental report'.[79] However, an anomaly exists in the omission of such a requirement in the case of transboundary consultations, so that notification of a party likely to be affected by a plan or programme need only

[73] Art. 3 EC Directive on environmental assessment. For a broader analysis of the potential of strategic environmental assessment, see R. Therivel and M. R. Partidario (eds.) *The Practice of Strategic Environmental Assessment* (London: Earthscan, 1996) and Partidario, 'Strategic Environmental Assessment'.

[74] P. Morgan, *EIA: A Methodological Perspective* (London: Kluwer, 1999), 425.

[75] Ch. 2, pp. 60–5.

[76] Art. 5(1), to be read in conjunction with Annex I of the 2001 Directive.

[77] Annex I(b) states that information shall be provided by the developer on, *inter alia*, 'the relevant aspects of the current state of the environment and the likely evolution thereof without implementation of the plan or programme'. There is nothing equivalent in the EIA Directive.

[78] Art. 9 Directive 2001/42/EC.

[79] Art. 7 UN/ECE Draft Protocol on Strategic Environmental Assessment (Kiev Protocol).

include information on the possible environmental effects and information regarding the decision-making procedure.[80] Notwithstanding these various provisions, a warning of the potential insignificance of strategic environmental assessment in terms of identifying and pursuing alternatives arises in the case of the Lewes Flood Defence Strategy,[81] in which the consideration of alternatives, even at the level of policy making, was curtailed because this inevitably took place within the broader context of a range of social, economic, and technical considerations. This became sharply apparent at a public meeting (of about 300 people) on the flood management strategy for the Ouse, in which the environmental considerations, analysed in some detail in the strategic environmental assessment, were overlooked in favour of other issues. These included the socio-economic injustice of the proposed plan for flood defence works which prioritized business areas, while less prosperous but equally vulnerable housing estates were accorded less priority. The chronology of events is also instructive, with a gradual broadening of considerations beyond the environmental taking place when policy alternatives were being considered, prior to a more specific environmental impact assessment then being undertaken, as described in the flood defence strategy:

The overall strategy option(s) is selected from the balance of technical, economic, and environmental issues . . . once approved, this would be subjected to project-level environmental impact assessment which would look at the specific environmental impacts of the option (e.g. location, size, and nature) in greater detail.[82]

The information derived from such project-based environmental assessments will then be fed into a broader decision-making process, constituting one material consideration amongst many others. Importantly, even strategic environmental assessment forms only a part of the policy and decision-making jigsaw, and possibly a marginal one at that.

Environmental Governance: The European Commission's Development of Internal Impact Assessment

The adoption of the SEA Directive represents the logical expansion of environmental assessment, beyond a concern with an individual project or site usually

---

[80] Art. 10 of the Draft Protocol. For related provisions, see Appendix VI.

[81] Discussed in Chapter 3, pp. 86–92. On a far larger scale, see the case of the Trans-European Network in Sheate, 'From Environmental Impact Assessment to Strategic Environmental Assessment', in which he describes a strategic environmental assessment of sorts of the trans-European network, but with the fatal flaw that the decision to sanction this policy, and the associated major development projects involved, had already been taken. See also, Royal Society for the Protection of Birds, *The Environment and the Structural Funds: the Role of Strategic Environmental Assessment—The Sicilian Experience* (Sandy, Beds: Birdlife International, RSPB, 1997).

[82] Environment Agency, Southern Region, *Sussex Ouse Flood Defence Strategy SEA*, Stage 2 Report, ch. 6.1.

representing the interests of a developer to encompass the assessment of policies and legislative proposals of more general interest. Within the European Commission, environmental assessment is similarly being expanded, so that a form of policy appraisal now operates to review the internal formulation of legislative and policy proposals. This provides an instructive case study on the uses and potential abuses of strategic environmental assessment, particularly in terms of how the consideration of alternatives is shaped in an organizational context, and against the background of broader integration attempts within the European Union.[83]

Directorate-General Environment of the European Commission has been the main driver of environmental assessment in Europe, although the European Council has provided political leadership and impetus to the progress of environmental integration.[84] DG Environment initially developed a mandatory system of environmental impact assessment within the Member States (in the form of the EIA Directive),[85] amended this,[86] and then extended its scope to take in plans and programmes (the SEA Directive),[87] all the while facing resistance from some Member States, and from within the Commission, particularly from the Directorates dealing with transport, agriculture, and structural funds. The long-standing external focus of activity by the Commission, the implementation and effectiveness of environmental assessment in the Member States, has led to considerable time being spent on monitoring and enforcement actions, often with limited results. For example, in its first quinquennial review of the amended EIA Directive,[88] the Commission acknowledged the variety of good and bad practice between, and even within, Member States. The Commission found unsystematic screening of Annex II projects, the exclusion of whole categories of project from thresholds and criteria designed to identify likely significant effects of development, poor practice in scoping, a lack of regard for cumulative effects, and inadequate consultation in the case of transboundary assessments, concluding, not surprisingly, that there is currently incomplete implementation of the Directive. When faced with similar difficulties in the implementation of the antecedent (unamended) EIA Directive, the Commission followed a quite restricted approach to ironing out some of its ambiguities and gaps in the amended version.

---

[83] On which, see N. Dhondt, *Integration of Environmental Protection into Other EC Policies: Theory and Practice* (Groningen: Groningen Law Publishing, 2003) which details applications of the principle of integration but does not consider internal decision making of the Commission.

[84] Lenschow, 'New Regulatory Approaches'. Note that the European Environment Agency has taken a backseat with regard to such development, its role being limited to conducting assessments, such as the Dobris Assessments, on the progress of internal measures designed to integrate policy areas.   [85] Directive 85/337/EEC.   [86] By Directive 97/11/EC.

[87] Directive 2001/42/EC.

[88] European Commission, *Five Years Report to the European Parliament and the Council on the Effectiveness of the EIA Directive* (Brussels: CEC, 2002), prepared by Oxford Brookes University School of Planning.

In response to the current problems being experienced with the effectiveness of the amended EIA, DG Environment seems instead to advocate the future development of 'sustainable development assessment' which will 'move towards a more holistic evaluation'[89] by taking into account social, economic, and environmental factors. The Commission's current development of just such an environmental assessment regime for its *internal* procedures, discussed below, provides a testing ground for the future application of a similar system in the Member States. It also suggests that the Commission recognized that it was untenable to require Member States to comply with the EIA Directive when it did not apply it to its own procedures. The initiative of applying environmental assessment standards to its internal procedures actually goes beyond the obligations imposed on Member States by the EIA Directive and fits well with the Commission's attempt to modernize environmental assessment in general. DG Environment describes the EIA Directive as conceptually dated,[90] and cites 'broader policy developments' and the need to further elaborate the role of environmental assessment in sustainable development as impulses for the expansion of environmental assessment to take in other policy sectors and other types of plan and programmes ('the Directive is sometimes criticised for being yesterday's tool as it does not clearly spell out the three pillars of sustainable development').[91] The Directorate foresees that the experience of applying a broad-ranging impact assessment procedure to its internal activities means that 'we will have practical experience of operating the Commission's own integrated assessment procedures and will thus also have the moral high ground' when it comes to promulgating a similar model for Member States.[92] This lends support to the idea of multi-level environmental assessment.[93]

Before reviewing the development of the internal impact assessment procedure in detail, it should first be mentioned that a form of assessment or *ex ante* evaluation[94] has been required of projects financed by the European Community's funds since 1993 when the principle of 'environmental compatibility' was established by the Framework Regulation[95] (although the European Regional Development Fund had been reformed earlier to reflect environmental concerns).[96] This Regulation required

---

[89] Internal note to the Policy Group, DG Environment, on European Commission, *Five Years Report on the Effectiveness of EIA*, 10.   [90] ibid.   [91] ibid.   [92] ibid.
[93] Discussed in Ch. 2.
[94] There are, however, key differences between (budgetary) *ex ante* evaluation and impact assessment in terms of functions and purposes: 'Ex ante evaluation focuses primarily on value for money, the cost-effectiveness for the Community budget of all expenditure programmes/actions proposed. In contrast, impact assessment is policy driven, it focuses upon whether the impact of major policy proposals is sustainable and conform to the principle of Better Regulation' (*Communication from the Commission on Impact Assessment*, COM(2002) 276 final, at p. 3).
[95] Art. 7(1) Regulation 2081/93/EC OJ 1993 L 193, p. 5 (the Framework Regulation) provides that 'measures financed by the structural funds or receiving assistance from the EIB or another existing financial instrument shall be in conformity with the provisions of the Treaties, with instruments adopted pursuant thereto and with Community policies, including those concerning . . . environmental protection'. See generally also Regulation 2082/93/EC OJ 1993 L 193, p. 21 (the coordination framework).   [96] Lenschow, 'New Regulatory Approaches', at 29.

that measures financed by the Community from the structural or cohesion funds were to conform to Community policies, including environmental protection.[97] Environmental assessment was central to the integration of environmental policy into structural funding decisions, as the Commission explained:

... development plans ... must in the future include an *appraisal* of the environmental situation of the region concerned and an *evaluation of the environmental impact* of the strategy and operations planned, in accordance with the principles of sustainable development and in agreement with the provision of Community law in force.[98]

This form of environmental assessment therefore introduced some parity between the rules imposed on Member States by the EIA Directive and the internal appraisal procedure to which the Community institutions were subject in order to further environmental policy integration. The *Handbook*[99] accompanying the 1993 Framework Regulation presents the ensuing assessments as to 'environmental compatibility' as methodologically limited, highly technicist—with references to cost-benefit analysis, environmental baselines, and impact matrices—and with scant regard to the involvement of those likely to be affected by the projects funded.

The general system of granting Community funds was revised[100] to require a specific *'ex ante* evaluation of the environmental situation of the region concerned, including an estimate of the existing environmental situation and an estimate of the expected impact of the strategy and assistance on the environmental situation'.[101] This offers an indirect and rudimentary means of assessing the environmental implications of Community-funded developments in the Member States. Importantly, this evaluation lies alongside *ex ante* evaluations of 'the social and economic situation, mainly trends in the national labour market, including regions encountering particular employment problems' and 'the situation in terms of the equality of men and women with regard to labour market opportunities and treatment at work'.[102] As with the assessment of 'environmental compatibility' required under the 1993 Regulation, considerable discretion is enjoyed by the Member States in carrying out this evaluation, particularly concerning project selection and methodology.

---

[97] See Scott, EC *Environmental Law*, ch. 7 and on the detail of the application process for funding, including scrutiny of likely environmental impacts of projects in the context of a case study on development in the Highlands and Islands, see J. Scott, 'From Rio to Inverness: Environment and Development in the Highlands and Islands Objective 1 Enterprise Area', in Holder, *Impact of EC Environmental Law*, 319–26.

[98] European Commission, *Community Structural Funds: 1994–1999, Revised Regulations and Comments* (Brussels: CEC, 1993), cited in Lenschow, 'New Regulatory Approaches', at 29, with emphasis added.

[99] European Commission, *A Handbook on Environmental Assessment of Regional Development Plans and EU Structural Funds Programmes* (London: Environmental Resources Management, 1998).

[100] By Regulation 1260/1999/EC OJ 1999 L 161, p. 1 laying down general provisions on the Structural Funds.   [101] Art. 41(2)(b).   [102] Art. 41(2)(a) and (c).

In summary, having put in place an environmental assessment regime in each Member State, the Commission adopted a *laissez-faire* approach to supervising the environmental assessment of projects funded by the European Community, seemingly ignoring the fact that such assessments inevitably take place in the context of a hefty financial leg-up, and despite an ostensible obligation to monitor compliance with the principle of environmental compatibility.[103] This suggests that Community-funded projects should be more fully assessed at the Community level, in recognition that such projects should not be entirely regarded as the Member State's responsibility, even though this may depart from ideas of devolved governance and subsidiarity.[104] The danger at present is inadequate assessment at both national and Community levels. For example, plans and programmes supported by structural funds currently fall outside the scope of the SEA Directive,[105] whilst policy options for structural funds are not subject to the new system of internal policy appraisal, discussed below, precisely because of the presence of environmental impact assessment, and now strategic environmental assessment, regimes in the Member States. The result is uncertainty about responsibility (and accountability) for ensuring 'environmental compatibility' through environmental assessment, which may be explained as a negative by-product of 'quite dramatically new forms of shared (or multi-level) governance'.[106]

In general, this state of affairs produces asymmetry between the considerable demands of the Commission and the European Court of Justice about what is expected of Member States in terms of the scrutiny of general classes of development (as compared with Community-funded projects), and that applied internally, prior to the funding of projects often highly damaging to the environment. Even allowing for the rules introduced in 1999, the current review procedures for funded projects is remote from the iterative, fully consultative process demanded of the Member States by the European Court of Justice in some of its more expansive judgments,[107] in line with culture theories of environmental assessment. In contrast, the use of environmental assessment to judge structural funds applications conforms more to information theories of environmental assessment, in which basic information on the likely effects of a proposed project is fed into

[103] For example, as exists in Regulation 2064/97/EC OJ 1997 L 290, p. 1, Art. 4.

[104] Scott, *EC Environmental Law*, 145. One effect of this approach was the legal débâcle of the Mullaghmore interpretative centre, financed by general European Community funds for tourism, leading to inadequate assessment at Community or national level of the likely environmental consequences; Case T-461/93 *An Taisce* v *European Commission* [1994] ECR II-733 (CFI) and Case C-325/94P *An Taisce* v *European Commission* [1996] ECR I-3727 (ECJ) in which the Court found that there was not a reviewable decision because of the nature of operational programmes. Such a finding highlights the criticism that, in excluding structurally funded plans and programmes, the 2001 SEA Directive has left an important gap (although showing some awareness of the difficulty of retrospectively applying environmental assessment procedures to projects which have been embarked upon).   [105] For the reasons discussed above, Ch. 2, p. 65.

[106] Scott, *EC Environmental Law*, 146.

[107] See e.g. Ch. 4, pp. 116–20 on the European Court of Justice's interpretation of significance.

decision making, typified by a form-filling, box-ticking approach to environmental assessment.[108]

During the 1990s, the Commission's strong adherence to the form of environmental assessment in the external dimension of Member States' land use systems, encouraged by the instrument's easy alliance with the concept of sustainable development and its reflection of new forms of governance, began to jar with some of the decisions taken by the European Union institutions. Examples include, most famously, the Community's reluctance to intervene in French nuclear testing in Polynesia,[109] the financial support of power station construction in Gran Canaria,[110] and the disintegrated policy on the Trans-European transport network.[111] This disjuncture was recognized explicitly in the European Commission's Sixth Environmental Action Programme which pledged internal, as well as external, obligations towards the environment,[112] as an expression of the principle of integration.[113] These, together with other influences, have led to the application of assessment procedures to the internal workings of the Commission, to give practical effect to the European Union's strategy on governance, particularly instrument choice, enhanced participation, and better access to Community environmental information.[114] This development also appears to fall squarely within the Commission's conception of sustainable development as 'the central objective of all sectors and policies', and means that '[C]areful assessment of the full effects of a policy proposal must include estimates of its economic, environmental, and social impacts inside and outside the EU'.[115] In this respect there are high hopes for the use of impact assessment as a plank of 'better regulation', interpreted as an 'improved and simplified regulatory environment'.[116] The development of new forms of governance to achieve sustainable development may therefore be recognized in an amended and expanded form of environmental assessment. This also highlights the gradual convergence of aims

[108] For example, see European Commission, *Structural Funds Major Projects Request for Confirmation of the Rate of Assistance*, pursuant to Regulation 1260/1999/EC, which includes a form, Annex I of which concerns environmental impact assessment, including a declaration that the project is not likely to have significant effects on a Natura 2000 site.

[109] The subject of Case T-219/95 *Danielsson* v *Commission* OJ 1996 C 77, p. 12 (CFI).

[110] Challenged in Case C-321/95P *Greenpeace* v *Commission* [1998] ECR I-1651.

[111] See Sheate, 'From Environmental Impact Assessment to Strategic Environmental Assessment'.

[112] As formally recorded in Declaration No. 12 Protocol, annexed to the Treaty of Amsterdam: 'The Conference notes that the Commission undertakes to prepare environmental impact assessment studies when making proposals which may have significant environmental implications'.

[113] Articles 3 and 6 EC Treaty call for the integration of environmental issues into policy making. DG Environment, cites 'environmental assessment as an ideal tool for this', in *Impact Assessment Environment Guide* (Brussels: DG Environment, 2002), 39.

[114] European Commission, *White Paper on European Governance*, COM(2001) 428 final (Brussels: CEC, 2001).

[115] European Commission, *Proposal for an EU Sustainable Development Strategy*, COM(2001) 264 (Brussels: CEC, 2001).

[116] European Commission, *Action Plan on Simplifying and Improving the Regulatory Environment*, COM(2002) 278 (Brussels: CEC, 2002).

of the European Union (sustainable development, integration, equality, better regulation) which lay behind the initial plans to align the integration principle with other horizontal principles in the EU's draft constitution. DG Environment is confident about the role of internal impact assessment in achieving specific goals relating to these principles: 'Impact Assessment will be a test case for putting into practice the principles of Governance, the requirements of the Aarhus Convention, the Sixth Environmental Action Programme prescriptions, and the proposed communication on minimum standards for consultation.'[117]

The key development currently taking place in the Commission is the amalgamation of existing sectoral assessment procedures (business impact assessment, gender assessment, regulatory impact assessment, and, of course, environmental impact assessment) into a new integrated and standardized assessment process, encompassing environmental, social, and economic impacts of all major policy and legislative initiatives.[118] The result is a new form of assessment, labelled 'sustainability' or 'impact' assessment,[119] which is far broader than environmental assessment, and is to be applied to all policy and legislative proposals, including white papers, expenditure programmes, and international agreements that have an economic, social, or environmental impact. This form of impact assessment follows the pattern of the trio of *ex-ante* evaluations, conducted for the purpose of structural-fund allocations.[120]

The Commission's new integrated assessment procedure (embarked upon in early 2003) is a two-stage affair. A preliminary assessment is carried out of policy options and legislative proposals to identify possible options and sectors affected. This serves as a filter to help the Commission identify the policies and proposals that will be subjected to an extended impact assessment. In DG Environment preliminary *fiches d'impact* have been produced on water (action on river-basin management), and strategies for the protection of soils, the protection of the marine environment, and the sustainable use of pesticides, amongst others. An important aspect of these relatively short documents is that in each case the lead Directorate must identify what policy options are available to reach certain objectives, and what range of alternatives will be considered. This statement on policy options must also include an account of how the principles of subsidiarity and proportionality have been taken into account. The following example of these requirements is taken from a preliminary *fiches d'impact* of a proposed Directive on the biological treatment of biodegradable waste.[121] This demonstrates the

[117] DG Environment, *Impact Assessment—Operational Proposals for DG Environment*, 3.7.02.

[118] A development working against the overall approach of convergence of assessment procedures, is the compilation of guidelines on state aid for specifically *environmental protection* objectives, described by Vedder, 'The New Community Guidelines'.

[119] European Commission, *Communication from the Commission on Impact Assessment*, COM(2002) 272 final (Brussels: CEC, 2002), 2.

[120] Governed by Regulation 1260/1999/EC, discussed above, p. 167.

[121] European Commission, *Preliminary Impact Assessment on Directive on the Biological Treatment of Biodegradable Waste* (Brussels: CEC, 2002).

twin concerns of flexibility of implementation for the competent authority, and compatibility with internal market objectives.

Policy Options

What policy options are available to reach the objective? What range of alternatives will be considered?
The measures to be proposed will take the form of a Directive, so as to leave as much freedom as possible to the Member States in organising the biological treatment of biodegradable waste according to local conditions. Three aspects would need to be addressed at Community level: collection standards, treatment standards and end-product standards. As to collection standards, it could be envisaged to oblige Member States to offer a separate collection service for biodegradable waste in those areas where it makes economical and environmental sense (not, for instance, in rural areas with scattered dwellings). As for treatment standards, the adoption of EU rules would harmonise existing measures in a number of Member States and ensure that measures are adopted also in those Member States that at present have none. As for end-product standards, the requirements of the Internal Market would only be fulfilled if end-product standards are harmonised across the EU.

How have the principles of subsidiarity and proportionality been taken into account?
This Directive is partially related to Internal Market provisions, insofar as it would lay down product requirements for compost to be used on land. As such, it is necessary to ensure a high level of uniformity in the application of key measures relating to treatment standards, product requirements, sampling methods and labelling. The action of Member States alone under these respects would not be sufficient to achieve the proposed aim of a free circulation of compost products across the EU.

The Directive will only contain proportionate measures to the objectives to be achieved. In particular, any requirements for separate collection of biodegradable waste that may be decided would have to be carefully drafted in order to allow the necessary flexibility to the competent authority.

Of these preliminary impacts (approximately 170 a year are anticipated) the most potentially significant proposals and policies will then be subject to a further round of more detailed, and extended impact assessment, the test for which is whether the proposal will result in substantial economic, environmental, and/or social impacts on a specific sector or several sectors; will have a significant impact on major interested parties; and represents a major policy reform of one or several sectors.[122] The current plan is for 41 such extended assessments to take place on a broad range of proposals or acts, including transport, asylum, criminal justice, tropical forests, fisheries, gender equality, and tourism, which reflects the diversity and prevalence of contemporary Community action. The Commission envisages that such extended impact assessments will be conducted according to the principle of proportionate analysis, so that the depth of analysis will be in accordance with

---

[122] European Commission, *Communication on Impact Assessment*, 8.

the likely significance of the impacts. The assessments, flagged up by DG Environment as currently having most relevance, and on which work has already begun, are policies on the tobacco and sugar regimes, and the sustainability of European tourism. DG Environment is responsible or closely involved (with other DGs) for the conduct and compilation of these and almost every other extended impact assessment listed, the assessment process thereby offering an opportunity to include environmental factors and criteria in previously separate, and environmentally remote, policy areas. This illustrates well the process of integrating or 'mainstreaming' the environment into European governance, and means that DG Environment may be more capable of advancing an environmental agenda throughout the Commission. This point was made by DG Environment, which, on the face of it, views the extended assessment process as having some advantages, including 'reviving and boosting environmental integration within the Commission'.[123] It recommends seizing the opportunities presented by this development, while minimizing the main risks that 'environmental objectives may be diluted', 'the extra workload will slow down the legislative process', and 'excessive environmental input may be counterproductive with other DGs'.[124] The Directorate particularly expressed concern in its internal documents that the 'environment dimension' may not be properly integrated into the process overall, and suggested the development of practical guidance (a tools guide to environmental assessment)[125] to enable other Directorates to better integrate the environmental dimension in policy making,[126] in recognition that '[T]he proposed interaction between environmental assessment and the overall impact assessment is complex'.[127]

Whatever eventually happens in practice, this development of a broad assessment procedure which draws together impact analysis of policy areas (including, but not restricted to, environmental policy) may be understood using a hybrid of the two prevailing theories of environmental assessment, referred to throughout this book.[128] First, in terms of theories of information provision, the process is presented by the Commission as contributing information to decision making, rather than as 'a substitute for political judgment'.[129] However, this form of impact assessment clearly extends the traditional remit of environmental assessment, providing in addition information on the social and economic effects of the policy or proposal (as well as allowing a discussion of considerations such as political and ethical issues), as reflected in the non-specific 'Impact Assessment' nomenclature. This is an explicit example of the trend to extend the scope of the

[123] Internal note for DG Environment Policy Group, 'Impact Assessment: Operational Proposals for DG ENV', 3.7.03, p. 1.   [124] ibid. 1.   [125] DG Environment, *Impact Assessment*.
[126] Internal note for DG Environment, *Guide on Impact Assessment/Public Participation*, 11.6.02.
[127] DG Environment, Internal note, 'Environmental Impact Assessment: Environment Guide (ex 'Better Policies' Guide), 3.7.02, p. 1.   [128] For an initial discussion, see Ch. 1, pp. 22–9.
[129] European Commission, *Communication on Impact Assessment*, 9.

subject matter of environmental assessment, which reaches its apogee with the form of 'sustainability environmental assessment' advocated by Sadler.[130] In terms of information theories underpinning the development of environmental assessment the (as yet) minor role of the European Environment Agency in compiling and evaluating such assessments is curious, particularly considering the information-gathering (though admittedly not evaluative) remit of this body.

A further rationale for the Commission's impact assessment procedure is that it will force cultural change within the institutions of the European Union (akin to the action-forcing nature of the United States' NEPA 1969). However, this function does not entirely accord with culture theories of environmental assessment because the impact assessment procedure is broadly credited with strengthening the Commission's 'evaluation culture', as part of a 'Better Regulation' package,[131] and reinforcing the culture of consultation and dialogue with interested parties,[132] rather than instilling specifically environmental values throughout the Commission. This is a product of the nature of this form of assessment, since the potential environmental impacts of a particular policy constitute just one factor or 'pillar' amongst more wide-ranging assessments of the social and economic dimensions of a policy or legislative choice.

Taking into account the highly political context of decision making at European Union level (particularly Member States' related sensitivities about national sovereignty and EU competence), the form of impact assessment advanced by the Commission performs a further function of justifying particular proposals, which hitherto has not been adequately represented by either of the previous (information and culture) theoretical models of environmental assessment. Although this justificatory role of environmental assessment is not unique to this setting of supranational governance,[133] here it creates ambiguity about the purpose of the internal assessment process. For example, in its *Communication on Impact Assessment*, the Commission states:

As to the final policy choice, the final options will emerge through the Impact Assessment process. Sometimes the impact assessment may point towards a preferred basic approach and the optimal policy instrument early in the process. Subsequent analysis will then focus on improving the effectiveness of the proposal in terms of changes introduced to key design parameters or stringency levels. It may also identify accompanying measures to

---

[130] See Ch. 2, pp. 58–9.

[131] European Commission, *Better Regulation*, COM(2002) 276 final (Brussels: CEC, 2002). See also European Commission, *Simplifying and Improving the Regulatory Environment* COM(2001) 726 final (Brussels: CEC, 2001).

[132] As advanced in European Commission, *Towards a Reinforced Culture of Consultation and Dialogue—Proposal for General Principles and Minimum Standards for Consultation of Interested Parties by the Commission*, COM(2002) 277 (Brussels: CEC, 2002) which details minimum standards for public consultation and enhanced information access provision.

[133] e.g. the justificatory role of environmental assessment is apparent in several of the case studies, particularly the Kentish Flats windfarm case study, Ch. 4, pp. 140–6, and the Cairngorm funicular railway case study, Ch. 7, pp. 272–81.

maximise positive and minimise negative impacts . . . The reasons for the most preferred policy option will be clearly outlined in the Impact Assessment Report. Alternative instruments that meet the same set of policy objectives should always be considered at an early stage in the preparation of policy proposals.[134]

This passage suggests an iterative and deliberative process. But the *Communication* continues: 'The assessment report will justify the chosen policy option, after having examined alternatives'.[135] This suggests a legitimatory role for environmental assessment in terms of specific proposals or policies, but also for regulatory intervention in a broader sense. The role of impact assessment as a way of 'substantiating and improving communication on Commission policy-making'[136] is similarly emphasized by DG Environment:

Thinking through all the implications of a policy proposal before it is agreed will mean that the policy is more likely to succeed. Making policy in this way means that the adverse side effects are identified and addressed before they become real problems. It will be possible to demonstrate to the public, NGOs, Member States, Council and the European Parliament that the policy has been carefully considered. This is especially important for the Parliament and Council since they increasingly expect to see information about the environmental implications of all policies. A policy that has been subject to an environmental assessment is therefore more likely to be acceptable to the Council and Parliament than one that has not. Providing such information would also respond to NGO concerns and interests that are normally expressed during the policy development process.[137]

Avowedly, the main impetus to develop an internal impact assessment procedure is to create an integrated policy and legislative appraisal procedure which allows for broad, and cross-sectoral, consideration of alternative policy choices by regulating decision-making processes. The inherently integrated, and interdisciplinary, nature of environmental assessment offers an ideal opportunity to pursue this. However, this development does not come without some cost. DG Environment recognize that the consequence of merging existing assessments in a single instrument, allowing for the overall consideration and assessment of impacts, is the identification of trade-offs between competing objectives,[138] rather than a wholesale shift in the culture of decision making in favour of environmental protection interests. This suggests the potential marginalization of an integrated, but diluted, environmental policy, reduced to a material consideration in the decisions taken by the institutional and financial heavyweights of the European Commission Directorates concerned with transport, competition, the internal market, and agriculture. An example of this was the attempt to reorient

---

[134] e.g. the justificatory role of environmental assessment is apparent in several of the case studies, particularly the Kentish Flats windfarm case study, Ch. 4, pp. 140–6, and the Cairngorm funicular railway case study, Ch. 7, pp. 272–81.   [135] ibid. 10.
[136] DG Environment, 'Information note on the Communication on Impact Assessment (IA)', 14.6.02.   [137] DG Environment, *Impact Assessment* 6–7.
[138] DG Environment, 'Information Note on the Communication on Impact Assessment', 14.6.02.

the Common Agricultural Policy,[139] which, whilst having some influence, did not change fundamentally the culture of decision making in a Directorate influenced by farming, petrochemical, and certain Member States' interests.[140]

The concern that an enlarged impact assessment procedure will facilitate the identification and making of trade-offs between policy objectives is borne out by the methodological principles guiding the Commission's internal impact assessment procedure. In its *Communication on Impact Assessment* (2002), the Commission states:

> The economic, social and environmental impacts identified for the proposed option should be analysed and presented in a format that facilitates a better understanding of the trade-offs between competing economic, social, and environmental objectives. To show the different impacts, make comparisons easier and identify trade-offs and win-win situations in a transparent way, it is desirable to quantify the impacts in physical and, where appropriate, monetary terms (in addition to a qualitative appraisal).[141]

The Commission then acknowledges that impacts that cannot be expressed in quantitative or monetary terms should not necessarily be seen as less important. Notwithstanding this brief acknowledgement of the role of 'qualitative appraisal', the methods of assessment advocated by the Commission are largely reductionist and simplistic. Surprisingly, few lessons appear to have been learnt about the discrediting of neoclassical economic models of valuation in recent years, particularly cost-benefit analysis, or the surpassing of economist methodology with techniques more sensitive to the unique quality of environmental values. Perhaps more surprisingly, DG Environment also closely adheres to this outmoded approach of identifying and valuing impacts in its *Impact Assessment: Environment Guide*, distributed throughout the Commission to ensure adequate account is taken of environmental impacts in the new cross-policy impact assessment procedure:

> Quantifying the effects that a policy proposal has on the environment is extremely useful and effective. Giving figures or values to the impacts, perhaps in monetary terms, means that they can be more easily compared with economic benefits for instance. The Commission should be provided with a clear idea of the scale of the implications of any policy. For example, the policy proposal may bring 500,000 extra tourists to a region of

---

[139] See, for example, Art. 13 of Regulation 1257/99/EC on support for rural development, OJ 1999 L 160, p. 80 which seeks, through various means, to promote sustainable farming systems. See also, European Commission, Communication from the Commission, *Indicators for the Integration of Environmental Concerns into the Common Agricultural Policy* COM(2000) 20 final (Brussels: CEC, 2000).

[140] For a broad critique of this and similar attempts to 'green EU governance', see D. Wood, 'Challenging the Ethos of the European Union: A Green Perspective on European Union Policies and Programmes for Rural Development and the Environment', in J. Holder and D. McGillivray (eds.) *Locality and Identity: Environmental Issues in Law and Society* (Aldershot: Ashgate, 1999). On more recent developments in reorienting the CAP, see M. O'Neill, 'Agriculture, the EC and the WTO: A Legal Critical Analysis of the Concepts of Sustainability and Multifunctionality' (2002) 4 *Env L Rev* 144.   [141] European Commission *Communication on Impact Assessment*, 16.

the Community but at a cost of a 20% worsening of air quality in those urban areas which is likely to cause 6,000 early deaths a year. By being as precise as possible about the effects, the Commission will have the best possible information on which to take the decision . . . For the more strategic policies, the impacts will probably need to be expressed in qualitative ways rather than quantitative ways since meaningful figures (e.g. a 15% loss of a specific habitat across the Community) are unlikely to be possible.[142]

The search for 'meaningful figures', described by DG Environment in its guide to impact assessment from an environmental perspective, suggests instead the 'economisation of environmental values'[143] by which to better identify and secure trade-offs between policy sectors and policies. Such a critique applies generally to balancing exercises, such as that implicit in sustainable development. More specifically, this methodological approach is out of step with the Commission's drive to further encourage lay participation in decision making. This inevitably produces judgments about the significance of impacts which are difficult to quantify in economic terms. A related issue is that as plans stand consultation will take place after the environmental assessment report is complete. According to DG Environment, this situation does not adequately reflect the requirement of the Aarhus Convention,[144] and commitments under the proposed minimum standards on consultation[145] to provide for public participation at an early stage in decision making,[146] even taking into account that in any event decision making at the European Union level produces difficulties for engaging the public and interested parties, other than professional lobbyists. A key point is that the methodologies advanced for the impact assessment procedure appear likely to give weight to economic factors, by fitting environmental values into crude economic models (such as cost-benefit analysis) and adopting economic language, objectives, and methods, all of which may have the effect of excluding alternative values and policy choices.

Role of Alternatives in Internal Impact Assessment

The consideration of alternatives is a guiding principle of the Commission's internal impact assessment procedure, along with consideration of the principles of subsidiarity and proportionality. As mentioned above, all preliminary impact assessments must document which policy options are available to reach a particular objective, and what range of alternatives will be considered (as well as demonstrating how the principles of subsidiarity and proportionality have been taken into account). An enhanced duty to consider alternatives is imposed at the second stage of assessment, the compilation of an extended impact assessment, so that: '[W]here the environmental assessment process shows that there will be substantial

---

[142] European Commission *Communication on Impact Assessment*, 20.

[143] D. McGillivray, 'Valuing Nature: Economic Value, Conservation Values and Sustainable Development' (2002) 14 *JEL* 85, at 100.   [144] See Appendix VI.   [145] ibid.

[146] DG Environment, *Internal Note: Impact Assessment: Environment Guide* (ex 'Better Policies Guide'), 3.7.02.

adverse impacts on the environment, different ways of achieving the policy objectives might need to be considered. As these new ideas are developed, the environmental assessment process should continue in parallel.'[147]

This emphasis upon the consideration of alternatives is not restricted to the development of the Commission's internal impact assessment procedure, as the above discussion on alternatives in EC conservation law suggests.[148] It already exists in several other areas of European law. In the field of chemicals,[149] the Court of Justice has approved national legislation on the basis that no safer replacement product was available and provided that alternative, less harmful (to public health and the environment) solutions were sought, in accordance with the 'substitution' principle derived from health and safety law[150] which seeks to eliminate or reduce risks by replacing dangerous substances with less dangerous substitutes. In this case also, the Court applied the familiar proportionality test, that national rules are compatible with the EC Treaty only to the extent that they are necessary for the effective protection of the health and life of humans, and not if the health and life of humans may be protected just as effectively by measures which are less restrictive of intra-Community trade. The evaluation of alternatives is also seen clearly in typical trade/environment dilemmas, such as in *Commission v Denmark*[151] in which a choice of alternatives justified by EC law was clearly considered by the Court as part of its judgment on the proportionality, or otherwise, of the national rules requiring a deposit and return scheme for bottles (thus encouraging recycling) and the re-use of approved containers, the latter conferring an enhanced environmental benefit, but deemed disproportionate by the Court. In this case, the need to consider alternatives may be understood to be a variant of the principle of proportionality, since both principles set up the conditions for inquiry into other (less restrictive or less harmful) means of achieving a desired aim. The similarity of the inquiry pursued by the two principles[152] suggests that judgments about alternatives may be subject to similar criticism to those levelled against the Court's intuitive application of the principle of proportionality.[153] Most forthrightly, Scott states:

[P]roportionality should be viewed as art not science. It demands not only a necessarily subjective assessment of the degree of environmental worth attaching to Member State

---

[147] European Commission, *Impact Assessment: Environment Guide* (2002).
[148] See pp. 158–62.
[149] In Case C-473/98 *Kemikalieinspektionen* v *Toolex Alpha* [2000] ECR I-5681.
[150] Directive 89/391/EEC on the introduction of measures to encourage improvement in the safety and health of workers at work (OJ 1989 L 183, p. 1) and Directive 90/394/EEC on the protection of workers at work (OJ 1990 L 196, p. 1).
[151] Case 302/86 [1988] ECR 4607. See also Case C-131/93 *German Crayfish* [1994] ECR I-3303.
[152] Nollkaemper similarly considers that the alternative solutions test is directly related to the proportionality (the least drastic means) test, 'Habitat Protection', at 281.
[153] L. Kramer, *Casebook on EC Environmental Law* (London: Sweet and Maxwell, 1st edn., 1993), 98–9, in which he criticizes the Court's judgment in *Danish Bottles* as sanctioning an insufficient level of environmental protection, via its decision about the proportionality of the national rule.

action, and of the costs associated with this in terms of market fragmentation, but also a balancing of competing, and arguably incommensurable, goals (integration and environment) . . . Such language of necessity, proportionality and alternative means sounds, or ought to sound, warning bells in the minds of environmental lawyers.[154]

Scott's main concern is that the method of ascertaining the proportionality of a measure 'appears to be predicated upon a naïve faith in the revelationary potential of science, and an assumption of knowledge, pertaining especially to the existence, magnitude and origins of environmental risk'.[155] Although this view of the 'naïve faith' in science belongs to an earlier period, and recent judgments such as *Pfizer*[156] show much greater subtlety in appreciating scientific uncertainty, the critique remains relevant to an analysis of the need to consider alternatives. This is that apparently scientific, or technical, assessments of alternatives may equally be informed by the need to secure political or institutional advantage, or to pursue a political agenda such as deregulation.

Returning to the development of an internal impact assessment procedure within the Commission, a possible future development is the subtle rearranging of the requirement to consider alternatives, in order to ensure that DG Environment, and other Directorates, justify a particular choice of instrument, as opposed to alternative, and less onerous instruments, such as market mechanisms, or even the 'do-nothing' alternative of not regulating an area (or not regulating it further).[157] This possibility is clarified by the Commission: 'The reasons for the most preferred policy option will be clearly outlined in the Impact Assessment Report. Alternative instruments that meet the same set of policy objectives should always be considered at an early stage in the preparation of policy proposals'.[158] A long list of the generic types of policy instruments, or 'regulator's toolbox',[159] that should be considered then follows: 'prescriptive regulatory actions; co-regulatory approaches (e.g. social dialogue); market-based instruments (e.g. emission trading, taxation); financial interventions (e.g. subsidies, co-financing, seed or risk financing), action aiming at Voluntary Agreements or self-regulation; Information, networking or co-ordination activities',[160] and so on. This supports Weiner's argument on the nature of instrument choice in response to global environmental problems that 'the economics of instrument choice are embedded in and contingent on the underlying legal system',[161] and are thus quite different from the sorts of choices operating at the national level.

---

[154] Scott, *EC Environmental Law*, 70.   [155] ibid.

[156] T-13/99 *Pfizer Animal Health SA* v *Council of the EU* [2002] ECR II-3305.

[157] Pers. comm. Ludwig Kramer, 10.4.03.

[158] European Commission, *Communication from the Commission on Impact Assessment*, 9.

[159] See, on the 'toolbox' idea, Bell and McGillivray, *Environment Law, passim* (see e.g p. 6); J. Weiner, 'Global Environmental Regulation: Instrument Choice in Legal Context' (1999) 108 *Yale LJ*, 679, and in the European context, L. Fisher, 'Unpacking the Toolbox: Or Why the Public/Private Divide is Important in EC Environmental Law', forthcoming.

[160] European Commission, *Communication on Impact Assessment*, 9.

[161] Weiner, 'Global Environmental Regulation', at 681.

The European Union offers a further, and different legal context, as demonstrated by Fisher,[162] which has proved highly amenable to market-based mechanisms, in part because of the habitual problem of ensuring the effectiveness of more uniform, 'classical' instruments, such as licensing regimes, applying set quality or emission standards. The message from the Commission from a number of sources is that the flexibility and other apparent advantages offered by market mechanisms should now be seriously considered in the impact assessment process.

This approach is illustrated by the range of alternatives considered in a preliminary impact assessment on a thematic strategy on the prevention and recycling of waste[163] under the heading 'What policy options are available to reach the objective? What range of alternatives will be considered?'[164] Under review is an environmental protection measure, but the considerations relating to alternatives are clearly broader, including competition and flexibility.

There is a wide range of policy options discussed in a draft communication which is currently being debated. These concern on the one hand potential targets for waste prevention and recycling and policy approaches with which such targets can be achieved on the other hand. As regards targets, this is intended to address in particular the potential role and effectiveness of material-oriented targets; the possibility of introducing greater flexibility to take into account local conditions by setting targets for the Community as a whole. This would also have implications for competition in the recycling industry; and the scope for using tradable permit systems to implement recycling schemes at Community level. As regards waste prevention, policy approaches put to the debate are waste prevention plans, pay-as-you-throw schemes and qualitative prevention in line with the principles of the Chemicals Strategy. As regards waste recycling, particular instruments mentioned include economic instruments such as landfill taxes, producer responsibility and tradable certificates as well as refinement of definition and setting of standards for recycling to ensure a level playing field for recycling. The role of R&D and demand-side measures will be discussed. The European institutions and stakeholders will be invited to comment and present any alternatives they consider useful.

This example demonstrates the enlargement of the scale of environmental assessment, from individual projects on particular sites, to the assessment of diverse policy choices, and consideration of a range of regulatory instruments. But the explicit need to consider alternatives in the impact assessment process may be extended still further, as a means of questioning the need to regulate at all. Borrowing from environmental assessment, in which the consideration of an inherently anti-development, 'do-nothing', option is generally considered good practice, the Commission's form of impact assessment requires a similar assessment, but with regard to regulatory activity. This is a shift from the purpose of impact assessment, as conceived by the European Commission, of improving and simplifying the 'regulatory environment' to one of justifying the decision to

---

[162] Fisher, 'Unpacking the Toolbox'.
[163] European Commission, *Preliminary Impact Assessment on the Thematic Strategy on the Prevention and Recycling of Waste* (Brussels: CEC, 2002). [164] ibid.

regulate in the first place. Arguably, this form of assessment is a continuation of the Commission's concern with better and simpler regulation, and is consequently a result of a different political logic to that of ecologization, discussed earlier, except that it additionally fulfils the role of integrating previously disparate concerns, including environmental protection. The duality of impact assessment is emphasized by guidelines for Commission staff on 'How to Assess Impacts' which opens with a quotation from the White Paper on *European Governance*, revealing the priorities being pursued:

Proposals must be prepared on the basis of an effective analysis of whether it is appropriate to intervene at EU level and whether regulatory intervention is needed? If so, the analysis must also assess the potential economic, social and environmental impact, as well as the costs and benefits of that particular approach. A key element in such an assessment is ensuring that the objectives of the proposal are clearly defined.[165]

Such an approach is to be welcomed as a means of ruling out regulation which may be more costly than it needs to be, or regulation which is too prescriptive. But it also suggests that the requirement to consider alternatives to regulation may in future operate as a brake on legislative proposals, particularly as a result of inter-institutional pressure, whilst offering some assurance that environmental factors have been taken into account. There are two dimensions to the potentially justificatory function performed by the need to consider alternatives in the European Commission's form of impact assessment, which tally with the related principles of proportionality and subsidiarity: first, as justification for a particular instrument choice, or the appropriate form of regulation, as enshrined in the principle of proportionality; and second, as a means to justify the decision not to regulate in an area at all, related to subsidiarity-type concerns about competence. The consideration of 'alternatives' in both cases is suggestive of the rationality of decision making using assessment procedures. But the consideration of alternatives (as with judgments of proportionality) is a highly political act of decision making, and illustrates how impact assessment, as a technique of modern European governance, may be used to gloss over decisions about deregulation, and appropriate instrument choice, however benignly these may be portrayed, particularly in terms of their compatibility with sustainable development.[166]

To sum up the key points arising from this case study, the Commission's development of an expanded form of impact assessment, reliant upon the need to consider alternatives, demonstrates that environmental assessment is clearly capable of affecting decision making on different scales. This study also suggests that the

---

[165] European Commission, *White Paper on European Governance* COM(2001) 428 final, quoted in internal document, European Commission, *How to Assess Impacts: Guidelines for Commission Staff* (Brussels: CEC, 2002).
[166] For example in the Fifth Environmental Action Programme, *Towards Sustainability: A European Community Programme of Policy and Action in Relation to the Environment and Sustainable Development*, COM(92) 23 final which focuses upon 'instrument choice'.

experience of internal impact assessment is likely to shape the future development of environmental assessment regimes at the national level. Thus, although to some extent the developments in the Commission replicate those having occurred elsewhere,[167] the Commission's particular initiative reflects current developments in environmental assessment[168]—the convergence of the *form* of environmental assessment, combined with the expansion of its *scope*, to embrace the sustainability criteria of social, environmental, and economic impacts and interrelations. In particular, the latter development of a type of 'sustainability assessment' is an example of the exploitation of the integrated nature of environmental assessment. An irony revealed by this case study is that the integrative and interdisciplinary quality of environmental assessment may lessen the importance of environmental assessment, in a broader, and more integrated, policy sweep. Related to this, perhaps the most important aspect of this practical example of the extension of environmental assessment as a means to integrate a broader spectrum of concerns is that it reflects the key conceptual weaknesses of sustainable development—that undue emphasis may be placed upon developmental imperatives, with consideration, though not necessarily protection, given to the environmental dimension. A very real concern is that the enlargement of assessment procedures to take account of various dimensions of policy and law making will facilitate trade-offs between competing policy objectives. Although it is still very early days, the European Commission's development of an internal environmental assessment regime demonstrates the potential sharp end of the drive for integration of environmental protection in a broader policy context.

At this point it is useful to reflect on the different contexts of environmental assessment under discussion, in particular the strength or validity of an analogy between the Commission's proposals on impact assessment and the development of the EIA and SEA Directives which have the purpose of governing decision making in the Member States. Environmental impact assessment, at least, is a precursor to administrative or judicial decisions, whereas impact assessment precedes a political decision (to adopt particular legislation). An obvious difficulty is that 'rationality' in political decision making is not the same as might be expected from a local planning authority in making a determination under the EIA Directive. Hence, the (political) reasons for adopting the proposal may be quite different from those produced by the impact assessment. However, analysis of other case studies in this book[169] suggest that all kinds of decision making involving environmental assessment can be political, even though set in different legal contexts. This apart, the Commission's development of impact assessment is highly relevant because of the likelihood of a similar form of sustainability analysis being introduced in the Member States' legal systems in the near future.

---

[167] For example, a form of regulatory impact assessment is now commonplace in the United Kingdom, as encouraged by HM Government, *Policy Appraisal and the Environment* (London: HMSO, 1992).   [168] Discussed initially in Ch. 2, but also by way of conclusion in Ch. 8.
[169] Particularly the Cairngorm funicular railway case study, Ch. 7, pp. 272–81.

Conclusions

I began this chapter by considering legal resistance to the consideration of alternatives, due to a traditional emphasis upon developers' rights of exploitation of their property, enshrined in planning law, and the associated restricted definition of alternatives in terms of locations or sites. I suggested that this resistance is now under some strain from the influence of precautionary approaches to development, and broader acceptance of the conceptual underpinnings of environmental assessment, particularly the necessary disengagement with a particular site, in favour of considering broader ecological effects, especially by strategic environmental assessment. Nevertheless, as I suggested when reviewing the case study on the Kentish Flats windfarm, the need to consider alternatives remains capable of being exploited by developers wishing to demonstrate the 'need for' a certain project, rather than viable alternatives to it, and may be restricted by technological concerns.

In the second part of the chapter I considered the development of internal impact assessment procedures in the European Commission, designed with the express intention of making the consideration of alternatives (alongside compliance with the principles of proportionality and subsidiarity) more explicit. Analysing this case study suggests a function of environmental assessment, beyond that of providing information or changing the culture of decision making—its justificatory role, both in terms of appropriate instrument choice, and the decision to legislate in the first place. The deliberate consideration of alternatives proves central to this role.

In relation to the public–private divide, referred to throughout this book, the case study on the European Commission's development of impact assessment procedures places under some strain the thesis that reflexive and procedural techniques of environmental law, such as environmental assessment,[170] are 'in safe hands' in public institutions, or the non-industrial sector, far from the temptation of bias or persuasion,[171] and as a complement to public law regulation. The main significance of the internal application of environmental assessment in the European Commission is that it marks a shift from the identification of environmental assessment as a self-regulatory mechanism[172] capable of being used by private developers to their advantage,[173] to the use of the instrument in public administration as a braking and possibly deregulatory mechanism. Importantly, this is justified in the name of 'better', 'simpler' regulation and governance. When applied internally the impact assessment procedure may be used as a means to

[170] See further Ch. 7, pp. 249–50.
[171] The main argument of Gaines and Kimber, 'Redirecting Self-Regulation'.
[172] See further, Bregman and Jacobsen, 'Environmental Performance Review'.
[173] See Elworthy and Holder, *Environmental Protection*, ch. 10, which discusses this role of assessment in the context of a by-pass scheme.

demonstrate the ecological rationality of decisions about policy and legislative proposals, but also as a political lever by the Directorates. The neutral and indeed beneficial use of environmental assessment within public organizations, in particular the requirement to consider alternatives, should be subject to greater scrutiny in the light of the Commission's development of an overarching impact assessment model. An important aspect of the European Commission's development of a form of impact assessment is the relative lack of opportunity for public participation. This is discussed in general terms in the following chapter.

6

Participation and Protest

'Environmentalism as democratic reform'[1] is a phrase used to describe developments relating to environmental assessment, emphasizing that the regulation of decision-making procedures has entered the 'big picture' of law and politics, as well as having informed judicial thinking.[2] This tendency is identified in the first two chapters of this book[3] which outline how the evolution of environmental assessment has mirrored, and to some extent directed, certain developments in environmental law. These include an increasing reliance upon reflexive strategies, such as requiring information on the likely impacts of activities upon the environment, and conferring responsibility for the alleviation of these on a broader range of groups and individuals than hitherto. These regulatory developments correspond to methods of governance which rely upon enhanced coordination, communication, and above all participation, of groups and individuals. However, having analysed the role of science, particularly ecological science, in the prediction of impacts of development on the environment,[4] I concluded that although environmental assessment is an inherently interdisciplinary exercise the emphasis upon modelling and quantitative information and the objectification of information in developers' environmental statements mean that a range of values and viewpoints are not fully represented by the environmental assessment process. As Lee and Abbott surmise of environmental decision making as a whole, a technicist approach can 'crowd out' public participation.[5]

In this chapter I return to these considerations but focus on individual rights to participate in the assessment process under the EC EIA Directive[6] which, in

---

[1] In the United Kingdom, see McCracken, 'Environmental Assessment'. See also R. McCracken, 'EIA and Judicial Review: Some Recent Trends' (2003) 8 *JR* 31. In the United States, see C. Sabel, A. Fung and B. Karkkainen, 'After Backyard Environmentalism': Towards a Model of Information-Based Environmental Regulation' (1999) 25 *Boston Review* 4, and in the context of EU governance, H. Heinelt, T. Malek, R. Smith, and A. E. Toller (eds.), *European Union Environmental Policy and New Forms of Governance* (Aldershot: Ashgate, 2001).

[2] For example in *Richardson v North Yorkshire County Council and Secretary of State* [2003] EWCA Civ 1860 (CA) the applicants were granted leave to appeal by Richard J in the following terms: 'The case raises issues of some importance concerning the EIA regime and the workings of local democracy that in my view provide a compelling reason why an appeal should be heard' (as discussed in the Court of Appeal at para. 4). [3] Ch. 1, pp. 5–6, and Ch. 2, pp. 56–7.

[4] Ch. 3.

[5] M. Lee and C. Abbot, 'The Usual Suspects? Public Participation under the Aarhus Convention' (2003) 66 MLR 80, at 84.

[6] Directive 85/337/EEC on the assessment of the effects of certain public and private projects on the environment (the EIA Directive). See Appendix II.

common with the development of other human rights approaches to environmental protection, are in the form of procedural rather than substantive rights.[7] This Directive, which represented the European Community's main legislative initiative to improve public participation of decision making when it was first adopted, is now subject to the requirements of the Directive on participation[8] which implements the relevant parts of the Aarhus Convention[9] and is designed to further enhance participation in environmental assessment and other contexts. This Directive concretizes new governance approaches to participation in environmental decision making.

In this chapter theories of participation are related to new approaches to governance and regulatory strategies therein. The main question addressed is whether the more varied forms of participation described in contemporary deliberative theories and increasingly deployed by the European Union are capable of substantially reducing the reliance upon apparently objective or quantitative information in environmental assessment. This and several other issues relating participation to decision making regulated by environmental assessment are analysed in a case study on the Dibden Bay port development in which the contribution of the public to decisions about the environmental effects of the development was limited by the complexity of scientific information elicited in the course of the environmental assessment process and public planning inquiry. This leads me to consider the place and role of environmental information derived from the environmental assessment process in the more traditional forum of the public planning inquiry where a range of considerations beyond environmental protection are addressed.

Having outlined the requirements for participation in environmental assessment, I examine claims made generally for deliberation. I apply these to environmental assessment by mapping instrumental and dignitarian theories of participation onto information and cultural theories of environmental assessment. This discussion takes place within an apparent consensus about the benefits of decision making by deliberation in terms of outcomes and increasingly as a means to link environmental justice with environmental democracy, although arguments in favour of authoritativeness and technicism in decision making still exist. The practical experience of participation in environmental assessment procedures is taken into account, contrasting the recent attempts to engage the public with still 'unheard voices' in decision making, particularly the planning system.[10] Case law concerning revived permissions and reserved matters provides further examples of the circumvention of participation in

---

[7] This distinction forms the subject of Ch. 7. I also briefly consider the relationship between environmental assessment and human rights in Ch. 8, pp. 291–4.

[8] Directive 2003/35/EC providing for public participation in respect of the drawing up of certain plans and programmes relating to the environment and amending with regard to public participation and access to justice Council Directives 85/337/EEC and 96/61/EC OJ L 156, p. 17. See Appendix VIII.   [9] Arts. 6 and 7. See Appendix VI.

[10] On this point, note Clause 17 Planning and Compulsory Purchase Bill requires the compilation of 'statements of community involvement'. Also of relevance here is the issue of developers charging

practice. Also relevant to the use of environmental assessment procedures by the public is the judicial aligning of the public interest with developmental interests of preventing costly delay in decisions whether to exercise discretion to uphold a grant of development consent. In considering these aspects of participation the overall aim is not so much to uncover whether participation is capable of delivering a 'better' substantive outcome in decisions governed by environmental assessment procedures,[11] as to highlight the disparity between rules relating to participation in environmental assessment and practical experience. This arises whenever the deliberative ideal of public participation is made to bend to the reality of everyday decision making. For example, time constraints significantly influence the quality of assessment in ecological and deliberative terms.

The gap between the ideal and practical experience of participation (as well as the current lack of opportunity given to third parties to contest decisions in the planning system) almost inevitably produces dissatisfaction amongst participants of environmental assessment processes, particularly those engaged in challenging development. Echoing Pugh-Smith's soundbite of environmental assessment, '[I]t is a potential snare for local planning authorities, a pitfall for developers, and a potent weapon in the hands of third party objectors',[12] I address an alternative use of environmental assessment as a protest strategy. Rather than participating in the process in accordance with deliberative ideals, invoking environmental assessment may 'buy' protesters time to publicize their case, as illustrated by the case of the Newbury bypass.

The issue of participation in environmental assessment raises a theme of the appropriate scale or level of decision making. I have argued throughout this book that environmental assessment has developed as a response to the extension of environmental concern and the recognition of the interrelated nature of the causes and effects of environmental problems, so that environmental considerations are properly examined beyond an individual project or site. This is seen clearly in the generic requirements to take account of the cumulative effects of a project,[13] or to consider alternatives.[14] However, the logical expression of such concerns in the Directive on SEA (the assessment of plans and programmes) and transboundary environmental assessment poses problems for active public participation because of the difficulty of defining a constituency of interested

---

a reasonable cost for a copy of the environmental statement, and the practice of charging for making representations about an environmental statement, on which see A. Ryall, 'The EIA Directive and the Irish Planning Participation Fee' (2002) 14 *JEL* 317.

[11] On the practical difficulty of this issue see Ch. 1, p. 11. Although a case has been made for participation as a means of achieving sustainable development, see J. Chun, 'A Critical Analysis of the Contribution to Sustainable Development of the Law and Practice on Public Participation in the Authorisation of Radioactive Waste Disposal' Ph.D. (London: UCL, 2003). Steele, in 'Participation and Deliberation in Environmental Law', pursues the argument that participation tends to improve the outcomes of decision making.

[12] Pugh-Smith, 'Environment Impact Assessments', at 1316.

[13] See Ch. 4, pp. 130–6.   [14] See Ch. 5, pp. 149–50.

participants. There are further practical matters of information provision, given that some of the advantages of providing local knowledge are lost in cases in which environmental assessment operates on a greater geographical scale. Some of these effects are captured by Chalmers who argues that in adopting the EIA Directive the EC created a space between the state and its citizens in national territories. Within this space the Directive established new political structures and forms of engagement by granting the public a formal right to be informed and the opportunity to express an opinion on the developments covered by the Directive and that this has intruded directly on Member States' traditional ability to control the political praxis within their territories.[15] The advent of transboundary environmental assessment requires this analysis to be extended to accommodate citizen action having effects upon the praxis of states to which they may be linked geographically but not politically. Macrory and Turner, for example, hold up this sort of transboundary procedural right as an emergent requirement of good environmental governance in Europe.[16]

A further trend is that a human rights dimension to protecting individual rights granted by the EIA Directive is superseding the less powerful function of informing the public about a development, which has hitherto been a prevailing rationale for environmental assessment. This sense of legal empowerment by participation in environmental assessment procedures may be discerned in Brooke LJ's judgment in *ex parte Huddleston*,[17] concerning whether an individual could enforce the Directive in the case of a mining permission 'revived' by the imposition of conditions. This method of revival had had the practical effect of circumventing rights of participation in the decision whether quarrying should proceed. Having dismissed the argument that Huddleston (who had lived for eighteen years in a house close to the quarry) was prevented from relying on the Directive because his case fell into the 'horizontality trap' (according to which an individual is prevented from relying upon rights contained in EC directives as against another individual) Brooke LJ continued:

> In my judgment, Mr Huddleston is entitled to say to the court: 'I, an individual citizen, should have had a valuable opportunity to take part in an informed consultation in relation to an extraction project which will detrimentally affect my home and the environment in which I live. Because the state has failed to comply with its obligations under the Directive, I am entitled to ask the court to give direct effect to the Directive. It is a matter of indifference to me that it was a different emanation of the state that created my dilemma when it enacted the provisions as to deemed consent (without a prior environmental impact assessment) for conditions relating to dormant old mining permissions

---

[15] Chalmers, 'Inhabitants in the Field of EC Environmental Law', 673.

[16] R. Macrory and S. Turner, 'Participation Rights, Transboundary Environmental Governance and EC Environmental Law' (2002) 39 *CML Rev* 489. On transboundary assessment, see Ch. 2, p. 54.

[17] *R v Durham County Council ex parte Huddleston* [2000] 1 WLR 1484. See further, below, pp. 208–9.

that are contained in paragraph 2(6)(b) of Schedule 2 to the 1991 [Planning and Compensation] Act. The state has failed to afford me my rights, and I am entitled to ask for an order which will give the 1985 Directive direct effect.[18]

This rights-based reading of participation in the environmental assessment process is derived from European Court of Justice authorities on the direct effect of the EIA Directive, most clearly the judgment in *Bozen*[19] in which the Court held that the Directive confers directly enforceable rights upon citizens of the Member State. This means that in a case in which discretion conferred by the provisions of the Directive had been exceeded (as by omitting altogether to consider whether an environmental impact assessment should take place), individuals may rely upon the Directive before a court of a Member State to require 'the setting aside of the national . . . measures incompatible with those provisions'.[20] This further developed Advocate-General Elmer's point in *Kraaijeveld*[21] that '[W]here a member state's implementation of the Directive is such that projects which are likely to have significant effects on the environment are not made the subject of an environmental impact assessment, the citizen is prevented from exercising his right to be heard'.[22] Underlying these pronouncements of 'directly enforceable rights'[23] conferred by the EIA Directive is a concern with the effectiveness of European Community environmental law, particularly because this instrument has proved notoriously difficult to implement. This casts the European Union's current emphasis upon participatory strategies and new governance approaches to regulation in a different light than purely giving effect to international obligations such as the Aarhus Convention (which similarly expresses individual procedural rights, and access to justice to protect these). Furthermore, these examples of respect for individual rights in environmental decision making raise the question of how this may be translated into environmental protection in the public interest, other than acceding to the view that 'the general public interest is the sum of many individual concerns'.[24]

The judgments in *Kraaijeveld* and *Bozen* have had profound effects on the extent to which rights to participate in the environmental assessment process have been upheld by the British courts. As well as the judgment in *Huddleston*, the most obvious expression of this is Lord Hoffmann's judgment in *Berkeley No. 1*:[25]

[T]he directly enforceable right of the citizen which is accorded by the Directive is not merely a right to a fully informed decision on the substantive issue. It must have been

---

[18] Para. 43.
[19] Case C-435/97 *World Wildlife Fund (WWF)* v *Autonome Provinz Bozen* [2000] 1 CMLR 149.
[20] At para. 71.
[21] Case C-72/95 *Aannemersbedrijf P.K. Kraaijeveld* v *Gedeputeerde van Staten Zuid-Holland* [1996] ECR I-5403.					[22] Para. 70 Opinion of A-G.
[23] Interestingly, the Court of Justice in *Kraaijeveld* avoided the terminology of 'direct effect'.
[24] A. Mathieson, 'Public Participation and Access to Justice' (2003) *EEL Rev* 37, at 38.
[25] *Berkeley* v *Secretary of State for the Environment (Berkeley No. 1)* [2000] 3 WLR 420, [2001] AC 603, (2001) 13 *JEL* 89.

adopted on an appropriate basis and that requires the inclusive and democratic procedure prescribed by the Directive in which the public, however misguided or wrongheaded its views may be, is given an opportunity to express its opinion on the environmental issues.[26]

Lord Hoffmann's elaboration of European Court of Justice authority meant that the House of Lords could no longer avail itself of the long-standing approach of the courts to retrospectively dispense with the requirement of environmental assessment on the ground that the outcome would have been the same or that the local planning authority or Secretary of State had all the information necessary to enable them to reach a proper decision on the environmental issues. This had amounted to a practical denial of the role of participation in decision making.[27] Hence, any infringement of this directly enforceable right precluded the Court from exercising its discretion to uphold the planning permission, a point I return to below.[28]

Taking participation seriously, whether from a rights perspective or because of a shift in regulatory theory and practice, involves considering the role of litigation in defining, constraining, and informing participation practices. This includes questioning the legitimacy associated with judicial review and the participation of the courts in planning decisions, even though the 'proper' role of the courts in these respects depends upon the normative basis ascribed to participation. Thus, for example, for advocates of deliberative democracy, judicial review serves as a means of policing the proper functioning of political decision-making processes and access to these, thus ensuring the inclusiveness of such processes. In this chapter I question this function by also considering judicial discretion to override environmental protection interests with a conception of the public interest which habitually prioritizes the financial rather than environmental interests at stake in new development.

Participation Requirements

Previously I have examined the prediction of environmental effects for the purpose of determining whether a full assessment should take place and as a matter of determining whether a project, plan, or policy should proceed, considerations both of which are based upon a judgment of the likely significance of effects on the environment. I have also considered the onus on the proponent of a project, plan, or policy to consider alternatives, and for the decision maker to take these into account.[29] Participation (or more accurately consultation) of a range of

---

[26] At 430.

[27] e.g. *Berkeley No. 1* [1998] Env LR 741 (CA); *R v Poole Borough Council ex parte Beebee* [1991] 2 PLR 27; *Wychavon District Council v Secretary of State for the Environment and Velcourt* [1994] Env LR 239. This point, including the important proviso of the 'substantial compliance' doctrine, is discussed further in Ch. 7, pp. 258–62.   [28] See pp. 218–22.

[29] Ch. 3, Ch. 4, and Ch. 5.

individuals and groups in order to elicit views on the proposal and the developer's environmental statement forms the next stage of the model environmental assessment process.[30] In the context of the regime under the EC EIA Directive, public participation in decision making is required by law and thus operates as a condition of the legality of the decision.[31] Article 6 is the key provision, establishing rules for the participation of the public in the assessment procedure, whilst also granting Member States discretion to establish the 'detailed arrangements' for the provision of information and consultation.[32] In greater detail, the Directive requires that Member States must ensure that any application for development consent and the accompanying environmental statement (compiled by the developer, according to guidance in Article 5 and Annex IV) 'are made available to the public within a reasonable time in order to give the public concerned the opportunity to express an opinion before the development consent is granted'.[33] It is then left up to the Member States to establish the arrangements for such information and consultation, including (and depending upon the particular characteristics of the projects or sites concerned) determining who are the 'public concerned', the places where the information can be consulted, the way in which the public may be informed, the manner in which the public is to be consulted, and to fix time limits for the stages of the procedure.[34]

These requirements are the result of amendments brought about by the 1997 EIA Directive which also included some textual changes and closed a loophole which had allowed the public concerned to 'express an opinion before the project is initiated' rather than 'before development consent is granted', as now. An important reform concerned the transboundary assessment of projects. The previously weak provision (requiring only that a Member State forward information provided by a developer to the other, likely to be affected, Member State at the same time that it makes it available to its own nationals) was strengthened by imposing an onus on the potentially 'affected' Member State to ensure that the public are given an opportunity to express their opinions on the project to the consenting authority in the Member State in which the project might be carried out. This deepens the obligations on Member States whilst also broadening the geographical range of the Directive's requirements. The strengthening of the transboundary assessment provisions makes it more difficult for Member States to pursue an 'island mentality'[35] with regard to other affected areas, and thus

---

[30] See process in outline, Ch. 2, p. 36.
[31] Steele, 'Participation and Deliberation in Environmental Law', at 415. On current good practice in the area, see Institite of Environmental Management and Assessment, *Perspectives: Guidelines on Participation in Environmental Decision Making* (Lincoln: IEMA, 2002).   [32] Art. 3(2).
[33] Art. 6(2).   [34] Art. 6(3).
[35] As demonstrated by the United Kingdom's original failure to implement Art. 7 at all (in the Town and Country Planning (Assessment of Environmental Effects) Regulations 1988 (SI 1988, No. 1199), a gap which was filled by the Town and Country Planning (Environmental Impact Assessment) (England and Wales) Regulations 1999 (SI 1999, No. 293) ('the 1999 Regulations')).

exploit an external accountability gap, by which environmental effects are disregarded when they fall in areas which are geographically remote from the source of the effects, and there are no formal or direct avenues of accountability.[36]

These provisions on information provision and consultation are mirrored almost exactly in the EC SEA Directive,[37] except for an additional reference to the public being given 'an early and effective opportunity . . . to express their opinion on the draft plan or programme or its submission to the legislative procedure' in the latter.[38] The large scale, and potentially abstract nature of the plans and programmes which form the subject of this Directive, raise considerable problems in 'identifying the public' for the purpose of securing effective participation.[39] This appears to be recognized in the inclusion of non-governmental organizations in the category of the 'public affected' since these are more likely to operate on the national and regional levels which form the subject of plans and programmes. Thus the criterion for defining the public (affected or likely to be affected by the plan or programme) is broadened to include 'having an interest' in a plan or programme.[40]

Notwithstanding the promulgation of provisions on participation in the EC Directives on EIA and SEA, these instruments describe a passive public, receiving a narrow category of information (the developer's environmental statement) and being consulted upon this rather than shaping the process through active participation. This suggests that the policy ethos of the original 1985 EIA Directive remains intact, notwithstanding its amendment in 1997. For example, there is no mention of participation in the preamble to the amended Directive, which might be compared with its revised focus upon the input of the developer and expert authorities in the process. The opportunities that the Directive carves out for consultation (rather than participation) are out of step with ideas of deliberation as a function of environmental assessment. As discussed further below, deliberation requires more extensive mechanisms than traditional consultation, since it moves beyond models of decision making based upon expertise, which use consultation primarily to provide information for decision makers.[41]

In general terms, European Community environmental law is increasingly influenced by the general rise of deliberative politics and a related 'consensus on the importance of public involvement in environmental decision-making'.[42]

---

[36] This is a term more usually applied in the context of law relating to trade, for example, see J. Scott, 'GMOs: The WTO and the EC' (2004) 56 *CLP* (forthcoming).

[37] Directive 2001/42/EC on the assessment of the effects of certain plans and programmes on the environment OJ 2001 L 197, p. 30. See Appendix III.

[38] Art. 6(2) of the EC Directive on SEA.

[39] Other areas of difficulty are considered in detail by Mathieson, 'Public Participation and Access to Justice'. [40] Art. 6(4).

[41] This state of affairs might be contrasted with the duty to 'encourage' participation under the Water Framework Directive.

[42] Lee and Abbott, 'The Usual Suspects?', at 80. Discussed below, pp. 195–9.

This has been given legal form in international law in the Aarhus Convention[43] which aims to improve participation in a range of decision-making activities.[44] The Directive on participation[45] forms part of a set of legislation and policy proposals aimed at bringing Community law into line with the Convention.[46] Compared to the EC Directives on EIA and SEA, this represents a reorientation from information provision and consultation, to giving the public 'early and effective opportunities to participate in decision-making procedures'[47] (as also stated in the SEA Directive, but with some important areas of elaboration). In addition to introducing standards for public participation in the drawing up of plans and programmes relating to the environment (not covered by the SEA Directive which is deemed Aarhus-compatible),[48] the Directive on participation amends several provisions of the EIA Directive and introduces several further measures. A key amendment significantly broadens the categories of information that the Member States shall make available to the public. In addition to information gathered by the developer in the form of an environmental statement, as already provided for, and the main reports and advice issued to the competent authority or authorities at the time when the public is informed of the request for development consent,[49] information which comes to light after this initial notification, and which is considered relevant to the final decision, must also be conveyed to the public. Such a provision may possibly cover the type of planning agreement reached between the developer and Highland Council in the Cairngorm funicular

[43] UN/ECE Convention on access to information, public participation in decision making and access to justice in environmental matters, Aarhus, 25 June 1998 (the Aarhus Convention) Arts. 6 and 7. See Appendix VI, full document available at http://www.unece.org/env/pp/documents/cep43e.pdf. An exception to the Community's upholding of the deliberative ideal is seen with regard to its own decision-making processes, and, related to this, the discrepancy between the provisions in Aarhus on access to justice and the routes to judicial review by the European Court of Justice defined in Arts. 230 and 232 of the EC Treaty. This is, belatedly, addressed in European Commission, Proposal for a Regulation of the European Parliament and of the Council, on the application of the provisions of the Aarhus Convention on access to information, public participation in decision-making and access to justice in environmental matters to EC institutions and bodies COM(2003) 622 final, which is relevant to internal impact assessment of policy and legislation (although the proposal does not currently apply to Community-financed projects in the Member States). On this last point, see further Ch. 5, pp. 164–81.

[44] Certain listed activities or other activities likely to have a significant effect on the environment (Art. 6), plans, programmes, and policies relating to the environment (Art. 7), and the preparation of regulations and/or generally applicable legally binding normative instruments (Art. 8).

[45] Directive 2003/35/EC. See Appendix VIII.

[46] Directive 2003/4/EC of the European Parliament and the Council on public access to environmental information and repealing Directive 90/313/EEC OJ 2003 L 41, p. 26; Directive 2003/35/EC; European Commission, Proposal for a Directive of the European Parliament and of the Council on access to justice on environmental matters, COM(2003) 624 final; and European Commission, Proposal for a Council Decision on the conclusion, on behalf of the European Community, of the Convention on access to information, public participation in decision making and access to justice regarding environmental matters, COM(2003) 625 final.

[47] Art. 3(4) of Directive 2003/35/EC which amends Art. 6.

[48] As expressed in Commission proposal for the amendment of Directive 85/337/EEC and Directive 96/61/EC, COM (2000) 839 (Brussels: CEC, 2000), though Mathieson, 'Public Participation and Access to Justice', at 46 ff. doubts this.

[49] Art. 6(4)(b) of the EC Directive on EIA as amended by the EC Directive on participation.

case, which was negotiated well after a formal application for planning permission and accompanying environmental statement was submitted.[50] This suggests that the framers of this Directive conceive of environmental assessment as a process, with participation a feature of several stages of this, at least when compared to the more simplistic approach of the current EIA Directive which lays open for scrutiny by the public just the initial application for development consent and the developer's environmental statement.

The Directive aims generally at inclusiveness, for example by the requirement that the arrangements for public participation be notified to the public likely to be affected by the proposed project. Importantly, it revises existing procedures by entitling the public 'to express comments and opinions when all options are open to the competent authority or authorities before the decision on the request for development consent is taken'.[51] This potentially engages the public in the consideration of alternatives, before options have become fixed. Nevertheless the space for public involvement remains within existing boundaries to the extent that there are no opportunities for public participation on the initial screening decision, nor the scoping of the assessment to be conducted (precedents for which exist in the system of environmental assessment in the Netherlands).[52]

Some expansion of the categories of information to be made available also applies to transboundary environmental assessment, with the notable exception of information which comes to light in the course of the assessment.[53] A guarantee of sorts exists in the requirement that detailed arrangements for such assessments shall 'be such as to enable the public concerned in the territory of the affected Member State to participate effectively in the environmental decision-making procedures',[54] although there is no parallel provision entitling the public in an affected Member State to be given '*early* and effective opportunities to participate', in particular by commenting upon possible options open to the authorities before a final decision is made, as now exists in the case of assessment procedures which do not have a transboundary dimension.[55]

The opportunity for the consenting authority to overlook the results of participation is narrowed slightly by a new Article 9. This extends the information to be made available to the public when a decision is reached.[56] Currently this includes the content of the decision and any conditions attached to this, the main reasons and considerations on which the decision is based, and a description of the main measures to avoid, reduce, and, if possible, offset the major adverse effects. The amended article requires information about the public participation process, alongside an oblique requirement that the main reasons and considerations

[50] See Ch. 7, pp. 272–82.
[51] New Art. 6(4) of Directive 85/337/EEC, as amended by Art. 3 of Directive 2003/35/EC.
[52] Sheate, *Environmental Impact Assessment* ch. 6.
[53] Art. 7.   [54] New Art. 7(5) inserted by Art. 3 of Directive 2003/35/EC.
[55] New Art. 6(4) inserted by Art. 3 of Directive 2003/35/EC.
[56] Art. 9. On the duty to give reasons, see further Ch. 7, pp. 269–72.

should be expressed 'having examined the concerns and opinions expressed by the public concerned'. This due process requirement potentially requires the decision maker to internalize the participatory elements of environmental assessment. It may also be seen as giving effect to the 'therapy', or legitimacy functions of environmental assessment.[57]

These provisions are strengthened by an enforceable right of access to judicial review to challenge the substantive or procedural legality of decisions, acts, and omissions subject to the public participation provisions of the Directive.[58] Some doubts exist about the actual meaning and the potential effect of this provision, particularly in terms of empowering non-governmental organizations. In relation to the regulatory nature of environmental assessment[59] the right of access to a review procedure to challenge the *substantive* or procedural legality of decisions, acts, or omissions subject to the public participation provisions of the Directive on environmental assessment is vital. Although it has been suggested that the introduction of a merits review by the courts on the basis of this provision would be a constitutional innovation and that, more likely, such a review would be satisfied by a proportionality test, or *Wednesbury* unreasonableness, it may well increase pressure for a third party right of substantive appeal, possibly by some form of environmental tribunal.[60]

In summary, the Directive on participation which will amend the existing EIA Directive in several important ways aims at a more inclusive, less technicist, environmental assessment procedure, with public involvement in decision making expressed in the manner of an entitlement to participate (and for the first time, a right of access to the courts to enforce its provisions). This is an advance on the more restricted information disclosure and consultation provisions of current forms of assessment. Such developments have been explained as arising from the application of theories of deliberative democracy to new governance approaches to regulation.

Theories of Participation and New Approaches to Governance

The basic claim for participation in environmental assessment as with other environmental decision-making procedures is that it contributes to the correctness or validity of decisions, by allowing assertions to be checked against the views of those who have local knowledge of an area, or are interested parties. This function of participation was expressly acknowledged in *Hardy No. 2*,[61] in which

---

[57] Discussed below, pp. 204–5.

[58] Art. 10a of the Directive on EIA, inserted by Art. 7 of the Directive on participation. See Appendix VIII.   [59] Discussed throughout this book, but particularly Ch. 7, pp. 237–43.

[60] Lee and Abbott, 'The Usual Suspects?', at 103.

[61] *Hardy No. 2* [2002] EWHC 1056 (Admin).

an application to challenge the grant of planning permission on the basis that the developer's environmental statement on the effects on conservation of the extension of a landfill site contained insufficient or inaccurate information was refused. Sullivan J commented that there is a clear distinction between a failure to comply with the 1999 Regulations and the provision of an environmental statement which is criticized by some parties. He stated that '[T]he whole purpose of the procedure under the Regulations is that the environmental statement being made public, parties may comment upon it, correct it, supplement it, and provide the council with additional environmental information which it may then consider'.[62]

More fundamental claims for participation now rest upon a deliberative ideal that better outcomes may be arrived at and, furthermore, that the process of deliberation is capable of inculcating environmental values which may encourage an ongoing sense of environmental responsibility in those involved in decision making—both participants and decision makers. Notwithstanding that such claims represent a considerable advance on the information gathering function traditionally ascribed to environmental assessment, the increasing identification of environmental assessment with this deliberative ideal, at least in terms of reflexive theory, suggests the need for some elaboration of this premise.

The Deliberative Ideal

The theoretical basis for the appreciation of participation and the accretion of legal instruments to secure this lies in deliberative politics. At the centre of this is the Habermasian ideal of 'deliberative democracy', or decision making by discussion, among a range of stakeholders whose lives are materially affected by these decisions. A strong claim for deliberation is that this improves the outcomes of decision making (possibly in favour of environmental protection) by reflecting more accurately the range of values present in multicultural society (beyond that offered by representative democracy), particularly about the acceptability of a particular risk. This recognizes the need for a broader range of knowledge, particularly local knowledge, to balance or question the prevalence of scientific technicism frequently employed to address the complexity and uncertainty of many environmental problems, and to encourage the communication and internalization of environmental values.[63] This form of decision making therefore provides a marked contrast to the instrumental rationality of decision making (and clashes of interests) which tends to result in the public being excluded from many decision-making fora.[64]

---

[62] At para. 34.

[63] J. Dryzek, *Discoursive Democracy: Politics, Policy and Political Science* (Cambridge: Cambridge University Press, 1990). See also F. Fischer, *Citizens, Experts and the Environment: The Politics of Local Knowledge* (Durham, NC and London: Duke Press, 2000).

[64] On the unchallengeability of scientific information in designation of land for conservation purposes, see D. Brock, 'Is Nature Taking Over?' [2003] JPL Occ. Papers No. 31, 50.

The encouragement of more collaborative forms of planning is a measure of the practical effect of the deliberative ideal, related to concerns about the mutual importance of local environmental democracy and sustainability in Local Agenda 21.[65] For example, in their experience of environmental plan-making, Burgess and Harrison found that the negotiated outcome of deliberation is more consistent with sustainable development than a set of pre-given, 'objective' solutions arrived at by experts, because of the importance of local knowledge in decisions about land use.[66] Participative decision making also contributes to trust being placed in those decisions, although from a critical perspective this raises the issue of undue legitimacy or 'symbolic reassurance' via proceduralization.

In the relationship between deliberative theory and environmental governance, enhancing participation is consistent with reducing the interventionist and regulatory role of the state (including developing local political structures through devolution) and replacing traditional, autonomous forms of bureaucracy and expertise in response to actual and perceived failures of expert regulation by public administration.[67] One example of a new approach to regulation which relies upon participation for its effectiveness is performance-based regulation (or the 'rolling rule regime') in the United States in which the constant reformulation of standards is based on information provided by local participants. As described by Sabel, Fung, and Karkkainen:[68]

... this emergent regulatory regime owes its success precisely to a counterintuitive but durable form of practical deliberation between and among environmentalists, developers, farmers, industrialists, and officials from distinct, perhaps competing, subdivisions of government—parties who are conventionally thought to be antagonists. In this problem-solving process, disciplined consideration of alternative policies leads protagonists to discover unanticipated solutions provisionally acceptable to all. Further deliberation leads to successive re-definitions of self-interest that permit robust collaborative exploration, including revision of institutional procedures, and even what is feasible.[69]

This form of deliberation is described as a novel form of democracy that combines localism and decentralism with national coordination. The centrality of information for establishing and revising environmental standards in this regime suggests a parallel with environmental assessment. However, the contexts in which environmental standard setting and environmental assessment take place are quite different because making a decision finalizes the assessment process, bringing deliberation to an end. There are also very few examples of ongoing

---

[65] e.g. Department of the Environment, Transport and the Regions, *Modernising Local Government: In Touch with the People* (London: DETR, 1998). See further P. Healey, *Collaborative Planning: Shaping Places in Fragmented Societies* (Basingstoke: Macmillan, 1997).

[66] Burgess and Harrison, 'Capturing Values for Nature'. C. Harrison and T. Bedford, 'Environmental Gains? Collaborative Planning, Planning Obligations, and Issues of Closure in Local Land-Use Planning in the UK', in J. Holder and C. Harrison (eds.) *Law and Geography* (Oxford: Oxford University Press, 2002).   [67] Lee and Abbot, 'The Usual Suspects?', at 80.

[68] 'After Backyard Environmentalism'.   [69] At p. 4.

monitoring in environmental assessment by which to engage the public in performance review. This tends to result in a snapshot approach to the regulation of behaviour which may be criticized as inimical to ecological principles.[70] This is less the case with strategic environmental assessment, in which case a series of assessment, procedures may be embarked upon as part of a continuous policy review (clearly when strategic environmental assessment is focused upon particular plans and programmes being considered for adoption, adoption will bring deliberation to an end at least until these are revised). Although finality (or discontinuity) is clearly a central feature of environmental impact assessment, ongoing adjustment of behaviour and standards which may contribute to organizational or social learning has been identified as a feature of the assessment process.

Social Learning and Awareness

A prominent theme of this book is the role of the developer in decision making, particularly the influence of developers' information provided in the form of an environmental statement. Related to this is the question of how motive and interests influence deliberative processes and may be supplanted by more general interests as a result of exposure to other values and information. The achievement of the latter has been attributed to new forms of governance which seek to stimulate environmental learning or awareness that will achieve shared responsibility for structural and institutional change amongst public and private groups and individuals, rather than merely making 'the best possible decision in advance'.[71] Accordingly, the view that participation encourages social learning is a central claim made for reflexive legal mechanisms. In this context, 'social awareness' describes the internalization of values as well as the accretion and assimilation of knowledge.

   In broad terms, learning is supposed to take place when individuals and organizations appreciate that their private interests are closely linked with broader social interests such as environmental protection. In turn this may lead to a greater awareness of how to alter behaviour in order to achieve this. The *process* of deliberation itself is thought to encourage the development of such awareness. As Cohen describes:

. . . participants in the ideal case will need to appeal to considerations that are quite generally recognised as having considerable weight and as a suitable base for collective choice, even

---

[70] See further Ch. 3, at pp. 92–4. Heinelt *et al.*, *European Union Environmental Policy*, 22 compare this aspect of EIA with EMAS (Eco-Management and Audit Scheme) which is characterized by continuity of decision making.

[71] D. J. Fiorino, 'Rethinking Environmental Regulation: Perspectives on Law and Governance' (1999) 23 *Harv Env L Rev* 441, at 452. Fiorino sets out a pattern of learning in policy making in the United States, the general premise of which may be applied to learning experiences in the case of environmental assessment.

among people who disagree about the right result: agreement on political values is not agreement on the proper combination of them. But when people do appeal to considerations that are quite generally recognised as having considerable weight, then the fact that a proposal has majority support will itself commonly count as a reason for endorsing it. Even people who disagree may, then, accept the results of a deliberative procedure as legitimate.[72]

More expansive claims for deliberation also appear to hinge upon the (specifically social) learning opportunities provided by enhanced public participation in environmental decision making. For example, since participation locates environmental issues in a public realm, this may mean that civil society is increasingly well informed[73] about potential environmental impacts or risks and are thus better able to contribute to decision making. However, this is to describe the public meeting on the expert's 'home ground'. The more telling test is when decision makers are being asked to accommodate 'irrational' (not scientifically based) activities as 'material considerations'. The fostering of civil society in the more limited 'home ground' manner is now a pervasive feature of European Union governance, including (increasingly) internal decision making.[74]

Expanding the opportunities for participation to encourage social learning has also led to a growing concern with environmental justice. This is related to environmental assessment to the extent that it relies upon identifying the disproportionate burden of predicted impacts imposed upon particular groups and areas. Along these lines Kuehn criticizes quantitative risk assessment on which environmental assessment methodology is most frequently based for making it more difficult for minority and low income communities to participate fully and effectively in deliberations about environmental risks. The related argument that environmental justice cannot be realized until those communities affected by environmental regulations have a voice in decision making equivalent to that of industry[75] (or, not so much 'having a voice' as speaking the same language) links distributive outcomes and exclusion from decision-making processes.[76]

The case for enhancing participation is therefore made by those who consider that deliberation broadens knowledge and values and helps to arrive at reasoned

[72] J. Cohen, 'Democracy and Liberty', in J. Elster (ed.) *Deliberative Democracy* (Cambridge: Cambridge University Press, 1998), 197–8.

[73] Steele, 'Participation and Deliberation', at 437.

[74] See European Commission, *European Governance—A White Paper* COM (2001) 428 final, as discussed in J. Scott and D. M. Trubeck, 'Mind the Gap: Law and New Approaches to Governance in the European Union' (2002) 8 *ELJ* 1, at 3. See also Proposed Regulation on the application of the provisions of the Aarhus Convention on access to information, public participation in decision making and access to justice in environmental matters in EC institutions and bodies COM (2003) 622 final.

[75] S. Kuhn, 'Expanding Public Participation is Essential to Environmental Justice and the Decision Making Process' (1995) 25 *Ecology LQ* 647, at 647. This linkage is also made by S. Foster, 'Justice from the Ground Up: Distributive Inequities, Grassroots Resistance and the Transformative Politics of the Environmental Justice Movement' (1998) 86 *Cal L Rev* 775.

[76] R. R. Kuehn, 'The Environmental Justice Implications of Quantitative Risk Assessment' (1996) *Univ of Ill L Rev* 103.

arguments, through the narrowing and final eclipse of personal or organizational interest. A critique of the deliberative ideal, based upon claims of social learning, is that interests inevitably continue to shape information and its communication in the process of ostensible deliberation. For example, deceptive 'pseudo-preferences' may be generated among people supposedly in deliberation, but generally seeking to manipulate the issues involved.[77] Such an observation may be related to the practice of presenting certain 'alternatives' and mitigating measures in developers' environmental statements. Against this is Steele's view that the discursive nature of deliberation actually broadens the range of possible solutions by emphasizing the power of reason. She suggests that 'rational dialogue of the relevant form supports those holding critical views to the extent that it seeks to infiltrate *prudential* thinking into economic rationality—for example, to introduce ecological rationality into economic activity'.[78] This provides a variant on Dryzek's prescription that ecological rationality should trump all other forms because these depend on an ecological resource base.[79] The thrust of this argument about the reality of interests and power relations is picked up by Lee and Abbotts with respect to the Aarhus Convention that '[A] move to participation needs to be informed by an awareness of the existing distribution of power and how participation will affect that power'.[80] One obvious way in which power relations may be masked and even sustained by deliberation is by the legitimatory function of participation. This is a potential problem in environmental assessment as discussed below.

Applying Public Participation Claims to Environmental Assessment: Instrumentalism and Dignitarianism

In applying deliberative models to decision making using environmental assessment (and other regulatory mechanisms), instrumentalism[81] stresses the need for strict procedural requirements to ensure accurate decision making. This traditional claim that the accuracy of decision making will improve from the contribution of local knowledge arising from participation roughly correlates to information theories of environmental assessment which emphasize the type and range of

---

[77] P. Fitzpatrick, 'Consolations of the Law: Jurisprudence and the Constitution of Deliberative Politics' (2001) 14 *Ratio Juris* 281, at 283.

[78] J. Steele, 'The Role of the Citizen: From Preferences and Values, to Deliberation?' Paper given at the Environmental Citizenship conference, University of Aberdeen, 2000.

[79] Dryzek, *Rational Ecology*, 59–60.

[80] 'The Usual Suspects?', at 107.

[81] For example, M. Bayles, *Procedural Justice: Allocating to Individuals* (Dordrecht: Kluwer, 1990); J. Mashaw, 'Administrative Due Process: The Quest for a Dignitary Theory' (1981) 61 *Boston Uni L Rev* 885, discussed by G. Richardson in 'The Legal Regulation of Process' in G. Richardson and H. Genn (eds.) *Administrative Law and Government Action* (Oxford: Clarendon, 1994). In the United States such an exercise is conducted by Hertz, 'Parallel Universes', comparing environmental assessment under NEPA and 'new property' tribunals.

information elicited by participation.[82] More fundamentally, the degree of participation is considered to affect the quality of the environmental impact analysis process which in turn affects the *quality* of the decision making.[83] In the context of environmental assessment this is because participation tends to result in a range of alternatives being presented to decision makers.[84]

A distinction may be made here with dignitarian approaches to participation which consider that procedures exist to foster and protect values, even independently of the final outcome.[85] At first sight, dignitarian approaches to participation relate to culture theories of environmental assessment. However, such theories rely more precisely on an idea that values in favour of environmental protection inform decision making and cannot and should not exist independently from the outcome. Furthermore, both instrumental and dignitarian approaches emphasize the importance of rights. In the case of the former (instrumental) approaches, the possession of a substantive right may trigger a secondary right to procedural protection; the latter dignitarian approaches are grounded in natural rights theory, and emphasize individual rights and autonomy. This focus upon rights means that the dual analysis (instrumental and dignitarian) of procedural requirements here departs from information and culture theories of environmental assessment since in the case of environmental assessment there is no clearly defined, individualized, *substantive* 'right' to be protected. The procedural right of participation in decision making which is increasingly recognized with regard to environmental assessment (primarily by the European Court of Justice) may more accurately be seen as a means, rather than an end or 'right' in itself.[86] This should make clear that environmental assessment procedures do not give expression to rules of natural justice, as is the case with some criminal and administrative law procedures. Rather, they accommodate a more limited form of due process. This is not to deny that human rights approaches to environmental law are gaining currency and may in future encourage a more rights-based approach to the enforcement of environmental assessment regimes.[87]

An argument more in line with culture theories of environmental assessment is that by broadening the range of information and values (about a proposal and alternatives to this), participation in environmental assessment encourages environmental learning or awareness amongst the decision maker, developer, and participants.

For analytical purposes, different types of learning may be advanced depending upon theoretical understandings of environmental assessment. In Table 6.1 the

---

[82] See an outline of information theories, Ch. 1, pp. 23–7.

[83] W. A. Tilleman, 'Public Participation in the Environmental Impact Assessment Process: A Comparative Study of Impact Assessment in Canada, the United States and the European Community' (1995) 33 *Colum J Trans L* 337, at 337.   [84] ibid.

[85] As described by Richardson, 'The Legal Regulation of Process', 111 ff. in the context of procedural requirements in administrative law.   [86] See Ch. 7, pp. 238–9.

[87] See Ch. 8, pp. 291–4.

Table 6.1 Participation, learning, and theories of environmental assessment[1]

Learning strategy	Organizational learning		
	Technical learning	Conceptual learning	Social learning/awareness
Characteristics/claims of participation	Expert-led: technical prediction of impact; fact-based methodologies	Lay participation: local knowledge	Civil dialogue; communication; cultural change; expression of values
	Consultation	Redefinition of goals	Structural openness; change in participant roles
	'Option alternatives'	'Alternative options'	Collective decision making
Model of deliberation	Instrumentalism: ensuring accurate decision making	Instrumentalism: ensuring broad base of information on which decision is based	Dignitarian: respect for values coupled with expression of values in outcome of decision
		Learning 'loops'	
		Redefining objectives/goals	
Corresponding theories of environmental assessment	←———— Information theories ————→		←———— Cultural theories ————→

[1]Applying the categories of social learning discussed by Fiorino, 'Rethinking Environmental Regulation', at 459.

key characteristics of technical, conceptual, and social learning are represented as corresponding to these theories, although there are clearly some overlaps between the categories of learning and the corresponding theoretical 'set'. For example, I have previously outlined that information theories of environmental assessment emphasize the prediction of impacts, using fact-based (rather than values-based, deliberative) methodologies such as modelling, and GIS.[88] Such learning is technical, consisting of the application of methodologies or instruments within the context of a relatively fixed set of objectives. Based upon Fiorino's analysis, building a capacity for technical learning is the first response of policy systems to the recognition of environmental problems: problems are placed in manageable categories; expertise forms around specific issues and technologies; and the legal system is mobilized to respond to the apparent threats, largely from industrial pollution. In this category, change may occur but within a narrow range, with limited discussion of alternative strategies and little attempt to use novel instruments or methods.[89]

A second category of organizational learning (conceptual learning) describes how perspectives on problems change and challenge 'bounded rationality'. Fiorino describes the onset of this category of learning as a consequence of signs of dissatisfaction with technical learning, for example instruments that focus only on pollution control are seen as too narrow and legalistic strategies produce more conflict than useful dialogue. Policy makers therefore adapt by working to improve their capacity for conceptual learning and integrate this with technical learning. In this phase of learning, policy makers reassess their goals (e.g. from pollution control to pollution prevention, risk management, or sustainable development), apply novel policy instruments, consider how to integrate across environmental programmes and policy sectors, and attempt to think more ecologically and globally. Decision making becomes less a process of choosing among alternatives ('option alternatives'), but rather a process of generating new alternatives ('alternative options' or 'brainstorming'!). This search for real alternatives arises because of greater appreciation of the integration of environmental problems, both in terms of environmental media, and policy making associated with conceptual forms of learning. In this category also, providing information on the likely effects of a project (and its alternatives) from an environmental perspective may create learning 'loops' in the form of systems, rules, or organizational memory of important experiences, lodged with particular members of that organization.[90] A similar point is that assessment procedures may have precedent value, providing guidance to developers, environmental consultants, or decision makers in the future. This may help to foster environmental values (as considerations that are recognized as having considerable weight) amongst developers (and decision makers) with the consequence that public and private interests and duties are

---

[88] Ch. 2, pp. 39–40 and Ch. 3, pp. 94–6.
[89] Fiorino, 'Rethinking Environmental Regulation', at 458.
[90] Heinelt *et al.*, *European Union Environmental Policy*, 16–17.

repositioned. This description of conceptual learning rests upon the deliberative ideal. However, as already discussed, the creation of learning loops in environmental assessment procedures is inevitably limited by the finality of decision making. This is particularly the case with project-based environmental assessment because of the place of environmental impact assessment within a development consent system, the immediate aim of which is to sanction or refuse planning permission.[91]

The account of the Dibden Bay port below[92] suggests that these categories of technical and conceptual learning describe the current state of participative 'learning'. The *future* development of environmental assessment in a more deliberative direction might foster cultural change in the form of *social awareness* or environmental education. Along these lines, culture theories of environmental assessment (and other mechanisms displaying reflexive tendencies) support the capability of institutions, organizations, and individuals to modify existing beliefs and practices, in other words to internalize values by their involvement in the assessment process. This may arise by being held responsible for providing information and by monitoring impacts and by improving conduct in the light of these. The key features of this last category of learning include structural openness (whereby public and private entities interact), related to changes in the roles performed by the participants, particularly in cases in which developers are expected to participate in the search for the collective good, rather than just asserting their own economic or political interests.[93] At this stage of development, newly vocal interests (advocates of environmental justice domestically and developing nations internationally) demand greater equity, both in their access to policy processes and the processes' substantive outcomes.[94]

Considering this last category of *social* learning more specifically, it may be argued that cooperative behaviour and mutual adjustment stem from the participation of lay participants or interest groups in the environmental assessment process. Wilkins, for example, suggests that common understandings of community and environmental needs evolve by engaging in discourse since this exposes individuals to new experiences and beliefs.[95] Steele similarly argues that the participatory elements of decision making ('a habit of deliberation') may contribute to strengthening the public realm and the possibilities for collective control, in particular the promotion of a broader range of possible solutions from one case to the next.[96] Even though one may broadly adhere to such an educational or culture-changing function of environmental assessment, it remains difficult

---

[91] This issue is addressed in relation to the role of the developer in environmental assessment procedures in the context of the Cairngorm railway funicular case study on the regulation of decision making. See Ch. 7, at pp. 272–81.   [92] See pp. 227–32.

[93] Fiorino, 'Rethinking Environmental Regulation', at 461.   [94] ibid. at 466.

[95] Wilkins, 'The Need for Subjectivity in Environmental Impact Assessment'.

[96] Steele, 'Participation and Deliberation', at 436.

to conceptualize, let alone empirically explore, whether such collective processes of learning are occurring.[97] In addition the varying claims about environmental protection, or even 'the environment', make it difficult to generalize about fostering environmental protection values among individuals and groups taking part in the assessment process. In the *Congestion Charges* case,[98] for example, applicants challenged the introduction of traffic controls in central London aimed at reducing air pollution with a competing vision of their local environment marred by 'street furniture' and the removal of some trees.

Aside from these doubts, a further critique is that environmental assessment is used as a means of allaying the public's (unjustified) fears and giving credence or legitimatory force to the final decision. These roles were recognized by the Department of the Environment in the early days of the Directive's implementation in its description of the information provision function of environmental assessment:[99]

The general public's interest in a major project is often expressed as concern about the possibility of unknown or unforeseen effects. By providing a full analysis of the project's effects, an environmental statement can help to allay fears created by a lack of information. At the same time it can help to inform the public on the substantive issues which the local planning authority will have to consider in reaching a decision. It is a requirement of the Regulations that the environmental statement must include a description of the project and its likely effects together with a summary in non-technical language. One of the aims of a good environmental statement should be to enable readers to understand for themselves how its conclusions have been reached, and to form their own judgments on the significance of the environmental issues raised by the project.

This policy statement stops well short of encouraging lay judgments to be fed directly into decision-making processes,[100] supporting instead a view of participation as communication, therapy even. This role is similarly described (seemingly uncritically) by Tilleman:

Environmental assessment is a process that relies on the expression of public communication. Discussion and dialogue are key. The process has merit as a therapy, or a relief valve to give voice to dissension among minorities and to expose differing opinions. One must admit that it is difficult to predict accurately future impact. But as long as the public has a chance to become involved in the process, their opinions will at least be communicated and expressed.[101]

Some support for this legitimatory function of environmental assessment is found in statistics which suggest a reduction in litigation in cases in which

---

[97] Heinelt *et al.*, *European Union Environmental Policy*, 15.

[98] *R v Mayor of London ex parte Preece and Adamson* [2002] EWHC 2440. See further Ch. 1, pp. 1–2.

[99] Department of the Environment, *Environmental Assessment: A Guide to the Procedures* (London: HMSO, 1989), p. 4.   [100] As I argue in Ch. 4, at pp. 146–7.

[101] 'Public Participation', 346.

extensive public participation took place in the environmental assessment process.[102] However, the sheer quantity of cases currently being generated and reported suggests that this argument is now a little dated.[103]

In summary, in current environmental assessment procedures such as the EIA Directive participation takes the form of eliciting representations about a developer's environmental statement and taking these into account. Whilst this brings an element of deliberation to the environmental assessment process, it does not seriously disrupt the flow of information from expert (and developer) to decision maker. Vitally, public participation does not directly influence either judgments about the significance of potential impacts on the environment or the final decision. This leads to the basic point that the very nature of the environmental assessment procedure means that it fails to contribute to *collective* decision making, considered to be the hallmark of deliberative decision making. As Steele notes:

[D]eliberation is not just about decision-making which takes account of all perspectives, but (ideally) it includes all perspectives in the process itself. Citizens therefore are deliberates; they are not simply called to inform those with greater expertise in decision-making. There is a crucial difference between this sort of active deliberation by citizens, and expert decision-making on the basis of a broad range of evidence.[104]

Instead, as presently formulated, law relating to environmental assessment fosters a model of expert decision making on the basis of a broad range of evidence which has the potential to encourage only limited forms of learning on the part of decision makers and participants (technical or conceptual learning). This jaundiced view of the process of engaging the public through environmental assessment procedures arises from the case of the Dibden Bay port development, discussed below.[105] Support is also lent by the Lewes Flood Defence Strategy[106] in which initial involvement of the public in the identification of objectives for the strategy gave way to expert and objective assessment of the weight to be given to the various options identified, largely on the basis of a predetermined hierarchy of legal norms. A more extensive consultation programme was a feature of the Kentish Flats windfarm development.[107] However this consultation took place within geographical boundaries set by the developer, which had the effect of diluting local concerns about the significance of the project on the landscape.[108] These examples suggest that the practical experience of participants in planning decisions is as yet remote from theories of participation and approaches to governance which seek to encourage social learning.

---

[102] A. Ureta, 'Prevention Rather than Cure: The EC EIA Directive and its Impact in Spain and the UK' (1992) *Envtl Liab* 61, at 62.   [103] Cf. comments Ch. 1, p. 7.

[104] 'Participation and Deliberation', at 428.   [105] Discussed below, pp. 227–32.

[106] Ch. 3, at pp. 86–92.   [107] As described at www.kentishflats.co.uk.

[108] As discussed in Ch. 4, pp. 140–6.

Circumventing Participation and Planning Practice

There are clearly strong claims made for public participation in environmental assessment. In contrast a pragmatic approach to the public participation requirements of the EIA Directive has been adopted by local planning authorities[109] and the courts. The long-standing, though now discredited, approach of the courts, is that the participation requirements of the Directive are deemed to be fulfilled if environmental information comes to light, notwithstanding the absence of a formal environmental impact assessment procedure.[110] A critique of this approach, on the grounds that it effectively overlooks the potential contribution of public participation to the outcome of decisions, does not necessarily mean that a pragmatic approach is misplaced in all cases. Obviously deliberation is incapable of engaging all interests or an unlimited plurality of participants,[111] and inevitably falls short of Cotterrell's description of a fully democratic polity as 'one in which the aspirations, interests, values and beliefs of all citizens could be asserted fully, in all their richness and variety, in many different kinds of processes of deliberation and decision'.[112] A practical reality is that deliberation in environmental assessment is constrained by the need to make a decision in a certain period of time, which severely curtails the opportunity for continuous improvement and learning.[113] However, as I consider below in the context of case law on revived permissions and reserved matters, opportunities for participation may also be unduly restricted by an emphasis on the singular and discrete nature of decision making, overlooking that this may take place at several stages of consideration. A similar point may be made about the changes to environmental assessment advocated from an ecological perspective, such as long-term baseline surveys which capture the flow and flux of natural systems, but which do not fit easily within temporal boundaries established by systems for development consent.

Recognition that the practical circumstances of decision making are capable of involving a deviation from the Habermasian ideal of deliberation is stretched, by circumstances in which participation is effectively circumvented. Case law on revived or extended permissions and reserved matters[114] focuses on the seemingly

---

[109] As I discuss in the account of the Dibden Bay port development, below, pp. 227–32.

[110] As discussed in Ch. 7, pp. 258–63.   [111] Fitzpatrick, 'Consolations of the Law', at 284.

[112] R. Cotterrell, 'Judicial Review and Legal Theory', in G. Richardson and H. Genn (eds.) *Administrative Law and Government in Action* (Oxford: Clarendon, 1994).

[113] J. Elster, 'Introduction', in Elster, *Deliberative Democracy*, 14. I make a similar point about the changes to environmental assessment advocated from an ecological perspective, such as long-term baseline surveys which capture the flow and flux of natural systems, but which do not fit easily within the boundaries established by systems for development consent; cf. Ch. 3, pp. 92–4.

[114] See also cases in which mitigating measures are taken into account prematurely at the screening stage, in order to judge whether a project should be made subject to a full assessment procedure (in the course of which mitigating measures would then be analysed by experts and the public, as discussed in Ch. 4, pp. 136–40).

technical and related matters of the meaning of 'development consent' for the purposes of the EIA Directive, and the adequacy of information available to a local authority to allow it to make a decision whether or not to grant planning permission, both of which strongly influence public involvement in decision making.

Revived Permissions

The circumvention of participation requirements was first challenged in *Brown*,[115] which brought to light the possible incompatibility of a power to impose conditions upon the operation of a quarry which revived a grant of planning permission[116] with the EIA Directive. This arose because it was not originally envisaged that the attachment of conditions to a dormant mining permission might be interpreted as a grant of development consent for the purpose of the EIA Directive, Article 2 of which states that 'before development consent is given, projects likely to have significant effects on the environment by virtue, inter alia, of their nature, size or location are made subject to a requirement for development consent and an assessment with regard to their effects'. A legal irony is that the regime for registering the existence of old mining permissions and attaching conditions thereto was designed expressly to flush out plans to mine the quarries (the commencement or resumption of which sometimes came as an unpleasant surprise to people who had bought property in the area many years after the permission had been granted) and to control the working of mines for the protection of the local environment. In *Brown* Lord Hoffmann considered that the nature of this regime was sufficient to bring it within the European Community concept of 'development consent' as defined by the EIA Directive (as a decision of the competent authority or authorities which entitles the developer to proceed with the project).[117] He gave a purposive interpretation of the Directive as a means to ensure that planning decisions which may affect the environment are made on the basis of full information. Possibly mindful of the implications of this judgment for authorities which grant outline planning permission subject to reserved matters,[118] he said: 'The principle in this and similar cases seems to me to be clear: the directive does not apply to decisions which involve merely the detailed regulation of activities for which the principal consent raised in the substantial environmental issues, has already been given'.[119]

---

[115] *R v North Yorkshire CC ex parte Brown* [1999] 2 WLR 452, [1999] JPEL 616, [2000] 1 AC 404. First instance judgment reported [1997] Env LR 391.

[116] As provided for by s. 22 and Schedule 2 of the Planning and Compensation Act 1991.

[117] Art. 1 of the EC EIA Directive. Having established that a determination to revive a mining permission is development consent for the purposes of the Directive in this case, legislation was introduced requiring an environmental impact assessment as a precondition of making this determination; the Town and Country Planning (Environmental Impact Assessment) (England and Wales) (Amendment) Regulations 2000 (SI 2000, No. 2867).   [118] Discussed below, pp. 211–18.

[119] At 458.

Lord Hoffmann's reasoning in *Brown* relies more on the destructive and disruptive potential of mining work than a concern with rights of participation under the Directive (or the relationship between these). Although he later extended this analysis in *Berkeley No. 1*,[120] by expressing a concern about participatory rights conferred by the Directive being overlooked, this was in the sense that the public must be 'given an opportunity to express its opinion on the environmental issues',[121] rather than safeguarding participation in decision making in order to improve outcomes and foster awareness about the value of environmental protection.

The Court of Appeal was faced with a similar issue in *Huddleston*,[122] but with the additional complication that the applicant potentially fell within the 'forbidden territory' of horizontal direct effect in European law because of the imposition on a private entity (a mining company) of the duty to conduct an environmental impact assessment in line with the EC Directive.[123] In this case, however, Sedley LJ described the purpose of the assessment as enabling 'informed consultation' (such as by Mr Huddleston, a retired quarry engineer living nearby) to take place about the conditions which needed to be annexed by the mineral planning authority to the permission.[124] He concluded that the Court's (and Council's) hands were not tied in this case by the need to avoid the horizontal effect of EC directives. Rather, the character of the relationship between the applicant and the mining company (concerning the rights and duties of the citizen as against the State) meant that the Court had a power and duty to give effect to the Directive.[125] To elaborate, the public law nature of the applicant's claim, based upon his interest in the legal protection of the environment, and his interest in the State's failure to give effect to this, additionally gave him the necessary standing to trigger the State's obligation to give effect to the obligations contained in the Directive. Sedley LJ therefore followed the principle established by the European Court of Justice in *Bozen*[126] that an individual could call the State to account for the non-implementation of the requirements of the Directive on EIA in a case in which a developer was directly and adversely affected by the intervention. The significance of rights of participation in the environmental assessment process was pointed out by Brooke LJ who had read the non-technical summary of an environmental statement which had been prepared for the mining company several months after permission was deemed to have been granted subject to conditions: 'It is sufficient to say that this

---

[120] *Berkeley v Secretary of State for the Environment (Berkeley No. 1)* [2000] WLR 420, [2001] AC 603, (2001) 13 *JEL* 89.   [121] At 430.

[122] *R v Durham County Council ex parte Huddleston* [2000] 1 WLR 1484.

[123] On this point see also Case C-201/02 *R (Wells) v Secretary of State for Transport, Local Government and the Regions*, Opinion of Advocate-General Leger, 25 September 2003 in which the A-G considers that previous authority of the ECJ does not prevent this result.   [124] At para. 1.

[125] ibid., at para. 1.

[126] Case C-435/97 *World Wildlife Fund v Autonome Provinz Bozen* [2000] 1 CMLR.

summary contains information which would have enabled Mr Huddleston, whose amenities (both in his home and in the environment close to his home) would be detrimentally affected by the proposed quarrying, to have taken a much more informed part in the consultation process, as was his right if the Directive had been effectively implemented'.[127]

The applicant in *Prokopp*[128] similarly alleged the bypassing of the public consultation elements of the EIA Directive by the making of an agreement under which conditions attached to a previous grant of planning permission were made effective once again, thus revising the planning permission. The permission had been granted to London Underground Limited to build the East London Line Extension which was likely to 'affect the setting' of a viaduct listed as a building of architectural interest. The effect of this was described by English Heritage as a 'conservation tragedy' but in an understated manner by Schiemann LJ: 'Bishopsgate Goods Yard through which a couple of hundred metres of the line were planned to run . . . was built in the nineteenth century and, although much ravaged by time and fire and no longer in use, nevertheless contains a number of features of interest to those knowledgeable about railway architecture'.[129] The applicant's argument was that the decision by the London Boroughs not to take enforcement action against London Underground Limited (for failure to carry out building work in the period specified in planning permission) amounted to development consent for the purposes of the Directive, thus triggering the 1999 EIA Regulations. The Court of Appeal refused to countenance this. Schiemann LJ advanced a (technically correct, but limited) snapshot view of environmental assessment:

The fact is that the Directive does not attempt to impose on Member States detailed control throughout the implementation of a project . . . Thus it can happen that the execution of a properly authorised project suddenly causes more environmental problems than were envisaged at the time of authorisation. There is nothing in the Directive which deals with that situation.[130]

A concern with national autonomy over development projects informed this part of the judgment. Schiemann LJ failed to accept that the purpose of the Directive would be undermined if Member States were 'left free to police, in whatever manner they regard as appropriate, the progress of a project once it has started'.[131]

On whether there was substantial compliance with the EIA Directive,[132] particularly in terms of the practical fulfilment of participation requirements in conformity with Article 6(2) of the EIA Directive, Buxton LJ (giving the second

---

[127] At para. 39.
[128] *R (Prokopp)* v *London Underground Limited and Strategic Rail Authority* [2003] EWCA Civ 960.   [129] At paras. 6–7.
[130] At paras. 39 and 40.   [131] At para. 42.   [132] See further Ch. 7, p. 262.

judgment) was satisfied that the public concern about the viaduct had had ample opportunity to express itself. Rather dismissively, he stated:

As to consultation, the only persons who have shown an active interest in these matters are English Nature and Mr Prokopp. English Nature has expressed itself content, however reluctantly, that the ELLX [extension line] should proceed as proposed. Mr Prokopp is not of the same mind as English Nature, but he can hardly say that he has not had an opportunity to put his point of view.[133]

Having rejected the applicant's argument that implicit in the Directive is an obligation to have a national development consent in force throughout the implementation of a project, Buxton LJ characterized the Directive as concerned with prior assessment and approval of the project, not with continuous assessment of it in the light of developments in the course of its completion.[134]

This rather narrow view of the meaning of development consent must now be reviewed following the European Court of Justice's judgment in *Wells*.[135] In this case operators of a quarry had obtained planning permission to work the quarry in 1947 but as this permission was dormant (quarrying had not taken place in the two years prior to the 1991 Planning and Compensation Act) new conditions were required before operations could be resumed. The Court was asked whether the determination of planning conditions constitutes development consent within the meaning of the EIA Directive. A complication was that the planning conditions for the quarry were determined in two stages: first, the Secretary of State's decision to impose conditions on the planning permission (thus permitting extraction at the quarry) and second, the mineral planning authority's approval of certain reserved matters such as the monitoring of noise and blasting on the site. Hence a further question was which of these decisions properly constituted development consent. The Court of Justice decided that the decision determining new conditions and the decision approving reserved matters for the working of the quarry amounted to development consent and thus required an environmental assessment to be carried out.[136] The Court elaborated that where a consent procedure comprises several stages, that assessment must in principle be carried out as soon as it is possible to identify and assess all the effects which the project may have on the environment.[137] This interpretation of the Directive follows Advocate General Leger's opinion that although the national law of each Member State establishes the moment from which the developer is granted the right to proceed with the project, development consent is not a national concept.[138] The Advocate General appeared influenced by the premise that the resumption of extraction of minerals at the quarry was likely to have significant

---

[133] At para. 74.   [134] At para. 59.
[135] Case C-201/02 *R (Wells)* v *Secretary of State for Transport, Local Government and the Regions*, nyr Judgment 7.1.04, A-G Leger's Opinion 25.9.03.   [136] At para. 47.   [137] At para. 54.
[138] Consistent with previous case law, for example Case C-81/96 *B en W Haarlemmerliede en Spaarnwoude* v *GS van Noord-Holland* [1998] ECR I-3923 on pipeline projects.

effects on the environment, which called for a purposive reading of the Directive in line with previous case law of the Court giving the Directive a broad scope.[139] The Court's judgment is similarly shaped by concerns about the effectiveness of the Directive, stating that this would be undermined by regarding the adoption of decisions which replace the terms and substance of prior consent, such as the old mining permission, as mere modifications of an existing consent. The Court related this finding to the enforceable nature of participatory rights, confirming the Advocate General's opinion that the provisions of the Directive entitling individuals to express their opinion of the likely significance of a project are sufficiently precise and enforceable as a matter of the principle of direct effect. Furthermore the Court clarified that the limits it had laid down previously on the (horizontal) direct effect of directives do not apply in cases in which the adverse repercussions for third parties are merely of the order of this case—the halting of mining operations awaiting the results of an environmental assessment.[140]

Reserved Matters

As suggested by *Wells,* further problems with the meaning of development consent giving effect to the participation requirements of the EIA Directive arise in the conceptually related area of reserved matters cases because granting outline permission (subject to a later decision on certain matters) confuses the meaning of development consent for the purposes of complying with the EIA Directive. Whilst a grant of outline permission gives the developer a right to develop (in accordance with conditions), work cannot commence until the authority has considered certain reserved matters. The problem is that the authority is bound to act in accordance with the principle of development, or otherwise face paying compensation, even though the reserved matters may result in (possibly significant) effects on the environment. This widespread practice in effect breaks the decision to award consent into more than one stage. This is not envisaged by the Directive which seemingly presents 'development consent' as a single stage in which planning permission is applied for and a decision is made. This underlines that the absorption of the Directive's provisions—including rights of participation—within existing planning law and practice has proved more difficult than originally foreseen.[141]

The practice of granting outline planning permission with later approval of reserved matters was first challenged as incompatible with the EIA Directive by the CPRE,[142] because a planning authority had failed to require an environmental assessment for a 40-acre urban regeneration project at White City (including

---

[139] e.g. Case C-72/95 *Kraaijeveld* [1996] ECR I-5403.   [140] At paras. 62 and 71.

[141] On various explanations for this, including the nature of the pre-existing environmental assessment requirements in planning law, see Ch. 2, pp. 47–52.

[142] *R v London Borough of Hammersmith and Fulham ex parte CPRE London Branch* [2000] Env LR 532.

leisure and retail facilities, and parking for 4,500 cars). It was also argued that the anticipated approval of reserved matters would be unlawful because of this failure, despite the developer voluntarily providing an environmental assessment *after* the grant of outline permission. At first instance the CPRE's difficulty was that it was assumed that the Directive had been correctly transposed which confined them to remedies under domestic law. On the matter of the applicability of the Directive to the reserved matters stage, Richard J said:

> For my part I do not see how Community law could confound the entire planning process and enable or require a Local Planning Authority to reopen the principle of the development at the reserved matters stage. To my mind the argument advanced simply does not get off the ground. It seems to me that the effect of the Directive and the Regulations made to implement it, is to require the question of Environmental Assessment to be considered at the stage of the initial planning decision, in this case the outline consent. It is the outline consent which constitutes development consent for the purposes of the Directive in implementing provisions.[143]

The Court of Appeal[144] refused an application for leave to apply for judicial review of the local authority's decisions on broadly similar grounds, dismissing the argument that the need for an environmental assessment (or environmental survey as the Court referred to it) followed from taking a purposive approach to the Directive.[145] Giving the main judgment, Singer J advanced a simplistic solution to the question of what constitutes development consent. This was arrived at by holding that for the purposes of the Directive this was the outline planning permission, and the fact that there were conditions subsequent which were capable of precluding the project did not have the effect of elevating the approval of reserved matters to the status of an 'entitling' (i.e. activating and enabling) decision.[146] To extend the decision whether an 'environmental survey' is needed at the reserved matters stage would 'turn our planning system on its head and would (I add) produce total uncertainty and manifest absurdity'[147], which view contrasts with the Advocate General's more nuanced approach to staged decision making in *Wells*.

The issue has been similarly raised in the *Tew* cases.[148] In *Tew 1* residents living near to a planned business park successfully challenged a grant of 'bare' outline planning permission for this (with all detailed matters reserved for subsequent approval) on the ground that there had been a failure to provide environmental information required under the 1988 Regulations.[149] The developer had provided only an 'illustrative masterplan' of the project (which was to be developed in several phases). Sullivan J concluded that whilst the Council had taken this

---

[143] At 541.   [144] [2000] Env LR 549.   [145] Paras. 31–3 per Singer J.
[146] Para. 54.   [147] Para. 56.
[148] *R v Rochdale Metropolitan Borough Council ex parte Tew* (*Tew 1*) [2000] Env LR 1 and *R v Rochdale Metropolitan Borough Council ex parte Milne* (*Tew 2*) [2001] Env LR 22.
[149] Town and Country Planning (Assessment of Environmental Effects) Regulations 1988 (SI 1988, No. 1199).

information into account, there was nothing to tie this information to the actual development proposed, nor to the permission which was granted.[150] In addition, insufficient information about mitigating measures had been provided.

Following this judgment, the developers substantially revised their application for the business park and accompanied this with an environmental statement. The Council then granted outline permission, but this decision was again subject to judicial review on the grounds that although the revised application detailed the scale and size of the project, the 'details' of landscaping, design, and external appearance of all the buildings were reserved. More generally, the applicants asserted that outline planning permission could not be granted for a project which required environmental assessment. In 'round 2 of the battle for Kingsway Park' (*Tew 2*), also heard by Sullivan J, the application was refused. The judge considered that in circumstances other than the extreme case of a grant of bare outline permission (as in *Tew 1*), it is for the decision maker to decide whether the information provided about the proposed development is sufficient for the purposes of the (by then) 1999 Regulations,[151] rather than for the court as a matter of primary fact. This judgment appeals to pragmatism given the economic reality of phased projects such as this (reliant upon uptake of business units over a period of time, and the varying nature of these) so that in this case 'full knowledge' was taken to mean as much information as can reasonably be expected from the developer at the time the application for planning permission was made. Whilst some account was taken of the role of the public in contributing environmental information in this judgment,[152] greater attention was paid to the fear of environmental assessment procedures obstructing the development of such projects for 'no good purpose'.[153] For example, Sullivan J commented testily that projects such as industrial estate developments and urban development projects have been placed in a 'legal straitjacket' by the assessment regulations.[154]

In contrast, other judges have expressed concern about the effects of similar practices on participation. In *Hardy No. 1*[155] Harrison J displayed understanding of environmental impact assessment as a process, an element of which is information adduced by consultation and participation, as well as from the developer's environmental statement. The case had arisen because the local planning authority had granted planning permission to extend an existing landfill site subject to a condition that the applicant undertake further nature conservation surveys and prepare appropriate mitigation measures. The authority imposed this condition, following the advice of English Nature and the Cornish Wildlife Trust that

---

[150] Followed in *Elmbridge Borough Council* v *Secretary of State for the Environment, Transport and the Regions* [2002] Env LR 1.
[151] Town and Country Planning (Environmental Impact Assessment) (England and Wales) Regulations 1999, (SI 1999, No. 293).   [152] At para. 101.   [153] At para. 135.
[154] At para. 91.
[155] *R* v *Cornwall County Council ex parte Hardy* (*Hardy No. 1*) [2001] Env LR 25. Discussed more fully in the context of prediction of likely effects, Ch. 3, pp. 78–9.

further information (beyond that provided in the developer's environmental statement) was necessary to establish the impact of the proposed development upon nature conservation interests on the site. The environmental statement (containing an ecological survey) had raised the possibility of the effect of the development upon badgers, the scarce liverwort plant, and lesser horseshoe bats, although the liverwort and badger sett were 'only' found on the edge of the site and bats had not been found (the statement had said only that their roosting places might be found in the mine shafts if surveys were carried out). The applicant maintained that it was impermissible to leave the information arising from the surveys to the reserved matters stage, because it would by then be too late to prevent the development and also because there was no requirement for publicity or public consultation on the impact arising from the surveys or the mitigation measures that might be envisaged. On these points Harrison J stated:

> [Counsel for the local planning authority] laid emphasis upon the fact that the local planning authority felt that, in imposing conditions, it had ensured that adequate powers would be available to it at the reserved matters stage. That, in my view, is no answer. At the reserved matters stage there are not the same statutory requirements for publicity and consultation. The environmental statement does not stand alone. Representations made by consultees are an important part of the environmental information which must be considered by the local planning authority before granting planning permission. Moreover, it is clear from the comprehensive list of likely significant effects in paragraph 2(c) of Schedule 3, and the reference to mitigation measures in paragraph 2(d), that it is intended that in accordance with the objectives of the Directive, the information contained in the environmental statement should be both comprehensive and systematic, so that a decision to grant planning permission is taken 'in full knowledge' of the project's likely significant effects on the environment. If consideration of some of the environmental impacts and mitigation measures is effectively postponed until the reserved matters stage, the decision to grant planning permission would have been taken with only a partial rather than a 'full knowledge' of the likely significant effects of the project . . . It will be for the local planning authority to decide whether a particular effect is significant, but a decision to defer a description of a likely significant adverse effect and any measures to avoid, reduce or remedy it to a later stage would not be in accordance with the terms of Schedule 3, would conflict with the public's right to make an input into the environmental information and would therefore conflict with the underlying purpose of the Directive.[156]

Whilst upholding the view of Sullivan J (in *Tew 1* and *2*) that it is for the planning authority to judge the adequacy of the environmental information, subject to *Wednesbury* unreasonableness, Harrison J decided that the environmental information specified by the 1999 Regulations must be provided and considered by the authority before planning permission was granted. He concluded that at least so far as the bats were concerned, the environmental statement was deficient. It therefore became vital whether the nature conservation aspects relating to the

---

[156] At para. 41.

bats, badgers, and liverwort involved 'significant adverse effects'.[157] The non-technical summary of the developer's environmental statement had concluded that there would be no significant adverse environmental effects which should prevent the proposal from gaining planning permission, and this also formed the basis of the recommendation put to the planning committee of the Council. However, Harrison J found it difficult to see how this could have been accepted by the Council, given the advice from the conservation bodies that further surveys should be carried out to ensure that the bats (and other species) would not be adversely affected by the development.[158] The case was finally decided on the basis that bats are protected species under the Habitats Directive. This meant that since there was evidence that bats or their resting places might be found in the mine shafts if further surveys were carried out, if it were found that they were likely to be adversely affected, this finding would constitute a 'significant adverse effect' for the purpose of the 1999 Regulations. This should then be considered by the planning committee before deciding to grant planning permission. The surveys which might have revealed significant adverse effects on the bats and their resting places could therefore not be left to the reserved matters stage when the same requirements for publicity and consultation (as for the usual EIA procedure) do not apply.[159]

The state of law on the appropriateness of leaving environmentally relevant decisions to the reserved matter stage in cases concerning environmental assessment was the subject of a reference to the European Court of Justice in *Barker*,[160] in which a grant of outline planning permission to redevelop Crystal Palace park by building a hotel, shops, and restaurant was challenged by a mother who used the park for recreation with her child. The applicant and other protesters (who staged a round the clock vigil) had argued that the development would infringe various aspects of environmental and planning law, including the Wildlife and Countryside Act 1981.[161] The specific grounds of the case raised whether the consideration of reserved matters is a stage of the consent procedure for the purposes of the Directive to which environmental information may be relevant. Relying on the House of Lords' interpretation of the legislative scheme for revised mining permissions considered in *Brown*, the applicant argued that where there has been a decision in principle, any later consideration of conditions as reserved matters amounts to a stage in the development consent process requiring an environmental impact assessment. The Court of Justice was called upon to

---

[157] As a matter of paras. 2 and 3 of Part II of Schedule 4 of the 1999 Regulations.
[158] Paras. 59–60.   [159] Para. 62.
[160] *R (Barker)* v *London Borough of Bromley* [2002] Env LR 638.
[161] In *Mayor and Burgesses of the London Borough of Bromley* v *Susanna (a Female)* [1999] Env LR D 13, the Court of Appeal held that these considerations were irrelevant to the proceedings. All that mattered was whether the Borough had title to the site, whether the occupants were trespassers, and whether the formal requirements of possession proceedings had been complied with. On environmental protests involving environmental assessment, see further below, pp. 222–6.

decide whether development consent has an autonomous meaning for the purposes of the EIA Directive and to which national laws and courts must give effect, but the judgment of the Court of Justice in *Wells* has now provided this. A postscript is that the developers agreed to abandon the project because of the protracted High Court battle, but the European Commission has remained keen to take enforcement action against the United Kingdom over the Council's failure to require an environmental impact assessment in these circumstances.

Concern with the effect of planning practices such as these on public participation was expressed by Sedley LJ in *Smith*.[162] This dealt with the exension of planning permission for extracting stone from a quarry in the green belt, and the respective obligations of the local authority and other bodies to mitigate the environmental effects of this. The applicant's main argument was that the conditions imposed by a planning inspector in effect allowed the local authority to later reassess the impact on the environment and alter plans which were intended to mitigate any adverse effects, without requiring an environmental impact assessment. This was considered to be possibly in contravention of Article 4(2) of the EIA Directive and gave the appearance of having passed the environmental 'buck' to the authority. Although it was finally decided that the inspector was entitled to consider that the authority would deal with the details (landscaping and so on) in such a way that any adverse effects of the development would be mitigated, so that the appeal was dismissed,[163] Sedley LJ entertained some doubts about this practice. In a sharply observed judgment, he identified two apparent results of the inspector's action: 'One was that the content of the conditions could thereafter be set by private negotiation between developer and local authority and become known to the public only when a fait accompli. The second was that the negotiated content might modify significant elements of the consent'.[164] In the event, such effects were considered not to flow from the circumstances in *Smith*, and more generally may do so only when what is being left over to be decided by the authority is capable of modifying or disrupting the terms on which planning permission is being granted.[165] As Sedley LJ noted of the facts of this case: 'sensing the proximity of the wall to their backs, counsel for both the Secretary of State and the developer stressed how little was being left by the inspector in the local planning authority's hands—matters only of detail . . . none of them capable of aggravating the environmental impact of the development or impeding its remediation'.[166] In contrast, '[I]f there are significant environmental elements (not, that is, matters of detail arising within a comprehensive grant of permission) it might seem in principle more appropriate that the Secretary of State through his inspectorate, should reserve them to himself and thereby keep the public in

---

[162] *Smith* v *Secretary of State for the Environment, Transport and the Regions* [2003] EWCA Civ 262 (CA).

[163] The issues in this case relating to mitigating measures are further discussed in Ch. 4, pp. 136–40.   [164] At para. 54.   [165] At para. 55.   [166] At para. 56.

the picture'.[167] He also raised a related concern about the planning inspector's reliance in this case on certain measures—including £40,000 to the city council for traffic safety measures, local landscape management of the site and its surroundings, and the establishment of a local liaison committee—offered by the developer in mitigation for the impact of the development.[168] The offer of such 'significant community and environmental benefits' (as described by the inspector) recollects the type of questions raised in *Tesco*[169] about whether such 'mitigating measures' should be related in scale or kind to the likely damage to the environment; indeed whether they constitute mitigating measures at all. The possible exclusion from public discussion of the adequacy and relatedness of such mitigating measures was left unexplored.

The sets of cases on revived permission and reserved matters suggest that the deceptively simple European definition of development consent ('the decision of the competent authority or authorities which entitles the developer to proceed with the development') does not reflect planning practice which has developed to accommodate developers' contradictory demands for flexibility and pragmatism (in the provision of environmental information) and certainty that environmental considerations will not be revisited at a late stage in the development consent process. Appreciating this, Sedley LJ urged 'consideration whether the full extent of the practice, which appears for many years to have been to remit the amplification of conditions to the local planning authority, is appropriate under the modern regime of environmental protection', and noted that '[I]t would be odd if such a carefully structured regime could be circumvented by the surrender of public judgment to private negotiation'.[170] (A conceptually similar problem arises with large-scale developments operating within long timescales, during which environmental standards and methods may undergo changes).[171] The underlying issue is whether environmental considerations should inform each stage of the development consent process (for example, the setting of conditions, as in *Brown*, *Huddleston*, *Wells*, and *Smith*, and decisions about reserved matters, as in *CPRE*, *Barker*, and the *Tew* cases) and thus reflect the practical reality that decision making reaches over several stages, each requiring differing standards of environmental information, and involving varying levels of uncertainty about the likely significant effects of development and the likely effectiveness of mitigating measures. With respect to case law on reserved matters, a key issue is whether an environmental impact assessment has taken place at the stage of granting outline permission, which is governed by judgments of significance.[172] In the courts' consideration of the applicability of environmental assessment rules at this and other stages

---

[167] At para. 58.
[168] As a unilateral undertaking under s. 106 of the Town and Country Planning Act 1990, as amended.
[169] *Tesco Stores Ltd* v *Secretary of State for the Environment* (1995) 2 All ER 636 (HL).
[170] At para. 58.   [171] See the 'Dam cases', in Ch. 2, pp. 55–6.
[172] See Ch. 4.

of decision making, the possibility of rights of participation being infringed is recognized, but criticism of this is relatively muted (at least when compared to European Court of Justice judgments in cases such as *Bozen*).[173] As mentioned above, Harrison J in *Hardy No. 1* neatly pinpointed the problem of securing effective participation in reserved matters cases,[174] Sedley LJ has appealed to 'keeping the public in the picture', and Lord Hoffmann has argued that a correct interpretation of the EIA Directive requires that the public be 'given an opportunity to express its opinion on the environmental issues'. Although these statements are to be welcomed as moving in the right direction, an appreciation of the public's potential role in decision making, such as strengthening the public realm through engagement with the environmental assessment process, is not obviously apparent and there is a danger of confusion on the part of the public as to the point at which their input is needed.

Discretionary Relief: Misaligning Public and Environmental Interests, and Putting *Berkeley No. 1* in its Place

In exercising discretion in cases concerning the review of environmental assessment decisions,[175] as in planning law more generally, courts rarely align the public interest with environmental interests, so that rights of development tend to predominate.[176] This reflects the importance of developmental interests in a parcel of land for the purposes of development consent, as a matter of planning law.[177] The exercise of discretion in this respect is relevant to the issue of participation in the decision-making process because of the potential irrelevance of making a challenge by way of judicial review based upon upholding environmental assessment procedures, particularly individual rights of participation. An early example is *Swale*,[178] in which the applicants, the RSPB, were not regarded as

[173] Case C-435/97 [2000] 1 CMLR.
[174] *R v Cornwall County Council ex parte Hardy* [2001] Env LR 25, at para. 41.
[175] Under s. 288(5)(b) of the Town and Country Planning Act 1990 which provides that a court 'may' quash an ultra vires planning decision.
[176] As first observed by Alder, 'Environment Impact Assessment'.
[177] As discussed in Ch. 5, pp. 153–4. Further examples of the favouring of specific, developmental interests include the fact that third parties are given few rights to parallel those conferred on developers to appeal to the Secretary of State against a grant of permission, or to challenge a decision of the planning authority in the ordinary courts (on which see CPRE, RSPB, WWF *et al.*, *Third Party Rights of Appeal in Planning*). There are also restrictions on the scope of environmentally beneficial conditions, with the courts adopting the attitude that conditions that take away private property rights and which are not compensated are ultra vires. See *Hall v Shoreham Urban Development Corporation* [1964] 1 WLR 240; however, policy guidance in Circular 1/85, *The Use of Conditions in Planning Permission* (London: HMSO, 1985), para. 59 (development of contaminated sites) and Planning Policy Guidance Note 23, *Planning and Pollution Control* (London: HMSO, 1992) paras. 3.23–3.27 tended to be more amenable to the use of environmentally beneficial conditions.
[178] *R v Swale Borough Council and Medway Ports Authority ex parte the Royal Society for the Protection of Birds* (1991) 3 JEL 135. See further Ch. 4, pp. 111–14.

representing the 'public interest'. Simon Brown J refused to quash a grant of planning permission (for a storage area for a nearby trading port to be built upon the mudflats of the Medway Estuary) on the ground that the financial interests of the developer outweighed the applicants' environmental concerns, which were considered to be at most a right to be consulted.[179] In a similar vein, in *Velcourt*[180] the local planning authority was considered incapable of acting 'for the promotion and protection of the interests of the inhabitants of their area' in opposing the applicant's development.

The judicial tendency to prioritize developmental interests was particularly marked in the *Twyford Down* case[181] in which McCullogh J allied the 'public interest' with the developer's interests in building the road as quickly as possible so that they did not lose a Department of Transport grant for its construction. This was pitched against the applicants' argument that this would result in the loss of an important site in ecological and archaeological terms. McCullogh J's opinion was that 'to have quashed this scheme would have occasioned considerable further delay to the building of this much needed section of road which would have been contrary to the interests of the wider public'.[182] Such a categorical statement glossed over the controversy occasioned by the proposal, which centred upon the validity of judgments about the need for the road. McCullogh J had held in this case that the road which was proposed to be built through Twyford Down had been in the 'planning pipeline' before even the adoption of the EC EIA Directive, and that therefore the requirements of the Directive and the 1988 Regulations[183] did not apply.[184] However, he held that even if this was not the case, no right of action could arise because the applicants had not suffered as a result of the alleged failure to implement the Directive. This was to impose an additional test of 'harm suffered' to that imposed at the stage of applying for standing. McCullogh stated:

In my judgment no prejudice, let alone any substantial prejudice, to the applicants has been shown . . . The complaint here . . . is one of form, not substance. None of the applicants has asserted that there was any relevant piece of environmental information of which he was in ignorance or which was made in too complex a form so that he could not understand it or its significance . . . The highest [counsel] was able to put it was to say, as he did, in his closing submissions, that an environmental statement and a non-technical summary might have saved the applicants time, trouble and money. But this is speculative.[185]

This judicial approach (which was reconsidered in the light of *Berkeley No. 1* and *Brown*) suggests that in the early case law at least environmental assessment was

---

[179] At 149–50.
[180] *Wychavon District Council* v *Secretary of State for the Environment and Velcourt Ltd* (1994) 6 *JEL* 352, at 354.
[181] *Twyford Parish Council and Others* v *Secretary of State for Transport* (1992) 4 *JEL* 273, [1992] 1 CMLR 276.   [182] At 282.
[183] The Highways (Assessment of Environmental Effects) Regulations 1988 (SI 1988, No. 1241).
[184] This aspect of the judgment is discussed further in Ch.7, pp. 257–8.   [185] At 281.

perceived as primarily a means of conveying information to the public, rather than a means by which participants might contribute to the decision-making process. It is also based upon what was (even then) rather dated European Court of Justice authority on the nature and protection of financial or employment rights (sex equality, employment rights, and so on) contained in directives,[186] in which evidence of harm to individual rights was self-evident. Such substantive rights are not easily compared with the procedural rights of participation in the environmental assessment process from which less tangible effects flow.

Since the *Twyford Down* case, the development of European case law on environmental law and particularly environmental assessment has led to greater recognition of the self-standing nature of environmental policy,[187] rather than as an adjunct to the internal market, so that difficult analogies with financial and social rights are less frequently applied. This development was seemingly recognized by the House of Lords in *Berkeley No. 1* in which the very infringement of Article 6(2) of the EIA Directive defined the nature of prejudice to the applicant, without any need for the applicant to demonstrate further harm suffered. A further, more recent, development is the European Court of Justice's judgment in *Wells*[188] which additionally imposes an obligation on Member States to take measures necessary to ensure that projects are examined in order to determine whether they are likely to have significant effects on the environment, including revoking or suspending a consent already granted for a project which has not been subject to an assessment.[189] The recognition of harm suffered by the failure to carry out an environmental impact assessment is clear in the related requirement that a Member State is 'to make good any harm caused by the failure to carry out an environmental impact assessment'.[190]

These examples apparently provide a mark of how judicial views or understanding of environmental assessment have developed since *Twyford Down*, except that the House of Lords judgment in *Berkeley No. 1* may possibly be considered to be atypical (although initially influential), arising after lengthy and well-publicized proceedings and demanding considerable legal stamina and resources on the part of the applicant. Returning to the Court of Appeal's judgment in *Berkeley No. 1*,[191] the Court's exercise of its discretion so as not to quash the Secretary of State's decision to grant planning permission to Fulham Football Club to redevelop their premises was fatal to the applicant's case. This was because, although the Court held that there had been a failure to comply with the 1988 Regulations because the planning authority and the Secretary of State had not considered whether an environmental impact assessment should be

---

[186] e.g. Case 8/81 *Becker* v *Finanzamt Munster-Innenstadt* [1982] ECR 53.
[187] e.g. in cases such as *Kraaijveld* and *Bozen*.   [188] Case C-201/02.   [189] At para. 65.
[190] At para. 66.
[191] *Berkeley* v *Secretary of State for the Environment and Fulham Football Club* [1998] Env LR 741 (CA). For the facts, see Ch. 1, p. 2, and on the implications of this in terms of procedural decision making, see Ch. 7, pp. 258–62.

required,[192] and thus that the grant of planning permission was unlawful, this was not considered to have had any material effect on the decision reached by the authority. Pill LJ, for example was unpersuaded that an environmental impact assessment 'could have had any effect on the course of events or was prejudicial to objectors or the quality of the decision'[193] because certain information had come to light in the course of a planning inquiry into the development. This aspect of the judgment had the effect of negating the role of public participation in the environmental assessment process, adhering instead to a narrow view of the process as concerned primarily with the gathering of a 'vast amount of information'.[194] Thorpe LJ's judgment is particularly striking for its lack of references to the role of participation in the environmental assessment process. He stated:

[T]he existence of the discretion necessarily entails some review of the probable outcome had the proper procedures been observed throughout. On the facts of this case I am left with the clear conviction that the procedures adopted, though flawed, were thorough and effective to enable the inspector to make a comprehensive judgment on all the environmental issues affecting the Thames . . .[195]

The reversal of this finding by the House of Lords was considered something of a triumph for the claims for participation. Lord Hoffmann's reasoning, mentioned above,[196] was that the right to participate in the environmental assessment process contained in Article 6 of the Directive on EIA is directly enforceable as a matter of European law. The planning permission, granted contrary to the provisions of the Directive, was thus ultra vires. As Lord Hoffmann notes: 'It is exceptional even in domestic law for a court to exercise its discretion not to quash a decision which had been found to be ultra vires'.[197]

At the time of the House of Lords judgment it was considered that this point was no longer a live issue. As Carnwath LJ later stated of *Berkeley*: 'the developer was not represented in the House and there was no reference to any evidence of actual prejudice to his or any other interest',[198] suggesting that this factor had conferred some freedom on the court to uphold the principle of participation over pragmatism. Carnwath LJ emphasized: '[T]he speeches [in *Berkeley*] need to be read in context . . . Care is needed in applying the principles there decided to other circumstances such as cases where as here there is clear evidence of a pressing public need for the scheme which is under attack'.[199] He reiterated this point in *Jones*,[200] and extended the caution (the Court of Appeal had not been asked to dismiss the appeal on discretionary grounds) by commenting upon the protracted nature of the case: '[W]ith hindsight it might have saved time if there had been

---

[192] Reg. 4(2) of the 1988 Regulations.   [193] At 757.   [194] Per Pill LJ, at 757.
[195] At 758.   [196] See above, pp. 188–9.   [197] At 431.
[198] Per Carnwath LJ in *Bown* v *Secretary of State* [2003] EWCA Civ 170, para. 47, concerning a challenge to orders authorizing a new bypass, alleged to be in conflict with Directive 79/404/EEC on wild birds.   [199] ibid.
[200] *R (Jones)* v *Mansfield District Council* [2003] EWCA Civ 1408 (CA), para. 59. For analysis of this case, see Ch. 4, pp. 125–6.

an EIA from the outset. However, five years on, it is difficult to see what practical benefit, other than delaying the development, will result to [the applicant] or to anyone else from putting the application through this further procedural hoop'.[201] Having urged against further delay, Carnwath LJ raised the issue of the role of legal challenges, based upon environmental assessment, which are intended as an 'obstacle race', rather than 'an aid to efficient and inclusive decision-making in *special* cases'.[202] Similar views were expressed by the Court of Appeal in *Prokopp*.[203] As mentioned above, London Underground Limited had refused to submit a new application for permission to develop a site on the ground that preparing an environmental statement as required by the 1999 Regulations would cause delay which could prejudice the funding and completion of the scheme. Schiemann LJ agreed: '[T]here is to put it no higher, a perfectly tenable case that it is more in the public interest for the project to proceed than for it to be held up for yet further consultation or consideration'.[204] Buxton LJ concurred, stating: '[T]he need for and benefits of the ELLX (East London Line Extension) are undisputed . . . there is nothing that the court can properly put in the scales against the overwhelming weight of evidence in favour of permitting the ELLX to proceed without further delay'.[205]

This, and the various other episodes in the judicial exercise of discretion conferred by statute, suggest that the review of decision making subject to environmental assessment procedures does not fundamentally disturb support for developmental interests, particularly when involved in major infrastructure works. In particular, the courts do not appear unduly influenced by circumstances in which considerable environmental costs *are* weighed in the balance.[206]

Protest: Environmental Assessment as Strategy

The discussion above suggests that relying upon environmental impact assessment rules as a basis for launching a legal challenge to development (by way of statutory appeal[207] in the case of decisions by or on behalf of the Secretary of State, or judicial review[208] in the case of local authority decisions) is frequently unsuccessful from the perspective of securing environmental protection. More generally, I have explored the use of environmental assessment as a means to mediate conflict, often between competing interests in land, by improving information and communication.[209] A further use of environmental assessment is as a strategy, whereby groups and individuals attempt to invoke environmental

---

[201] Para. 57.   [202] Para. 58 (emphasis added).

[203] *R (Prokopp)* v *London Underground Limited* [2003] EWCA (Civ) 960.   [204] At para. 24.

[205] At para. 88.   [206] These costs are described more fully in Ch. 7, pp. 256–63.

[207] S. 78 Town and Country Planning Act 1990.

[208] S. 288 Town and Country Planning Act 1990.

[209] As above, pp. 197–9.

assessment procedures to stall a project, with a view to freeing up sufficient time and popular interest in the project and thus influence the decision whether it should be permitted to go ahead or not. Invoking environmental assessment as an 'obstacle race' in this way is a highly functional, defensive, and costly use of the procedure which may be related to the current lack of third-party appeals since environmental assessment rules potentially provide a hook for challenging unwanted development. Although procedural in nature, such a challenge may have substantive effects.

The deployment of environmental assessment rules as a protest strategy[210] (in a broad sense so as to include obstruction and delay) originated in the United States where decisions not to produce an environmental statement for a particular development and the adequacy of many statements have been challenged successfully by environmental groups. *Calvert Cliffs*[211] was particularly influential, the litigious aftermath of which saw groups bringing legal actions and securing court review of federal agencies' actions in the light of an environmental impact statement[212] (an experience European legislators were wary of replicating). As Hertz confirms: '[T]he need to produce an EIS (or the threat that a court will discover such a need well down the road) gives project opponents a real-world bargaining tool that is artificially powerful'.[213] This motivation has been similarly described by Kunzlik in his account of the legal battle (action for judicial review and complaint to the European Commission) embarked upon by the Twyford Down Association:

> Partly it was because they [the Association] sincerely believed that if the proper procedures had been followed public opinion would be better informed as to the environmental consequences of the scheme, so that it would have been politically difficult for the Government to confirm the route. Secondly, the making of the complaint and subsequent steps in the enforcement procedure were important elements of a campaign to recruit public opinion against the project and make it politically difficult for the Government to proceed with it.[214]

Invoking environmental impact assessment as a strategy to secure delay and to publicize the cause of the Association was ultimately unsuccessful in the *Twyford Down* case. This did not prevent a similar strategy being adopted in the case of the Newbury bypass in the Thames Valley. This bypass, which became the subject of local and national controversy, mass letter writing, European lobbying, non-violent direct action ('The Third Battle of Newbury'), and criminal damage, was proposed following a public inquiry in 1988. As with most bypasses, the exact route was highly contested with alternatives centred upon two main routes—an

---

[210] See generally, S. Tromans, 'Environmental Protest and the Law' [2003] JPL 367.

[211] *Calvert Cliffs' Coordinating Committee* v *Atomic Energy Commission* 449 F2d 1109. See analysis of this case, Ch. 7, pp. 252–4.   [212] Brooks *et al., Law and Ecology*, 159.

[213] Hertz, 'Parallel Universes'.

[214] P. Kunzlik, 'The Lawyer's Assessment', in B. Bryant, *Twyford Down: Roads, Campaigning and Environmental Law* (London: Spon, 1996), 237.

eastern route which was likely to cause damage to an SSSI and a Local Nature Reserve, and a western route likely to damage attractive landscape. The western route was chosen by the Department of Transport, even though an environmental impact assessment had not been carried out on this option. It was argued, for example, that the presence of otters, dormice, badgers, and other protected animals along the route had been overlooked or underplayed.[215] The road was finally given the go-ahead after another inquiry in 1994 (at which wildlife matters were not discussed on the grounds that these had been covered at an earlier inquiry).

A spate of cases followed. In the context of challenging the Department of Transport's possession proceedings against protesters, the Court of Appeal in *Haughian*[216] clarified that a trespasser could not challenge the right of the local authority to possession of land compulsorily acquired for a road scheme on the grounds that the scheme had not been the subject of an environmental impact assessment. This has been criticized in strong terms:[217]

Its effect is to elevate the public policy interest in the certainty of a particular decision . . . above the rights to participate in that decision, and to information both facilitating that participation and rendering the decision transparent. It also reinforces the perception that the possibilities in this country of legal redress for the vast majority of those concerned with breaches of environmental law are more academic than real.[218]

In any event, the Court in *Haughian* found that an unlawful failure to conduct an environmental impact assessment would render the relevant decision *voidable*, rather than void. This meant that the decision would not necessarily be quashed on the grounds that assessment procedures had not been complied with (which is now questionable after *Berkeley No. 1*).

Famously, colonies of Desmoulin's whorl-snail (a tiny, rare, and endangered species) were discovered in the floodplains of the rivers Kennet and Lambourn during initial clearance and building work. English Nature had considered that a major stronghold for the snail might have existed in the path of the proposed road, which indicated the presence of ancient habitat, but had not acted upon this, suggesting a tendentious and 'weak official conservation effort'.[219] Since the snail was listed as a species under the EC Habitats Directive, the area might well have qualified as a Special Area of Conservation, meaning that an environmental impact assessment would have had to be conducted on the impact of the road on

---

[215] P. Marren, *Nature Conservation* (London: HarperCollins, 2002), 218. This is an unusual example of species with public appeal or 'charisma' not being selected to mobilize public support, when compared to the discovery of the less 'cuddly' Desmoulin's whorl-snail, discussed below. On bias in the selection of species for study by environmental impact assessment, see Treweek, *Ecological Impact Assessment*, 95.

[216] *Secretary of State for Transport* v *Haughian* (CA) unreported, 27.2.1996, [1996] *JR* 126 and *Goillon*, unreported, 12.2.1996. Both cases discussed in P. Roderick, 'The Newbury Bypass Litigation: Part I' [1996] *JR* 252.   [217] Roderick, 'The Newbury Bypass Litigation', at 253.

[218] ibid. at 253–4.

[219] P. Roderick, 'The Newbury Bypass Litigation: Part 2' [1997] *JR* 54, at 55.

the site and its wildlife and alternative schemes considered. This opportune finding halted work and gave those opposed to the bypass the basis for a further legal challenge. In *Fillingham*[220] the applicant protesters argued that as the clearance operations would damage the snail's habitat, the Secretary of State was in breach of obligations contained in the Habitat Regulations 1994,[221] and that the protection of the habitat in the wider public interest outweighed the private rights of the Crown to have immediate possession of the site. Sedley J held that the Secretary of State was not in breach of his duty because the relevant parts of the Directive were not effective at that time (even though a precautionary approach would have been to treat submitted candidate SACs as designated SACs, as outlined in government policy). He also commented that by starting to build the road at the same time that its environmental impact was being determined, the government was apparently foreclosing the possible answers to its own question. In effect, though, the judgment makes clear that even though the government's environmental obligations may be real and enforceable, this should not be by way of defending possession proceedings.[222]

English Nature belatedly recommended that the site of snail populations on and near the route of the proposed road be submitted by the government to the European Commission as a candidate SAC (on the same day as the Department of Transport announced the award of the contract for building the road). A final challenge to the award of the construction contract was made by the local wildlife trust and local residents, but leave to apply for judicial review of this decision was refused.[223] Marren takes up the account of the case:

The snail story now moves into realms of farce. The Environment Agency in consultation with English Nature came up with a plan to move the snail out of harm's way, along with chunks of its habitat, by digging up giant turves and transporting them to a prepared site further upstream. It did not seem to matter than no one knew anything about the snail's life cycle or ecology.[224]

The *Newbury* case has been described as a hollow 'moral victory',[225] because whilst making it more difficult for breaches of the EIA Directive to be raised in possession proceedings and further encouraging direct rather than legal action, it also prompted (short-lived) changes to road-building policy. In addition, following the controversy and direct action which was a feature of both the *Twyford Down* and *Newbury* cases (as well as cases concerning extensions to airports and the building of incinerator facilities) the government proposed that major

---

[220] *Secretary of State for Transport* v *Fillingham* [1997] Env LR 73.
[221] Reg. 3(4) of the Conservation (Natural Habitats, &c.) Regulations 1994 (SI 1994, No. 2716).
[222] On this and similar cases, see Tromans, 'Environmental Protest and the Law', at 1314.
[223] *R* v *Secretary of State for Transport and Secretary of State for the Environment ex parte BBONT, Friends of the Earth, the Wildlife Trusts and WWF (UK)* [1997] Env LR 80.
[224] *Nature Conservation*, 119–220.
[225] Roderick, 'The Newbury Bypass Litigation: Part II', 55.

infrastructure works such as these should be scrutinized and approved by Parliament before a further inquiry stage and finally authorized by the appropriate Secretary of State.[226] Amongst many criticisms of this proposal were doubts about how the new procedure could accommodate the requirements of the EIA Directive, particularly because of the proposed split between a parliamentary and inquiry process, and how effective participation could be secured in parliamentary procedures, since the approval of a project in advance would preclude discussion on matters settled by Parliament, such as alternative options.[227]

The proposed parliamentary scrutiny of major developments represented an unusual direction in the more general development of multi-level governance strategies based upon enhancing citizen participation, decentralization, and devolution. But to some extent the proposals were merely an extension of current procedures—private and hybrid bills and special development orders—which involve Parliament in the review and authorization of projects. Importantly, the EIA Directive does not apply to such projects, the 'details of which are adopted by a specific act of national legislation, since the objectives of this Directive, including that of supplying information, are achieved through the legislative process'.[228] As well as putting objectors in an unfair position, this means that there are no legal requirements about the content of environmental statements provided as part of parliamentary procedures.[229]

The proposal that Parliament scrutinize all major infrastructure development has now been abandoned in favour of the existing public inquiry framework,[230] but even this volte-face has not stemmed debate about major project authorization and the current practice of assessing environmental effects in Parliament.[231] Specifically, the proposal highlighted that the appreciation that participation should take place at different levels of decision making has its limits, in this case that the corresponding pattern of multi-level environmental assessment (of policies, plans, and projects)[232] might be ignored in favour of high-level (and exclusionary) scrutiny, even when concerned with much of the detail of major developments. Continuing concern about the effectiveness of participation in environmental impact assessment procedures for major infrastructure projects, as well as the potential use of environmental assessment as a protest strategy, are illustrated by the following case study.

[226] DTLR, Planning Green Paper, *New Parliamentary Procedures for Major Infrastructure Projects* (London: HMSO, 2001). See more recent proposals in the Planning and Compulsory Purchase Bill.
[227] P. Thompson, 'Major Infrastructure Projects: Where to Now?' [2002] JPL 25.
[228] Art. 1(5)   [229] Popham and Purdue, 'The Future of the Major Inquiry', at 144.
[230] Town and Country Planning (Major Infrastructure Project Inquiries Procedure) (England) Rules 2002 (SI 2002, No. 1624). Major infrastructure projects are defined in the rules by using the 1999 EIA Regulations, which list in Sch. 1 to the Regulations those development projects for which environmental impact assessment is mandatory.
[231] For e.g. Royal Commission on Environmental Pollution, Twenty-Third Report, *Environmental Planning* (Cm 5459) recommends that 'the national need for additional infrastructure should be probed in an open and participatory process, which where practicable should engage local communities which may be affected' (para. 8.50).   [232] See Ch. 2, pp. 60–4.

Science and Deliberation: The Case of Dibden Bay 'Global' Port

The high-profile anti-road campaigns of the early 1990s have given way to protests against the building or extension of ports (and airports) as the highly visible consequence of global trade. Several of the legal cases concerned with port development, in both national and European fora, have clustered around nature conservation and environmental impact assessment issues.[233] This case study concerns a proposed 202 hectare container terminal (referred to as a 'superport' by opponents) on the New Forest side of Southampton Water, in an undeveloped gap between two villages. The application has been the subject of an environmental assessment process and a planning inquiry (held for a year from November 2001). The inspector's report was submitted to the Secretary of State for the Environment, Transport and the Regions in October 2003, and a final decision is awaited.[234] The site and area around the proposed terminal is the subject of international, national, and local designations. For example, the Solent and Southampton Water Ramsar site and Special Protection Area support internationally important wintering waterfowl, breeding gull and tern populations, and an important assemblage of rare invertebrates and plants. The Solent Maritime candidate Special Area of Conservation is considered to be one of the most important areas for Atlantic salt meadow in the United Kingdom. Dibden Bay itself is designated as a Site of Special Scientific Interest due to providing one of the richest sites around the Solent for nationally rare and nationally scarce bird species, including breeding lapwing.[235] Under the Habitats Directive, designation of the site as an SPA and candidate SAC means that development can only be approved in the absence of alternatives and for reasons of overriding public interest (which may include social or economic reasons).[236]

In the main environmental statement[237] which accompanied the applications for various authorizations,[238] Associated British Ports concluded that the Dibden Bay development would have direct effects, both adverse and beneficial, on the site

---

[233] For e.g. Case C-44/95 *R* v *Secretary of State for the Environment ex parte RSPB* (*Lappel Bank*) [1996] ECR I-3805, prior national proceedings reported at (1995) 7 JEL 245 and Case C-371/98 *R* v *Secretary of State for the Environment, Transport and the Regions ex parte First Corporate Shipping* [2001] ECR I-9235.   [234] See Epilogue, p. 300.

[235] Friends of the Earth, 'A New Superport for the New Forest?' Briefing paper.

[236] Art. 6(4) EC Directive 92/43/EC on the conservation of natural habitats and of wild flora and fauna OJ 1992 L 206, p. 7. If either of the sites hosts a priority natural habitat type and/or priority species, the only considerations which may be raised are those relating to human health or public safety, to beneficial consequences of primary importance for the environment, or further to an opinion from the Commission, to other imperatives of overriding public interest. See further Ch. 2, pp. 68–70 and Ch. 5, pp. 158–9.

[237] Adams Hendry, 'Dibden Terminal: Environmental Statement, Non-technical Summary' (Winchester, 2000), para. 100. See further critique of the environmental statement in J. Walker, 'Dibden Bay Port: the Quality of Life Questions' (2001) 22 *ECOS* 65.

[238] The applications comprised a Harbour Revision Order for the main port development; a Transport and Works Act Order for works to a railway line, Stopping Up Orders for roads and

and surrounding areas, but that considering the balance of effects of the port facility and its habitat restoration proposals, this would not have a significant adverse
effect on the estuarine systems of Southampton Water and the Solent. ABP
arrived at this conclusion because of the intertidal recharge of an area of the foreshore with cleaner sediment, and its planned creation and management of other
coastal sites, notably a new creek and a nature conservation area likely to provide
sufficient alternative habitat for waterfowl that regularly feed and breed on the
Dibden foreshore.

Hampshire County Council disagreed with this key conclusion of the developer's
environmental statement, asserting that the proposals would have a considerable
adverse effect on nature conservation. The Council detailed the direct loss of
42 hectares of intertidal mudflat along the Dibden foreshore (designated as an SPA),
the further loss of 34 hectares of intertidal foreshore and wet grassland which is
important for birds using the foreshore. It expressed concerns about the appropriateness of the ecological assessment methodologies used by ABP, in particular the
assumption that the proposed creek (designed as mitigation) might adequately
replace the foreshore as it did not represent 'like for like', and that the habitats would
become functional within the timescales put forward by ABP (English Nature considered that it could take up to 20 years for colonization to be achieved), concluding
that the development was likely to lead to a serious decline in waterfowl populations
in the Bay. In terms of the 'appropriate assessment' for the purpose of the
Conservation Regulations 1994[239] the Council considered that the sequence of
analysis was flawed because ABP took into account mitigation measures as part of its
assessment as to whether the project was likely to have a significant effect on a nature
conservation site of European importance.[240] Aside from degradation of the designated conservation sites and effects on landscape, opponents argued that the predicted 5,000 further vehicle movements and nearly 50 more train movements per
day generated by the development were likely to affect pollution levels in the area.[241]

Hampshire County Council objected to the proposal for predominantly environmental reasons because its structure plan acknowledged that port development
might be permitted if it could be demonstrated that the need for the port outweighed
its impact on nature conservation, the New Forest, and local communities and

footpaths, and Compulsory Purchase Orders (submitted to the Secretary of State for the
Environment, Transport and the Regions); two planning applications for roadworks and for noise
barriers along a railway line (submitted to the District Council, although these have now been called
in by the Secretary of State) and various Food and Environment Protection Act Licences (submitted
to the Ministry of Agriculture, Fisheries and Food). Numerous documents accompanied the proposal, including two Environmental Statements (one for the port development and one for the railway line works), an 'appropriate assessment' under Reg. 48 of the Conservation (Natural Habitats,
&c.) Regulations 1994 (SI 1994, No. 2716) (the Conservation Regulations 1994), as well as technical reports and various plans.

[239] ibid.
[240] The assessment of significance should precede analysis of the effects of mitigation and compensatory measures, as discussed further in Ch. 4, pp. 136–40.
[241] Adams Hendry, 'Dibden Terminal', para. 100.

if sufficient mitigation were provided. The Council considered that this requirement had not been discharged and summarized the likely environmental effects in the following terms:

6.5 The environmental impact of the proposed development is dramatic. On nature conservation grounds it affects the integrity of European sites. The proposed creek should be viewed as compensation and not mitigation as put forward by ABP. The creek does not represent 'like for like' replacement of the foreshore. The recharge may also need to be considered as compensation. The recharge is a solution on an untested scale and doubts are raised on its feasibility. There are major implications on National Park and landscape grounds—there will be a detrimental effect on the New Forest.[242]

This assessment was based only in part on ABP's Environmental Statement because the Council considered that this was inadequate, in particular that ABP had not fully assessed alternatives to the project, including improving efficiency at the existing port and other sites.[243] As the Harbour Authority for the Port of Southampton, ABP was considered a statutory body for the purposes of the EIA Directive.[244] This enabled it to assess the adequacy of its own environmental statement. The Environment Agency (a statutory consultee for the purpose of scrutinizing the application, including the environmental statement) criticized the potential for a conflict of interest that this occasioned in its statement of case for the planning inquiry:

The Agency questions the adequacy of the investigations undertaken, the methodology adopted and the reliability of the conclusions reached. The Agency does not understand the basis upon which ABP can have felt able to conclude that a commercial development involving major engineering operations and a permanent change to a material proportion of the Sites is unlikely to have any significant effect and it has seen no written justification for that stance.[245]

In this case environmental impact assessment procedures formed a part of a planning inquiry into the application. This leads to questions of the priority or otherwise given to information arising from environmental impact assessment procedures in a more wide-ranging and adversarial inquiry procedure.

The Place and Role of Environmental Assessment in Planning Inquiries: Implications for Participation

Prior to the implementation of the EC EIA Directive in the United Kingdom, the planning inquiry offered the main means by which potential environmental

---

[242] Hampshire County Council Policy and Resources Committee and Transportation Committee, 'ABP's Proposal for Dibden Bay: Overall Response Report of the County Planning Officer and County Surveyor', 12.2.01.

[243] Friends of the Earth, 'A New Superport for the New Forest?'.

[244] Note, there is no statutory provision to prevent this.

[245] Environment Agency, Statement of Case, submitted for the purposes of the planning inquiry, November 2001.

effects of developments could be assessed and considered. It remains one of the major vehicles for public participation in the planning system. However, at the time that the EIA Directive was being negotiated, optimism for the new system of environmental impact assessment was partly born out of the perceived failure of several high-profile public inquiries.[246] At the time of the initial implementation effort there was little consideration of how environmental assessment procedures could be integrated practically into planning inquiry procedures, even though the same projects were likely to be subject to both statutory assessment rules and inquiry rules.[247] The interrelation of environmental assessment and the planning inquiry is now the subject of guidance which explains that the Secretary of State may use the 1999 Regulations[248] to request further information for the purposes of a local inquiry under the 1990 Act,[249] in which case that information is regulated by rules relating to the submission of evidence to local planning inquiries.[250]

It was initially considered that integration of the EC EIA Directive with the British model of inquiry had important implications for public participation because of the possible dissipation of effort on the part of protesters who might spend a disproportionate amount of time challenging environmental statements which make up only one aspect of the inquiry. There was also the concern that the specialist knowledge elicited from environmental impact assessment procedures was likely to be swamped by the wide-ranging considerations of the planning inquiry. These concerns are borne out to some extent by 'exploratory' research conducted by Jones and Wood,[251] on the use of environmental assessment by planning inspectors. They describe that the importance of the developer's environmental statement to inspectors lies in evaluating the information about a case, and that this is generally less than the additional evidence given (and the subsequent examination) at the inquiry. But the results from consultations based upon the statement were found to be often as important (and sometimes more so) in making a decision as information derived from the developer's environmental statement. However, neither the environmental statement nor the results of consultations based upon this were given great prominence in the inspectors' reports. Rather, Jones and Wood conclude that the environmental statement is important

---

[246] As discussed in Ch. 2, pp. 45–7.

[247] Although C. Wood and C. Jones, *Monitoring Environmental Assessment and Planning* (London: HMSO, 1990), 45–6 raised this issue: 'public inquiry decisions will inevitably have significant ramifications for the adequacy of environmental statements generally' and 'the use made in public inquiries of environmental statements by the various parties should be investigated to determine whether environmental assessment is being integrated appropriately in the call-in and appeal procedures'.

[248] Reg. 19 Town and Country Planning (Environmental Impact Assessment) Regulations 1999 (SI 1999, No. 293).   [249] Town and Country Planning Act 1990.

[250] Town and Country Planning (Major Infrastructure Projects Inquiries Procedure) (England) Rules 2000 (SI 2000, No. 1624) and the Town and Country Planning Appeals (Determination by Inspectors) (Inquiries Procedure) (England) Rules 2000 (SI 2000, No. 1626).

[251] C. Jones and C. Wood, 'The Impact of Environmental Assessment on Public Inquiry Decisions' [1995] JPL 890.

at the start of the public inquiry procedure as a means to place on the agenda environmental issues arising from a particular development.

A unique feature of the Dibden Bay inquiry[252] was the establishment of working groups on specific areas of concern, for example birds, sedimentation, contaminated land, and marine navigation. These were set up by planning inspectors to encourage agreement to be reached on methodologies and, if possible, the potential impacts of the development, and to feed information into pre-inquiry meetings, thus saving time in the actual inquiry. In practice, the groups were used to discuss the more complex environmental implications of the development, outside formal environmental impact assessment procedures. The groups were highly significant as a way of circumventing public participation because, although membership of the groups was self-selecting, in practice only parties to the inquiry with financial interests were able to devote time and other resources. This meant that the groups were largely composed of scientific experts and lawyers retained by the developer and interest groups (the RSPB) with little representation from local residents and the wider public. In addition, the material discussed was highly technical and practically incapable of being scrutinized or supplemented by non-experts (and even lawyers!). The discussions, as well as the structure of the groups, were based upon the areas of concern identified in the Environmental Statement, but the material discussed superseded information provided in the Statement. For example, as a result of discussions on the impacts of the proposed development on the local bird population, data was recast and represented along different timelines. Importantly, the groups were coordinated by the developer, who gained a complete picture of progress on the application, as well as potential 'troublespots', prior to the inquiry taking place. This meant that ABP were able to anticipate criticism and use this to inform their response to evidence at the inquiry.

In summary, the environmental impact assessment process helped to place environmental issues arising from the development on the inquiry agenda. But information contained in the developer's environmental statement was superseded by information elicited by specialist working groups, in which there was little participation or scrutiny by local participants. The operation of the groups meant that the environmental impact assessment procedure was sidelined as a means of securing effective public participation. This contributed to the 'professionalization' of assessment and inquiry procedures, to the exclusion of third parties. The expert and discrete handling of complex scientific information in this case supports a view that a technical approach to decision making ousts values and concerns that do not fit within a technical perspective, even when environmental procedures are

---

[252] In terms of public participation, a further, basic problem was that the inquiry was due to take place at Southampton Docks, on premises owned by the applicant. The lack of public transport discouraged the attendance of local residents owing to the time and cost of travel. This formed the subject of a parliamentary petition organized by the 'Residents against Dibden Bay Port', HC, 19.11.2001, col. 148.

involved. Appreciation of environmental protection concerns was inevitably limited to the category of technical learning.[253] A feature of this is limited discussion of alternatives, in this case restricted to options to alleviate harm, for example by the artificial replication of wetland areas for waterfowl.

The limited nature of the alternatives discussed raises the issue of the appropriate policy and political context in which projects such as this should be decided, as well as the level of decision making.[254] In this case, there was no central strategic overview of ports' capacity at the time of the inquiry,[255] which might have helped assess whether this port was needed, particularly when compared to other applications for extending port capacity around the country. Instead, the question of need was aired in Parliament in the form of a memorandum submitted by local residents to the Committee for Environment, Transport and Regional Affairs.[256] The gist of this was that demand for port development in the United Kingdom could be satisfied at alternative locations where the environmental and social impact would be less than with the development of Dibden Bay. This, however, raises the question of the level at which need should be addressed, for example, port capacity in Europe should also have been taken into account.

The Dibden Bay development suggests that the more varied forms of participation described in contemporary deliberative theories have not substantially reduced the reliance upon quantitative information in decision making involving environmental assessment. The impact of this on the outcomes of decision making is explored by Kuehn,[257] who concludes that impacts which can be measured receive more weight in decision making than less tangible, though perhaps more important, non-quantifiable results. This is especially important when the centrality of the attribution of weight in decision making governed by environmental assessment is considered.[258]

Conclusions

The existence of procedural rules establishing opportunities for participation is a key characteristic of environmental assessment.[259] In this chapter I outlined the ways in which such opportunities are currently being strengthened, apparently underpinned by an appreciation of fundamental rights involved in public participation in decision making. At least in policy, the participatory elements of environmental assessment appear to have overcome an original rationale for this

---

[253] Discussed above, pp. 197–203.

[254] On this and similar issues, see Ch. 5, pp. 162–4.

[255] Although such a strategic overview was due to be published at the time that the inquiry took place.

[256] Minutes of Evidence, Committee for Environment, Transport and Regional Affairs, 28.3.01.

[257] 'The Environmental Justice Implications of Quantitative Risk Assessment'.

[258] Ch. 7 at pp. 237–43.   [259] Ch. 1, pp. 18–19, and Ch. 7, pp. 237–43.

procedure, the generation of more accurate scientific information about the effects of development on the environment to be fed into political decision making.[260] For example, Taylor analysed the influence of NEPA in terms of how far it accorded to a science model of generating scientific knowledge.[261] However, the application of environmental assessment procedures in the Dibden Bay planning inquiry tends to accord more with this original rationale than modern governance strategies of participation and coordination of decision making. This reveals an understanding of environmental assessment as primarily for information generation (information theories) rather than more culturally based understandings of the process (culture theories). It is relevant that although there appears to be a political consensus about deliberation, the desirability of a technicist approach to assessing risks is still expressed in the literature on participation in decision making. This advances the view that effective public involvement in environmental decision making is difficult to achieve, not necessarily constructive, and more fundamentally, that 'the chaos of uninformed public involvement is not democracy'.[262] The implication is that decision-making systems should not be developed which rely on an assumption of deep citizen interest or learning, but rather that the public's role should be restricted to reviewing the generation of 'good data' and the most scientific and technical information possible.[263] The practice of participation in environmental assessment procedures suggests that this is curtailed in key, sensitive, areas of decision making such as the screening and scoping stages of the assessment process, and that the expression of the deliberative ideal in environmental assessment procedures should not be overplayed.[264] This jars with the attention given to inclusive decision making in the planning system, originally prompted by concerns about the mutual importance of local environmental democracy and sustainability in Local Agenda 21. Equally important is a perception of exclusion (and scepticism about the efficacy of participation) which may provide some explanation for the largely marginal role played by the general public in environmental impact assessment and other planning processes such as development plan formation.[265] This suggests that the widespread problem of non-participation is more than one of 'process' that can be resolved simply by providing more channels of participation. The high profile and strategic use of environmental assessment as a hook for challenging unwanted development

---

[260] On fundamental rights and environmental assessment, see Ch. 8, pp. 291–4.

[261] Taylor, *Making Bureaucracies Think*, 305–6.

[262] D. C. Esty, 'Toward Optimal Environmental Governance' (1999) *NYU L Rev* 1495, at 1566.

[263] ibid.

[264] The Royal Commission on Environmental Pollution, *Environmental Planning*, Twenty-third Report, para. 7.31 concluded that current informal arrangements for public participation were far from satisfactory. For example, the Commission cited a 1998 review of environmental statements which found that the public was involved in scoping in only about 40 per cent of cases and influenced the content of the environmental statement in only a proportion of these.

[265] C. Wood, 'Environmental Assessment', in C. Miller (ed.) *Planning and Environmental Protection* (Oxford: Hart, 2001), 167.

similarly highlights that dilemmas about land use are clearly not being resolved by participation at the plan-making stage.[266]

Nevertheless, in theory and policy the regulatory pillar of environmental governance continues to rest upon the participation of a range of sectors, groups, and individuals, so that a mix of the public and private may be achieved in pursuing certain goals aimed at environmental protection. The many claims for participation in environmental assessment—that it ensures coordination and communication, information disclosure, social awareness, and education—mean that it provides a test for reflexive models of regulation. Most notably, effective participation (rather than consultation or supervision) in environmental assessment procedures may contribute to a state of regulatory pluralism in which no single proponent or participant has a monopoly over the provision of information and its interpretation. On this point, in the following chapter I focus on developers' use of environmental assessment procedures in the context of the regulation of decision making and thus analyse a further claim of reflexivity, shared responsibility for environmental problems.

[266] This was the original aim of the Skeffington Report 1968 which recommended greatly enhanced public participation in plan-making.

7

Regulation of Decision Making

In the previous chapter I analysed the ideal and practice of deliberation, as reflected in the participation requirements of the environmental assessment process. Such deliberation is brought to an end by a decision, for example the grant of development consent, the sanctioning of a contract for foreign assistance, or an opinion on the survival of a threatened habitat. Otherwise, deliberation would be 'interminably unresolved'.[1] The decision therefore provides the denouement of environmental assessment and also its rationale. But, in formal terms at least, the final decision may not be determined by environmental assessment procedures. This is made clear by the requirement (and no more) in the EC EIA Directive that '[T]he results of consultations and the information gathered . . . must be taken into consideration in the development consent procedure'.[2] This requirement, mirrored in the EC SEA Directive,[3] is striking for its simplicity and apparent lack of substantive content.[4] It means in practice that environmental assessment does not provide an enforceable or positive means by which a grant of planning permission or other authorization may either be refused or made conditional. The consequences of this may be seen in increased environmental pollution and exploitation of natural resources which flow from the granting of such licences.

This procedural aspect of environmental assessment is central to its regulatory character, and relates directly to the conceptual underpinnings of environmental assessment as a route by which to feed information to decision makers, or in a broader sense as an organ for cultural change in administrations and organizations. In this chapter I give an account of the way in which courts in the United States and the United Kingdom[5] (and other jurisdictions) have distinguished between procedural control exercised by environmental assessment and its potential to shape substantive outcomes. Recently, the English higher courts have begun to recognize the related nature of these two functions. The European

---

[1] Fitzpatrick, 'Consolations of the Law', at 285.

[2] Art. 8 Directive 85/337/EEC, OJ 1985 L 175, p. 40, as amended by Directive 97/11/EC, OJ 1997 L 73, p. 5. See Appendix II.

[3] Art. 8 Directive 2001/42/EC, OJ 2001 L 197, p. 30. See Appendix III.

[4] McAuslan, *Ideologies of Planning Law,* 47, considered this also to be the case with the progressive public participation agenda in the late 1970s.

[5] For a comparative analysis, see W. M. Tubb, 'Environmental Impact Assessment in the European Community: Shaping International Norms' (1999) 73 *Tul L Rev* 923.

Commission is also tentatively exploring the means by which a more substantive element may be introduced into the Member States' environmental assessment regimes by obliging authorities to refuse consent for a project that is likely to have negative impacts on the environment.[6]

Considering the procedural (and possibly more substantive) effects of environmental assessment highlights the difficulty of demarcating responsibility for environmental decision making between administrators as decision makers, and the courts. It is also an example of the universal predicament of decision making invoking due process requirements, that a balance must be struck, often through compromises being made, between strict compliance with the prescribed procedures designed to steer decision making in a certain direction and the reality of everyday decision making, shaped by particular circumstances and also inevitably influenced by particular interests.

The common presentation of environmental assessment as primarily a procedural mechanism, and thus most easily explained by information theories, is now allied to theories of reflexivity in environmental law. Reflexivity describes the increasing reliance upon indirect, abstract, and procedural forms of law, which may also have the capacity to encourage social learning.[7] A key purpose of this chapter is to challenge the restricted portrayal of environmental assessment as a procedural mechanism by applying theories of reflexivity in law to the reality of decision making, and by examining the claims of cultural change brought about by environmental assessment. The Cairngorm funicular railway case study offers an account of the use of environmental assessment within planning practices which are heavily influenced by private interests. It also provides a practical example of the way in which some of the guiding ideas of ecological modernization[8]— partnership (between regulator and regulated), shared responsibility for environmental protection, and reconciliation of economic and environmental costs and benefits—may manifest themselves in a particular set of events, through engagement with the environment assessment process. In the light of this case study, I relate information provision theories of environmental assessment to the procedural control exercised by the instrument, and compare this to the more substantive outcomes envisaged by proponents of cultural change theories.

The following quotation from Advocate-General Elmer's Opinion in *Grosskrotzenburg*,[9] on the procedural nature of environmental assessment, sets the scene for this chapter, not least because of its repercussions in national courts:[10]

It must be emphasised that the provisions of the directive are essentially of a procedural nature. By the inclusion of information on the environment in the consent procedure it is ensured that the environmental impact of the project shall be included in the public

---

[6] As discussed below, pp. 268–9.   [7] As discussed in Ch. 6, pp. 195–9.
[8] As discussed in Ch. 2, p. 59.
[9] Case C-431/92, *Commission v Germany* [1995] ECR I-2209, para. 35 of A-G Opinion.
[10] For example, the European Court of Justice's judgment strongly influenced the judgment of the Court of Appeal in *Berkeley No. 1;* see further below, pp. 258–68.

debate and that the decision as to whether consent is to be given shall be adopted on an appropriate basis. The directive on the other hand can scarcely serve as an instrument for monitoring the content of the consents issued on the basis of environmental criteria. Even though the expression 'must be taken into consideration' in Article 8 of the directive must mean that the information gathered is to be subjected to an independent, critical examination, the directive does not prevent the competent authority's giving consent to a project, even though the environmental impact assessment shows that the project will have negative effects on the environment.

This expresses a once commonplace judicial understanding. But clearly this purely procedural and thus narrow take on environmental assessment is not the whole story, and now represents a simplistic view of the instrument that has to some extent been overtaken by recognition of its broader functions, particularly those which reflect environmental governance strategies of participation and social learning.

As is the case with judgments of significance,[11] environmental assessment procedures influence the discretion exercised by the final decision maker, in terms of the information available to be considered, but not the relative weight to be granted to environmental considerations (as against the weight attached to developmental considerations) which may arise from this information. This remains the preserve of the decision maker, subject only to principles of good administration. As Hertz notes: 'the whole idea [of environmental assessment] is to inform discretion, making sure that where there are no substantive constraints on the government, that decision will at least be thought through and subject to public input'.[12] That said, the development of a duty to give reasons[13] narrows discretion on the part of the decision maker to disregard environmental factors and possibly further encourages the internalization of information about environmental harm and the value of environmental protection.

Characterizing the Regulatory Form of Environmental Assessment

The regulation exercised by environmental assessment has several important characteristics. The key characteristic, already mentioned, is that environmental assessment does not directly determine the outcome of a decision-making process. Rather, information gathered in the course of the environmental assessment process must be taken into account by the decision-making body. The basic legal form of environmental assessment therefore sets procedural requirements for considering the predicted effects of development on the environment and in this way regulates the creation and gathering of environmental knowledge and

---

[11] As discussed in Ch. 4.   [12] Hertz, 'Parallel Universes', at 1669.
[13] See below, pp. 269–72.

decision making based upon this. The conceptual underpinning of the regulatory nature of environmental assessment is that 'process substitutes for (substantive) standards by ensuring thoughtful and well-informed exercises of discretion'.[14] This characteristic is well illustrated by the form of environmental assessment exercised in the United States under NEPA 1969. This does not mandate particular results, but simply prescribes the necessary process. As Hertz forcefully comments: 'Notice what NEPA is not. It is not a pollution control statute. It does not forbid any form of environmentally harmful activity. It does not directly protect a single tree or in any way tie agencies' hands'.[15] Put simply, 'NEPA merely prohibits uninformed—rather than unwise—agency action'.[16]

In terms of law and policy, the procedural control exercised by environmental assessment is similarly apparent in Article 8 of the EC EIA Directive,[17] quoted above, which in turn is replicated in the 1999 Regulations:[18] 'The relevant planning authority or the Secretary of State or an inspector shall not grant planning permission pursuant to an application to which this regulation applies unless they have first taken the environmental information into consideration, and they shall state in their decision that they have done so.' [19] Circular 02/99 elaborates:

Where the EIA procedure reveals that a project will have an adverse impact on the environment, it does not follow that planning permission must be refused. It remains the task of the local planning authority to judge each planning application on its merits within the context of the Development Plan, taking account of all material considerations, including the environmental impacts.[20]

As a procedure intended to enable decision makers to make informed choices between environmental protection and other objectives (and for the public to be informed about these), environmental assessment does not appear to contain substantive, or positive, goals. Rather, by setting out common and abstract procedural requirements and establishing programmes of administration governing decision makers, environmental assessment rules relate to the style and structure of decision making. It does not control future action according to specific standards but by a presumption that environmental harm may occur, in particular by setting rules by which information about the effects of development on the environment is to be gathered and taken into account in decision making. Alder's oft-quoted summary of the functions of environmental assessment is worth reiterating here: 'Environmental impact assessment is not, as such, an environmental protection measure with positive goals. Environmental impact assessment is

---

[14] But, see below, pp. 239–40.   [15] 'Parallel Universes', at 1681.

[16] *Marsh* v *Oregon Natural Resources Council*, 490 US 360, 371 (1989).

[17] Directive 85/337/EEC, as amended. This requires that '[T]he results of consultations and the information gathered . . . must be taken into consideration in the development consent procedure'.

[18] Town and Country Planning (Environmental Impact Assessment) (England and Wales) Regulations 1999 (SI 1999, No. 293).   [19] Reg. 3(2) of the1999 Regulations.

[20] Department of Environment, Transport and the Regions, Circular 02/99, *Environmental Impact Assessment*, para. 13.

intended to enable decision makers to make an informed choice between environmental and other objectives and for the public to be consulted'.[21]

Although these examples suggest that environmental assessment is a strongly procedural technique of environmental law, it is more accurate to consider the procedural control exercised over decision making and the substantive outcomes of those decisions as mutually enforcing. Following Nonet, one function of procedural rules is to gain recognition of substantive rights in administration; once a decision maker becomes accountable to a *procedural* rule, the *content* of the decision arrived at also becomes an issue for debate.[22] Selznick similarly describes how new (procedural) rules create a critical spirit which entails a scrutiny of both the integrity of the rules' administration and the quality of the rules themselves. In other words, the rules are assessed 'in the light of the substantive ends'.[23] Jowell reinforces the fine distinction between procedural due process (affecting the propriety of the procedure involved in reaching a decision) and substantive due process (affecting the quality of the decision reached). He stresses that, although not positive or substantive measures, procedural rules have a number of important functions which bear upon the substance of the decision arrived at in a decision-making process. Procedural rules may, for example, serve the function of achieving congruence between officially determined ends (for example, environmental protection) and official decision making, particularly by excluding or reducing the possibility of arbitrary decisions.[24] Upholding environmental assessment as a procedural form of law, unrelated to the substance or outcome of decisions, is to artificially bifurcate procedural and substantive rules. Procedural rules are capable of 'speaking' very clearly to the shape of the final decision by ensuring participation by those interested in the result. Decision makers may therefore recognize a spectrum of interests via the style and structure of the decision-making procedures.

In relation to these questions about the substantive or procedural nature of regulation by environmental assessment, an important issue is whether environmental assessment operates to satisfy standards, (for example, quality standards formulated for controlling pollution). Whilst a cynic would say that it does not operate *at all* to satisfy standards, there is a view that, practically speaking, the boundary between procedural rules and substantive outcomes contained in standards is more vague and that potentially environmental assessment may be used to identify the likelihood of future compliance with existing standards. Thus, whether an impact is judged to be significant is in part a question of whether standards (for example, quality standards) are likely to be infringed by a proposed project (this being less the case with policy). Hertz concurs: 'It is an oversimplification to say that NEPA operates independently of and in place of substantive

---

21 Alder, 'Environmental Impact Assessment', at 211.
22 P. Nonet, *Administrative Justice* (New York: Russell Sage Foundation, 1969), at 170.
23 Selznick, *Law, Society and Industrial Justice*, 30.
24 Jowell, 'The Legal Control of Administrative Discretion', at 216.

standards. In practice the EIS process is tied to the application of those standards'.[25] More generally, an important argument in favour of moving to more reflexive methods of law is that environmental assessment and other instruments may reach even beyond the satisfaction of existing standards.

A similar point may be made about procedural requirements in administrative law more generally, in which a distinction is crafted for the purpose of analysis between instrumental approaches, stressing the need for strict procedural requirements to ensure accurate decision making (which roughly correlate to information theories of environmental assessment) and dignitarian approaches which consider that procedures exist to foster and protect values, even independently of the final outcome.[26]

Returning specifically to the regulatory characteristics of environmental assessment, the main consequence of the various procedural requirements is that a 'burden of proof' is imposed on the developer or proponent to demonstrate that a proposed project is acceptable in environmental terms at the planning stage, that alternatives have been considered, and that adverse effects may be mitigated. This imposes a duty on the developer to take account of environmental protection when proposing development which interferes with an idea of the desirability of untrammelled rights of development. In the United Kingdom, this 'burden of proof' was introduced into the land use planning system by the implementation of the EC EIA Directive.[27] This in effect qualified the presumption in favour of development which had long prevailed in planning policy (at least before the shift to plan-led development)[28] and began to encourage a general perception of development as potentially environmentally harmful, even in a policy climate favouring entrepreneurial planning. By bearing primary responsibility for providing information about the effects of a project in this way, the developer acquires partial responsibility for environmental protection. In the land use planning system, the significance of this information is disproportionate to the developer's traditional status in planning law and policy. This is particularly relevant when considering the role of environmental assessment in this setting: the developer's developmental (or property) interest in a parcel of land provides a receptive base for the advancement of environmental issues by providing information about the likely effects of development, but only to the extent, and in a manner, determined by the developer. For example, the illustrative case studies of the Kentish Flats windfarm[29] and the Cairngorm funicular railway[30] suggest that the developer may benefit from defining the boundaries of assessment studies and narrowly identifying alternatives, as well as highlighting any (economic and/or environmental)

---

[25] Hertz, 'Parallel Universes', at 1683.   [26] As discussed in Ch. 6, pp. 199–205.

[27] Directive 85/337/EEC, as amended.

[28] The nature of this shift and the implications for environmental protection (brought about by s. 54A Town and Country Planning Act 1990, as amended) are considered in Elworthy and Holder, *Environmental Protection*, ch. 7.   [29] See Ch. 4, pp. 140–6.

[30] See below, pp. 272–81.

benefits that flow from development and prescribing certain measures to alleviate potential harm. The roles of the developer and decision maker may therefore become fused in terms of gathering information and identifying mitigating measures, although the local authority or Secretary of State still remains responsible, and accountable, for the final decision.

Taking the case of the EIA Directive, the local planning authority or other competent authority should carry out an assessment *on the basis of* information provided by the developer.[31] In practice, the developer (by engaging an environmental consultant) conducts a *de facto* environmental assessment of the proposed development, a very real example of information asymmetry between developer and decision maker. This sets up the conditions for deeply contradictory roles for the developer—as proponent, and as information provider—and a conflict between developmental interests (including freedom of enterprise) in a specific parcel of land and broader communitarian interests in environmental protection.[32] The unequal economic (as well as information-gathering) resources possessed by the public and private sectors is also clearly relevant. Whilst private developers can afford to secure environmental consultants to compile a favourable, or at least visually attractive, environmental statement, it appears that few public authorities can do the same for an evaluation of the statement, although to some extent statutory consultees provide expertise analogous to consultants.[33] In addition, the reliance in environmental assessment procedures upon scientific and expert opinion appears to offer objectivity in terms of prediction of likely effects and impacts.[34] The governing role of the developer as information provider, and the weight accorded to this information, means that the more general identification of assessment with objectivity may operate in favour of private interests. Environmental assessment may therefore allow the private sector to become excessively influential in the planning system.[35] Coupled with this is the practice of developers providing voluntary statements because they consider that this may facilitate a grant of planning permission. For example, in the *London Congestion Charges* case,[36] in which

[31] Fifth recital to the preamble of the unamended Directive 85/337/EEC: 'whereas this assessment must be conducted on the basis of the appropriate information supplied by the developer which may be supplemented by the authorities and by the people who may be concerned by the project in question'. This formulation no longer appears in the Directive as amended by Directive 97/11/EC, OJ 1997 L 73, p. 5.

[32] Ost, 'A Game Without Rules?', at 351, extends this analysis by describing a tension in environmental assessment between the public logic of publicity, freedom of information, and the carrying out of a 'public service' and the prevailing private logic of the promoter's freedom of enterprise.

[33] On the role of statutory consultees, see Ch. 2, pp. 41–2. Clause 52 of the Planning and Compulsory Purchase Bill, presently before Parliament, places a duty upon statutory consultees to respond to planning applications within a given period. This may shift the balance of information provision away from the developer.   [34] Discussed further in Ch. 3, pp. 94–7.

[35] For a discussion—and defence—of the process of 'privatization' in the planning system through developers' contributions, see *Tesco Stores Ltd* v *Secretary of State for the Environment* [1995] 2 All ER 636, per Lord Hoffman at 659.

[36] *R* v *Mayor of London ex parte Preece and Adamson* [2002] EWHC 2440 (Admin), [2002] 2 All ER (D) 494 (Jul). See further, Ch. 1, pp. 1–2 and Ch. 4, p. 114.

the actions of a *public* authority were reviewed, the desirability of the Mayor producing an environmental statement was commented upon by the judge even though this was not strictly necessary as a matter of law.

These regulatory characteristics point to the sharing of responsibility for environmental protection between the regulator and the regulated through environmental assessment processes, particularly within the domain of development planning. Arguably, this is qualitatively different from the relationship between developer and local planning authority in 'ordinary' planning cases, not involving environmental assessment.[37] This is indicative of the regulatory space metaphor which describes 'the fact that regulatory authority and responsibility are frequently dispersed between a number of organisations, public and private'.[38] Scott elaborates, tying responsibility and authority to the holding of resources such as information, a factor which is highly apposite when considering the influence that may be brought to bear on decision-making processes by information contained in a developer's environmental statement:

These resources are not restricted to formal, state authority derived from legislation or contracts, but also include information, wealth and organisational capacities. The possession of these resources is fragmented among state bodies, and between state and non-state bodies. The combination of information and organisational capacities may give to a regulated firm considerable informal authority, which is important in the outcome even of formal rule formation or rule enforcement processes. Put another way, capacities derived from possession of key resources are not necessarily exercised hierarchically within the regulatory space, regulator over regulatee. We recognise the presence within the regulatory space not just of regulators and regulatees, but of other interested organisations, state and non-state, possessing resources to a variable degree. Relations can be characterised as complex, dynamic, and horizontal, involving negotiated interdependence. This re-conceptualisation of regulatory processes is important in understanding the limits of law within regulation. The dispersed nature of resources between organisation in the same regulatory space means regulators lack a monopoly both over formal and informal authority.[39]

The application of regulatory space analysis to environmental assessment suggests that developers and proponents, as regulated actors, should be held within the accepted and legal limits of the regime. However, this may only be done by considering 'the whole configuration of resources and relations within the regulatory space',[40] for example the opportunities available for effective public participation, in order to bring about genuine 'regulatory pluralism', rather than the currently limited opportunities for interdependence.[41] Scott suggests that normative approaches to law and regulation which argue for greater responsiveness or reflexivity may be capable of enhancing or constraining capacities within regulatory

---

[37] This is the view of Bregman and Jacobsen, 'Environmental Performance Review', although it is a difficult proposition to support empirically.   [38] Scott, 'Analysing Regulatory Space', at 31.
[39] ibid. 30.   [40] ibid. 31.
[41] See further Ch. 6. The independent review of developers' information contained in environmental statements provides a further means of balancing the leeway given to developers in such documents to cast a project in a favourable light, discussed in Ch. 8, pp. 296–7.

spaces,[42] such as in the case of decision making regulated by environmental assessment. Understood in this way, environmental assessment offers a good example of the current theoretical re-evaluation of regulatory processes, in the pursuance of environmental governance.

In general, the relevance of these characteristics lies in advancing an idea of the rematerialization of environmental law, as illustrated by the way in which modern environmental assessment procedures may be used to import particular interests or values into decision making. As an example of procedural law, environmental assessment may not be accurately described as a neutral, restrained, legal form. Environmental assessment engages the proponent, or developer, of a particular project in the decision-making process to a high degree. In considering the case studies in this book,[43] environmental assessment procedures are clearly capable of advancing and legitimizing a particular project, on a particular site. This provides a sharp contrast with the potential of environmental assessment to bring about fundamental changes in the culture of decision making. To summarize, in terms of regulatory form, environmental assessment possesses self-regulatory elements whilst operating within a broader, and more traditional, regulatory system, such as the licensing regime of the town and country planning system. The regulatory form of the procedure means that it additionally provides an avenue for publicity or advocacy for the developer, balanced to some extent by the public disclosure of internal decision-making processes, opportunities for public participation, and the potentially important and expert role of statutory consultees.[44]

Environmental Governance and Regulatory Theories

The development of environmental assessment as a means of controlling and shaping decision making relates to broader theories of environmental governance and regulation. The regulatory characteristics of environmental assessment referred to above as the dispersal of regulatory responsibility and authority—conferring responsibility for environmental protection on a range of participants, particularly by requiring information to be provided on the likely effects of a project or policy and judgments made about this—describes also the tendency of environmental regulation in recent years. This may be summed up as a transition from 'first generation' to 'second generation' environmental laws, in which apparently rigid, standards-based, regulation gave way to more accommodating, and flexible forms. In the United States, this transition has been described as a 'reinvention'

---

[42] Scott, 'Analysing Regulatory Space', at 31.   [43] As summarized in Ch. 8, pp. 287–9.

[44] Although this role appears to be stronger as a matter of theory than it may turn out to be in practice. (In the case of one appeal (the Dargate Dump) the inspector actually criticized the Environment Agency for its lack of involvement over failing to send along a representative to answer points that had been raised about its assessment of the project.)

of environmental law.[45] Although the form of regulation represented by environmental assessment is now commonplace,[46] at the time of its inception, environmental assessment was considered a unique regulatory form ('a procedural invention')[47] because it set certain procedural requirements for decision making. Simplistically, environmental assessment was portrayed as forging a new class of procedural law which fell between the existing, and supposedly well-established, categories of 'command and control' type regulation,[48] and so-called alternative approaches, such as the use of economic incentives and environmental agreements or covenants.[49]

The impetus for the development of new forms of regulation such as environmental assessment came from the perceived inadequacies of command and control regulation. These were further enhanced by the nature of environmental problems. For example, Dryzek's identification of the core features of ecosystems (instability, dynamism, interpenetration) may be seen as unresponsive to traditional rules of law, force, or the deployment of markets.[50] For this reason, he advanced an idea of ecological rationality as a rationality of living systems (an order of relationships among living systems and their environments) which emphasizes particularly the interrelationship and mutual dependency of a system's individual components. The inherently interdisciplinary quality of environmental assessment[51] meant that it was considered to provide a fitting level of flexibility, coordination, and appreciation of ecological interrelationships to deal with the nature of ecological systems and disturbances to these. However, the development of environmental assessment departs from Dryzek's idea of ecological rationality because it ultimately fails to uphold this as a more fundamental kind of reason when compared to other forms, for example economic and political rationality. He states: '[T]he

[45] B. A. Ackerman and R. B. Stewart, 'Reforming Environmental Law' [1985] *Stanford L Rev* 1333. For a party political perspective on such regulatory shifts in environmental law, and other areas, see T. O. McGarity, 'The Expanded Debate over the Future of the Regulatory State' [1996] *U Chicago L Rev* 1463, particularly 1499 ff., at 1500: 'The modern mugwumps generally favour broadly participatory administrative decision making of the sort that encourages debate among regulators, regulatees, and regulatory beneficiaries. Although very reluctant to position themselves in debates over substantive regulatory reform, the modern mugwumps tend to side with the free marketeers because, like their nineteenth century counterparts, they are still devoted to the free market paradigm'.

[46] For example, eco-management and audit systems, and labelling schemes, deploy similar methods of information gathering, and public disclosure. See, for example, Regulation 1836/93/EC on a Community Eco-Management and Audit Scheme OJ L 1993 L 168, p. 1 and Regulation 1980/2000/EC on a Community Eco-labelling Scheme OJ 2000 L 237, p. 1. However, there are some major contrasts to be drawn between environmental assessment and these regulatory regimes, particularly in terms of their predominantly voluntary and ongoing nature.

[47] L. Caldwell, *Science and the National Environmental Policy Act: Redirecting Policy through Procedural Reform* (Alabama: Alabama University Press, 1982), 1.

[48] As summed up nicely by Fiorino, 'Rethinking Environmental Regulation', 441, at 448: 'Regulatory agencies issue rules that are binding on defined classes of entities. Agencies create systems of inspections and reporting to monitor compliance with their rules. Entities that fail to comply are subject to penalties'.

[49] For example S. Taylor, *Making Bureaucracies Think: The Environmental Impact Statement Strategy of Administrative Reform* (Stanford, Calif.: Stanford University Press, 1984).

[50] Dryzek, *Rational Ecology*.   [51] As discussed in Ch. 2, pp. 80–3.

preservation and promotion of the integrity of the ecological and material under-pinning of society—ecological rationality—should take priority over competing forms of reason in collective choices with an impact upon that integrity'.[52] This is because long-term conflict between ecological and other forms of rationality will result in the elimination of the other forms.[53]

In addition, doubts remain about the effectiveness of environmental assess-ment when working within the constraints of more prevalent and traditional, regu-latory structures such as development consent regimes. This is highlighted by the restrictive opportunities for social learning (through feedback loops) as a result of environmental assessment taking place within development consent regimes organized around the making of a final decision.[54]

A complex picture of regulatory mechanisms now exists, so that the slippage between rules and their implementation, once seen as problematic in command and control methods and indicative of the failure of standards-based regulation, may now more accurately be seen as a necessary part of the process, acting as guid-ance in negotiations between the regulators and regulated, rather than immovable goals.[55] This insight fundamentally undermines critiques of this type of regulation: 'command and control regulation does not really exist in the first place . . . [I]nstead, what looks like a regulatory command is only one stage in a larger and more flex-ible process',[56] with almost a built-in reliance upon slippage of various types. By the same token, alternative methods (for example, emissions trading, taxation) often reliant upon using the market rather than constraining it, are now more commonly located within the regulatory mainstream. These methods are supposed-ly characterized by more flexible and coordinated (between regulator and regu-lated) legal forms, such as contract, which encourage negotiation and deliberation between government, industry, and the public. This regulatory realignment has been examined comprehensively in the United States,[57] and at the European Union level.[58] For example, Scott[59] focuses upon the increasingly procedural dimension of European environmental regulation, using as a case study the Directive on Integrated Pollution Prevention and Control (IPPC).[60] The IPPC Directive deploys a mix of regulatory instruments which produces flexibility in the form of implementation, and substantive differentiation in environmental standards across Europe, but which also prescribes certain procedures for consultation and public participation. A qualification to this argument is that the assessment

---

[52] *Rational Ecology*, 59–60.

[53] As discussed by Bartlett, 'Ecological Reason in Administration'.

[54] As discussed in Ch. 6, pp. 199–203.   [55] Farber, 'Taking Slippage Seriously', at 315.

[56] ibid., at 318.   [57] e.g. Esty, 'Toward Optimal Environmental Governance'.

[58] Heinelt *et al.*, *European Union Environment Policy*. See also Fisher, 'Unpacking the Toolbox', forthcoming. For a critique of alternative approaches in the United Kingdom, see R. Macrory, 'Regulating in a Risky Environment' (2001) 54 *CLP* 619. For an excellent overview and interweav-ing of legal theory and regulatory practice, see J. Black, 'Decentring Regulation: Understanding the Role of Regulation and Self-Regulation in a Post-Regulatory World' (2001) 54 *CLP* 103.

[59] Scott, 'Flexibility, "Proceduralisation", and Environmental Governance in the EU'.

[60] Directive 96/61/EC OJ 1996 L 257, p. 6.

procedures within IPPC and environmental assessment regimes tend in practice to confer rather greater flexibility upon Member States with regard to participation than may be inferred from the legal requirements.[61]

These major shifts in regulatory theory and method have been strongly influenced by the development of new approaches to environmental governance which, in turn, are a response to an advanced state of complexity of environmental problems and the lack of a single authority to deal with this, so that governing and problem solving becomes necessarily shared. New governance approaches appear to rely upon flexible, horizontal, and contingent regulatory forms which influence and coordinate behaviour through negotiation and debate between sectors in society, politics, and law, at least when compared to traditional patterns of regulation by 'government'. The general change in the pattern of governance is summed up well by Fiorino: 'from one- to two-way communications; from vertical to horizontal relationships; from directing to learning strategies; from adversarial relationships to relationships based on trust; and from conflict to cooperation'.[62] In the search for corresponding regulatory instruments, as broadly defined, environmental assessment appears well fitted to new governance approaches.[63] For example, Heinelt *et al.* collectively identify environmental impact assessment and eco-management and audit regimes 'as instruments of a new policy approach (or paradigm) which reflects horizontal forms of coordination through processes of negotiation and debate between societal and political actors rather than relying on command and control mechanisms laid down by the state'.[64]

This identification relies upon several points. First, environmental assessment is capable of responding to environmental problems of different scales and levels. As Esty simply states: 'Environmental problems come in many shapes and sizes',[65] in much the same way as new governance approaches seek to encourage multi-tier governance structures that correspond to a diversity of issues.[66] A broad range of participants within the environmental assessment process also helps to secure information from diverse sources and at various geographic scales, upon which effective governance is dependent.[67] This is seen particularly clearly by the development of strategic environmental assessment.[68] (Of course, against this 'problem-response' analysis it could be suggested that environmental assessment is actually being used to *define* what is capable of constituting an 'environmental problem'.) A second precondition of environmental governance is transparent

---

[61] In this regard it is relevant that the IPPC Directive is, along with the EIA Directive, to be amended to further enhance participation. See further Ch. 6, pp. 192–4.

[62] Fiorino, 'Rethinking Environmental Regulation', at 465. Although forms of governance have been categorized in a more precise way, for example, Scott and Trubeck, 'Mind the Gap' in the context of EU law.

[63] Recall the shift from 'first generation' to 'second generation' environmental laws, discussed above, at pp. 243–4.

[64] Heinelt *et al.*, *European Union Environmental Policy*, 1. Though note the important areas of contrast, mentioned above, n. 46.

[65] 'Toward Optional Environmental Governance', at 1520.   [66] ibid. at 1501.

[67] ibid., at 1502.   [68] As discussed in Ch. 2, pp. 60–5.

policy-making processes in which the prevailing wisdom of government and organizations is subject to scrutiny and ongoing review.[69] Such critical scrutiny, especially of notions of 'development', is a function of the enhanced opportunities for participation by individuals and groups in the environmental assessment process (although such opportunities may not be realized in practice) so that 'policy making may be seen not as something to be done by autonomous regulators, but rather as a process of mutual problem-solving among stakeholders from government and the private sector, from different levels of government'.[70] The participation requirements in environmental assessment may also stimulate learning (akin to cultural change) that may lead to cooperation and a sharing of responsibility between those involved in the process.[71] A third element of modern environmental governance is the proceduralization of decision making,[72] which, as discussed above, describes the defining characteristic of environmental assessment.

The alliance of environmental assessment with new governance approaches suggests that it is in the vanguard of regulatory techniques. However, environmental assessment is also sufficiently flexible and (in formal terms at least) lacking in substantive content that it may be reinterpreted to serve various regulatory strategies, or policy movements (sometimes simultaneously). As discussed previously,[73] environmental assessment has proved highly responsive to the vagaries of the environmental movement. At first it was considered to be a legal application of ecological thought and method.[74] Later, environmental assessment was allied with the economic and institutionalist discourse of sustainable development, and ecological modernization approaches to this, which rest on the claim that economic growth can take on new, more environmentally friendly, forms, through partnership arrangements and shared responsibility for environmental regulation.[75] When viewed from the perspective of developments in environmental regulation, this adaptability means that environmental assessment has been able to ride out the regulatory paradigm shift which has accompanied both the ascendance of new methods of governance, and the dominance of sustainable development as a policy framework. As Bartlett notes, 'EIA can be adapted to a changing political and economic climate and can be an active agent in changing that climate'.[76]

Related to these obvious points of correspondence between environmental assessment and new governance approaches, environmental assessment has been interpreted in regulatory terms as a reflexive mechanism. This is because of its predominantly procedural quality, combined with its supposed capacity for

---

[69] Esty, 'Toward Optional Environmental Governance', at 1501.   [70] Scott and Trubeck, 'Mind the Gap', at 5.   [71] As discussed in greater detail in Ch. 6, pp. 197–9.

[72] Described in the context of the EC by Scott, 'Flexibility, "Proceduralisaton", and Environmental Governance in the EU'.   [73] Ch. 2, pp. 42–5.

[74] On which, see Ch. 3, pp. 197–203.

[75] On environmental assessment and ecological modernization, see Ch. 2, pp. 59–60. On the more general ecological modernization justification of environmental policy, see Weale *et al.*, *Environmental Governance in Europe*, 75 ff.   [76] 'Ecological Reason in Administration', at 90.

encouraging self-referential learning,[77] which promises to eclipse the apparent distinction between purely procedural requirements (the information provision function of environmental assessment) and more substantive influences upon the outcomes of decisions (through changing the culture of decision making). The advancement of different regulatory approaches, outlined above in relation to environmental assessment, neatly fits Teubner's schema of legal rationality,[78] which teases out as reflexivity a distinction identified in the third element of Nonet and Selznick's typology of law—responsive law.[79]

Applying analysis of stages of law to environmental assessment, the formal and rational nature of environmental assessment is expounded in Taylor's work on the influence of the environmental assessment requirements in NEPA 1969 in the United States.[80] Taylor finds the *procedural* form of environmental assessment capable of changing the culture of decision making in a number of federal agencies. Nevertheless, he distinguishes rigidly between procedure and substance in law. In his view, procedural duties have an indirect effect on decision making and relate to essential procedural measures or due process. On the other hand, substantive duties or rules have a direct effect on decision making and generally relate to essential principles of law, such as equality and fairness: '[P]rocedural rules do not speak as directly to the shape of the final decision as "substantive" rules and are less powerful and efficient in influencing policy outcomes but they have greater generality'.[81] Applying this distinction, regulating for environmental protection by direct and *centrally* set standards or substantive rules typically involves setting technological or behavioural parameters and detecting deviations from these standards. The promulgation of set standards, or regulation by 'command and control' means that 'in the ideal case it is clear what the regulatory organisation should be doing and when they are complying'.[82] In contrast, environmental assessment replaces substantive standards with centrally set procedures for eliciting and analysing information about specific projects, primarily at a *local* level. Some accommodation between these two positions with regard to environmental assessment is proposed by Bartlett in his critique of the administrative state.[83] From an environmental politics, rather than legal, perspective, he identifies environmental impact assessment as a means by which the form of ecological rationality—the ecological rationality of living systems identified by Dryzek[84]—may be institutionalized in government and in wider society. His conception of ecological rationality engages both formal, and substantive elements:

[B]y requiring and encouraging political actors, as individuals and as organisations, to think ecologically and to consider environmental values, EIA embeds procedural

[77] Orts, 'Reflexive Environmental Law', 1232.

[78] Teubner, 'Substantive and Reflexive Elements in Modern Law', at 255.

[79] P. Nonet and P. Selznick, *Law and Society in Transition: Towards Responsive Law* (New York: Harper Torch, 1978; reprinted 2001).   [80] Taylor, *Making Bureaucracies Think*.

[81] ibid. 230.   [82] ibid. 296.   [83] Bartlett, 'Ecological Reason in Adiministration'.

[84] *Rational Ecology*.

ecological rationality in political institutions. By establishing, continuously reaffirming, and progressively legitimating, environmental values and ecological criteria as standards by which individual actions are to be structured, chosen, and evaluated, EIA institutionalises substantive ecological rationality.[85]

Returning to Teubner's regulatory schema, it is worth noting that the first two stages of law are, he argues, historically material. He describes the portents of a third stage of legal development, reflexive law.[86] This stage is 'characterised by a new kind of legal self-restraint'. Instead of taking over regulatory responsibility for the outcome of social processes, reflexive law restricts itself to the installation, collection, and redefinition of democratic self-regulatory mechanisms.[87] The legal control exercised is 'indirect and abstract, for the legal system determines the organisational and procedural premises of future action'.[88] It provides an arena into which information will enter, but within the limits of which 'the parties are free to strike whatever bargain they will . . . unlike substantive law it does not hold that certain outcomes are desirable'.[89] Instead, law creates incentives and procedures that induce entities to act in certain ways and to engage in internal reflection about what form behaviour and decision making should take. Reflexive law thereby relies upon 'the self-referential capacities of social systems and institutions outside the legal system, rather than direct intervention of the legal system itself, through agencies, highly detailed statutes, or delegation of great power to the courts'.[90]

In terms of recognizing such elements in environmental assessment, the most important general feature of reflexive law is that it relies upon norms that regulate processes, organizations, and the distribution of rights and competencies. Environmental assessment similarly determines the organizational and procedural premises of decision making but, in theory at least, not the outcomes of such procedures. The significance of identifying environmental assessment as procedural or reflexive law lies in the assertion that this is an emerging kind of law which offers an alternative both to formal legal rationality, and to substantive,[91] or purposive law. This raises questions about how far procedural, or 'restrained', law is a realistic interpretation of the practical application of environmental assessment and therefore to what extent procedural rules affect the quality and substance of the decision reached. The key concern, for the purposes of this book, is whether the substantive and reflexive elements of law (which very roughly translate as 'substance' and 'procedure') are irreconcilable. For example, Teubner separates 'responsive law' into its 'substantive' and 'reflexive' elements, thus differentiating between procedure and substance. Bregman and Jacobson consider that the environmental review process combines these elements since, when applied to private projects requiring approval,

---

[85] At 91.
[86] As defined by Teubner in 'Substantive and Reflexive Elements in Modern Law', at 256.
[87] ibid., at 239.   [88] ibid. at 255.   [89] ibid.
[90] Orts, 'Reflexive Environmental Law', at 1232.
[91] See G. Teubner, 'After Legal Instrumentalism? Strategic Models of Post-Regulatory Law', in G. Teubner (ed.) *Dilemmas of Law in the Welfare State* (Berlin: Walter de Gruyter, 1986), 299–325, at 299.

the public officials significantly influence the substantive decisions.[92] This is also the main finding of the Cairngorm funicular railway case study discussed below,[93] in which the private entity was found also to influence the substantive decision by identifying measures in the environmental statement which then formed part of an environmental agreement such that objections to the project were overcome. This underlines that the environmental assessment procedure may be used to give expression to particular (public or private) interests, and that these may have a bearing upon the final decision about whether to grant development consent or not. In short, it is difficult to reconcile the theory of responsive law with the tendency for developers to 'take control' of the environmental assessment process.

The association of environmental assessment with what has been labelled reflexive law has been much commented upon,[94] particularly in the United States. Orts, for example, identifies (admittedly inchoate) reflexive elements in the establishment of procedural mechanisms for self-referential administrative decision making that takes into account environmental impact under NEPA, although he admits that overall, '[T]he reflexive lesson of NEPA is problematic',[95] partly because it applies only to the actions of government agencies. Others more stridently describe the environmental impact assessment process (particularly as applied to governmental permitting of private activity) as a 'quite pure example of responsive, or, more narrowly, reflexive law'.[96] In this context it is highly relevant that there is a sharp political edge to the development of reflexive mechanisms such as environmental assessment as a response to the limits of direct intervention of the legal system by agencies, legislation, and the courts (particularly in terms of environmental problems). For example, the development of reflexive law mechanisms in environmental law may be set against a backdrop of continued dissatisfaction with environmental regulation.[97] In the United States this has been translated into a political agenda of 'rolling back' environmental programmes,[98] and one of deregulation, simplification, and flexibility, in the European Union.[99]

Procedural Regulation and Substantive Outcomes: The View from the Courts

In the above discussion I identified the procedural quality of environmental assessment as its primary regulatory characteristic, and related this to broader

---

[92] Bregman and Jacobsen, *'Environmental Performance Review'*.   [93] At pp. 272–81.

[94] Orts, 'Reflexive Environmental Law'; Hertz, 'Parallel Universes'; and Gaines and Kimber, 'Redirecting Self-Regulation'.   [95] Orts, 'Reflexive Environmental Law', at 1275.

[96] Hertz, 'Parallel Universes', at 1692; see also Bregman and Jacobsen, 'Environmental Performance Review', who consider this to be the case with environmental review procedures such as environmental assessment.   [97] Fiorino, 'Rethinking Environmental Regulation', at 441.

[98] Hertz, 'Parallel Universes'.

[99] e.g. European Commission, *Better Regulation* COM(2002) 276 final, and *Action Plan on Simplifying and Improving the Regulatory Environment* COM(2002) 278 final.

theories of environmental governance and regulation, particularly the development of reflexive mechanisms in law. Here, I further examine the relationship between procedural control and substantive outcomes as this has been interpreted by courts in various jurisdictions. It is worth reiterating that focusing upon the procedural function of environmental assessment emphasizes the quality and type of information entering the process. This accords with the idea of environmental assessment as a process that does not necessarily determine the outcomes of decisions. In contrast, recognizing that environmental assessment may have important substantive effects upon the outcome of a decision may lead to a greater emphasis upon the range of information entering the system, particularly that qualitative assessments of the likelihood of certain impacts may act as testimony to the application of values to facts. Theoretical approaches to the nature of the procedure/substance dichotomy in environmental assessment, discussed above, are commonly and simplistically translated into questions before the courts, for example, what is a court to do when an authority has granted authorization for a project for which an environmental assessment was required but for which no assessment was conducted?

The judicial attribution of procedural and substantive functions (or a combination of the two) to environmental assessment in such circumstances has occurred in practice in the context of NEPA. This contains aspirational and vaguely drafted declarations of national policy in section 101,[100] for example that the Federal Government are to 'use all practicable means and measures, including financial and technical assistance, in a manner calculated to foster and promote the general welfare, to create and maintain conditions under which man and nature can exist in productive harmony, and fulfil the social, economic, and other requirements of present and future generations of Americans'. Policy aspirations such as this are to be implemented by the environmental assessment procedure, the key requirement of which is that all federal agencies prepare environmental impact statements before undertaking major federal projects significantly affecting the environment.[101] This was the intention of Caldwell who drafted these sections of the Act: '[T]he impact statement was required to force the agencies to take the substantive provisions of NEPA seriously, and consider the environmental policy directives of the Congress in the formulation of agency plans and procedures'.[102] This duty on federal agencies has been considered indicative of the substantive core of the Act.[103] However, it would appear that the federal judiciary has strictly interpreted the procedural provisions on environmental impact assessment in the Act, effectively overlooking its potential to require more extensive consideration

---

[100] See Appendix I.   [101] S. 102(2)(C).

[102] L. K. Caldwell, 'The National Environmental Policy Act: Retrospect and Prospect' (1976) 6 *Envtl L Reptr* 50, at 50, cited in M. Ferester, 'Revitalising the National Environmental Policy Act: Substantive Law Adaptions from NEPA's Progeny' (1992) *Harv Env L Rev* 207, at 223.

[103] NEPA, although, more usually, substantive measures describe the use of standards. As Hertz, 'Parallel Universes', at 1680, states: 'While substantially important, this is not a standard'.

of the merits of a particular decision, in order to comply with the Act's substantive provisions. This has contributed to criticism of the impact statement requirements as necessitating 'nothing more than full disclosures of future environmental degradation'.[104]

In contrast, the substantive foundation of environmental assessment, and other environmental planning laws, has been expanded by several of the state laws enacted in parallel to NEPA. This has had the effect of encouraging the judiciary to review the merits of administrative decisions made following an environmental impact statement,[105] as first, and famously, established in *Calvert Cliffs*.[106] This case concerned a challenge to the granting of a development consent for a nuclear power plant and more broadly the apparent inadequacy of the Atomic Energy Agency's consideration of environmental issues. The DC Circuit found that the aspirational declarations of national environmental policy ('to avoid environmental degradation' and so on) in NEPA imposed substantive duties on agencies. Having prophetically stated 'these cases are only the beginning of what promises to become a flood of new litigation—litigation seeking judicial assistance in protecting our natural environment',[107] Judge Skelly Wright interpreted the Act's procedural measures on environmental impact assessment as 'action-forcing', requiring the agency not merely to prepare the report for the Council on Environmental Quality, but to 'consider environmental issues just as they consider other matters within their mandate'.[108] Consideration of environmental matters under the 1969 Act must therefore be more than a pro forma ritual, or 'paper tiger'.[109] As Judge Skelly Wright stated: 'a purely mechanical compliance with the particular measures required[110] will not satisfy the Act if they do not amount to full good faith consideration of the environment'.[111] Implicitly, the Circuit Court made the fulfilment of this requirement by agencies subject to judicial review. Furthermore, Judge Skelly Wright's judgment demonstrates a profound awareness of the potential of environmental impact assessment, beyond a procedural requirement to be complied with. A (necessarily fulsome) extract from his spirited judgment reveals his view of the significance of environmental assessment in substantive terms, as well as his view of the 'judicial role' in the fulfilment of this (this contrasts with the tepid cognizance of the 'action-forcing' nature of the instrument in Advocate-General Elmer's Opinion in *Grosskrotzenburg*, mentioned above):[112] Judge Skelly Wright commenced his judgment, stating:

Several recently enacted statutes attest to the commitment of the Government to control, at long last, the destructive engine of material 'progress'. But it remains to be seen whether the promise of this legislation will become a reality. Therein lies the judicial role. In these cases, we must for the first time interpret the broadest and perhaps most important of the

---

[104] Ferester, 'Revitalising the National Environmental Policy Act'.　　　[105] ibid., at 210.
[106] *Calvert Cliffs' Coordinating Committee* v *Atomic Energy Commission* 449 F2d 1109 (DC Circ 1971).　　　[107] At 1111.
[108] At 1114.　　　[109] At 1114.　　　[110] S. 102(C) and (D). See Appendix I.
[111] At 1113.　　　[112] Case C-431/92 *Commission* v *Germany*. See pp. 236–7.

recent statutes: the National Environmental Policy Act 1969 (NEPA). We must assess claims that one of the agencies charged with administration has failed to live up to the congressional mandate. Our duty, in short, is to see that important legislative purposes, heralded in the halls of Congress, are not lost or misdirected in the vast hallways of the federal bureaucracy.[113]

The judge continued:

The question here is whether the Commission is correct in thinking that its NEPA responsibilities may 'be carried out in toto outside the hearing process'—whether it is enough that environmental data and evaluations merely 'accompany' an application through the review process, but receive no consideration whatever from the hearing board.

We believe that the Commission's crabbed interpretation of NEPA makes a mockery of the Act. What possible purpose could there be in the Section 102(2)(C) requirement (that 'the detailed statement' accompany proposals through agency review processes) if 'accompany' means no more than physical proximity—mandating no more than the physical act of passing certain folders and papers, unopened, to reviewing officials along with other folders and papers? What possible purpose could there be in requiring the 'detailed statement' to be before hearing boards, if the boards are free to ignore entirely the contents of the statement? NEPA was meant to do more than regulate the flow of papers in the federal bureaucracy. The word 'accompany' in Section 102(2)(C) must not be read so narrowly as to make the Act ludicrous. It must rather, be read to indicate a congressional intent that environmental factors, as compiled in the 'detailed statement', be *considered* through agency review processes.[114]

From here, the Court considered the importance of the declarations of national policy on environmental protection contained in s. 101 of the Act. The Court concluded:

Section 102 of NEPA mandates a particular sort of careful and informed decision making process and creates judicially enforceable duties. The reviewing courts probably cannot reverse a substantive decision on its merits, under Section 101, unless it be shown that the actual balance of costs and benefits that was struck was arbitrary or clearly gave insufficient weight to environmental values. But if the decision was reached procedurally without individualised consideration and balancing of environmental factors—conducted fully and in good faith—it is the responsibility of the courts to reverse.[115]

On the facts of the case, the Atomic Energy Commission's decision to grant development consent was judged not to be arbitrary and capricious. But the decision in *Calvert Cliffs* that strongly indicated that the judiciary's proper role under NEPA extended to a review of the merits of administrative decisions has proved to be the 'high water mark for substantive review'.[116]

Recognizing the great opportunities this case afforded for extensive judicial intervention in administrative decision making, the Supreme Court appear to have transformed NEPA into what many contend is merely a procedural requirement,

---

[113] At 1111.   [114] At 1117–18.   [115] At 1115.
[116] Ferester, 'Revitalising the National Environmental Policy Act', at 215.

rather than a substantive mandate for environmental protection. *Stryker's Bay*[117] is emblematic of the Supreme Court's 'extinguishing of substantive review'[118] under NEPA. Plaintiffs who sought to challenge the building of luxury housing on land which had been earmarked for low-income housing failed to prove that the government department for housing should have done more than merely consider the environmental and social issues arising from the development. NEPA was found not to confer upon residents a right to be free from environmental damage. Rather it creates only procedural rights for residents of an area affected by federal action,[119] thus reversing the decision of the Second Circuit which held that the *consideration* of environmental consequences does not by itself satisfy NEPA.

This aspect of the *Stryker's Bay* judgment was confirmed in *Robertson* v *Methow Valley Citizens Council*,[120] in which the Forest Service's decision to issue a permit for a ski resort was challenged. The Forest Service claimed that the resort's environmental impact on wildlife and air quality could be mitigated, however the environmental impact statement (or 'study') accompanying the proposal failed to assess any specific mitigation measures. The Ninth Circuit found that the environmental statement was inadequate as a matter of law, having interpreted s. 102 of NEPA as charging the Service with the development and assessment of mitigating measures, as well as the further substantive requirement to go on and actually mitigate the adverse effects of major federal actions having significant environmental impacts. Reviewing this judgment, the Supreme Court effectively narrowed the purpose of NEPA to two functions: to ensure that agencies consider environmental impacts, and to ensure they disclose the relevant information to the public.[121] Justice Stevens opined that the environmental impact statement must contain only a 'reasonably complete' discussion of possible mitigation measures in order to fulfil these functions. Summing up the Supreme Court's approach to environmental assessment, and elaborating upon the procedural/substantive nature of environmental assessment, Judge Stevens stated:

The sweeping policy goals announced in s. 101 of NEPA are thus realised through a set of 'action-forcing' procedures that require that agencies take a 'hard look' at environmental consequences and that provide for broad dissemination of relevant environmental information. Although these procedures are almost certain to affect the agency's substantive decision, it is now well settled that NEPA itself does not mandate particular results, but simply prescribes the necessary process. If the adverse environmental effects of the proposed action are adequately identified and evaluated, the agency is not constrained by NEPA from deciding that other values outweigh the environmental costs. In this case, for example, it would not have violated NEPA if the Forest Service, after complying with the Act's procedural prerequisites, had decided that the benefits to be derived from downhill skiing at Sandy Butte justified the issuance of a special use permit, notwithstanding the

---

[117] *Stryker's Bay Neighbourhood Council Inc* v *Karlen* 444 US 223 (1980).
[118] Ferester, 'Revitalising the National Environmental Policy Act', at 217.
[119] *Stryker's Bay*, at 1543.   [120] 490 US 332, 104 LEd2d 351 (1989).
[121] At 349.

loss of 15 per cent, 50 per cent or even 100 per cent of the mule deer herd. Other statutes may impose substantive environmental obligations on federal agencies, but NEPA merely prohibits uninformed—rather than unwise—agency action.[122]

There is a fundamental distinction . . . between a requirement that mitigation be discussed in sufficient detail to ensure that environmental consequences have been fairly evaluated, on the one hand, and a substantive requirement that a complete mitigation plan be actually formulated and adopted, on the other . . . [I]t would be inconsistent with NEPA's reliance on procedural mechanisms—as opposed to substantive, result-based standards—to demand the presence of a fully developed plan that will mitigate environmental harm before an agency can act . . . We thus conclude that the Court of Appeals erred, first, in assuming that 'NEPA requires that action be taken to mitigate the adverse effects of major federal actions', and second, in finding that this substantive requirement entails the further duty to include in every EIS 'a detailed explanation of specific measures which *will* be employed to mitigate the adverse impacts of a proposed action'.[123]

In summary, the Supreme Court has not judicially reviewed the substantive outcomes of environmental assessment processes by scrutinizing projects which are subject to the procedures, notwithstanding contra-indications in early case law in the state courts. The discretionary nature of decision making on the part of the agency has remained undisturbed by NEPA. This stance on environmental assessment's substantive consequences has apparently meant that agency practice has not been fundamentally affected by environmental assessment. Stewart writes:

One is left with the impression that NEPA has not deterred agencies from following their bent in most cases after going through the motions of devising an impact statement. It is perhaps surprising that any different outcome should have been expected. As long as agency discretion to set substantive policy is unrestrained by legislative discretion or any other exogenous limits, formal procedures may serve to delineate conflicting claims, but procedures alone cannot resolve them.[124]

This is an early criticism. The more recent appreciation of reflexive elements in environmental law means that the very weakness of the procedural character of various instruments, including environmental assessment, may be reinterpreted as important to their functioning as indirect but self-referential, mechanisms. In terms of specific interpretations of NEPA, Ferester considers that there remains a substantive core to environmental assessment, due largely to the enunciation of environmental policies in the related sections of the Act and the imposition of a duty on the federal agencies to accord with these, and also the potential for linking judgments of significance of impacts to the fulfilment, or otherwise, of legislative standards. This has led him to make the argument that the substantive effect of NEPA can, and should, be strengthened ('the renaissance of NEPA'),[125] especially by creating stronger substantive mandates to guide federal agencies to select projects

[122] 490 US 332, 104 LEd2d 351 (1989), at 350–1.   [123] At 353.
[124] R. Stewart, 'The Reformation of American Administrative Law' (1975) 88 *Harv L Rev* 1667, at 1780–1, as cited in Hertz, 'Parallel Universes', at 1699.
[125] Ferester, 'Revitalising the National Environmental Policy Act', at 255.

with lesser environmental impacts, and encouraging a more rigorous approach to judicial review, thus building upon some of the more far-reaching examples of case law in the area.

United Kingdom Judicial Approaches

In the United Kingdom, thinking about the procedural or substantive content of environmental assessment has been interpreted along slightly different lines— the adequacy of the information provision function of environmental assessment, and particularly whether a body of environmental information will suffice to fulfil national legislative requirements and, ultimately, the EC Directive on environmental assessment which promoted these. A clutch of early cases offers an indication of the initial judicial view which was that the procedural requirements of the Directive were deemed to have been fulfilled if environmental information had come to light, notwithstanding the absence of a formal environmental assessment procedure. In *ex parte Beebee*,[126] which took place in the immediate post-implementation period of the EC EIA Directive, the local planning authority granted itself planning permission for a housing development on Canford Heath, a Site of Special Scientific Interest and habitat to a number of protected species. The applicants, who represented the British Herpetological Society, applied for judicial review of the Council's decision on the grounds that the authority had failed to consider whether an environmental assessment should have been carried out. The authority had, however, considered some relevant information on the environmental effects of the development, some of which had been provided by the applicants. Schiemann J refused to revoke the planning permission (though the Secretary of State later did) on the following grounds:

In my judgment, this point can be disposed of when one remembers that the purpose, in circumstances such as the present, of any environmental assessment, is to draw to the attention of the authority material relevant to the coming to a decision. In the present case it seems to me that the relevant bodies, the Nature Conservancy Council and the British Herpetological Society drew the significant factors to the attention of the authority, so the authority had in their possession the substance of what they would have had had they applied their minds to the 1988 Regulations and had prepared such an environmental statement. The substance of all the environmental information which was likely to emerge by going through the formal process envisaged by the regulation had already emerged and was apparently present in the Council's mind.[127]

In so doing, the judge ignored the participatory aspects of environmental assessment and the likelihood that the results of formal participation procedures bear on the substance of decision making. There is also some question about the quality of information available as some evidence was missing.[128]

---

[126] *R v Poole Borough Council ex parte Beebee* [1991] JPL 643.   [127] At 650.
[128] S. Ball and S. Bell, *Environmental Law: The Law and Policy Relating to the Environment* (London: Blackstones, 2nd edn., 1994), 361.

A similar approach was adopted in the *Twyford Down* case,[129] in which two parish councils and three individuals sought judicial review of the Secretary of State's decision to allow the M3 (a six-lane motorway) to be built, requiring a cut across Twyford Down, without an environmental assessment being conducted. The Down was an important area in conservation terms (comprising two Sites of Special Scientific Interest and two scheduled ancient monuments and part of an area of outstanding natural beauty), but this listing of designations gives only an imperfect description of the value of the site. The landscape was marked by medieval field patterns, dewponds and water meadows, all creating the 'genius loci of the place'.[130] The road was clearly an Annex I project for the purpose of the EC EIA Directive and therefore, the applicants argued, should have been subject to mandatory environmental assessment. The applicants relied on the ground that there had been no opportunity for public information and consultation in breach of the Directive. Having considered that the project had been in the 'planning pipeline' for several years before the date for implementing the Directive (in 1988), McCullogh decided that the Directive did not apply (in line with a strict textual reading of the Directive). McCullogh J additionally failed to uphold the need to provide a non-technical summary, a basic procedural requirement of the environmental assessment procedure,[131] stating that:

The complaint . . . is one of form and not substance. None of the applicants have asserted that there was any relevant piece of environmental information which he was in ignorance of, or which was not made available in too complex a form so that he was not unable to understand it, or its significance.[132]

This approach was also adopted by the European Commission in the course of enforcement action against the government concerning this and other infrastructure projects.[133] Invoking a concept of 'equivalent guarantees', apparently developed by the Commission, the case on Twyford Down was closed because 'the documentation provided in the UK's response . . . included an equivalent to the non-technical summary, acceptable on the facts of this case, which had not previously been submitted to the Commission'.[134] Questions posed to the Environment Commissioner later failed to pinpoint the exact nature of the 'equivalence',[135] (for example the 'non-technical summary' ran to 322 pages) and fuelled the idea that the soft approach to infringements adopted by the Commission with regard to Twyford Down (and other projects) was politically motivated: the height of the exchanges between the Commission and the Secretary of State took place against a background of the United Kingdom opting out of the Social Chapter of the Treaty on European Union and invoking the subsidiarity principle in an attempt

---

[129] *Twyford Parish Council and Others* v *Secretary of State for Transport* (1992) 4 *JEL* 2, 273.

[130] B. Bryant, *Twyford Down: Roads, Campaigning and Environmental Law* (London: Spon, 1996), 38.   [131] Now contained in Art. 5(3) of the EC EIA Directive.

[132] At 281.   [133] See Ch. 2, p. 50.

[134] Cited in P. Kunzlik, 'EIA: The British Cases' [1995] *EEL Rev* 336, at 342.

[135] OJ 1993 C 86, p. 22, 26.3.1993.

to persuade the Commission that planning matters, such as in this tranche of cases, were the exclusive concern of the Member States.[136]

There was a similar failure to appreciate the contribution of the participatory elements of environmental assessment in decision making in *Velcourt*.[137] This is apparent in Tucker J's *obiter* comments on the exercise of discretion in this case:

> . . . it became apparent that there was material available to the Inspector which, although not put in the form of an environmental impact assessment, covered all matters that such a statement would have provided . . . the Applicants did not themselves argue that the contents or substance of the Directive would or should have affected the outcome of the appeal process or as to the effect of the Regulations.[138]

Such a decision, Macrory considered, 'underlines the reluctance of the courts to quash planning decisions where they feel that the grounds of challenge are essentially based on procedural arguments, rather than issues of substance'.[139]

Such judgments were influential, and were apparently (but misguidedly) strengthened by the European Court of Justice's approach in *Grosskrotzenburg*[140] in which the Court sanctioned an environmental assessment of sorts (in compliance with national law), even though the more exacting procedures of the EIA Directive had not been satisfied. This elicited the opinion from Advocate General Elmer that environmental assessment is 'essentially procedural'.[141] The Court of Justice clearly followed the approach taken by the Commission on 'equivalent guarantees' in its earlier infringement proceedings against the United Kingdom concerning Twyford Down. The special circumstances of the *Grosskrotzenburg* case (that the Commission had failed to specify the points of non-compliance, and the hasty, *ex post facto*, integration of the information gathered) did not prevent the Court of Appeal relying on this approach in *Berkeley No. 1*.[142]

Berkeley (*No. 1*)[143] raised the issue whether the gathering of a body of environmental information is capable of fulfilling the requirement to conduct a formal environmental assessment procedure, as required by national and Community law. The case was brought to challenge the Secretary of State's grant of planning permission to Fulham Football Club for new stands, together with the building of parking areas, access roads, and a new riverside wall and riverside walk, with encroachment onto the River Thames. The effects of these developments on the ecology of the river were to be offset by the provision of a wetland shelf planted with reeds along the foreshore. The Secretary of State accepted that there was a failure to comply with

---

[136] See account by P. Kunzlick, 'The Lawyer's Assessment', in Bryant, *Twyford Down*, 256–79.

[137] *Wychavon District Council* v *Secretary of State for the Environment and Velcourt Ltd* (1994) 6 *JEL* 352.   [138] At 357.

[139] R. Macrory, 'Environmental Assessment and the "Direct Effect" Doctrine' (1994) 228 *ENDS Report* 44.   [140] Case C-431/92 *Commission* v *Germany* [1995] ECR I-2189, paras. 44–5.

[141] See above, pp. 236–7.

[142] Although a distinction may be drawn between invoking the equivalence guarantee when comparing documentation (for example, whether a 322-page report can be taken for a non-technical summary), and when comparing public participation in the environmental assessment procedure and, say, public meetings and planning inquiries; the latter being more difficult to gauge.

[143] *R* v *Secretary of State ex parte Berkeley* (*No. 1*) [2000] WLR 420, AC 603, (2001) 13 *JEL* 89.

the requirements of the 1988 Regulations[144] (the project was an urban development project which was likely to have significant effects on the environment by
virtue of its sensitive location) but argued that even if an Environmental Statement
had been required, it would have made no difference to the outcome, since all relevant environmental matters had been considered in the course of a public inquiry,
and it was not established that the planning authority had failed to take anything
specific into account. Mr Justice Tucker agreed at first instance,[145] as did the Court
of Appeal.[146] In the course of his judgment to this effect, Lord Justice Pill, giving
the leading judgment, interpreted the European Court of Justice's decision in
Grosskrotzenburg[147] as recognizing a degree of flexibility in how the EIA Directive's
obligations might be discharged, and included a lengthy excerpt from the case to
illustrate the point (paying rather less attention to the European Court's more
emphatic judgment on the need to subject certain projects to an assessment of their
effect upon the environment in *Kraijeveld*).[148] The heart of Pill LJ's judgment
focused on the matter of discretion—the discretion of the local planning authority
to require an assessment, and the discretion of the Court to uphold a grant of planning permission in cases in which assessment procedures had not been complied
with as a matter of planning law.[149] He dealt with the latter point as follows:[150]

The court must be satisfied that the objectives of the Directive are met. However, the court
retains a discretion, notwithstanding the absence (which I assume without deciding) of a
Schedule 3 (of the 1988 Regulations) statement properly so-called, to decline to quash a
decision if the objectives are in substance achieved by the procedure followed. These
objectives include the provision of appropriate information in a comprehensible form,
making the public aware of the environmental implications of a project, giving an opportunity to the public to express opinions about it; and the decision-maker taking account of
opinions expressed and making an overall assessment when reaching a conclusion . . .
While an environmental statement should, of course, be provided in the form required by
Schedule 3 of the Regulations, it is legitimate upon an s. 288 application to have regard to
all the circumstances. I am satisfied that Community law does not require the elimination
of the discretion available to an English court under s. 288(5)(b) of the 1990 Act.[151]

On the facts, Pill LJ was persuaded that the environmental issues were fully
considered at the inquiry held into the planning application—a 'vast amount of
information was available and available in a comprehensible form'.[152] Remarkably,
he considered that there was in substance almost certainly a better compliance with

---

[144] Town and Country Planning (Assessment of Environmental Effects) Regulations 1988 (SI 1988,
No. 1199).   [145] Unreported 26 March 1997.
[146] [1998] Env LR 741.
[147] Case C-431/92 *Commission* v *Germany (Grosskotzenburg)* [1995] ECR I-2189.
[148] C-72/95 *Aannemersbedrijf P. K. Kraaijeveld B.V.* v *Gedeputeerde Staten van Zuid-Holland
(Dutch Dykes)* [1996] ECR I-5403. On the facts, see Ch. 4, pp. 117–18.
[149] S. 288 Town and Country Planning Act 1990, as amended; on the nature of this discretion,
see further Ch. 6, at pp. 218–22.
[150] At 756. Cited with approval by Simon Brown LJ in *ex parte Moses* [2000] Env LR 443 (CA),
see Ch. 4, p. 134.   [151] The Town and Country Planning Act 1990, as amended.
[152] At 757.

the objects of the Directive and the Regulations than if a statement had been supplied or requested at the time of the application for planning permission,[153] and
was therefore not convinced by the argument that an environmental statement
would have made a difference to the course of the procedures, or their outcomes.

Two problems exist with this judgment. First, the judgment conflates the entire
environmental assessment *process* with the submission of an environmental statement by the developer, which forms just one (albeit important) part of the process.
Pill LJ therefore downplays the significance of participation in the environmental
assessment process by those likely to be personally affected by the decision, and by
those representing conservation interests. Although inquiry procedures undoubtedly fulfil this function to some extent, they are broad-ranging affairs, concerned
with social and economic effects of development, particularly when compared to
the specificity of concern in the environmental assessment procedure—the likelihood, scale, and integration of environmental impacts of a proposed development.
Second, Pill LJ overlooks that, had the Directive been complied with, the developer would have had to consider different options, mitigating measures, and the
cumulative impact on the river of this development. Rather, he appears impressed
with the sheer amount of information gathered—a veritable 'library of numerous
relevant documents made available at the inquiry',[154] which suggests a rather blunt
understanding of environmental assessment as an information-gathering tool, in a
similar vein to Schiemann J's judgment in *ex parte Beebee*.[155] Finally, it is possible
to discern, as a subtext of the Lord Justice's judgment, distaste with a late appeal to
the EC Directive by the applicant, suggesting its employment as a delaying tactic,
whatever the merits of the argument. Comments by Thorpe LJ that '[T]he existence of the discretion necessarily entails some review of the probable outcome had
the proper procedures been observed throughout',[156] are also apposite when considering the procedural nature of environmental assessment. On the facts of the
case, Thorpe LJ was convinced that the procedures adopted, though flawed, were
thorough and effective enough to enable the inspector to make a comprehensive
judgment on all the environmental issues affecting the Thames.[157] On this basis,
the decision in the Court of Appeal was authority for the proposition that even
though a formal assessment was required under the Regulations (as conceded
by the Secretary of State), the decision to require an assessment remained a matter
for the discretion of the local planning authority.[158] This had the effect of down-
playing the procedural requirements of the Regulations in cases in which adequate
environmental information is available to enable a decision to be made.[159]

---

[153] At 756.   [154] ibid.
[155] *R v Poole Borough Council ex parte Beebee* [1991] 2 PLR 27, [1991] JPL 643.
[156] At 758.   [157] At 758.
[158] This extends the principle as to discretion established in *R v Swale BC ex parte RSPB* (1991)
3 *JEL* 135, a point made in the commentary to *Berkeley 1* (CA), at 759. See further Ch. 4, pp. 110–16.
[159] This approach may also be seen in *Berkeley v Secretary of State for the Environment, Transport
and the Regions (Berkeley No. 3)* (2002) 14 *JEL* 331 (on the facts of which see Ch. 4, at pp. 121–3
and 133–4, concerning the compatibility with the requirements of the EIA Directive of the decision

Lady Berkeley persevered ('guiding herself through legal territory of some obscurity and considerable technicality', in the words of Thorpe LJ),[160] reaching the House of Lords.[161] There, the House, with Lord Hoffmann giving judgment, offered a closer and more respectful reading of the Directive and authority of the European Court of Justice. Lord Hoffmann disagreed that the absence of a proper environmental assessment procedure would have had no effect on the outcome of the inquiry and was not prejudicial to the objectors or the quality of the decision. Building on his judgment in *Brown*[162] that the purpose of the Directive was 'to ensure that planning decisions which may affect the environment are made on the basis of full information',[163] Lord Hoffmann elaborated: '[T]he Directive requires not merely that the planning authority should have the necessary information, but that it should have been obtained by means of a particular procedure, namely that of an EIA'.[164] He continued to describe as an essential element of this procedure that an environmental statement by the developer should have been made available to the public and that the public, 'however misguided or wrongheaded its views may be',[165] should have been given the opportunity to express an opinion in accordance with Article 6(2) of the Directive. This is to give effect to 'the inclusive and democratic procedure prescribed by the Directive'[166] and thus allow individuals to exercise their directly enforceable rights arising from this ('the consultative purpose of the Directive').[167] For this reason, Lord Hoffmann decided that:

[A] court is therefore not entitled retrospectively to dispense with the requirement of EIA on the ground that the outcome would have been the same or that the local planning authority or Secretary of State had all the information necessary to enable them to reach a proper decision on the environmental issues.[168]

To do so would be inconsistent with the Court's obligation to comply with Community law, as made clear by the judgment of the European Court of Justice in *Bozen*,[169] that it was for the authorities of Member States to 'take all the general or particular measures necessary to ensure that projects are examined in order to determine whether they are likely to have significant effects on the environment and, if so, to ensure that they are subject to an impact assessment'.[170]

that a development (lying outside statutory thresholds) would not have significant effects, notwithstanding the potential for cumulative effects). Apparently rejecting a purposive approach to interpreting the Directive, Schiemann LJ stated: 'certainly so far as the present application is concerned, there seems to us no reason to suppose that the quality of the decision making process in relation to this block of flats would be significantly improved by the carrying out of an EIA' (at para. 51).

[160] *Berkeley No. 3*, at 759.   [161] [2000] WLR 420; [2001] 2 AC 603.
[162] *R v North Yorkshire County Council ex parte Brown and Cartwright* [2000] 1 AC 397. The House of Lords held that the Directive applied to the determination of conditions for old mineral permissions even though no transposing legislation required this as a matter of English law. See further, Ch. 6, pp. 207–8.   [163] At 404.
[164] [2000] WLR 420, at 430.   [165] At 430.   [166] ibid.   [167] At 431.
[168] At 431.
[169] Case C-435/97 *World Wildlife Fund (WWF)* v *Autonome Provinz Bozen* [2000] 1 CMLR 149.
[170] At para. 70.

Lord Hoffmann countenanced one proviso—substantial compliance with the Directive could enable the planning permission in the case to be upheld.[171] This meant that a procedure of sorts could be considered an EIA by any other name and would therefore suffice, so long as it was *in substance* an EIA. This is now referred to as the doctrine of 'substantial compliance',[172] which approximates to the Commission's approach of 'equivalent guarantees' in the *Twyford Down* case, which was seemingly adopted by the European Court of Justice in *Grosskrotzenburg*. Lord Hoffmann decided in *Berkeley No. 1* that the various reports, statements, and proofs of evidence did not amount to a single and accessible compilation, produced by the applicant at the start of the application process, of the relevant environmental information and summarized in non-technical language (although they were available to the public).[173] It was instead a 'paper chase' (reminiscent of Judge Skelly Wright's warning that environmental assessment should not become a 'paper tiger').[174] In summary, 'the Secretary of State did not comply with his basic obligation to consider whether the UK machinery for implementation of the Directive should be put into motion'.[175]

In this judgment Lord Hoffmann adhered to a culture theory interpretation of environmental assessment—that the process makes a difference to the outcome of a decision because of the exposure to information on predicted effects of interested parties and decision makers, who may then change their attitude towards development, possibly in favour of environmental protection interests. He also showed a related concern with the effectiveness of directly enforceable rights by citizens, derived from European law. He cited as authority Advocate-General Elmer's Opinion in *Kraaijeveld*: 'Where a member state's implementation of the Directive is such that projects which are likely to have significant effects on the environment are not made the subject of an environmental impact assessment, the citizen is prevented from exercising his right to be heard'.[176] This interpretation comes from a purposive and 'Eurocentric' reading of the Directive, but is also informed by a rights-based approach to environmental protection.[177]

The House of Lords unanimous decision in *Berkeley No. 1*, that an environmental impact assessment must be conducted in cases such as this, was extended in *Lebus*[178] to the obligation on the part of the local authority to carry out screening opinions.[179] The local authority had not wanted to be drawn into requesting an environmental statement 'purely to get information it should rightfully expect anyway', and produced no more than a composite screening opinion, in much the same way as the Secretary of State had accepted a composite environmental

---

[171] At 431.
[172] *R (Prokopp)* v *London Underground Ltd and London Borough of Tower Hamlets and London Borough of Hackney* [2003] EWCA Civ 960 (CA), para. 70. See further, pp. 209–10.
[173] At 432.　　　[174] In *Calvert Cliffs*, at 1114.　　　[175] At 433.
[176] Case C-72/95 *Kraaijeveld* [1996] ECR I-5403, at para. 70.
[177] On this aspect, see further Ch. 6, pp. 187–9 and Ch. 8, pp. 291–4.
[178] *R (Lebus)* v *South Cambridgeshire DC* [2002] EWHC 2009 (Admin).
[179] On which, see Ch. 2, pp. 35–6.

statement in *Berkeley No. 1*. Sullivan J considered that this followed from the 'impermissible premise that it is unnecessary to obtain a formal environmental statement if the information will be received in sufficient detail as part and parcel of the material one might expect with an application'.[180] Such a premise now amounted to an error of law.

A reassessment of the obligation to interpret the broad purpose of the EIA Directive, as Lord Hoffman had required in *Brown*[181] was made (by Schiemann LJ and Buxton LJ) in *Prokopp*.[182] As mentioned previously,[183] this concerned the application of the EIA Directive to the building of the East London Line Extension, the planning permission for which had lapsed (and, arguably, the environmental assessment with it). When the project was resumed, the local planning authority requested that London Underground Limited submit an application for planning permission accompanied by an updated or new EIA. When this was declined, the London Boroughs decided not to take enforcement action, preferring instead to accept a unilateral obligation which replicated the original planning conditions, even though this action did not take account of up-to-date knowledge about the effects of the project on the cultural heritage and thus arguably side-stepped the environmental assessment procedure. The Court of Appeal refused to countenance that the decision by the London Boroughs not to take enforcement action amounted to a grant of development consent (as defined by the Directive), and thus required a new environmental assessment. The applicant had argued that implicit in the Directive was an obligation to have a national development consent in force throughout the implementation of the project, supported by the purposive reading of the Directive by the European Court of Justice in *Kraaijeveld*. The main issue in this context was whether the principle of 'substantial compliance' (as described by Lord Hoffmann in *Berkeley 1*) could be extended to permit breaches of the Directive. Buxton LJ considered (rather for the sake of argument) that it could, stating of the sources and analyses which supplemented the original environmental assessment, 'Common sense cries out that everything reasonably necessary has been achieved'.[184] The updated environmental impact assessment in this case was thereby distinguished from a paperchase of the kind criticized by Lord Hoffmann in *Berkeley No. 1*, and for that reason, in Buxton LJ's words: 'Even if the premise is accepted that EIAs can be required iteratively during the life of a project, it really would be a victory of technicality over reason not to permit the new EIA to take the form of the old EIA plus accessible analysis of the new developments'.[185]

---

[180] At 377.   [181] *R v North Yorkshire County Council ex parte Brown and Cartwright*.

[182] *R (Prokopp)* v *London Underground Ltd and London Borough of Tower Hamlets and London Borough of Hackney*.   [183] Ch. 6, at pp. 209–10.

[184] Para. 74.

[185] Para. 73. Although the European Court of Justice's judgment in Case C-201/02 R (*Wells*) v *Secretary of State for Transport, Local Government and the Regions*, Judgment 7.1.04 on the autonomous meaning of development consent calls for a reassessment of this judgment. See further, Ch. 6, pp. 210–11.

In European jurisdictions, the courts have adopted various approaches to the exercise of their discretion in similar cases. The Dutch Council of State, for example, considers that any violation of the obligation to submit an environmental assessment will result in the annulment of the underlying grant of development consent, as has occurred in several cases.[186] The question whether the lack of an environmental assessment would have resulted in a materially different decision is thus irrelevant in the Dutch context and has not been examined by the courts.[187] In contrast, in the German federal administrative court,[188] procedural errors do not in themselves entitle those affected by a project to have the permit set aside or annulled. The consent will only be annulled where the error was obvious and influenced the outcome of the decision. Regional courts have tended to follow this lead, rejecting the intensification of substantive criteria in assessing environmental interests, but have nevertheless accentuated the autonomous importance of the formal environmental assessment process.[189] Jans identifies a further approach to dealing with the consequences of a defective, or absent, environmental assessment procedure in the judgment of the Swedish Supreme Administrative Court concerning a consent to operate a nuclear power reactor.[190] With respect to a possible minor procedural defect (the failure to provide a non-technical summary), the Swedish Supreme Administrative Court ruled: 'it is evident in the view of the court . . . that a publication of a non-technical summary would not have contributed anything new to the matter and that accordingly the defect that can be considered as having existed in relation to the requirements of the Directive lacked significance for the Government decision . . . In this situation the Government decision shall not be revoked on the basis of lack of compliance with the directive'. However, Jans considers that this divergent case law fails to relate to the decisions of the Court of Justice in *Kraaijeveld*,[191] and *Bozen*,[192] both cases in which the Court ruled, in a deceptively simple manner, that if the Member States have exceeded their discretion under the environmental assessment Directive, the national provisions must be set aside and that national courts have a duty to inquire into this.

The procedural and/or substantive nature of environmental assessment, and the practical consequences that flow from this distinction, has led to a substantial,

---

[186] For example *Aramide* [1992] AB 122, Dutch Council of State, 11.12.1991, and *Aramide* [1992] MR 9, Dutch Council of State, 12.5.1992.

[187] J. Jans, *European Environmental Law* (Groningen: Europa, 2000) 199–200.

[188] As discussed by Jans, *European Environmental Law* 190–1; he refers particularly to German Bundesverwaltungsgericht 23.2.1994 [1994] DVBL 763 and German Bundesverwaltungsgericht 17.2.1997 [1997] *Natur und Recht* 305.

[189] K. Ladeur and R. Prelle, 'Environmental Assessment and Judicial Approaches to Procedural Errors: A European and Comparative Law Analysis' (2001) 13 *JEL* 185, at 186.

[190] Judgment of the Swedish Supreme Administrative Court on 16 June 1999, case no. 1424–1998, 2397–1998 and 2939–1998, nyr (see Jans, *European Environmental Law*).

[191] Case C-72/95, at para. 61. See Ch. 4, pp. 117–18.

[192] Case C-435/97 *World Wildlife Fund* v *Autonome Provinz*, at para. 70. See Ch. 4, pp. 118–19.

diverse, and sometimes inconclusive body of case law.[193] To summarize, in the United States the potential for environmental assessment to have a substantive effect was first highlighted in the *Calvert Cliffs* judgment and subsequent case law, although this interpretation of the effects of NEPA was later sidelined by the Supreme Court, so that a criticism of the Act is that it has not really effected real change.[194] In the United Kingdom courts,[195] an inverse development has taken place. The early, narrow emphasis on the purely procedural character of environmental assessment, which was strongly criticized, has given way to enhanced recognition of the potentially substantive effects of the entire environmental assessment process, particularly the role of public participation in shaping the outcome of a decision governed by environmental assessment,[196] a judicial path summed up as 'Technocratic Paternalism to Participatory Democracy'.[197] This does not, however, amount to a review of the merits of decision making shaped by environmental assessment. To extend the courts' power of review in this way, on the back of the scrutiny of the adequacy of environmental assessment procedures, would be to strain at the inherent boundaries of judicial review.[198]

The difference between the United States' and the United Kingdom's experience of environmental assessment in this respect can be accounted for by factors other than chronology. Primarily it is important to note that NEPA was the product of the first wave of environmental concern, when environmental rights were gaining recognition in US law. This resulted in statutes such as the Clean Air Act 1970 and the Clean Water Act 1972 and progressive judgments such as *Sierra Club* v *Morton*.[199] In contrast, the EC EIA Directive was agreed at a time of legislative stagnation in the European Community and crises about its legitimacy (in land use planning issues as well as more generally). From the perspective of the United Kingdom, the Directive was then implemented into a planning system directed by policy aims of fostering entrepreneurship and lifting the burden on developers. A possible consequence of the different legal and policy contexts is that the United States' environmental assessment procedures were introduced

---

[193] Such that the Office of the Deputy Prime Minister has issued 'A Government Note on the Environmental Impact Assessment Directive' [2002] *JPL* 1067 which, whilst not substituting Circular 02/99, is 'designed as an aide-memoire (for developers and local authorities) on how to avoid potential pitfalls'. [194] Brookes *et al., Law and Ecology.*

[195] In Scotland, *Swan* v *Secretary of State for Scotland* (1999) 11 *JEL* 177, amongst other cases, concerned the extent to which courts are prepared to refuse to consider cases relating to environmental assessment when it is argued that there can be no practical outcome from their deliberations.

[196] For example as expressed in the UN/ECE Convention on Access to Information, Public Participation in Decision Making and Access to Justice in Environmental Matters (Aarhus Convention), See Appendix VI.

[197] The title of a paper given by R. McCracken, at the Centre for European Law, Enforcement of EC Environmental Law Seminar, 6 June 2003. On environmental assessment and environmental democracy, see further Chs. 6 and 8.

[198] See similar point made with regard to judgments of significance in Ch. 4, at pp. 127–30.

[199] 405 US 727 (1972). In this case the Supreme Court recognized environmental damage as a basis for injury in fact sufficient to secure standing for the Club's members. Justice Douglas argued for the unique standing of inanimate objects (although this was not endorsed by his colleagues).

alongside explicit policy objectives and the imposition from the outset of duties to accord with these. This substantive content of NEPA was then read into its procedural requirements for environmental assessment so that it proved relatively easy to interpret NEPA as having substantive effects on decision making, which could be subjected to review, as decided in *Calvert Cliffs* (although the potentially far-reaching consequences of this led the Supreme Court to interpret NEPA's provisions on environmental assessment more timidly). By contrast, in the United Kingdom the manner of implementation of formal environmental assessment by its absorption into existing planning legislation,[200] with no clearly defined policy aims with respect to environmental protection other than a broad appeal to 'sustainable development' in planning guidance, has meant that any substantive content has been much harder to infer.[201] Furthermore, this transposition took place against a background of official confidence that the Directive would make little difference because normal planning procedures already required the consideration of environmental information.[202] This made the occurrence of early decisions such as *Twyford Down*,[203] *Beebee*,[204] and *Swale*[205] practically inevitable. The deceptive smoothness and subtlety of the form of implementation obscured the real changes to planning culture that had to take place to render the Directive's provisions effective.[206] From this perspective, the reticence of the local planning authority and developers to fully give effect to environmental assessment in recent cases (as upheld by the Court of Appeal in *Berkeley No. 1* and *Prokopp*) may be marked out as about fifteen years out of date.

Weight Given to Environmental Information

The decision whether or not to conduct an environmental assessment should be based exclusively on the prediction whether a project, plan, or programme is likely to have a significant effect upon the environment (prior assessment).[207] The information derived from the environmental statement or report, and representations upon this, is then fed into the decision whether or not to grant development consent in the case of projects, or accede to the plan, programme (assessment *in concreto*). At this stage of decision making, the prediction as to the likely significant

---

[200] Using a raft of secondary legislation. On this method of implementation and its consequences, see Ch. 2, pp. 49–51.

[201] For example, the Royal Commission on Environmental Pollution recommended in its Twenty-Third Report, *Environmental Planning*, Cm 5459 that the town and country planning system should be given a statutory purpose 'to facilitate the achievement of legitimate economic and social goals while ensuring that the quality of the environment is safeguarded and wherever appropriate enhanced' (para. 8.33).

[202] N. Haigh, 'The EC and Land Use: An Incoming Tide' [1990] JPL 58.

[203] (1992) 4 *JEL* 273.   [204] [1991] 2 PLR 27.

[205] (1991) 3 *JEL* 135. See further Ch. 4, pp. 111–14.

[206] This point has also been made by C. Miller, 'The Environmental Roles of Town and Country Planning', in C. Miller (ed.) *Planning and Environmental Protection* (Oxford: Hart, 2001).

[207] Rather than considerations as to whether mitigating measures may render effects insignificant, as discussed in Ch. 4, pp. 136–40.

effects of the proposal does not determine the final outcome. The weight accorded to environmental information, arising in the main from the environmental assessment process, then becomes vital, as this will be balanced against any number of probably conflicting economic and social interests and values. The generally low priority accorded to environmental interests, as seen in several of the (particularly early) environmental assessment cases mentioned above, is therefore one consequence of information about the effects of development on the environment constituting one material consideration amongst many others in decision-making processes, most obviously the development consent system. No special weight is thus attributed to this category of environmental information. This reflects the traditional flexibility of the planning system to take account of a number of often conflicting material considerations, which the implementation of the EC EIA Directive has not fundamentally disturbed.

There are, however, several precedents for giving special 'weight' to information arising from the environmental assessment process.[208] Perhaps the clearest is in the case of the Habitat Regulations 1994[209] which require that a local planning authority make an 'appropriate assessment' of the implications of a project or plan for the conservation status of a site,[210] before deciding whether to grant planning permission for a project which is likely to have a significant effect on a 'European site' (although this requirement for an assessment is not restricted to planning authority decisions).[211] Notwithstanding a negative assessment of the implications of the site, a local planning authority may grant planning permission for a project if they are satisfied that it must be carried out for imperative reasons of overriding public interest, which may be of a social or economic nature, and

---

[208] e.g. s. 54A Town and Country Planning Act 1990, as amended by the Planning and Compensation Act 1991 which requires that planning permission be determined 'in accordance with the relevant development plan unless material considerations indicate otherwise', thus giving rise to a relatively weak presumption in favour of the development plan, and one that is clearly capable of being rebutted. Policies relating to environmental protection which are incorporated into a development plan, as required in current planning policy, might thereby be granted greater weight by the local planning authority in determining an application for planning permission. Similarly, in listed buildings and conservation areas law, in addition to having regard to the relevant development plan, the local planning authority must 'pay special regard to the desirability of preserving or enhancing the character or appearance of that area' when considering applications for development consent in conservation areas. This objective of preservation has been deemed by the courts to be of 'great importance' as a material consideration when in conflict with development plan policy; *Heatherington UK Ltd* v *Secretary of State for the Environment* [1994] 2 PLR 9.

[209] Reg. 48 Conservation (Natural Habitats, &c.) Regulations 1994 (SI 1994, No. 2716). See also Planning Policy Guidance Note 9, *Nature Conservation* (London: HMSO, 1994). See description of this form of assessment, and contrast with the EIA regime in Ch. 2, pp. 68–70.

[210] The term 'European site' includes both Special Protection Areas, as defined by Directive 79/409 on the conservation of wild birds, OJ L 103, 25.12.1979, and Special Areas of Conservation designated for the purposes of Directive 92/43 on the conservation of natural habitats and of wild fauna and flora, OJ L 206, 21.5.1992.

[211] The term 'European site' includes both Special Protection Areas, as defined by Directive 79/409/EC on the conservation of wild birds, OJ L 103, 25.12.1979, and Special Areas of Conservation designated for the purposes of Directive 92/43/EC on the conservation of natural habitats and of wild fauna and flora, OJ L 206, 21.5.1992.

if compensatory measures are taken. However, where the site concerned hosts a so-called priority, or particularly endangered, natural habitat type or species, then the planning authority may only grant planning permission for reasons relating 'to human health or public safety, to beneficial consequences of primary importance for the environment, or further to an opinion from the Commission, to other imperative reasons of overriding public interest'.[212] A two-tier system of protection therefore operates with the effect that greater weight is given to information relating to a priority European habitat site or species, thus making development consent more difficult to obtain. But the main point to take from this is that species and habitats of European conservation importance are accorded substantive respect and protection.

In the main, though, decisions arising from the environmental assessment process are not constrained by a requirement that environmental protection must be secured. The *Cairngorm Funicular Railway* case suggests in addition that the environmental assessment process may help to identify mitigating measures, which may allow objections to a project or policy to be overcome, whilst also making decision makers aware of the consequences of development.[213] In the context of environmental assessment law in the United States, Ferester writes: '[I]t is now clear that mere procedural recognition of environmental impacts is insufficient to alter the substance of agency decision making'.[214] This is also now recognized by the European Commission. In an internal note on its Five Year Report on the working of environmental assessment,[215] DG Environment states:

[T]here is no obligation to refuse consent for a project that will have negative impacts on the environment. At the moment the authorities have the duty to take into account only the outcomes of the EIA process when formulating their decision. But it is consistent with the principles of sustainable development that economic and social implications should also be taken into account in deciding whether a project should receive consent.

An option to '[A]mend the EIA Directive so that competent authorities could be obliged to refuse a project, which could cause significant environmental damage' has been proposed by DG Environment. The Directorate reasoned that requiring authorities to refuse consent for projects in some circumstances is consistent with the requirement of the EC Treaty that Community policy aim at a high level of protection of the environment,[216] but admitted that it would be politically contentious and possibly contrary to the subsidiarity principle because in effect the EU would be narrowing the discretion available to authorities to attribute weight to factors relevant to their jurisdiction. Such an amendment would also fundamentally alter the regulatory character of environmental assessment.

---

[212] Art. 6(4) of the Habitats Directive. On the Commission's Opinion on imperative reasons, see Ch. 5, pp. 158–62.   [213] See below, pp. 272–81.

[214] Ferester, 'Revitalising the National Environmental Policy Act', at 269.

[215] Internal note accompanying European Commission, *Five Years Report to the European Parliament*, which considers the progress made by Directive 97/11/EC, [1997] OJ L 73, p. 5.

[216] Consistent with Arts. 2 and 174(1) EC.

A less far-reaching and possibly more politically acceptable option is to strengthen the regard which competent authorities must have to environmental protection, for example by amending the preamble and Articles 8 or 9 of the EIA Directive so as to require that a high level of environmental protection must be promoted, and that decisions must be judged in the light of such a criterion. In any event, national case law post-*Berkeley No. 1* indicates that the environmental assessment process itself is being given more weight by the courts in judicial review decisions than previously. In particular, following Hoffmann's declaration that the courts' discretion is confined within the 'narrowest possible bounds' it remains questionable whether the courts will exercise their discretion to overcome defaults in the environmental assessment process.[217] This is because of the potential for incompatibility between the duty of the court under European Community law to ensure the fulfilment of the obligations arising out of the EC Treaty or arising from action taken by the institutions of the Community (Article 10 EC), and the courts' upholding of planning permission which had been granted contrary to the provisions of the EIA Directive, a decision which is almost certainly *ultra vires*. As Jans sums up, 'the EIA Directive provides a very good example of how EC Directives can influence national rules of procedural and administrative law. In particular, where a directive, like the EIA Directive, is primarily of a procedural nature, the room for applying "standard" national rules can be very limited indeed'.[218] Recent signs, however, suggest that the progressive aspect of the House of Lords judgment in *Berkeley No. 1* is being subject to critical review in cases of judicial discretion which are, arguably, harder to decide because of the developmental interests at stake.[219]

Internalizing Environmental Information: The Duty to Give Reasons

Environmental assessment procedures generally include a duty to give reasons for the final decision taken. This tests whether the decision maker has internalized the findings of the process and narrows the discretion available to disregard information arising from the environmental assessment process. This duty also provides others with an opportunity to challenge the decision on the basis that relevant information has not been taken into account. A requirement to give reasons for decisions following an environmental assessment has had important effects in the United States. The California Environmental Quality Act 1970, for example, seeks to promote compliance with its provisions by requiring a 'findings statement' when approving projects subject to the Act's processes. This compels agencies to

---

[217] *Berkeley No. 1*, at 431. A point made by Winter, 'EIA', at 19.

[218] J. Jans and M. de Jong, 'Somewhere between Direct Effect and Rewe/Comet: Some Remarks on Dutch Public Law, Procedural Defects and the EIA Directive', Workshop on Member States Administrative Procedural Law and its Impact on the European Harmonisation Process, Florence, 20.11.1999. [219] See further, Ch. 6, pp. 218–22.

disclose the rationale behind their decisions; for example, should a decision maker find alternative options unfeasible, specific explanations must be given as to which considerations led them to favour the proposed project. This provision ensures that at a minimum agencies have to consider alternatives to a project, and mitigating measures, but it also infuses the assessment procedures with the Act's substantive aspirations, giving them greater practical effects.[220]

In the European Union, the EIA Directive was amended[221] to enhance provisions on giving reasons for a decision. Article 9 of the EIA Directive now requires: '[W]hen a decision to grant or refuse development consent has been taken, the competent authority or authorities shall inform the public' (and any Member State which has been consulted with regard to any possible transboundary effects), and 'make available information on the content of the decision and any conditions attached thereto; the main reasons and considerations on which the decision is based; and a description of the main measures to avoid, reduce, and, if possible, offset the major adverse effects'. This provision challenges a tradition of granting discretion to administrations to make decisions, without necessarily providing rationales.

This traditional approach still informs decision making, as seen in the judgment in *ex parte Marson*,[222] a case brought prior to the implementation of Directive 97/11/EC.[223] This concerned the decision whether an environmental assessment should be conducted in the first place rather than the decision arising from a full environmental assessment process as to whether development consent should be granted or refused. The applicant challenged Parcelforce's plan to develop for sorting and handling a large site, served by air and road, on the basis that he had an individual right in certain cases to require that a planning application should not be considered without the benefit of an environmental impact assessment, a right that must be protected by the English courts under Community law. Without reasons being given for declining to require an environmental assessment, it was argued, the applicant was unable to properly make an application to the courts, and was thus deprived of this right. The Court of Appeal held that under the 1988 Regulations the Secretary of State was not subject to a duty to give reasons for his decision that a formal environmental impact assessment should not take place, since no general duty had been established under Community or national law to give reasons for all decisions by competent authorities of Member States. Concluding his judgment with several 'bullet points', Pill LJ rejected the applicability of the various European Community authorities which concerned fundamental rights, holding that the right in question was some way removed from this category of right, since environmental assessment was only part of the planning

---

[220] Ferester, 'Revitalising the National Environment Policy Act', at 235.
[221] By Directive 97/11/EC.
[222] *R v Secretary of State for the Environment, Transport and the Regions and Parcelforce, ex parte Marson* [1998] JPL 869. Marson's case has also been taken to the ECHR, but judgment is still awaited.   [223] OJ 1997 L73, p. 5.

process, and development consent could be refused even if there were no systematic environmental assessment. This made clear that an applicant has no right to an environmental impact assessment, but only to a decision from the Secretary of State as to whether such an assessment is required. To elaborate, applicants have a right to a decision whether an assessment is required on valid grounds (and if it is clear that invalid grounds have been applied, then their right will be given effect to). In *Marson*, the Secretary of State did give a reason for his decision not to require a full environmental assessment, albeit that this was in a summary form derived from the wording of Article 2 of the Directive, that 'the development proposed would not be likely to have a significant effect on the environment by virtue of such factors as its nature, size or location'. Such a reason was deemed adequate.[224] The duty to give reasons for decisions regulated by the Directive was therefore restricted to the decision whether to grant or refuse development consent under Article 9. It does not extend to the determination of whether an environmental assessment should be conducted in the first place, based upon the likely significant effects of the project, which is properly the subject of Articles 2 and 4 of the Directive. It should be noted, however, that *Marson* was decided according to the old version of Article 9. As mentioned above, the EIA Directive currently contains tighter guidance on the duty to give reasons.

The *Marson* approach has been reviewed, but not markedly altered in *Richardson*,[225] which was heard in the light of the House of Lords' purposive reading of the Directive in *Berkeley 1*.[226] The applicant in *Richardson* questioned the extent of a local authority's duty to make available for public inspection a statement containing the main reasons and considerations on which a decision is based when an environmental impact assessment procedure has been carried out. Whilst it was accepted that North Yorkshire Council had failed to comply with this requirement under the 1999 Regulations,[227] it was not clear what the consequences of that failure should be, particularly because of the Council's attempt at restrospective compliance. The applicants' argument that the failure rendered the decision to grant planning permission *ultra vires* and/or that having regard to *Berkeley No. 1* the Court had no alternative but to quash it and no discretion to withhold relief was dismissed by the Court of Appeal. Simon Brown LJ was much persuaded by the fact that the duty to give reasons looks to the position *after* the grant of planning permission: 'It is concerned with making information available

---

[224] Although Office of the Deputy Prime Minister, 'A Government Note on the Environmental Impact Assessment Directive' [2002] JPL 1067 counsels against relying on this approach. Related to this point, see also *Jones v Mansfield District Council* [2003] EWCA 1408 Civ (CA), which makes clear that at this stage of screening proposals, *Wednesbury* rationality applies. See further Ch. 4, pp. 125–6.

[225] *Richardson v North Yorkshire County Council and Secretary of State* [2003] EWCA Civ 1860 (CA).

[226] This is particularly the case because of the repercussions of *Berkeley No. 1*, as seen, for example, in the Court of Appeal's decision in *ex parte Lebus*, that the Directive's requirement for a complete, rather than composite, assessment, applies also to the screening stage of the process.

[227] Reg. 21.

to the public as to what has been decided and why it has been decided, rather than laying down requirements for the decision-making process itself'.[228] The nature of this duty was distinguished from the situation in *Berkeley No. 1* in which the failure to follow procedures was found likely to have an effect upon the decision arrived at. This led to the view that the breach of the duty to give reasons ought not to lead necessarily to the quashing of the decision, in favour of requiring the authority to put the information in place before the public. Whilst not eroding *Berkeley No. 1*, this judgment narrows its potential application as a benchmark against which shortfalls in the practice of environmental impact assessment may be measured. It also misconceives the purpose of the duty to give reasons in environmental assessment procedures. Rather than being a technicality after the event (the decision having been made at the time that the statement of reasons is made public) merely to afford the public with an opportunity to challenge the decision on the grounds of inaccurate information or illegality, the knowledge on the part of the decision maker that they must justify a decision on environmental grounds plays a part in shaping that decision. The requirement ensures that the environmental information and representations made about this have been thoroughly internalized by the decision maker. For this reason Figure 2.1.[229] properly shows the decision whether the proposal should proceed, be rejected, or accepted subject to modifications on a par with giving reasons for the decision.

Rematerialization: The Case of the Cairngorm Funicular Railway

The Cairngorm range of mountains contains several of the highest summits in Scotland, including Cairn Gorm. It has inspired literature, poetry, and art, as artists have attempted to capture what the Save the Cairngorms Campaign describes as a 'supreme landscape' with particular importance for Scottish identity. It is also a prime location for skiing (although climate change appears to be altering this).[230] The general area of the Cairngorm range has been the subject of SSSI (Site of Special Scientific Interest) notifications, and also procedures for the designation of the land as a Special Protection Area, under the Wild Birds Directive,[231] and a Special Area of Conservation under the Habitats Directive,[232] (collectively known as European sites). Following several legal battles,[233] in 1994

---

[228] At para. 49.   [229] Above, p. 36.

[230] Diversification of activities seems inevitable after several years of poor snowfall.

[231] Directive 79/409/EEC on the conservation of wild birds, OJ 1979 L 103, p. 1.

[232] Directive 92/43/EEC on the conservation of natural habitats and of wild flora and fauna, OJ 1992 L 206, p. 7. Indeed, the timetable for classification of a SAC in the area was still running at the time when the planning permission was granted.

[233] Described by Marren, *Nature Conservation*, 229–33.

the Cairngorm Chairlift Company applied to the Highland Regional Council for permission to develop the skiing area. This involved replacing the existing chairlift in Coire Cas with a funicular railway (as well as catering and exhibition facilities, offices and workshops, and the use of land for the disposal of spoil).

To place this case study in context, in Chapter 6 I discussed the importance of a statutory framework for public participation in the environmental assessment process, particularly as this appears to serve new governance approaches. Case studies, considered previously in this book, have demonstrated the role of environmental assessment in giving voice to competing interests in land.[234] This case study, concerning the deeply contested development of a remote and ecologically rich natural environment, provides a quite different view by sharply illustrating the involvement of private interests in the development consent regime, via the environmental assessment process and related planning procedures and mechanisms, and under the auspices of 'partnership' programmes. Most notable of these was the Cairngorms Partnership Board ('care.consensus.continuity') which at the time that this development was proposed comprised 23 individuals who represent nine local authorities in the area, local communities, land managers, business and tourism, conservation interests, recreation, agriculture, and forestry. Scott and Trubeck[235] consider such partnership arrangements to be a manifestation of new governance, particularly the forms that emerged with responsibility for implementing Community structural funding. The Cairngorm Partnership made clear that it held no statutory responsibilities in this case. Opinions differ, however, about the exact involvement of the group (as expressed by Scottish Natural Heritage in its Position Statement on the Cairngorm Funicular Railway in decision-making procedures), as well as the breadth of its composition (portrayed by the Partnership as including a range of stakeholders). The case study also suggests the potential for the convergence of different forms of environmental assessment, since the proposed development was subject to assessment procedures required as a matter of both planning[236] and conservation[237] laws. In addition, doubts about the adequacy of assessment procedures for the purposes of development consent and conservation attracted the attention of the European Commission because the area was the subject of an application for EU Objective 1 funds (requiring a further form of 'environmental' assessment).[238]

The nub of the case study is that, the developer having complied (more or less) with the *process* of environmental assessment, as required by Community and

---

[234] See Lewes Flood Defence case study, Ch. 3, pp. 86–92 and Dibden Bay case study, Ch. 6, pp. 227–32.   [235] 'Mind the Gap', at 4.

[236] Environmental Assessment (Scotland) Regulations 1988 (SI 1988, No. 1221), as amended by the Environment Assessment (Scotland) Amendment Regulations 1994 (SI 1994, No. 2102) (the '1988 Regulations').

[237] Reg. 48 The Conservation (Natural Habitats, &c.) Regulations 1994 (SI 1994, No. 2716) (the '1994 Regulations'), which requires an 'appropriate assement'. This implements Art. 6 of the Habitats Directive.   [238] For analysis of this form of assessment, see Ch. 5.

national law, the decision reached was unassailable, the merits of this being purely a matter of discretion on the part of the decision maker. As Lord Nimmo Smith stated in the preamble to his judgment on the legality of the grant of planning permission for the funicular:[239] 'At the outset I must emphasise that I am concerned not with the merits of any of these decisions'.[240] However, the relationship between the planning procedures and the outcome of the decision whether to grant or refuse planning permission was more subtle in practice because the developer's environmental statement proposed mitigating measures which later formed the subject of a planning agreement. This allowed objections to the development on the part of Scottish Natural Heritage to be overcome. The content of the environmental statement therefore had considerable bearing upon the substance of the decision reached, but not in terms of furthering protection of the sites at issue, the fragility of which was accepted by the Company in a remarkably blunt and less than insightful comment: 'Redevelopment of the top station at Ptarmigan would include the construction of new catering facilities together with a new exhibition and Interpretive Centre. This part of the development would be designed to increase people's enjoyment of their visit to Cairngorm, explaining the area's history and fragile environment'.[241] For the Royal Society for the Protection of Birds (Scotland), the *adequacy* of the environmental statement was not the main issue in this case, since the Statement duly identified the potential environmental effects of the development, as it was designed to do (although there was some concern that alternatives to the proposed scheme had not been adequately addressed, as required specifically by Article 6 of the Habitats Directive).[242] Rather the RSPB's main objection was the manner in which the Statement was *interpreted* by Scottish Natural Heritage and Highland Council as proof that certain measures could mitigate the undeniably adverse consequences of the development.[243] Arriving at such an interpretation was, quite rightly, a matter of discretion on the part of the authorities because of the fundamentally procedural nature of environmental assessment.

To return to the main events, the Cairngorm Chairlift Company submitted an environmental statement with their application for planning permission as required by the 1988 Regulations.[244] Extensive consultation and lengthy negotiations on a planning agreement followed.[245] The main concern was that large

[239] *WWF-UK and RSPB* v *Secretary of State for Scotland* [1999] Env LR 632, Court of Session.
[240] At 640.
[241] Cairngorm Chairlift Company, Non-technical Summary, *Environment Statement*, 153.
[242] e.g. Scottish Wildlife and Countryside Link and Save the Cairngorms Campaign published *The Northern Cairngorms: An Alternative Approach* (1996). The Chairlift Company's *Environment Statement* specifically stated that the developer had not considered the environmental effects of the other options, and only dealt with the selected funicular proposals (CCC, *Environmental Statement*, 153). The Planning Committee considered such alternatives more carefully (Meeting of the Highland Regional Council Planning Committee, March 1996).
[243] Lloyd Austin, RSPB (Scotland) pers. comm.
[244] Environmental Assessment (Scotland) Regulations, as amended.
[245] Under s. 50 of the Town and Country Planning (Scotland) Act 1972 and s. 49A of the Countryside (Scotland) Act 1967.

numbers of the estimated 200,000 visitors per year would be able to gain access to the Cairn Gorm-Ben Macdui plateau area and the Northern Corries SSSI from the funicular, all of which fell into the Cairngorms Special Protection Area, with resulting environmental damage. Interestingly, the RSPB invited discussion on a package of stringent mitigation measures, the acceptance of which would have led to the withdrawal of the organization's strong objections to the proposal. Planning permission for the funicular and associated development was granted in 1997, following the conclusion of a planning agreement between the Company and various government departments and agencies, including Scottish Natural Heritage. The agreement was made the subject of a condition attached to the grant of planning permission, along with a requirement that a baseline survey document the existing condition of the area to be affected by the development, and that the area be continuously monitored. The key provision in the agreement was a draft 'Visitor Management Plan', which advocated a 'closed system' at the summit of the funicular, preventing public access to the protected summit areas. Such a plan had been outlined as a mitigating measure in the Chairlift Company's environmental statement which accompanied the application for planning permission.[246] The non-technical summary of this statement details such measures, *prior* to the environmental effects of the development being described in any detail:

The Cairngorm Chairlift Company anticipate that the funicular and its related facilities would greatly increase the attraction of the ski area during the non-ski season and are planning on the basis of between 200,000 and 250,000 non-skiing visitors per annum. This figure would place the proposed Cairngorm Funicular amongst Scotland's top ten visitor attractions . . . Such an increase in non-skiing visitors clearly has potential implications for the fragile environment of the Cairn Gorm plateau. The Cairngorm Chairlift Company plan to manage the increase in visitor numbers at Ptarmigan so as to reduce the number of people walking onto the plateau. The provision of an Interpretive Centre at the top station would play an important part in this plan. It would help to minimise any feeling that a visit to Cairngorm is incomplete without walking to the summit. It would also provide the means to communicate the message that the Cairn Gorm plateau is a special and fragile place which is being brought to the visitor by the Interpretive Centre, so that he or she can appreciate it without endangering it.[247]

The environmental statement then provides an assessment of sorts of the impact of the development on flora and fauna, as well as water, air quality, landscape, and

---

[246] This is now a familiar feature of grants of planning permission for developments which have been subject to environmental assessment. For example, in *R v Rochdale Metropolitan BC ex parte Tew* [1993] 3 PLR 74 (discussed further in Ch. 6, pp. 212–13), mitigating measures set out in the environmental statement formed the basis of conditions for the grant of planning permssion, described as such: 'The development shall be carried out in accordance with the mitigation measures set out in the Environmental Statement submitted within the application unless provided for in any other condition attached to this permission'.

[247] CCC, *Environmental Statement*, paras. 216–18.

so on. The opportunity is taken in this context to outline again the mitigation of effects arising from the development:

The most significant potential effect arising from the operation of the proposed funicular is the damage to flora and fauna that would result if there was an increase in the numbers of people walking from Ptarmigan to the summit of Cairn Gorm and further afield on to the plateau and into the Northern Corries. Much of the area that would be affected is of international importance for nature conservation. However, the funicular project is put forward within the context of the Tourism Management Programme (TMP) that has been devised for the summit of Cairn Gorm. The TMP requires that measures are put in place to manage usage and to reduce the numbers visiting the plateau, the ultimate (though possibly undesirable) measure being to prevent visitors leaving the Ptarmigan. We believe that strict adherence to the TMP would ensure that any adverse effects on flora and fauna from increased visitor use were slight.[248]

In order to comply with both the EIA Directive and the Habitats Directive, the potential environmental effects of the development had to be evaluated, based upon information provided by the developer, and representations, and, importantly, preceding the consideration of mitigating measures.[249] Otherwise, as in this case, the developer may be capable of unduly emphasizing mitigating or compensatory action that may be taken, thus marginalizing the potential effects of the project upon the environment. This is particularly a concern in cases in which such mitigating measures form the basis of planning agreements negotiated (in private) between the developer and the planning authority. The adequacy of mitigating measures is properly a judgment for the authorities to make, having considered the developer's information and representations from statutory consultees and the public. This case study provides an example of the developer's influence in this evaluation, although this is strictly not out of line with recent case law.[250] The problem in the Cairngorm case is centred more on the inclusion of mitigation measures (and the acceptance of these by the planning authority) within a planning agreement, the negotiation of which remains outside public scrutiny.

A further significant feature of the Chairlift Company's environmental statement was that it detailed the potential impact of the development on skiers and non-skiers (a category unfamiliar to the EC Directive on environmental assessment or implementing Regulations) in terms of disruption to their leisure activities as well as visual intrusion and dust and noise from construction. Under the heading 'Tourism and Recreation', the Environmental Statement considers this and other overtly social and economic factors, focusing upon the benefits, rather than the costs, of tourism:

Operation of the funicular would result in major positive tourism and recreation effects both for skiing and non-skiing visitors. Given the important role of Cairngorm, we consider

---

[248] CCC, *Environmental Statement*, 159.

[249] Referring to the description of the model environmental assessment process in Ch. 2, pp. 35–42.

[250] For example, *Bellway Urban Renewal Southern* v *Gillespie* [2003] EWHC (Civ) 400 quite reasonably allows the decision maker to have regard to (standard and uncontroversial) mitigation measures, Ch. 4, pp. 137–40.

that these benefits would be of regional if not Scottish importance, benefiting visitors to the Cairngorm Northern Corries and Glen More corridor. However, we acknowledge that for some people the replacement of the chairlift with the funicular (with its associated visitor facilities and visitor management measures) is likely to have an adverse effect on their experience of 'untamed' Cairngorm. On the other hand, we assess the number of people affected in this way would be small when compared to those who would benefit from the new recreational opportunities.[251]

The Statement also considers economic criteria such as job creation, concluding that this 'is a benefit of some significance'. The respective treatment of potential environmental impacts and mitigating measures in this manner,[252] as well as the publicizing of certain social and economic 'benefits', departs from the required process and content of environmental statements. More important is that such information, avowedly of the environmental impacts of the development, was fed into the decision-making process as such. This information provided the basis for the final decision to grant planning permission, since it formed an important part of the minute of agreement which secured the withdrawal of serious objections, especially on the part of SNH, to the development. The influence of the Environmental Statement in this context highlights the potential role of environmental assessment within private planning activities such as the negotiation of planning agreements, particularly when these are used to secure development consent, with the side-effect that developers may unduly influence the appearance, and quality, of public space.

The World Wildlife Fund and the Royal Society for the Protection of Birds challenged several decisions, or omissions, relating to this grant of permission.[253] These included the exclusion of areas, such as the summit area of Cairn Gorm (vital for skiing), from the boundaries of the Special Area of Conservation (for the purposes of the Habitats Directive), the failure of the Secretary of State to notify the proposed Special Area to the European Commission, the (tardy) decision of Scottish Natural Heritage to withdraw its objections to the grant of planning permission, and the failure by Scottish Natural Heritage and the Highland Council to carry out a proper assessment of the implications of the project for European conservation sites. In summary, the petitioners claimed that the grant of planning permission was unlawful because approval of the project was made possible by drawing inappropriate boundaries for the European conservation site. As the Save the Cairngorms Campaign argued, 'the funicular site is virtually surrounded by land proposed for designation, and yet in ecological terms is very similar to the surrounding, soon to be protected, land'.[254] The specific question before the Court of Session on the application of Article 6(3) of the Habitats Directive,[255]

---

[251] CCC, *Environmental Statement*, 162.
[252] Discussed also in Ch. 4, pp. 136–40 with regard to judgments of significance.
[253] *WWF-UK and RSPB* v *Secretary of State for Scotland* [1999] Env LR 632. Court of Session.
[254] Save the Cairngorm Campaign, 'Cairn Gorm: Potential for Conflict with Europe' (1997).
[255] Art. 6(3) requires that 'Any plan or project not directly connected with or necessary to the management of the site but likely to have a significant effect thereon, either individually or in combination with other plans or projects, shall be subject to appropriate assessment of its implications for

as implemented,[256] was whether an assessment on the effects of the project entailed the need for an absolute guarantee that the integrity of the site would not be affected by the proposed development. WWF (Scotland) and the RSPB argued that the *draft* nature of the (closed system) plans for controlling visitors meant that such an assurance could not be given, and therefore planning permission should not have been granted.

In the Court of Session, Lord Nimmo Smith first rejected the petitioners' arguments about the exclusion of land used for skiing (including the funicular development) from the areas notified to the European Commission as candidate Special Protection Areas and Special Areas of Conservation on the basis of his interpretation of the Birds and Habitats Directives, specifically that these Directives require that a discretion be exercised in the determination of boundaries, as in other respects.[257] This means that so long as the criteria applied are ornithological or ecological, in line with European Court of Justice authority on this matter, then there is a discretion to be exercised in identifying the boundaries of the site, as an integral part of the process of identifying the site itself. On the need for absolute guarantees that the 'integrity of the sites' (the coherence of its ecological structure and function that enables it to sustain the habitat, complex of habitats, and levels of populations of species for which it was classified) would not be adversely affected by the funicular development, as required under Article 6(3) of the Habitats Directive, the judge accepted that the planning agreement and visitor management plan imposed real controls; the funicular could not be brought into use until the visitor plan had been finalized and implemented, thus giving Scottish Natural Heritage a 'stranglehold' over the commercial enterprise. The judge also made clear the potential for reviewing Highland Council's interpretation of the efficacy of this guarantee: 'The question whether the way in which the development would be operated would prevent adverse effects was a question of fact for the authority carrying out the assessment. It was speculation to suggest that controls would not be used'.[258] He further stated, pragmatically, that there need not be an absolute guarantee that the integrity of the site would not be adversely affected because '[T]here never can be an absolute guarantee about what will happen in the future, and the most that can be expected of a planning authority . . . is to identify the potential risks, so far as they may be reasonably

---

the site in view of the site's conservation objectives. In the light of the conclusions of the assessment of the implications for the site and subject to the provisions of paragraph 4, the competent national authorities shall agree to the plan or project only after having ascertained that it will not adversely affect the integrity of the site concerned and, if appropriate, after having obtained the opinion of the general public'. See further Ch. 2, pp. 68–70. Art. 6 is reproduced in full in Appendix IX.

[256] Implemented by Reg. 48(5) of the 1994 Regulations. Reg. 54(2) of the 1994 Regulations provides that this provision applies in Scotland in relation to granting planning permission on an application under Part III of the Town and Country Planning (Scotland) Act 1972 (now amended). Reg. 49 of the 1994 Regulations contains provisions authorizing agreement to a plan or project, notwithstanding a negative assessment for the site, for imperative reasons of overriding public interest.

[257] [1999] Env LR 632, at 672.   [258] At 699.

foreseeable in light of such information as can reasonably be obtained, and to put in place a legally enforceable framework with a view to preventing these risks from materialising'.[259]

The petitioner finally challenged the grant of planning permission on the basis that the Highland Council had not made the planning agreement, and the draft visitor management plan annexed to this, available for public consultation before the agreement was entered into. Lord Nimmo Smith considered it relevant that the operation of the funicular railway as a closed system was an option that was described in the environmental statement submitted by the Chairlift Company with its application for planning permission, which was freely available to the public. This option then formed the basis of the draft visitor management plan which was advertised and was the subject of a public hearing. The Highland Council then requested further information in the context of negotiating the planning agreement and the visitor management plan annexed to it. Arguably, this was 'information gathered' on a measure 'envisaged in order to avoid, reduce or remedy' significant adverse effects on the environment of the proposed development for the purposes of Article 6(2) of the EIA Directive which was required to be made available to the public. This was not done, even though it was this information about the operation of the visitor management programme which caused SNH to withdraw its objection to the development. The question was whether there existed a duty to consult further on an amended proposal which had itself emerged from the consultation process, that is whether consultation should take place at every stage of the process. On this, Lord Nimmo Smith stated that he could find 'nothing in the Directive which requires the 1988 regulations to be interpreted as imposing a procedure of the kind desiderated by the petitioners . . . which appears to me to go far beyond what would normally be regarded as consultation, as it would in effect amount to a requirement to secure each and every one of the consultees' approval of the final draft before the process was complete'.[260] Having overstated, and misrepresented, the petitioner's argument in this way, the judge adopted Pill LJ's limited interpretation of the objectives of the environmental assessment process in the Court of Appeal's judgment in *Berkeley No. 1*[261] as including the provision of appropriate information in a comprehensible form, making the public aware of the environmental implications of a project, giving an opportunity to the public to express opinions about it, and the decision maker taking account of opinions expressed and making an overall assessment when reaching a conclusion.[262] He further cited with approval the approach of the European Court of Justice in *Grosskrotzenburg*[263] on which Pill LJ's judgment was based. He concluded:

The situation in the present case appears to me to be *a fortiori* of that in *Grosskrotzenburg* and *Berkeley*, in each of which cases the Court had regard to the substance of the information

---

[259] At 700.   [260] At 712.
[261] *Berkeley* v *Secretary of State for the Environment* [2001] AC 603.   [262] At 712.
[263] Case C-431/92 *Commission* v *Germany*.

which was made available to the public, even if not in the form specified in the EA Directive or in regulations implementing it. In the present case it was not suggested that the environmental statement and the addendum thereto did not comply, either in form or in substance, with the statutory requirements. For these reasons I reject the interpretation of the EA Directive and the 1988 Regulations advanced by the petitioners, and I reject the submission that the planning process has been vitiated by the procedure which was adopted in respect of the final draft of the . . . agreement and visitor management plan.[264]

This judgment draws upon an earlier, more limited, interpretation of the Directive than that which currently prevails in the light of the House of Lords' judgment in *Berkeley No. 1*. For example, it is telling that Lord Nimmo Smith refers twice to a Scottish Circular issued in 1988 which states:

[I]t has been the Government's aim in implementing the requirements to ensure that no additional burdens are placed on either developers or authorities. The process of EA should not be imposed where it is not required by the Directive . . . While such [environmental] statements will need to comply with the requirements of the Directive, it is important that they should be prepared on a realistic basis and without undue elaboration; and that the additional costs imposed on developers by the requirement to provide information about environmental effects should be kept to a reasonable minimum.[265]

This also informed the judge's outdated view of the purpose of the Directive and Regulations within planning decisions as striking a balance between the interests of applicants who are required to prepare environmental statements, and the interests of those who might wish to make representations about them.

To conclude, this case study provides a test of the operation of environmental assessment as a procedure within broader systems of control, particularly whether it secures a fundamental change in the culture of decision making, as opposed to providing the developer with opportunities to advance mitigating measures, and publicize any potential beneficial aspects of the project. As Orts notes about the NEPA regime of environment assessment in the United States, '[R]eflexive procedures added around the edges of a morass of substantive law are unlikely to yield systematic change'.[266] In the context of this case study, it is clear that procedural rules are not entirely abstract, formal and immune from partisanship. Instead, the environmental assessment procedures offered a means by which the developer could, by the identification of mitigating measures, help to secure development consent. This pinpointing of measures to offset the predicted adverse effects contributed to the planning agreement by which objections to the project were overcome. Such measures might well have been identified in the course of normal planning procedures, but the manner of presentation in a formal environmental statement is arguably more persuasive, because of the apparent objectivity of the document.[267]

---

[264] At 713.

[265] Scottish Circular No. 13/88 *Environmental Assessment: Implementation of EC Directive: The Environmental Assessment (Scotland) Regulations 1988*, para. 7.

[266] Orts, 'Reflexive Environmentol Law', at 1274.

[267] As discussed in Ch. 3, pp. 94–7.

This case study also suggests that modern environmental governance methods, such as environmental assessment, extend and dignify the role of the developer, although this may not serve environmental protection so much as economic and developmental interests. I describe these features as indicating the rematerialization of environmental assessment[268] since the developer, engaged in the decision-making process, may use environmental assessment to pursue a particular outcome, in this case the grant of planning permission, following the acceptance of mitigating measures. Such a state of affairs may be criticized in the light of the public–private distinction in law. For example, Ost warns that '[W]hile one should certainly welcome the involvement of a greater number of actors in the concern for environmental protection, that does not mean abandoning all critical vigilance or sacrificing overhastily the legal mechanisms that age old knowledge of the ways and byways of human and social games have made it possible to develop'.[269] This view is undeniably cautious and possibly distrustful of the part to be played by private (and public) developers in protecting the broader public interest. It is, however, reinforced by Fisher in her critique of the European Union's 'new' approach to environmental governance which promotes the idea that private actors should have a central role to play in environmental regulation. In advancing an administrative and constitutional perspective of this approach, she construes questions of the role of private actors in terms of fairness, participation by third parties, and implementation problems, concluding that in 'new' governance approaches, the relative legitimacy of the role of private and public actors is far messier than the concept of 'shared responsibility' suggests,[270] and that consequently there is a danger of ignoring the public law nature of many environmental problems. In relation to the theme of public versus private interests in environmental assessment, Fisher notes, 'recognition of the actual or potential influence of private actors (in environmental regulation) raises a series of legal questions concerning how and whether they should be accommodated into a decision making process'.[271] Such a critique differs fundamentally from the optimism displayed by Sabel, Fung, and Karkkainen about how new forms of regulation, such as information disclosure via environmental assessment, may lead to 'a form of participatory democracy in environmental regulation—and elsewhere as well'.[272]

Conclusions

In this chapter I have used environmental assessment, taking place in various decision-making procedures, as a focal point between theories of regulation and environmental governance. The pronounced procedural quality of environmental

---

[268] As defined in Ch. 1, p. 8.   [269] 'A Game without Rules?', 344.
[270] 'Unpacking the Toolbox'.   [271] ibid.
[272] Sabel *et al.*, '*After Backyard Environmentalism*'. See discussion on this, Ch. 6, pp. 196–7.

assessment suggests that it typifies the replacement of substantive standards with rules governing decision-making processes, which fosters scrutiny of internal decision making, possibly in the light of substantive outcomes, but does not impinge fundamentally on the discretion available to decision makers. One example of this form of reflexive regulation is that exercised by the European Commission with regard to its internal procedures for policy formation and making legislative proposals.[273] The main case study in this chapter, the Cairngorm funicular railway project, confirms the importance of the role of environmental assessment as a reflexive law mechanism within decision making in the town and country planning system, but also makes clear that environmental assessment may nevertheless have substantive effects upon the outcome of a decision, and not necessarily in terms of environmental protection. This may be explained in the broader terms of autopoiesis theory which seeks to explain the rise of reflexive mechanisms by asserting that legal structures reinterpret themselves in the light of external factors and forces, so encompassing the internal dynamics of the legal order and the impact of social or external change.[274] This suggests also that whilst law is not merely an expression of economic structures and interests, it may remain influenced by (particularly economic) conditions and factors, external to the legal system.

The regulatory impact of environmental assessment rests with the influence that it brings to bear upon authorities' discretion in decision making. The EIA Directive and the principal 1999 Regulations confer considerable discretion on planners to determine the application of the procedural rules, the adequacy of environmental statements submitted by developers with an application for planning permission, and, of course, the final decision as to whether development consent should be granted or not. However, unlike the informal procedures which existed prior to the transposition of the EIA Directive, this discretion is now subject to certain statutory boundaries, and control by the courts. The implementation of the Directive is therefore an example of legalization in which broad, discretionary, and non-binding standards of environmental assessment have become transformed into procedural rules having a definite legal consequence. In theory, this has the effect of increasing administrative accountability to the public because, once policies and standards are taken out from under the ambit of discretionary application and exposed as rules, they are no longer hidden from public scrutiny.[275] However, these formal environmental assessment procedures also grant considerable discretion to the developer, in terms of the selection and presentation of information on the effects of development on the environment. Theories of 'regulatory space' underline that such discretion is an important resource, particularly in cases in which the developer's environmental statement is treated as though it were a full account of the environmental assessment process.

---

[273] See Ch. 5, pp. 164–82.
[274] Teubner, 'Substantive and Reflexive Elements in Modern Law'.
[275] Jowell, 'The Legal Control of Administrative Discretion', at 183.

Underlying critiques of the regulation of decision making by environmental assessment, particularly in the United States, are concerns about the ability of procedural reform in general to deliver environmental protection. Sax, for example, colourfully doubts the regulatory quality of environmental assessment for this reason: 'I know of no solid evidence to support the belief that requiring articulation, detailed findings or reasoned opinions enhances the integrity or propriety of the administrative decisions. I think the emphasis on the redemptive quality of procedural reform is about nine parts myth and one part coconut oil.'[276]

More recently, such criticisms have been glossed over by the identification of environmental assessment as an example of reflexive law, defined by its procedural character, and aligned with modern strategies of participation and social learning. This chapter suggests that the environmental assessment process departs from theories of reflexivity because in practice it is not always an indirect and abstract means of governing decision making, but rather may be used to express interests in favour of development, even of the supreme or showcase environment of the Cairngorms. In the concluding chapter I pursue the argument that in practice forms of procedural law such as environmental assessment fail to conform to the characteristics of reflexive law.

[276] J. L. Sax 'The (Unhappy) Truth about NEPA' (1973) 26 *Okl L Rev* 239, at 239.

8

Conclusions

In this book I have sought to combine a conceptual analysis of environmental assessment with a structural understanding of the process. To this effect, I have examined the key elements (and stages) of environmental assessment—prediction (primarily of the significance of impacts of development),[1] the consideration of alternatives,[2] scrutiny of environmental information by a range of participants,[3] and decision making shaped by environmental considerations.[4] This has shown environmental assessment to be multifaceted, and thus capable of fulfilling several (sometimes contradictory) functions. The main functions are first, ascertaining and introducing information about the effects of development or policies on the environment into political decision-making processes, and second, encouraging environmental awareness or learning. These functions accord with the theoretical premises (information theories and culture theories) applied throughout the book to help better understand environmental assessment and its legal development.

Considering these potential functions, it is perhaps unsurprising that there were great expectations about the regulation of decision making by environmental assessment, particularly in terms of eliciting expert and public opinion and 'rationalizing' decision making. For example, adhering to information theories of environmental assessment, Goode and Johnstone considered (writing at roughly the time that a formal system of environmental impact assessment was introduced into United Kingdom planning law by the EC EIA Directive) that 'EIA can present information in a form that permits logical and rational decisions to be made, and provides a platform for the planning of the substantive use of resources'.[5] In line with theories which stress cultural change and environmental awareness arising from environmental assessment, Bartlett attributed a radical edge to the process: '[B]y requiring, fostering and reinforcing ecological rationality, both inside and outside of government, environmental impact assessment may well be subversive of the traditional administrative state'.[6] From this perspective, the outcome of a decision subject to environmental assessment is less important than the sense of responsibility and openness that it may trigger.

---

[1] Ch. 3, and Ch. 4.   [2] Ch. 5.   [3] Ch. 6.   [4] Ch. 7.
[5] P. M. Goode and A. Johnstone, 'EIA: Its Potential Application to Appropriate Technology in Developing Countries' (1988) 8 *The Environmentalist* 57–66, at 57.
[6] Bartlett, 'Ecological Reason in Administration', 83.

Taylor, for example, has argued that environmental assessment is not merely a question of ensuring that technically better information is used by decision makers, but that it is inextricably linked to questions about how political and administrative institutions are fashioned according to environmental criteria.[7] More generally, the core function of environmental assessment may be summed up as offering a means by which environmental concerns about a development or policy may be expressed and upon which conflict is focused, but ultimately mediated in favour of reaching a decision. This function, derived from the lack of substantive content of environmental assessment, is viewed by its proponents as the key to its effectiveness (since this relies upon learning and responsibility rather than the imposition of standards). In this respect, environmental assessment can be adapted to changing political and economic climates, and can even be influential in changing these.[8]

In contrast, critical approaches highlight that environmental assessment may function as a conduit for information which the developer wishes to make public so that a project may be presented in a favourable light.[9] The process may be used to identify mitigation measures which mask the ecologically unacceptable effects of development and thus allow objections to be overcome. Such measures may justify the loss of plants and animals on the basis that they will be replicated or moved elsewhere, effectively ignoring the irreplaceable nature of some places and some things.[10] Finally, rather than fundamentally reorienting decision making through social learning or environmental awareness, the participatory function of environmental assessment may legitimize development and help to quell public disquiet. In these various ways, environmental assessment may disguise or contain conflict about development.

In the following set of conclusions, I elaborate a critical approach to environmental assessment based upon the illustrative case studies discussed previously in this book and analysis of relevant case law. This approach relies upon a reinterpretation of environmental assessment as an exemplar of modern environmental governance strategies designed to proceduralize and democratize decision making, and foster learning and shared responsibility for environmental protection. Within law, these strategies have been conceived as examples of reflexivity. However, rather than operating neutrally (as expected of reflexive mechanisms), environmental assessment procedures have in certain circumstances been used to express developmental interests or particular substantive outcomes, thus displaying some of the signs of 'rematerialization'. Below, I review the implications of this conclusion for environmental law, and outline several means by which the imbalance in favour of the developer in the provision and use of environmental information in the assessment process may be redressed.

---

[7] Taylor, *Making Bureaucracies Think*, 246.

[8] Bartlett, 'Ecological Reason in Administration', 91.

[9] Notwithstanding examples of good practice highlighted by the Institute of Environmental Management and Assessment, Lincoln.   [10] See discussion in Ch. 1, pp. 25–6.

Relating Governance and Law through
Environmental Assessment

Analysis of the environmental assessment process in this book has revealed a functional fit between environmental governance and environmental assessment because of the way in which the assessment process is capable of dealing with the varying scale of environmental problems and engaging a range of public and private individuals and groups in decision making, thus encouraging environmental awareness. Using environmental assessment as a neat focal point for theories of environmental governance and the regulation of decision making, I have examined the correspondence between the multi-level nature of modern governance structures (post-devolution, and in the case of partnership experiments) and the development of different levels of environmental assessment to provide information on varying scales, for example on the impacts of policy initiatives and draft legislation in the case of strategic environmental assessment. With this form of environmental assessment, the consideration of impacts is clearly not restricted to a particular site or project, but may range over space and time. Transboundary environmental assessment provides a further practical example of the expansion of environmental concern across jurisdictional boundaries.[11] The legal accommodation of this expansion comes from the basic requirement of project-based environmental impact assessment that the effects of a particular project must be considered beyond a particular site. I have also considered how environmental assessment conforms to the demands of modern governance strategies by mandating opportunities for participation,[12] within procedural structures for decision making.[13]

Each of these characteristics of modern environmental governance—multiple levels of decision making, participation, and proceduralization—are reactions to the legitimacy problems experienced with 'traditional' and unresponsive (command and control-type) environmental regulation.[14] This development of reflexive mechanisms in law, within which environmental assessment has recently been grouped,[15] implements these characteristics with the aim of changing the learning capabilities of public and private organizations (developers, proponents, and authorities) and enhancing their ability to adapt to complex and changing problems.[16] Importantly, though, the idea of environmental assessment as reflexive law depends upon culture theories of environmental assessment, particularly that carrying out assessment processes changes attitudes towards the need for and design of new development by raising environmental awareness and conferring

---

[11] See Ch. 2, p. 54 and Ch. 6, pp. 190–1.   [12] Ch. 6, pp. 189–99.
[13] Ch. 7, pp. 237–50.   [14] See Ch. 7, pp. 243–50.
[15] Most notably by Heinelt *et al., European Union Environmental Policy,* although the identification is also made by Orts, 'Reflexive Environmental Law'. For further analysis of this categorization, see Ch. 7, pp. 249–50.   [16] As argued by Taylor, *Making Bureaucracies Think,* 323.

a sense of environmental responsibility. This requires the (hitherto) prime function of environmental assessment espoused by information theories—the gathering and introduction of scientific information into political decision-making processes—to be redefined and made secondary to the change of values in favour of environmental protection. Recently, there has been a shift in judicial thinking along these lines.[17]

A sceptical view is that presenting environmental assessment in this manner serves to fit environmental law into a broader spectrum of academic concern, with the result that a 'common sense' procedure which has existed for centuries[18] is dignified with the label 'reflexive law'. The development of environmental assessment may equally be seen as a good example of law's response to modern problems, particularly when these form part of new methods of governance. For example, using the law to strengthen 'reflexion mechanisms' (information disclosure, management systems, auditing, and environmental assessment) may stimulate institutions—corporations, authorities, educational establishments—to be sensitive to the external effects of their attempts to maximize (economic and scientific) internal rationality.[19]

The illustrative case studies in this book suggest that the apparent functional and conceptual compliance of environmental assessment with modern or 'new' environmental governance strategies is not straightforward. Several difficulties are revealed, clustered around the enhanced role of the developer or proponent in the provision and presentation of information about environmental effects which is conferred by some environmental assessment instruments, and particularly arises from the manner of implementation of the EC EIA Directive in the United Kingdom.[20] This enhanced role takes place within the regulatory space opened up by environmental assessment for the exchange of information between developer or proponent and the authority.[21] In such circumstances, information becomes a valuable resource in terms of the ability to select and present information and to determine the boundaries of an environmental assessment process. For example, the delimitation of boundaries was a determining factor in the Kentish Flats windfarm case study[22] because of the influence of distance upon judgments about the likely significance of changes to the coastal landscape. Very simply, the broader the study of the impact of the windfarm upon the landscape, the less significant this impact became. The importance of such 'frames' for studying impacts appears not to be addressed by the usual scoping exercises carried out prior to an assessment being conducted, since these tend to focus upon the range

---

[17] See below, pp. 291–4, and Ch. 7, pp. 261–3.

[18] See F. Bosselmans' work on medieval and early environmental assessment (the *ad quod damnum* writ) described in Ch. 1, pp. 3–5.

[19] Fiorino, 'Rethinking Environmental Regulation', at 445.

[20] Discussed in Ch. 2, pp. 97–9, and Ch. 7, pp. 240–3.

[21] See analysis of this aspect of environmental assessment by Bregman and Jacobsen, 'Environmental Performance Review', and on regulatory space theory, see Scott, 'Analysing Regulatory Space'. Discussed in Ch. 7, pp. 242–3.   [22] Discussed in Ch. 4, pp. 140–6.

of likely impacts. This case study also highlighted the use of the environmental statement by the developer to make a case for the 'need' for the particular development, rather than considering a range of suitable alternatives. Although operating in the different context of policy making, the European Commission's development of a system of impact assessment further suggests the possible omission or manipulation of the requirement to consider alternatives, in this case alternatives to the proposed policy or legislative act. With this system of impact assessment, there is also some concern that the need to consider 'alternatives' currently operates as a brake on legislation, so that rather than constituting a justification for the particular proposed development (as in the windfarm case), this requirement may equally justify a critical review of existing legislation in favour of simplification, or encourage the use of more flexible, or 'non-legislative', instruments. This aspect of the case study offers an important example of the broadening remit of environmental assessment, with potential implications for environmental law.[23]

The Cairngorm funicular railway project,[24] designed to further facilitate leisure activities on the mountain, raised the issue of the persuasive role of mitigation measures identified in a developer's environmental statement. The measures, presented as a 'visitor management plan' restricting visitor access to the summit of Cairn Gorm, had considerable bearing upon the decision to grant planning permission for the railway, and became the subject of a planning agreement reached between the developer and authorities. Communication between the developer and authority about the likely impacts of the project and appropriate mitigation measures were removed from the scope of the environmental assessment process to the realm of private negotiations with little opportunity for public scrutiny. This case study highlighted also the political (as well as ecological) nature of mitigation measures, the description of which is considered an essential and desirable part of the environmental assessment process. The main point is that the developer placed great emphasis upon the likely effectiveness of mitigation measures in the environmental statement accompanying the application for development consent, with the consequence that these may have prematurely informed the authority's judgment of the significance of the likely impacts of the project, and marginalized information about the adverse effects of the development upon the sensitive ecological state of the mountain habitat.

On the public scrutiny of projects subject to environmental impact assessment procedures, the Dibden Bay global port case[25] suggested that this may be circumvented in practice by the conduct of planning inquiries in which the information ascertained from environmental assessment procedures is inevitably overtaken by broader and more detailed information. In this case, the developer's role in presenting and advancing the project was not adequately balanced by input from participants (although this was admittedly an extreme case because of the highly complex and technical nature of this project's likely effects).

---

[23] See below, pp. 294–6.   [24] Ch. 7, pp. 272–81.
[25] Discussed in Ch. 6, pp. 227–32.

These examples of environmental assessment in practice suggest that environmental assessment procedures have been used as a means of expressing developmental interests. Most notably, the responsibility to produce an environmental statement also confers considerable freedom upon the developer to present a project in a particular way and to shape responses to it. This is an example of the rematerialization of environmental assessment law, not in the sense used by legal theorists to describe legal rationality defined by substantive law (for example, the growth of statute law in the early twentieth century),[26] but rather to describe law that pursues a particular purpose. This is in opposition to the defining character of reflexive law—the delimitation of spheres for autonomous private action, within which decisions may be made, but outcomes are not prescribed. In practice, then, attempts to foster cultural change via reflexive regulatory instruments which confer responsibility upon developers and proponents to collect and present environmental information according to their interests may compromise the information function of assessment—the gathering of accurate, impartial information, according to theories of rational decision making. Put another way, the emergence of new governance strategies, and their expression in law as reflexive mechanisms, may be explained in part by the contested legitimacy of traditional command and control methods of regulation, but this may also have created further legitimacy problems because of the direct role of the developer in presenting and evaluating information about possible environmental harm (and benefits).[27] Whilst reflecting what has been described as a welcome 'move away from the chimera of neutral and purely technical administrative government'[28] by advocating openness, coordination, and transparency, new methods of governance can also act as a medium for the predominance of developmental interests. This means that critical analysis of environmental assessment necessarily leads to questioning the co-joining of categories of procedural law and reflexive law.[29]

Environmental assessment further departs from reflexive mechanisms forming part of new governance approaches because in practice the process rarely includes post-assessment monitoring which may encourage learning through 'feedback loops' and thus foster environmental awareness amongst its participating actors. Instead, the finality of decision making (particularly when culminating in a grant of development consent) serves to locate environmental assessment within more traditional regulatory systems based upon authorization and compliance.

[26] Teubner, 'Substantive and Reflexive Elements in Modern Law', at 253.
[27] This irony is examined in the *European Union* by Scott and Trubeck, 'Mind the Gap', at 17.
[28] ibid., at 16.
[29] An admittedly narrow set of case studies has been analysed, in line with the methodological premises of this book (see Ch. 1, pp. 8–9). It remains to be seen whether the rematerialization theory holds for other sites of assessment, e.g. 'appropriate assessments' under the Conservation (Natural Habitats, &c.) Regulations 1994 (SI 1994, No. 2716), 'BPEO assessments' under Part I of the Environmental Protection Act 1990, and in the case of assessments for the purpose of development assistance. A description of each of these assessment types is given in Ch. 2, pp. 65–72. Although, see comments below about the convergence of these forms of assessment, pp. 295–6.

An important and related critique is that although the initial impetus to develop environmental assessment came from the perceived need to integrate ecological principles and knowledge in political decision making,[30] the law relating to environmental assessment currently fails to reflect this. For example the EC EIA Directive contains relatively weak provisions on such 'ecological' requirements as predicting cumulative and indirect effects, which testify to the complex nature of relationships between species and habitats and the resilience or otherwise of these.[31] Factors which work against an ecological approach to environmental assessment include the frequent need to reach a decision on a particular application for development consent which prevents the use of generous timescales to establish baseline conditions. In addition, regulatory timescales tend to make the ecological success of compensatory mitigation, such as the creation of a wetlands, difficult to evaluate. Nevertheless, an important development was suggested by the Lewes Flood Defence Strategy case study in which the environmental assessment process triggered further ecological studies. In this case extensive baseline studies were commissioned to determine the local existence of similar ecological conditions to those at stake from plans to flood freshwater levels with seawater. These additional studies were carried out, not as part of the environmental assessment process itself, but as a consequence of the Environment Agency's initial strategic environmental assessment for a flood defence strategy. A similar development was seen in the Dibden Bay case study, in which working groups were established as part of the public planning inquiry into the building of the container port, to further discuss and reach agreement on the likely impacts and methodologies identified in the developer's environmental statement.

These various legal and ecological problems identified with the practice of environmental assessment are compounded by the legitimatory force of the 'due process' nature of assessment systems. This comes from the accepted conceptual basis of environmental assessment, that the introduction of environmental information from diverse sources into a decision-making process encourages an informed choice between environmental and other objectives, possibly resulting in less environmentally harmful decisions. This in turn relies upon a presumption that the effects on the environment can be *objectively* predicted and their significance measured. From the perspective of information theories, environmental assessment is perceived as a 'one-way system' in which information flows in a single direction towards a decision maker.[32] In practice the process is more complex than that because it makes use of a set of assumptions about the prediction of harm by using scientific methods, and the nature of causes and effects of harm, all of which are subject to different interpretations and may, at times, prove unsupportable. An appearance of objectivity which legitimizes expertise results from the use of scientific methodologies and language, and, importantly, from the legal

---

[30] Discussed in Ch. 3, pp. 80–3.   [31] As explained in Ch. 3, pp. 92–4.
[32] de Jongh, 'Uncertainty in Environmental Impact Assessment', 64–7.

control of the process. Furthermore, the public participation and consultation requirements contribute to a perception that the environmental assessment procedure is distanced from the proponent of a particular project.[33] Rather than operating as a 'one-way' flow of information, environmental assessment accommodates flows of information from different directions. This means that the procedure may be influenced by the needs of the decision maker or the proponent of the project to secure development consent; either might choose methods for eliciting, selecting, and presenting information on this basis. So, although I have described the environmental assessment process as pluralistic in the sense of the disciplinary influences which have shaped it, and the diversity of actors involved,[34] analysis of the case studies suggests that environmental assessment offers a means of 'developmental advocacy'.

In summary, the case studies illustrate a disjuncture between the practice and aspiration of decision making. This is a familiar legal predicament. As Ladeur and Prelle identify in the context of European Community environmental law, the difficulty of implementing environmental impact assessment reflects 'a transnational problem, common to the legal systems involved, of coping with complex decision making through new procedural forms'.[35] The United Kingdom courts in particular have had to cope with the implementation of a formal environmental impact assessment regime overlaid upon already existing procedures for assessment. The survey in this book of judgments on key aspects of environmental assessment—significance,[36] alternatives,[37] and reasons for a decision made subject to assessment procedures,[38] suggests that there is some judicial resistance to the potentially far-reaching aspects of environmental assessment, most notably the need to take into account the cumulative and indirect effects of development, but there are also signs that this is abating.

Human Rights and the Rule of Law

A key shift in judicial thinking has recently taken place with regard to the role of public participation in environmental assessment.[39] This is best illustrated by Lord Hoffmann's elaboration of the importance of this in *Berkeley No. 1*,[40] having based his judgment on the need to uphold participation requirements as a matter of European Community law.[41] This approach appears to have infiltrated judicial thinking so that, for example, the importance of environmental impact assessment for the working of local democracy has recently been

---

[33] As I discuss in Ch. 6, pp. 232–4.   [34] See Ch. 3, pp. 80–6.

[35] Ladeur and Prelle, 'Environmental Assessment and Judicial Approaches to Procedural Errors', at 195.   [36] Ch. 4.   [37] Ch. 5.   [38] Ch. 7, pp. 269–72.

[39] Ch. 6, pp. 187–9.

[40] *Berkeley* v *Secretary of State for the Environment and Fulham Football Club* (*Berkeley No. 1*) [2003] 3 WLR 420, [2001] AC 603, (2001) *JEL* 89, HL.

[41] Compare this to his judgment (on similar grounds) in *R* v *North Yorkshire County Council ex parte Brown and Cartwright* [1999] 2 WLR 452, [1999] JPL 616, [2001] 1 AC 404.

Conclusions

remarked upon.[42] The potentially far-reaching recognition of environmental assessment as a form of participatory democracy[43] (espoused in several international law instruments) suggests that a human rights dimension to protecting individual rights granted by the EIA Directive may be capable of superseding the less powerful function of eliciting information about the likely effects of development and informing the public about these—hitherto the main rationale for the environmental assessment procedure.[44] This glimpse appears fleeting when *Adlard*[45] is considered. In this case, concerning the long-running dispute about the demolition and rebuilding of Fulham Football Club's stadium (although specifically concerned with challenging the Secretary of State's refusal to 'call in' and set up a public inquiry to consider the application for planning permission on the grounds of Article 6 ECHR), Colin J revisited the House of Lords decision in *Alconbury*,[46] that it is only in the case of disputes of fact that judicial review may not be adequate to comply with Article 6 ECHR. He also cited with approval Forbes J's view in *Friends Life*[47] that 'the assessment of such matters as the likely impact of the proposed development on Norwich City Centre and its associated traffic issue is clearly very different from findings of facts, or the evaluation of facts such as arises on the question whether there has been a breach of planning control'.[48] This suggests that a human rights review of judgments of significance (other than purely factual application of thresholds and indicative criteria judgments) is unlikely. Against this, in *BT*,[49] Elias J stated that 'there are limits to the ability of the courts to review facts on the merits, and I suspect there may well be cases where the lack of safeguards provided by a quasi judicial inquiry will make it difficult for the claimant to be able to identify precisely what facts have been thought relevant and how judgments on important issues have been made'. There was in this opinion some movement in the direction of a human rights approach to environmental assessment.[50]

A related development is the judgment of the Privy Council in a case concerned with the construction of the Chalillo Dam in Belize[51] to provide a permanent source of water for the generation of electricity. This has aroused strong opposition from environmentalists because the dam will cause the loss of a biologically rich floodplain. The Environmental Alliance challenged the decision to build the dam as unlawful because environmental assessment procedures, contained in the Environmental Protection Act 2000 and the Environmental Impact Assessment

[42] *Richardson* v *North Yorkshire CC and Secretary of State* [2003] EWCA Civ 1860, CA, Richards J.
[43] With possible implications for the status of third party rights.
[44] R *(Adlard)* v *Secretary of State for the Environment, Transport and the Regions* [2002] EWHC 7.
[45] On the background to this case, see *Berkeley No. 1*, Ch. 1, pp. 2–3.
[46] R *(Alconbury Developments)* v *Secretary of State for the Environment, Transport and the Regions* [2001] 2 WLR 1389. [47] At para. 93. [48] Paras. 23–5.
[49] *BT* v *Gloucester City Council* [2001] EWHC Admin 1001.
[50] This appears to have been taken up, albeit unsuccessfully, by the applicants in *Kathro*: R *(Kathro)* v *Rhondda Cynon Taff County Borough Council* [2002] JPL 304, [2001] EWHC Admin 527.
[51] *Belize Alliance of Conservation Non-Governmental Organisations* v *Department of the Environment and the Belize Electric Company Ltd*, Judgment of the Privy Council, 29.1.04.

Regulations 1995, provide that anyone undertaking a project which may 'significantly affect the environment' must carry out an environmental impact assessment and submit it to the Department of the Environment. The 1500-page environmental statement was deemed to be inadequate by the Alliance, largely because it contained an error about the geological state of the bed of the river on which the dam was to be built (which raised safety issues). The majority judgment of the Privy Council (given by Lord Hoffmann) detailed other deficient provisions of the environmental impact assessment, but decided that this did not mean that it necessarily failed to comply with statute and regulations. In this, the majority apeared to be persuaded by the opportunity for follow-up programmes to continue to exercise control over the project and the fact that the Department of the Environment had considered representations, other than those of the developer. The Privy Council concluded that in arriving at the decision to approve the dam, the Department was making a political decision about the public interest. It was not exercising a judicial and reviewable function.[52] However, the dissenting judgments are significant in that they pay greater attention to the deficiencies of the environmental statement and assessment procedures, including the lack of public consultation. Lord Walker, for example, accepted that the appellant's case was:

. . . stronger than that of the successful applicant in *Berkeley* v *Secretary of State for the Environment* [2001] 2 AC 603. In that case all the relevant information was (one way or another) in the public domain, but only if the public embarked on a 'paper chase'. Here not even the most protracted and determined paper chase could have got at the true facts.[53]

The judge would have allowed the appeal on the ground that the EIA was so flawed by important errors about the geology of the site as to be incapable of satisfying the requirements of the Act and the Regulations, and that to overlook this would be to sacrifice the rule of law:[54]

Belize has enacted comprehensive legislation on environmental protection and direct foreign investment, if it has serious environmental implications, must comply with that legislation. The rule of law must not be sacrificed to foreign investment, however desirable . . . It is no answer to the erroneous geology in the EIA to say that the dam design would not necessarily have been different. The people of Belize are entitled to be properly informed about any proposals for alterations in the dam design before the project is approved and before work continues with its construction.[55]

This judgment suggests that the majority's view that this case raises no issue of human rights[56] is not sustainable.

To conclude, despite some reticence on the part of the judiciary about the far-reaching impact of the House of Lords judgment in *Berkeley No. 1*,[57] (as expressed in the majority opinion in *Challilo Dam*), references to environmental assessment

---

[52] Para. 82.   [53] Para. 117.   [54] Paras. 118–20.   [55] At para. 120.
[56] At para. 9.
[57] e.g. in *Bown* v *Secretary of State* [2003] EWCA Civ 170, on which see Ch. 6, pp. 221–2.

as a form of local or participatory democracy suggest some accommodation of culture theories of environmental assessment by the judiciary, particularly recognizing the potential role of participation in shaping the outcome of decision making governed by environmental assessment. In contrast, the practice of environmental assessment revealed by the case studies discussed in this book may better be understood as reflections of information theories because of a common emphasis upon the gathering and dissemination of data to be fed into decision making. The particular insight gained from these case studies is that the environmental assessment process is equally capable of being used as a means to publicize projects in the interests of the developer, through the presentation and selection of information in the environmental statement, and that this may not be adequately balanced by contributions from other interested actors in the process.

Implications for Environmental Law

An important theme of this book is that the development of environmental assessment is a specific application of advances in environmental law to identify and manage the impacts of development to which the environment is exposed. As with environmental assessment, the interdisciplinary basis of environmental law is now recognized, with an associated emphasis on integrated methods of regulation (both in terms of cross-media pollution controls and, more fundamentally, the integration of policy areas). Environmental assessment also operates as a practical evocation of the sustainable development concept which informs environmental law more generally. In conceptual terms, it represents a method of regulation which is not restricted to protecting a particular sector or site. Instead, environmental assessment stresses the interdependence of ecological systems by a presumption that the effect of environmental harm will be felt beyond its immediate source, particularly by the requirement that cumulative effects and indirect effects of development and policies should be taken into account in decision making. This process of broadening out inquiries in environmental assessment is responsible also for the need to consider alternative options or sites to those proposed or planned. In addition, as an integrated method of regulation, environmental assessment represents a more preventative approach to environmental protection than that found in more traditional techniques of environmental law. These characteristics reflect the legal acceptance of integrated methods of pollution control and the precautionary principle in environmental law and the broadening range of regulatory instruments beyond those employing substantive and prescriptive standards. For these reasons, environmental assessment is an important part of the machinery of environmental law.

Given these points of comparison between environmental assessment and environmental law, two key developments in environmental assessment identified in this book are likely to have implications for the future shape of environmental law.

The first is the convergence of different forms of environmental assessment so that they begin to share similar procedures, leading to the possibility of shared, or coordinated, procedures as a matter of habitat protection, land use, and pollution control.[58] This process has led to a set of European administrative principles established by the UNECE[59] and the European Court of Justice.[60] These provide an 'ordering idea'[61] for adapting national law to the procedural requirements of environmental assessment (which proved to be anathema to those wishing to maintain informal and national methods of environmental assessment in the initial period following the implementation of the EC EIA Directive in the United Kingdom). This convergence of forms of environmental assessment, accompanied by governing principles, is emblematic of the broader convergent evolution of environmental law,[62] increasingly gathered around the principles and techniques expressed by environmental assessment. In the development of environmental assessment may therefore be seen a more general search for common administrative principles for the regulation of decision making within European law and international law.

The second key development is the expansion of the remit of environmental assessment, particularly in the form of 'sustainability analysis' which includes a full cost-benefit analysis of legislation, policies, or activities. This means that the form of environmental assessment may be used as a means of evaluating the economic and social impacts of development or policy alongside environmental criteria, as a logical consequence of the overarching concept of sustainable development. The case study on the European Commission's internal application of impact assessment suggested the possibility of environmental criteria being sidelined in favour of the weightier concerns of the Commission—trade and competition.[63] This realizes the concern expressed by the Royal Commission on Environmental Pollution that sustainability appraisal can in fact marginalize the environmental appraisals that it is supposed to bolster as a counterpoint to dominant financial or economic appraisals.[64] Such a concern led the Royal Commission to recommend strengthening the environmental component in line with the EC SEA Directive

---

[58] See Ch. 2, pp. 65–72.

[59] UN/ECE Convention on environmental impact assessment in a transboundary context (Espoo Convention) (1992) 31 ILM, UN/ECE Draft Protocol on strategic environmental assessment to the Convention on environmental impact assessment in a transboundary context (Kiev, 2003) and UN/ECE Convention on access to information, public participation in decision making and access to justice (Aarhus Convention).

[60] See particularly Case C-72/95 *Aannemersbedrijf P.K. Kraaijeveld B. V.* v *Gedeputeerde Staten van Zuid-Holland* [1996] ECR I-5403 and Case C-435/97 *World Wildlife Fund* (*WWF*) v *Autonome Provinz Bozen* [2000] 1 CMLR 149, discussed Ch. 4, pp. 117–19.

[61] J. Schwarze, 'The Convergence of the Administrative Laws of the EU's Member States' (1998) *European Public Law* 191. See also Ladeur and Prelle, 'Environmental Assessment and Judicial Approaches to Procedural Errors'.

[62] Houck, 'Of Bats, Birds and B-A-T'. See discussion of this argument, Ch. 2, pp. 72–3.

[63] Ch. 5, pp. 164–81.

[64] Royal Commission on Environmental Pollution, *Environmental Planning*, Twenty-Third Report, Cm 5459, para. 7.47.

(as well as incorporating health impacts within the purview of the environmental impact assessment process). One way in which this might be achieved is by conducting specialist environmental assessment studies in certain cases, for example on habitats and biodiversity, so long as these comply with existing participation requirements and are taken into account in decision making.[65]

Redressing the Imbalance

The interdependence of actors in environmental assessment is built upon the provision and sharing of information.[66] Whilst desirable in terms of communication and shared responsibility this also creates problems by granting developers and proponents latitude in their presentation of information in the environmental statement (or report in the case of strategic environmental assessment). Such problems include emphasizing the 'need' for the specific project, omitting a 'do-nothing' comparator and the elaboration of sometimes inappropriate mitigation and compensatory measures, often without a full assessment of their chances of 'success' in ecological terms. A prescription for good governance relevant to this area is to dilute the authority of those rich in information and other resources by dispersing information more widely and encouraging the participation of non-governmental organizations in decision-making procedures,[67] all of which suggests the potential importance of an independent commission to oversee the compilation and evaluation of environmental statements. One such commission operates in the Netherlands to provide advice on scoping guidelines for the content of environmental statements and review environmental statements drawn up by applicants. The EIA Commission consists of a group of experts appointed by Royal Decree who are invited to take part in working groups on a project-by-project basis depending upon expertise required,[68] with detailed involvement made possible by the relatively small number of proposals passing thresholds for environmental assessment to take place.[69] Whilst the Commission is unable to prevent authorization being granted even in cases of inadequate compliance with environmental impact assessment rules,[70] Dutch legislation forces developers to tighten up the claims made in environmental statements. Consenting authorities are required to carry out post-assessment monitoring of projects, report the findings of this to the EIA Commission and statutory consultees, and take remedial action as is necessary, for example by revising licence conditions if impacts are much more severe than anticipated on the basis of the environmental statement when consent was given.[71] A related development is the initiative

---

[65] On specialist ecological assessments, see Ch. 3, pp. 85–6.
[66] See Ch. 6, pp. 189–94, and Ch. 7, pp. 237–43.
[67] Scott, 'Analysing Regulatory Space', at 347–8.
[68] As described by the Royal Commission on Environmental Pollution, *Environmental Planning*, Twenty-Third Report, 94.   [69] Sheate, *Environmental Impact Assessment*, 106.
[70] ibid.
[71] Royal Commission on Environmental Pollution, *Environmental Planning*, Twenty-Third Report, 94. Compare this position with the less stringent treatment of mitigation measures in the

this Commission to establish an international commission to advise upon, and evaluate, environmental assessment procedures in developing countries faced with large-scale infrastructure projects, as first suggested by the World Commission on Environment and Development in 1987.[72]

A better balance between the information resources held by developers and those of other groups may also be encouraged by securing public participation, although in this context such participation is still likely to fall short of the Habermasian deliberative ideal. Referring once again to the far-reaching recommendations of the Royal Commission on Environmental Pollution, there is a sound case for public involvement at the scoping stage of environmental assessment. More controversially this argument may be extended to judgments of the potential significance of a project or policy at the initial screening stage, and possibly to aspects of decision making, such as the acceptability or otherwise of mitigation measures (although the final decision will rest with an accountable authority). This suggestion draws on the inclusive approach taken to judgments of significance of listed buildings and monuments in heritage policy.[73]

To summarize, whilst clearly capable of steering decisions in the general direction of environmental protection, the practice of environmental assessment is problematic at times, in particular by providing a medium for the expression of developmental interests. Even though environmental impact assessment was initially described as 'the theft of political decision making by technical experts',[74] empirical research suggests that 'few "yes's" become "no's" or vice versa' as a consequence of carrying out an environmental assessment.[75] Whilst not going so far as to suggest that 'Pseudo-EIAs'[76] are in fact commonplace, a difficulty is that the law relating to environmental assessment in the United Kingdom is still in its formative stages. Case law is currently establishing the 'zone of acceptability' of developers and authorities in terms of their duties and powers under the various assessment regimes. Working on the basis of the development of environmental assessment in the United States, once this has been established, popular and possibly judicial concern may shift instead to the remaining difficulty of settling specific environmental disputes underpinned by competing values. As Taylor has noted, it is at this point in the evolution of environmental assessment, when it is recognized

1999 Regulations (Ch. 2, pp. 40–2), and particularly as a matter of determining significance (Ch. 4, pp. 136–40).

[72] World Commission on Environment and Development, *Our Common Future* (the Brundtland Report) (Oxford: Oxford University Press, 1987), 222.

[73] Ch. 4, pp. 145–6.   [74] Wood, 'Environmental Assessment', 148.

[75] ibid. 149. Although Wood does point out that as a result of environmental assessment procedures, 'projects were better designed initially, that planners felt much more certain about the wisdom of their recommendations, that better quality projects ensued and that conditions on operation were more effective' (at 149).

[76] 'Pseudo-EIAs' indicates those environmental assessments which are carried out with the single objective of getting the project cleared, irrespective of the true environmental costs, as discussed by Perez in the context of large infrastructure projects in developing countries; Perez, 'Using Private-Public Linkages to Regulate Environmental Conflicts', at 94.

that disputes pitting environmental against other values still arise, 'that the absence of more substantive rules begins to chafe'.[77] It is also at this point that the more difficult and possibly unresolvable question 'What difference has environmental assessment made?' will need to be addressed more fully. In the meantime, the very idea of environmental assessment—of rational decision making on the basis of accurate predictions about the environmental consequences of development or policy—still has remarkable force in case law and policy. To borrow from Fitzpatrick's analysis of the Habermasian legacy of the 'ideal speech situation':[78]

[I]n such a situation we cannot discern an ultimate truth and endow it with any specific content. Nor can we ever certainly know what is properly rational, impartial and unco-erced. Yet the search for truth, the efficacy of reason, and so on, all operate still as impelling ideals. They may be unattainable, but they can still somehow have an always anticipatory operation in the here and now. They act as if an autonomous impartiality were possible, as if everything relevant could be brought to bear on the decision—could be 'taken into account'. All of which places Habermas in the tradition of an anomalous but convenient liberal political philosophy where an idea which simply cannot be can nonetheless have a potent and pervasive existential purchase.[79]

For now, though, the inauguration of environmental assessment as an impelling means (rather than idea) of dealing with the ecological dilemmas and limits which arise from the respective values attributed to environmental protection and development has not been realized.

---

[77] Taylor, *Making Bureaucracies Think*, 329.   [78] Discussed in Ch. 6, pp. 195–7.
[79] Fitzpatrick, 'Consolations of the Law', at 283.

Epilogue

The analysis of environmental assessment in this book was advanced by several case studies. The following provides a brief update of these.

LEWES FLOOD DEFENCE STRATEGY

The flood defence strategy[1] options outlined in a strategic environmental assessment have been the subject of studies carried out by consultants to determine engineering feasibility. A final decision has yet to be agreed upon by the Department of the Environment, Food, and Rural Affairs. However, funding difficulties have meant that it will have taken at least five years since the October 2000 flood to put in place flood protection.

KENTISH FLATS WINDFARM

Development consent for this project[2] was granted by the Energy Minister in March 2003. The actual installation of the foundations is expected to begin in the summer of 2004. Until then surveys will be carried out on the site to establish the final design of the windfarm, especially the dimensions of the foundations which will support the offshore turbines. The project should be completed, subject to final tests, by July 2005. SOS Whitstable, a local conservation group, maintains that local opinion remains split over the desirability of the windfarm.

EUROPEAN COMMISSION IMPACT ASSESSMENT

This book details the early stages of the Commission's development of an internal system of impact or sustainability analysis for all major Commission proposals.[3] Further research has now been conducted by the Institute for European Environmental Policy. IEEP[4] found that the criteria for the selection of proposals for extended impact assessments have been unclear, and that the system as a whole has not been transparent, with many of the assessments not readily available to the public. The quality of the extended assessments has been uneven and several of them have been poor, although IEEP attributes this in part to the circumstances of the first year of operation of the system. Most importantly, there appears to be no institutional framework within which 'learning by doing' can take place. Such criticisms will need to be addressed before the implementation of such a system of assessment in the Member States.

---

[1] Discussed in Ch. 3, pp. 86–92.   [2] Discussed in Ch. 4, pp. 140–6.
[3] In Ch. 5, pp. 164–81.
[4] Institute for European Environmental Policy, *Sustainable Development in the European Commission's Integrated Impact Assessments for 2003* (London: IEEP, 2004).

DIBDEN BAY PORT

In April 2004 the Secretary of State for Transport decided that Associated British Ports' application for development consent to build a container port at Dibden Bay[5] should be refused. In deciding this, the Secretary of State accepted the recommendations of the Inspector who had conducted an inquiry into the proposed development. The central reason for refusing development consent was the likely environmental effects of the development. The Inspector stated in his report of the inquiry that, contrary to the view put forward by the Applicant, the proposals would be likely to have an adverse effect upon the integrity of the designated conservation sites. In particular, the Inspector found against the Applicant's 'functional approach' towards assessing environmental impact. He considered the Applicant's assessment fundamentally flawed in that it treated compensatory measures as mitigation and wrongly relied on proposed habitat creation outside the European sites in concluding that the development would not adversely affect their integrity.

CAIRNGORM FUNICULAR RAILWAY

The future operation of the Cairngorm funicular railway[6] appears doubtful following the recent doubling of its losses (to almost £2 million). The losses are blamed upon limited snow cover, possibly the result of climate change. Environmental groups have also attacked the funicular's operators for failing to prevent passengers from straying near fragile areas near the summit of Cairn Gorm, triggering a review of the 'closed system' of visitor management in the area.

The designation of the Cairngorms National Park was recently celebrated by the Cairngorm Partnership at the restaurant at the top of Cairn Gorm, the subject of so much controversy.

[5] Ch. 6, pp. 227–32.   [6] Ch. 7, pp. 272–81.

Bibliography

Ackerman, B. A. and Stewart, R. B. 'Reforming Environmental Law' (1985) *Stanford L Rev* 1333.

Alder, J. 'Environmental Impact Assessment: The Inadequacies of English Law' (1993) 5 *JEL* 203.

Ashby, E. 'Background to Environmental Impact Assessment', in O'Riordan, T. and Hey, R. D. (eds.) *Environmental Impact Assessment* (Farnborough: Saxon House, 1976).

Ayres, I. and Braithwaite, J. *Responsive Regulation: Transcending the Deregulation Debate* (Oxford: Oxford University Press, 1992).

Ball, S., and Bell, S. *Environmental Law: The Law and Policy Relating to the Environment* (London: Blackstone, 2nd edn., 1994).

Barrow, C. J. *Environmental and Social Impact Assessment* (London: Arnold, 1997).

Bartlett, R. V. 'Ecological Reason in Administration: Environmental Impact Assessment and Administrative Theory', in Paehlke, R. and Torgerson, D. (eds.) *Managing the Leviathan: Environmental Politics and the Administrative State* (London: Belhaven, 1990).

Bateman, I. J. 'Environmental Impact Assessment, Cost-Benefit Analysis and the Valuation of Environmental Impacts', in Petts, J. (ed.) *Handbook of Environmental Impact Assessment: Vol. 1 Process, Methods and Potential* (Oxford: Blackwell, 1999).

Bates, G. 'Environmental Assessment: Australia's New Outlook under the Environment and Biodiversity Conservation Act 1999' (2000) 4 *Env L Rev* 203.

Bayles, M. *Procedural Justice: Allocating to Individuals* (Dordrecht: Kluwer, 1990).

Beattie, R. 'Everything You Already Knew about EIA (But Don't Often Admit)' (1995) 15 *EIA Rev* 109.

Becker, J. and Wood, G. *Scoping Decision Making under the Town and Country Planning (Environmental Impact Assessment) (England and Wales) Regulations 1999* (Oxford: Oxford Brookes University, 2003).

Beggs, J. 'Combating Biospheric Degradation: International Environmental Impact Assessment and the Transboundary Pollution Dilemma' (1995) *Fordham Env L J* 379.

Bell, S. and McGillivray, D. *Environmental Law* (Oxford: Oxford University Press, 5th edn., 2000).

—— —— *Ball and Bell on Environmental Law* (Oxford: Oxford University Press, 6th edn., 2005).

Billot, M. 'Implementing the Effective Treatment of Alternatives into the UK EIA Process' (2002) MA dissertation, EIA Centre, University of Manchester.

Bissett, R. and Tomlinson, P. 'Monitoring and Auditing of Impacts', in Wathern, P. (ed.) *Environmental Impact Assessment: Theory and Practice* (London: Routledge, 1988).

Black, J. 'Decentring Regulation: Understanding the Role of Regulation and Self-Regulation in a "Post-Regulatory" World' (2001) 54 *CLP* 103.

Blowers, A. (ed.) *Planning for a Sustainable Future* (London: Earthscan, 1993).

Boch, C. 'The Enforcement of the Environmental Assessment Directive in the National Courts: A Breach in the "Dyke"?' (1997) 9 *JEL* 129.

Bohman, J. *Public Deliberation* (Boston: MIT Press, 2000).

Bosselman, F. P. 'Limitations in the Title to Wetlands at Common Law' (1996) 15 *Stan LJ*‡247.

Bosselman, F. P. and Tarlock, A. D. 'The Influence of Ecological Science on American Law' (1994) 69 *Chicago-Kent L Rev* 847.

Botkin, D. B. *Discordant Harmonies: A New Ecology for the Twenty-First Century* (Oxford: Oxford University Press, 1990).

Boucher, S. and Whatmore, S. 'Green Gains? Planning by Agreement and Nature Conservation' (1993) 36 *JEPM* 33.

Bregman, E. and Jacobsen, A. 'Environmental Performance Review: Self-Regulation in Environmental Law', in Teubner, G. Farmer, L. and Murphy, D. (eds.) *Environmental Law and Ecological Responsibility: The Concept and Practice of Ecological Self-Organisation* (Chichester: Wiley, 1994).

Brock, D. 'Is Nature Taking Over?' [2003] JPL Occ Papers No. 31, 50.

Bronstein, D. A. (ed.) *Environmental and Social Impact Assessment* (Chichester: Wiley, 1995).

Brookes, E. 'On Putting the Environment in its Place: A Critique of Environmental Impact Assessment', in O'Riordan, T. and Hey, R. D. (eds.) *Environmental Impact Assessment* (Farnborough: Saxon House, 1976).

Brooks, R. O., Jones, R. and Virginia, R. A. *Law and Ecology: The Rise of the Ecosystem Regime* (Aldershot: Ashgate, 2002).

Bryant, B. *Twyford Down: Roads, Campaigning and Environmental Law* (London: Spon, 1996).

Búrca, G. de and Scott, J. (eds.) *The Changing Constitution of the EU: From Uniformity to Flexibility?* (Oxford: Hart, 2000).

Burgess, J. and Harrison, C. 'Capturing Values for Nature: Ecological, Economic, and Cultural Perspectives', in Holder, J. and McGillivray, D. (eds.) *Locality and Identity: Environmental Issues in Law and Society* (Aldershot: Ashgate, 1999).

Butler, C. 'The Judicial Interpretation of the EIA Directive in Ireland' (LLM dissertation, UCL, 2002).

Caldwell, L. K. 'The National Environmental Policy Act: Retrospect and Prospect' (1976) 6 *Envtl L Reptr* 50.

—— *Science and the National Environmental Policy Act: Redirecting Policy through Procedural Reform* (Alabama: Alabama University Press, 1982).

—— *Between Two Worlds: Science, the Environmental Movement and Policy Choice* (Cambridge: Cambridge University Press, 1992).

Callis, R. *Reading upon the Statute of Sewers* 137 (William John Broderip ed., 4th edn., 1824).

Carnwath, R. 'The Planning Lawyer and the Environment' (1991) 3 *JEL* 56.

Centre for Environment, Fisheries and Aquaculture Science, *Offshore Wind Farms: Guidance Note in Respect of Food and Environment Protection Act 1985 and Coast Protection Act 1949* (London: DEFRA, 2001).

Chalmers, D. 'Inhabitants in the Field of EC Environmental Law', in Craig, P. and de Búrca, G. (eds.) *The Evolution of EU Law* (Oxford: Oxford University Press, 1999).

Chun, J. 'A Critical Analysis of the Contribution to Sustainable Development of the Law and Practice in Public Participation in the Authorisation of Radioactive Waste Disposal', Ph.D. (London: UCL, 2003).

Clark, B. D. 'Environmental Impact Assessment: Scope and Objectives', in Clark, B. D. Bissett, R., and Gilad, A. (eds.) *Perspectives on Environmental Impact Assessment* (New York: Reidel, 1984).

—— Bissett, R. and Gilad, A. *Perspectives on Environmental Impact Assessment* (New York: Reidel, 1984).

—— —— —— 'Methods of Environmental Analysis' (1978) 4 *Built Env* 111.

Clark, M. 'Environmental Impact Assessment: An Ideology for Europe' (1978) *TCP* 395.

—— and Herington, J. (eds.) *The Role of Environmental Impact Assessment in the Planning Process* (London: Mansell, 1988).

Clarke, T. 'Environmental Assessment and Sustainable Development' (1991) 6 *EIA* 2.

Cohen, J. 'Democracy and Liberty' in Elster, J. (ed.) *Deliberative Democracy* (Cambridge: Cambridge University Press, 1998).

Commoner, B. *The Closing Circle* (London: Cape, 1972).

Council for the Protection of Rural England, *Sense and Sustainability: Land Use Planning and Environmental Sustainable Development* (London: CPRE, 1993).

—— RSPB, WWF *et al.*, *Third Party Rights of Appeal in Planning* (London: CPRE, 2002).

Cotterrell, R. 'Judicial Review and Legal Theory', in Richardson, G. and Genn, H. (eds.) *Administrative Law and Government in Action* (Oxford: Clarendon, 1994).

Countryside Commission, *Environmental Assessment: The Treatment of Landscape and Countryside Recreation Issues* (Manchester: Countryside Commission, 1991).

Curran, J. M., Wood, C., and Hilton, M. 'Environmental Appraisal of UK (Local) Plans: Current Practice and Future Directions' (1998) 25 *Environment and Planning B: Planning and Design* 411.

Dalal-Clayton, B. *Getting to Grips with Green Plans: National Level Experience in Industrial Countries* (London: Earthscan, 1996).

Delaney, D. *Law's Nature* (Cambridge: Cambridge University Press, 2003).

Department of Culture, Media and Sport, *The Historic Environment: Force for our Future* (London: HMSO, 2001).

Department of the Environment, Circular 4/79 *Memorandum on Structure and Local Plans* (London: HMSO, 1979).

—— *Implementation of the European Directive on Environmental Assessment* (London: HMSO, 1986).

—— Circular 15/88 (Welsh Office 23/88) *Environmental Assessment* (London: HMSO, 1988).

—— *Environmental Assessment: A Guide to the Procedures* (London: HMSO, 1989).

—— *Monitoring Environmental Assessment and Planning* (London: HMSO, 1990).

—— *Policy Appraisal and the Environment* (London: HMSO, 1992).

Department of the Environment, Transport and the Regions, Circular 1/97, *Planning Obligations* (London: HMSO, 1997).

—— *Modernising Local Government: In Touch with the People* (London: DETR, 1998).

—— Circular 02/99, *Environmental Impact Assessment* (London: HMSO, 1999).

—— *Proposals for a Good Practice Guide on Sustainability Appraisal of Regional Planning Guidance* (GPG 25) (London: DETR, 2000).

DG Environment, *Impact Assessment Environment Guide* (Brussels: DG Environment, 2002).

Dhondt, N. *Integration of Environmental Protection into Other EC Policies: Theory and Practice* (Groningen: Groningen Law Publishing, 2003).

DTLR, Planning Green Paper, *New Parliamentary Procedures for Major Infrastructure Projects* (London: HMSO, 2001).

—— Planning: Delivering a Fundamental Change (London: HMSO, 2002).

Dryzek, J. S. Rational Ecology: Environment and Political Ecology (New York: Basil Blackwell, 1987).

—— Discoursive Democracy: Politics, Policy and Political Science (Cambridge: Cambridge University Press, 1990).

Dugdale, W. The History of the Imbanking and Drayning of Divers Fenns and Marshes (London: Alice Warren, 1662).

Edwards, R. A. 'Judicial Deference under the Human Rights Act' (2002) 65 MLR 859.

Elster, J. (ed.) Deliberative Democracy (Cambridge: Cambridge University Press,1998).

—— 'Deliberation and Constitution Making', in Elster, J. (ed.) Deliberative Democracy (Cambridge: Cambridge University Press, 1998).

Elworthy, S. and Holder, J. Environmental Protection: Text and Materials (London: Butterworths, 1997).

English Heritage, Power of Place (London: HMSO, 2000).

English Nature, Baseline Biological Survey of the Lower Ouse Valley (Lewes: English Nature, 2002).

—— RSPB, WWF, BWEA, Windfarm Development and Nature Conservation (Peterborough: English Nature, 2001).

English, P. 'The Genius Loci of Ancient Places', in Holder, J. and Harrison, C. (eds.) Law and Geography (Oxford: Oxford University Press, 2002).

Environment Agency, Southern Region, Sussex Ouse Flood Defence Strategy SEA, Stage 2 Report (Worthing: Environment Agency, 2002).

—— Sussex Ouse Flood Management Strategy Executive Summary (Worthing: Environment Agency, 2002).

Environmental Data Services Ltd, Environmental Consultants in the UK: A Market Analysis (London: ENDS Ltd, 1995).

Esty, D. C. 'Toward Optimal Environmental Governance' [1999] NYU L Rev 1495.

European Commission, Fourth Environmental Action Programme, COM(86) 485 final (Brussels: CEC, 1987).

—— Fifth Environmental Action Programme, Towards Sustainability: A European Community Programme of Policy and Action in Relation to the Environment and Sustainable Development, COM(92) 23 final, (Brussels: CEC, 1992).

—— Report from the Commission on the Implementation of Directive 85/337/EEC on the Assessment of the Effects of Certain Public and Private Projects on the Environment, COM(93) 28, 2.4.1993 (Brussels: CEC, 1993).

—— Community Structural Funds: 1994–1999, Revised Regulations and Comments (Brussels: CEC, 1993).

—— Eleventh Annual Report to the European Parliament on Commission Monitoring and Application of Community Law OJ C 154, 6.6.1994 (Brussels: CEC, 1994).

—— A Handbook on Environmental Assessment of Regional Development Plans and EU Structural Funds Programmes (London: Environmental Resources Management, 1998).

—— Guidelines for the Assessment of Indirect and Cumulative Impacts as well as Impact Interactions (Brussels: CEC, 1999).

—— Managing Natura 2000 Sites (Brussels: CEC, 2000).

—— Indicators for the Integration of Environmental Concerns into the Common Agricultural Policy, COM(2000) 20 final (Brussels: CEC, 2000).

—— *Proposal for an EU Sustainable Development Strategy*, COM(2001) 264 (Brussels: CEC, 2001).

—— *White Paper on European Governance*, COM(2001) 428 final (Brussels: CEC, 2001).

—— *Simplifying and Improving the Regulatory Environment*, COM(2001) 726 final (Brussels: CEC, 2001).

—— *SEA and the Integration of the Environment into Strategic Decision Making* (Brussels: CEC, 2001).

—— *Guidance on Indirect, Cumulative and Impact Interactions* (Brussels: CEC, 2001).

—— *Communication on Precaution* (Brussels: CEC, 2001).

—— *Internal Preliminary Impact Assessment on the Thematic Strategy on the Prevention and Recycling of Waste* (Brussels: CEC, 2002).

—— *Preliminary Impact Assessment on Directive on the Biological Treatment of Biodegradeable Waste* (Brussels: CEC, 2002).

—— *Impact Assessment: Environment Guide* (Brussels: CEC, 2002).

—— *How to Assess Impacts: Guidelines for Commission Staff* (Brussels: CEC, 2002).

—— *Five Years Report to the European Parliament and the Council on the Effectiveness of the EIA Directive* (Brussels: CEC, 2002).

—— *Better Regulation*, COM(2002) 276 final (Brussels: CEC, 2002).

—— *Communication from the Commission on Impact Assessment*, COM(2002) 276 final (Brussels: CEC, 2002).

—— *Towards a Reinforced Culture of Consultation and Dialogue—Proposal for General Principles and Minimum Standards for Consultation of Interested Parties by the Commission*, COM(2002) 277 final (Brussels: CEC, 2002).

—— *Action Plan on Simplifying and Improving the Regulatory Environment*, COM(2002) 278 (Brussels: CEC, 2002).

—— *Indirect and Cumulative Impacts and Impact Interactions* (Brussels: CEC, 2002).

—— *Proposal for a Directive of the European Parliament and of the Council on Access to Justice on Environmental Matters*, COM(2003) 624 final (Brussels: CEC, 2003).

—— *Proposal for a Council Decision on the Conclusion, on Behalf of the European Community, of the Convention on Access to Information, Public Participation in Decision Making and Access to Justice regarding Environmental Matters*, COM(2003) 625 final (Brussels: CEC, 2003).

Evernden, N. *The Social Creation of Nature* (Baltimore: Johns Hopkins University Press, 1993).

Fairfax, S. K. 'A Disaster in the Environmental Movement' (1978) 99 *Science* 743.

Farber, D. 'Taking Slippage Seriously: Noncompliance and Creative Compliance in Environmental Law' (1999) 23 *Harv Env L Rev* 297.

—— *Eco-Pragmatism* (Chicago: Chicago University Press, 1999).

Ferester, M. 'Revitalising the National Environmental Policy Act: Substantive Law Adaptions from NEPA's Progeny' [1992] *Harv Env L Rev* 207.

Fiorino, D. J. 'Rethinking Environmental Regulation: Perspectives on Law and Governance' (1999) 23 *Harv Env L Rev* 441.

Fischer, F. *Citizens, Experts and the Environment: The Politics of Local Knowledge* (Durham, NC and London: Duke Press, 2000).

Fisher, L. 'Is the Precautionary Principle Justiciable?' (2001) 13 *JEL* 315.

—— 'Unpacking the Toolbox: Or Why the Public/Private Divide is Important in EC Environmental Law' (forthcoming).

Fitzpatrick, B. 'Redressing the Late Implementation of the Environmental Impact Assessment Directive' (1994) 6 *JEL* 351.

Fitzpatrick, P. 'Consolations of the Law: Jurisprudence and the Constitution of Deliberative Politics' (2001) 14 *Ratio Juris* 281.

Foster, S. 'Justice from the Ground Up: Distributive Inequities, Grassroots Resistance and the Transformative Politics of the Environmental Justice Movement' (1998) 86 *Cal L Rev* 775.

Gaines, S. E. and Kimber, C. 'Redirecting Self-Regulation' (2001) 13 *JEL* 157.

Garner, J. and O'Riordan, T. 'Environmental Impact Assessment in the Context of Economic Recession' (1982) 148 *Geog J* 343.

Gibson, R. B. 'Respecting Ignorance and Uncertainty', in Lykke, E. (ed.) *Achieving Environmental Goals: The Concepts and Practice of Environmental Performance Review* (London: Belhaven, 1992).

Gilpin, A. *Environmental Impact Assessment: Cutting Edge for the Twenty-First Century* (Cambridge: Cambridge University Press, 1995).

Giroult, E. 'World Health Organisation Interest in Environmental Health Impact Assessment', in Wathern, P. (ed.) *Environmental Impact Assessment: Theory and Practice* (London: Routledge, 1988).

Global Renewable Energy Partners, *Environmental Statement: Kentish Flats Offshore Windfarm* (Durley, Hants: GREP, 2002).

Goldstein, R. 'Putting Environmental Law on the Map: A Spatial Approach to Environmental Law Using GIS', in Holder, J. and Harrison, C. (eds.) *Law and Geography* (Oxford: Oxford University Press, 2002).

Goode, P. M. and Johnstone, A. 'EIA: Its Potential Application to Appropriate Technology in Developing Countries' (1998) 8 *The Environmentalist* 57.

Gouge, E. 'The UK Implementation of Environmental Assessment: Organisational and Political Implications' [1989] *Local Government Policy Making* 55.

Grant, M. 'Implementation of the EC Directive on Environmental Impact Assessment', (1989) 4 *Conn J of Int L* 463.

—— 'Development and the Protection of Birds: The *Swale* Decision' (1991) 3 *JEL* 150.

Gray, K. 'International Environmental Impact Assessment: Potential for a Multilateral Environmental Agreement' [2000] *Col J of Int Env L and Policy* 83.

Greenpeace, *North Sea Offshore Wind—A Powerhouse for Europe: Technical Possibilities and Ecological Considerations* (London: Greenpeace, 2000).

Habermas, J. *Towards a Rational Society* (London: Heinemann,1971).

Haigh, N. 'The EEC Directive on Environmental Assessment of Development Projects' [1983] *J of Plg and Env Law* 585.

—— 'The EC and Land Use: An Incoming Tide' [1990] JPL 58.

Hajer, M. A. *The Politics of Environmental Discourse: Ecological Modernisation and the Policy Process* (Oxford: Oxford University Press, 1997).

Harrison, C. and Bedford, T. 'Environmental Gains? Collaborative Planning, Planning Obligations and Issues of Closure in Local Land-Use Planning in the UK', in Holder, J. and Harrison, C. (eds.) *Law and Geography* (Oxford: Oxford University Press, 2002).

Harvey, D. *Justice, Nature and the Geography of Difference* (Oxford: Blackwell, 1996).

Healey, P. *Collaborative Planning: Shaping Places in Fragmented Societies* (Basingstoke: Macmillan, 1997).

Heinelt, H., Malek, T., Smith, R., and Toller, A. E. (eds.) *European Union Environmental Policy and New Forms of Governance* (Aldershot: Ashgate, 2001).

Herington, J. 'Environmental Values in a Changing Planning System', in Clark, M. and Herington, J. (eds.) *The Role of Environmental Impact Assessment in the Planning Process* (London: Mansell, 1998).

Hertz, M. 'Parallel Universes: NEPA Lessons for the New Property' (1993) 93 *Columbia L Rev* 1668.

HM Government, *Policy Appraisal and the Environment* (London: HMSO, 1992).

Hobday, S. R. *Coulson and Forbes on the Law of Waters* (6th edn., 1952).

Holder, J. *'An Analysis of Council Directive 85/337/EEC on the Assessment of the Effects of Certain Public and Private Projects on the Environment and the Development of Environmental Law in the United Kingdom'* (Ph.D., University of Warwick, 1995).

—— and D. McGillivray (eds.) *Locality and Identity: Environmental Issues in Law and Society* (Aldershot: Ashgate, 1999).

—— 'New Age: Rediscovering Natural Law' (2000) 53 *CLP* 151.

Holling, C. S. (ed.) *Adaptive Environmental Assessment and Management* (Chichester: John Wiley, 1978).

Houck, O. A. 'Of Bats, Birds and B-A-T: The Convergent Evolution of Environmental Law', (1994) 63 *Miss L J* 403.

House of Commons Environment Committee, Fifth Report, *Planning Appeals and Call-in and Major Public Inquiries*, Session 1985–86 HC 181, Cm 43.

House of Lords Select Committee on the European Communities, Eleventh Report, *Environmental Assessment of Projects*, Session 1980–81 (London: HMSO, 1981).

Howarth W. *Flood Defence Law* (Crayford: Shaw and Sons, 2002).

—— and McGillivray, D. *Water Pollution and Water Quality Law* (Crayford: Shaw and Sons, 2001).

Htun, M. N. 'Development of United Nations Environment Programme Guidelines for Assessing Industrial Criteria for the Siting of Industry', in Clark, B. D., Bissett, R., and Gilad, A. (eds.) *Perspectives on Environmental Impact Assessment* (New York: Reidel, 1984).

Hutton, N. *Lay Participation in a Public Inquiry: A Sociological Case Study* (London: Gower, 1986).

Hyman, E. L. *Combining Facts and Values in Environmental Impact Assessment* (NY: Westview Publications, 1986).

IMPEL, *Report on the Interrelationship between IPPC, EIA and SEVESO Directives and EMAS Regulation* (Brussels: CEC, 1998).

Institute of Environmental Assessment, *Practical Experience of Environmental Assessment in the United Kingdom* (East Kirkby: Institute of Environmental Assessment, 1993).

Institute of Environmental Management and Assessment, *Perspectives: Guidelines on Participation in Environmental Decision Making* (Lincoln: IEMA, 2002).

Institute for European Environmental Policy, *Sustainable Development in the European Commission's Integrated Impact Assessments for 2003* (London: IEEP, 2004).

Jacobs, M. *The Green Economy* (London: Pluto Press, 1993).

Jacobs, P. *et al.*, *Sustainable Development and Environmental Assessment: Perspectives on Planning for a Common Future* (Quebec: Canadian Environmental Research Council, 1980).

Jans, J. *European Environmental Law* (Groningen: Europa, 2nd edn., 2000).

—— and de Jong, M. 'Somewhere between Direct Effect and Rewe/Comet: Some Remarks on Dutch Public Law, Procedural Defects and the EIA Directive', Workshop on Member States Administrative Procedural Law and its Impact on the European Harmonisation Process, Florence, 1999.

Jardine, L. *Ingenious Pursuits: Building the Scientific Revolution* (London: Little, Brown and Co., 1999).

Jasanoff, S. *The Fifth Branch: Science Advisers as Policy Makers* (Cambridge, Mass.: Harvard University Press, 1989).

Jones, C. and Wood, C. 'The Impact of Environmental Assessment on Public Inquiry Decisions' [1995] JPL 890.

—— —— and Dipper, B. 'Environmental Assessment in the Planning Process' (1998) 69 *T P Rev* 315.

Jongh, P. de 'Uncertainty in Environmental Impact Assessment', in Wathern, P. (ed.) *Environmental Impact Assessment: Theory and Practice* (London: Routledge, 1988).

Jowell, J. 'The Legal Control of Administrative Discretion' [1977] *PL* 178.

Kemp, R. 'Planning, Legitimation and the Development of Nuclear Power: A Critical Theoretic Analysis of the Windscale Inquiry' (1986) 14 *Policy and Politics* 350.

Kennedy, W. V. 'Environmental Impact Assessment and Bilateral Development Aid: An Overview', in Wathern, P. (ed.) *Environmental Impact Assessment: Theory and Practice* (London: Routledge, 1988).

Kramer, L. *Casebook on EC Environmental Law* (London: Sweet and Maxwell, 1st edn., 1993).

Kuehn, R. R. 'The Environmental Justice Implications of Quantitative Risk Assessment' [1996] *Univ of Ill L Rev* 103.

Kuhn, S. 'Expanding Public Participation is Essential to Environmental Justice and the Decision Making Process' (1995) 25 *Ecology LQ* 647.

Kunzlik, P. 'The Lawyer's Assessment' in B. Bryant, *Twyford Down: Roads, Campaigning and Environmental Law* (London: Spon, 1996), 'EIA: The British Cases' (1995) 8 *EEL Rev* 336.

Ladeur, K. and Prelle, R. 'Environmental Assessment and Judicial Approaches to Procedural Errors: A European and Comparative Law Analysis' (2001) 13 *JEL* 185.

Lawrence, D. 'Quantitative versus Qualitative Evaluation: A False Dichotomy' (1993) 13 *EIA Rev* 2.

Ledger, M. J. 'An Assessment of the Effectiveness of Land Use Planning Powers to Control Pollution', Unpublished Ph.D. thesis (University of Manchester, 1982).

Lee, M. and Abbott, C. 'The Usual Suspects? Public Participation under the Aarhus Convention' (2003) 66 *MLR* 80.

Lee, N. and Wood, C. 'Environmental Impact Assessment: A European Perspective', (1978) 4 *Built Env* 101.

Lenschow, A. 'New Regulatory Approaches in "Greening" EU Policies' (2002) 8 *ELJ* 19.

Lichfield, N. *Community Impact Evaluation: Principles and Practice* (London: University College Press, 1996).

McAuslan, P. *Ideologies of Planning Law* (Oxford: Pergamon Press, 1980).

McCracken, R. 'EIA and Judicial Review: Some Recent Trends' (2003) 8 *JR* 37.

—— 'Environmental Assessment: From Technocratic Paternalism to Participatory Democracy?', Paper given at the Enforcement of EC Environmental Law Seminar, Kings College London, June 2003.

McGarity, T. O. 'The Expanded Debate over the Future of the Regulatory State' (1996) 63 *U Chicago L Rev* 1463.

McGillivray, D. 'Valuing Nature: Economic Value, Conservation Values and Sustainable Development' (2002) 14 *JEL* 85.

—— and Holder, J. 'Locating EC Environmental Law' (2001) 20 *Yearbook of European Law*, 139.

McKibben, W. T. *The End of Nature* (Random House, 1989).

Macrory, R. 'Environmental Assessment: Critical Legal Issues in Implementation', in Vaughan, D. (ed.) *EC Environmental and Planning Law* (London: Butterworths, 1986).

—— 'Environmental Assessment and the "Direct Effect" Doctrine' (1994) 228 *ENDS Report* 44.

—— 'Regulating in a Risky Environment' (2001) 54 *CLP* 619.

—— and Turner, S. 'Participation Rights, Transboundary Environmental Governance and EC Environmental Law' (2002) 39 *CML Rev* 489.

Marren, P. *Nature Conservation* (London: HarperCollins, 2002).

Mashaw, J. 'Administrative Due Process: The Quest for a Dignitary Theory' (1981) 61 *Boston Uni LR* 885.

Mathieson, M. 'Public Participation and Access to Justice' [2003] *EEL Rev* 37.

Miller, C. 'The Environmental Roles of Town and Country Planning', in Miller, C. (ed.) *Planning and Environmental Protection* (Oxford: Hart, 2001).

—— and Wood, C. *Planning and Pollution: An Examination of the Role of Land Use Planning in the Protection of Environmental Quality* (Oxford: Oxford University Press, 1983).

Millichap, D. 'Sustainability: A Long-Established Concern of Planning' [1992] *Journal of Planning and Environmental Law*, 1111.

Mitchell, J. C. 'Case and Situation Analysis' [1983] *Sociol Rev* 188.

Montini, M. 'Habitats Impact Assessment: An Effective Instrument for Biodiversity Conservation' (2001) 9 *Env Liab* 182.

Morgan, B. 'The Economisation of Politics' (2003) 12 *SLS* 489.

Morgan, R. K. *Environmental Impact Assessment: A Methodological Perspective* (Dordrecht: Kluwer, 1999).

Morris, P. and Therivel, R. (eds.) *Methods of Environmental Impact Assessment* (London: Spon, 2nd edn., 2001).

Munn, R. E. (ed.) *Environmental Impact Assessment: Principles and Procedures* (New York: John Wiley, 1979).

Myerson, G. and Rydin, Y. 'Environment and Planning: A Tale of the Mundane and Sublime' (1994) 12 *Environment and Planning D: Space and Society* 432.

Nollkaemper, A. 'Habitat Protection in European Community Law: Evolving Conceptions of a Balance of Interests' (1997) 9 *JEL* 271.

Nonet, P. *Administrative Justice* (New York: Russell Sage Foundation, 1969).

—— and Selznick, P. *Law and Society in Transition: Towards Responsive Law* (New York: Harper Torch, 1978).

Office of the Deputy Prime Minister, 'A Government Note on the Environmental Impact Assessment Directive' [2002] JPL 1067.

O'Neill, M. 'Agriculture, the EC and the WTO: A Legal Critical Analysis of the Concepts of Sustainability and Multifunctionality' (2002) 4 *Env L Rev* 144.

Organization for Economic Cooperation and Development, *Coordinated Methods of Assessing the Potential Environmental Effects of Chemical Compounds*, C(74)215 (Paris: OECD, 1974).

—— *Environmental Consequences of Significant Public and Private Projects*, C(74)216 (Paris: OECD, 1974).

—— *Coordination Guidelines in Respect of Procedures and Requirements for Anticipating the Effects of Chemicals on Man and the Environment*, C(77)97 final (Paris: OECD, 1977).

—— *The Assessment of Projects with Significant Impact on the Environment*, C(79)116 (Paris: OECD, 1979).

—— *Recommendation of the Council on Measures Required to Facilitate the Environmental Assessment of Development Assistance Projects and Programmes*, C(86)26 (Paris: OECD, 1986).

O'Riordan, T. and Hey, R. D. (eds.) *Environmental Impact Assessment* (Farnborough: Saxon House, 1976).

Orts, E. 'Reflexive Environmental Law' (1995) 89 *Northwestern ULR* 1227.

Ost, F. 'A Game without Rules? The Ecological Self-Organisation of Firms', in Teubner, G., Farmer, L. and Murphy, D. (eds.) *Environmental Law and Ecological Responsibility: The Concept and Practice of Ecological Self-Organisation* (Chichester: Wiley, 1994).

Parkin, J. *Judging Plans and Projects* (Aldershot: Avebury, 1993).

Partidario, M. 'Strategic Environmental Assessment: Principles and Potential', in Petts, J. (ed.) *Handbook of Environmental Impact Assessment: Vol. 1 Process, Methods and Potential* (Oxford: Blackwell, 1999).

Pearce, D. W., Markandya, A. and Barbier, E. *Blueprint for a Green Economy* (London: Earthscan, 1989).

Pelizzoni, L. 'Sociological Aspects of Environmental Impact Assessment', in Columbo, A. G. (ed.) *Environmental Impact Assessment* (Dordrecht: Kluwer, 1992).

Percival, R. V. *Environmental Regulation, Law, Science and Policy* (New York: Little Brown, 1992).

Perez, O. 'Using Private-Public Linkages to Regulate Environmental Conflicts: The Case of International Construction' (2002) 29 *JLS* 77.

Peters, H. J. 'The Significance of Environmental Precaution in the Environmental Impact Assessment Directive' [1996] *EEL Rev* 210.

Petts, J. (ed.) 'EIA: Overview of Purpose and Process', in Petts, J. (ed.) *Handbook of Environmental Impact Assessment: Vol. 1 Process, Methods and Potential* (Oxford: Blackwell, 1999).

Plant, G. 'Offshore Wind Energy Development: The Challenges for English Law' [2003] *JPL* 939.

Popham, J. and Purdue, M. 'The Future of the Major Inquiry' [2002] *JPL* 137.

Pugh-Smith, J. 'Environmental Impact Assessments: The Continuing Jurisprudence' [2002] *JPL* 1316.

Purdue, M. 'Integrated Pollution Control in the Environmental Protection Act 1990: A Coming of Age of Environmental Law?' (1991) 54 *MLR* 534.

—— 'The Case for Third Party Planning Appeals' (2001) 3 *Env L Rev* 83.

Redclift, M. and Woodgate, G. 'Sociology and the Environment: Discordant Discourse', in Redclift, M. and Benton, T. (eds.) *Social Theory and the Global Environment* (London: Routledge, 1994).

Richardson, G. 'The Legal Regulation of Process', in Richardson, G. and Genn, H. (eds.) *Administrative Law and Government Action* (Oxford: Clarendon, 1994).

Roderick, P. 'The Newbury Bypass Litigation: Part I' [1996] *JR* 252.

—— 'The Newbury Bypass Litigation: Part II' [1997] *JR* 55.

Rodriguez-Bachiller, A. and Wood, G. 'Geographical Information Systems (GIS) and EIA', in Morris, P. and Therivel, R. (eds.) *Methods of Environmental Impact Assessment* (London, Spon, 2nd edn., 2001).

Royal Commission on Environmental Pollution, *Air Pollution Control: An Integrated Approach* Cmnd 6371 (London: HMSO, 1976).

—— *Setting Environmental Standards*, Twenty-First Report, Cm 4053 (London: HMSO, 1998).

—— *Environmental Planning*, Twenty-Third Report, Cm 5459 (London: HMSO, 2002).

Royal Institute of Chartered Surveyors, *Environmental Assessments* (London: RICS, 1989).

Royal Society for the Protection of Birds, *The Environment and the Structural Funds: The Role of Strategic Environmental Assessment—The Sicilian Experience* (Sandy, Beds: Birdlife International, RSPB, 1997).

Ryall, A. 'The EIA Directive and the Irish Planning Participation Fee' (2002) 14 *JEL* 317.

Sabel, C., Fung, A., and Karkkainen, B. 'After Backyard Environmentalism: Towards a Model of Information-Based Environmental Regulation' (1999) 25 *Boston Review* 4.

Sadler, B. *The Place of Negotiation in Environmental Assessment* (Quebec: Canadian Environmental Assessment Research Council, 1987).

—— *Environmental Assessment in a Changing World: Evaluating Practice to Improve Performance*, Final Report of the International Study of the Effectiveness of Environmental Assessment and Canadian Environmental Assessment Agency, Ministry of Supply and Services (Ottawa, 1996).

—— 'Environmental Sustainability Assessment and Assurance' in Petts, J. (ed.) *Handbook of EIA: Vol. 1 Process, Methods and Potential* (Oxford: Blackwell, 1999).

Salter, J. 'EIA: The Question of Implementation' [1992] JPL 313.

—— 'EIA: The Challenge from Brussels' [1992] JPL 14.

Sandbach, F. *Environmental, Ideology and Policy* (Oxford: Basil Blackwell, 1980).

Sands, P. *Principles of International Environmental Law* (Cambridge: Cambridge University Press, 2nd edn., 2003).

Save the Cairngorm Campaign, 'Cairn Gorm: Potential for Conflict with Europe (1997).

Sax, J. L. 'The (Unhappy) Truth About NEPA' (1973) 26 *Okl L Rev* 239.

Schwarze, J. 'The Convergence of the Administrative Laws of the EU's Member States' [1998] *European Public Law* 191.

Scott, C. 'Analysing Regulatory Space: Fragmented Resources and Institutional Design' [2001] *PL* 329.

Scott, J. 'From Rio to Inverness: Environment and Development in the Highlands and Islands Objective 1 Enterprise Area', in Holder, J. (ed.) *The Impact of EC Environmental Law in the United Kingdom* (Chichester: Wiley, 1997).

—— *EC Environmental Law* (London: Longmans, 1998).

—— 'Flexibility, "Proceduralisation" and Environmental Governance in the EU', in de Búrca, G. and Scott, J. (eds.) *The Changing Constitution of the EU: From Uniformity to Flexibility?* (Oxford: Hart, 2000).

—— and D. Trubeck, 'Mind the Gap: Law and New Approaches to Governance in the European Union' (2002) 8 *ELJ* 1.

—— 'GMOs: The WTO and the EC' (2004) 57 *CLP* (forthcoming).

Scottish Executive, Circular No. 13/88, *Environmental Assessment: Implementation of EC Directive: The Environmental Assessment (Scotland) Regulations 1988* (Edinburgh: Scottish Executive, 1988).

Scottish Wildlife and Countryside Link and Save the Cairngorms Campaign, *The Northern Cairngorms: An Alternative Approach* (1996).

Selman, P. H. 'The Use of Ecological Evaluations by Local Planning Authorities' (1982) 15 *J of Env Plg and Management* 1.

Selznick, P. *Law, Society and Industrial Justice* (New York: Russell Sage, 1969).

Shackley, S. 'Mission to Model Earth', in Elworthy, S. *et al.* (eds.) *Perspectives on the Environment 2* (Aldershot: Avebury, 1995).

Sheate, W. *The Environmental Assessment Directive: Five Years On* (London: Council for the Protection of Rural England, 1991).
—— *Environmental Impact Assessment: Law and Policy* (London: Cameron May, 1996).
—— 'From Environmental Impact Assessment to Strategic Environmental Assessment: Sustainability and Decision-Making', in Holder, J. (ed.) *The Impact of EC Environmental Law in the United Kingdom* (Chichester: Wiley, 1997).
Sifakis, A. 'Precaution, Prevention, and the EIA Directive' [1998] *EEL Rev* 349.
Simenstad, C. A. and Thom, R. M. 'Functional Equivalency Trajectories of the Restored Gog-le-Hi-Te Estuarine Wetland' (1996) 6 *Ecological Applications* 38.
Sippe, B. 'Criteria and Standards for Assessing Significant Impact', in Petts, J. (ed.), *Handbook of Environmental Impact Assessment: Vol. 1 Process, Methods and Potential* (Oxford: Blackwell, 1999).
Skegly, S. I. *The Human Rights Obligations of the World Bank and Monetary Fund* (London: Cavendish, 2001).
Smith, R. 'The Implementation of EIA in Britain', in Heinelt, H., Malek, T., Smith, R. and Toller, A. E. (eds.) *European Union Environment Policy and New Forms of Governance* (Aldershot: Ashgate, 2001).
Sontag, N. C. and Everitt, R. R. *et al.*, *Cumulative Effective Assessment: A Context for Further Development and Research* (Quebec: Canadian Environmental Assessment Research Centre, 1987).
Stallworthy, M. *Sustainability, Land Use and Environment: A Legal Analysis* (London: Cavendish, 2002).
Steele, J. 'The Role of the Citizen: From Preferences and Values, to Deliberation?' Paper given at the Environmental Citizenship conference, University of Aberdeen, 2000.
—— 'Participation and Deliberation in Environmental Law: Exploring a Problem-Solving Approach' (2001) 21 *OJLS* 415.
Stewart, R. 'The Reformation of American Administrative Law' (1975) 88 *Harv L Rev* 1667.
Tabb, W. M. 'Environmental Impact Assessment in the European Community: Shaping International Norms' (1999) 73 *Tul L Rev* 923.
Taylor, S. *Making Bureaucracies Think: The Environmental Impact Statement Strategy of Administrative Reform* (Stanford, Calif.: Stanford University Press, 1984).
Teubner, G. 'Substantive and Reflexive Elements in Modern Law' [1983] *L and Soc Rev* 239.
—— 'Regulatory Law: A Chronicle of a Death Foretold', in Lenoble, R. (ed.) *The Crisis of the Welfare State* (Berlin: Walter de Gruyter, 1984).
—— 'After Legal Instrumentalism? Strategic Models of Post-Regulatory Law', in G. Teubner (ed.) *Dilemmas of Law in the Welfare State* (Berlin: Walter de Gruyter, 1986), 229–325.
—— Farmer, L. and Murphy, D. (eds.) *Environmental Law and Ecological Responsibility: The Concept and Practice of Ecological Self-Organisation* (Chichester: Wiley, 1994).
Therivel Directory of Environmental Statements 1988–1991
Therivel, R. and Partidario, M. R. (eds.) *The Practice of Strategic Environmental Assessment* (London: Earthscan, 1996).
—— and Wilson, E. *et al.*, *Strategic Environmental Assessment* (London: Routledge, 1993).
Thompson, P. 'Major Infrastructure Projects: Where to Now?' [2002] JPL 25.
Tilleman, W. A. 'Public Participation in the Environmental Impact Assessment Process: A Comparative Study of Impact Assessment in Canada, the United States and the European Community' (1995) 33 *Colum J Trans L* 337.

Treweek, J. *Ecological Impact Assessment* (Oxford: Blackwell, 1999).

Tromans, S. and Roger-Machart, C. 'Strategic Environmental Assessment: Early Evaluation Equals Efficiency?' [1997] JPL 993.

—— 'Environmental Protest and the Law' [2003] JPL 1367.

—— and Fuller, K. *Environmental Impact Assessment: Law and Practice* (London, Butterworths, 2003).

Tubb, W. M. 'Environmental Impact Assessment in the European Community: Shaping International Norms' (1999) 73 *Tul L Rev* 923.

UKELA (United Kingdom Environmental Law Association), *Overlaps in the Requirements for Environmental Assessment* (London: UKELA, 1993).

Unger, R. M. *Law in Modern Society: Towards a Criticism of Social Theory* (New York: Free Press, 1976).

United Nations Environment Programme, *Guidelines for Assessing Industrial Environmental Impact and Criteria for the Siting of Industry* (Paris: UNEP, 1980).

Upton, W. 'The EIA Process and the Directly Enforceable Rights of Citizens' (2001) 13 *JEL* 98.

—— 'The Use of Minimum Size Thresholds in EIA' (2002) 14 *JEL* 346.

Ureta, A. 'Prevention Rather than Cure: The EC EIA Directive and its Impact in Spain and the UK' [1992] *Envtl Liab* 61.

Vanclay, F., and Bronstein, D. A. (eds.) *Environmental and Social Impact Assessment* (Chichester: Wiley, 1995).

Vedder, H. 'The New Community Guidelines on State Aid for Environmental Protection: Integrating Environment and Competition' [2001] *Eur Comp Rev* 365.

Von Moltke, K. 'Environmental Impact Assessment in the United States and Europe', in Clarke B. D., Bissett R., and Gilad, A. (eds.) *Perspectives on Environmental Impact Assessment* (New York: Reidel, 1984).

Walker, J. 'Dibden Bay Port: The Quality of Life Questions' (2001) 22 *ECOS* 65.

Wandesforde-Smith, G. and Kerbavaz, J. 'The Co-evolution of Politics and Policy: Elections, Entrepreneurship and EIA in the United States', in Wathern, P. (ed.) *Environmental Impact Assessment: Theory and Practice* (London: Routledge, 1988).

Ward, A. 'The Right to an Effective Remedy in European Community Law and Environmental Protection: A Case Study of United Kingdom Judicial Decisions concerning the Environmental Assessment Directive' (1993) 5 *JEL* 221.

Wathern, P. (ed.) *Environmental Impact Assessment: Theory and Practice* (London: Routledge, 1988).

—— 'The EIA Directive of the European Community', in Wathern, P. (ed.) *Environmental Impact Assessment: Theory and Practice* (London: Routledge, 1988).

—— 'Implementing Supranational Policy: Environmental Impact Assessment in the United Kingdom', in Bartlett, R. V. (ed.) *Policy through Impact Assessment: Institutionalised Analysis as a Policy Strategy* (New York: Greenwood Press, 1989).

Weale, A. *The New Politics of Pollution* (Manchester: Manchester University Press, 1992).

—— Pridham, G. *et al.* (eds.) *Environmental Governance in Europe: An Ever Closer Ecological Union* (Oxford: Oxford University Press, 2000).

Weber, M. 'Power and Bureaucracy', in Thompson, K. and Turnstall, J. (eds.) *Sociological Perspectives* (London: Harmondsworth, 1971).

Westman, W. E. *Ecology, Impact Assessment and Environmental Planning* (Chichester: John Wiley, 1985).

Wiener, J. 'Global Environmental Regulation: Instrument Choice in Legal Context' (1999) 108 *Yale L J* 679.

Wilkins, H. 'The Need for Subjectivity in Environmental Assessment' (2003) 23 *EIA Rev* 401.

Wilkinson, D. 'Using Environmental Ethics to Create Ecological Law', in Holder, J. and McGillivray, D. (eds.) *Locality and Identity: Environmental Issues in Law and Society* (Aldershot: Ashgate, 1999).

Williams, R. 'Twyford Down' [1991] *CLJ* 382.

Wilson, E. 'Progress towards Strategic Environmental Assessment of Policies, Plans and Programmes', paper delivered at the IRNES conference on Perspectives on the Environment, September 1992.

Winter, P. 'EIA: Getting it Right' [2000] JPL 18.

Wolfe, D. 'A Duty to Find the Least Worst Option?' (2004) 17 e-law (u.k. environmental law association e-journal) 8.

Wood, C. *Planning Pollution Prevention: A Comparison of the Siting Controls over Air Pollution in Great Britain and the USA* (Oxford: Heinemann Newnes, 1989).

—— 'Five Years of British Environmental Assessment', in Cross, D. and Whitehead, C. (eds.) *Development and Planning* (Cambridge: Cambridge University Press, 1994).

—— 'Environmental Assessment', in C. Miller (ed.) *Planning and Environmental Protection* (Oxford: Hart, 2001).

—— and Jones, C. 'The Impact of Environmental Assessment on Local Planning Authorities' (1992) 35 *JEPM* 115.

—— —— and Lee, N. *Environmental Statements 1988–1990: An Analysis* (Manchester: University of Manchester, 1990).

Wood, D. 'Challenging the Ethos of the European Union: A Green Perspective on European Union Policies and Programmes for Rural Development and the Environment', in Holder, J and McGillivray, D. (eds.) *Locality and Identity: Environmental Issues in Law and Society* (Aldershot: Ashgate, 1999).

Wood, G. and Becker, J. *Screening Decision Making under the Town and Country Planning (Environmental Impact Assessment) Regulations 1999* (Oxford: Oxford Brookes University, 2003).

World Bank, *The World Bank and the Environment: First Annual Report* (Washington: World Bank, 1990).

—— *Mainstreaming the Environment: The World Bank Group and the Environment since the Rio Earth Summit* (Washington: World Bank, 1995).

World Commission on Environment and Development, *Our Common Future* (Oxford: Oxford University Press, 1987).

—— WCED Experts Group on Environmental Law, *Legal Principles for Environmental Protection and Sustainable Development* (Dordrecht: Martinus Nijhoff, 1987).

World Health Organization, *Rapid Assessment of Sources of Air, Water and Land Pollution Resolution* WHO/35.17 (Geneva: WHO, 1982).

Wynne, G. (ed.) *Biodiversity Challenge: An Agenda for Conservation Action in the UK* (Sandy: RSPB, 1993).

APPENDIX I

The National Environmental Policy Act of 1969, as amended

(Pub. L. 91–190, 42 U.S.C. 4321–4347, January 1, 1970, as amended by Pub. L. 94–52, July 3, 1975, Pub. L. 94–83, August 9, 1975, and Pub. L. 97–258, § 4(b), Sept. 13, 1982)

TITLE I

Declaration of National Environmental Policy

Sec. 101. (a) The Congress, recognizing the profound impact of man's activity on the interrelations of all components of the natural environment, particularly the profound influences of population growth, high-density urbanization, industrial expansion, resource exploitation, and new and expanding technological advances and recognizing further the critical importance of restoring and maintaining environmental quality to the overall welfare and development of man, declares that it is the continuing policy of the Federal Government, in cooperation with State and local governments, and other concerned public and private organizations, to use all practicable means and measures, including financial and technical assistance, in a manner calculated to foster and promote the general welfare, to create and maintain conditions under which man and nature can exist in productive harmony, and fulfill the social, economic, and other requirements of present and future generations of Americans.

(b) In order to carry out the policy set forth in this Act, it is the continuing responsibility of the Federal Government to use all practicable means, consistent with other essential considerations of national policy, to improve and coordinate Federal plans, functions, programs, and resources to the end that the Nation may —

(1) fulfill the responsibilities of each generation as trustee of the environment for succeeding generations;
(2) assure for all Americans, safe, healthful, productive, and esthetically and culturally pleasing surroundings;
(3) attain the widest range of beneficial uses of the environment without degradation, risk to health or safety, or other undesirable and unintended consequences;
(4) preserve important historic, cultural, and natural aspects of our national heritage, and maintain, wherever possible, an environment which supports diversity and variety of individual choice;
(5) achieve a balance between population and resource use which will permit high standards of living and a wide share of life's amenities; and
(6) enhance the quality of renewable resources and approach the maximum attainable recycling of depletable resources.

(c) The Congress recognizes that each person should enjoy a healthful environment and that each person has a responsibility to contribute to the preservation and enhancement of the environment.

Sec. 102. The Congress authorizes and directs that, to the fullest extent possible: (1) the policies, regulations, and public laws of the United States shall be interpreted and administered in accordance with the policies set forth in this Act, and (2) all agencies of the Federal Government shall—

(A) utilize a systematic, interdisciplinary approach which will insure the integrated use of the natural and social sciences and the environmental design arts in planning and in decisionmaking which may have an impact on man's environment;

(B) identify and develop methods and procedures, in consultation with the Council on Environmental Quality established by title II of this Act, which will insure that presently unquantified environmental amenities and values may be given appropriate consideration in decisionmaking along with economic and technical considerations;

(C) include in every recommendation or report on proposals for legislation and other major Federal actions significantly affecting the quality of the human environment, a detailed statement by the responsible official on—
  (i) the environmental impact of the proposed action,
  (ii) any adverse environmental effects which cannot be avoided should the proposal be implemented,
  (iii) alternatives to the proposed action,
  (iv) the relationship between local short-term uses of man's environment and the maintenance and enhancement of long-term productivity, and
  (v) any irreversible and irretrievable commitments of resources which would be involved in the proposed action should it be implemented. Prior to making any detailed statement, the responsible Federal official shall consult with and obtain the comments of any Federal agency which has jurisdiction by law or special expertise with respect to any environmental impact involved. Copies of such statement and the comments and views of the appropriate Federal, State, and local agencies, which are authorized to develop and enforce environmental standards, shall be made available to the President, the Council on Environmental Quality and to the public as provided by section 552 of title 5, United States Code, and shall accompany the proposal through the existing agency review processes;

(D) study, develop, and describe appropriate alternatives to recommended courses of action in any proposal which involves unresolved conflicts concerning alternative uses of available resources;

(E) recognize the worldwide and long-range character of environmental problems, and where consistent with the foreign policy of the United States, lend appropriate support to initiatives, resolutions, and programs designed to maximize international cooperation in anticipating and preventing a decline in the quality of mankind's world environment;

(F) make available to States, counties, municipalities, institutions, and individuals advice and information useful in restoring, maintaining, and enhancing the quality of the environment;

(G) initiate and utilize ecological information in the planning and development of resource-oriented projects; and

(H) assist the Council on Environmental Quality established by title II of this Act.

Sec. 103. All agencies of the Federal Government shall review their present statutory authority, administrative regulations, and current policies and procedures for the purpose of determining whether there are any deficiencies of inconsistencies therein which prohibit full compliance with the purposes and provisions of this Act and shall propose to the President not later than July 1, 1971, such measures as may be necessary to bring their authority and policies into conformity with the intent, purposes and procedures set forth in this Act.

Sec. 104. Nothing in Section 102 or 103 shall in any way affect the specific statutory obligations of any Federal agency (1) to comply with criteria or standards of environmental quality, (2) to coordinate or consult with any other Federal or State agency, or (3) to act, or refrain from acting contingent upon the recommendations or certification of any other Federal or State agency.

Sec. 105. The policies and goals set forth in the Act are supplementary to those set forth in existing authorizations of Federal agencies.

Council Directive 97/11/EC of 3 March 1997 amending Directive 85/337/EEC of 27 June 1985 on the Assessment of the Effects of Certain Public and Private Projects on the Environment (Consolidated Version)

1. Whereas Council Directive 85/337/EEC of 27 June 1985 on the assessment of the effects of certain public and private projects on the environment aims at providing the competent authorities with relevant information to enable them to take a decision on a specific project in full knowledge of the project's likely significant impact on the environment; whereas the assessment procedure is a fundamental instrument of environmental policy as defined in Article 130r of the Treaty and of the Fifth Community Programme of Policy and action in relation to the environment and sustainable development;

2. Whereas, pursuant to Article 130r(2) of the Treaty, Community policy on the environment is based on the precautionary principle and on the principle that the preventive action should be taken, that environmental damage should as a priority be rectified at source and that the polluter should pay;

3. Whereas the main principles of the assessment of environmental effects should be harmonized and whereas the Member States may lay down stricter rules to protect the environment;

4. Whereas experience acquired in environmental impact assessment, as recorded in the report on the implementation of Directive 85/337/EEC, adopted by the Commission on 2 April 1993, shows that it is necessary to introduce provisions designed to clarify, supplement and improve the rules on the assessment procedure, in order to ensure that the Directive is applied in an increasingly harmonized and efficient manner;

5. Whereas projects for which an assessment is required should be subject to a requirement for development consent; whereas the assessment should be carried out before such consent is granted;

6. Whereas it is appropriate to make additions to the list of projects which have significant effects on the environment and which must on that account as a rule be made subject to systematic assessment;

7. Whereas projects of other types may not have significant effect on the environment in every case; whereas these projects should be assessed where Member States consider they are likely to have significant effects on the environment;

8. Whereas Member States may set thresholds or criteria for the purpose of determining which such projects should be subject to assessment on the basis of the significance of their environmental effects; whereas Member States should be required to examine projects below those thresholds or outside those criteria on a case-by-case basis;

9. Whereas when setting such thresholds or criteria or examining projects on a case-by-case basis for the purpose of determining which projects should be subject to assessment on the basis of their significant environmental effects, Member States should take account of the relevant selection criteria set out in this Directive; whereas, in accordance with the Subsidiarity principle, the Member States are in the best position to apply these criteria in specific instances;

10. Whereas the existence of a location criterion referring to special protection areas designated by Member States pursuant to Council Directive 79/409/EEC of 2 April 1979 on the conservation of wild birds and 92/43/EEC of 21 May 1992 on the conservation of natural habitats and of wild fauna and flora does not imply necessarily that projects in those areas are to be automatically subject to an assessment under this Directive;

11. Whereas it is appropriate to introduce a procedure in order to enable the developer to obtain an opinion from the competent authorities on the content and extent of the information to be elaborated and supplied for the assessment; whereas Member States, in the framework of this procedure, may require the developer to provide, *inter alia*, alternatives for the projects for which it intends to submit an application;

12. Whereas it is desirable to strengthen the provisions concerning environmental impact assessment in a transboundary context to take account of developments at international level;

13. Whereas the Community signed the Convention on Environmental Impact Assessment in a Transboundary Context on 25 February 1991,

HAS ADOPTED THIS DIRECTIVE:

. . .

Article 2

1. Member States shall adopt all measures necessary to ensure that, before consent is given, projects likely to have significant effects on the environment by virtue, *inter alia*, of their nature, size or location are made subject to a requirement for development consent and an assessment with regard to their effect. These projects are defined in Article 4.

2. The environmental impact assessment may be integrated into the existing procedures for consent to projects in the Member States, or, failing this, into other procedures or into procedures to be established to comply with the aims of this Directive.

2a. Member States may provide for a single procedure in order to fulfil the requirements of Council Directive 96/61/EC of 24 September 1996 on integrated pollution prevention and control.[1]

3. Without prejudice to Article 7, Member States may, in exceptional cases, exempt a specific project in whole or in part from the provisions laid down in this Directive.

In this event, the Member State shall:

  (a) consider whether another form of assessment would be appropriate and whether the information thus collected should be made available to the public;
  (b) make available to the public concerned the information relating to the exemption and the reasons for granting it;

[1] OJ No. L 257, 10.10.1996, p. 126.

(c) inform the Commission, prior to granting consent, of the reasons justifying the exemption granted, and provide it with the information made available, where applicable to their own nationals.

The Commission shall immediately forward the documents received to the other Member States.

The Commission shall report annually to the Council on the application of this paragraph.

ARTICLE 3

The environmental impact assessment shall identify, describe and assess in an appropriate manner, in the light of each individual case and in accordance with Articles 4 to 11, the direct and indirect effects of a project on the following factors:

- human beings, fauna and flora;
- soil, water, air, climate and the landscape;
- material assets and the cultural heritage;
- the interaction between the factors mentioned in the first, second and third indents.

ARTICLE 4

1. Subject to Article 2(3), projects listed in Annex I shall be made subject to an assessment in accordance with Article 5 to 10.

2. Subject to Article 2(3), for projects listed in Annex II, the Member States shall determine through:

    (a) a case-by-case examination;

or

    (b) thresholds or criteria set by the Member State,

whether the project shall be made subject to an assessment in accordance with Articles 5 to 10.

Member States may decide to apply both procedures referred to in (a) and (b).

3. When a case-by-case examination is carried out or thresholds or criteria are set for the purpose of paragraph 2, the relevant selection criteria set out in Annex III shall be taken into account.

4. Member States shall ensure that the determination made by the competent authorities under paragraph 2 is made available to the public.

ARTICLE 5

1. In the case of projects which, pursuant to Article 4, must be subjected to an environmental impact assessment in accordance with Articles 5 to 10, Member States shall adopt the necessary measures to ensure that the developer supplies in an appropriate form the information specified in Annex IV inasmuch as:

    (a) the Member State consider that the information is relevant to a given stage of the consent procedure and to the specific characteristics of a particular project or type of project and of the environmental features likely to be affected;

(b) the Member States consider that a developer may reasonably be required to compile this information having regard *inter alia* to current knowledge and methods of assessment.

2. Member States shall take the necessary measures to ensure that, if the developer so requests before submitting an application for development consent, the competent authority shall give an opinion on the information to be supplied by the developer in accordance with paragraph 1. The competent authority shall consult the developer and authorities referred to in Article 6(1) before it gives its opinion. The fact that the authority has given an opinion under this paragraph shall not preclude it from subsequently requiring the developer to submit further information.

Member States may require the competent authorities to give such an opinion, irrespective of whether the developer so requests.

3. The information to be provided by the developer in accordance with paragraph 1 shall include at least:

- a description of the project comprising information on the site, design and size of the project;
- a description of the measures envisaged in order to avoid, reduce and, if possible, remedy significant adverse effects;
- the data required to identify and assess the main effects which the project is likely to have on the environment;
- an outline of the main alternatives studied by the developer and an indication of the main reasons for his choice, taking into account the environmental effects;
- a non-technical summary of the information mentioned in the previous indents.

4. Member States shall, if necessary, ensure that any authorities holding relevant information, with particular reference to Article 3, shall make this information available to the developer.

ARTICLE 6

1. Member States shall take the measures necessary to ensure that the authorities likely to be concerned by the project by reason of the specific environmental responsibilities are given an opportunity to express their opinion on the information supplied by the developer and on the request for development consent. To this end, Member States shall designate the authorities to be consulted, either in general terms or on a case-by-case basis. The information gathered pursuant to Article 5 shall be forwarded to those authorities. Detailed arrangements for consultation shall be laid down by the Member States.

2. Member States shall ensure that any request for development consent and any information gathered pursuant to Article 5 are made available to the public within a reasonable time in order to give the public concerned the opportunity to express an opinion before the development consent is granted.

3. The detailed arrangements for such information and consultation shall be determined by the Member States, which may in particular, depending on the particular characteristics of the projects or sites concerned:

- determine the public concerned;
- specify the places where the information can be consulted;

- specify the way in which the public may be informed, for example by bill-posting within a certain radius, publication in local newspapers, organization of exhibitions with plans, drawings, tables, graphs, models;
- determine the manner in which the public is to be consulted, for example by written submissions, by public enquiry;
- fix appropriate time limits for the various stages of the procedure in order to ensure that a decision is taken within a reasonable period.

ARTICLE 7

1. Where a Member State is aware that a project is likely to have significant effects on the environment in another Member State or where a Member State likely to be significantly affected so request, the Member State in whose territory the project is intended to be carried out shall send to the affected Member State as soon as possible and no later than when informing its own public, *inter alia*:

    (a) a description of the project, together with any available information on its possible transboundary impact;

    (b) information on the nature of the decision which may be taken,

and shall give the other Member State a reasonable time in which to indicate whether it wishes to participate in the Environmental Impact Assessment procedure, and may include the information referred to in paragraph 2.

2. If a Member State which receives information pursuant to paragraph 1 indicates that it intends to participate in the Environmental Impact Assessment procedure, the Member State in whose territory the project is intended to be carried out shall, if it has not already done so, send the affected Member State the information gathered pursuant to Article 5 and relevant information regarding the said procedure, including the request for development consent.

3. The Member State concerned, each insofar as it is concerned, shall also:

    (a) arrange for the information referred to in paragraphs 1 and 2 to be made available, within a reasonable time, to the authorities concerned in the territory of the Member State likely to be significantly affected; and

    (b) ensure that those authorities and the public concerned are given an opportunity, before development consent for the project is granted, to forward their opinion within a reasonable time on the information supplied to the competent authority in the Member State in whose territory the project is intended to be carried out.

4. The Member State concerned shall enter into consultations regarding, *inter alia*, the potential transboundary effects of the project and the measures envisaged to reduce or eliminate such effects and shall agree on a reasonable time frame for the duration of the consultation period.

5. The detailed arrangements for implementing the provisions of this Article may be determined by the Member States concerned.

ARTICLE 8

The results of consultations and the information gathered pursuant to Articles 5, 6 and 7 must be taken into consideration in the development consent procedure.

ARTICLE 9

1. When a decision to grant or refuse development consent has been taken, the competent authority or authorities shall inform the public thereof in accordance with the appropriate procedures and shall make available to the public the following information:

- the content of the decision and any conditions attached thereto;
- the main reasons and considerations on which the decision is based;
- a description, where necessary, of the main measures to avoid, reduce and, if possible, offset the major adverse effects.

2. The competent authority or authorities shall inform any Member State which has been consulted pursuant to Article 7, forwarding to it the information referred to in paragraph 1.

Directive 2001/42/EC of the European Parliament and of the Council on the Assessment of the Effects of Certain Plans and Programmes on the Environment

of 27 June 2001

THE EUROPEAN PARLIAMENT AND THE COUNCIL OF THE EUROPEAN UNION

Having regard to the Treaty establishing the European Community, and in particular Article 175(1) thereof,

Having regard to the proposal from the Commission,

Having regard to the opinion of the Economic and Social Committee,

Having regard to the opinion of the Committee of the Regions,

Acting in accordance with the procedure laid down in Article 251 of the Treaty, in the light of the joint text approved by the Conciliation Committee on 21 March 2001,

Whereas:

(1) Article 174 of the Treaty provides that Community policy on the environment is to contribute to, inter alia, the preservation, protection and improvement of the quality of the environment, the protection of human health and the prudent and rational utilisation of natural resources and that it is to be based on the precautionary principle. Article 6 of the Treaty provides that environmental protection requirements are to be integrated into the definition of Community policies and activities, in particular with a view to promoting sustainable development.

(2) The Fifth Environment Action Programme: Towards sustainability 'A European Community programme of policy and action in relation to the environment and sustainable development',[1] supplemented by Council Decision No 2179/98/EC[2] of its review, affirms the importance of assessing the likely environmental effects of plans and programmes.

(3) The Convention on Biological Diversity requires Parties to integrate as far as possible and as appropriate the conservation and sustainable use of biological diversity into relevant sectoral or cross-sectoral plans and programmes.

(4) Environmental assessment is an important tool for integrating environmental considerations into the preparation and adoption of certain plans and programmes which are likely to have significant effects on the environment in the Member

---

[1] OJ C 138, 17.5.1993, p. 5.   [2] OJ l 275, 10.10.1998, p. 1.

States, because it ensures that such effects of implementing plans and programmes are taken into account during their preparation and before their adoption.

(5) The adoption of environmental assessment procedures at the planning and programming level should benefit undertakings by providing a more consistent framework in which to operate by the inclusion of the relevant environmental information into decision making. The inclusion of a wider set of factors in decision making should contribute to more sustainable and effective solutions.

(6) The different environmental assessment systems operating within Member States should contain a set of common procedural requirements necessary to contribute to a high level of protection of the environment.

(7) The United Nations/Economic Commission for Europe Convention on Environmental Impact Assessment in a Transboundary Context of 25 February 1991, which applies to both Member States and other States, encourages the parties to the Convention to apply its principles to plans and programmes as well; at the second meeting of the Parties to the Convention in Sofia on 26 and 27 February 2001, it was decided to prepare a legally binding protocol on strategic environmental assessment which would supplement the existing provisions on environmental impact assessment in a transboundary context, with a view to its possible adoption on the occasion of the 5th Ministerial Conference 'Environment for Europe' at an extraordinary meeting of the Parties to the Convention, scheduled for May 2003 in Kiev, Ukraine. The systems operating within the Community for environmental assessment of plans and programmes should ensure that there are adequate transboundary consultations where the implementation of a plan or programme being prepared in one Member State is likely to have significant effects on the environment of another Member State. The information on plans and programmes having significant effects on the environment of other States should be forwarded on a reciprocal and equivalent basis within an appropriate legal framework between Member States and these other States.

(8) Action is therefore required at Community level to lay down a minimum environmental assessment framework, which would set out the broad principles of the environmental assessment system and leave the details to the Member States, having regard to the principle of subsidiarity. Action by the Community should not go beyond what is necessary to achieve the objectives set out in the Treaty.

(9) This Directive is of a procedural nature, and its requirements should either be integrated into existing procedures in Member States or incorporated in specifically established procedures. With a view to avoiding duplication of the assessment, Member States should take account, where appropriate, of the fact that assessments will be carried out at different levels of a hierarchy of plans and programmes.

(10) All plans and programmes which are prepared for a number of sectors and which set a framework for future development consent of projects listed in Annexes I and II to Council Directive 85/337/EEC of 27 June 1985 on the assessment of the effects of certain public and private projects on the environment,[3] and all plans and programmes which have been determined to require assessment pursuant to Council Directive 92/43/EEC of 21 May 1992 on the conservation of

[3] OJ L 175, 5.7.1985, p. 40. Directive as amended by Directive 97/11/EC (OJ L 73, 14.3.1997, p. 5).

natural habitats and of wild flora and fauna,[4] are likely to have significant effects on the environment, and should as a rule be made subject to systematic environmental assessment. When they determine the use of small areas at local level or are minor modifications to the above plans or programmes, they should be assessed only where Member States determine that they are likely to have significant effects on the environment.

(11) Other plans and programmes which set the framework for future development consent of projects may not have significant effects on the environment in all cases and should be assessed only where Member States determine that they are likely to have such effects.

(12) When Member States make such determinations, they should take into account the relevant criteria set out in this Directive.

(13) Some plans or programmes are not subject to this Directive because of their particular characteristics.

(14) Where an assessment is required by this Directive, an environmental report should be prepared containing relevant information as set out in this Directive, identifying, describing and evaluating the likely significant environmental effects of implementing the plan or programme, and reasonable alternatives taking into account the objectives and the geographical scope of the plan or programme; Member States should communicate to the Commission any measures they take concerning the quality of environmental reports.

(15) In order to contribute to more transparent decision making and with the aim of ensuring that the information supplied for the assessment is comprehensive and reliable, it is necessary to provide that authorities with relevant environmental responsibilities and the public are to be consulted during the assessment of plans and programmes, and that appropriate time frames are set, allowing sufficient time for consultations, including the expression of opinion.

(16) Where the implementation of a plan or programme prepared in one Member State is likely to have a significant effect on the environment of other Member States, provision should be made for the Member States concerned to enter into consultations and for the relevant authorities and the public to be informed and enabled to express their opinion.

(17) The environmental report and the opinions expressed by the relevant authorities and the public, as well as the results of any transboundary consultation, should be taken into account during the preparation of the plan or programme and before its adoption or submission to the legislative procedure.

(18) Member States should ensure that, when a plan or programme is adopted, the relevant authorities and the public are informed and relevant information is made available to them.

(19) Where the obligation to carry out assessments of the effects on the environment arises simultaneously from this Directive and other Community legislation, such as Council Directive 79/409/EEC of 2 April 1979 on the conservation of wild birds,[5]

---

[4] OJ L 206, 22.7.1992, p. 7. Directive as last amended by Directive 97/62/EC (OJ L 305, 8.11.1997, p. 42).

[5] OJ L 103, 25.4.1979, p. 1. Directive as last amended by Directive 97/49/EC (OJ L 223, 13.8.1997, p. 9).

Directive 92/43/EEC, or Directive 2000/60/EC of the European Parliament and the Council of 23 October 2000 establishing a framework for Community action in the field of water policy,[6] in order to avoid duplication of the assessment, Member States may provide for coordinated or joint procedures fulfilling the requirements of the relevant Community legislation.

(20) A first report on the application and effectiveness of this Directive should be carried out by the Commission five years after its entry into force, and at seven-year intervals thereafter. With a view to further integrating environmental protection requirements, and taking into account the experience acquired, the first report should, if appropriate, be accompanied by proposals for amendment of this Directive, in particular as regards the possibility of extending its scope to other areas/sectors and other types of plans and programmes,

HAVE ADOPTED THIS DIRECTIVE:

ARTICLE 1

Objectives

The objective of this Directive is to provide for a high level of protection of the environment and to contribute to the integration of environmental considerations into the preparation and adoption of plans and programmes with a view to promoting sustainable development, by ensuring that, in accordance with this Directive, an environmental assessment is carried out of certain plans and programmes which are likely to have significant effects on the environment.

ARTICLE 2

Definitions

For the purposes of this Directive:

(a) 'plans and programmes' shall mean plans and programmes, including those co-financed by the European Community, as well as any modifications to them:

- which are subject to preparation and/or adoption by an authority at national, regional or local level or which are prepared by an authority for adoption, through a legislative procedure by Parliament or Government, and
- which are required by legislative, regulatory or administrative provisions;

(b) 'environmental assessessment' shall mean the preparation of an environmental report, the carrying out of consultations, the taking into account of the environmental resport and the results of the consultations in decision-making and the provision of information of the decision in accordance with Articles 4 to 9;

(c) 'environmental report' shall mean the part of the plan or programme documentation containing the information required in Articles 5 and Annex I;

(d) 'The public' shall mean one or more natural or legal persons and, in accordance with national legislation or practice, their associations, organisations or groups.

[6] OJ L 327, 22.12. 2000, p. 1.

ARTICLE 3

Scope

1. An environmental assessment, in accordance with Articles 4 to 9, shall be carried out for plans and programmes referred to in paragraphs 2 to 4 which are likely to have significant environmental effects.

2. Subject to paragraph 3, an environmental assessment shall be carried out for all plans and programmes,

(a) which are prepared for agriculture, forestry, fisheries, energy, industry, transport, waste management, water management, telecommunications, tourism, town and country planning or land use and which set the framework for future development consent of projects listed in Annexes I and II to Directive 85/337/EEC; or

(b) which, in view of the likely effect on sites, have been determined to require an assessment pursuant to Articles 6 or 7 of Directive 92/43/EEC.

3. Plans and programmes referred to in paragraph 2 which determine the use of small areas at local level and minor modifications to plans and programmes referred to in paragraph 2 shall require an environmental assessment only where the Member States determine that they are likely to have significant environmental effects.

4. Member States shall determine whether plans and programmes, other than those referred to in paragraph 2, which set the framework for future development consent of projects, are likely to have significant environmental effects.

5. Member States shall determine whether plans or programmes referred to in paragraphs 3 and 4 are likely to have significant environmental effects either through case-by-case examination or by specifying types of plans and programmes or by combining both approaches. For this purpose Member States shall in all cases take into account relevant criteria set out in Annex II, in order to ensure that plans and programmes with likely significant effects on the environment are covered by this Directive.

6. In the case-by-case examination and in specifying types of plans and programmes in accordance with paragraph 5, the authorities referred to in Article 6(3) shall be consulted.

7. Member States shall ensure that their conclusions pursuant to paragraph 5, including the reasons for not requiring an environmental assessment pursuant to Articles 4 to 9, are made available to the public.

8. The following plans and programmes are not subject to this Directive:

- plans and programmes the sole purpose of which is to serve national defence or civil emergency;
- financial or budget plans and programmes.

9. This Directive does not apply to plans and programmes co-financed under the current respective programming periods[7] for Council Regulations (EC) No 1260/99[8] and No 1257/99.[9]

---

[7] The 2000–2006 programming period for Council Regulation (EC) No 1260/99 and the 2000–2006 and 2000–2007 programming periods for Council Regulation (EC) No 1257/99.

[8] Council Regulation (EC) No 1260/99 of 21 June 1999 laying down general provisions on the Structural Funds. (OJ L 161, 26.6.1999, p. 1.)

[9] Council Regulation (EC) No 1257/99 of 17 May 1999 on support for rural development from the European Agricultural Guidance and Guarantee Fund (EAGGF) and amending and repealing certain regulations. (OJ L 160, 26.6.1999, p. 80.)

ARTICLE 4

General Obligations

1. The environmental assessment referred to in Article 3 shall be carried out during the preparation of a plan or programme and before its adoption or submission to the legislative procedure.

2. The requirements of this Directive shall either be integrated into existing procedures in Member States for the adoption of plans and programmes or incorporated in procedures established to comply with this Directive.

3. Where plans and programmes form part of a hierarchy, Member States shall, with a view to avoiding duplications of the assessment, take into account the fact that the assessment will be carried out, in accordance with this Directive, at different levels of the hierarchy. For the purpose of, inter alia, avoiding duplication of assessment, Member States shall apply Article 5(2) and (3).

ARTICLE 5

Environmental Report

1. Where an environmental assessment is required under Article 3(1), an environmental report shall be prepared in which the likely significant effects on the environment of implementing the plan or programme, and reasonable alternatives taking into account the objectives and the geographical scope of the plan or programme, are identified, described and evaluated. The information to be given for this purpose is referred to in Annex I.

2. The environmental report prepared pursuant to paragraph 1 shall include the information that may reasonably be required taking into account current knowledge and methods of assessment, the contents and level of detail in the plan or programme, its stage in the decision-making process and the extent to which certain matters are more appropriately assessed at different levels in that process in order to avoid duplication of the assessment.

3. Relevant information available on environmental effects of the plans and programmes and obtained at other levels of decision-making or through other Community legislation may be used for providing the information referred to in Annex I.

4. The authorities referred to in Article 6 (3) shall be consulted when deciding on the scope and level of detail of the information which must be included in the environmental report.

ARTICLE 6

Consultations

1. The draft plan or programme and the environmental report prepared in accordance with Article 5 shall be made available to the authorities referred to in paragraph 3 of this Article and the public.

2. The authorities referred to in paragraph 3 and the public referred to in paragraph 4 shall be given an early an effective opportunity within appropriate time-frames to express their opinion on the draft plan or programme and the accompanying environmental report before the adoption of the plan or programme or its submission to the legislative procedure.

3. Member States shall designate the authorities to be consulted which, by reason of their specific environmental responsibilities, are likely to be concerned by the environmental effects of implementing plans and programmes.

4. Member States shall identify the public for the purposes of paragraph 2, including the public affected or likely to be affected by, or having an interest in, the decision-making subject to this Directive, including relevant non-governmental organizations, such as those promoting environmental protection and other organizations concerned.

5. The detailed arrangements for the information and consultation of the authorities and the public shall be determined by the Member States.

ARTICLE 7

Transboundary Consultations

1. Where a Member State considers that the implementation of a plan or programme being prepared in relation to its territory is likely to have significant effects on the environment in another Member State, or where a Member State likely to be significantly affected so requests, the Member State in whose territory the plan or programme is being prepared shall, before its adoption or submission to the legislative procedure, forward a copy of the draft plan or programme and the relevant environmental report to the other Member State.

2. Where a Member State is sent a copy of a draft plan or programme and an environmental report under paragraph 1, it shall indicate to the other Member State whether it wishes to enter into consultations before the adoption of the plan or programme or its submission to the legislative procedure and, if it so indicates, the Member States concerned shall enter into consultations concerning the likely transboundary environmental effects of implementing the plan or programme and the measures envisaged to reduce or eliminate such effects.

Where such consultations take place, the Member States concerned shall agree on detailed arrangements to ensure that the authorities referred to in Article 6(3) and the public referred to in Article 6(4) in the Member State likely to be significantly affected are informed and given an opportunity to forward their opinion within a reasonable time-frame.

3. Where Member States are required under this Article to enter into consultations, they shall agree, at the beginning of such consultations, on a reasonable time-frame for the durations of the consultations.

ARTICLE 8

Decision Making

The environmental report prepared pursuant to Article 5, the opinions expressed pursuant to Article 6 and the results of any transboundary consultations entered into pursuant to Article 7 shall be taken into account during the preparation of the plan or programme and before its adoption or submission to the legislative procedure.

ARTICLE 9

Information on the Decision

1. Member States shall ensure that, when a plan or programme is adopted, the authorities referred to in Article 6(3), the public and any Member State consulted under Article 7 are informed and the following items are made available to those so informed:

(a) the plan or programme as adopted;

(b) a statement summarizing how environmental considerations have been integrated into the plan or programme and how the environmental report prepared pursuant to Article 5, the opinions expressed pursuant to Article 6 and the results of consultations entered into pursuant to Article 7 have been taken into account in accordance with Article 8 and the reasons for choosing the plan or programme as adopted, in the light of the other reasonable alternative dealt with; and

(c) the measures decided concerning monitoring in accordance with Article 10.

2. The detailed arrangements concerning the information referred to in paragraph 1 shall be determined by the Member States.

ARTICLE 10

Monitoring

1. Member States shall monitor the significant environmental effects of the implementation of plans and programmes in order, inter alia, to identify at an early stage unforeseen adverse effects, and to be able to undertake appropriate remedial action.

2. In order to comply with paragraph 1, existing monitoring arrangements may be used if appropriate, with a view to avoiding duplication of monitoring.

UN/ECE Convention on Environmental Impact Assessment in a Transboundary Context (Espoo Convention)

ARTICLE 2

General Provisions

1. The Parties shall, either individually or jointly, take all appropriate and effective measures to prevent, reduce and control significant adverse transboundary environmental impact from proposed activities.

2. Each Party shall take the necessary legal, administrative or other measures to implement the provisions of this Convention, including, with respect to proposed activities listed in Appendix I that are likely to cause significant adverse transboundary impact, the establishment of an environmental impact assessment procedure that permits public participation and preparation of the environmental impact assessment documentation described in Appendix II.

3. The Party of origin shall ensure that in accordance with the provisions of this Convention an environmental impact assessment is undertaken prior to a decision to authorize or undertake a proposed activity listed in Appendix I that is likely to cause a significant adverse transboundary impact.

4. The Party of origin shall, consistent with the provisions of this Convention, ensure that affected Parties are notified of a proposed activity listed in Appendix I that is likely to cause a significant adverse transboundary impact.

5. Concerned Parties shall, at the initiative of any such Party, enter into discussions on whether one or more proposed activities not listed in Appendix I is or are likely to cause a significant adverse transboundary impact and thus should be treated as if it or they were so listed. Where those Parties so agree, the activity or activities shall be thus treated. General guidance for identifying criteria to determine significant adverse impact is set forth in Appendix III.

6. The Party of origin shall provide, in accordance with the provisions of this Convention, an opportunity to the public in the areas likely to be affected to participate in relevant environmental impact assessment procedures regarding proposed activities and shall ensure that the opportunity provided to the public of the affected Party is equivalent to that provided to the public of the Party of origin.

7. Environmental impact assessments as required by this Convention shall, as a minimum requirement, be undertaken at the project level of the proposed activity. To the extent appropriate, the Parties shall endeavour to apply the principles of environmental impact assessment to policies, plans and programmes.

8. The provisions of this Convention shall not affect the right of Parties to implement national laws, regulations, administrative provisions or accepted legal practices protecting

information the supply of which would be prejudicial to industrial and commercial secrecy or national security.

9. The provisions of this Convention shall not affect the right of particular Parties to implement, by bilateral or multilateral agreement where appropriate, more stringent measures than those of this Convention.

10. The provisions of this Convention shall not prejudice any obligations of the Parties under international law with regard to activities having or likely to have a transboundary impact.

ARTICLE 3
Notification

1. For a proposed activity listed in Appendix I that is likely to cause a significant adverse transboundary impact, the Party of origin shall, for the purposes of ensuring adequate and effective consultations under Article 5, notify any Party which it considers may be an affected Party as early as possible and no later than when informing its own public about that proposed activity.

2. This notification shall contain, *inter alia*:

    (a) Information on the proposed activity, including any available information on its possible transboundary impact;

    (b) The nature of the possible decision; and

    (c) An indication of a reasonable time within which a response under paragraph 3 of this Article is required, taking into account the nature of the proposed activity;

    and may include the information set out in paragraph 5 of this Article.

3. The affected Party shall respond to the Party of origin within the time specified in the notification, acknowledging receipt of the notification, and shall indicate whether it intends to participate in the environmental impact assessment procedure.

4. If the affected Party indicates that it does not intend to participate in the environmental impact assessment procedure, or if it does not respond within the time specified in the notification, the provisions in paragraphs 5, 6, 7 and 8 of this Article and in Articles 4 to 7 will not apply. In such circumstances the right of a Party of origin to determine whether to carry out an environmental impact assessment on the basis of its national law and practice is not prejudiced.

5. Upon receipt of a response from the affected Party indicating its desire to participate in the environmental impact assessment procedure, the Party of origin shall, if it has not already done so, provide to the affected Party:

    (a) Relevant information regarding the environmental impact assessment procedure, including an indication of the time schedule for transmittal of comments; and

    (b) Relevant information on the proposed activity and its possible significant adverse transboundary impact.

6. An affected Party shall, at the request of the Party of origin, provide the latter with reasonably obtainable information relating to the potentially affected environment under the jurisdiction of the affected Party, where such information is necessary for the preparation of the environmental impact assessment documentation. The information shall be furnished promptly and, as appropriate, through a joint body where one exists.

7. When a Party considers that it would be affected by a significant adverse transboundary impact of a proposed activity listed in Appendix I, and when no notification has taken place in accordance with paragraph 1 of this Article, the concerned Parties shall, at the request of the affected Party, exchange sufficient information for the purposes of holding discussions on whether there is likely to be a significant adverse transboundary impact. If those Parties agree that there is likely to be a significant adverse transboundary impact, the provisions of this Convention shall apply accordingly. If those Parties cannot agree whether there is likely to be a significant adverse transboundary impact, any such Party may submit that question to an inquiry commission in accordance with the provisions of Appendix IV to advise on the likelihood of significant adverse transboundary impact, unless they agree on another method of settling this question.

8. The concerned Parties shall ensure that the public of the affected Party in the areas likely to be affected be informed of, and be provided with possibilities for making comments or objections on, the proposed activity, and for the transmittal of these comments or objections to the competent authority of the Party of origin, either directly to this authority or, where appropriate, through the Party of origin.

ARTICLE 4

Preparation of the Environmental Impact Assessment Documentation

1. The environmental impact assessment documentation to be submitted to the competent authority of the Party of origin shall contain, as a minimum, the information described in Appendix II.

2. The Party of origin shall furnish the affected Party, as appropriate through a joint body where one exists, with the environmental impact assessment documentation. The concerned Parties shall arrange for distribution of the documentation to the authorities and the public of the affected Party in the areas likely to be affected and for the submission of comments to the competent authority of the Party of origin, either directly to this authority or, where appropriate, through the Party of origin within a reasonable time before the final decision is taken on the proposed activity.

ARTICLE 5

Consultations on the Basis of the Environmental Impact Assessment Documentation

The Party of origin shall, after completion of the environmental impact assessment documentation, without undue delay enter into consultations with the affected Party concerning, *inter alia*, the potential transboundary impact of the proposed activity and measures to reduce or eliminate its impact. Consultations may relate to:

(a) Possible alternatives to the proposed activity, including the no-action alternative and possible measures to mitigate significant adverse transboundary impact and to monitor the effects of such measures at the expense of the Party of origin;

(b) Other forms of possible mutual assistance in reducing any significant adverse transboundary impact of the proposed activity; and

(c) Any other appropriate matters relating to the proposed activity.

The Parties shall agree, at the commencement of such consultations, on a reasonable time-frame for the duration of the consultation period. Any such consultations may be conducted through an appropriate joint body, where one exists.

ARTICLE 6

Final Decision

1. The Parties shall ensure that, in the final decision on the proposed activity, due account is taken of the outcome of the environmental impact assessment, including the environmental impact assessment documentation, as well as the comments thereon received pursuant to Article 3, paragraph 8 and Article 4, paragraph 2, and the outcome of the consultations as referred to in Article 5.

2. The Party of origin shall provide to the affected Party the final decision on the proposed activity along with the reasons and considerations on which it was based.

3. If additional information on the significant transboundary impact of a proposed activity, which was not available at the time a decision was made with respect to that activity and which could have materially affected the decision, becomes available to a concerned Party before work on that activity commences, that Party shall immediately inform the other concerned Party or Parties. If one of the concerned Parties so requests, consultations shall be held as to whether the decision needs to be revised.

ARTICLE 7

Post-project Analysis

1. The concerned Parties, at the request of any such Party, shall determine whether, and if so to what extent, a post-project analysis shall be carried out, taking into account the likely significant adverse transboundary impact of the activity for which an environmental impact assessment has been undertaken pursuant to this Convention. Any post-project analysis undertaken shall include, in particular, the surveillance of the activity and the determination of any adverse transboundary impact. Such surveillance and determination may be undertaken with a view to achieving the objectives listed in Appendix V.

2. When, as a result of post-project analysis, the Party of origin or the affected Party has reasonable grounds for concluding that there is a significant adverse transboundary impact or factors have been discovered which may result in such an impact, it shall immediately inform the other Party. The concerned Parties shall then consult on necessary measures to reduce or eliminate the impact.

United Nations/Economic Commission for Europe Draft Protocol on Strategic Environmental Assessment (Kiev Protocol)

...

ARTICLE 4

Field of Application Concerning Plans and Programmes

1. Each Party shall ensure that a strategic environmental assessment is carried out for plans and programmes referred to in paragraphs 2, 3 and 4 which are likely to have significant environmental, including health, effects.

2. A strategic environmental assessment shall be carried out for plans and programmes which are prepared for agriculture, forestry, fisheries, energy, industry including mining, transport, regional development, waste management, telecommunications, tourism, town and country planning or land use, and which set the framework for future development consent for projects listed in annex I and any other project listed in annex II that requires an environmental impact assessment under national legislation.

3. For plans and programmes other than those subject to paragraph 2 which set the framework for future development consent of projects, a strategic environmental assessment shall be carried out where a Party so determines according to article 5, paragraph 1.

4. For plans and programmes referred to in paragraph 2 which determine the use of small areas at local level and for minor modifications to plans and programmes referred to in paragraph 2, a strategic environmental assessment shall be carried out only where a Party so determines according to article 5, paragraph 1.

5. The following plans and programmes are not subject to this Protocol:

   (a) Plans and programmes whose sole purpose is to serve national defence or civil emergencies;
   (b) Financial or budget plans and programmes.

ARTICLE 5

Screening

1. Each Party shall determine whether plans of programmes referred to in article 4, paragraphs 3 and 4, are likely to have significant environmental, including health, effects either through a case-by-case examination or by specifying types of plans and programmes or by combining both approaches. For this purpose each Party shall in all cases take into account the criteria set out in annex III.

2. Each Party shall ensure that the environmental and health authorities referred to in article 9, paragraph 1, are consulted when applying the procedures referred to in paragraph 1 above.

3. To the extent appropriate, each Party shall endeavour to provide opportunities for the participation of the public concerned in the screening of plans and programmes under this article.

4. Each Party shall ensure timely public availability of the conclusion pursuant to paragraph 1, including the reasons for not requiring a strategic environmental assessment, whether by public notices or by other appropriate means, such as electronic media.

ARTICLE 6

Scoping

1. Each Party shall establish arrangements for the determination of the relevant information to be included in the environmental report in accordance with article 7, paragraph 2.

2. Each Party shall ensure that the environmental and health authorities referred to in article 9, paragraph 1, are consulted when determining the relevant information to be included in the environmental report.

3. To the extent appropriate, each Party shall endeavour to provide opportunities for the participation of the public concerned when determining the relevant information to be included in the environmental report.

ARTICLE 7

Environmental Report

1. For plans and programmes subject to strategic environmental assessment, each Party shall ensure that an environmental report is prepared.

2. The environmental report shall, in accordance with the determination under article 6, identify, describe and evaluate the likely significant environmental, including health, effects of implementing the plan or programme and its reasonable alternatives. The report shall contain such information specified in annex IV as may reasonably be required, taking into account:

   (a) current knowledge and methods of assessment;
   (b) the contents and the level of detail of the plan or programme and its stage in the decision-making process;
   (c) the interests of the public; and
   (d) the information needs of the decision-making body.

3. Each Party shall ensure that environmental reports are of sufficient quality to meet the requirements of this Protocol.

ARTICLE 8

Public Participation

1. Each Party shall ensure early, timely and effective opportunities for public participation, when all options are open, in the strategic environmental assessment of plans and programmes.

2. Each Party, using electronic media or other appropriate means, shall ensure the timely public availability of the draft plan or programme and the environmental report.

3. Each Party shall ensure that the public concerned, including relevant non-governmental organizations, is identified for the purposes of paragraphs 1 and 4.

4. Each Party shall ensure that the public referred to in paragraph 3 has the opportunity to express its opinion on the draft plan or programme and the environmental report within a reasonable time frame.

5. Each Party shall ensure that the detailed arrangements for informing the public and consulting the public concerned are determined and made publicly available. For this purpose, each Party shall take into account to the extent appropriate the elements listed in annex V.

ARTICLE 9

Consultation with Environmental and Health Authorities

1. Each Party shall designate the authorities to be consulted which, by reason of their specific environmental or health responsibilities, are likely to be concerned by the environmental, including health, effects of the implementation of the plan or programme.

2. The draft plan or programme and the environmental report shall be made available to the authorities referred to in paragraph 1.

3. Each Party shall ensure that the authorities referred to in paragraph 1 are given, in an early, timely and effective manner, the opportunity to express their opinion on the draft plan or programme and the environmental report.

4. Each Party shall determine the detailed arrangements for informing and consulting the environmental and health authorities referred to in paragraph 1.

ARTICLE 10

Transboundary Consultations

1. Where a Party of origin considers that the implementation of a plan or programme is likely to have significant transboundary environmental, including health, effects or where a Party likely to be significantly affected so requests, the Party of origin shall as early as possible before the adoption of the plan or programme notify the affected Party.

2. This notification shall contain, inter alia:

   (a) The draft plan or programme and the environmental report including information on its possible transboundary environmental, including health, effects; and

   (b) Information regarding the decision-making procedure, including an indication of a reasonable time schedule for the transmission of comments.

3. The affected Party shall, within the time specified in the notification, indicate to the Party of origin whether it wishes to enter into consultations before the adoption of the plan or programme and, if it so indicates, the Parties concerned shall enter into consultations concerning the likely transboundary environmental, including health, effects of implementing the plan or programme and the measures envisage to prevent, reduce or mitigate adverse effects.

4. Where such consultations take place, the Parties concerned shall agree on detailed arrangements to ensure that the public concerned and the authorities referred to in article 9, paragraph 1, in the affected Party are informed and given an opportunity to forward their opinion on the draft plan or programme and the environmental report within a reasonable time frame.

ARTICLE 11

Decision

1. Each Party shall ensure that when a plan or programme is adopted due account is taken of:
   (a) the conclusions of the environment report;
   (b) the measures to prevent, reduce or mitigate the adverse effects identified in the environmental report; and
   (c) the comments received in accordance with articles 8 to 10.

2. Each Party shall ensure that when a plan or programme is adopted the public, the authorities referred to in article 9, paragraph 1, and the Parties consulted according to article 10 are informed, and that the plan or programme is made available to them together with a statement summarizing how the environmental, including health, considerations have been integrated into it, how the comments received in accordance with articles 8 to 10 have been taken into account and the reasons for adopting it in the light of the reasonable alternatives considered.

ARTICLE 12

Monitoring

1. Each Party shall monitor the significant environmental, including health, effects of the implementation of the plans and programmes, adopted under article 11 in order, inter alia, to identify, at an early stage, unforeseen adverse effects and to be able to undertake appropriate remedial action.

2. The results of the monitoring undertaken shall be made available, in accordance with national legislation, to the authorities referred to in article 9, paragraph 1, and to the public.

ARTICLE 13

Policies and Legislation

1. Each Party shall endeavour to ensure that environmental, including health, concerns are considered and integrated to the extent appropriate in the preparation of its proposals for policies and legislation that are likely to have significant effects on the environment, including health.

2. In applying paragraph 1, each Party shall consider the appropriate principles and elements of this Protocol.

3. Each Party shall determine, where appropriate, the practical arrangements for the consideration and integration of environmental, including health, concerns in accordance with paragraph 1, taking into account the need for transparency in decision-making.

4. Each Party shall report to the Meeting of the Parties to the Convention serving as the Meeting of the Parties to this Protocol on its application of this article.

United Nations/Economic Commission for Europe Convention on Access to Information, Public Participation in Decision-Making and Access to Justice in Environmental Matters (Aarhus Convention)

ARTICLE 1

Objective

In order to contribute to the protection of the right of every person of present and future generations to live in an environment adequate to his or her health and well-being, each Party shall guarantee the rights of access to information, public participation in decision-making, and access to justice in environmental matters in accordance with the provisions of this Convention.

. . .

ARTICLE 6

Public Participation in Decisions of Specific Activities

1. Each Party:
    (a) shall apply the provisions of this article with respect to decisions on whether to permit proposed activities listed in annex I;
    (b) shall, in accordance with its national law, also apply the provisions of this article to decisions on proposed activities not listed in annex I which may have a significant effect on the environment. To this end, Parties shall determine whether such a proposed activity is subject to these provisions; and
    (c) may decide, on a case-by-case basis if so provided under national law, not to apply the provisions of this article to proposed activities serving national defence purposes, if that Party deems that such application would have an adverse effect on these purposes.

2. The public concerned shall be informed, either by public notice or individually as appropriate, early in an environmental decision-making procedure, and in an adequate, timely and effective manner, *inter alia*, of:
    (a) the proposed activity and the application on which a decision will be taken;
    (b) the nature of possible decisions or the draft decision;
    (c) the public authority responsible for making the decision;
    (d) the envisaged procedure, including, as and when this information can be provided:
        (i) the commencement of the procedure;
        (ii) the opportunities for the public to participate;

    (iii) the time and venue of any envisaged public hearing;

    (iv) an indication of the public authority from which relevant information can be obtained and where the relevant information has been deposited for examination by the public;

    (v) an indication of the relevant public authority or any other official body to which comments or questions can be submitted and of the time schedule for transmittal of comments or questions; and

    (vi) an indication of what environmental information relevant to the proposed activity is available; and

  (e) the fact that the activity is subject to a national or transboundary environmental impact assessment procedure.

3. The public participation procedures shall include reasonable time-frames for the different phases, allowing sufficient time for informing the public in accordance with paragraph 2 above and for the public to prepare and participate effectively during the environmental decision-making.

4. Each Party shall provide for early public participation, when all options are open and effective public participation can take place.

5. Each Party should, where appropriate, encourage prospective applicants to identify the public concerned, to enter into discussions, and to provide information regarding the objectives of their application before applying for a permit.

6. Each Party shall require the competent public authorities to give the public concerned access for examination, upon request where so required under national law, free of charge and as soon as it becomes available, to all information relevant to the decision-making referred to in this article that is available at the time of the public participation procedure, without prejudice to the right of Parties to refuse to disclose certain information in accordance with article 4, paragraphs 3 and 4. The relevant information shall include at least, and without prejudice to the provisions of article 4:

  (a) a description of the site and the physical and technical characteristics of the proposed activity, including an estimate of the expected residues and emissions;

  (b) a description of the significant effects of the proposed activity on the environment;

  (c) a description of the measures envisaged to prevent and/or reduce the effects, including emissions;

  (d) a non-technical summary of the above;

  (e) an outline of the main alternatives studied by the applicant; and

  (f) in accordance with national legislation, the main reports and advice issued to the public authority at the time when the public concerned shall be informed in accordance with paragraph 2 above.

7. Procedures for public participation shall allow the public to submit, in writing or, as appropriate, at a public hearing or inquiry with the applicant any comments, information, analyses or opinions that it considers relevant to the proposed activity.

8. Each Party shall ensure that in the decision due account is taken of the outcome of the public participation.

9. Each Party shall ensure that, when the decision has been taken by the public authority, the public is promptly informed of the decision in accordance with the appropriate procedures.

Each Party shall make accessible to the public the text of the decision along with the reasons and considerations on which the decision is based.

10. Each Party shall ensure that, when a public authority reconsiders or updates the operating conditions for an activity referred to in paragraph 1, the provisions of paragraphs 2 to 9 of this article are applied *mutatis mutandis*, and where appropriate.

11. Each Party shall, within the framework of its national law, apply, to the extent feasible and appropriate, provisions of this article to decisions on whether to permit the deliberate release of genetically modified organisms into the environment.

ARTICLE 7

Public Participation Concerning Plans, Programmes And Policies Relating to the Environment

Each Party shall make appropriate practical and/or other provisions for the public to participate during the preparation of plans and programmes relating to the environment, within a transparent and fair framework, having provided the necessary information to the public. Within this framework, article 6, paragraphs 3, 4 and 8, shall be applied. The public which may participate shall be identified by the relevant public authority, taking into account the objectives of this Convention. To the extent appropriate, each Party shall endeavour to provide opportunities for public participation in the preparation of policies relating to the environment.

Town and Country Planning (Assessment of Environmental Effects) Regulations 1999 (SI 1999, No. 293), Schedules 2, 3 and 4

SCHEDULE 2

REGULATION 2(1)

Descriptions of Development and Applicable Thresholds and Criteria for the Purposes of the Definition of 'Schedule 2 Development'

1. In the table below —

'area of the works' includes any area occupied by apparatus, equipment, machinery, materials, plant, spoil heaps or other facilities or stores required for construction or installation;

'controlled waters' has the same meaning as in the Water Resources Act 1991;

'floorspace' means the floorspace in a building or buildings.

2. The table below sets out the descriptions of development and applicable thresholds and criteria for the purpose of classifying development as Schedule 2 development.

Table

Column 1	*Column 2*
Description of development	*Applicable thresholds and criteria*
The carrying out of development to provide any of the following —	
1. ***Agriculture and aquaculture***	The area of the development exceeds 0.5 hectare.
(a) Projects for the use of uncultivated and or semi-natural areas for intensive agricultural purposes;	
(b) Water management projects for agriculture, including irrigation and and drainage projects;	The area of the works exceeds 1 hectare.
(c) Intensive livestock installations (unless included in Schedule 1);	The area of new floorspace exceeds 500 square metres.
(d) Intensive fish farming;	The installation resulting from the development is designed to produce more than 10 tonnes of dead weight fish per year.
(e) Reclamation of land from the sea.	All development.

Table (*Continued*)

Column 1	*Column 2*
2. **Extractive industry**	All development except the construction of buildings or other ancillary structures where the new floorspace does not exceed 1,000 square metres.
(a) Quarries, open-cast mining and peat extraction (unless included in Schedule 1);	
(b) Underground mining;	
(c) Extraction of minerals by fluvial dredging;	All development.
(d) Deep drillings, in particular —	(i) In relation to any type of drilling, the area of the works exceeds 1 hectare; or
(i) geothermal drilling;	(ii) in relation to geothermal drilling and drilling for the storage of nuclear waste material, the drilling is within 100 metres of any controlled waters.
(ii) drilling for the storage of nuclear waste material;	
(iii) drilling for water supplies;	
with the exception of drillings for investigating the stability of the soil.	
(e) Surface industrial installations for the extraction of coal, petroleum, natural gas and ores, as well as bituminous shale.	The area of the development exceeds 0.5 hectare.
3. **Energy industry**	The area of the development exceeds 0.5 hectare.
(a) Industrial installations for the production of electricity, steam and hot water (unless included in Schedule 1);	
(b) Industrial installations for carrying gas, steam and hot water;	The area of the works exceeds 1 hectare.
(c) Surface storage of natural gas;	(i) The area of any new building, deposit or structure exceeds 500 square metres; or
(d) Underground storage of combustible gases;	(ii) a new building, deposit or structure is to be sited within 100 metres of any controlled waters.
(e) Surface storage of fossil fuels;	
(f) Industrial briquetting of coal and lignite;	The area of new floorspace exceeds 1,000 square metres.
(g) Installations for the processing and storage of radioactive waste (unless included in Schedule 1);	(i) The area of new floorspace exceeds 1,000 square metres; or
	(ii) the installation resulting from the development will require an authorisation or the variation of an authorisation under the Radioactive Substances Act 1993.
(h) Installations for hydroelectric energy production;	The installation is designed to produce more than 0.5 megawatts.
(i) Installations for the harnessing of wind power for energy production (wind farms).	(i) The development involves the installation of more than 2 turbines; or
	(ii) the hub height of any turbine or height of any other structure exceeds 15 metres.

Column 1	Column 2

4. **Production and processing of metals**
(a) Installations for the production of pig iron or steel (primary or secondary fusion) including continuous casting;
(b) Installations for the processing of ferrous metals —
  (i) hot-rolling mills;
  (ii) smitheries with hammers;
  (iii) application of protective fused metal coats.
(c) Ferrous metal foundries;
(d) Installations for the smelting, including the alloyage, of non-ferrous metals, excluding precious metals, including recovered products (refining, foundry casting, etc.);
(e) Installations for surface treatment of metals and plastic materials using an electrolytic or chemical process;
(f) Manufacture and assembly of motor vehicles and manufacture of motor-vehicle engines;
(g) Shipyards;
(h) Installations for the construction and repair of aircraft;
(i) Manufacture of railway equipment;
(j) Swaging by explosives;
(k) Installations for the roasting and sintering of metallic ores.
	The area of new floorspace exceeds 1,000 square metres.

5. **Mineral industry** (a) Coke ovens (dry coal distillation); (b) Installations for the manufacture of cement; (c) Installations for the production of asbestos and the manufacture of asbestos-based products (unless included in Schedule 1); (d) Installations for the manufacture of glass including glass fibre; (e) Installations for smelting mineral substances including the production of mineral fibres; (f) Manufacture of ceramic products by burning, in particular roofing tiles, bricks, refractory bricks, tiles, stonewear or porcelain.	The area of new floorspace exceeds 1,000 square metres

Table (*Continued*)

Column 1	Column 2
6. *Chemical industry (unless included in Schedule 1)*	The area of new floorspace exceeds 1,000 square metres.
(a) Treatment of intermediate products and production of chemicals;	
(b) Production of pesticides and pharmaceutical products, paint and varnishes, elastomers and peroxides;	(i) The area of any new building or structure exceeds 0.05 hectare; or
(c) Storage facilities for petroleum, petrochemical and chemical products.	(ii) more than 200 tonnes of petroleum, petrochemical or chemical products is to be stored at any one time.
7. *Food industry*	The area of new floorspace exceeds 1,000 square metres.
(a) Manufacture of vegetable and animal oils and fats;	
(b) Packing and canning of animal and vegetable products;	
(c) Manufacture of dairy products;	
(d) Brewing and malting;	
(e) Confectionery and syrup manufacture;	
(f) Installations for the slaughter of animals;	
(g) Industrial starch manufacturing installations;	
(h) Fish-meal and fish-oil factories;	
(i) Sugar factories.	
8. *Textile, leather, wood and paper industries*	The area of new floorspace exceeds 1,000 square metres.
(a) Industrial plants for the production of paper and board (unless included in Schedule 1);	
(b) Plants for the pre-treatment (operations such as washing, bleaching, mercerisation) or dyeing of fibres or textiles;	
(c) Plants for the tanning of hides and skins;	
(d) Cellulose-processing and production installations.	
9. *Rubber industry* Manufacture and treatment of elastomer-based products.	The area of new floorspace exceeds 1,000 square metres.
10. *Infrastructure projects*	The area of the development exceeds 0.5 hectare.
(a) Industrial estate development projects;	

Column 1	*Column 2*
(b) Urban development projects, including the construction of shopping centres and car parks, sports stadiums, leisure centres and multiplex cinemas;	
(c) Construction of intermodal trans-shipment facilities and of intermodal terminals (unless included in Schedule 1);	
(d) Construction of railways (unless included in Schedule 1);	The area of the works exceeds 1 hectare.
(e) Construction of airfields (unless included in Schedule 1);	(i) The development involves an extension to a runway; or (ii) the area of the works exceeds 1 hectare.
(f) Construction of roads (unless included in Schedule 1);	The area of the works exceeds 1 hectare.
(g) Construction of harbours and port installations including fishing harbours (unless included in Schedule 1);	The area of the works exceeds 1 hectare.
(h) Inland-waterway construction not included in Schedule 1, canalisation and flood-relief works;	The are of the works exceeds 1 hectare.
(i) Dams and other installations designed to hold water or store it on a long-term basis (unless included in Schedule 1);	
(j) Tramways, elevated and underground railways, suspended lines or similar lines of a particular type, used exclusively or mainly for passenger transport;	
(k) Oil and gas pipeline installations (unless included in Schedule 1);	(i) The area of the works exceeds 1 hectare; or,
(l) Installations of long-distance aqueducts;	(ii) in the case of a gas pipeline, the installation has a design operating pressure exceeding 7 bar gauge.
(m) Coastal work to combat erosion and maritime works capable of altering the coast through the construction, for example, of dykes, moles, jetties and other sea defence works, excluding the maintenance and reconstruction of such works;	All development.
(n) Groundwater abstraction and artificial groundwater recharge schemes not included in Schedule 1;	The area of the works exceeds 1 hectare.

Table (*Continued*)

Column 1	Column 2
(o) Works for the transfer of water resources between river basins not included in Schedule 1; (p) Motorway service areas.	The area of the development exceeds 0.5 hectare.
11. *Other projects* (a) Permanent racing and test tracks for motorised vehicles;	The area of the development exceeds 1 hectare.
(b) Installations for the disposal of waste (unless included in Schedule 1);	(i) The disposal is by incineration; or (ii) the area of the development exceeds 0.5 hectare; or (iii) the installation is to be sited within 100 metres of any controlled waters.
(c) Waste-water treatment plants (unless included in Schedule 1);	The area of the development exceeds 1,000 square metres.
(d) Sludge-deposition sites; (e) Storage of scrap iron, including scrap vehicles;	(i) The area of deposit or storage exceeds 0.5 hectare; or (ii) a deposit is to be made or scrap stored within 100 metres of any controlled waters.
(f) Test benches for engines, turbines or reactors; (g) Installations for the manufacture of artificial mineral fibres; (h) Installations for the recovery or destruction of explosive substances; (i) Knackers' yards.	The area of new floorspace exceeds 1,000 square metres.
12. *Tourism and leisure* (a) Ski-runs, ski-lifts and cable-cars and associated developments;	(i) The area of the works exceeds 1 hectare; or (ii) the height of any building or other structure exceeds 15 metres.
(b) Marinas;	The area of the enclosed water surface exceeds 1,000 square metres.
(c) Holiday villages and hotel complexes outside urban areas and associated developments; (d) Theme parks;	The area of the development exceeds 0.5 hectare.
(e) Permanent camp sites and caravan sites;	The area of the development exceeds 1 hectare.
(f) Golf courses and associated developments.	The area of the development exceeds 1 hectare.

Column 1	Column 2
13.	
(a) Any change to or extension of development of a description listed in Schedule 1 or in paragraphs 1 to 12 of Column 1 of this table, where that development is already authorised, executed or in the process of being executed, and the change or extension may have significant adverse effects on the environment;	(i) In relation to development of a description mentioned in Column 1 of this table, the thresholds and criteria in the corresponding part of Column 2 of this table applied to the change or extension (and not to the development as changed or extended).
	(ii) In relation to development of a description mentioned in a paragraph in Schedule 1 indicated below, the thresholds and criteria in Column 2 of the paragraph of this table indicated below applied to the change or extension (and not to the development as changed or extended):

Paragraph in Schedule 1	Paragraph of this table
1	6(a)
2(a)	3(a)
2(b)	3(g)
3	3(g)
4	4
5	5
6	6(a)
7(a)	10(d) (in relation to railways) or 10(e) (in relation to airports)
7(b) and (c)	10(f)
8(a)	10(h)
8(b)	10(g)
9	11(b)
10	11(b)
11	10(n)
12	10(o)
13	11(c)
14	2(e)
15	10(i)
16	10(k)
17	1(c)
18	8(a)
19	2(a)
20	6(c).

Table (*Continued*)

Column 1	Column 2
(b) Development of a description mentioned in Schedule 1 undertaken exclusively or mainly for the development and testing of new methods or products and not used for more than two years.	All developoment.

SCHEDULE 3

REGULATION 4(5)

Selection Criteria for Screening Schedule 2 Development

1. Characteristics of development   The characteristics of development must be considered having regard, in particular, to —

- (a) the size of the development;
- (b) the cumulation with other development;
- (c) the use of natural resources;
- (d) the production of waste;
- (e) pollution and nuisances;
- (f) the risk of accidents, having regard in particular to substances or technologies used.

2. Location of development   The environment sensitivity of geographical areas likely to be affected by development must be considered, having regard, in particular, to —

- (a) the existing land use;
- (b) the relative abundance, quality and regenerative capacity of natural resources in the area;
- (c) the absorption capacity of the natural environment, paying particular attention to the following areas —
  - (i) wetlands;
  - (ii) coastal zones;
  - (iii) mountain and forest areas;
  - (iv) nature reserves and parks;
  - (v) areas classified or protected under Member States' legislation; areas designated by Member States pursuant to Council Directive 79/409/EEC on the conservation of wild birds and Council Directive 92/43/EEC on the conservation of natural habitats and of wild fauna and flora;
  - (vi) areas in which the environmental quality standards laid down in Community legislation have already been exceeded;

(vii) densely populated areas;

(viii) landscapes of historical, cultural or archaeological significance.

3. Characteristics of the potential impact   The potential significant effects of development must be considered in relation to criteria set out under paragraphs 1 and 2 above, and having regard in particular to —

(a) the extent of the impact (geographical area and size of the affected population);

(b) the transfrontier nature of the impact;

(c) the magnitude and complexity of the impact;

(d) the probability of the impact;

(e) the duration, frequency and reversibility of the impact.

SCHEDULE 4

REGULATION 2(1)

Information for Inclusion in Environmental Statements

Part 1

1. Description of the development, including in particular —

(a) a description of the physical characteristics of the whole development and the land-use requirements during the construction and operational phases;

(b) a description of the main characteristics of the production processes, for instance, nature and quantity of the materials used;

(c) an estimate by type and quantity, of expected residues and emissions (water, air and soil pollution, noise, vibration, light, heat, radiation, etc.) resulting from the operation of the proposed development.

2. An outline of the main alternatives studied by the applicant or appellant and an indication of the main reasons for his choice, taking into account the environmental effects.

3. A description of the aspects of the environment likely to be significantly affected by the development, including, in particular, population, fauna, flora, soil, water, air, climatic factors, material assets, including the architectural and archaeological heritage, landscape and the inter-relationship between the above factors.

4. A description of the likely significant effects of the development on the environment, which should cover the direct effects and any indirect, secondary, cumulative, short, medium and long-term, permanent and temporary, positive and negative effects of the development, resulting from:

(a) the existence of the development;

(b) the use of natural resources;

(c) the emission of pollutants, the creation of nuisances and the elimination of waste, and the description by the applicant of the forecasting methods used to assess the effects on the environment.

5. A description of the measures envisaged to prevent, reduce and where possible offset any significant adverse effects on the environment.

6. A non-technical summary of the information provided under paragraphs 1 to 5 of this Part.

7. An indication of any difficulties (technical deficiencies or lack of know-how) encountered by the applicant in compiling the required information.

Directive 2003/35/EC of the European Parliament and of the Council of 26 May 2003 Providing for Public Participation in respect of the Drawing Up of Certain Plans and Programmes relating to the Environment and Amending with regard to Public Participation and Access to Justice Council Directives 85/337/EEC and 96/61/EC

THE EUROPEAN PARLIAMENT AND THE COUNCIL OF THE EUROPEAN UNION

Having regard to the Treaty establishing the European Community, and in particular Article 175 thereof

Having regard to the proposal from the Commission,

Having regard to the opinion of the European Economic and Social Committee,

Having regard to the opinion of the Committee of the Regions,

Acting in accordance with the procedure laid down in Article 251 of the Treaty, in the light of the joint text approved by the Conciliation Committee on 15 January 2003,

Whereas:

(1) Community legislation in the field of the environment aims to contribute to preserving, protecting and improving the quality of the environment and protecting human health.

(2) Community environmental legislation includes provisions for public authorities and other bodies to take decisions which may have a significant effect on the environment as well as on personal health and well-being.

(3) Effective public participation in the taking of decisions enables the public to express, and the decision-maker to take account of, opinions and concerns which may be relevant to those decisions, thereby increasing the accountability and transparency of the decision-making process and contributing to public awareness of environmental issues and support for the decisions taken.

(4) Participation, including participation by associations, organisations and groups, in particular non-governmental organisations promoting environmental protection, should accordingly be fostered, including inter alia by promoting environmental education of the public.

(5) On 25 June 1998 the Community signed the UN/ECE Convention on Access to Information, Public Participation in Decision-Making and Access to Justice in Environmental Matters (the Århus Convention). Community law should be properly aligned with that Convention with a view to its ratification by the Community.

(6) Among the objectives of the Århus Convention is the desire to guarantee rights of public participation in decision-making in environmental matters in order to contribute to the protection of the right to live in an environment which is adequate for personal health and well-being.

(7) Article 6 of the Århus Convention provides for public participation in decisions on the specific activities listed in Annex I thereto and on activities not so listed which may have a significant effect on the environment.

(8) Article 7 of the Århus Convention provides for public participation concerning plans and programmes relating to the environment.

(9) Article 9(2) and (4) of the Århus Convention provides for access to judicial or other procedures for challenging the substantive or procedural legality of decisions, acts or omissions subject to the public participation provisions of Article 6 of the Convention.

(10) Provision should be made in respect of certain Directives in the environmental area which require Member States to produce plans and programmes relating to the environment but which do not contain sufficient provisions on public participation, so as to ensure public participation consistent with the provisions of the Århus Convention, in particular Article 7 thereof. Other relevant Community legislation already provides for public participation in the preparation of plans and programmes and, for the future, public participation requirements in line with the Århus Convention will be incorporated into the relevant legislation from the outset.

(11) Council Directive 85/337/EEC of 27 June 1985 on the assessment of the effects of certain public and private projects on the environment, and Council Directive 96/61/EC of 24 September 1996 concerning integrated pollution prevention and control should be amended to ensure that they are fully compatible with the provisions of the Århus Convention, in particular Article 6 and Article 9(2) and (4) thereof.

(12) Since the objective of the proposed action, namely to contribute to the implementation of the obligations arising under the Århus Convention, cannot be sufficiently achieved by the Member States and can therefore, by reason of the scale and effects of the action, be better achieved at Community level, the Community may adopt measures in accordance with the principle of subsidiarity as set out in Article 5 of the Treaty. In accordance with the principle of proportionality, as set out in that Article, this Directive does not go beyond what is necessary in order to achieve that objective,

HAVE ADOPTED THIS DIRECTIVE:

ARTICLE 1

Objective

The objective of this Directive is to contribute to the implementation of the obligations arising under the Århus Convention, in particular by:

(a) providing for public participation in respect of the drawing up of certain plans and programmes relating to the environment;

(b) improving the public participation and providing for provisions on access to justice within Council Directives 85/337/EEC and 96/61/EC.

ARTICLE 2

Public participation concerning plans and programmes

1.   For the purposes of this Article, 'the public' shall mean one or more natural or legal persons and, in accordance with national legislation or practice, their associations, organisations or groups.

2.   Member States shall ensure that the public is given early and effective opportunities to participate in the preparation and modification or review of the plans or programmes required to be drawn up under the provisions listed in Annex I.

To that end, Member States shall ensure that:

(a) the public is informed, whether by public notices or other appropriate means such as electronic media where available, about any proposals for such plans or programmes or for their modification or review and that relevant information about such proposals is made available to the public including inter alia information about the right to participate in decision-making and about the competent authority to which comments or questions may be submitted;

(b) the public is entitled to express comments and opinions when all options are open before decisions on the plans and programmes are made;

(c) in making those decisions, due account shall be taken of the results of the public participation;

(d) having examined the comments and opinions expressed by the public, the competent authority makes reasonable efforts to inform the public about the decisions taken and the reasons and considerations upon which those decisions are based, including information about the public participation process.

3.   Member States shall identify the public entitled to participate for the purposes of paragraph 2, including relevant non-governmental organisations meeting any requirements imposed under national law, such as those promoting environmental protection.

The detailed arrangements for public participation under this Article shall be determined by the Member States so as to enable the public to prepare and participate effectively.

Reasonable time-frames shall be provided allowing sufficient time for each of the different stages of public participation required by this Article.

4.   This Article shall not apply to plans and programmes designed for the sole purpose of serving national defence or taken in case of civil emergencies.

5.   This Article shall not apply to plans and programmes set out in Annex I for which a public participation procedure is carried out under Directive 2001/42/EC of the European Parliament and of the Council of 27 June 2001 on the assessment of the effects of certain plans and programmes on the environment or under Directive 2000/60/EC of the European Parliament and of the Council of 23 October 2000 establishing a framework for Community action in the field of water policy.

ARTICLE 3

Amendment of Directive 85/337/EEC

Directive 85/337/EEC is hereby amended as follows:

1. in Article 1(2), the following definitions shall be added:

    ' "the public" means: one or more natural or legal persons and, in accordance with national legislation or practice, their associations, organisations or groups;
    "the public concerned" means: the public affected or likely to be affected by, or having an interest in, the environmental decision-making procedures referred to in Article 2(2); for the purposes of this definition, non-governmental organisations promoting environmental protection and meeting any requirements under national law shall be deemed to have an interest;'

2. in Article 1, paragraph 4 shall be replaced by the following:

    '4. Member States may decide, on a case-by-case basis if so provided under national law, not to apply this Directive to projects serving national defence purposes, if they deem that such application would have an adverse effect on these purposes.';

3. in Article 2(3), points (a) and (b) shall be replaced by the following:

    '(a) consider whether another form of assessment would be appropriate;
    (b) make available to the public concerned the information obtained under other forms of assessment referred to in point (a), the information relating to the exemption decision and the reasons for granting it.';

4. in Article 6, paragraphs 2 and 3 shall be replaced by the following paragraphs:

'2. The public shall be informed, whether by public notices or other appropriate means such as electronic media where available, of the following matters early in the environmental decision-making procedures referred to in Article 2(2) and, at the latest, as soon as information can reasonably be provided:

(a) the request for development consent;
(b) the fact that the project is subject to an environmental impact assessment procedure and, where relevant, the fact that Article 7 applies;
(c) details of the competent authorities responsible for taking the decision, those from which relevant information can be obtained, those to which comments or questions can be submitted, and details of the time schedule for transmitting comments or questions;
(d) the nature of possible decisions or, where there is one, the draft decision;
(e) an indication of the availability of the information gathered pursuant to Article 5;
(f) an indication of the times and places where and means by which the relevant information will be made available;
(g) details of the arrangements for public participation made pursuant to paragraph 5 of this Article.

3. Member States shall ensure that, within reasonable time-frames, the following is made available to the public concerned:

(a) any information gathered pursuant to Article 5;

(b) in accordance with national legislation, the main reports and advice issued to the competent authority or authorities at the time when the public concerned is informed in accordance with paragraph 2 of this Article;

(c) in accordance with the provisions of Directive 2003/4/EC of the European Parliament and of the Council of 28 January 2003 on public access to environmental information, information other than that referred to in paragraph 2 of this Article which is relevant for the decision in accordance with Article 8 and which only becomes available after the time the public concerned was informed in accordance with paragraph 2 of this Article.

4.   The public concerned shall be given early and effective opportunities to participate in the environmental decision-making procedures referred to in Article 2(2) and shall, for that purpose, be entitled to express comments and opinions when all options are open to the competent authority or authorities before the decision on the request for development consent is taken.

5.   The detailed arrangements for informing the public (for example by bill posting within a certain radius or publication in local newspapers) and for consulting the public concerned (for example by written submissions or by way of a public inquiry) shall be determined by the Member States.

6.   Reasonable time-frames for the different phases shall be provided, allowing sufficient time for informing the public and for the public concerned to prepare and participate effectively in environmental decision-making subject to the provisions of this Article.'

5.   Article 7 shall be amended as follows:

(a) paragraphs 1 and 2 shall be replaced by the following:

'1. Where a Member State is aware that a project is likely to have significant effects on the environment in another Member State or where a Member State likely to be significantly affected so requests, the Member State in whose territory the project is intended to be carried out shall send to the affected Member State as soon as possible and no later than when informing its own public, inter alia:

(a) a description of the project, together with any available information on its possible transboundary impact;

(b) information on the nature of the decision which may be taken, and shall give the other Member State a reasonable time in which to indicate whether it wishes to participate in the environmental decision-making procedures referred to in Article 2(2), and may include the information referred to in paragraph 2 of this Article.

2.   If a Member State which receives information pursuant to paragraph 1 indicates that it intends to participate in the environmental decision-making procedures referred to in Article 2(2), the Member State in whose territory the project is intended to be carried out shall, if it has not already done so, send to the affected Member State the information required to be given pursuant to Article 6(2) and made available pursuant to Article 6(3)(a) and (b).'

(b) paragraph 5 shall be replaced by the following:

'5.   The detailed arrangements for implementing this Article may be determined by the Member States concerned and shall be such as to enable the public concerned in the territory of the affected Member State to participate effectively in the environmental decision-making procedures referred to in Article 2(2) for the project.'

6. Article 9 shall be amended as follows:

(a) Paragraph 1 shall be replaced by the following:

'1. When a decision to grant or refuse development consent has been taken, the competent authority or authorities shall inform the public thereof in accordance with the appropriate procedures and shall make available to the public the following information:

- the content of the decision and any conditions attached thereto;
- having examined the concerns and opinions expressed by the public concerned, the main reasons and considerations on which the decision is based, including information about the public participation process;
- a description, where necessary, of the main measures to avoid, reduce and, if possible, offset the major adverse effects.'

(b) Paragraph 2 shall be replaced by the following:

'2. The competent authority or authorities shall inform any Member State which has been consulted pursuant to Article 7, forwarding to it the information referred to in paragraph 1 of this Article.

The consulted Member States shall ensure that that information is made available in an appropriate manner to the public concerned in their own territory.';

7. the following Article shall be inserted:

ARTICLE 10a

Member States shall ensure that, in accordance with the relevant national legal system, members of the public concerned:

(a) having a sufficient interest; or alternatively,
(b) maintaining the impairment of a right, where administrative procedural law of a Member State requires this as a precondition,

have access to a review procedure before a court of law or another independent and impartial body established by law to challenge the substantive or procedural legality of decisions, acts or omissions subject to the public participation provisions of this Directive.

Member States shall determine at what stage the decisions, acts or omissions may be challenged.

What constitutes a sufficient interest and impairment of a right shall be determined by the Member States, consistently with the objective of giving the public concerned wide access to justice. To this end, the interest of any non-governmental organisation meeting the requirements referred to in Article 1(2), shall be deemed sufficient for the purpose of subparagraph (a) of this Article. Such organisations shall also be deemed to have rights capable of being impaired for the purpose of subparagraph (b) of this Article.

The provisions of this Article shall not exclude the possibility of a preliminary review procedure before an administrative authority and shall not affect the requirement of exhaustion of administrative review procedures prior to recourse to judicial review procedures, where such a requirement exists under national law. Any such procedure shall be fair, equitable, timely and not prohibitively expensive.

In order to further the effectiveness of the provisions of this article, Member States shall ensure that practical information is made available to the public on access to administrative and judicial review procedures.';

8.   in Annex I, the following point shall be added:

'22.   Any change to or extension of projects listed in this Annex where such a change or extension in itself meets the thresholds, if any, set out in this Annex.';

9.   in Annex II, No 13, first indent, the following shall be added at the end:

'(change or extension not included in Annex I)'.

Directive 92/43/EC on the Conservation of Natural Habitats and of Wild Fauna and Flora, OJ 1992 L 206, p. 7, Art. 6

1. For special areas of conservation, Member States shall establish the necessary conservation measures involving, if need be appropriate management plans specifically designed for the sites or integrated into other development plans, and appropriate statutory, administrative or contractual measures which correspond to the ecological requirements of the natural habitat types in Annex I and the species in Annex II present on the sites.

2. Member States shall take appropriate steps to avoid, in the special areas of conservation, the deterioration of natural habitats and the habitats of species as well as disturbance of the species for which the areas have been designated, in so far as such disturbance could be significant in relation to the objectives of this Directive.

3. Any plan or project not directly connected with or necessary to the management of the site but likely to have a significant effect thereon, either individually or in combination with other plans or projects, shall be subject to appropriate assessment of its implications for the site in view of the site's conservation objectives. In the light of the conclusions of the assessment of the implications for the site and subject to the provisions of paragraph 4, the competent national authorities shall agree to the plan or project only having ascertained that it will not adversely affect the integrity of the site concerned and, if appropriate, after having obtained the opinion of the general public.

4. If, in spite of a negative assessment of the implications for the site and in the absence of alternative solutions, a plan or project must nevertheless be carried out for imperative reasons of overriding public interest, including those of a social or economic nature, the Member States shall take all compensatory measures necessary to ensure that the overall coherence of Natura 2000 is protected. It shall inform the Commission of the compensatory measures adopted.

Whereas the site concerned hosts a priority natural habitat type and/or a priority species, the only considerations which may be raised are those relating to human health or public safety, to beneficial consequences of primary importance for the environment, or further to an opinion from the Commission, to other imperatives of overriding public interest.

Regulations in Force in the United Kingdom and Gibraltar

England and Wales

Regulation	Date In Force
The Transport and Works (Assessment of Environmental Effects) Regulations 1995 SI no. 1541	1 August 1995
The Transport and Works (Assessment of Environmental Effects) Regulations 1998 SI no. 2226	7 October 1998
The Channel Tunnel Rail Link (Assessment of Environmental Effects) Regulations 1999 SI no. 107	17 February 1999
The Highways (Assessment of Environmental Effects) Regulations 1999 SI no. 369	13 March 1999
The Town and Country Planning (Environmental Impact Assessment) (England and Wales) Regulations 1999 SI no. 293	14 March 1999
The Environmental Impact Assessment (Land Drainage Improvement Works) Regulations 1999 SI no. 1783	21 July 1999
The Environmental Impact Assessment (Forestry) (England and Wales) Regulations 1999 SI no. 2228	6 September 1999
The Electricity Works (Environmental Impact Assessment) (England and Wales) Regulations 2000 SI no. 1927	1 September 2000
The Town and Country Planning (Environmental Impact Assessment) (England and Wales) (Amendment) Regulations 2000 SI no. 2867	15 November 2000
The Transport & Works (Application and Objections Procedure) Rules 2000 SI no. 2190	16 October 2000
The Transport and Works (Assessment of Environmental Effects) Regulations 2000 SI no. 3199	1 January 2001
The Environmental Impact Assessment (Uncultivated Land and Semi-Natural Areas) (England) Regulations 2001 SI no. 3966	1 February 2002
The Environmental Impact Assessment (Uncultivated Land and Semi-Natural Areas) (Wales) Regulations 2002 Welsh SI no. 2127 (W.214)	19 August 2002
The Water Resources (Environmental Impact Assessment) (England and Wales) Regulations 2003 SI no. 164	1 April 2003

Scotland

Regulation	Date In Force
The Environmental Impact Assessment (Scotland) Regulations 1999 SI no. 1	1 August 1999
Environmental Impact Assessment (Forestry) (Scotland) Regulations 1999 SI no. 43	6 September 1999
The Electricity Works (Environmental Impact Assessment) (Scotland) Regulations 2000 SI no. 320	5 October 2000
The Environmental Impact Assessment (Uncultivated Land and Semi-Natural Areas) (Scotland) Regulations 2002 SI no. 6	4 February 2002
The Environmental Impact Assessment (Scotland) Amendment Regulations 2002 SI no. 324	23 September 2002
The Environmental Impact Assessment (Water Management) (Scotland) Regulations 2003 SI no. 341	30 September 2003

Great Britain

Regulation	Date In Force
The Environmental Impact Assessment (Fish Farming in Marine Waters) Regulations 1999 SI no. 367	14 March 1999
The Public Gas Transporter Pipe-line Works (Environmental Impact Assessment) Regulations 1999 SI no. 1672	15 July 1999
Nuclear Reactors (Environmental Impact Assessment for Decommissioning) Regulations 1999 SI no. 2892	19 November 1999
The Harbour Works (Environmental Impact Assessment) Regulations 1999 SI no. 3445	1 February 2000
The Pipe-line Works (Environmental Impact Assessment) Regulations 2000 SI no. 1928	1 September 2000
The Harbour Works (Environmental Impact Assessment) (Amendment) Regulations 2000 SI no. 2391	2 October 2000

Northern Ireland

Regulation	Date In Force
The Planning (Environmental Impact Assessment) Regulations (Northern Ireland) 1999 SR no. 73	14 March 1999
Roads (Environmental Impact Assessment) Regulations (Northern Ireland) 1999 SR no. 89	14 March 1999
Environmental Impact Assessment (Fish Farming in Marine Waters) Regulations (Northern Ireland) 1999 SR no. 415	8 November 1999

Northern Ireland (*Continued*)

Regulation	Date In Force
Environmental Impact Assessment (Forestry) Regulations (Northern Ireland) 2000 SR no. 84	1 May 2000
Drainage (Environmental Impact Assessment) Regulations (Northern Ireland) 2001 SR no. 394	26 November 2001
The Environmental Impact Assessment (Uncultivated Land and Semi-Natural Areas) (Northern Ireland) Regulations 2001 SR no. 435	11 February 2002
Environmental Impact Assessment (Forestry) (Amendment) Regulations (Northern Ireland) 2002 SR no. 249	27 September 2002
The Harbour Works (Environmental Impact Assessment) Regulations (Northern Ireland) 2003 SR no. 136	14 April 2003

United Kingdom

Regulation	Date In Force
The Offshore Petroleum Production and Pipe-lines (Assessment of Environmental Effects) Regulations 1999 SI no. 360	14 March 1999

Gibraltar

Regulation	Date In Force
Town Planning (Environmental Impact Assessment) Regulations (Gibraltar) 2000 Legal Notice no. 13	17 February 2000
Town Planning (Environmental Impact Assessment) Amendment Regulations (Gibraltar) 2003 Legal Notice no. 129	18 December 2003

Index

Abbott, C. 184, 199
ad quod damnum 3–5, 42
adversarial inquiry systems 45
afforestation 120
agriculture 50
airports 155, 162
Alder, J. 238–9
alternatives to proposed projects 15–18,
    148–52, 288
  assessment of other sites 152–8
  European Commission's internal impact
      assessment 176–83
  geographical boundaries 153–8, 287–8
  Habitats Directive 158–62
  off–site issues 153–4
  protection of property rights 152–3, 182
  strategic environmental assessment 162–4
ancient monuments 145, 257
Antarctica 65
anthropocentricity 104
aquatic plant species 90
architectural heritage 209
Associated British Ports (ABP) 227, 228,
    229, 231
Atlantic salt meadow 227

badgers 78, 214–15, 224
balance of nature 60, 84
Bartlett, R.V. 7, 28, 247, 248, 284
bats 78–9, 214–15
Beattie, R. 96
Belize 292–3
Bell, S. 116
Best Practicable Environmental Option 16
bias 97–9, 240–1, 285, 287, 289
biological diversity 68–70, 85, 90
birdlife 227, 231, 232
  see also Royal Society for the Protection of Birds
    (RSPB)
bogland 120
Bosselman, F.P. 3, 5, 60
bounded rationality 202
breeding birds 227
Bregman, E. 25, 249
British Herpetological Society 256
Brooks, R.O. 94

brownfield sites 137
burden of proof 240
Burgess, J. 196

Cairngorm funicular railway 272–81, 288, 300
Caldwell, L.K. 81, 251
Callis, Robert 5
Canary Islands 102, 169
Canford Heath 256
Canterbury County Council 141
car parks 155–6
car traffic controls 1–2, 204, 241–2
carbon dioxide emissions 143–4
case law 10
Chalillo Dam 292–3
chemicals 177
chicken litter 153–4
citizens' juries 40
climate change 65, 88, 89, 141
coastal projects 140
Cohen, J. 197
command and control mechanisms 20, 244, 245
Common Agricultural Policy 175
common good 28
compensation 58–9
  writ of *ad quod damnum* 3–5
conceptual learning 201, 202, 203
congestion charges 1–2, 204, 241–2
consensus conferences 40
conservation
  biological diversity 68–70, 90
  European conservation sites 158, 267–8, 272
conservationist groups 46
  Royal Society for the Protection of Birds
      (RSPB) 111, 112, 132, 218–9, 231,
      274, 275, 277, 278
  whale strandings 103
  World Wildlife Fund 277, 278
consultation 40, 41
  see also participative decision making
contaminated land 137
control mechanisms 20
Cornish Wildlife Trust 213
cost–benefit analysis 42
Cotterell, R. 206
Countryside Commission 95